Contents

BUSINESS LAW

With UCC Applications

Seventh Edition

Gordon W. Brown
Professor of Business Law
North Shore Community College
Beverly, Massachusetts

Edward E. Byers
Former Editor in Chief, Business Management
Gregg Division
McGraw-Hill Book Company

Mary Ann Lawlor
Chairman/Chief Executive Officer
Drake Business Schools
New York, New York

Contributing Author
Paul Sukys
Professor of Law and Legal Studies
North Central Technical College
Mansfield, Ohio

McGRAW-HILL BOOK COMPANY

New York Atlanta Dallas St. Louis San Francisco
Auckland Bogotá Guatemala Hamburg Lisbon
London Madrid Mexico Milan Montreal New Delhi
Panama Paris San Juan São Paulo Singapore
Sydney Tokyo Toronto

Sponsoring Editor: Robert B. Nirkind
Editing Supervisor: Melonie Parnes
Design and Art Supervisor: Meri Shardin
Production Supervisor: Catherine Bokman

Text Designer: Suzanne Bennett & Associates
Cover Designer: Jennifer Dossin

Library of Congress Cataloging-in-Publication Data
Brown, Gordon W., date.
Business law.
Rev. ed. of: Business law / R. Robert Rosenberg . . . [et al.]. 6th ed. 1983.
Bibliography: p.
Includes index.
1. Commercial law—United States. I. Byers, Edward Elmer. II. Lawlor, Mary Ann. III. Title.
KF889.3.B84 1989 346.73'07 88-12865
ISBN 0-07-053919-7 347-3067

The manuscript for this book was processed electronically.

Business Law: With UCC Applications, *Seventh Edition*

3 4 5 6 7 8 9 0 HALHAL 8 9 5 4 3 2 1 0

ISBN 0-07-053919-7

Preface

As the law evolves and expands to encompass new applications and trends, so too has the Seventh Edition of *Business Law: With UCC Applications* been improved and enlarged to meet the greater needs of today's business students. This program has been restructured, rewritten, and revised to emphasize teachability and learnability. Our goal has been to present business law concepts accessibly and coherently, and to provide the most up-to-date coverage of essential business law topics.

New to This Edition

Four major additions have been made to the Seventh Edition text. First, five new chapters have been added. These chapters focus on criminal law, bankruptcy, and in a new part entitled "Emerging Trends and Issues," professional legal liability, computer law, and ethics.

Second, an abridged version of the Uniform Commercial Code and the complete U.S. Constitution have been added to the back of this book. To encourage a practical application of both documents, marginal references to specific articles and sections tie the text to the documents themselves.

Third, to provide an overview and cohesion to each chapter, a new chapter opener and chapter summary have been added to the Seventh Edition. Each chapter begins with an outline; it is followed by a commentary, or introductory paragraph relating the chapter topic to a real-world application; and then a list of chapter objectives, all of which are reviewed in the end of chapter activities. Each summary returns to the numbering system of the chapter outline to restate each major topic discussed in the chapter.

Fourth, a new two-page feature entitled "Case Study" has been added to the end of each part in the text. The "Case Study" summarizes an actual litigated case, presents a lengthy extract from the judge's decision, and provides a series of follow-up questions both pertinent to the case and effective as a review of legal concepts studied.

Expanded and Updated Topics

In addition to the features added in the Seventh Edition, information has been expanded and updated. Chapters retained from previous editions have been substantially revised and restructured to give greater emphasis to subjects such as the elements of a contract, the remedies available to buyer and seller for breach of a sales contract, and security devices.

Information concerning legislation, case law, and uniform law relating to today's business world has been fully expanded as well. Included is coverage of the broad effects of, among others, the Computer Software Copyright Act of 1980, the Subchapter S Revision Act of 1982, the Revised Model Business Corporation Act of 1984, the Counterfeit Access Devise and Computer Fraud Act of 1984, and the Used Car Rule of 1985.

In a further effort to enhance the usefulness and ease of learning of the Seventh Edition of *Business Law: With UCC Applications,* many new case examples and cited case problems have been added to this text. The illustration program has also been expanded in this edition, as has the glossary, which has now been improved by the inclusion of pronunciation guides for difficult legal terms and phrases.

Teaching and Learning Resources

The Seventh Edition of *Business Law: With UCC Applications* is a complete introductory program, and to ensure that completeness we have added two components and improved two others.

New to this program is a *Cases From the People's Court* video. Ten cases have been selected from the popular syndicated television series starring Judge Joseph A. Wapner. These ten cases are correlated with chapters in the text and may be used with review exercises provided in the student *Study Guide,* which is a suggested accompaniment to this program. *Cases From the People's Court* presents students with the opportunity to summarize the facts in a case and then to apply legal principles to those facts.

Also new to this edition is a *Microcomputer Test Bank.* The Test Bank provides a quick and easy means of generating more than 1000 test questions. It may be tailored to the instructor's needs by allowing questions to be added or deleted. Three types of tests may be created: (1) Random—questions randomly selected from specified chapters; (2) nonrandom—questions selected by the instructor; or (3) alternate—either even-numbered or odd-numbered questions from specified chapters. Multiple versions of a test may be generated with the same questions in different orders. Twenty-five question tests are included for each of the 41 chapters in the text.

Revised for the Seventh Edition is the student *Study Guide.* Included for the first time is a full-page fill-in outline for each chapter in the text. This outline is correlated to the outline provided in each chapter opener, and it may be used as a study aid or as an indicator of subject mastery. New to this edition as well are review exercises correlated to the ten cases chosen for the *Cases From the People's Court* video. These exercises may be used to illustrate legal concepts studied in the text and to gauge the students' ability to summarize facts presented in a case. Also included in the *Study Guide* are student activities designed to encourage competence in legal vocabulary and legal principles as well as to provide practice in solving case problems through the application of legal principles and the use of reasoning and judgment. Answers to all *Study Guide* exercises are provided in the back of the book.

Helping to meld these teaching and learning resources into a coherent and effective instructional system is the *Instructor's Manual.* New to this edition are classroom suggestions provided for teaching each chapter in the text and the answers to all *Cases From the People's Court* exercises. Also included are suggested syllabi for teaching the program, keys to all review and discussion questions and cases in the text, and answers to all chapter tests.

Acknowledgments

We wish to gratefully acknowledge the contributions of the following reviewers, without whose considerable efforts, suggestions, ideas, and insights the Seventh Edition would not be the program it is.

Marlene E. Barkin, Ithaca College, Ithaca, New York

Brian J. Beck, Harding Business College, Youngstown, Ohio

Roger C. Crowe, State Technical Institute at Knoxville, Knoxville, Tennessee

Era Boone Ferguson, Sullivan Jr. College, Louisville, Kentucky

Susan Flashner, Stautzenberger College, Toledo, Ohio

William M. Friedman, Fontbonne College, St. Louis, Missouri

George C. Leef, Northwood Institute, Midland, Michigan

Howard Douglas Morgan, Jr., State Technical Institute at Memphis, Memphis, Tennessee

William G. Ott, Goldey Beacom College, Wilmington, Delaware

Bettye T. Spence, Columbus Area Technical College, Columbus, Georgia

Brenda J. Schwamberger, Assistant Auditor for the State of Ohio, Mansfield, Ohio

Gloria B. Walker, Fayetteville Technical Institute, Fayetteville, North Carolina

Donald A. Wiesner, University of Miami, Florida

Gordon W. Brown
Edward E. Byers
Mary Ann Lawlor

About the Authors

Gordon W. Brown is a professor with over 20 years of experience teaching business law, real estate law, and legal terminology at North Shore Community College in Beverly, Massachusetts, where he has served as Business Division chairman. He is a coauthor of *Understanding Business and Personal Law,* and contributes articles to *Business Education World.* In addition, he is a speaker at workshops and conferences on methods of law instruction. Mr. Brown is a practicing attorney and a member of the Massachusetts Bar.

Edward E. Byers, now retired, served as editorial director and editor in chief of business management and supervision publications in the Gregg Division of the McGraw-Hill Book Company. In his many years with the company, Dr. Byers authored books in the areas of general and specialized secretarial procedures as well as medical secretarial reference works. He also taught at both the high school and the college levels and served as an academic dean at a business college.

Mary Ann Lawlor is chairman and chief executive officer of the Drake Business Schools Corporation, which operates four postsecondary career schools in New York City. Ms. Lawlor has served as chairman of the board of the Association of Independent Colleges and Schools (AICS) and is a recipient of the association's Distinguished Service Award. She is a trustee of St. John's University and earned her J.D. from the Fordham University School of Law. A practicing attorney, Ms. Lawlor is a member of the New York Bar and is also admitted to practice in Connecticut.

Contributing Author

Paul A. Sukys is a professor of law and legal studies at North Central Technical College in Mansfield, Ohio, and an adjunct professor at Cuyahoga Community College in Cleveland. He is also a coauthor of *Understanding Business and Personal Law.* Mr. Sukys received his law degree from Cleveland State University. He is a member of the Ohio Bar.

PART 1
Law and the Judicial System

CHAPTER 1
Objectives and Sources of the Law

OUTLINE

COMMENTARY

If a nuclear war were to destroy civilization as we know it and only one person were left alive, this person would be free to act without external restraint. Perhaps our mythical survivor would choose to speed down the street at 100 miles per hour or to drive on the wrong side of the road or even on the sidewalk. Since no one could be injured or even inconvenienced, there would be no reason to refrain from that behavior, unwise as it might seem. However, as soon as another person appeared, each survivor would have to restrict certain activities in order to respect the other person's rights. The two survivors would have to sit down and map out rules governing their conduct. They would have to decide what types of activities would be prohibited as a means of protecting themselves and preserving harmony. They might also establish guidelines for settling disputes between themselves. Our survivors would, in effect, be *making law*. In our society, the details are more complex, but the process of lawmaking is basically the same. In this chapter we'll see what the law is and where it originates.

OBJECTIVES

1. Defend the view that sees our legal system as a balancing act between order and justice.
2. Outline the content of the various parts of the U.S. Constitution.
3. State the principle of constitutional supremacy and explain the relationship between federal and state law.
4. Defend the need to set up a system of uniform state laws.
5. Trace the development of common law as a method of settling legal disputes.
6. Describe how the principle of *stare decisis* serves as an instrument of stability in our legal system.
7. Explain statutory interpretation and distinguish it from judicial review.
8. Identify the elements of a case citation and explain how lawyers determine whether a case has been cited by other courts.
9. Account for the legislature's need to establish administrative agencies.
10. Outline the objectives of the Administrative Procedures Act.

1-1 OBJECTIVES OF THE LAW

The law is a set of rules created by the governing body of a society to ensure the orderly maintenance of that society. Ideally, the two primary objectives of the law are to promote justice and harmony. In everyday life, this balance is not always easy to maintain. Often justice is sacrificed for order. Sometimes, the opposite is true.

Swann sued the Charlotte-Mecklenburg Board of Education, charging that the board maintained a segregated school system. Such deliberate segregation had been outlawed by the United States Supreme Court 17 years before Swann's lawsuit. Since the school board had not created a satisfactory desegregation plan, the trial court set up its own plan. Part of the plan provided that elementary school children would have to be bused across the county. On appeal, the school board argued that the court-ordered busing would cause disorder in the school system and hardship for the students. Nevertheless, the U.S. Supreme Court upheld the plan. The Supreme Court ruled that for years the school system had been unfair to black students because it had separated them from the mainstream and given them an inferior education. Now this injustice would have to be corrected, despite the disorder that would result from the busing.

The law is often a balancing act. One person's rights are enforced while another's are not. One group is allowed to act, which restrains the freedom of another group. One company's contract rights are upheld at the expense of another's. Balancing like this occurs frequently. Generally, the two objectives of harmony and justice are kept in mind as such decisions are made.

Because the law is made by people, it is not perfect. Legislators and judges bring their own personal prejudices and biases into the process. Nevertheless, most of them try to apply the law as objectively as possible. Imperfect as it may be, the law is still better than letting individuals settle their own disputes in a haphazard or in a violent or coercive manner. Thus, it is safe to say that we live in a *law-centered society.*

1-2 CONSTITUTIONAL LAW

The **law** has been defined as rules created by the governing body of a society. This definition sounds adequate but is somewhat limited. It does not explain where this governing body comes from or who gives it the power to make those rules. The governing body of a society is established by its constitution. A **constitution** is the basic law of a nation or state. The U.S. Constitution provides the organization of the federal government. Each state also has a constitution that sets up the state's governmental structure. That body of law which involves a constitution and its interpretation is known as **constitutional law.**

The U.S. Constitution

The Constitution of the United States was written by the Founding Fathers in the summer of 1787 at a Constitutional Convention held in Philadelphia. The purpose of the convention was to revise the nation's first constitution, the Articles of Confederation. However, the Articles were so weak that the delegates decided, instead, to come up with a brand new constitution. This new constitution is still in effect today. Basically, the U.S. Constitution is divided into two parts: the articles and the amendments. The articles establish the organization of the federal government. The amendments change provisions in the original articles and add ideas that the Founding Fathers did not include in those articles.

U.S. Const., Articles I–VII (see pp. 599–608)

The Articles The first three articles of the U.S. Constitution distribute power among the legislative, executive, and judicial branches of the federal (national) government. Article I establishes Congress as the legislative (statute making) branch of the government. Article II gives executive power to the President, and Article III gives judicial power to the Supreme Court and other courts set up by Congress. Article IV explains the relationships among the states, while Article V outlines methods for amending the Constitution. Article VI establishes the U.S. Constitution, federal laws, and federal treaties as the supreme law of the land. Finally, Article VII outlines how the original 13 states would go about approving the new Constitution (see Table 1-1).

The Amendments The U.S. Constitution may be changed by amendment. Amendments can be proposed in one of two ways. One method requires a two-thirds vote by both the House and the Senate. The second method requires a national convention called by Congress. The Constitution also provides two techniques for approving amendments. Approval can be made by either three-fourths of the state legislatures or by three-fourths of special state conventions.

Table 1-1 ARTICLES OF THE U.S. CONSTITUTION

Articles	*Content*
Article I	Establishes the legislative branch of the federal government (the Congress) Defines the duties and powers of each House Outlines how Congress must conduct its business Lists legislative powers granted to Congress Lists powers denied to Congress Lists powers denied to the states
Article II	Gives executive power and responsibilities to the President Outlines President's term of office, qualifications, and manner of election Identifies President as Commander-in-Chief Gives President power to make treaties
Article III	Establishes the Supreme Court and authorizes the establishment of other federal courts Provides for trial by jury for crimes. Defines treason against the United States.
Article IV	Defines interstate relations Sets up the full faith and credit clause obligating each state to recognize the public acts and proceedings of other states Provides for extradition of those accused of crimes in other states
Article V	Outlines the methods of amending the Constitution
Article VI	Establishes the Constitution, federal laws, and federal treaties as the supreme law of the land
Article VII	Provides for the original ratification of the Constitution

---

In 1971 two-thirds of the House and of the Senate proposed adding an Equal Rights Amendment to the U.S. Constitution. The amendment stated that "equality or rights under the law shall not be denied or abridged by the United States or by any state on account of sex." The next step in the process was to have the amendment approved. Congress elected to have the state legislatures approve the amendment. While many state legislatures voted their approval, the three-fourths mark was never reached. As a result, the amendment was never approved.

The U.S. Constitution has a total of 26 amendments. The first ten make up the Bill of Rights and were added soon after ratification of the Constitution by the 13 original states. Table 1-2 gives a more detailed look at the amendments. For convenience, the table divides the amendments into six categories: The Bill of Rights, pre-Civil War amendments, the Civil War amendments, early twentieth-century amendments, depression era amendments, and modern amendments.

Table 1-2 AMENDMENTS TO THE U.S. CONSTITUTION

The Bill of Rights	*Pre-Civil War Amendments*	*Civil War Amendments*	*Early Twentieth Century Amendments*	*Depression Era Amendments*	*Modern Amendments*
Amendment 1: Freedom of religion, speech, press, assembly	*Amendment 11*: Lawsuits against the states	*Amendment 13*: Slavery is abolished	*Amendment 16*: The income tax is established	*Amendment 20*: Terms of President, Vice President, Senators and Representatives altered	*Amendment 22*: President's terms limited to two
Amendment 2: The right to bear arms and set up a militia	*Amendment 12*:* President and Vice President elected together	*Amendment 14*: Equal protection of the law, due process, citizenship	*Amendment 17*: Senators elected by direct election	*Amendment 21*: Prohibition repealed	*Amendment 23*: Washington, D.C. gets electors
Amendment 3: The quartering of soldiers in homes is prohibited		*Amendment 15*:† Voting rights guaranteed	*Amendment 18*:‡ Prohibition established		*Amendment 24*: Poll taxes outlawed
Amendment 4: Search and seizure by probable cause			*Amendment 19*: Women given right to vote		*Amendment 25*: Disability of the President, vacancies in the Vice Presidency
Amendment 5: Grand juries, double jeopardy, self-incrimination, due process and eminent domain					*Amendment 26*: Vote extended to 18-year-olds
Amendment 6: Procedures allowed in criminal cases					
Amendment 7: Jury trials in common law cases guaranteed					
Amendment 8: Bill rights guaranteed, cruel and unusual punishment prohibited					
Amendment 9: People retain other rights					
Amendment 10: Powers reserved to states					

*Altered somewhat by the 20th Amendment.

†Voting age changed by 26th Amendment.

‡Repealed by 21st Amendment.

State Constitutions

Each state in the union also adopts its own constitution. A state constitution establishes a state's government. It also establishes principles to guide the state government in making state laws and conducting state business. Most state constitutions are patterned after the U.S. Constitution. However, state constitutions tend to be longer and more complex than the U.S. Constitution since they must deal with local as well as statewide matters.

Principle of Supremacy

U.S. Const., Article VI (see p. 604)

A basic principle of constitutional law is that the U.S. Constitution is the supreme law of the land. This principle of **constitutional supremacy** means that all other laws must be in line with Constitutional principles. If a law somehow conflicts with the provisions of the Constitution, that law is said to be unconstitutional.

U.S. Const., Amendment 8 (see p. 605)

> Furman had been sentenced to death under the Georgia state death penalty statute. Furman contested his death sentence by arguing that the statute under which he was condemned to die was administered arbitrarily. This arbitrary enforcement generally meant that poor people and minority members ended up on death row, whereas rich, white criminals received less severe sentences. This basic unfairness violated the U.S. Constitution. The U.S. Supreme Court agreed and ruled that the Georgia death penalty law was unconstitutional. The Georgia law has since been amended and has been held to be constitutional.

State constitutions represent the supreme law in the state. Consequently, all other state laws must be in keeping with the state constitution.

1-3 STATUTORY LAW

U.S. Const., Articles I & II (see pp. 599–603)

The laws passed by a legislature are known as **statutes.** At the federal level, these are the laws passed by Congress and signed by the President. They include, among others, tax laws, labor laws, product safety laws, and civil rights laws. At the state level, statutes are enacted by state legislatures such as the Ohio General Assembly or the Oregon Legislative Assembly. Broadly interpreted, the term statute also includes the ordinances and resolutions of the subdivisions of the states such as cities, towns, and villages. That body of law which includes statutes, ordinances, and resolutions along with their interpretation is known as **statutory law.** All forms of statutory law must conform to the U.S. Constitution. However, statutes can be used to change the effect of court decisions.

Statutory Organization

Statutes must be arranged, cataloged, and indexed for easy reference. This is done by compiling state and federal codes. A **code** is a compilation of all the statutes of a particular state or of the federal government. Generally, codes are subdivided into **titles,** which are groupings of statutes that deal with a particular area of the law.

Uniform Law

Because many different statutes are passed each year by the Congress and by the 50 separate state legislative bodies, there are important differences in state statutory law throughout the nation. This lack of similarity does not present a problem when the parties to a dispute live in the same state. However, when a buyer from state A does business with a seller in state B, a problem can arise if the statutory law in state A differs from the statutory law in state B. This problem has been addressed by the National Conference of Commissioners on Uniform State Laws.

The National Conference of Commissioners One solution to the problem of inconsistent state statutory law is for the legislatures of all the states to adopt the same statutes affecting business. To this end, a group called the National Conference of Commissioners on Uniform State Laws (NCCUSL) was created in the latter years of the nineteenth century. After proposed uniform acts are created by the NCCUSL, they are recommended to the state legislatures for adoption. The first such act was the Uniform Negotiable Instruments Act which was first proposed in 1896. The most important development in uniform state legislation has been the Uniform Commercial Code.

The Uniform Commercial Code The **Uniform Commercial Code (UCC)** is a unified set of statutes designed to govern almost all commercial transactions. It superseded a number of prior unified acts including the Sales Act, the Negotiable Instruments Act, and the Bills of Lading Act. The basic principles of commercial law were not changed by the UCC provisions. By defining and clarifying often misunderstood business and legal terms, the UCC helps parties construct their contracts. It also provides rules that specify what transactions people can and cannot conduct. All the states, the District of Columbia, and the Virgin Islands have now adopted the UCC (except Louisiana, which has only adopted four articles). For all practical purposes, therefore, the rules governing commercial transactions are the same throughout all the states because of the UCC. Table 1-3 lists the articles and contents of the UCC.

Santavicca moved from San Diego, California, to Portland, Oregon, where he opened a new computer outlet. Before leaving San Diego, he had ordered a series of letterheads, envelopes, business cards, advertising posters, and invoices from Von Striker Printing. The order, which would cost Santavicca $1,749.50, was never placed in writing. Three weeks later when Von Striker attempted to deliver the goods, Santavicca, refused to take them. Santavicca said he was not bound by the contract because it was not in writing. Since both Oregon and California have adopted the Uniform Commercial Code, the law governing this situation would be the same in both states. Both states would rule against Santavicca because the UCC states that orders for specially manufactured goods do not have to be in writing once the seller has made "a substantial beginning of their manufacture or commitments to their procurement."

1-4 COURT DECISIONS

When most people think of the law, they think of the Constitution or of statutes passed by Congress and state legislatures. While these two sources are

Table 1-3 THE UNIFORM COMMERCIAL CODE

Article	*Content*
Article 1: General provisions	Presents purposes and policies of the UCC Purposes are (1) to simplify, clarify, and modernize the law of commercial transactions; (2) to permit the continued expansion of commercial practice; and (3) to make uniform the law among the various states
Article 2: Sales	Supersedes the Uniform Sales Act Unifies rules governing transactions in sale of personal property and goods See Part 3 of this text
Article 3: Commercial paper	Revision of the Uniform Negotiable Instruments Law Deals with form and interpretation of negotiable instruments such as checks and drafts See Part 5 of this text
Article 4: Bank deposits and collections	Classifies many of the rules of the American Bankers Association Code Deals with rules and liabilities relating to bank deposits and collections
Article 5: Letters of credit	A codification of decided cases Applies to credit issued by a bank or a person other than a bank
Article 6: Bulk transfers	Uniform consolidation of bulk sales statutes enacted by the states Deals with rules governing transfer of a major part of a business's inventory not in the ordinary course of business
Article 7: Documents of title	A consolidation and revision of the Uniform Bills of Lading Act and the Warehouse Receipts Act Sets down rules governing the negotiation of documents of title
Article 8: Investment securities	A revision of the Uniform Negotiable Instruments Law and the Uniform Stock Transfer Act Presents rules affecting issue/issuer of, purchase of, and registration of securities (stocks)
Article 9: Secured transactions	A codification of various statutes dealing with security interests in personal property See Chapter 30 of this text
Articles 10 and 11	Present effective date of UCC/lists inconsistent statutes

important, they are not the only part of the government that creates law. The courts also make law. Courts make law through common law, through the interpretation of statutes, and through judicial review.

Common Law The term **common law** comes from the attempts made by early English kings to eliminate confusion in the courts by establishing a body of law that all the courts in the kingdom would hold in common. At that time judges were sent out to the towns and villages of the kingdom with instructions to settle all disputes in as consistent a manner as possible. The judges maintained consistency by relying on previous legal decisions whenever they faced a similar set of circumstances. In this way they began to establish a common law throughout England.

As the process continued, more and more decisions became part of the tradition. Judges began to write down decisions and compare notes on a yearly basis. They would then take this record of previous decisions with them on subsequent trips throughout their assigned territory. Each time they faced a dispute, they would look for an established case that was similar and render a decision based on that past case. This body of recorded legal decisions became known as common law. The process of relying on past decisions is known as *stare decisis*. The past decisions themselves are called precedents.

Stare Decisis Although today's judges do not ride around on horseback in the outer provinces, they do make decisions in the same way their ancient predecessors did, according to the principle of *stare decisis*. The principle of ***stare decisis*** ("let the decision stand") allows a court to rely on the rules of law applied in previous decisions when deciding a similar case. *Stare decisis* serves as an instrument of stability in the legal system. It helps ensure consistency by its reliance on long-accepted legal principles and well-established rules.

Precedent A model case that a court can follow when facing a similar situation is known as a **precedent.** There are two types of precedent, binding precedent and persuasive precedent. **Binding precedent** is a previous case that a particular court must follow. **Persuasive precedent** is a case that a court is free to follow or ignore. Generally, whether a given precedent is binding or persuasive is determined by a court's location. For example, decisions made by the Supreme Court of Ohio would be binding on all state courts in Ohio but would be persuasive for courts in all other states. U.S. Supreme Court decisions are binding, of course, on all federal and state courts.

Zuern published a weekly newspaper, named the *Indianapolis Reporter*. The paper was a highly controversial investigative vehicle for radical writers. After several hard-hitting stories that exposed government corruption, the city law director asked a state judge to issue a court order shutting down the paper. The judge issued the order under an Indiana statute allowing judges to close newspapers considered a "public nuisance." Zuern's attorney looked to records of the U.S. Supreme Court to see if it had faced any similar situations in any previous cases. She located a case called *Near v. Minnesota* in which the U.S. Supreme Court had labeled a similar Minnesota statute as unconstitutional. *Near v. Minnesota* is a binding precedent which the Indiana state court must follow. When Zuern's attorney presented this case to the state appellate court, it reversed the trial court's order closing the newspaper.

Statutory Interpretation

A second way that court decisions operate to make law is in the interpretation of statutory law. When legislators enact a statute, they cannot predict how people will react to the new law. They also cannot foresee all the ramifications and implications of that statute. Thus, when two parties read a statute, they may have different notions as to what is meant by that new law. Also, legislators often leave gaps in the language of statutes. These gaps must be filled by someone. The job of reacting to unforeseen circumstances and filling in the gaps falls to the courts. As a result, a judge may be called upon to determine how a certain statute should be interpreted.

Copley decided to plead not guilty by reason of insanity when he was charged with the murder of his neighbor. The state statute which set up the insanity defense did not define "insanity." Copley said insanity meant that he should be found not guilty if his crime resulted from any kind of mental disturbance. The court disagreed, ruling that Copley should be found not guilty only if he had a mental disease that rendered him incapable of knowing the difference between right and wrong when he committed the crime.

In this case the court had to interpret what the legislature meant by insanity by providing the definition that the legislators had left out of the statute. Courts, however, are not free to interpret statutes at random. A court cannot interpret a statute unless it is faced with a case involving that statute. In interpreting statutes, courts look to a variety of sources. These sources include the legislative history of the statute, any other court ruling on the statute, and the old statute that the new statute replaced. A specialized form of statutory interpretation is known as judicial review.

Judicial Review

U.S. Const., Article VI **(see p. 604)**

A third way that courts make law is through judicial review. **Judicial review** is the process of determining the constitutionality of various legislative statutes, administrative regulations, or executive activities. In exercising the power of judicial review, a court will look at the statute, regulation, or activity and compare it to the Constitution. If the two are compatible, no problem exists. If they are contradictory, one of the two must be declared void. Since the Constitution is the supreme law of the land, the Constitution always rules, and the statute, regulation, or activity is declared void or unconstitutional.

Court Decisions and Legal Research

Court decisions are put in writing so that lawyers and judges can refer to them in preparing or hearing a lawsuit. Once written down, these decisions, also known as cases, are published in books called reporters. A case is identified by a **citation,** which consists of the names of the parties followed by the volume number, the name of the reporter, and the beginning page number of the case.

Darling broke his leg playing college football. He was treated by a physician who was a general practitioner. The physician made several serious errors which led to the eventual amputation of Darling's leg. Darling sued the hospital. The final court to rule on the case was the Supreme Court of Illinois. In *Darling v. Charleston Community Memorial Hospital,* 211 N.E.2d 253, the court held that the hospital had been negligent in not reviewing the physician's work and in not requiring the physician to consult with other doctors more experienced in the field.

Darling brought this suit in the state courts of Illinois. As the abbreviation after the case name above states, the case is reported in volume 211 of the *Northeastern Reporter, Second Series*, on page 253.

Analysis of Subsequent Cases Attorneys getting ready for trial must research related cases to strengthen their position. Some cases are followed in later court decisions; others are discussed and disregarded; still others are overruled by a higher-level court or by the same court that made the decisions in the first place. To determine whether a case is cited in a later case, attorneys use a set of books called *Shepard's Citations,* published by Shepard's/McGraw-Hill, Inc. Each book is called a **citator,** and together they show every instance in which a case has been referred to by any state or federal court decision.

The Shepardizing Process Using this method of legal research is referred to by lawyers as **shepardizing** a case. After compiling the list of citations, a legal researcher would locate and read the cases indicated. After locating these later cases, the researcher would find out what the court had to say about the original case being researched. Because much law is based on previous decisions, shepardizing is an essential step in preparing a case for court (see Figure 1-1).

1-5 ADMINISTRATIVE LAW

Neither legislators nor judges can deal with all aspects of today's society. Moreover, legislators are generalists. They know a little about a lot, but are rarely, if ever, experts in all areas under their power. Since legislators are generalists and since today's problems are so complex, statutory law, created by legislators, is very limited in what it can do. To broaden the power of statutory law, legislators delegate their power to others. They do this when they create administrative agencies.

Administrative Agencies

Federal administrative agencies administer statutes enacted by Congress in specific areas including commerce, communication, aviation, social security, labor relations, and so on. For example, the Interstate Commerce Commission (ICC) regulates truck and railroad transportation between the states while the Securities and Exchange Commission (SEC) regulates the sale of stocks and bonds. Similar agencies have been designated by the states to supervise and regulate internal state activities. These agencies create rules, regulate and supervise, and render decisions that have the force of law. Their decrees and decisions—the whole body of law that they generate—are known as **administrative law.**

Vol. 211 NORTHEASTERN REPORTER, 2d SERIES

Reprinted here is a page from Shepard's *Northeastern Reporter, 2nd Series, Citations*. In this chapter, *Darling v. Charleston Community Memorial Hospital*, 211 N.E.2d 253, is mentioned as a citation example. To locate other cases citing *Darling*, an attorney would open Shepard's *Northeastern Reporter, 2d Series Citations* at Volume 211 (shown at the top of the page) and find page 253 (in bold type near the bottom of the page). The attorney would find that all of the cases that are shaded in color cite the *Darling* case.

(33 I112d 326) Parenthesis indicate this is a "parallel cite." A parallel cite indicates where the case was originally reported in the official Illinois reporter.

(14 AL[3] 860) This indicates that the case was the subject of a report in American Law Reports 3d, a legal encyclopedia.

US cert den in 383 US 946. This citation indicates that one of the litigants asked the U.S. Supreme Court to hear the case. However, the Supreme Court declined to file a writ of certiorari. (See Chapter 2)

s 200 NE2 149. The small "s" means that this is the same case but at a lower level in the court system. This probably refers to the case as it decided by an intermediate state appellate court. (See Chapter 2)

215 NE2[9] 256. The raised number refers to the paragraph in the case that is cited.

d 218 NE2[2] 866. The "d" means that the case found at 218 N.E.2d 866 is distinguished, or different, either in law or in fact from *Darling*.

f 236 NE2[1] 138. The "f" means that the *Darling* case was followed by the court in the case found at 236 NE2d138.

250 NE2[4] 896. This is an Ohio case.

495 P2d 540. This is an Arizona case.

58 CaR 140. This is a California case.

– 99 –
(4M43)
273NE[3]156
303NE[1]480
303NE[3]480

– 130 –
(63IIA128)
295NE[1]731
73A2439s
85A21150s

– 134 –
(63IIA117)
a229NE504
292NE[5]556

– 139 –
(63IIA178)
256NE[3]144

– 141 –
(64IIA165)
222NE[2]345
251NE[1]731

– 144 –
(62IIA414)
221NE333
267NE[1]361

– 147 –
(63IIA19)
287NE[2]348
297NE[3]804
301NE[2]203
304NE[8]807
8A21248n

– 162 –
(247Ind39)
212NE[1]392
215NE[1]61
217NE[1]597
248NE[1]411
250NE[1]609
250NE[2]609
251NE[1]684
251NE[2]684
261NE[1]877
24A21127s

– 164 –
(247Ind51)
s207NE220
230NE[8]415
238NE493
267NE[8]395
290NE[1]755
290NE[2]757
290NE[3]757
290NE[4]757

296NE[1]908
15A21270s
283NE886

– 186 –
(247Ind126)
239NE[9]579
j239NE[8]584

– 193 –
(138InA554)
s209NE909

– 194 –
(138InA7)
228NE[3]436
79A2890s
2A312s

– 197 –
(140InA255)
s210NE378
256NE599

– 198 –
(40S13)
US cert den
in383US918
in383US951
s258NE258
213NE[2]181

j213NE[1]182
f214NE[2]230
216NE[1]453
217NE[1]776
218NE[1]121
221NE[1]221
237NE[1]57
241NE[1]850
246NE[1]809

– 226 –
(349Mas585)
260NE[1]152
269NE[2]681

– 228 –
(349Mas593)
256NE[2]310
Ill
264NE[5]220
NH
276A2d258

– 230 –
(349Mas589)
e216NE[1]439

– 231 –
(349Mas590)
440F2d[1]220
64A28s

– 233 –
(33Il2d301)

– 247 –
(33Il2d316)
s199NE265
f213NE[3]134
f213NE[4]134
f217NE[2]556
218NE[2]36
j218NE[7]38
219NE[2]395
e221NE[2]103
e221NE[8]104
221NE[3]635
223NE[1]443
225NE[2]72
226NE[2]639
227NE[2]106
228NE[3]109
228NE[2]110
228NE[1]112
230NE[9]59
232NE[2]47
d232NE[2]545
232NE[4]545
234NE581
f235NE[1]332
f235NE[2]332
f235NE[3]332
f235NE[4]335

236NE[1]726
j236NE[6]728
d243NE[2]321
d243NE[8]321
245NE[2]624
f250NE[2]836
f256NE[1]130
f256NE[2]130
f256NE[6]134
264NE[2]250
265NE[2]137
266NE[2]130
266NE[3]178
267NE[4]24
j267NE[2]25
j267NE[3]25
268NE[2]906
268NE[3]906
272NE[2]863
274NE[3]191
275NE[4]910
275NE[5]910
282NE[3]725
j282NE[3]727
j282NE[4]727
285NE[1]540
287NE[8]693
288NE[5]643
289NE[1]17
289NE[2]17
289NE[3]18
e290NE[2]24
e290NE[3]24
290NE[3]335
295NE[8]50
296NE323
297NE[2]723
297NE[4]723
j297NE[2]739
298NE[2]333
300NE[2]5
j300NE[4]9
300NE[3]516
302NE[3]56
302NE67
302NE[6]648
305NE[5]710
419F2d[7]1032
431F2d[2]828
452F2d[2]183
343FS[6]1272
Alk
445P2d935
64A21296s

– 253 –
(33Il2d326)
(14A3860)
US cert den
in383US946
s200NE149
215NE[9]256
d218NE[2]866
d222NE[6]238
222NE[17]707
223NE[1]269
232NE[1]544
232NE[16]779
235NE[1]334
235NE[15]674
f236NE[1]138
f236NE[2]138
237NE[1]765
241NE[1]223
243NE[1]564
246NE[6]904
249NE[3]736
250NE[2]838
f251NE[10]735
254NE[10]437
257NE[2]226
257NE[4]241
257NE[7]241
257NE[8]242
261NE[1]745
266NE[10]902
266NE[8]904
268NE[2]566
271NE[10]55
f273NE686
273NE810
f273NE[2]813
j273NE[6]813
274NE[2]517
h283NE[1]91
283NE[6]515
289NE[1]232
f290NE[2]26
290NE335
d299NE[4]328
299NE390
301NE492
f302NE[2]264
303NE[4]397
407F2d[8]1040
411F2d[10]904
Ohio
250NE[4]896
Ariz
495P2d497
500P2d1157
Calif
58CaR140
426P2d540
Colo
419P2d314
Haw
497P2d573
Idaho
421P2d747
Iowa
173NW884
175NW596
Mich
200NW203
200NW214
Mo
476SW484
Mont
498P2d141
Nebr
141NW855
Nev
495P2d608
495P2d610
NJ
260A2d528
262A2d436
278A2d203
NC
152SE495
Wis
206NW401
25A229s
60A277s
66A21334s
66A21382s
10A31386n
10A31423n
14A328n
35A31074n
36A3451n
38A3498n
38A3508n

– 261 –
(33Il2d357)
US cert den
in385US854
d215NE155
222NE[4]21
d227NE[2]163
227NE[2]523
229NE[4]927
f244NE[1]844
246NE[2]31
248NE[2]334
249NE[1]170
253NE[1]558
263NE[1]608
263NE[4]713
270NE[1]108
271NE[2]101
e274NE[1]924
275NE[2]396
14A3772n

– 265 –
(33Il2d246)
s220NE639
213NE[1]292
d233NE375
254NE[1]477
272NE[1]14
281NE[1]677
281NE[1]874

– 266 –
(33Il2d248)
268NE[3]225

– 269 –
(33Il2d252)
(14A3887)
219NE[4]523
245NE[1]606
245NE[4]606
245NE[5]606
245NE[6]606
Kan
453P2d86
453P2d88
35A2355s
77A21216s

– 273 –
(33Il2d264)
235NE[2]613
Tenn
412SW642

– 276 –
(33Il2d268)
230NE[1]265
d231NE[2]596
305NE[2]534
Mo
481SW553

– 279 –
(33Il2d274)
US cert den
in383US912
226NE[2]853
226NE[2]862
230NE[2]199
230NE[2]219
268NE[2]34

1320 •Illinois Appellate Court Cases when Certiorari or Appeal Denied or Dismissed

Figure 1-1

Administrative Procedures Act Problems sometimes come up because the people who run the agencies make the rules, enforce the rules, and judge those who break the rules. To help prevent any conflict of interest that could arise from these overlapping responsibilities, Congress passed the federal Administrative Procedures Act. Similarly, most states have adopted a uniform law known as the Model State Administrative Procedures Act. Under these acts, an agency planning a new regulation must notify those affected and hold hearings at which those people can express their views. These acts also allow the courts to review what agencies do.

SUMMARY

1-1. The law is a set of rules created by the government of a society to ensure that the society runs in an orderly manner. Sometimes the law must balance the objectives of justice and harmony. Most legislators and judges try to apply the law as objectively as possible to guarantee that we remain a law-centered society.

1-2. A constitution is the basic law of a nation or state. The U.S. Constitution establishes the organization of the federal government. Each state in the union also has its own constitution that sets up the state's government. The U.S. Constitution is the supreme law of the land. This means that all other laws must be in line with constitutional principles.

1-3. Laws passed by a legislature are known as statutes. At the federal level, they include laws passed by Congress and signed by the President. At the state level, statutes are enacted by state legislatures. Statutes are compiled into codes. The National Conference of Commissioners on Uniform State Laws was created to develop uniform laws that all states could adopt to diminish inconsistencies from state to state. One major achievement of the National Conference of Commissioners is the Uniform Commercial Code, a unified set of statutes designed to govern almost all commercial transactions.

1-4. Courts make law through common law, the interpretation of state statutes, and through judicial review. The common law tradition goes back to the attempts by early English kings to establish a body of law that all courts in the kingdom would hold in common. The principle of *stare decisis* allows a court to rely on the rules of law applied in previous decisions when deciding a similar case. These previous decisions or past cases are known as precedent. Courts also make law by interpreting statutes passed by the legislature and by judicial review, that is, determining the constitutionality of legislative statutes and executive actions.

1-5. To broaden the power of statutory law, legislators delegate their power to others. They do this when they create administrative agencies. The decrees, decisions, and rules made by administrative agencies comprise what is known as administrative law. Activities of federal agencies are monitored by the Administrative Procedures Act. Most states have adopted a uniform law known as the Model State Administrative Procedures Act which governs state agencies.

Understanding Key Legal Terms

administrative law (p. 11)
binding precedent (p. 9)
citation (p. 10)
citator (p. 11)
code (p. 6)
common law (p. 9)
constitution (p. 3)
constitutional law (p. 3)
constitutional supremacy (p. 6)
judicial review (p. 10)
law (p. 3)
persuasive precedent (p. 9)
precedent (p. 9)
shepardizing (p. 11)
stare decisis (p. 9)
statute (p. 6)
statutory law (p. 6)
titles (p. 6)
Uniform Commercial Code (UCC) (p. 7)

Questions for Review and Discussion

1. Explain the relationship between order and justice, and point out why they are not always necessarily compatible.
2. Briefly outline the content of the first three articles of the U.S. Constitution. Identify six categories of amendments to the U.S. Constitution.
3. What is the principle of constitutional supremacy, and what effect does this principle have on other laws?
4. Why was the National Conference of Commissioners on Uniform State Laws founded, and what is its purpose?
5. Discuss the origin of common law as a method for making legal decisions.
6. Distinguish between *stare decisis* and precedent.
7. How does statutory interpretation differ from judicial review?
8. Identify the elements in the following case citation, and note how a lawyer could find out if this case has been cited by other courts. The case citation is 472 N.E.2d 1046.
9. Defend the need for the administrative agencies created by Congress and by various state legislatures.
10. Explain how the Administrative Procedures Act helps prevent conflicts of interest within administrative agencies.

Analyzing Cases

1. Fitzgerald went to his physician for a routine examination. The doctor discovered that Fitzgerald's vision was failing. To prevent further problems, Fitzgerald would have to have special lighting installed in his office at work. He would also have to change his work schedule so that he would not have to drive after dark. When Fitzgerald told his employers about the changes, they fired him claiming that the alterations in his office and in his work schedule would cause too much disorder at work. Angered by this mistreatment, Fitzgerald sued his employers. He argued that a federal statute, the Rehabilitation Act of 1973, says that employers must try to meet the individual needs of workers who are handicapped even if these changes cause some inconvenience and disorder. Which of the two primary objectives of the law does this statute address? Which objective does it hurt? In your opinion, how should the judge decide this case? Explain your reasons.

2. Hardy was treated for an ear problem by Dr. Ver Meulen. Ten years later Hardy began to have ear trouble again. Examinations indicated that the new problem had been caused by Dr. Ver Meulen's treatment, which had been poorly done. Hardy sued Ver Meulen. The doctor tried to stop the lawsuit by arguing that Hardy had not sued him within the 4-year limit set up by state statute. Hardy argued that the statute which set up the 4-year limit conflicted with the state's constitution. He said this because the state constitution guaranteed that anyone injured by another person can bring a lawsuit. Assuming that Hardy is correct, will the court allow him to sue Ver Meulen even though the statute says that he can't? Explain. *Hardy v. Ver Meulen,* 512 N.E.2d 626 (Ohio).

3. Koepke and Wood invested some money in the Continental Longview Motor Inn. Under a Texas statute, investors like Koepke and Wood could not be sued by people who have a case against the business if the investors fill out the appropriate paperwork with the Texas secretary of state. Unfortunately, Koepke and Wood failed to file their paperwork. When Continental got into financial trouble, Koepke and Wood were sued by Garrett. Koepke and Wood argued that the only purpose of the statute is to use the paperwork to notify people that they are only investors and cannot be sued. Since Garrett already knew they were only investors, Koepke and Wood said their failure to finish the paperwork didn't matter. Since the statute fails to mention this issue, can the court intervene and try to figure out what the legislature meant? If you were the judge, what sources of information would you look at to figure out if the legislature would agree with Koepke and Wood? *Garrett v. Koepke,* 569 S.W.2d 568 (Texas Ct. App.).

4. Jones and Pridemore were injured while working on a VIP Development construction site. They collected their workers' compensation insurance checks and then sued VIP. In court, VIP argued that Jones and Pridemore could either collect the insurance or sue the company, but not both. The court disagreed saying that Jones and Pridemore could collect their insurance and also sue the company. The state legislature did not like the decision of the court. Legislators were worried that too many businesses would be afraid of being sued by their own workers and would, therefore, leave the state. What can the legislators do to fix what they see as a very bad court decision? *Jones v. VIP Development,* 472 N.E.2d 1046 (Ohio Sup.).

5. Station WWWX (3WX), a Washington, D.C., hard rock station, had begun a political editorial campaign that attacked the current administration in Washington. The Federal Communication Commission (FCC), a federal regulatory agency, instituted a new regulation prohibiting such conduct. To prevent opposition, the FCC announced the new regulation on Monday morning, and by Tuesday afternoon had shut down 3WX for violating the new regulation. The management of 3WX claimed that the FCC had overstepped its authority. Are the managers of 3WX correct? Explain.

6. The U.S. Supreme Court has ruled that racial segregation in education is unconstitutional because school children who are segregated cannot be treated equally. After the ruling, the Arkansas state constitution was amended. The amendment ordered the state legislature to oppose all desegregation attempts. The legislature obeyed the state constitution and passed legislation designed to keep schools segregated. The governor of Arkansas also got into the act by ordering the state national guard to stop black students from attending predominantly white schools. Are the state statutes legally binding? Are the governor's actions legally valid? Explain. *Cooper v. Aaron,* 78 S. Ct. 1401 (U.S. Sup. Ct.).

CHAPTER 2
The Judicial Process

OUTLINE

2-1 The Court System
- Court Jurisdiction
- Federal Court System
- State Court Systems

2-2 Alternatives to Litigation
- Compromise
- Mediation
- Arbitration
- Mandatory Arbitration

2-3 Litigation Procedure
- Commencement of the Action
- Service of Process
- The Answer
- Pretrial Stage
- The Trial
- The Appeal
- Execution of the Judgment

COMMENTARY

Court procedure is determined by a set of rules known as procedural law. Procedural law tells people what steps to follow when they are involved in a lawsuit. Substantive law, on the other hand, creates, defines, and regulates the rights and duties of those people as well as every other member of society. Sometimes an understanding of procedural law is even more important than an understanding of substantive law. In one instance, for example, three German freight hauling companies sued an American company in an American court. Once the American company found itself in an American courtroom, it turned around and sued the German companies on another matter. The lawyers for the American company were aware of procedural law and knew that the German case did really not belong in that particular court. When they brought this to the judge's attention, he agreed and threw the German case out of court. However, he allowed the American lawsuit against the Germans to remain. The jury awarded the American company $1.5 million. A misunderstanding of procedural law had cost the German companies a great deal of money. This chapter will explore some general issues in court procedure.

OBJECTIVES

1. Distinguish between original jurisdiction and appellate jurisdiction and between general jurisdiction and special jurisdiction.
2. Outline the structure of the federal court system, and judge whether the federal court in a given situation has jurisdiction over a particular case.
3. Recognize those cases which are likely to be heard by the U.S. Supreme Court.
4. Determine the law that the federal courts will apply when trying a case with parties from different states.

5. Identify the typical structure found in most state court systems.
6. Explain the alternative procedures outside the litigation process for settling disputes.
7. Describe a typical legal process from the filing of the complaint, through pretrial, trial, verdict, and enforcement of the judgment.
8. Contrast the three most commonly used discovery tools: deposition, interrogatories, and requests for real evidence.
9. Explain how the procedures of an appellate court differ from the procedures of a trial court.
10. Indicate why a court may need to issue a writ of execution.

2-1 THE COURT SYSTEM

The laws of our government are interpreted and enforced by a system of courts established by legislative authority. **Courts** are judicial tribunals that meet in a regular place and apply laws in an attempt to settle disputes fairly. Each of these official bodies is a forum for the party who presents a complaint, the party who answers the complaint, and the jury and/or judge who settles the dispute.

Court Jurisdiction

The authority of a court to hear and decide cases is called the court's **jurisdiction.** It is fixed by law and is limited as to territory and type of case. A court of **original jurisdiction** has authority to hear a case when it is first brought to court. Courts having power to review a case for errors are courts of **appellate jurisdiction.** Courts that have the power to hear any type of case are said to exercise **general jurisdiction.** Those with power to decide only certain kinds of cases have **special jurisdiction.** Examples of courts with special jurisdiction are juvenile courts and bankruptcy courts.

Federal Court System

U. S. Const., Article III **(see p. 603)**

The federal court system is authorized by Article III of the U.S. Constitution which states, "The Judicial Power of the United States, shall be vested in one supreme Court, and in such inferior Courts as the Congress may from time to time ordain and establish." The present system of federal courts includes the Supreme Court of the United States, the courts of appeals, and the U.S. district courts.

U.S. District Courts Each state and territory in the United States has at least one U.S. district court. U.S. district courts are also known as federal district courts. The district courts are the courts of original jurisdiction in the federal system. In general, most federal cases are filed in the district courts. Not all cases, however, belong in federal district court. To qualify for federal district court, a case must involve either federal law or diversity of citizenship.

Federal district courts have original jurisdiction over cases involving federal law. In this context, federal law includes the U.S. Constitution, federal statutes, and U.S. treaties. A state law issue can be included in a suit involving federal law if the state claim involves the same situation that created the federal law violation. If the federal claim is thrown out by the federal court, the state law issue usually cannot stand by itself. The people bringing the state law claim would have to take that claim to state court.

When the United States Football League (USFL) sued the National Football League (NFL), the suit was brought in a federal district court in New York City. The federal court had jurisdiction over the case because the USFL claimed that the NFL had violated a federal law, the Sherman Anti-Trust Act. The USFL was also allowed to bring several state law claims in the same case because the state claims involved the same situation that gave rise to the federal law violations.

Federal district courts can also hear cases that involve diversity of citizenship even when no federal law claims are present. **Diversity cases** include lawsuits that are between citizens of different states, between citizens of a state and a foreign government as plaintiff, or between citizens of a state or of different states and citizens of a foreign nation. For legal purposes, corporations are considered citizens of the state where they were formed and the state where they are headquartered. Diversity cases must involve an amount over $10,000.

In the commentary at the beginning of this chapter, three German corporations sued an American corporation in federal court even though no federal law was violated. The German firms were considered citizens of a foreign country. The American firm was a citizen of Texas and, therefore, a citizen of the United States. Since the amount they were fighting over was more than $10,000, the federal district court had jurisdiction.

U.S. Courts of Appeals Presently, 13 U.S. courts of appeals exist within the federal court system (see Figure 2-1). Eleven of these appellate courts cover geographical groupings of states. For example, the Sixth Circuit Court of Appeals includes Michigan, Ohio, Kentucky, and Tennessee, whereas the Fifth Circuit Court of Appeals includes Texas, Louisiana, and Mississippi. There is also a special appellate court for the District of Columbia called the U.S. Court of Appeals for the District of Columbia.

In addition to these 12 appellate courts, organized on a geographical basis, there is a thirteenth appellate court which has special jurisdiction over certain types of cases. This court is known as the U.S. Court of Appeals for the Federal Circuit. This court hears cases appealed from the Court of International Trade (formerly the U.S. Customs Court), the U.S. Claims Court (formerly the Court of Claims), and the International Trade Commission, among others. This court can also hear certain types of appeals from the U.S. District Courts.

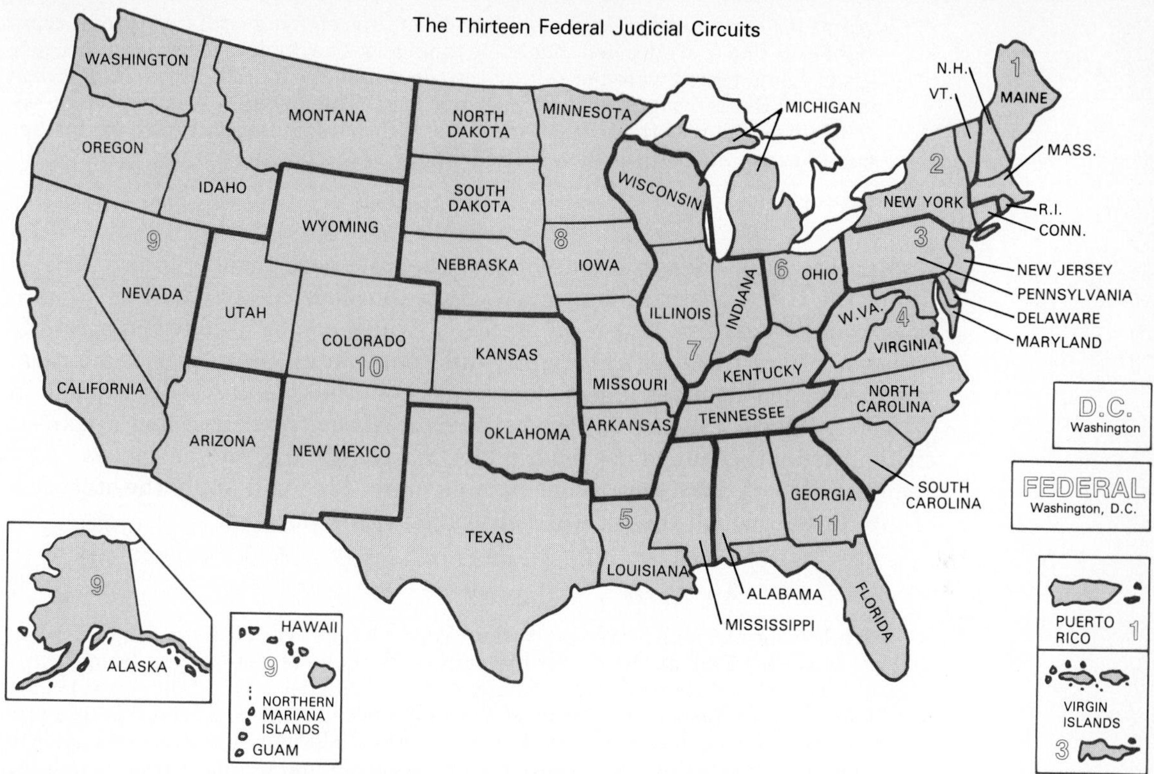

Figure 2-1 The U.S. federal court system is divided into 13 "circuits," including the D.C. and federal circuits. Each circuit has several district courts.

Supreme Court of the United States Established by the Constitution, the U.S. Supreme Court is the court of final jurisdiction in all cases appealed from lower federal courts and in cases coming from state supreme courts. It has original jurisdiction in cases affecting ambassadors or other public ministers and consuls, and in cases in which a state is a party. The Supreme Court is composed of a chief justice and eight associate justices. They are appointed by the President of the United States with the advice and consent of the Senate and hold office during good behavior.

In many situations, a case will reach the U.S. Supreme Court only if the Court agrees to issue a writ of certiorari. A **writ of certiorari** is an order to a lower court to deliver its records to the U.S. Supreme Court for review. The Court will issue a writ of certiorari if the case involves an issue that affects a large segment of society or if the case involves a constitutional issue. The Court will also issue a writ if several of the lower courts have dealt with an issue, but cannot agree on how it should be handled.

The U.S. Supreme Court agreed to hear the case of *Sony Corporation of America v. Universal City Studios, Inc.* because it involved an issue that had an enormous impact on many people. The issue was whether the home taping of television programs for later viewing (a process known as time shifting) violated federal copyright law. The court decided that home taping does not violate federal law, because the at-home tapers were not selling the tapes to make a profit. Since no sale was involved, the copyright holders were not hurt. This decision was important because it put to rest the fears of many VCR owners and encouraged the further manufacture and sale of such VCRs by Sony and other companies.

Applicable Law When a federal court hears a case involving only federal law or the U.S. Constitution, it must follow that federal law, the U.S. Constitution, and/or any line of federal precedent which can be used to interpret the situation. Circumstances are slightly different in a diversity case or a federal law case which includes a state law issue. For example, if a federal judge in Wisconsin hears a diversity case between a Wisconsin citizen and a Kansas citizen, would that judge use federal law, Wisconsin law, or Kansas law? As a general rule, a federal court hearing a diversity case will apply the state law of the state in which the federal court is physically located.

While walking along a railroad track in Pennsylvania, Tompkins was injured when he was struck by an open door protruding from one of the passing freight cars. Tompkins sued the railroad company in federal district court. The federal court had diversity jurisdiction because Tompkins was a citizen of Pennsylvania and the railroad company was formed in New York. Under Pennsylvania common law, Tompkins would have been considered a trespasser and would, therefore, lose the case. Tompkins urged the court to ignore Pennsylvania law and apply what he called "general law." General law included principles of law that are of a universal nature and thus not tied to any one state. The trial court and the appellate court agreed with Tompkins. The U.S. Supreme Court did not. The court held that attempts to enforce this unwritten "general law" were confusing and inconsistent, and thus ruled that federal courts in diversity cases must use state substantive law.

State Court Systems

The courts of each state are organized according to the provisions of the state constitution. Despite differences from state to state, such as the names for similar types of courts, there are basic similarities. For instance, each state has an arrangement of inferior, or lower, courts that serve as limited-jurisdiction trial courts. Higher-level trial courts with broader jurisdiction are also provided. In addition, each state has appellate courts to which questions of law (not questions of fact) may be appealed. (Figure 2-2 gives a general outline of the federal and state court system.)

State Trial Courts The general jurisdiction trial court has the power to hear any type of case. It is often known as the circuit court, the court of common pleas, or the superior court. Most states have other trial courts that are lower than the general jurisdiction courts. These trial courts usually hear only certain types of cases. For instance, courts with jurisdiction limited to a county or a city are often called county courts or municipal courts. Courts may also be

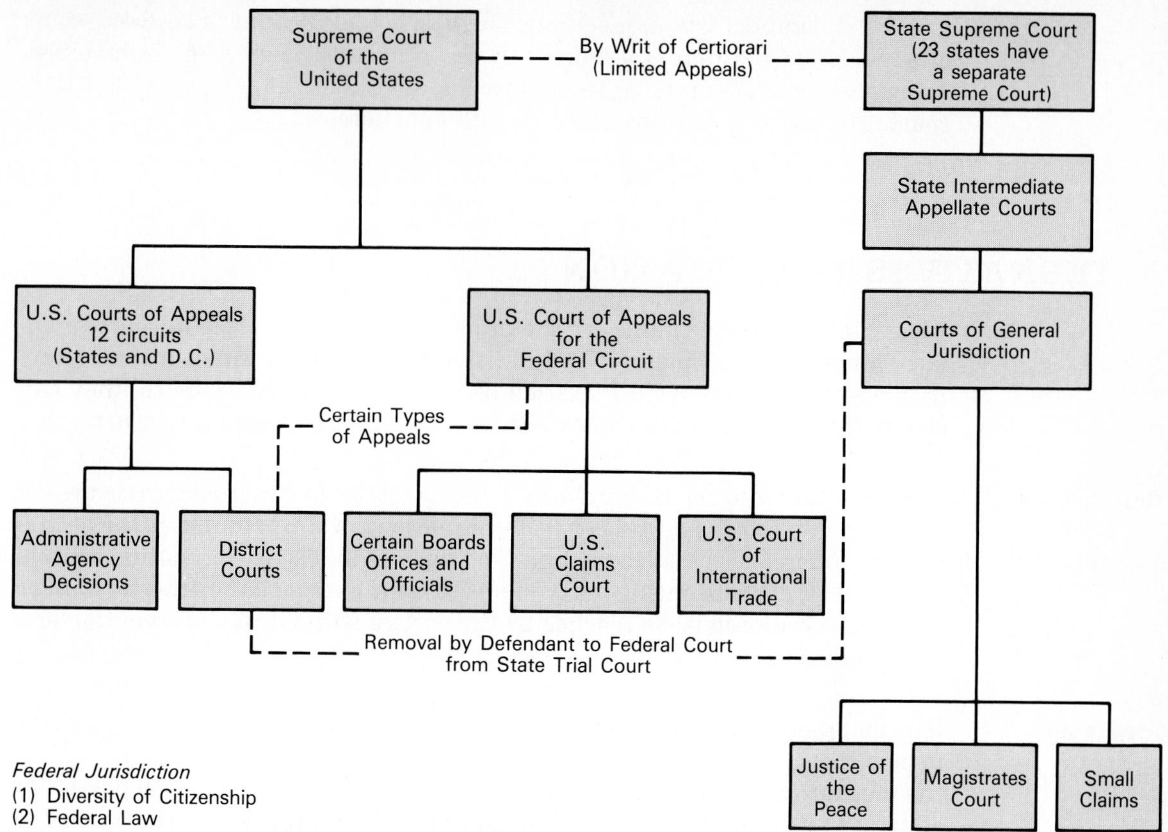

Figure 2-2 Federal and state court systems.

limited to specific subjects. For example, probate courts deal only with wills and estates of deceased persons, whereas family courts or domestic relations handle divorces, family relations, and juveniles. Many localities have small claims courts that hear civil cases involving small dollar amounts ranging from $500 to $5,000 depending on state law.

State Intermediate Appellate Courts State court systems provide for appeals to appellate courts on questions of law that arise during trial court proceedings. A panel of judges, usually three in number, examines the records of proceedings before the trial court, and the lawyers file arguments and make their statements orally before the judges. If the appellate court disagrees on the meaning on the points of the law raised, it may set aside or modify the action of the trial court. It may enter such judgment as it concludes the trial court should have taken, or it may send the case back to the trial court for a new trial.

State Supreme Courts Difficult questions of law may be appealed to the supreme court of the state. Although a person is entitled to one trial and one appeal, another review may be obtained if the supreme court of appeals agrees to review the case. A panel of three to nine judges generally hears the lawyers argue the points of law in question. The decision of the state's supreme court of appeals is final unless a federal issue or constitutional right is involved. Twenty-seven states rely on their state supreme court as their only appellate court. These states have no intermediate appellate courts.

2-2 ALTERNATIVES TO LITIGATION

Litigation is another name for the process of bringing a case to court to enforce a right. The people involved in litigation are called the **litigants.** Many people would like to avoid litigation as much as possible. To do so, they can choose from several ways to settle their dispute without going to court.

Compromise

A compromise solution to simple civil disputes is often a more logical course of action than a costly and time-consuming lawsuit. **Compromise** is the settlement of differences or the adjustment of matters in dispute by mutual concession; that is, each disputing party yields to some extent to the other's claim or demand. A compromise is reached by the parties without the intervention of a third person.

Mediation

If a compromise cannot be reached, the parties sometimes invite a third party to help them find a solution. This is called **mediation.** The third party is called the **mediator.** The job of the mediator is to convince the contending parties to adjust or settle their dispute. The mediator will try to persuade the parties to reach some sort of compromise but cannot decide what the parties will do.

Arbitration

Sometimes the parties invite a third party to settle their dispute. This is known as **arbitration.** The third party is known as an **arbitrator.** The procedures governing arbitration are generally more flexible than those followed in a lawsuit. The rules are either set by law or agreed upon in an arbitration agreement. The hearing may be relaxed, with the arbitrator receiving informal testimony from the parties, or it may be rigidly controlled, with the arbitrator following strict rules of evidence and requiring lengthy explanations.

When the National Football League (NFL) players went on strike, they had many demands that they carried to the bargaining table. The owners of the various professional football teams around the country found that they could not agree with most of those demands. After several weeks of frustrating negotiations, the players asked the owners to submit to arbitration. The owners refused because they did not want an outside third party to have the authority to decide their dispute. Instead, the owners suggested the use of a mediator. The owners were willing to submit to mediation because the mediator would not actively decide the dispute. Instead, the mediator would act as a go-between who would try to persuade the parties to reach a compromise.

Mandatory Arbitration

Some states require arbitration prior to trial in certain cases. Required arbitration is also called **mandatory arbitration.** Some litigants have challenged mandatory arbitration, arguing that it violates their constitutional rights to a jury trial and to equal protection under the law. Most courts have disagreed with these arguments as long as the arbitration does not replace the jury trial and the motives for establishing mandatory arbitration are reasonable.

2-3 LITIGATION PROCEDURE

Although litigation procedures differ from state to state, the following examination of common elements can simplify the task of analyzing the cases presented in this text. Keep in mind that this process involves a civil case, rather than a criminal case. In a criminal case, an individual is accused of committing an offense against the community-at-large. In a civil case, one individual brings suit against another. Figure 2-3 illustrates the steps in the litigation process.

Commencement of the Action

The principal parties to a lawsuit are the **plaintiff** and the **defendant.** The **plaintiff** is the person who begins a legal suit by filing a complaint in a trial court of original jurisdiction. The **defendant** is the person against whom relief or recovery is sought in the lawsuit. The **complaint** sets forth the names of the parties and the facts in the case. The complaint will also contain a request for relief. Usually, the request for relief asks for money from the defendant. However, sometimes it will ask the court to order the defendant to do something or to stop doing something.

Service of Process

The complaint is presented to the appropriate court officer, generally the clerk. The clerk will then see that a summons is issued. The **summons** names the court of jurisdiction, describes the nature of the action, and demands that the defendant answer the complaint within a given period of time. A copy of the complaint and the summons must be given to the defendant so that the defendant will know about the lawsuit and can therefore exercise the right to be heard. Giving the summons and complaint to the defendant is called **service of process.**

The Answer

After the complaint and summons are properly served, the defendant has a set period of time in which to file an answer. An **answer** is the defendant's official response to the allegations in the complaint. In the answer, the defendant will admit or deny the allegations made in the complaint. The defendant's answer may include counterclaims, cross-claims, and third-party complaints. A **counterclaim** is a claim that the defendant has against the plaintiff. A **cross-claim** is a claim filed by a defendant against another defendant in the same case. A

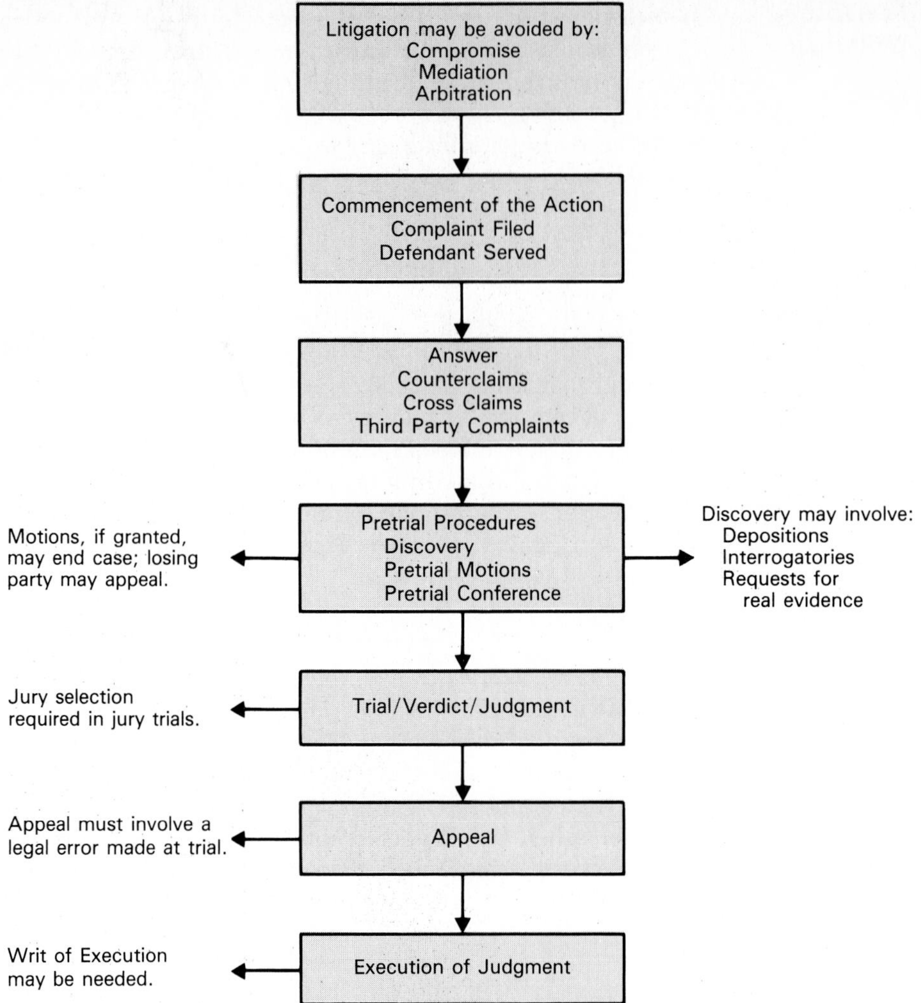

Figure 2-3 Steps in the litigation process.

third-party complaint reaches outside the original circle of parties and brings in a party that heretofore was not a part of the suit.

Shaefer posed for a photo layout in a fashion magazine called *The Leader*. When the photos appeared they were very unflattering. Because she had evidence that her career was hurt by the photographs, Shaefer sued the photographer and *The Leader*. *The Leader* filed an answer denying most of what Shaefer said in the complaint. In addition, *The Leader* filed a counterclaim against Shaefer because she had broken her contract and gone to work for another magazine. *The Leader* also filed a cross-claim against the photographer for not letting Shaefer select the photographs. Finally, the magazine filed a third-party complaint against the printing company which printed *The Leader,* claiming that an incompetent printing job contributed to the poor quality of the photos in that issue.

Pretrial Stage

After the answer has been filed, the parties must await trial. During this waiting period, dubbed the pretrial stage, several activities can be carried out including a pretrial conference, discovery, and the filing of pretrial motions.

Pretrial Conference Some courts require cases to go to a pretrial conference after the complaint and the answer have been filed. At this meeting, the judge and the lawyers attempt to get the parties to settle their dispute without a formal trial or to clarify and narrow the issues. If a settlement is not forthcoming, a date for the trial is set.

Discovery **Discovery** is the process by which the parties to a civil action search for information relevant to the case. The objective is to simplify the issues and to avoid unnecessary arguments and surprises in the subsequent trial. Discovery techniques or tools include depositions, interrogatories, and the requests for documents and other items of evidence for inspection or copys.

Depositions are oral statements made under oath by witnesses or parties to the action in response to questions from the opposing lawyers. The answers are recorded by a court stenographer and can be used for later reference.

Interrogatories are written questions to be answered in writing under oath by the opposite party. Interrogatories cannot be given to witnesses. Only defendants and plaintiffs can be required to answer interrogatories.

A **request for real evidence** will ask the other party to produce papers, accounts, correspondence, photographs, or other tangible evidence.

Pretrial Motions Several motions may be filed during the pretrial stage. A **motion** is a request for the court to rule on a particular issue. One motion available at this time is a motion for **summary judgment.** Such a motion asks the court for an immediate judgment for the party filing the motion because both parties agree on the facts and under the law the party who introduced the motion is entitled to a favorable judgment.

The Trial

Upon completion of discovery, the pretrial conference, and any hearings held on the pretrial motions, the case is ready for trial. A trial by jury is an adversary proceeding in which the judge's role is secondary to that of the jury. Competition between lawyers permits the jury to sort out the truth and arrive at a just solution of the dispute.

Jury Selection Once it is decided that the case will involve a jury, the process of *voir dire* (to speak the truth) begins. In this process, the lawyers for both parties question prospective jurors to determine whether they will be allowed to sit on the jury. Prospective jurors may be rejected if they are unable to render an impartial judgment because they have a relationship of some kind with the litigants or their witnesses.

Prospective jurors might also be rejected if they have a financial interest in the outcome of the trial. However, the financial interest must be a direct, substantial interest. Remote financial interests in a trial will not disqualify a juror. Thus, the fact that the outcome of a trial might result in higher insurance rates would not disqualify a juror who has an insurance policy.

While walking by a skyscraper in Oklahoma City, Zypperstein was hit by a window washer's platform that had dislodged from the building and fallen to the ground. The owner of the building, a major insurance company, was eventually sued by Zypperstein. While examining the jury, Zypperstein's attorney asked the judge to dismiss all jurors who had insurance policies. He argued that any juror with an insurance policy had a financial interest in the outcome of the trial because insurance rates might go up if the insurance company lost the case. The judge disagreed and refused to disqualify any jurors based solely on the fact that they had insurance policies. She concluded that the financial interest was neither direct, nor substantial. In fact, she said, the interest was both remote and minor.

Direct Examination The trial begins when each lawyer makes an opening statement outlining the case and the evidence to be introduced. Evidence and witnesses are then presented to prove each of the disputed issues of fact. The examination of witnesses by the lawyers who call them is called **direct examination.**

Cross-Examination Opposing lawyers have the right to challenge the truthfulness of each piece of evidence presented. In this process of **cross-examination,** the witnesses answer the cross-questions of the opposing lawyer.

Closing Statements After each side completes its presentation of evidence and the cross-examination, each lawyer makes a closing statement. In this statement the lawyers emphasize aspects of the testimony and other evidence they believe are most meaningful to their arguments.

Jury Instruction Since juries are composed of people who are not familiar with many aspects of the law, someone must explain the law to the jury. This job falls to the judge. Both attorneys may suggest to the judge what the instructions ought to be. However, the final instructions come from the judge. These instructions explain the rules of law which the jurors are to apply to the facts in reaching their decision.

Verdict and Judgment After receiving the judge's instructions, the members of the jury retire to a private room, where they apply the rules stated by the judge to the evidence presented by the witnesses. The jury eventually reaches a **verdict** (a finding of fact) as to **liability** and **damages.** Liability means that the defendant is held legally responsible for his or her actions. The term **damages** refers to the money recovered by the plaintiff for the injury or loss caused by the defendant. The verdict is entered by the judge in the court records, and the case is now said to be decided. By the terms of the judgment, the defeated party is required to pay the amount specified or to do a specific thing. Court costs are usually paid by the loser.

The Appeal Either party in a lawsuit may appeal a judgment if that party believes an error was made during the trial that unfavorably influenced the verdict. An **appeal** is the referral of a case to a higher court for review. For an appeal to be granted, it must be shown that some legal error (not an error in fact-finding) occurred. For example, a party may claim that the verdict was excessive or inadequate or that it was not supported by evidence. A party could also claim that evidence that should have been admitted was rejected, that the judge refused to instruct the jury as it should have been instructed, or that the judge instructed the jury in an incorrect or inappropriate manner.

Appellate Procedure Appellate procedures differ from those governing trial courts. Lawyers for both parties are usually allowed to appear to answer questions asked by the appellate court judges and to argue the merits of the issues presented. All presentations to the appellate court are made on the basis of the record of the lower court, without the examination of witnesses or the presentation of new evidence.

Appellate Judges The appellate judges listen to the arguments, review trial records, conduct legal research, vote, and reach a decision. They support their decision with reasons for the ruling. If either party is dissatisfied with the result, that party may seek a ruling from the court of last appeal, the supreme court of the state, or federal system.

Execution of the Judgment In civil cases, if the judgment is not paid, the court will order the loser's property to be sold by the sheriff to satisfy the judgment. This order by the court is known as a **writ of execution.** Any excess from the sale must be returned to the loser.

Execution of the judgment may also be issued against any income due the loser, such as wages, salaries, or dividends. This is known as execution against income, or **garnishment**, and the proceedings are known as **garnishee proceedings**. Checking accounts in a bank are also subject to garnishment.

SUMMARY

2-1. The court system in the United States is actually a dual system. The Federal Court System is divided into three levels: the district courts, the courts of appeals, and the U.S. Supreme Court. State systems vary in structure but will often consist of several levels including lower-level limited-jurisdiction trial courts, higher-level trial courts, intermediate appellate courts, and state supreme courts.

2-2. Litigation is another name for the process of bringing a case to court to enforce a right. The four legally appropriate alternatives to litigation include: compromise, mediation, arbitration, and mandatory arbitration. A compromise is the settlement of differences by each side's yielding to some extent to the other side's claim or demand without the aid of any outside third party. Mediation is the intervention of a third party who tries to lead the parties to a compromise but who has no power to decide the case. Arbitration is the process of submitting disputes to a third party who has the power to decide the case. Some states require arbitration in particular suits. Required arbitration is generally called mandatory arbitration.

2-3. Litigation begins when the plaintiff files a complaint with the appropriate trial court. The defendant must then be given a copy of the complaint and a summons. The defendant then files an answer which may contain counterclaims, cross-claims and third-party complaints. During the pretrial stage, conferences can be held, motions can be made, and discovery can be conducted. The trial includes both direct and cross-examination of witnesses. The judge explains the law and issues the instructions to the jury which renders a verdict. Either party may appeal the case if that party believes legal error was made during the trial that influenced the verdict unfavorably. If a judgment is not paid, the court may issue a writ of execution.

Understanding Key Legal Terms

answer (p. 23)
appellate jurisdiction (p. 17)
arbitration (p. 22)
complaint (p. 23)
compromise (p. 22)
cross-examination (p. 26)
damages (p. 26)
defendant (p. 23)
direct examination (p. 26)
discovery (p. 25)
diversity cases (p. 18)
general jurisdiction (p. 17)
jurisdiction (p. 17)
litigation (p. 22)
mandatory arbitration (p. 23)
mediation (p. 22)
original jurisdiction (p. 17)
plaintiff (p. 23)
service of process (p. 23)
special jurisdiction (p. 17)
summary judgment (p. 25)
verdict (p. 26)
writ of certiorari (p. 19)
writ of execution (p. 27)

Questions for Review and Discussion

1. What is the difference between original jurisdiction and appellate jurisdiction? Between general jurisdiction and special jurisdiction?
2. Explain the basic structure of the federal court system. Over what two types of cases do the federal trial courts have jurisdiction?
3. Under what circumstances might the U.S. Supreme Court grant a writ of certiorari?
4. When dealing with a claim filed under diversity jurisdiction, do federal courts follow a state or federal law?
5. Outline the structure of a typical state court system.
6. Contrast compromise with the processes of arbitration and mediation.
7. Summarize the steps in the litigation process beginning with the commencement of the action, up through the execution of the judgment.
8. Differentiate between a deposition, an interrogatory, and a request for real evidence.
9. How does the procedure followed in a trial court differ from the procedure in an appellate court?
10. Explain why a court would issue a writ of execution.

Analyzing Cases

1. Members of the Cleveland Typographical Union had a multiemployer contract with the *Cleveland Press* and the *Cleveland Plain Dealer*. In essence, the agreement guaranteed lifelong employment to members of the union. When the *Press* closed down operation, 89 employees lost their jobs and benefits under the contract. The former employees sued the *Press* and the *Plain Dealer* in the federal court in Cleveland alleging violations of federal law and Ohio state law. Before trial, the court dismissed the federal law claims. Can the employees continue to pursue their state claim in the federal court? Explain. *Province v. Cleveland Press Publishing Co.,* 605 F. Supp. 945 (N.D. Ohio).
2. Lynch became upset when the city where he lived used tax dollars to set up a nativity scene in the downtown area. The nativity scene was located on public property along with other Christmas decorations, including Santa Claus and a Christmas tree. When city hall refused to remove the scene, Lynch brought suit in federal court arguing that the use of tax money to set up the religious scene violated the first amendment to the U.S. Constitution. On what grounds did the U.S. Supreme Court agree to issue a writ of certiorari in this case? *Lynch v. Donnelly,* 104 S. Ct. 1355 (U.S. Sup. Ct.).
3. Zelig, a citizen of Idaho, worked as a chemist for Benhauer-Westendorf Pharmaceuticals (BWP). The corporation, which had its headquarters in Oregon, had been formed in Delaware. The Tortorello Chemical Company of Oklahoma lured Zelig away from BWP with promises of job security, bonuses, and promotions. When Zelig left BWP, he took several formulas with him that he had been working on at the time. BWP sued Tortorello in federal district court in Oklahoma. The case does not involve federal law. Rather it involves a state common law principle that forbids one employer to lure employees from another employer under certain circumstances. Which state's law should the federal court consider in settling the dispute? The law of Idaho, Oregon, Delaware, or Oklahoma? Explain.
4. The Beattys sued the Akron City Hospital and Dr. Walker in state court. They claimed that Dr. Walker had performed an operation on Mrs. Beatty without her consent. Under state law, the case was submitted for mandatory arbitration before the trial. The Beattys lost the arbitration hearing. The case then went to a jury trial. At trial the hospital asked the court to allow the results of the arbitration hearing into evidence. The Beattys attempted to block the submission of the arbitration results. They argued that the mandatory arbitration of such claims is an unconstitutional violation of their right to an impartial jury trial and an unconstitutional violation of their right to equal protection under the law. Are the Beattys correct? Explain. *Beatty v. Akron City Hospital,* 424 N.E.2d 586 (Ohio).
5. Bell fell on a sidewalk in the city of Bay St. Louis, Mississippi, and broke both her legs. She sued the city for failing to take proper care of its sidewalks. During jury selection, Bell's attorney challenged all city residents on the jury. Bell's attorney argued that city residents had a financial interest in seeing his client lose. His argument was based on the fact that all city residents were taxpayers and that the city treasury, which came from the taxpayers, would have to pay any judgment awarded by the court. This, he said, would make city residents biased against his client. Is Bell's attorney correct? Explain. *Bell v. City of Bay St. Louis,* 467 So.2d 657 (Mississippi).

CHAPTER 3
Criminal Law

OUTLINE

3-1 Definition of a Crime

3-2 Classes of Crimes

3-3 Elements of a Criminal Liability
- A Criminal Act
- Requisite Mental State
- The Element of Motive

3-4 Defenses to Criminal Liability
- The Insanity Defense
- Mistake
- Entrapment
- Self-Defense
- Defense of Others

3-5 Specific Crimes
- Crimes against the Government
- Crimes against the People
- Crimes against Property
- Business Crimes

COMMENTARY

While Benjamin Eaton and Juan Rodriquez were working at the bottom of a 27-foot trench on a Sabine Consolidated construction site, the walls gave way, burying them. Before rescue workers could reach the trapped men, they had smothered. When a Travis County Texas prosecutor visited the construction site, he found deplorable working conditions. More importantly, he uncovered evidence that the Sabine company had been criminally negligent in its maintenance of the trench that had become Rodriquez and Eaton's tomb. The prosecutor charged Sabine's president with criminally negligent homicide. Fifteen months later, the president was found guilty and sentenced to jail. Such stories are becoming more and more common today. Business people, who used to think of criminal law only in terms of violent crime, are beginning to learn that it can also affect them in many ways.

OBJECTIVES

1. Enumerate the various categories and classifications of crime.
2. Describe the nature of an "act" within the meaning of criminal liability.
3. Identify the four mental states that can be found in state criminal codes.
4. Distinguish motive from the required elements of criminal liability.
5. Explain the three standards for the insanity defense found in criminal law.
6. Outline the requirements of other criminal defenses including mistake, entrapment, self-defense, defense of others, and defense of property.
7. Differentiate between crimes against the government, crimes against the people, and crimes against property.
8. Classify the major business crimes, and judge the extent of liability that may be imposed for particular crimes.

3-1 DEFINITION OF A CRIME

A **crime** is an offense against the public at large. As such, it is punishable by the official governing body of a state or nation. Since crimes are considered very serious transgressions and since the prosecution of an alleged criminal can result in imprisonment or death, criminal liability is outlined quite specifically in criminal law statutes. Although the criminal statutes of the states generally resemble one another, the exact definitions and penalties may differ from jurisdiction to jurisdiction. The exact charges may also differ; that is, petty larceny in one state may be grand larceny in another. Since a criminal act or the failure to perform a duty required by statutory law is a violation of public law, legal action is always taken in the name of the state or the federal government.

3-2 CLASSES OF CRIMES

Under common law, crimes were dealt with in the order of their seriousness—treason, felonies, and misdemeanors. Most states divide offenses into only felonies and misdemeanors. Some states cite murder as a separate category. Such states may have as many as four separate categories including aggravated murder, murder, felonies, and misdemeanors. States may also list infractions or minor misdemeanors (i.e., minor traffic and local ordinance violations) as another category of crime.

Under federal and most state laws, a **felony** is a crime punishable by death or by imprisonment in a federal or state prison for a term exceeding one year. A few strategies define a felony as a crime subject to "punishment by hard labor," "an infamous crime," or a crime subject to "infamous punishment." Manslaughter, armed robbery, and arson are examples of felonies. A **misdemeanor** is a less serious crime that is generally punishable by a jail sentence for not more than 1 year. Included in this category of lesser crimes against society are offenses such as disorderly conduct, exceeding speed limits, and simple assault.

3-3 ELEMENTS OF CRIMINAL LIABILITY

The two elements necessary to create criminal liability are (*a*) an act and (*b*) the requisite state of mind. Although it is difficult to generalize about both these concepts, certain characteristics are common to each, regardless of jurisdiction. Nevertheless, keep in mind that criminal law is largely statutory in nature. Consequently, specific statutory definitions may vary from state to state.

A Criminal Act

Under American law, a crime cannot be committed unless some overt act has occurred. An individual cannot be accused of a crime for merely "thinking" of the criminal activity in question. The element of action is so important to criminal liability that defendants may avoid or overturn convictions if they can show that the statute under which they were prosecuted is ambiguous in its description of the act.

McBoyle moved a stolen airplane from Illinois to Oklahoma. He was convicted, fined, and imprisoned under a federal statute which prohibited the transportation of stolen "motor vehicles" in interstate commerce. The statute's explanation of the criminal act specifically detailed several types of motor vehicles including cars, trucks, and motorcycles. Airplanes were not mentioned. The U.S. Supreme Court overturned McBoyle's conviction stating that a court cannot expand the statutory definition of a criminal act even to include what appears to be a similar act.

Status versus Possession The courts have consistently held that mere "status" cannot be the type of act which gives rise to criminal liability. For example, a criminal statute cannot make drug addiction by itself a crime. Drug addiction is a status rather than an act. In contrast, the courts have held that "possession" is an act within the meaning of criminal law. While possession may be passive rather than active, the fact that an individual exercises control over an item of contraband is enough to constitute an act.

Refusal to Act At times a refusal to act may also be considered criminal. Generally, however, such a refusal must be coupled with a legally imposed duty. An air traffic controller's refusal to warn two planes of an impending collision could be a criminal act, even though, strictly speaking, the controller has not acted, but has instead failed to act.

Involuntary Acts Many states specifically exclude involuntary acts from their general definition of criminal act. Convulsions, reflexes, movements during sleep or unconsciousness, and conduct during hypnosis are all considered involuntary acts falling outside the limits of criminal liability.

Requisite Mental State

Generally speaking, a crime cannot be committed unless the criminal act named in the statute is performed with the requisite state of mind. Many state criminal codes include four possible states of mind: (1) purpose, (2) knowledge, (3) recklessness, and (4) negligence.

Purpose Individuals act with **purpose** when they act with the intention to cause the result that does, in fact, occur. For example, if a young man were to purchase a gun with the intention of shooting his ex-girlfriend, and if he were to actually shoot her, he would have acted with purpose.

Knowledge When people act with an awareness that a particular result will probably occur, they act with **knowledge.** For instance, if a young wife were to find her husband with another woman, she might easily become enraged and attack the woman or her husband with whatever weapon she might find handy. If she were, for example, to strike them both with an iron fireplace poker killing them, she would have acted with knowledge. In other words, she would have known that striking someone with a heavy iron poker might easily kill that person.

Recklessness **Recklessness** requires a perverse disregard for a known risk of negative consequences. People act recklessly when they are indifferent to a serious risk they know to exist. If two drivers were to challenge one another to an illegal drag race on a public highway, they would be acting recklessly. In other words, they would have disregarded the possible serious consequences of their illegal race.

Negligence People act with **negligence** when they fail to see the possible negative consequences of their conduct. A young woman who cleans a hunting rifle without checking it thoroughly to see if it is loaded would be acting with negligence. This is because she has not bothered to look for any possible negative consequences that could result from her actions. Criminal negligence should not be confused with negligence in tort law. Negligence in tort law is concerned with the compensation of accident victims. (See Chapter 4, pages 47–50.) In contrast, negligence in criminal law is concerned with punishing the wrongdoer.

The Element of Motive

Motive in criminal law is the wrongdoer's reason for committing a crime. One common misconception about the law is that motive is an element of criminal liability. Such is not the case. Establishing motive may help investigators pinpoint the guilty party, but proving an evil motive is not necessary for a criminal conviction. Conversely, establishing the existence of a good motive will rarely absolve a defendant of criminal liability.

Father Berrigan and several other demonstrators invaded a draft office, broke into files, and poured blood on draft records to protest the war in Vietnam. At trial, Father Berrigan argued that he and the others believed that the conflict in Vietnam was immoral and illegal and that the United States was violating constitutional law by waging an undeclared war. Berrigan characterized the mutilation of the draft records as an attempt to prevent an illegal act. He argued further that he and the others acted with good motive and had, therefore, lacked the appropriate mental state needed for criminal culpability. The court disagreed, saying that "once the commission of a crime is established—the doing of a prohibited act with the necessary intent—proof of a good motive will not save the accused from conviction."

3-4 DEFENSES TO CRIMINAL LIABILITY

Since the essence of criminal law lies within the two essential elements of act and mental state, a logical defense would be aimed at eliminating either or both of those elements. Most defenses attempt to do just that. The most common defenses include insanity, mistake, entrapment, self-defense, defense of others, and defense of property (see Table 3-1).

The Insanity Defense

Typically, insanity statutes involve two levels. On one level, the defendants who plead insanity plead that they are incompetent to stand trial. On the second level, the defendants may plead **not guilty by reason of insanity (NGRI).** A defendant can plead one or the other, or both.

Competence to Stand Trial Criminal defendants are generally presumed to be mentally competent to stand trial. However, the issue of competency can be raised if the court, the defense attorney, or the prosecutor suspects that the defendant is not competent. If the issue is raised, the defendant will undergo psychiatric examinations to determine the level of competence. Generally, defendants are considered competent to stand trial if they understand the nature and purpose of the trial and if they are capable of aiding their attorneys. When defendants are found to be incompetent, they are usually given treatment to improve their competency level so that they can understand what is going on and can assist in their defense.

Eckener was about to stand trial for the murder of a local disk jockey whom he believed had been out to "get him" by playing rock music that "robbed him of his soul." When Lehrmann, Eckener's court appointed attorney, questioned him, she began to suspect that he did not really understand what was going on. Lehrmann asked the court for a psychiatric examination to determine whether Eckener was competent to stand trial. At Eckener's competency hearing, the court psychiatrist testified that the defendant did not understand the nature and the purpose of the trial and could not, in any way, assist his attorney in his defense. The court ordered Eckener to undergo psychiatric treatment to improve his competency level. Three months later after treatment, Eckener was declared competent and stood trial for the disk jockey's murder.

Not Guilty by Reason of Insanity While the incompetency question involves the question of the defendant's mental condition at the time of trial, NGRI involves the question of the accused's mental condition at the time of the crime. Three tests exist for determining the insanity of a defendant pleading NGRI. They are the M'Naughten Rule, the irresistible impulse test, and the American Law Institute test.

The **M'Naughten Rule** is the oldest test for determining a criminal defendant's insanity. Under M'Naughten, defendants would be considered insane if, at the time of a criminal act, they suffered from a mental disease

Table 3-1 CRIMINAL LIABILITY AND DEFENSES

Criminal Liability	*Criminal Defenses*
The act:	Defenses to the act:
Criminal behavior specifically outlined by statute	Act as defined is "status" only
	Act as defined is ambiguous
	Act as defined is overbroad
The mental state:	Defenses to the mental state:
Mental state specifically outlined by statute	Insanity
Purpose	Mistake
Knowledge	Self-defense
Recklessness	Defense of others
Negligence	Defense of property

which prevented them from understanding the difference between right and wrong.

A second test for determining a criminal defendant's insanity is the **irresistible impulse test**. Under this test, criminal defendants would be judged insane if at the time of the offense they suffered from a mental disease that either prevented them from knowing right from wrong or compeled them to commit the criminal act.

The third test for insanity, adopted by the American Law Institute (ALI), steps away from the total impairment requirement under the M'Naughten Rule and the irresistible impulse test, requiring instead only substantial impairment. The **American Law Institute test** states that defendants will be found not guilty by reason of insanity if the mental disease from which they suffered prevented them from fully understanding just how wrong their actions were or stopped them from conforming their conduct to the law.

Guilty but Mentally Ill In reaction to strong public protest against the insanity defense, some states have enacted a new plea, **guilty but mentally ill (GMI).** Under GMI, defendants are sentenced to prison for a set number of years. Generally, they then get treatment at a state hospital. When they are cured, they are returned to prison to finish out their sentences.

Mistake

Mistake is a defense to charges of criminal liability as long as the mistake destroys one of the elements necessary to that crime. If a mistake does not destroy an element, then it is not a defense.

Zenger brought his car into the Melrose Auto Shop for repairs. Sanchez, the shop manager, told Zenger that he could pick up the keys to his loaner car at the front desk. By mistake, Zenger took the keys to Biaggi's Toyota Corolla. When Biaggi could not find his car in the lot, he called the police and reported it stolen. In this situation, Zenger has committed the criminal act of car theft. However, his honest mistake would absolve him of criminal liability because it negates an element necessary to the offense of theft, that is, the mental state of knowledge. Zenger did not knowingly deprive Biaggi of his car.

To be a successful defense, the mistake must be based on a reasonable belief. It would be no defense for a defendant to say that he shot his wife because he believed she was an invader from Mars. Note also that the mistake must destroy the criminal nature of the act in the mind of the accused. It would be no defense for an accused woman to argue that she had shot a man by mistake, thinking he was her husband. Finally, it is not a defense for an accused to say that he did not know that this particular conduct was prohibited by law. For instance, it is not a defense to a gambling charge for the defendant to argue that he did not know that the gambling law applied to him.

Entrapment

Entrapment will absolve a defendant of criminal liability if he would not have committed the criminal act without being invited to do so by a government agent, usually a police officer acting under cover. **Entrapment** occurs when a previously law-abiding citizen is led into an illegal situation by a government agent. In contrast, if a known criminal is searching for an accomplice to commit a crime, then that known criminal would not be able to use entrapment as a defense if the accomplice turned out to be a police officer. For example, if a known thief sells stolen goods to a police officer acting undercover as a fence, that thief would not be able to use entrapment as a defense.

Self-Defense

Generally, **self-defense** is available to defendants if they can demonstrate (1) that they did not start the altercation, (2) that they believed they were in danger of death or severe bodily injury, (3) that this belief was reasonable, and (4) that they used only enough force to repel the attack. One issue which frequently accompanies a determination of self-defense is the question of retreat. Stated simply, the question asks whether an intended victim is required to retreat before answering force with force. In all states, if the attack is nondeadly in nature, no retreat is necessary. Similarly, in most states, no retreat is necessary even in the face of a deadly attack. However, a few states require the intended victim to retreat "to the wall" if the attack is deadly. Not even these states, however, require a retreat in one's own home or a retreat that is inherently unsafe.

While riding on a New York subway, Goetz was approached by three young men who demanded money from him. Goetz pulled out a gun and shot all three youths. Goetz was later charged with attempted murder. In order to demonstrate that he acted in self-defense, Goetz would have to show (1) that he did not start the confrontation with the four young men, (2) that he believed he was in danger of death or severe bodily injury, (3) that this belief was reasonable, and (4) that he did not use excessive force, but only enough force to stop the attack. It was this last element which caused much of the controversy in this case. Eventually, Goetz was acquitted of the attempted murder charges. However, he was convicted of the illegal possession of a weapon.

Defense of Others

In most states, defending another person who is under attack is a valid defense, as long as the nonvictim acted under the reasonable belief that the intended victim was in danger of severe bodily harm or death. A few states do not allow defendants to use deadly force to protect other people unless the intended victims really had the right to defend themselves. In these minority states, the perceptions of the defendant do not matter.

The Nelson Financial Bank was in the process of being robbed by Henderson. Unknown to Henderson, Kristoff, a teller, set off an alarm that notified Nelson's private security department of the robbery. Two plain-clothes security officers arrived on the scene, drew their weapons, and entered the bank. Startled, Henderson ran out the back door of the bank. One of the officers gave chase while the other remained in the bank with his weapon drawn and pointed in Kristoff's direction. A passerby, Slater, saw the officer through the window and thought he was about to shoot and kill Kristoff. She attacked the officer and killed him. In most states, Slater could absolve herself, if she could convince the court that her actions were reasonable. In a minority of the states, however, she could not use defense of others because Kristoff was not, in reality, threatened with death by the officer.

3-5 SPECIFIC CRIMES

Statutory definitions and classifications of crimes vary from jurisdiction to jurisdiction. Nevertheless, several generalities can be drawn to simplify an examination of specific crimes. In general, crimes can be classified as crimes against the government, crimes against the people, crimes against property, and business crimes.

Crimes Against the Government

U.S. Const., Article III, Sec. 3 (see p. 603)

In the U.S. Constitution, **treason** is defined as the levying of war against the United States or giving aid and comfort to the nation's enemies. For conviction, a confession in open court or the testimony of two witnesses to the same overt act is required. Federal statutes define **espionage** as the gathering or transmitting of information pertaining to the national defense of the United States for the political or military use of any foreign nation.

Crimes Against the People

Crimes against the people, most often referred to as felonies, include homicide, maiming, and kidnapping.

Homicide Any killing of one human by another may be defined as **homicide.** Criminal homicide is either murder or manslaughter. When the unlawful killing is done with deliberate purpose (intent) the crime is defined as **murder.** In contrast to murder, **manslaughter** is an unlawful killing without the intent to kill. A killing that results when a person acts in a state of extreme fright, terror, anger, or blind rage that destroys reason is known as **voluntary manslaughter.** When an unintended killing results from negligence, the homicide becomes **involuntary manslaughter.**

Rosetti arrived home to find his wife in the arms of another man. In a state of extreme rage, Rosetti killed the man. The court would probably find Rosetti guilty of voluntary manslaughter. While Rosetti's actions were clearly intentional, they were performed in a state of extreme anger that destroyed his ability to reason. Note in this case that the extreme anger was the result of reasonable provocation. Had the man simply smiled at Rosetti's wife or tipped his hat to her, the rage would not be considered reasonable and Rosetti would have found himself facing murder charges instead.

Maiming Maiming is one of the most serious crimes committed against a person. **Maiming** includes acts done with the intent to injure or disfigure the victim's person—for example, cutting off part of the body or inflicting a wound that breaks the skin, whether by some kind of instrument or by corrosive acid.

Kidnapping The unlawful abduction of an individual against that person's will is known as **kidnapping**. It constitutes false imprisonment, with the additional element of removal of the victim to another place. Most state laws distinguish between simple kidnapping and the more serious offenses involving child stealing or demands for ransom.

Crimes Against Property

Burglary, arson, robbery, larceny, and extortion are among the most common crimes against property.

Burglary **Burglary** consists of a break-in of a dwelling or building for the purpose of carrying out a felony or theft. The slightest forced entry, such as turning a doorknob, qualifies as a break-in. Inserting a stick through a window while remaining outside constitutes entry. Entry through an open door or window does not alone establish the act of burglary, but once the person is inside, the opening of an interior door would constitute a break-in.

Arson **Arson** is the willful and malicious act of causing the burning of another's property. Under rules established in the common law tradition, arson included only the burning of a person's home. Modern criminal statutes, however, have expanded the crime of arson to include the burning of other structures as well. In some states, arson also includes the burning of a house by its owner. The willful burning is often motivated by the intent to defraud an insurer of the property.

Robbery The act of taking personal property from the possession of another against that person's will and under threat to do great bodily harm or damage is **robbery.** When force is not used, robbery is committed when the victim is subjected to extreme fear.

Larceny A person who takes and carries away the personal property of another without the right to do so is guilty of **larceny.** The value of the property taken—$50 in many states, as high as $200 in others—determines whether the theft is grand larceny and a felony or petty larceny and a misdemeanor.

Extortion **Extortion** is taking another's property with consent when such consent is coerced by threat to injure the victim's person, property, or reputation. Extortion is sometimes called blackmail.

Business Crimes

Nonviolent in nature, business crimes are those carried out by a business or individual in the course of doing business to obtain a business-related advantage. Covering a wide range of illegal practices, business crimes are directed against individuals, other businesses, the government, or the public at large.

Embezzlement Individuals who wrongfully take property entrusted to their care have committed the crime of **embezzlement.** In contrast to larceny, in which the offender takes the property without permission, the embezzler gains possession of the property or the money by legitimate means in the ordinary course of business. The embezzler then either keeps the property or puts it to personal use. It is no defense for the embezzler to argue that the intention was to return the property after using it or when the rightful owner requested its return.

Bribery The crime of **bribery** involves a corrupt agreement induced by an offer of reward. Central to the offense is the offering, giving, receiving, or soliciting of something of value to influence official action or the discharge of legal or public duty. Whether the recipient knows that a bribe is being offered or whether the recipient accepts or rejects it does not release the person who offered the bribe from liability. If the intended recipient accepts the bribe then that recipient would be guilty of bribery acceptance.

Racketeer Influenced and Corrupt Organizations Act One of the most controversial business-related criminal statutes today is the Racketeer Influenced and Corrupt Organizations Act (RICO). In an attempt to prevent a criminal invasion of legitimate businesses, Congress passed RICO in 1970. Under terms of the statute, conducting a legitimate business with funds acquired from "a pattern of racketeering activities" can give rise to both criminal and civil liability. Many of the offenses that fall within the scope of "racketeering activities"—such as arson and robbery—are serious crimes. Others, however, are less sinister. For example, both mail fraud and wire fraud fall within the definition of racketeering activities.

SUMMARY

3-1. A crime is an offense against the public at large. It is, therefore, punishable by the government of the nation or state.

3-2. Crimes were classified under common law as treason, felonies, and misdemeanors. Today most states have two major categories: felonies and misdemeanors.

3-3. The two elements necessary for criminal liability are an act and the requisite state of mind. The mental states may include:

purpose, knowledge, recklessness, and negligence.

3-4. Defenses to criminal liability include: the insanity defense, mistake, entrapment, self-defense, and defense of others.

3-5. Specific crimes can be categorized as: crimes against the government, crimes against the people, crimes against property, and business crimes.

Understanding Key Legal Terms

American Law Institute test (p. 35)
arson (p. 38)
bribery (p. 39)
burglary (p. 38)
crime (p. 31)
embezzlement (p. 39)
entrapment (p. 36)
espionage (p. 37)
extortion (p. 39)
felony (p. 31)
homicide (p. 37)
irresistible impulse test (p. 35)
kidnapping (p. 38)
knowledge (p. 33)
larceny (p. 38)
maiming (p. 38)
misdemeanor (p. 31)
M'Naughten Rule (p. 34)
negligence (p. 33)
purpose (p. 32)
recklessness (p. 33)
robbery (p. 38)
self-defense (p. 36)
treason (p. 37)

Questions for Review and Discussion

1. Although most states classify crimes as felonies and misdemeanors, some states include additional categories. Name three of these additional categories.
2. Indicate which of the following can be considered acts within the meaning of criminal law: (*a*) status, (*b*) possession, (*c*) a refusal to act.
3. Discuss the four mental states often included in criminal liability statutes.
4. To secure a conviction, must a prosecutor prove that a defendant had an evil motive for committing the crime? Can a defendant escape criminal liability by demonstrating a good motive for committing a crime?
5. Differentiate between a claim of incompetency to stand trial and a plea of not guilty by reason of insanity.
6. Describe the three most prominent tests for determining whether a criminal defendant should be held not guilty by reason of insanity.
7. Outline the circumstances under which entrapment might be used as a defense.
8. List the elements necessary for building a case based on self-defense.
9. Compare and contrast crimes (*a*) against the people, (*b*) against property, and (*c*) against the government.
10. Explain how business crimes differ from other crimes such as robbery.

Analyzing Cases

1. Robinson was arrested by Los Angeles police officers for violating a California criminal statute making it a misdemeanor for a person "either to use narcotics or to be addicted to the use of narcotics" (California Health and Safety Code §11721). Robinson

was convicted of this offense. The only evidence offered at trial was the existence of scar tissue and skin discoloration on the inside of his right arm. Robinson appealed his conviction, claiming that addiction was a "status" and could not, therefore, be prohibited by criminal law. Is Robinson correct? Explain. *Robinson v. State of California,* 82 S. Ct. 1417 (U.S. Sup. Ct.).

2. Katie Roberts was wasting away from the effects of an incurable disease. She asked her husband Frank to help her commit suicide. In response to her request, Roberts mixed poison with water and placed the mixture on a chair within her reach. She took the poison and died several hours later. Roberts admitted placing the poison within his wife's reach. However, he denied having the required state of mind for first-degree murder because he was responding to his wife's request and was, thus, motivated by love and mercy. Will Roberts prevail? Explain. *People v. Roberts,* 178 N.W. 690 (Michigan).

3. While at a party, Scott drank some punch which he did not know was laced with PCP. Subsequent to this event, he exhibited bizarre behavior and began to hallucinate. Believing that his life and the life of the President were in danger, he attempted to commandeer several motor vehicles. He was charged, tried, and convicted of two counts of attempted theft. Will Scott's conviction be overturned? Explain. *People v. Scott,* 194 Cal. Rptr. 633 (California).

4. Cowen had on many occasions in the past operated as a paid drug informant for the FBI and the Ventura Police Department. The Ventura police had asked Cowen to keep in touch with them should Cowen become involved in any future drug deals. Subsequently, Cowen asked Busby to introduce him to any drug dealers he knew. Busby introduced Cowen to Mandell, who sold Cowen several samples of cocaine in anticipation of a $41,500 deal. Cowen then contacted the Ventura police. A police officer posed as Cowen's buyer and both Busby and Mandell were arrested and eventually turned over to federal authorities. Busby was convicted of possession of cocaine with intent to distribute. He appealed this conviction, claiming that he had been entrapped by Cowen. Will Busby's entrapment defense succeed on appeal? Explain. *United States v. Busby,* 780 F.2d 804 (9th Cir. Ct.).

5. Dickinson was made guardian of Burgy, who had been declared incompetent by the court. Dickinson appropriated $10,000.22 from Burgy's account to her own use and was charged, tried, and convicted of embezzlement. On appeal, she argued that she had intended to return the funds to Burgy's account and would have done so had she been given a little more time. Will Dickinson's argument succeed on appeal? Explain. *State v. Dickinson,* 42 N.E.2d 196 (Ohio).

6. Wyland owned a construction company which was working on the construction of a skyscraper in downtown Shelby. When the project was a little more than half complete, Easterbrook, a state building inspector, investigated the construction site. In a private meeting, Easterbrook told Wyland that the building did not measure up to state building code specifications in several areas. At that point, Wyland offered Easterbrook $10,000 to "look the other way." Easterbrook refused the money and left the construction site immediately. The next day Wyland was arrested for bribery. Wyland argued that he could not be found guilty of bribery because Easterbrook had not accepted the $10,000. Is Wyland correct? Explain.

CHAPTER 4
Tort Law

OUTLINE

4-1 Tort Law Defined
- The Right to Damages
- The Right to an Injunction
- Tort Law versus Criminal Law
- *Respondeat Superior*

4-2 The Element of Duty
- The Existence of Duty
- Special Rights and Duties

4-3 Intentional Torts
- Assault
- Battery
- False Imprisonment
- Defamation
- Invasion of Privacy
- Trespass
- Nuisance
- Interference with a Contract

4-4 Negligence
- The Elements of Negligence
- Negligence Defenses

4-5 Strict Liability
- Grounds for Strict Liability
- Product Liability

COMMENTARY

Who is at fault and who has a right to sue when a disaster occurs? When an Amtrak passenger train collided with three Conrail locomotives just outside Baltimore, the crash killed 15 people and injured 176 others. Almost immediately suits were filed against Conrail and Amtrak. Most early suits were filed by injured passengers. However, the list of potential plaintiffs included injured employees and relatives of the crash victims. Decisions on who can sue in such cases are firmly grounded in tort law. When most people think of business law, they think of contracts, corporate law, and employment law. Such an approach ignores tort law a large portion of the law that affects business today.

OBJECTIVES

1. Differentiate between the objectives of tort law and of criminal law.
2. Discuss the concept of duty and explain how duties are related to rights.
3. Identify the principal intentional torts and outline the elements of each.
4. Determine the four elements that must be present in order to establish liability on grounds of negligence.
5. Contrast the defense of contributory negligence and the principle of comparative negligence in court actions for negligence.
6. Judge in particular cases whether the doctrine of strict liability applies.
7. Outline the circumstances under which the doctrine of product liability might be available to an injured party.

4-1 TORT LAW DEFINED

A **tort** is a private wrong that causes injury to another person's physical well-being, property, or reputation. The English word tort derives from the Latin word *tortus*, which may be translated as "twisted." A person who commits a tort is known as a **tortfeasor.** Generally, the other party is referred to as the victim, the innocent party, or the injured party.

The Right to Damages

Victims of torts have the right to sue the alleged tortfeasor to recover money to compensate them for the injuries received. This compensation is known as **damages.** Damages can include compensation for lost wages, medical bills, and any pain and suffering that the victim was forced to endure. If the tort involves property, the tortfeasor may have to pay for the repair or replacement of the property. If the tortfeasor's acts are notoriously willful and malicious, a court may impose **punitive damages.** These are damages above and beyond those needed to compensate the injured party. Punitive damages are designed to punish the tortfeasor and to make an example of the tortfeasor so that similar malicious actions are avoided by others.

The Right to an Injunction

If the tort involves a continuing problem, such as the dumping of chemical wastes into a river, the injured party may ask the court for an injunction. An **injunction** is a court order preventing someone from performing a particular act. If the tort involves some permanent fixture that harms the interest of the injured party, the court may order the wrongdoer to take positive steps to alleviate the problem. Thus, the court might order a company to clean up a landfill that has become a nuisance to neighborhood homes.

Tort Law Versus Criminal Law

The principal purposes of tort law are to compensate and to protect the victims of a tort by making up for any loss suffered or by deterring future tortious behavior. In contrast, criminal law involves a public rather than a private wrong, that is, a wrong that affects society as a whole. Since criminal law is concerned with protecting the public, its focus is different from that of tort law. When a crime is committed, government authorities begin legal actions designed to remove the offender from society. It is possible, however, for a single act to be both a tort and a crime.

Feeling he had been wronged by an unfair court ruling, Engel attacked the judge and held her hostage in the courthouse for several hours. Engel's wrongful acts were both a wrong against society (crime) and wrong against the judge (tort). The state can therefore punish Engel and remove him from society. Moreover, the judge can sue him for her injuries.

Respondeat Superior

Business people must be especially aware of tort law because of the doctrine of ***respondeat superior*** ("let the master respond"). The doctrine of *respondeat superior* may impose liability on employers and make them pay for torts committed by their employees within the scope of the employer's business. The theory behind this doctrine is that injuries to persons and property are the hazards of doing business, the cost of which the business should bear; the loss should not be borne by the innocent victim of the tort or by society as a whole. (See Chapter 32.)

4-2 THE ELEMENT OF A DUTY

One approach to the law is to think of legal liability in terms of elements. This approach emphasizes that no liability can be imposed against an individual unless all the elements are present. In tort law, the first element is duty. A **duty** is an obligation placed on individuals by law. The second element is a violation of that duty. A duty can be violated intentionally, through negligence, or under a theory of strict liability.

The Existence of a Legal Duty

Duty is best understood by looking first at rights. Legal rights arise because one of the objectives of the law is to promote justice. (See Chapter 1, page 2.). Justice demands that all people be allowed to enjoy their health, reputation, business, and property without unjust interference. Since another object of the law is to promote harmony, a duty corresponding to each right also arises within each member of our society. For example, since each member of society has a right to engage in business without interference, everyone else has the duty not to wrongfully interfere with that right.

Special Rights and Duties

Some rights and their corresponding duties are universal. For example, all people have the right to enjoy their property. Those who trespass on, take, or destroy property violate that right. In contrast, some special rights arise because of changing circumstances. When patients enter a health care facility, they have the right to expect professional care that meets appropriate standards of competence. Therefore, all health care providers who treat patients in health care facilities have a duty to perform according to a professional standard of care.

4-3 INTENTIONAL TORTS

Intentional violations of duty include a vast variety of intentional torts, all of which have their own individual elements. The principal intentional torts, however, include assault, battery, false imprisonment, defamation, invasion of privacy, trespass, nuisance, and intentional interference with a contract.

Assault

An **assault** occurs when the victim is placed in fear of immediate bodily harm. No contact is necessary for an assault. Thus when a security guard in the lobby of a major corporation pulled out a night stick and approached an innocent customer waving the stick menacingly, the guard had already committed an assault.

Battery

A **battery** involves an offensive unprivileged touching. Note that the touching need not be harmful. A physician who injects a patient with an antibiotic may be liable for battery, despite her intent to help the patient, if the patient has not consented to that injection. A battery does not always require the actual touching of a victim's person. If something closely associated with the victim, such as a hat, handbag, or chair, is touched by the tortfeasor, a battery may occur.

False Imprisonment

When one party prevents another from moving about freely, the first party has committed the intentional tort of **false imprisonment** (also known as false arrest). The victim of false imprisonment need not be locked in a prison or a jail cell. All that is required is that the person's freedom of movement is restricted in some fashion. For example, a patient who has been deprived of clothing removed for a physical examination has a cause of action for false imprisonment against the physician who refuses to return the patient's clothes until partial payment is received for a long overdue bill.

Defamation

Any false statement communicated to others that harms a person's good name or reputation may constitute the tort of **defamation.** To be defamatory, the statement must hold the person up to ridicule, contempt, or hatred. Defamation in a temporary form such as speech is **slander**; in a permanent form, such as writing, movies, or videotape, it is **libel.** The U.S. Supreme Court has given journalists the extra protection of the actual malice test when they write about public officials. Under this test, a public official must prove actual malice to win a libel suit. **Actual malice** means that the public official must prove that the statement was published either with the knowledge that it was false or with a reckless disregard for whether the statement was true or false. Later decisions expanded the actual malice requirements to include public figures such as show business celebrities and sports stars who seek out public fame and who are readily recognizable by the public at large. To be public figures, individuals must have gained such prominence that they have a great deal of persuasive power within their chosen fields. Local figures may not have this type of persuasive power, while national and state figures would. The actual malice test does not apply to most people. To win a libel suit, most people must simply prove that the damaging statement was false.

Invasion of Privacy

Invasion of privacy occurs when one person unreasonably denies another person the right to be left alone or intrudes into another's private affairs. Illegal wiretapping and unauthorized checking into one's investments or bank account are examples. Invasion of privacy can also occur when a person's face or name is used for advertising, publicity, or publication purposes without the person's consent.

Navarre, a young movie starlet, decided to have some cosmetic surgery done on her face by a famous plastic surgeon. Six months after the surgery, Ms. Navarre discovered that "before and after" photographs of her had appeared in a medical journal in an article written by her physician. The plastic surgeon had taken the photos while she was unconscious to use in the article, illustrating his new techniques. Ms. Navarre sued for $100,000 in damages, claiming humiliation, annoyance, and embarrassment as a result of the publication. The court would hold the unauthorized use of her photographs as an invasion of her right of privacy.

The invasion of privacy concept has been extended to information contained in data banks. This includes information in computers and in manual files, including company personnel files. Some courts have also held the use of lie-detector tests and drug tests by employers may be an invasion of privacy.

City officials pulled an unexpected midnight raid on the town's main fire station. The fire fighters, most of whom had been awakened from a sound sleep, were forced to submit to on-the-spot drug tests, including a urinalysis in the presence of a physician. Several of the fire fighters later sued the city for invasion of privacy. The court found that privacy rights of the fire fighters took priority over the right of the city to detect drug abuse in such a random manner. The court did not totally outlaw drug testing. It merely held that such testing must be done only in light of individualized, reasonable suspicion.

Trespass

Trespass is one of the most commonly committed intentional torts. **Trespass** involves a wrongful injury to or interference with the property of another. Generally, tort law recognizes two types of trespass: trespass to land and trespass to personal property.

Trespass to Land Traditionally, an individual enjoys the right to own and use land without interference. Even the simplest form of entry upon private property without the owner's consent, even if the property is unharmed, constitutes trespass. Examples include the intrusion of animals on one's property or using private property as a shortcut. More serious trespass results when the land or its owner is damaged. It is trespass to use land for an unauthorized purpose, to remain on land when permission to be there is denied, or to dump or abandon things on another's land.

Trespass to Personal Property The tort of trespass to personal property is the unlawful interference by one person with the control and possession of the personal property of another. Taking a lawn mower without the owner's permission would make the taker liable to the owner for the unauthorized acquisition of the lawn mower.

Nuisance

Anything that endangers life or health, offends the senses, violates the laws of decency, or obstructs the reasonable and comfortable use of property is a **nuisance.** A nuisance may be classified as either private or public.

Private Nuisance Interference with an individual's or a family's use or enjoyment of land can be classified as a **private nuisance.** The people who have been deprived of the peaceful use of their property may bring a lawsuit. Creating noise that disturbs another person is an example of a private nuisance. Blocking a right of way can also be considered a private nuisance.

Public Nuisance Annoyances which offend, interfere with, or damage the rights common to all are called **public nuisances.** Public nuisances include offenses to public morals; interference with the use of a public place; or endangerment or injury to property, health, safety, or comfort of a number of persons. The legal means to obtain relief from public nuisances are provided for under state statutes and city ordinances. Generally, only public authorities may begin a lawsuit for public nuisance.

Interference With a Contract

The law promotes a competitive market which allows individuals to bargain with one another on an equal basis. Once a contract has been entered, however, the agreement should not be broken by either party. People not involved in a contract cannot, out of ill will, entice one of the contractual parties into breaking the agreement. If they do, those outside people will be liable to the injured party for intentional **interference with a contract.** However, if the outside party has some justifiable reason for interfering with the contract, no liability will follow.

Lancaster and Mariott were coworkers at the Engle-VanPreuss Pharmaceutical Company. They were also engaged. When Lancaster broke her engagement with Mariott, he vowed revenge. He began to falsify reports to indicate that production was falling in Lancaster's department. He also staged shipping failures that seemed to be Lancaster's fault. Eventually, Lancaster lost her job. When she found out what Mariott had done, she sued him for the intentional interference with her contract. The court upheld her claim because she demonstrated that Mariott's behavior had caused the company to breach her employment contract. In addition, she demonstrated that Mariott had been motivated purely by ill will and had no legitimate interest to protect.

4-4 NEGLIGENCE

People and property are sometimes injured even though no one "intends" that the injury occur. Such an occurrence is usually labeled "an accident." Although no one acted with intent, someone was injured. The victim experienced pain and suffering, lost wages, and incurred medical bills. Justice demands that the injured party be compensated. That part of tort law which is concerned with the compensation of accident victims is called **negligence.**

The Elements of Negligence The issue before the court in a negligence action is "Under what circumstances can the actions of an alleged tortfeasor be labeled negligent so that the tortfeasor can be held liable?" Four elements must be present to establish negligence: legal duty, a breach of that duty, proximate cause, and actual harm.

Legal Duty A determination that a legal duty exists between the parties must be made in order to establish liability through negligence. This is solely a question of whether the tortfeasor should have reasonably foreseen a risk of harm to the injured party.

While traveling in Utah, DeMatteis, a citizen of Oregon, began to experience chest pains. Otero, his traveling companion, took him to the nearest hospital emergency room. Otero helped DeMatteis into the emergency room and went to find a nurse. The nurse, Sinclair, told Otero that hospital policy was to treat only patients whose physicians are staff members. She took a look at DeMatteis and suggested that Otero take him to the city hospital which was more than 20 miles away. Sinclair also told Otero to drive fast because DeMatteis looked pretty bad. When DeMatteis died on the way to the other hospital, his family sued Sinclair. The nurse argued that she owed no duty to DeMatteis because of the hospital's policy. The court disagreed, saying that it was reasonable to expect Sinclair to have foreseen a risk of harm to DeMatteis. This gave rise to a duty which Sinclair ignored. She was held liable for the death of DeMatteis.

Breach of Duty The judge or the jury must determine whether the person accused of negligence has breached the duty owed to the victim. A breach of duty occurs if the tortfeasor has not met the standard of care. This means that the alleged tortfeasor has failed to be careful enough under the circumstances. To determine if the alleged tortfeasor has met the standard of care, the court uses a **reasonable person test.** This test compares the actions of the tortfeasor with those of the reasonable person in a similar situation. If the reasonable person would not have done what the tortfeasor actually did, then the tortfeasor is liable. The reasonable person test is an objective measuring stick. Circumstances may change, but the reasonable person does not. How the reasonable person would behave in one set of circumstances may not be the same in another set of circumstances.

While test-driving a new Porsche on an interstate parkway, Newsome decided to take the car up to 120 mph and try several tricky maneuvers in heavy traffic. As a result, she lost control of the car and crashed into several automobiles and trucks. Newsome was sued by the other drivers. The question to the jury was, "Would a reasonable person drive a Porsche at 120 mph on a crowded interstate highway while attempting several tricky maneuvers?" The jury said no, and Newsome was held liable to the other drivers. Suppose, in contrast, that the car developed engine problems and caught fire while Newsome was driving within the speed limit. At the last possible moment Newsome jumped out of the Porsche, and the flaming car hit another auto. Under these circumstances, Newsome's actions were reasonable and she would not be held liable.

If the defendant in a particular case is a professional person, such as a physician or an engineer, the circumstances—not the test—change. To determine whether the defendant acted reasonably, the jury would have to know how the reasonable professional would act under similar circumstances. Determining this may require the use of expert witnesses to testify as to the reasonable professional's conduct under the circumstances.

Proximate Cause It is not enough to simply show that the tortfeasor's actions were unreasonable. In order for the tortfeasor to be held liable, the unreasonable conduct must also be the proximate cause of the victim's injury. **Proximate cause** is the connection between the unreasonable conduct and the resulting harm. In determining proximate cause, the court asks whether the harm which resulted from the conduct was foreseeable at the time of the original negligent action.

Two Transglobal Airline mechanics failed to properly repair the landing gear of a TGA747. As a result, the landing gear collapsed on takeoff and the plane caught fire. Several passengers were injured. While racing to the scene of the crash, an airport fire truck blew a tire and hit a light pole. The pole crashed onto Carbonari's car, smashing the trunk and damaging a CD player stored there. The injured passengers and Carbonari sued TGA and the mechanics. When the mechanics failed to properly repair the landing gear, it would have been easy for them to foresee that their unreasonable conduct could cause a crash that would injure passengers. However, it would have been impossible for them to foresee the damage to Carbonari's CD player. Therefore, their conduct is the proximate cause of the injuries to the passengers but not to the damage to the CD player.

Actual Harm The injured party in a lawsuit for negligence must show that actual harm was suffered. In most cases, the harm suffered is a physical injury and is visible. Harm suffered due to fright or humiliation is difficult to demonstrate. Courts often deny damages unless they can see an actual physical injury.

Reinhold was cleaning a .45 automatic on his front porch in a suburban area. He accidentally dropped the pistol, which then discharged. The bullet lodged in an old maple tree on Reinhold's property. Even though Reinhold's actions were negligent, he could not be sued because no one was injured and no damage was done.

Negligence Defenses

Several defenses can be used by the defendant in a negligence case. These defenses include contributory negligence, comparative negligence, and assumption of the risk.

Contributory Negligence The defense of **contributory negligence** involves the failure of the injured party to be careful enough to ensure personal safety. Contributory negligence completely prevents recovery by the injured party. In other words, if the injured party's negligence contributed to personal injury, the tortfeasor wins. **Last clear chance** is the injured party's defense to a charge of contributory negligence. Under this doctrine, a tortfeasor may be held liable if the injured party can show that the tortfeasor had the last chance to avoid injuring the victim.

Comparative Negligence To soften the harsh effects of contributory negligence, many states have adopted **comparative negligence** statutes that require courts to assign damages according to the degree of fault of each party. Rather than deny all recovery, the court weighs the relative degree of wrongdoing in awarding damages. If the tortfeasor was 80 percent negligent, the injured party may be allowed to recover for 80 percent of the losses suffered. Some states have adopted the "fifty percent rule." Under this rule, an injured party who was found to be more than 50 percent negligent cannot recover damages from the tortfeasor.

Assumption of the Risk Another defense to negligence is any voluntary exposure by the victim to a known risk. The injured party's awareness of the extent of the danger is the court's primary consideration in awarding or denying damages. The owner of a baseball stadium might present this defense against the negligence charge of a spectator injured by a foul ball. The charge of inadequate protection might not hold if it can be shown that the injured party was aware of the risks of injury that are associated with viewing such a sport.

4-5 STRICT LIABILITY

Under certain circumstances, the courts may judge a person liable for harm even though that person was not negligent and did not commit an intentional tort. This doctrine is known as **strict liability,** or absolute liability. In recent years, strict liability has also been applied to product liability cases.

Grounds for Strict Liability

Under strict liability the court will hold a tortfeasor liable for injuries to a victim even though the tortfeasor did not intend the harm and was not, in any way, negligent. Strict liability is generally applied when the harm results from an ultrahazardous, or very dangerous, activity. Such activities include using explosives, keeping wild animals, and storing toxic pollutants. A number of hazardous activities, such as flying an airplane, operating x-ray equipment, and laying public gas lines, are not subject to liability without fault. These activities are recognized as essential to the economic health and welfare of the public.

Product Liability

Product liability is a legal theory that imposes liability on the manufacturer and seller of a product produced and sold in a defective condition. Anyone who sells or produces a product in a **defective condition** (unreasonably dangerous to the user or to the consumer or to property) is subject to liability for physical or emotional injury to the ultimate consumer and for any physical harm to the user's property. The courts have regularly held that liability for defective products extends to the producer of the product, the wholesaler, and the retailer. The seller or producer must be engaged in the business of selling or manufacturing such products. In addition, the product manufactured or sold must be expected to reach the ultimate consumer without substantial change in conditions under which it was originally manufactured and sold.

Costanza purchased a hair dryer from the Burton Brothers Merchandising Outlet. The next morning she plugged it in and received a severe shock for which she was briefly hospitalized. Investigation revealed that the entire line of hair dryers had been manufactured based on a defective wiring diagram. Costanza sued the manufacturer, Murasaki Electronics, and the seller, Burton Brothers, under a theory of product liability. Costanza argued that the hair dryer had been sold to her in a defective condition. Since evidence indicated that the hair dryer was unreasonably dangerous and since it had reached Costanza without being changed in any way, she won her case against Murasaki and Burton.

In most states, product liability is not available as a cause of action if the only property damaged is the defective property itself. In such a situation, the product owner must seek a remedy in sales law for breach of warranty.

SUMMARY

4-1. A tort is a private wrong committed by one person, usually called the tortfeasor, against another person, often called the victim, the injured party, or the innocent party.

4-2. In all tort situations, the tortfeasor has allegedly breached a duty not to violate the rights of the injured party.

4-3. The major intentional torts include assault, battery, false imprisonment, defamation, invasion of privacy, trespass, nuisance, and intentional interference with a contract.

4-4. The four elements that must be present to establish negligence include legal duty, breach of duty, proximate cause, and actual harm. The primary defenses to negligence include contributory negligence, comparative negligence, and assumption of risk.

4-5. Under strict liability, the court will hold a tortfeasor liable for injuries to a victim even though the tortfeasor did not intend the harm and was not, in any way, negligent. The doctrine is applied when the harm results from an ultrahazardous activity.

Understanding Key Legal Terms

actual malice (p. 45)
assault (p. 45)
battery (p. 45)
comparative negligence (p. 50)
contributory negligence (p. 49)
damages (p. 43)
defamation (p. 45)
defective condition (p. 50)
duty (p. 44)
false imprisonment (p. 45)
injunction (p. 43)
interference with a contract (p. 47)
invasion of privacy (p. 45)

libel (p. 45)
negligence (p. 47)
nuisance (p. 47)
proximate cause (p. 49)
punitive damages (p. 43)
respondeat superior (p. 44)
slander (p. 45)
strict liability (p. 50)
tort (p. 43)
tortfeasor (p. 43)
trespass (p. 46)

Questions for Review and Discussion

1. Distinguish between a tort and a crime.
2. Discuss the legal relationship between duties and rights.
3. Differentiate between assault and battery.
4. Outline the actual malice test as it relates to defamation.
5. Identify the circumstances under which an invasion of privacy may occur.
6. Point out the differences between a private nuisance and a public nuisance.
7. Relate the reasonable person test as it is used to measure care in a negligence case.
8. Explain how proximate cause is determined in a negligence case.
9. What activities usually fall within the limits of strict liability?
10. Describe the legal doctrine of product liability.

Analyzing Cases

1. Five Commerce City police officers were summoned to break up a disturbance at a local party of teenagers. At the party, Ralph Crowe, who had consumed eight cups of beer and three cups of an alcoholic punch, became rowdy and had to be detained by the officers. After receiving assurances from Ralph's brother, Eddie, that he would drive Ralph home, the police released him. After leaving the party, Eddie allowed Ralph to take the wheel. Instead of going home, Ralph drove to the site of another party where he lost control of the car and ran down six people. The police officers were sued for negligence in the release of Ralph. Did the five police officers owe a duty to the six victims of Ralph's drunk-driving accident? Explain. *Leake v. Cain,* 720 P.2d 152 (Colorado Sup. Ct.).
2. When Milkovich, the head wrestling coach of Maple Heights High School in Cleveland, testified in court about a brawl at a wrestling meet, he was labeled a "liar" in a column written by Diadium for the *News-Herald*. Milkovich sued the *News-Herald* and Diadium for libel. The defendants claimed that, as head wrestling coach of a local high school, Milkovich was a public figure and that they were, therefore, entitled to the protection of the actual malice test. Are the defendants correct? *Milkovich vs. News-Herald,* 473 N.E.2d 1191 (Ohio Sup. Ct.).
3. The Nifty Foods Corporation (Nifty) had been supplying the Great Atlantic and Pacific Tea Company (A&P) with frozen waffles for several years. When Pet Incorporated entered the frozen waffle business, it, too, sought the A&P's business in order to boost its percentage of that particular market. After several years of trying, Pet eventually entered an agreement with A&P. Subsequently, the A&P notified Nifty that it would make no more contracts with

Nifty for frozen waffles. Nifty then sued A&P and Pet, alleging intentional interference with a contract. At trial, testimony indicated that there was no valid existing contract between Nifty and A&P at the time that Pet and A&P entered their frozen waffle contract. Will Nifty succeed with its claim? Explain. *Nifty Foods Corporation, The Great Atlantic and Pacific Tea Company, Inc.,* 614 F.2d 832 (2d Cir. Ct.).

4. Gorman was being treated with radiation at St. Francis Hospital for a skin ailment. Instead of improving, his condition worsened. Gorman theorized that he had been given an overdose of radiation. To vindicate the wrong, he brought suit against the radiologist and the hospital. Expert testimony indicated that a 5-minute treatment of 1,025 roentgens would have been within appropriate operating procedure. Testimony at trial revealed that Gorman had been exposed to 2,050 roentgens for 10 minutes. Further expert testimony confirmed that such a dosage could have resulted in the injuries Gorman suffered. Was the radiologist negligent in his treatment of Gorman? Explain the legal test used to arrive at your answer. *Gorman v. St. Francis Hospital,* 208 N.E.2d 653 (Ill. App. Ct.).

5. Burns was admitted to Forsyth Memorial Hospital to undergo several diagnostic tests. Ten days later, his physician ordered him moved to a private or semiprivate room for his nerves. The hospital failed to carry out this order. Two days later, Moore, a psychiatric patient, was moved into Burns's room. The next day, Moore struck Burns with a chair, injuring him. Burns sued, basing his claim on the hospital's negligence in failing to carry out Dr. DeLa Torre's order. Was the hospital's failure to carry out the order the proximate cause of Burns's injuries? Explain. *Burns v. Forsyth County Hospital Authority,* 344 S.E.2d 839 (North Carolina).

6. Queensway Tankers, Inc., Kingsway Tankers, Inc., East River Steamship Corporation, and Richmond Tankers, Inc., all chartered supertankers designed by Transamerican Delaval, Inc. Under terms of the charters, each shipping company was financially responsible for any repairs to the tankers. From the start, there were problems with the tankers' turbines, resulting in damage to the turbines themselves and necessitating costly repairs. The plaintiffs brought a product liability suit against Delaval. The suit alleged that manufacturing defects caused the damages. Should the shipping companies prevail in product liability against the manufacturer? Explain. *East River Steamship Corporation v. Transamerica Delaval, Inc.,* 106 S. Ct. 2305.

PART 1
CASE STUDY

Jones v. Hawkes Hospital of Mt. Carmel

Supreme Court of Ohio
196 N.E.2d 592

SUMMARY

Mrs. Jones was admitted to the maternity ward of Hawkes Hospital of Mt. Carmel in a delirious, agitated, and highly restless state. According to customary hospital procedure, nurses were supposed to keep a close watch on delirious patients because they can easily fall out of bed and injure themselves. Despite this customary practice, the nurse assigned to Mrs. Jones left the labor room for 5 minutes. While the nurse was out of the room, Mrs. Jones climbed out of bed, fell to the floor, and injured herself. Mrs. Jones and her husband sued the nurse and the hospital for negligence. The trial court decided the case in favor of Mrs. Jones. The appellate court reversed the decision because the trial court had allowed the jury to decide the case without expert testimony on the type of care that should be provided in hospital delivery rooms.

THE COURT'S OPINION: JUDGE HERBERT

The paramount question here arises from the holding of the Court of Appeals that:

"It was incumbent upon the plaintiff [appellant] to produce evidence proving the standard of care required to be exercised by the defendant [appellee] appropriate to the situation and surrounding circumstances shown to exist at the time and place of plaintiff's injury and consequent damage...."

Appellant was unattended for a period of from one to five minutes. There was substantial evidence for the consideration by a jury upon the question of negligence of the nurse...!

The doctrine of *respondeat superior* is applicable to hospitals in Ohio. See paragraph one of the syllabus of Avellone v. St. John's Hospital, 165 Ohio St. 467, 135 N.E.2d 410, which reads:

"A corporation not for profit, which has as its purpose the maintenance and operation of a hospital, is, under the doctrine of *respondeat superior,* liable for the torts of its servants.

In order to establish the standard of care exercised by hospitals in this community in the labor rooms of their obstetrical departments, it would be necessary to resort to expert opinion. But is resort to expert-opinion evidence necessary in this cause? Is proof of the standard of care maintained in other hospitals required? We think not.

21 Ohio Jurisprudence (2d), 450, Section 436, discusses expert-opinion evidence, as follows: "Broadly speaking, expert opinion evidence is admissible only where the inquiry involves a question of science or art, or of professional or mechanical skill, and is incompetent where the matter of inquiry is within the common knowledge of average general information..."

"To sum up: In everything pertaining to the ordinary and common knowledge of mankind jurors are supposed to be competent, and peculiarly qualified to determine the connection between the cause and effect established by common experience, and to draw the proper conclusions from the facts..."

It seems quite clear that the average juror from his own personal knowledge would be able to conclude that an expectant mother, delirious, drugged, restless and determined to climb out of her bed, would in all probability succeed unless she was closely supervised. Surely no testimony is necessary to establish cause and effect under the circumstances...

The court may take judicial notice that juries of today include women. Many of these women jurors are mothers and, in many instances, grandmothers. In the case at bar, there were six women. They know probably as much if not more about childbirth than many experts...

The jury, unaided by the opinion of experts, was sufficiently equipped with knowledge gained from everyday life to consider the facts and to return a verdict supported by competent evidence of proof of negligence proximately causing appellant's injuries.

It having been determined that the nurse was negligent, and that, as a proximate result of her negligence, the appellant was injured, it follows that, under the doctrine of *respondeat superior,* the hospital must respond in damages...

It may be contended that the conduct of the nurse or nurses was in a professional capacity, and that they, therefore, were independent contractors and not subject to the doctrine of *respondeat superior.*

Klema, Admx., v. St. Elizabeth's Hospital of Youngstown, 170 Ohio St. 519, 166 N.E.2d 765 disposes of that question:

"A corporation not for profit, which has as its purpose the maintenance and operation of a hospital, is, under the doctrine of *respondeat superior,* liable for the negligent acts of its employees..."

Therefore, the judgment of the Court of Appeals is reversed, and those of the Court of Common Pleas and of the Municipal Court are affirmed. Judgment reversed.

QUESTIONS FOR ANALYSIS

1. The final decision in this case was rendered by the highest court in the state. Outline the other courts which would have heard the case before it reached the state supreme court.
2. How would the procedure for hearing the case differ in the appellate courts as compared to the procedure at trial?
3. Who would have given the original instructions to jury members, telling them that they did not need expert testimony to come to a verdict?
4. State the test that would be used to determine whether the nurse was negligent.
5. Explain why the hospital would like the court to disregard the doctrine of *respondeat superior.*
6. The court's decision on the *respondeat superior* issue rests on an earlier decision in the case of *Klema vs. St. Elizabeth's Hospital.* This precedent is binding on all courts in the state of Ohio. With this fact in mind, determine which state court heard the *Klema* case.
7. Identify the elements of the *Klema* citation, 166 N.E.2d 765.

PART 2
Contract Law

CHAPTER 5
The Nature, Characteristics, and Status of Contracts

OUTLINE

5-1 The Nature of Contracts
- The Elements of a Contract
- Contracts and the UCC
- Contracts and Other Agreements
- Contracts and Privity

5-2 Contractual Characteristics
- Valid, Void, Voidable, and Unenforceable Contracts
- Unilateral and Bilateral Contracts
- Express and Implied Contracts
- Informal and Formal Contracts

5-3 Status of Contracts
- Executory Contracts
- Executed Contracts

COMMENTARY

Mary Beth Whitehead and William Stern made promises to one another whereby Whitehead agreed to carry Stern's baby for 9 months in exchange for $10,000. When the time came for Whitehead to give the baby to Stern, she refused to do so. Stern brought a lawsuit against her in a New Jersey state court. In his suit, Stern claimed that Whitehead had not lived up to her part of the agreement. Whitehead claimed that the contract was void because it was illegal in New Jersey to buy and sell babies. Stern argued that the agreement was not the sale of the baby because he, as the baby's father, already had a one-half interest in the baby. The baby was, therefore, his as well as Whitehead's. He was simply purchasing her half-interest which made the contract legal and her breach unacceptable. Who is correct here? Whitehead with her claim of illegality or Stern with his half interest argument? Answers to questions like these are found in contract law.

OBJECTIVES

1. Identify the six elements of a contract.
2. Distinguish contracts from other agreements made between different parties.
3. Explain the nature of valid, void, voidable, and unenforceable contracts.
4. Contrast unilateral and bilateral contractual arrangements.
5. Outline the difference between express and implied contracts.
6. State the nature of a formal contract in contrast to the nature of an informal contract.
7. Explain how executory contracts differ from executed contracts.

5-1 THE NATURE OF CONTRACTS

A **contract** is an agreement between two or more competent parties, based on mutual promises, to do or to refrain from doing some particular thing which is neither illegal nor impossible. The agreement results in an obligation or a duty that can be enforced in a court of law.

Bascombe Press, Inc., a leading publisher of novels, biographies, and best-selling "how-to" books, hired Greenhouse as an editor. Greenhouse agreed to perform all the duties of an editor in exchange for his annual salary. As one of his first duties as editor, Greenhouse contacted Garneau, who had just announced finding the long-lost private diaries of Napoleon. Bascombe Press agreed to pay Garneau $5.5 million for the exclusive right to publish and distribute the diaries. Garneau, in turn, agreed to refrain from selling the publishing and distribution rights to anyone else, including the rights to any movie or television miniseries based on the diaries.

Both of the agreements in this case resulted in legally enforceable contracts because the parties agreed to mutually satisfactory terms. In the agreement between Bascombe and Greenhouse, both parties agreed to do something they were legally entitled to do. In the agreement covering Napoleon's diaries, Garneau agreed not to do something he had a legal right to do, that is, sell the rights to the diaries to other publishers.

The contracting party who makes a promise is known as the **promisor;** the one to whom the promise is made is the **promisee.** The party who is obligated to deliver on a promise or to undertake some act of performance is called the **obligor.** The contracting party to whom this party owes an obligation is called the **obligee.**

The Elements of a Contract

A legally complete contract will arise between two parties when all six elements of a contract are present. These six elements include *offer, acceptance, mutual assent, capacity, consideration,* and *legality.* (See Table 5-1.) If any one of the six elements is missing, the transaction is not a legally complete con-

Table 5-1 THE SIX ELEMENTS OF A CONTRACT

Element	*Explanation*
Offer	A proposal made by one party (the offeror) to another party (the offeree) indicating a willingness to enter a contract.
Acceptance	The agreement of the offeree to be bound by the terms found in the offer.
Mutual Assent	Offer and acceptance go together to create mutual assent or "a meeting of the minds." Assent can be destroyed by fraud, misrepresentation, mistake, duress, or undue influence.
Capacity	The law presumes that anyone entering a contract has the legal capacity to do so. However, minors are generally excused from contractual responsibility, as are mentally incompetent and drugged or drunk individuals.
Consideration	Consideration is the thing of value promised to the other party in a contract in exchange for something else of value promised by the other party. This mutual exchange binds the parties together.
Legality	Parties are not allowed to enforce contracts that involve doing something that is illegal. Some illegal contracts involve agreements to commit a crime or a tort. Others involve activities made illegal by statutory law.

tract. Some contracts must also be *in writing* to be enforceable. However, even these contracts must involve the other six elements. In the next six paragraphs, each of these elements is explained briefly. Each element is also given in-depth treatment in later chapters of Part 2.

Offer An **offer** is a proposal made by one party to another indicating a willingness to enter into a contract. The person who makes an offer is called the **offeror.** The person to whom the offer is made is the **offeree.** The making of the offer is actually the first step in creating the contractual relationship between the two parties. Because of this position of importance, it must be seriously intended, clear and definite, and communicated to the offeree. If these requirements are met, it is then up to the offeree to accept or to reject the offer. (See Chapter 6.)

Acceptance In most cases, only the specifically identified offeree has the right to accept an offer. **Acceptance** means that the offeree agrees to be bound by the terms set up by the offeror in the offer. In many situations, if the offeree changes any of those terms, the acceptance is not really an acceptance. Instead, it is a **counteroffer.** (See Chapter 6.)

Mutual Assent If a valid offer has been made by the offeror and a valid acceptance has been made by the offeree, then the parties have agreed to the terms and **mutual assent** exists between them. Mutual assent is sometimes called a "meeting of the minds." It means that both parties know what the terms are and have readily agreed to be bound by those terms. Sometimes events or activities occur that destroy mutual assent. If mutual assent has been destroyed, the contract is said to be a **defective agreement**. A defective agreement can arise as a result of fraud, misrepresentation, mistake, duress, or undue influence. (See Chapter 7.)

Capacity Offer and acceptance go together to create mutual assent. However, three other additional elements must be present to make a contract complete. The first of these three is capacity. **Capacity** is the legal ability to enter into a contractual relationship. The law has established a general presumption that anyone entering a contractual relationship has the legal capacity to do so. However, this presumption can be attacked. Minors are generally excused from contractual responsibility. Persons deprived of the mental ability to comprehend and understand contractual obligations also have the right to abandon their contracts. People under the influence of alcohol or drugs may have this right as well. (See Chapter 8.)

Consideration The fifth element to any complete contract is the mutual exchange of benefits and sacrifices. This exchange is called **consideration.** Consideration is the thing of value promised to the other party in exchange for something else of value promised by the other party. It is this exchange of valued items or services that binds the parties together. If no consideration passes between the parties, then no contract exists. (See Chapter 9.)

Legality The final element of a binding contract is legality. Parties cannot be allowed to enforce a contract that involves doing something that is illegal. Some illegal contracts involve agreements to perform a crime or a tort. However, activities that are neither crimes nor torts have been made illegal by specific statutes. Among these activities are usurious agreements, wagering agreements, unlicensed agreements, unconscionable agreements, and Sunday agreements (See Chapter 10).

Contracts and the UCC

As discussed previously in Chapter 1, the Uniform Commercial Code (UCC) is a unified set of statutes designed to govern almost all commercial transactions. Article 2 of the UCC sets down the rules which govern sale-of-goods contracts. All other types of contracts, including employment contracts and real property contracts, are governed by common law rules and certain special statutory provisions. Fortunately, in many cases, common law rules and UCC provisions are the same. Moreover, those differences which do exist will be pointed out in this discussion of general contract law. In Part 3 we will discuss Article 2 of the UCC and sale-of-goods contracts. In Part 4 we will discuss property law contracts, and in Part 7 employment contracts.

Contracts and Other Agreements

All contracts contain agreements, but not all agreements are contracts. An agreement may or may not be legally enforceable. An agreement to take a friend to a football game would not be a legally enforceable agreement because the friend has not given you anything in exchange for that promise. However, an agreement to buy season tickets to all Cleveland Browns home games for a friend in exchange for his painting your house would be legally enforceable. In this case, there has been an exchange of value that binds each party to the other, creating the contract. To be enforceable, an agreement must conform to the law of contracts. The courts have never been agreeable to the enforcement of social agreements: dates, dinner engagements, or the like. Many states have extended this concept to include agreements to marry and agreements to live together without the benefit of a marriage contract.

Contracts and Privity

The general rule of contract law is that the parties to a contract must stand in privity to one another. **Privity** simply means that both parties must have a legally recognized interest in the subject of the contract if they are to be bound by it. Outside parties who do not have such an interest in the subject matter of the contract may not be bound by it. Their right to sue in the event of breach of contract (i.e., broken or violated) would also be called into question.

Blythedale opened a checking account with the Suffolk County National Bank by depositing $1,500. This created a contract between Blythedale and the bank. Under the contract, the bank agreed to pay money out, up to the amount of the deposit, whenever ordered to by Blythedale. Blythedale wrote out a $250 check and mailed it to the Rochelle Art Gallery for the purchase of a limited-edition Van Gogh print. Suffolk refused to pay the check and Rochelle refused to send the print. By the time the mess was straightened out, the cost of the print had gone up to $300. Blythedale could sue the bank for $50, the difference between the original price and the price he had to pay. Since the checking account created a contract between Blythedale and the bank, they were in privity to one another. When the bank refused to pay the check, it broke its agreement with Blythedale, giving him the right to sue the bank. If the price of the print had decreased and Rochelle had lost money because of the delay, the gallery could not sue the bank for failure to pay Blythedale's check in a timely manner.

Despite this privity rule, it is possible for two or more parties to provide benefits to a third party. Moreover, an exception to the general rule of privity exists in cases involving warranties and product liability (see Chapter 16).

5-2 CONTRACTUAL CHARACTERISTICS

Contractual characteristics fall into four different categories. These categories include: valid, void, voidable, and unenforceable; unilateral and bilateral; express and implied; informal and formal. Any given contract would be classifiable in all four ways. Thus a single contract could be said to be valid, bilateral, express, and formal.

Valid, Void, Voidable, and Unenforceable Contracts

A **valid contract** is one which is legally binding and fully enforceable by the court. In contrast, a **void contract** is one that has no legal effect whatsoever. A contract to perform an illegal act would be void.

In the opening commentary, the New Jersey Supreme Court held that the surrogate parent contract between Whitehead and Stern was a void contract.

The court stated that the agreement was void because it amounted to "baby selling" which was illegal in the state of New Jersey. (The court did, however, award custody of the baby to the Sterns, reasoning that they could provide her with a secure home.)

A **voidable contract** is one that may be avoided or canceled by one of the parties. Contracts made by minors and contracts that are induced by fraud or misrepresentation are examples of voidable contracts. An **unenforceable contract** is one which, because of some rule of law, cannot be upheld by a court of law. An unenforceable contract may have all the elements of a complete contract and still be unenforceable.

Unilateral and Bilateral Contracts

A **unilateral contract** is an agreement in which one party makes a promise to do something in return for an act of some sort. The classic example of a unilateral contract is a reward contract. A person who promises to pay the finder of his gold watch $10 does not expect a promise in return. Rather, the person expects the return of the watch. When the watch is returned, the contract arises and the promisor owes the finder $10. In contrast, a **bilateral contract** is one in which both parties make promises. Bilateral contracts come into existence at the moment the two promises are made. A **breach of contract** occurs when one of the two parties fails to keep the promise. When there is a breach of contract, the injured party has the right to ask a court of law to somehow remedy the situation. (Remedies and breach are discussed in detail in Chapter 13.)

Express and Implied Contracts

Contracts can be either express or implied. An **express contract** requires some sort of written or spoken expression indicating the desire to enter the contractual relationship. **Implied contracts** are created by the actions or gestures of the parties involved in the transaction.

Express Contracts When contracting parties accept mutual obligations either through oral discussion or written communication, they have created an express contract. Oral negotiations will, in many cases, be reduced to writing, but this is not always necessary.

Written contracts do not have to be long formal preprinted agreements. While such lengthy, preprinted forms are common in some businesses, other less formal written documents are frequently used to show that a contract exists. For example, a written contract may take the form of a letter, sales slip and receipt, notation, or memorandum. Written contracts may be typed, printed, scrawled, or written in beautiful penmanship. In some situations, state laws require certain types of contracts to be in writing. (These contracts are covered in Chapter 11.)

When the law does not require a written agreement, an **oral contract** resulting from the spoken words of the parties will be enough. Parties to such an agreement, however, should anticipate the difficulty of proving such agreements should disputes arise later. Nevertheless, expressing every agreement in writing, in anticipation of future need of proof is impractical in the fast-paced modern world of business.

Implied Contracts One who knowingly accepts benefits from another may be obligated for their payment even though no express agreement has been made. Pumping gas into a car at a self-service gas station is an example of an implied contract. Agreements of this type can either be implied in fact or implied in law.

Contracts implied by the direct or indirect acts of the parties are known as **implied-in-fact contracts.** Courts follow the objective concept rule in interpreting the acts and gestures of a party. Under this concept, the meaning of one's acts is determined by the impression they would make upon any reasonable person who might have witnessed them, not by a party's self-serving claim of what was meant or intended.

Van Dine watched workers employed by the Hairston Construction Company as they replaced the asphalt in his driveway. The asphalt was to have been laid in the driveway next door. Van Dine never stopped the work crew, even though he knew that a mistake had been made. Hairston Construction was within its rights to believe that the work was being done with Van Dine's consent. In assessing damages for the cost of the improvement, the court would apply the objective concept rule. A reasonable person who might have watched Hairston lay the asphalt would conclude that Van Dine consented to the work.

An **implied-in-law contract** can be imposed by a court when someone is unjustly enriched. It is used when a contract cannot be enforced or when there is no actual written, oral, or implied-in-fact agreement. Applying reasons of justice and fairness, a court may obligate one who has unfairly benefitted at the innocent expense of another. An implied-in-law contract is also called a **quasi-contract.**

Lichtenstein was found unconscious on the highway by a passing motorist who arranged to have her placed in a hospital for emergency treatment. When Lichtenstein regained consciousness, she refused to pay for the treatment, claiming that she was not aware of what was going on and had not agreed to what had been done to her. The case illustrates a quasi-contractual situation wherein it would be unfair to allow the injured person to benefit at the expense of the hospital. In any suit that might arise over this expense, a court would require Lichtenstein to pay the fair value of the services rendered.

The quasi-contract concept cannot apply, however, as a means of obtaining payment for an act that a party simply feels should be done. The concept will also not be applied where one party bestows a benefit on another unnecessarily or through misconduct or negligence. Note also that quasi-contracts are not contracts in the true sense of the word because they are created by the court. They do not arise as a result of the mutual assent of the parties as do express or implied-in-fact contracts.

Informal and Formal Contracts

The law sometimes requires that contracts follow formalities prescribed by statute or by common law. These are called formal contracts. All others are classified as informal.

Informal Contracts Any oral or written contract that is neither under seal nor a contract of record is considered an **informal contract.** An informal contract is also known as a **simple contract.** Informal contracts generally have no requirements as to language, form, or construction. They comprise those obligations entered into by parties whose promises are expressed in the simplest and usually most ordinary nonlegal language.

UCC 2-203 **(see p. 616)**

Formal Contracts Under common law principles, a **formal contract** differs from other types in that it has to be (1) written, (2) signed, witnessed, and placed under the seal of the parties, and (3) delivered. A **seal** is a mark or an impression placed on a written contract indicating that the instrument was executed and accepted in a formal matter. The UCC removed the requirement for the seal in sale of goods contracts. Some states, however, still require the use of the seal in agreements related to the sale and transfer of real property.

> Ballantine signed an agreement with Parker to buy two acres of beachfront property. Parker found another interested buyer who was willing to pay a higher price for the land. Ballantine had signed the sales agreement without including any representation of the seal. Ballantine would be helpless in attempting to enforce the contract in a state that required such formality in real property contracts.

Today a person's seal may be any mark or sign placed after the signature intended to be the signer's seal. In states still requiring the seal or formal contract, it is sufficient to write the word *seal* after the signature.

Contracts of Record A special type of formal contract having certain unique characteristics is known as a **contract of record.** Often, such a contract is one that has been confirmed by the court with an accompanying judgment issued in favor of one of the parties. The judgment is recorded, giving the successful litigant the right to demand satisfaction of the judgment. Contracts of record are not contracts in the true sense of the word because they are court-created. Although they do not have all the elements of a valid contract, they are enforced for public policy reasons.

> Prindergast installed new windows on Cain's porch at an agreed-upon price of $3,200. Prindergast then sent Cain a bill for $3,200. Cain sent Prindergast a check for $1,700, on which was written "in full payment of all money owed." These words were in very fine print and not seen by Prindergast. Prindergast sued Cain for the amount still owed. The court ruled in favor of Prindergast and entered a judgment against Cain for the money owed. Entry of the judgment created a contract of record, which was enforceable against Cain.

5-3 STATUS OF CONTRACTS

After a contract has been negotiated, all obligations must then be satisfactorily performed in order for the contract to be executed.

Executory Contracts

A contract that has not yet been fully performed by the parties is called an **executory contract.** Such a contract may be completely executory, in which case nothing has been done, or it may be partly executory, in which case the contract is partially complete.

Gillespie hired Bridgeman to ghostwrite Gillespie's memoirs for $20,000. Bridgeman completed the manuscript and delivered it to Gillespie. Gillespie read the manuscript and made numerous corrections, additions, and deletions. He then returned the manuscript to Bridgeman, who made the required changes. Once the changes had been made, Gillespie approved the manuscript for publishing. Bridgeman sent a bill to Gillespie. At this point, the contract is executory on the part of Gillespie and executed on the part of Bridgeman.

Executed Contracts

When a contract's terms have been completely and satisfactorily carried out by both parties it is an **executed contract.** Such contracts are no longer active agreements and are valuable only if a dispute about the agreement occurs.

SUMMARY

5-1. A contract is an agreement between two or more competent parties based on mutual promises to do or to refrain from doing some particular thing which is neither illegal nor impossible. The six elements of a contract include offer, acceptance, mutual assent, capacity, consideration, and legality. Article II of the UCC covers sale-of-goods contracts; common law and special statutory provisions cover employment and real property contracts. To be enforceable, an agreement must conform to the law of contracts. The courts have never been agreeable to the enforcement of social contracts. Finally, the general rule of contract law is that the parties to a contract must stand in privity to one another.

5-2. Contractual characteristics fall into four different categories. These categories are: valid, void, voidable, and unenforceable; unilateral and bilateral; express and implied; informal and formal.

5-3. A contract can also be executory or executed. An executory contract is one in which neither party has performed. A contract that is executory in part is one which has been partially performed. An executed contract is one whose terms have been carried out by both parties.

Understanding Key Legal Terms

bilateral contract (p. 61)
breach of contract (p. 61)
contract (p. 57)
contract of record (p. 63)
executed contract (p. 64)
executory contract (p. 64)
express contract (p. 61)
formal contract (p. 63)
informal contract (p. 63)
implied-in-fact contract (p. 62)
implied-in-law contract (p. 62)
obligee (p. 57)
obligor (p. 57)
privity (p. 60)
promisee (p. 57)
promisor (p. 57)
quasi-contract (p. 62)
unenforceable contract (p. 61)
unilateral contract (p. 61)
valid contract (p. 60)
voidable contract (p. 61)
void contract (p. 60)

Questions for Review and Discussion

1. List the six elements of a contract.
2. Explain the difference between a contract and an agreement.
3. What are the obligations of contracting parties under a valid contract?
4. What are the obligations of contracting parties under a voidable contract?
5. Contrast void contracts with unenforceable contracts.
6. Outline the nature of the promises made in regard to (*a*) unilateral contracts and in regard to (*b*) bilateral contracts.
7. How are the terms of an agreement in an implied contract determined? How are the terms of an express contract determined?
8. Give an example of an implied-in-fact contract and an implied-in-law contract, or quasi-contract. Also explain the differences between these two types of implied contracts.
9. What are the common law requirements as to formal and informal contracts? Are contracts of record really contracts? Explain.
10. When is a contract considered executed? When is a contract considered executory? Provide an example of each.

Analyzing Cases

1. One of Stewart's clients gave him a check for $185.48. The check had been drawn up by the client's corporate employer and properly indorsed by the client. Nevertheless, the bank refused to cash the check for Stewart even though there was enough money in the account to cover the $185.48. Can Stewart sue the bank for not cashing the check as he had requested? Explain. *J.E.B. Stewart v. Citizens and Southern National Bank,* 225 S.E.2d 761 (Georgia).
2. Vokes was told that she would become a professional dancer if she took a very expensive dancing course offered by Arthur Murray, Inc. She was also continually told that she had great talent. The contract called for payments amounting to a total of $31,000. As it turned out, she never became a professional dancer and, in fact, had little or no talent. She sued Arthur Murray claiming that the Arthur Murray people misrepresented the facts in order to entice

her to enter the contract. The court agreed and found in her favor. Does Vokes now have the right to void the contract? Ex plain. *Vokes v. Arthur Murray, Inc.*, 212 S.O.2d 906 (Florida).

3. Constantini asked Lucas to do some remodeling work on a building she intended to convert into a dinner club. Lucas and Constantini agreed on the terms of performance and the price, but did not put the agreement into writing. After Lucas spent 1,847 hours on the project, Constantini refused to pay him, claiming no contract had ever existed. The trial judge instructed the jury that the agreement between Lucas and Constantini was not an express contract. He did, however, suggest that it might be an implied contract. Should the appellate court rule that the trial court was wrong in these instructions? Explain. *Lucas v. Constantini* 469 N.E.2d 927 (Ohio).

4. Anderson, a farmer, orally agreed to buy a used tractor from the Copeland Equipment Company for $475. Copeland delivered the tractor to Anderson, who used it for 11 days. During this period Anderson could not borrow enough funds to cover the purchase price. Anderson therefore returned the tractor to Copeland. Both parties agree that their sales contract was canceled when the tractor was returned. However, Copeland now claims that under the doctrine of quasi-contract, Anderson is required to pay for the 11 days' use made of the tractor. Do you agree with Copeland? Explain your answer. *Anderson v. Copeland,* 378 P.2d 1006 (Oklahoma).

5. B.L. Nelson & Associates, Inc., entered into a contract with the city of Argyle. They agreed to design and construct a sanitary sewer collection and treatment facility for the city. The city attempted to get out of the contract by citing certain provisions of the state constitution. These provisions made it illegal for the city to enter a contract for services if it did not have the money to pay for these services. Since the city did not have the funds to pay Nelson, it argued that the contract was illegal and therefore void. Is the city correct? Explain. *B.L. Nelson & Associates, Inc. v. City of Argyle,* 535 S.W.2d 906 (Texas).

6. Peters entered into a contract to purchase Dowling's business. The following terms were agreed to: (*a*) Peters would take over all Dowling's executory contracts; (*b*) Peters would purchase Dowling's tools at an agreed-to price; (*c*) Peters would accept full responsibility for all warranties made by Dowling on previous contracts; (*d*) Dowling would remain as a consultant to the new firm for a period of 5 years. Analyze each part of this contract and classify each term according to whether it is executed or executory. *Wagstaff v. Peters,* 453 P.2d 120 (Kansas).

CHAPTER 6
Offer and Acceptance

OUTLINE

COMMENTARY

Richard Bay was the athletic director at Ohio State. Bay's excellent record attracted the attention of some people at the University of Michigan. They approached Bay several times and offered him a job as their athletic director. Each time Bay was offered the job, he turned it down. In 1987, Earle Bruce, the head football coach at Ohio State, was fired by Edward Jennings, the university's president. Since Bruce's overall record was 80 wins, 26 losses, and 1 tie, Bay felt that an injustice had been done. To protest, Bay resigned. At that point, could Bay have accepted Michigan's prior offer of a job or would he have to wait for a new offer? Could Michigan interpret Bay's resignation as an acceptance of their prior offers? Questions like these are addressed in this chapter.

OBJECTIVES

1. Identify the three requirements of a valid offer, and judge whether those requirements are present in any particular offer.
2. Differentiate between a public offer and an invitation to trade.
3. Explain acceptance of an offer in the case of (*a*) a unilateral contract and (*b*) a bilateral contract.
4. Outline the proper procedure for accepting an offer that has been sent by mail, telegram, telephone, or other means.
5. Discuss the mirror image rule and explain its status under the Uniform Commercial Code.
6. Relate the various means by which an offer can be revoked.
7. Explain what is meant by a firm offer.
8. Defend the proposition that an option is both a contract and an offer, and distinguish options from simple offers.

6-1 REQUIREMENTS OF AN OFFER

The first element of a valid contract is the existence of an offer. As explained in the previous chapter, an **offer** is a proposal made by one party to another indicating a willingness to enter a contract. The person who makes an offer is called an **offeror.** The person to whom the offer is made is called the **offeree.** An offer is valid only if it has (1) serious intent, (2) clear and reasonably definite terms, and (3) communication to the offeree. (See Table 6-1.)

Serious Intent

An offer is invalid if it is made as an obvious joke, during an emotional outburst of rage or anger, or under circumstances that might convey a lack of serious intent. The offeror's words or actions must give the offeree assurance that a binding agreement is intended. Serious intent is determined by the offeror's words and actions and by what the offeree had the right to believe was intended by those words and actions.

Adamson was having great difficulty with his automobile. First, the car needed a brake job. Then the transmission had to be replaced. Third, a new water pump had to be added. The fourth time Adamson brought the car into the repair shop the carburetor had to be rebuilt. At this point, he told Gunther, the mechanic, that he'd gladly sell the car for two cents and bus fare home. Under the unusual circumstances, Gunther would not have the right to believe that Adamson's offer to sell the car for two cents and bus fare was seriously intended.

Table 6-1 REQUIREMENTS OF AN OFFER

Requirement	*Explanation*
Serious intent	The offeror's words must give the offeree assurance that a binding agreement is intended.
Clarity and definiteness of terms	The terms of an offer must be sufficiently clear to remove any doubt about the contractual intentions of the offeror. Most courts require reasonable rather than absolute definiteness.
Communication to the offeree	The proposed offer must be communicated to the offeree by whatever means are convenient and desirable. The communication of the offer can be express or implied. Public offers are made through the media but are intended for one party whose identity or address is unknown. Invitations to trade are not offers.

Clarity and Definiteness of Terms

The communicated terms of an offer must be sufficiently clear to remove any doubt about the contractual intentions of the offeror. No valid offer will exist when terms are indefinite, inadequate, vague, or confusing.

The Parnassian Petroleum Company sent a telegram to the OYM Oil Company, Incorporated. The telegram stated, "Please consider this our offer to purchase 100 acres of your 1,200-acre South American oil field. Our offering price is $45,000 per acre. Please respond soon." This telegram would not be a legally effective offer. The terms are much too indefinite. The telegram does not specify which of OYM's 1,200 acres Parnassian wants to purchase.

Degree of Definiteness In general, an offer should include points similar to those covered in a newspaper story—who, what, when, where, how much—if it is to be clear, definite, and certain. This means that the offer should identify (1) the parties involved in the contract, (2) the goods or services that will be the subject matter of the contract, (3) the price the offeror is willing to pay or receive, and (4) the time required for the performance of the contract. Most courts require reasonable rather than absolute definiteness. Offers will be upheld as long as the language is reasonably definite enough to enable the court to establish what the parties intended the terms to be.

T'sura was working on a vaccine to combat a new strain of South American flu. The Spanier-Needledorf Pharmaceutical Corporation offered her a fair share of the profits if she would develop the vaccine for their exclusive use. At the same time the Puglisi Independent Chemical Company offered T'sura $500,000 to develop the vaccine for them. Since T'sura insisted on working in her private laboratory at home, Puglisi offered to reimburse T'sura for all expenses related to the development of the vaccine. Puglisi also offered her 20 percent of the profits during the first 5 years that the vaccine is on the market. The Spanier-Needledorf offer is too indefinite to be enforced. The Puglisi offer, however, is definite enough even though a final dollar amount has not been settled upon. This is because the court has a way to figure out what the parties intended and what the final amount should be.

UCC 2-204(3)
(see p. 616)

Offers and the UCC The UCC permits offers to omit certain information. It states that "even though one or more terms are left open a contract for sale does not fail for indefiniteness if the parties have intended to make a contract and there is a reasonably certain basis for giving an appropriate remedy." Under this section of the UCC, cost-plus contracts, output contracts, requirement contracts, and current market price contracts are enforceable even though they are not complete in certain matters. A **cost-plus contract** will not include a final price. Instead, that price is determined by the cost of labor and materials plus an agreed-to percentage markup. An **output contract** is one in which one party agrees to sell to the second party all the goods that party makes in a given period of time. A **requirement contract** is one in which one party agrees to buy all the goods it needs from the second party. Finally, a **current**

UCC 2-306
(see pp. 618–619)

UCC 2-305(1)(c) (see p. 618)

market price contract is an agreement in which prices are determined by reference to the market price of the goods as of a specified date.

Communication to the Offeree

An offer must be communicated to the offeree in order to be valid. The communication of the offeror's intentions may be by whatever means are convenient and desirable. It may be communicated orally, by letter, by telegram, or by any other means capable of transmitting the offeror's proposal. It may also be implied. Acts and conduct of the proposing party are in many cases successful in communicating an intention to make an offer to another party witnessing them. When acts and conduct are sufficient to convey an offeror's intentions, an implied offer results.

Public Offers At times, an offer must be communicated to a party whose name, identity, or address is unknown. In such cases, the public offer is made. A **public offer** is one made through the public media but which is intended for only one person whose identity or address is unknown to the offeror. The classic example of a public offer is an advertisement in a lost-and-found column in a newspaper. Although this is a public offer, it is no different legally from other types of offers.

Invitations to Trade By contrast, invitations to trade are not offers. An **invitation to trade** is an announcement published to reach many persons for the purpose of creating interest and attracting responses. Newspaper and magazine advertisements, radio and television commercials, store window displays, price tags on merchandise, and prices in catalogs come within this definition. In the case of an invitation to trade, no binding agreement develops until a responding party makes an offer which the advertiser accepts. Nevertheless, sometimes advertisements are held to be offers. However, such advertisements would have to contain very particular promises, use phrases like "first-come, first-served," or limit the number of items to be sold. Since the number of people who can buy the product is very limited, the advertisement becomes an offer.

6-2 ACCEPTANCE OF AN OFFER

The second major element in a binding contract is acceptance of the offer. As previously stated, **acceptance** means that the offeree agrees to be bound by the terms set up by the offeror in the offer. Only the offeree, the one to whom the offer is made, has the right to accept an offer. If another party attempts to accept, that attempt would actually be a new and independent offer.

Kosar sold computer equipment for the Stratmore High-Tech Corporation. Kosar met with executives from the Fantoni Aircraft Company and offered to sell them a new computer system. Nocenti, a computer technician for Racine Aircraft, learned that the computer system was for sale. He called Kosar and, after inspecting the computer system, bought it for $250,000. Kosar had mistakenly thought that Nocenti worked for Fantoni. When he found out Nocenti worked for Racine, he refused to deliver the computer. Racine sued. The court held that no contract resulted. Only Fantoni, the party to whom the offer was made, could accept it.

Unilateral contracts do not usually require communication of expressed acceptance. When the offeror makes a promise in a unilateral contract, the offeror expects an action, not another promise in return. Performance of the action requested within the time allowed by the offeror and with the offeror's knowledge creates the contract.

Fujimoto and Bravo were both employed by Rio Grande Pickle Company. When they expressed dissatisfaction with their jobs, their employer offered them a new contract whereby they would receive a 10 percent bonus on company profits if they remained with the firm. They did not respond with an expressed acceptance but remained on the job. At times they did discuss the terms of the new agreement with an official of Rio Grande. Rio Grande later refused to pay the 10 percent bonus, claiming that its offer had never been accepted. The court ruled this to be a unilateral agreement and that their performance in remaining with Rio Grande constituted acceptance.

In bilateral contracts, unlike unilateral ones, the offeree must communicate acceptance to the offeror. Bilateral contracts consist of a promise by one party in return for a promise by the other. Until the offeree communicates a willingness to be bound by a promise, there is no valid acceptance.

Suppose in the previous case Rio Grande Pickle Company had said to its two employees, "We will consider your written acceptance to this new proposal as binding us to the payment of the 10 percent bonus." There would have been the intention of creating a bilateral contract, supported by mutual promises by both Rio Grande and Fujimoto and Bravo.

Communication of Acceptance

Communication of acceptance of an offer may be either express or implied. In an express acceptance, the offeree may choose any method of acceptance, unless the offer states that an acceptance must be made in a particular manner. A stipulation such as "reply by Western Union" or "reply by express mail" included in the offer must be carried out to have an acceptance. (See Table 6-2.)

Face-to-Face and Telephone Communication No special problem as to the timing of acceptance usually arises if the parties are dealing face to face. The acceptance becomes complete and effective as soon as the offeror hears the words of acceptance spoken by the offeree. In a similar vein, if the parties are negotiating over the telephone, the acceptance becomes effective when the offeree

Table 6-2 COMMUNICATION OF ACCEPTANCE

Method Used	*Legal Effect*
Face-to-face communication	Acceptance complete and effective when offeror hears the words of acceptance.
Telephone communication	Acceptance complete and effective when offeror hears the words of acceptance.
Communication by same method used by offeror	Acceptance complete and effective when delivered to the offeror by that same medium (e.g., mailed offer is accepted when acceptance is dropped in the mail).
Communication by different method from that used by offeror	Acceptance is complete and effective when it actually reaches the offeror (e.g., acceptance by telegram if offer had been mailed is effective when telegram reaches the offeror).

speaks the words of acceptance into the telephone receiver. When the parties must negotiate by writing letters or sending telegrams, problems may arise and the law provides certain rules as to when acceptance occurs.

Communication by the Same Medium Used by the Offeror Under common law, if acceptance is made through the same medium that communicated the offer, acceptance is complete and effective when it is delivered to that same medium. Thus an offer made through the mail is accepted when the acceptance is mailed. Offers made by telegram are accepted and become effective when the acceptance is filed with the telegraph company. This ruling, of course, requires that the offeree properly address and deliver the acceptance to the forwarding agent. Otherwise, acceptance is not complete until actual delivery has been made to the offeror.

Bogdonovich sent a letter to Hassinger offering to purchase Hassinger's winter home in Florida for $150,000. Hassinger decided to sell and mailed an acceptance on the same day he'd received Bogdonovich's offer. In the meantime, Bogdonovich changed his mind about buying the land and withdrew the offer before receiving Hassinger's acceptance. In an action against Bogdonovich, the court ruled acceptance was complete when Hassinger mailed the acceptance.

Communication by Medium Different from That Used by Offeror Under common law, when the offeree selects a means of communicating acceptance different from that used by the offeror, acceptance is not complete and effective until it actually reaches the offeror. Accepting by telegram when the offer is made by mail would be illustrative of using a different medium. In these situations delivery is complete when the acceptance reaches the offeror's home, office, or other return address. It need not be proved that the offeror personally opened and read the communicated acceptance.

The Tsukiji Publishing Company mailed a letter to Asahi asking him to join their firm as an editor. Asahi accepted by sending a telegram to Tsukiji's main office in Tokyo. Asahi's decision to accept by telegram meant that acceptance would not occur until the telegram actually reached Tsukiji Publishing at its business office in Tokyo.

UCC 2-206(1)(a) **(see p. 616)**

The UCC has changed this rule in contracts for the sale of goods. This is explained in Chapter 14.

Unequivocal Acceptance

To be effective, an acceptance must be *unequivocal.* This means that the acceptance must not change any of the terms stated in the offer. Under common law this is known as the mirror image rule. The Uniform Commercial Code has changed the mirror image rule for sale-of-goods contracts.

The Mirror Image Rule Under the **mirror image rule,** the terms as stated in the acceptance must exactly "mirror" the terms in the offer. If the acceptance changes or qualifies the terms in the offer, it is not an acceptance. Instead, a qualified acceptance is actually a counteroffer. A **counteroffer** is a response to an offer in which the terms of the original offer are changed. No agreement is reached unless the counteroffer is accepted by the original offeror.

The board of trustees of Manoa University offered Wendover the job of president of the university. Wendover agreed to accept the position as president of Manoa University if the trustees would provide him with a new automobile each year and if they would add an annual $3,000 year-end bonus to his contract. Under the mirror image rule, Wendover's qualified acceptance is actually a counteroffer. The trustees of Manoa University are now free to accept or reject Wendover's counteroffer or to make a new offer.

UCC 2-207 **(see p. 617)**

Counteroffers under the UCC The UCC has altered the mirror image rule when contract negotiations are being carried on. In contracts for the sale of goods, a contract will come into existence even though an acceptance has different or additional terms. The different or additional terms are treated as proposals for additions to the contract if the parties are not both merchants. If the parties are both merchants, however, the different or additional terms become part of the contract unless (a) they make an important difference, (b) the offeror objects, or (c) the offer limits acceptance to its terms. This exception is discussed further in Chapter 14.

Implied Acceptance

Acceptance may result from the conduct of the offeree. Actions and gestures may indicate the offeree's willingness to enter into a binding agreement.

Mailing of Unordered Merchandise Delivery of unordered merchandise through the mails is now considered nothing more than an offer to sell. In the past, unethical sellers would attempt to treat the failure of the recipient to either return the goods or send money as an implied acceptance of the offer to sell goods. Complaints were made that this practice allowed unethical firms to use the mails to defraud consumers and to saddle recipients with unwanted merchandise. This led to corrective regulations which are now incorporated into the Postal Reorganization Act of 1970. By this act, the recipient of unordered merchandise delivered through the mails may treat such goods as a gift. The receiver has no obligation to pay for or return the goods or to communicate with the sender in any way.

Unordered Goods Not Delivered by Mail When unordered goods are delivered by agencies other than the post office, the common law rule is usually followed. The receiver generally is not obligated to contact the sender or pay for the goods. There is an implied obligation to retain the goods and give them reasonable care over a reasonable period of time. After that time the receiver may consider that the sender no longer claims the goods and may use or dispose of them as desired.

Silence as Acceptance

As a general rule, silence is not an acceptance. If, however, both parties agree that silence on the part of the offeree will signal acceptance, then such an acceptance is valid.

Bruzenak read an advertisement in a magazine inviting him to become a member of the Literary Guild. Bruzenak chose five books listed in the advertisement. He paid only $1 for those books and became a member of the Guild. In doing so, he also agreed to purchase four more books. Under terms clearly specified in the advertisement, Bruzenak knew he would receive a free magazine 14 times a year listing selections. The magazine would also identify the main selections which would be sent to him automatically unless he sent a reply form to stop the shipment. In effect, Bruzenak had agreed that whenever he did not return the reply card, that silence would amount to acceptance of the main selections.

Another exception to the general rule occurs when the offeree has allowed silence to act as an acceptance. Also, even though the offeror cannot force the offeree into a contract by saying silence will mean acceptance, the offeree can force the offeror into a contract if the offeror set up the silence condition.

Atwood wanted to sell his 1935 Dusenberg. He wrote a letter to Applebaum offering to sell the Dusenberg to Applebaum for $25,000. Atwood ended the letter by stating, "If I don't hear from you by September 9, I will take your silence to mean you accept my offer." Applebaum received the letter and did not reply. Although Atwood could not bind Applebaum to this contract, Applebaum could hold Atwood to his offer because Atwood set up the silence condition himself.

6-3 REJECTION OF AN OFFER

A **rejection** comes about when an offeree expressly or impliedly refuses to accept an offer. Rejection terminates an offer and all negotiations associated with it. Further negotiations could commence with a new offer by either party or a renewal of the original offer by the offeror. Rejection is usually achieved by communication of that intention by the offeree.

In the opening commentary, each time Michigan offered Bay the post of athletic director at the university, he rejected the offer. The rejection terminated the offer. In one instance, Bay even communicated his rejection in written form. After the Earle Bruce firing and Bay's own resignation, he could not expect to be allowed to accept the offer he had previously rejected. New negotiations could begin, however, with a new offer by either the University of Michigan or Bay or by a renewal of the original offer by Michigan.

6-4 REVOCATION OF AN OFFER

A **revocation** is the calling back of the offer by the offeror. With the exception of an option contract and a firm offer (discussed below), an offer may be revoked any time before it has been accepted. The offeror has this right, despite what might at times appear to be a strong moral obligation to continue the offer. Offers may be revoked by (1) communication, (2) automatic revocation, (3) passage of time, (4) death or insanity of the offeror, (5) destruction of the subject matter, or (6) the subsequent illegality of the contract.

Revocation by Communication

Offers may be revoked by the will of the offeror merely by communicating that intention to the offeree before the offer has been accepted. Revocation is ineffective if the acceptance has already been communicated, as by mailing the acceptance in response to a mailed offer. Direct communication of revocation is not required if the offeree knows about the offer's withdrawal by other means.

Wagner offered to sell a thoroughbred trotting horse to Simpers for $125,000. It was mutually agreed that the offer would remain open for 5 days. Three days later Simpers read that Wagner's horse had been sold to Chambers' Stables for $150,000. Having learned of the sale, Simpers would be aware that the offer had been withdrawn. Suppose in this same case that the offer had been made in a letter received by Simpers and that before any news of the sale to Chambers' Stables reached Simpers a letter of acceptance was mailed to Wagner. Although the acceptance may not reach Wagner for another day, acceptance was complete upon the mailing of the letter, and revocation would not apply.

Automatic Revocation

When the terms of an offer include a definite time limit for acceptance, the offer is automatically revoked at the expiration of the time stated.

Westendorf had just finished her new novel, *The Counterfeit Imposter,* when she offered to sell full publishing rights to Venezia Publishing for $2 million. Westendorf gave Venezia until July 20 to accept the offer. When Venezia did not accept Westendorf's offer by midnight on July 20, the offer was automatically revoked. Westendorf was not required to honor Venezia's acceptance on July 21. Instead, she was free to make a new offer to Venezia or to any other publisher.

Revocation by Passing of Time

When no time limit has been set, an offer will revoke automatically after the passing of a reasonable length of time. The time element is determined through a review of all facts and surrounding circumstances. Perishable characteristics of goods, price fluctuations, supply-and-demand factors, and all other surrounding circumstances will contribute to establishment of the reasonable time factor. For example, communicating an offer by telegram rather than by letter would ordinarily imply the need for haste in making acceptance.

Revocation by Death or Insanity

Death or insanity of an offeror automatically revokes an existing offer. Both death and insanity preclude the possibility of a meeting of the minds. Revocation in both situations is immediate. Communication to the offeree is not required.

Revocation by Destruction

Destruction of subject matter related to an offer automatically revokes that offer. Destruction of the subject matter removes any possibility of performance of an anticipated agreement.

Revocation by Subsequent Illegality

The passing of restrictive legislation that would make performance of an anticipated agreement impossible automatically revokes an existing offer. Any agreement resulting from an attempted acceptance of such offers would be unenforceable.

6-5 OPTION CONTRACTS

An **option contract** is an agreement that binds an offeror to a promise to hold open an offer for a predetermined or reasonable length of time. In return for this agreement to hold the offer open, the offeror receives money or something else of value from the offeree. Parties to an option contract often agree that the consideration may be credited toward any indebtedness incurred by the offeree in the event that the offer is finally accepted. Should the offeree fail to take up the option, however, the offeror is under no legal obligation to return the consideration.

Option contracts remove the possibility of revocation through death or insanity of the offeror. The offeree who holds an option contract may demand acceptance by giving written notice of acceptance to the executor or administrator of the deceased offeror's estate or to the offeror's legally appointed guardian.

Wrightson offered to sell Blackston a coin collection for $35,000. Blackston requested time to consider the offer, and Wrightson agreed to hold the collection for Blackston for 2 weeks in return for Blackston's payment of $50. Wrightson died several days later. When Blackston tendered the $35,000, the executor refused to deliver the collection, claiming that death had revoked the offer. The court ruled otherwise, with judgment given to the offeree based upon the option agreement between Blackston and the deceased.

UCC 2-205 **(see p. 616)**

A special rule has been developed under the UCC which holds that no consideration is necessary when a merchant agrees in writing to hold an offer open. This is called a **firm offer**.

SUMMARY

6-1. Contracts require mutual assent or a "meeting of the minds" between two parties. Agreement is reached when an offer made by one party is accepted by another party. An offer is valid if it has serious intent, clear and reasonably definite terms, and communication to the offeree.

6-2. The second major part of mutual assent is the acceptance of the offer. Only the offeree has the right to accept the offer. Communication of the acceptance may be either express or implied. Under common law principles, to be effective an acceptance must not change any of the terms of the offer. This is known as the mirror image rule. The UCC has altered the mirror image rule. Acceptance may result from the conduct or actions of the offeree. However, as a general rule, silence cannot be made acceptance by the offeror.

6-3. At any time prior to acceptance, the offeror can withdraw the offer. Offers may be revoked by communication, by an automatic revocation, by the passage of time, by the death or insanity of the offeror, by the destruction of the subject matter, or by the subsequent illegality of the contract.

6-4. Some types of offers cannot be revoked by the offeror. These involve irrevocable or firm offers and option contracts.

Understanding Key Legal Terms

acceptance (p. 70)
cost-plus contract (p. 69)
counteroffer (p. 73)
current market price contract (p. 69)
firm offer (p. 77)
invitation to trade (p. 70)
mirror image rule (p. 73)
offer (p. 68)
offeree (p. 68)
offeror (p. 68)
option contract (p. 76)
output contract (p. 69)
public offer (p. 70)
rejection (p. 75)
requirement contract (p. 69)
revocation (p. 75)

Questions for Review and Discussion

1. List the three requirements of a valid offer.
2. Must the courts automatically invalidate any contract which omits terms and conditions deemed important to the parties' obligations? Explain.
3. How does a public offer differ from an invitation to trade?
4. Explain how an acceptance comes about in answer to a unilateral offer and in answer to a bilateral offer.
5. Under common law, when does acceptance become effective if the offeree makes acceptance through the same method used by the offeror in communicating an offer?
6. Under common law, when does acceptance become effective if the offeree makes acceptance using an medium different from the one used by the offeror in communicating an offer?
7. What is the mirror image rule? How has the UCC altered the mirror image rule?
8. Identify the various ways that an offeror can revoke an offer.
9. What are the two special qualities of an option contract? How does an option contract differ from an ordinary offer?
10. Explain what is meant by a firm offer.

Analyzing Cases

1. The Great Minneapolis Surplus Store published the following advertisement in a Minneapolis newspaper: "Saturday 9 a.m. 2 Brand New Pastel Mink 3-Skin Scarfs selling for $89.50—Out they go Saturday. Each...$1.00. 1 Black Lapin Stole. Beautiful, Worth $139.50...$1.00. First Come First Served." Leftkowitz, the first customer admitted to the store on Saturday, tried to buy the Lapin stole. The store refused to sell, stating that the offer was for women only. Leftkowitz sued. Is the offer definite enough to allow Leftkowitz to tender a valid acceptance? Explain. *Leftkowitz v. Great Minneapolis Surplus Store,* 86 N.W.2d 689 (Minnesota).
2. An advertisement appeared in the *Chicago Sun-Times* for the sale of a Volvo station wagon at Lee Calan Imports, Inc., for $1,095. The advertisement had been misprinted by the *Sun-Times*. The actual price of the automobile was $1,795. O'Keefe showed up at Lee Calan and said he would buy the Volvo for $1,095. Lee Calan refused to sell the car for $1,095. O'Keefe sued claiming that the advertisement was an offer which he accepted, creating a binding agreement. Is O'Keefe correct? Explain. *O'Keefe v. Lee Calan Imports,* 262 N.E.2d 758 (Illinois).
3. Morrison wanted to sell certain described land to Thoelke. He decided to make an offer by sending Thoelke a letter. When he received the letter, Thoelke decided to accept. He wrote a letter to Morrison saying he would buy the land at the price quoted in the letter. Thoelke then mailed the letter. After the mailing but before he received the letter, Morrison changed his mind and withdrew the offer to Thoelke. When Thoelke found out Morrison would not sell the land to him, he sued. Was Thoelke's letter a valid acceptance, binding Morrison to the sale? Explain. *Morrison v. Thoelke,* 155 So.2d 889 (Florida).
4. Wholesale Coal Company ordered 25 carloads of coal from Guyan Coal and Coke Company. Guyan could not come up with 25 carloads. However, it did have seven car-

loads available. Before shipping the coal, Guyan wrote back to Wholesale stating, "You can be sure that if it is possible to ship the entire 25 carloads, we will do so. But under the circumstances, this is the best we can promise you." When Guyan heard nothing from Wholesale, it shipped the seven carloads. When Wholesale did not pay for the seven carloads, Guyan brought suit to compel payment. Wholesale countersued claiming Guyan had not yet delivered the remaining 18 carloads. Is Wholesale correct? Explain. *Guyan Coal and Coke Company v. Wholesale Coal Company,* 201 N.W. 194 (Michigan).

5. Tockstein wrote up an offer to purchase a house owned by Rothenbeucher. Tockstein signed the offer and personally delivered it to Rothenbeucher. The offer included a condition that acceptance must be made within 24 hours. At the end of that 24-hour period, the offer would be automatically revoked if Rothenbeucher had not accepted. Rothenbeucher signed the agreement within the 24-hour period. However, he did not deliver the acceptance to Tockstein personally as Tockstein had done with the offer. Instead, Rothenbeucher delivered the acceptance to his own real estate agent who delivered it to Tockstein after the automatic revocation time. Tockstein claims the offer was automatically revoked when Rothenbeucher did not deliver it within the specified time period. Is Tockstein correct? Explain. *Rothenbeucher v. Tockstein,* 411 N.E.2d 92 (Illinois).

6. Sessler was a representative of Tyler Stores. In that capacity, he wrote to Kiley and promised her that she would receive an agency store as long as she would follow instructions and advice in preparing to open the store. Sessler wrote in the letter that Kiley did not have to reply if she agreed to these terms. Kiley received the letter and, according to Sessler's instructions, did not bother to reply. Instead, she began to make arrangements to open her agency store. Unfortunately, Sessler and Tyler did not live up to the agreement. As a result, Kiley sued Sessler and Tyler. Tyler and Sessler denied the existence of a contract, claiming that Kiley's silence in not answering Sessler's letter could not be construed as acceptance. Are they correct?

CHAPTER 7
Mutual Assent and Defective Agreement

OUTLINE

COMMENTARY

Olivia Backus had been living on a plot of land for almost 20 years when the Holt family, who had previously owned the land, offered her $10,000 for it. In negotiating with Backus, the Holts failed to mention that they had discovered extensive oil deposits on the land. These oil deposits made the land worth millions of dollars. When Backus refused to sell, the Holts offered her $30,000 and permanent residence on the land. However, in return, they wanted drilling rights to the land. Again, they failed to tell her about the oil and, in fact, evaded all questions about the land's true value. When Backus still refused to sell, the Holts sued claiming Backus had no rights to the land in the first place. If the story sounds familiar, that's because it comes from the film *As Summers Die* starring Bette Davis and Jamie Lee Curtis. The movie has a happy ending and Olivia Backus keeps her land. However, if she had sold that million-dollar tract of land for $10,000, would she have a cause of action against the Holt family when she later found out that they had concealed the land's true value from her? This is the type of issue addressed in this chapter on mutual assent and defective agreements.

OBJECTIVES

1. Explain the nature of mutual assent, and indicate how mutual assent can be destroyed.
2. List the elements that must be proved to establish fraud, and judge whether those elements are present in a given contract situation.
3. Identify those situations which can give rise to claims of passive fraud.
4. Distinguish between fraud and misrepresentation, and contrast the remedies available for each.
5. Discuss the difference between unilateral and bilateral mistakes.

6. Judge which types of mistakes provide appropriate grounds for getting out of the contract.
7. Differentiate between physical, emotional, and economic duress, and recognize the remedies available to an injured party alleging duress.
8. Explain how the existence of a confidential relationship is a key factor in establishing undue influence.

7-1 MUTUAL ASSENT

As we have seen, a contract consists of six elements. The first element is the offer. An offer is a proposal made by one party, the offeror, to another party, the offeree. The proposal indicates the offeror's willingness to enter into a contract with the offeree. If the offer is seriously intended, clear and definite, and communicated to the offeree, then the offeree may accept or reject it. The second element of a contract is the acceptance. If the offeree does in fact accept the offer, then there is mutual assent between the parties. Mutual assent is the third element of a valid contract.

The Nature of Mutual Assent

As defined in Chapter 5, **mutual assent** means that the parties have had a "meeting of the minds." In other words, both parties know what the terms are and both have voluntarily agreed to be bound by those terms. Mutual assent may be reached quickly, as in buying a magazine at the local bookstore, or it may result from weeks of negotiations related to a multimillion dollar undertaking. Whatever the case, mutual assent evolves through the communication of an offer and an acceptance between the contracting parties.

The Destruction of Mutual Assent

After mutual assent has been reached, the law protects the contracting parties in their contractual relationship. If one party or the other discovers that he or she has been cheated or discovers that a mutual mistake placed the party at a great disadvantage, that party is no longer bound to the terms of the agreement. Each party to a contract is protected from the chicanery of the other or from certain mistakes that may have crept into their agreement and destroyed mutual assent. If mutual assent has been destroyed, the contract is said to be a defective agreement. A defective agreement can arise as a result of fraud, misrepresentation, mutual mistake, duress, or undue influence. The remainder of this chapter covers each of these potentially destructive forces.

7-2 FRAUD AND MISREPRESENTATION

Fraud is a wrongful statement, action, or concealment pertinent to the subject matter of a contract knowingly made to damage the other party. Fraud, if proved, destroys any contract and makes the wrongdoer **liable** (i.e., legally responsible) to the injured party for all losses that result.

The Elements of Fraud

To destroy mutual assent on a claim of fraud, the complaining or innocent party must prove the existence of five elements. First, the complaining party will have to show that the other party made a false representation about some **material fact** (i.e., an important fact; a fact of substance) involved in the contract. A material fact is one that is very crucial to the terms of the contract. Second, it must be shown that the other party made the representation knowing of its falsity. Third, it must be shown that the false representations were made with the intent that they be relied upon by the innocent party. Fourth, the complaining party must demonstrate that there was a reasonable reliance on the false representations. Finally, it must be shown that the innocent party actually suffered some loss by relying on the false representation after entering the contract. A case involving either active or passive fraud must be based on these five elements.

As director of the Comprehensive Learning Center (CLC) at Gillis Community College, Ekener purchased several software packages for mathematics and English enrichment. Teppler, owner and primary sales representative for Teppler Educational Services, told Ekener that the software packages were brand-new and in first-class condition. Teppler also told Ekener that the packages were compatible with the six different types of computer systems in the CLC. In reality, Teppler knew that the packages were not new, but had been previously used by another college. In addition, the packages were compatible with only one of the six computer systems in the CLC. Ekener and Gillis Community College could sue Teppler for a return of all the money paid to Teppler and for any other damages that resulted from the misrepresented facts.

In the Gillis Community College case noted above, all five elements of fraud are present. First, Teppler made false representations about several material facts. In the Gillis case, the condition of the software and its compatibility with the computer systems in the CLC were material to the contract. Second, Teppler made the representations knowing they were false. Third, the statements made by Teppler were designed to lead the Gillis College representative into relying on them. Fourth, the Gillis College representative reasonably relied on Teppler's statement in the purchase of the software. Finally, Gillis College actually suffered a financial loss because they paid a top price for used software that they could use in only one-sixth of their equipment.

Active Fraud

Active fraud occurs when one party to a contract makes a false statement intended to deceive the other party and thus leads that party into a deceptively based agreement. The false statements made by Teppler to the Gillis College representative would fall into this category. Thus, Teppler committed active fraud against Gillis College. False statements about material facts may also include illustrations and models that specifically relate to the description, condition, and characteristics of the subject matter of the contract. These "statements" need not be confined to oral or written representations. Actions designed to deceive, such as turning back a car's odometer or painting over rust spots, are considered statements about the condition of the subject matter of the contract.

Palencia ran a used-car lot on the outskirts of Wichita. Dujardin, who was new in town, needed a car quickly. Sensing that he could make a real killing on the deal, Palencia took one of the best-looking, but worst-running, cars on the lot and offered to let Dujardin take it for a test drive. Dujardin agreed. However, before turning the car over to Dujardin, Palencia had his mechanic put sawdust in the transmission so that it would run smoothly. Deceived by the apparently good condition of the car, Dujardin purchased it. Four days later the transmission fell out of the car. Even though Palencia never actually said anything to Dujardin about the transmission, he would still have committed fraud.

To be fraudulent, statements must involve facts. Opinions and **sales puffery** consist of the persuasive words and exaggerated claims made by salespeople to induce a customer to buy their product. As long as the comments are reserved to opinion and do not misstate facts, they cannot be considered fraud in a lawsuit even if they turn out to be grossly wrong.

Fitzwater, a sales clerk representing the Van Ryan Legal Publishing Company, was trying to sell a set of law books to Ortega. During the negotiations, Fitzwater told Ortega that (1) the set consisted of five cloth-bound volumes, (2) all references were supported by recent court decisions or sections from the UCC, (3) the books were printed in easily readable type, (4) a concentrated study of the five volumes would guarantee any student success in passing examinations in business law, and (5) the books would add a professional decor to the owner's library.

The first two statements are statements of material fact and could be the basis of a suit for fraud if they are proven to be false. The others are either opinions expressed by the seller or the persuasive puffing that might induce Ortega to buy the books and could not be used as the basis of a suit for fraud.

Passive Fraud

As noted above, active fraud occurs when one party actually makes a false statement intended to deceive the other party in a contract. In contrast, **passive fraud,** which is generally called **concealment,** or **nondisclosure,** occurs when one party does not say something about certain facts that he or she is under an obligation to reveal. If this passive conduct is intended to deceive and does, in fact, deceive the other party, fraud results. In general, a party is not required to reveal every known fact related to the subject matter of a contract. Certain facts may be confidential and personal. For instance, someone offering a VCR for sale need not disclose why it is being sold or how much profit will be realized. Hiding a fact becomes concealment, however, under certain circumstances. These circumstances include hidden problems and fiduciary relationships.

Hidden Problems As previously stated, in general a party is not under a duty to reveal everything about the subject matter of a contract. However, if the problem or defect is hidden and the other party cannot reasonably be expected to discover the defect, then, provided the problem involves some material fact, the offeror may be obliged to reveal it.

Plepler owned a house on Arlington Avenue which he was desperate to sell because he had been relocated from Swiftwater to St. Louis. Sheridan took a look at the house and made a rather thorough tour. What Sheridan did not know and, in fact, could not reasonably be expected to discover was that the foundation had been damaged by a recent earthquake. Plepler knew of the damage and knew that because of the damage, water leaked into the basement every time it rained. However, he did not reveal the problem to Sheridan. Plepler has committed passive fraud or concealment because he did not reveal a serious hidden problem that Sheridan could not reasonably be expected to discover on his own.

Some states have held that sellers are legally bound to reveal only problems so hidden that even an expert would not be able to uncover them. In these states, problems such as insect or rodent infestation would not be hidden problems because an expert could easily uncover them.

Fiduciary Relationships A **fiduciary relationship** is a relationship based upon trust. Such relationships exist between attorneys and their clients, guardians and wards, trustees and beneficiaries, and directors and the corporation, among others. If one party is in a fiduciary relationship with another party, then an obligation arises to reveal what otherwise might be withheld when the two parties enter an agreement.

Osborne was on the board of directors of Hawkes-VanBuren Chemical Corporation when he learned that the Laurel Valley Motel Company wanted to buy 50 acres of timberland owned by Hawkes-VanBuren. Osborne was the only one at Hawkes-VanBuren who knew that the new interstate interchange was going to be located on the acreage owned by the company. Moreover, Osborne knew that Laurel Valley wanted the land for a new luxury resort hotel and was willing to pay $10,000 per acre. Osborne made a deal with Laurel Valley agreeing to sell the land at that price. He then went to the rest of the board of Hawkes-VanBuren and offered to buy the timberland without revealing anything about the Laurel Valley deal. As a result, he purchased the acreage for $500 per acre and made a $9,500 profit on each acre he resold to Laurel Valley. Osborne will be liable to Hawkes-VanBuren because he concealed a material fact he was under a duty to reveal because of his fiduciary relationship to the company.

Misrepresentation

Misrepresentation is a false statement made innocently with no intent to deceive. Innocent misrepresentation makes an existing agreement voidable and

Table 7-1 AGREEMENTS MADE DEFECTIVE BY FALSEHOOD

Falsehood	*Definition*	*Remedy*
Active fraud	Active fraud occurs when one party to a contract makes a false statement intended to deceive the other party and thus lead that party into a deceptively based agreement.	Rescission and money damages
Passive fraud (concealment or nondisclosure)	Passive fraud occurs when one party does not say something about certain facts that he or she is obligated to reveal. Obligations arise in situations involving hidden problems and fiduciary relationships.	Rescission and money damages
Innocent misrepresentation	Misrepresentation occurs when a false statement is innocently made with no intent to deceive.	Rescission only

the complaining party may demand rescission. **Rescission** means that both parties are returned to their original positions, before the contract was entered into. Unlike cases based on fraud which allow rescission and damages, cases based on innocent misrepresentation allow only rescission and not money damages.

Malinowsky gave Cartwright of the Love and Glory Comics Shop $250 as a down payment on what Cartwright described as the June 1938 issue of *Action Comics,* featuring the first published story of Superman. Later, a careful examination revealed that the comic was actually a 1966 reprint of the original story. Without any indication of wrongdoing, Cartwright would be liable for nothing more than an innocent misrepresentation. Malinowsky can either rescind the agreement or demand delivery of the comic. In cases of this kind, the parties often renegotiate the purchase price if the agreement is affirmed.

If a party to an agreement makes an innocent misrepresentation and then later discovers that it is false, that party must reveal the truth. If the party does not reveal the truth, the innocent misrepresentation becomes fraud.

7-3 MISTAKE

When there has been no real meeting of the minds because of a mistake, mutual assent was never achieved and the agreement may be rescinded. As in misrepresentation, mistake permits rescission.

Unilateral and Bilateral Mistakes

A mistake made by only one of the contracting parties is a **unilateral mistake** and does not offer sufficient grounds for rescission or renegotiation. When both parties are mistaken, it is a **bilateral mistake.** A bilateral mistake, which is also called a **mutual mistake**, allows a rescission by either the offeror or the offeree.

Layton owned two farms in Sussex County. One of the farms was located near the waterfront and offered much potential for possible homesite and recreational development. The other was further inland and was equally valuable as a crop-producing venture. Baldt arranged to buy one of the properties, thinking that the agreement was for the waterfront acreage. Layton understood that the sale was for the other property. There had never been a true meeting of the minds since both parties were mistaken as to the other's intentions. The circumstances would support an action for rescission of this agreement.

The Nature of Mistakes

Mutual mistakes are of several kinds. Some are universally accepted as grounds for rescission. Others are not grounds for rescission. Still others can give rise to lawsuits, but not in all courts or in all states.

Mistakes as to Description When both parties are mistaken in the identification and description of subject matter, there is a real mutual mistake and rescission will be granted.

Mistakes as to Existence Proof that the subject matter had been destroyed before agreement was made gives grounds for rescission. Thus, if one accepted an offer to purchase a boat that both parties mistakenly believed to be berthed at a specified marina, the agreement would be voidable if it were proved that moments before acceptance the boat had been destroyed. Had the boat been destroyed after final acceptance, there would have been no mutual mistake and an enforceable contract would have resulted.

Mistakes as to Value When two parties agree on the value of the subject matter and later find they were both mistaken, this is a mutual mistake of opinion, not of fact. Mutual mistakes of opinion are not grounds for rescinding a contract.

Table 7-2 AGREEMENTS MADE DEFECTIVE BY MUTUAL MISTAKE

Mistake	*Legal Effect*
Mistake as to description	Rescission will be granted.
Mistake as to existence	Proof that subject matter was destroyed *before* the agreement was made gives grounds for rescission.
Mistake as to value	Rescission will not be granted since value is a matter of opinion, not fact.
Mistake through failure to read the document	Rescission will not be granted unless failure to read involves conditions printed on tickets and stubs.
Mistakes of law	Rescission usually will not be granted. Rescission may be granted when the mistake relates to the law of another state. This is interpreted as a mistake of fact. Some states have adopted statutes allowing rescission for mutual mistake of law.

Mistakes Through Failure to Read Document Failure to read a document or the negligent reading of a document does not excuse performance on the ground of a mistaken understanding of the document's contents. Exceptions may be made when conditions are printed on parking lot stubs, cleaner's tickets, hat check identifications, and the like. The law usually holds that these vouchers are given for identification purposes only. The courts generally are not favorable toward enforcing the fine-print conditions on the face or reverse side of such tickets.

Mistakes of Law Misunderstandings of existing laws do not give grounds for rescission. As often quoted, "Ignorance of the law is no excuse." Rescission may be allowed, however, when there have been mistakes related to the law of another state. In this way the courts interpret mistakes of law of a different state as mistakes of fact, not of law. Some states have now adopted statutes that completely remove the so-called ignorance-of-law concept. In those states any mutual mistake of law is sufficient to bring about a rescission.

7-4 DURESS AND UNDUE INFLUENCE

Duress and undue influence have only one thing in common. They both rob a person of the ability to make an independent, well-reasoned decision to freely enter a contractual relationship. **Duress** may be viewed as an action by one party which forces another party to do what need not otherwise be done. Duress forces a person into a contract through the use of physical, emotional, or economic threats. In contrast, undue influence merely involves the use of excessive pressure. Moreover, undue influence also requires the existence of a confidential relationship.

Physical and Emotional Duress

Physical duress involves either violence or the threat of violence against an individual or against that person's family, household, or property. If only threats are used, they must be so intense and serious that a person of ordinary prudence would be forced into the contract without any real consent. **Emotional duress** arises from acts or threats that would create emotional distress in the one on whom they are inflicted. Exposure to public ridicule, threatened attacks on one's reputation, or efforts to prevent employment might constitute emotional duress.

Economic Duress

Economic duress, also known as **business compulsion,** consists of threats of a business nature that force another party without real consent to enter a commercial agreement. In order to establish economic duress, the complaining party must demonstrate that the other party was responsible for placing the complainant in a precarious economic situation and that the other party acted wrongfully in doing so. The complainant must also show that there was no alternative other than to submit to the contractual demands of the wrongful party. As long as the innocent party acted reasonably in entering the contract, the court will rule the contract voidable on grounds of economic duress.

The Culver City Cavaliers renegotiated a five-year lease with Culver City for the use of the Culver City Municipal Coliseum for the Cavaliers' home hockey games. On the day before the opening game of the second season under the contract, Culver City officials locked the doors of the coliseum and told the Cavaliers they could not use the facilities unless they agreed to an enormous rent increase. The Cavaliers, who had already sold 35,000 tickets to the game and who could not find any other suitable ice skating facility within 250 miles of Culver City, agreed to the terms. Later the Cavaliers sued Culver City to have the rent increase rescinded. The court ruled that the rent increase was voidable on grounds of economic duress.

Undue Influence

Undue influence occurs when the dominant party in a confidential relationship uses excessive pressure to convince the weaker party to enter a contract that greatly benefits the dominant party. To prove undue influence, it must be shown that a confidential relationship existed between the parties. A **confidential relationship** involves the existence of trust and dependence between the two parties. Examples of confidential relationships include the relationships of parent to child, guardian to ward, husband to wife, attorney to client, physician to patient, pastor to parishioner, and so forth. In most cases involving undue influence, one party, with strength and leadership, dominates the other, who is obviously weaker and dependent.

Okoya was an 89-year-old invalid who needed daily care. He hired Rutherford, a live-in nurse who agreed to take care of Okoya. After one year in this arrangement, Rutherford began to pressure Okoya into signing over all his property to her in exchange for Rutherford's promise never to leave. Rutherford isolated Okoya from relatives and friends and told him that everyone had abandoned him and that only she, Rutherford, cared about him. Convinced he had been completely abandoned by his family and friends, Okoya signed over all his property. When Okoya's nephew found out what had happened, he fired Rutherford, hired a lawyer, and helped his uncle sue Rutherford. The court ruled that in Okoya's weakened condition, he had submitted to Rutherford's excessive pressure in signing over all his property.

Undue influence should not be confused with persuasion or some subtle form of inducement. Although one might be induced to enter into agreements through the urging of someone such as an employer, a professor, or an athletic coach, there is no undue influence if there is absence of the required confidential relationship. Persuasion and subtle inducement, while at times unethical, are not considered undue influence in the eyes of the law and do not, in and of themselves, provide a basis for rescinding agreements.

Table 7-3 AGREEMENTS MADE DEFECTIVE BY FORCE OR PRESSURE

Type of Force or Pressure	*Explanation*	*Legal Effect*
Physical duress	Violence or threat of violence to person, family, household, or property	Contract voidable; rescission allowed
Emotional duress	Acts or threats that create emotional distress in the one on whom they are inflicted	Contract voidable; rescission allowed
Economic duress or business compulsion	Threats of a business nature that force another party without real consent to enter a commercial agreement	Contract voidable; rescission allowed
Undue influence	Dominant party in a confidential relationship uses excessive pressure to convince the weaker party to enter a contract that greatly benefits the dominant party	Contract voidable; rescission allowed

SUMMARY

7-1. Offer and acceptance go together to create mutual assent. Mutual assent means that both parties know what the terms are and have agreed to be bound by those terms. If mutual assent has been destroyed, the contract is said to be a defective agreement. A defective agreement can arise as a result of fraud, misrepresentation, mutual mistake, duress, or undue influence.

7-2. Fraud involves a deliberate deception about some material fact that leads a party into an agreement that is damaging to that party. Active fraud occurs when one party makes a false statement intended to deceive the other party and thus lead that party into a deceptively based contract. The deception can involve an oral statement or an action that misleads the other party about a crucial fact. Passive fraud, or concealment or nondisclosure, occurs when one party does not say something that he or she is obligated to say. Misrepresentation is a false statement innocently made with no intent to deceive.

7-3. Unilateral mistakes, that is, mistakes made by one party, do not allow for rescission or renegotiation. When both parties are mistaken, it is a bilateral mistake. A bilateral mistake may allow for rescission by either party.

7-4. Duress and undue influence rob a person of the ability to make an independent, well-reasoned decision to freely enter into a contract. Physical duress involves violence or threats of violence. Emotional duress arises from acts or threats that would create emotional distress in the individual who is the object of the threats or acts. Economic duress consists of threats of a business nature that force another party without real consent to enter into a contract. Undue influence involves a confidential relationship. In most cases, undue influence involves the dominant party in the confidential relationship applying excessive pressure to the weaker party resulting in a contract that is of benefit to the dominant individual.

Understanding Key Legal Terms

active fraud (p. 82)
bilateral mistake (p. 85)
business compulsion (p. 87)
concealment (p. 83)
confidential relationship (p. 88)
duress (p. 87)
economic duress (p. 87)
emotional duress (p. 87)
fiduciary relationship (p. 84)
fraud (p. 81)
liable (p. 81)
material fact (p. 82)
misrepresentation (p. 84)
mutual assent (p. 81)
mutual mistake (p. 86)
nondisclosure (p. 83)
passive fraud (p. 83)
physical duress (p. 87)
rescission (p. 85)
sales puffery (p. 83)
undue influence (p. 88)
unilateral mistake (p. 85)

Questions for Review and Discussion

1. What is mutual assent and how can it be destroyed?
2. What five elements must be proved to establish that a contract is defective due to fraud? Does a salesperson's opinion and sales puffery constitute grounds for a lawsuit based on fraud?
3. Identify those situations which give rise to a duty not to conceal certain material facts when entering a contract.
4. What is the essential difference between fraud and misrepresentation? How do the remedies for each differ?
5. Does a unilateral mistake give grounds to a party to rescind a contract? Does a bilateral mistake give grounds for rescission? Explain.
6. Identify those types of mistakes which provide appropriate grounds for getting out of a contract.
7. How do physical and emotional duress differ from each other?
8. Explain what the complaining party must prove to demonstrate the existence of economic duress.
9. What is the meaning of confidential relationships in respect to a charge that a contract was obtained through undue influence? Give examples of parties who usually enjoy a confidential relationship and who may be particularly susceptible to charges of exercising undue influence.
10. In addition to the confidential relationship, what other elements are necessary to demonstrate the existence of undue influence?

Analyzing Cases

1. Walker and Cousineau were both in the gravel business. Walker advertised a tract of land claiming that he had an engineer's report indicating that the land held at least 80,000 cubic yards of gravel. In fact, Walker knew the land contained much less gravel. Cousineau purchased the land and began to excavate it. After only 6,000 cubic yards of gravel had been removed, the supply ran out. Cousineau sued Walker asking the court to rescind the contract. Will Cousineau win the case? Explain. *Cousineau v. Walker,* 613 P.2d 608 (Alaska).

2. Young sold a residential lot to Sorrell without revealing to Sorrell that the lot had been filled. The landfill was not obvious, and Sorrell could not have been reasonably expected to detect it. When Sorrell later discovered the landfill, he sued Young, asking the court to rescind the agreement. Young claimed he was under no obligation to reveal the fill to Sorrell. Is Young correct? Explain. *Sorrell v. Young,* 491 P.2d 1312 (Washington).

3. Boskett offered to sell a 1916 dime to Beachcomber Coins, Inc. Beachcomber examined the coin carefully and agreed to pay Boskett $500 for it. Later, Beachcomber asked a representative from the American Numismatic Society to examine the coin. The coin turned out to be counterfeit. No evidence existed to indicate fraud on Boskett's part. Beachcomber sued Boskett for rescission and a return of the $500. Beachcomber claims this bilateral mistake of fact creates grounds for a rescission. Is Beachcomber correct? Explain. *Beachcomber Coins, Inc. v. Boskett,* 400 A.2d 78 (New Jersey).

4. Prisoners rioted at the Iowa State Penitentiary. The rioting prisoners held prison staff members as hostages. The warden agreed in writing that no reprisals would be levied against the rioting inmates. In exchange, the prisoners released the hostages. After the hostages were released, several of the prisoners were punished for the riot. One prisoner, Wagner, was placed in solitary for 30 days. He also received 180 days of administrative segregation, and the loss of 1,283 days of good time earned. On what legal grounds can the warden refuse to keep his promise to the inmates? Explain. *Wagner v. State,* 364 N.W.2d 246 (Iowa).

5. Loral Corporation had a contract with the U.S. government to manufacture radar sets. Loral subcontracted with Austin Instrument for the production of precision parts to be used in the radar sets. In the middle of production, Austin told Loral that it would deliver no more parts unless Loral agreed to pay Austin a good deal more than originally agreed upon. Loral could not obtain the same parts in time from any other company. As a result, Loral agreed to the price increase. After delivering the radar sets, Loral sued Austin and asked the court to rescind the price increase. Will the court grant Loral's request? Explain. *Austin Instrument, Inc. v. Loral Corporation,* 272 N.E.2d 533 (New York).

6. Vargas, an artist, had been under contract with *Esquire* magazine for several years. When time came for a new contract, Vargas met with the president of the company and signed the new contract without reading it. Later, Vargas found out that the contract did not say what he thought it said. He sued *Esquire,* arguing that he signed the agreement only because he had relied upon the president of the company to look after his business affairs. Is this a case of undue influence? Explain. *Vargas v. Esquire, Inc.,* 166 F.2d 651 (7th Cir. Ct.).

CHAPTER 8
Contractual Capacity

OUTLINE

8-1 Minors' Rights and Obligations
- Definition of Minority
- Misrepresentation of Age

8-2 Contractual Capacity of Minors
- Contracts for Necessaries
- Other Contracts Not Voidable
- Disaffirmance of Minors' Contracts
- Ratification of Minors' Contracts

8-3 Mental Incompetents and Persons Drugged or Intoxicated
- Persons Mentally Infirm or Mentally Ill
- Persons Legally Insane
- Persons Drugged or Intoxicated

COMMENTARY

Kiefer was married and the father of one child. He was also one year shy of becoming an adult. Nevertheless, he contracted in writing to purchase a used car from Fred Howe Motors, Inc. The contract Kiefer signed included a preprinted statement right above his name which said that he was an adult. This, of course, was not true. Kiefer had a great deal of trouble with the car. The trouble was eventually traced to a cracked block that Kiefer said had existed at the time he purchased the car. Kiefer went back to Howe and told the dealer that he was a minor. He then demanded his money back. The dealer refused and Kiefer sued. Generally minors have the right to void their contracts. However, in this case, Kiefer had signed a document which said he was an adult. Should the court hold Kiefer to the agreement because of the document he signed? Should the fact that he is married make a difference? Should his parenthood make a difference in the court's decision? What about the fact that he is almost an adult? Does this make any difference? These questions are addressed in this chapter on contractual capacity.

OBJECTIVES

1. Describe the general legal presumptions in regard to a party's capacity to create a contract.
2. Explain why the law allows minors to void contracts for anything other than necessaries.
3. Differentiate between the age of minority and the age of majority under common law, and explain how Amendment 26 to the U.S. Constitution affects the age of majority.
4. Distinguish between emancipation and abandonment, and explain the meaning of each concept.
5. Assess the potential liability of minors who lie about their age when entering into a contract.
6. Contrast the legal liability of minors in contracts involving necessaries with their legal liability in contracts that do not involve necessaries.

7. Identify other types of contracts that the law may except from the general rule that contracts by minors are voidable by the minor.
8. Contrast the contractual capacity of persons declared legally insane with those not declared legally insane.
9. Discuss the contractual capacity of drugged or intoxicated persons.

8-1 MINORS' RIGHTS AND OBLIGATIONS

The fourth element essential to a legally effective contract is the legal ability to enter into a contractual relationship. This legal ability is known as **capacity.** The law has established a general presumption that anyone entering into a contractual relationship has the legal capacity to do so. This means that someone enforcing an agreement does not have to prove that the other party had contractual capacity when the contract was entered into. However, this is a **rebuttable presumption;** that is, a defending party (a minor, mental incompetent, or drunk) has the right to attack the presumption in order to rescind a contract. Minors are generally excused from contractual liability due to their incapacity; their contracts are voidable. The courts allow minors this privilege to protect them from adults who might take advantage of young people who might not fully understand their obligations. In effect, the privilege allows minors to get out of contracts they have entered before reaching adulthood.

Darmstedter and Yuan entered into a contract which obligated Darmstedter to sell her computer to Yuan. At the time, Darmstedter was only 17 years old. Before the computer was delivered or any money exchanged, Darmstedter changed her mind. Yuan brought suit against Darmstedter. It would not be necessary for Yuan to prove Darmstedter had contractual capacity because the law presumes that such capacity exists. However, since the presumption is rebuttable, Darmstedter could introduce evidence to show that, because she was a minor, she could rescind the contract.

When a minor **disaffirms** a contract, that is, indicates by a statement or act an intent not to live up to it, the minor is entitled to a return of everything given to the other party. This is true even when the property transferred to the minor under the contract has been damaged or destroyed. A few states will deduct something from the amount due back to the minor if the goods are damaged. Most states, however, deduct nothing.

Chandler was 17 years old when she purchased a VCR from Parrish Electronics. The VCR cost Chandler $349. After using it for one week, she decided to return it to Parrish. On the way to the store, Chandler dropped the VCR, damaging it. The store manager said it would take $100 to fix the machine. Most states would allow Chandler a full refund of $349 despite the damaged condition of the VCR. A minority of states would deduct $100.

Definition of Minority

Minority, under common law, was a term that described persons who had not yet reached the age of twenty-one. Upon reaching that age, a person was said to have reached **majority.** Ratification and adoption of Amendment 26 to the U.S. Constitution in 1971 lowered the voting age in federal elections from 21 to 18. To avoid the confusion that would result from having two voting ages, the states started to enact new laws that enabled 18-year-olds to vote in state and local elections. Then states began to lower the age of majority to 18 years for certain types of contracts. However, differences still exist within and between states as to the age requirements for achieving majority; this is so particularly in matters related to the use of alcoholic beverages, marriage, and the operation of motor vehicles. Recently, in response to outside influences from a variety of social organizations and governmental institutions, many states have raised the drinking age to 21.

Legal Age In most states, a person becomes an adult at the beginning of the day before his or her birthday. This is because the day on which a person is born is counted as the first day of life. The law does not consider fractions of days. For this reason, on a person's eighteenth birthday, the person is really 18 years and one day old.

Sutcliffe was born on February 28. State law required persons to be 21 before they could purchase and consume alcoholic beverages. Since Sutcliffe becomes 21 at any time on February 27, she would be legally allowed to celebrate at the local tavern on that date. Few bartenders and tavern owners know this rule, though, and so from a practical, not a legal, point of view, Sutcliffe would still probably have to wait until February 28 for her first drink.

Emancipation and Abandonment In some states, minors who became **emancipated,** that is, no longer under the control of their parents, are responsible for their contracts. Emancipated minors include those who are married as well as those who leave home and give up all right to parental support. They are said to have *abandoned* the usual protective shield given them. Although minors in these two categories are no longer protected from liability on their contracts, merchants are usually reluctant to deal with them on a credit basis, fearing that they may still attempt to *disaffirm,* or repudiate, their contracted debts. Again, for practical, not legal, reasons, merchants require that minors get the signature of a responsible adult who will agree to guarantee payment of money owed.

Misrepresentation of Age

Minors sometimes lie about their age when making a contract. Despite the misrepresentation of age, most states will allow the minor to disaffirm or get out of the contract. Some states, however, have enacted statutes which allow recovery against a minor when misrepresentation of age can be proved or when the minor is engaged in business. A number of states, for example, have statutes that deny disaffirmance if the minor has signed a written statement falsely asserting adult status. Without such a statute the minor will be allowed to get out of the contract despite her or his signature.

In the opening commentary, Kiefer signed a contract which indicated that he was an adult when, in actuality, he was still a minor. When the automobile he had purchased turned out to be worthless, Kiefer tried to get out of the contract, claiming he was a minor. Kiefer would have this right unless a state statute existed to take that right away. As it turned out, Kiefer's state had no such statute and he was allowed to disaffirm the agreement.

8-2 CONTRACTUAL CAPACITY OF MINORS

Executory contracts, those which have not been fully performed by both parties, may be repudiated by a minor at any time. A promise to deliver goods or render services at some future time need not be carried out by the minor who so decides. This privilege is not available to an adult who contracts with a minor. If goods delivered to a repudiating minor are still in the minor's possession, it is the minor's duty to return them to the other party. (See Figure 8-1).

Heinzmann, who was 17 years old, purchased a compact disk (CD) player from Spectrum Electronics. Heinzmann paid $50 down and agreed to pay the balance in 24 monthly installments. Three weeks later after he had taken the CD home, Heinzmann decided he didn't want it any longer. When Spectrum refused to take back the CD player, Heinzmann sued for the return of his down payment and the cancellation of the balance he still owed. In most states, Spectrum would be required to make the refund and cancel the debt. Heinzmann would have to return the CD player.

Contracts for Necessaries

Necessaries are those goods and services that are essential to a minor's health and welfare. A minor's contract covering necessaries is enforceable against the minor. The minor, however, is not required to pay the price agreed to on a contract for necessaries, but only the fair value, as determined by the court. If the necessaries had already been provided the minor by parents or others, they will not qualify under this rule.

Classified as necessaries are food, clothing, shelter, medical and dental services, and other goods and services reasonably required in protecting the minor's health and welfare. In determining whether goods and services qualify as necessaries, the court will inquire into the minor's family status, financial strength, and social standing or station in life. Necessaries, then, are not the same to all persons.

17810 Windward Rd.
Terre Haute, IN 47811
September 9, 19--

Seller's address

Spectrum Electronics
433 East 310th Street
Willowick, IN 47812

Minor's name and address

Date and place of contract

Please take notice that I, Andrew Heinzmann, of 17810 Windward Road, Terre Haute, Indiana, hereby disaffirm the contract made on August 19, for the purchase of a Kurasaki compact disk player, model S-5293, from Spectrum Electronics, 433 East 310th Street in Willowick, Indiana.

Statement of minority

On August 19, the date the contract was entered, I was seventeen years of age, a minor under the laws of Indiana.

Time and place to return goods

I also demand a return of the $50.00 downpayment which I gave you under the contract. I will return the compact disk player to your store at 1:00 p.m. on September 15.

Thank you for your understanding in this matter.

Sincerely,

Andrew Heinzmann

Andrew Heinzmann

Figure 8-1 Sample letter indicating minor's disaffirmance.

Casavetta had lived in southern California her entire life. Because she had started school one year before everyone else, she was only 17 when she graduated from high school and entered college. The college she attended was in North Dakota. Since she had never owned a winter coat, she purchased one from the Abrams Department Store in November, while she was still 17. This coat would be a necessary, and any attempt to repudiate the purchase would probably fail.

The rules related to necessaries apply only to executed contracts. Wholly executory contracts calling for a future delivery or rendering of services may be repudiated by the minor. Thus, in the foregoing case, had Casavetta's coat been ordered, but not delivered or paid for, she could have repudiated her agreement with no damages or monetary loss being assessed against her.

Technically, parents are not liable for contracts executed by minors, even for necessaries, unless the parents have cosigned the contracts. An exception exists, however, if the parent has neglected or deserted the minor. In such a situation, the parent may be held liable to a third person for the fair value of the necessaries supplied by the third party to the minor.

Other Contracts Not Voidable

By statute and court decision certain other types of contracts have been excepted from the general rule that the contracts of minors are voidable at the minor's option. For public policy reasons, minors may not at their option disaffirm a valid marriage or repudiate an enlistment contract in the armed forces based on a claim of incapacity to contract. Neither may a minor repudiate a contract for goods and services required by law; for example, minors may not repudiate payments for inoculations and vaccinations required for attendance at a university or college or required in securing a visa for travel in certain foreign lands.

Joan Williams, 14 years old, moved in and lived with Earl Johnson, Jr. Joan later testified at a trial for an unrelated cause that she was Johnson's common law wife. Johnson objected to her testimony, arguing that as a minor she could not consent to a marriage. Marriage laws in their state, Kansas, provided that a female must be at least 12 years old, and males at least 14, to marry. The court validated the marriage and would not permit rescission, as Kansas respected common law marriage and both parties were of ages that permitted marriage within their state.

Disaffirmance of Minors' Contracts

An individual may disaffirm an agreement made during minority before or within a reasonable time after reaching adulthood. The exact period of time will vary depending on the nature of the contract and on applicable state and local laws. Failure to disaffirm within a reasonable period of time would imply that the contract had been ratified. The method of disaffirmance is fundamentally the same as the method of ratification. Disaffirmance may be implied by the acts of the individual after achieving majority, as by a failure to make an installment payment. Similarly, an oral or written declaration of disaffirmance would achieve the same end.

Disaffirmance Related to Innocent Third Parties When anyone buys something from a minor, they have voidable ownership rights because the minor has the right to disaffirm the contract. The UCC permits one having voidable ownership rights to transfer valid ownership rights to an innocent third-party purchaser of those goods. Thus, disaffirmance by a minor will not require the innocent purchaser to return the goods.

UCC 2-403 (see p. 625)

Nikhazy, age 17, decided to sell her motorcycle to Autoquest Motor Sales, Inc. Autoquest then sold the cycle to Daugherty, an innocent third-party buyer. Before Nikhazy became an adult, she decided to get back her cycle from Daugherty by disaffirming her contract with Autoquest. Nikhazy would not be able to recover the cycle from Daugherty by disaffirming her contract with Autoquest.

The UCC rule refers only to the sale of personal property. In cases where a minor has sold real estate to one who subsequently sells it to an innocent third party, the minor, on reaching adulthood, may disaffirm the sale and recover the real property.

Ratification of Minors' Contracts

People may ratify their contracts made during minority only after reaching their majority—at age 18 or 21 or at any other age set by statute—or within a reasonable time thereafter. **Ratification,** or **affirmance,** the willingness to abide by contractual obligations, may be implied by using the item purchased, making an installment payment, paying off the balance of money owed on a previously voidable contract or continuing to accept goods and services being provided under a contract after becoming of full age. Affirmation may also result from the person's oral or written declaration to abide by the contract. These acts as well as others ratify an existing agreement and elevate it to the status of one that is enforceable against an adult.

8-3 MENTAL INCOMPETENTS AND PERSONS DRUGGED OR INTOXICATED

Persons deprived of the mental ability to comprehend and understand contractual obligations have the right to disaffirm their contracts. Their rights are, in many respects, the same as the rights of minors. Agreements of mental incompetents are either valid, voidable, or void, depending on the seriousness of their disability and on whether they have been declared insane.

Persons Mentally Infirm or Mentally Ill

A contract made by a person who is mentally infirm or who suffers from mental illness may be valid, if the person's infirmity or illness is not severe enough to rob that person of the ability to understand the nature, purpose, and effect of that contract. Thus mental retardation or mental illness does not necessarily reduce a person's ability to enter into contracts. The question will always be whether the mental problem was so serious that the person did not understand the nature of the contract. If that is the case, the mentally infirm or mentally ill person may disaffirm any contract except one for necessaries. The incompetent must return all consideration received, if he or she still has it.

Persons Legally Insane

Persons declared to be insane by competent legal authority are denied the right to enter contracts. Any contractual relationship with others results in nothing more than a void agreement. In most states persons who knowingly take advantage of one declared insane are subject to criminal indictment and prosecution.

Persons Drugged or Intoxicated

Contracts agreed to by persons under the influence of alcohol or drugs may be voidable. Incompetence related to either alcohol or drugs must be of such degree that a contracting party would have lost the ability to comprehend or to be aware of obligations being accepted under the contract. One who contracts while in this condition may either affirm or disaffirm the agreement at a later time. Disaffirmance here requires the return to the other party of all consideration that had been received. However, such a return may be refused when evidence indicates that one party took advantage of the other's drunken or weakened condition.

Sermolino attended a party at the home of a business executive in suburban Preston. Unknown to Sermolino, the punch at the party had been laced with several drugs including LSD. After drinking several glasses of the punch, Sermolino began to hallucinate. While hallucinating, he entered into a contract in which he sold his valuable stamp collection to Vandivert. When Sermolino recovered, he sought to disaffirm the contract. Because his involuntary drugged state had robbed Sermolino of his ability to comprehend the contract he was making with Vandivert, he would be allowed to get out of the agreement.

SUMMARY

8-1. The fourth element essential to a legally effective contract is the legal ability to enter into a contractual relationship. This legal ability is known as capacity. Under the law there is a rebuttable presumption that anyone entering a contract has the legal capacity to do so. Since the presumption is rebuttable, a party can attack it. Minors are allowed this privilege. Minority means that an individual has not yet attained the age of majority.

8-2. A contract made by a minor for necessaries is enforceable against the minor. Necessaries are food, clothing, shelter, medical and dental services, and other goods and services reasonably required in protecting the minor's health and welfare. Individuals may ratify or disaffirm their contracts on reaching majority or within a reasonable time thereafter.

8-3. Contracts of persons who are mentally infirm or mentally ill, but not legally declared insane, may be valid or voidable, depending on the seriousness of their mental problem. Persons declared to be insane by competent legal authority are denied the right to enter into contracts, and contracts entered into may be declared void. Incompetence related to alcohol or drugs must be of such a degree that the contracting party has lost the ability to comprehend or to be aware of the obligations being accepted under the contract.

Understanding Key Legal Terms

abandoned (p. 94)
affirmance (p. 98)
capacity (p. 93)
disaffirm (p. 93)
emancipated (p. 94)
majority (p. 94)
minority (p. 94)
necessaries (p. 95)
ratification (p. 98)
rebuttable presumption (p. 93)

Questions for Review and Discussion

1. What general presumption does the law make about a person's capacity to contract? Is this presumption the last word on the matter? Explain.
2. Why does the law allow minors to avoid contracts for anything other than necessaries?
3. Explain what minority and majority meant under common law, and note how Amendment 26 to the U.S. Constitution has affected the age at which minors achieve majority. How has the amendment affected rights and obligations of minors in regards to contracts?
4. Distinguish emancipation from abandonment, and note the legal effect of each on a minor's capacity to contract.
5. Identify the different ways the states have of dealing with minors who lie about their age when entering into contracts.
6. Contrast the legal responsibilities of minors for (*a*) contracts for necessaries and (*b*) contracts for items or services other than necessaries.
7. List three other types of contracts that the law may except from the general rule that minors may void their contracts.
8. What is the legal effect of contracts made by persons who are mentally infirm or mentally ill, but who have not been declared legally insane?
9. What is the legal effect of contracts made by persons declared legally insane?
10. When may an intoxicated or drugged person escape legal liability under a contract?

Analyzing Cases

1. Sperry Ford sold a car to Bowling when Bowling was only 16 years old. Once Bowling had paid the full purchase price in cash, Sperry turned over the car and the certificate of title. After driving the car for only a week, Bowling discovered that the main bearing was burned out. When Bowling found out that repair costs would almost equal the price he'd paid for the car, he left the car on Sperry's lot and asked for his money back. Sperry Ford refused to give Bowling his money. Is Sperry justified in this refusal? Explain. *Bowling v. Sperry*, 184 N.E.2d 901 (Indiana).
2. Quality Motors, Inc., refused to sell a car to Hays because he was only 16 years old. However, Quality told Hays that they would sell the car to an adult and then show Hays how to transfer title from the adult into his name. Hays agreed with the scheme and came back with a friend who was 23. Quality sold the car to Hays' friend. Quality then gave Hays the name of a notary public who would transfer title to Hays. After the transfer was accomplished, Hays' father found out about the deal and tried to get Quality Motors to take the car back. Quality would have nothing to do

with the car and claimed that since the car had been sold to an adult, Hays could not disaffirm the contract. Is Quality correct? Explain. *Quality Motors v. Hays,* 225 S.W.2d 326 (Arkansas).

3. The Bundy family entered a vinyl siding contract with Dalton. Dalton had assumed that the house belonged to the parents but later found out that it belonged to their daughter who was a minor. Dalton argued that the siding is a necessary and that the daughter should, therefore, be liable to him for its reasonable value. Is the vinyl siding a necessary? Explain. *Dalton v. Bundy,* 666 S.W.2d 443 (Missouri).

4. Lonchyna enlisted in the U.S. Air Force while still a minor. Three times he applied for and received educational delays that put off the beginning of his tour of duty. At that time, he claimed he could void the contract since he'd entered into it when he was a minor. Is Lonchyna correct? Explain. *Lonchyna v. Brown, Secretary of Defense,* 491 F. Supp. 1352 (N.D. Illinois).

5. Wayne was a dock worker. He was injured while working for the Global Steamship Line. Subsequent to the accident, Wayne signed an agreement with his employer that granted Wayne compensation in exchange for his promise not to sue. Wayne is now trying to have the agreement voided. Evidence introduced proved that Wayne had an IQ of 85 and that he dropped out of school at age 17. When he dropped out of school, he was in the eighth grade but was doing less than sixth-grade-level work. Will Wayne's "slowness" necessarily invalidate the contract? Explain.

6. Krasner had shared office space with Berk for many years. Periodically they renegotiated a contract which stipulated how rental payments would be divided between them. Before the most recent agreement was to be renegotiated, Krasner discovered that Berk was suffering from a serious case of senility that made him incapable of understanding the true nature of the agreement they were negotiating. Nevertheless, Krasner negotiated with Berk, and they entered into the new contract. Sixty days after the new agreement had been negotiated, Berk was forced to give up his business because of his mental problems. Berk then attempted to get out of the rental agreement based on his mental capacity. Will Berk succeed? *Krasner v. Berk,* 319 N.E.2d 897 (Massachusetts).

CHAPTER 9
Consideration

OUTLINE

COMMENTARY

When the Cuban inmates at a federal penitentiary in Atlanta learned that American authorities were planning to send them back to Cuba, they decided to prevent this action by taking the law into their own hands. They laid siege to the prison and took 89 people as hostages. These 89 people were held while the inmates negotiated with federal authorities. After 11 days of negotiation, an agreement was finally reached. As part of this pact, inmates agreed to release the hostages in return for amnesty for anything done during the siege of the prison and for a promise from authorities that each inmate's case would be reviewed on an individual basis. Clearly, each side in this situation gave up something while each side received something in return. Such an exchange of value is called consideration. Can an exchange based upon actions that are clearly illegal create a binding contract? Would a court of law uphold such an agreement? Questions like these are answered by the rules and principles surrounding the doctrine of consideration.

OBJECTIVES

1. Explain the term consideration, and identify the characteristics necessary for valid consideration.
2. Describe the attitude of the court when dealing with questions that involve the adequacy of consideration.
3. Discuss the types of consideration that can be used to bind parties to one another in a contractual situation.
4. Outline the procedure that a debtor and creditor may use to settle a claim by means of accord and satisfaction.
5. Identify those agreements which may be enforceable by a court of law even though they lack consideration.
6. Relate those agreements which, on the surface, appear to have consideration, but which the courts still refuse to enforce.

9-1 REQUIREMENTS OF CONSIDERATION

A fifth element essential to any valid contract is the mutual promise to exchange benefits and sacrifices between the parties. This promise to exchange things of value is called **consideration.** It is the thing of value promised to the other party in exchange for something else of value promised by that other party. It is this promise to exchange valued items or services that binds the parties together. If an agreement has no consideration, it is not a binding contract. For example, a promise to give someone a birthday present is not a contract. Instead, it is a promise to make a gift because the giver receives nothing in exchange for the birthday present.

The Nature of Consideration

Consideration consists of a mutual exchange of benefits and sacrifices between contracting parties. In the exchange, what is a benefit to the offeree is, at the same time, a sacrifice to the offeror. Likewise, the benefit bargained for by the offeror will finally result in a sacrifice by the offeree. The legal term used for this sacrifice is **detriment.** A detriment is any of the following: (1) doing something (or promising to do something) that one has a legal right not to do; (2) giving up something (or promising to give up something) that one has a legal right to keep; and (3) refraining from doing something (or promising not to do something) that one has a legal right to do. This last type of detriment is known as **forbearance.**

Jankowsky offered to pay his adult daughter, Marilyn, $1,000 if she would agree not to smoke cigarettes or drink alcoholic beverages for one year. Marilyn agreed and gave up both smoking and drinking for a year. At the end of that year, Jankowsky would be legally bound to give Marilyn the $1,000. Since she had the legal right to smoke and drink, her sacrifice in giving up both is a valid consideration. This is known as forbearance.

Note in the previous example that the act of giving up both smoking and drinking is actually beneficial to Marilyn's health. The fact that it is medically and physically beneficial does not change the fact that the sacrifice is a legal detriment since she has the right to do both.

The Characteristics of Consideration

Consideration has three characteristics: (1) Promises made during bargaining are dependent on the consideration to be received; (2) the consideration must involve something of value; (3) the benefits and detriments promised must be legal.

Bargained-for Exchange The law will not enforce an agreement that has not been bargained for. An agreement involves a **bargained-for exchange** when (1) a promise is made in exchange for another promise, or (2) a promise is made in exchange for an act, or (3) a promise is made for forbearance of an act. The concept of bargaining means that each party will be hurt in some way if the other party fails to keep a promise. Conversely, each party gains something when the promises are kept and the exchange is made.

Baudrillard agreed to loan Fairbridge his copy of the *Oxford Companion of American Literature* so that Fairbridge could finalize his research project on the works of the American poet James Magner. There was no understanding that Fairbridge would pay for the use of the reference book. Baudrillard now refuses to allow Fairbridge to use his book. Although Baudrillard might have a moral obligation to carry out the offer of the book, their agreement was not an enforceable one in that it contained no bargained-for promise.

Something of Value There are no specific requirements or qualifications, other than being legal, as to what one may promise in return for another's offer to deliver goods and services. The promise itself is consideration when it represents something of value. Thus, the promise to assist another to repair an automobile would be *something of value* promised. The value placed on goods and services need not be street or market value. It is important only that the parties freely agreed on the value and the price. In general, the courts do not look into the adequacy of consideration, that is, they do not look to see whether the value of the consideration was fair to both parties. Courts let people make their own agreements and then enforce those agreements. There is, however, an exception to this general rule.

Courts will at times give a party relief when the consideration is so outrageous that it shocks the conscience of the courts. A court may refuse to enforce a contract or any clause of that contract if it considers the contract or clause to be **unconscionable**, that is, where the consideration is ridiculously inadequate as to shock the court's conscience. This usually happens when there is a great inequality in bargaining power between the two parties. In very specific matters, usually related to taxes, some states have adopted statutes dealing with adequacy. In general, though, courts remain reluctant to disturb the promises made by parties to an enforceable contract.

Legality of Consideration Consideration requires that the benefits and sacrifices promised between the parties be legal. Absence of legality renders the consideration invalid. Thus, a party cannot agree to do something that he or she does not have the legal right to do. Similarly, a party cannot promise not to do something which he or she has no legal right to do. Also, a party cannot make valid consideration out of a promise to stop doing something that was illegal to do in the first place.

In the opening commentary, the Cuban inmates who held 89 hostages in the federal penitentiary in Atlanta agreed to free the hostages in exchange for a promise from the U.S. government to review each of their cases on an individual basis. Certainly the agreement was bargained for since it involved an exchange of benefits and detriments. Also, the promise by the inmates to release the hostages involved something of value. Nevertheless, since the inmates had no legal right to hold the hostages against their will in the first place, the consideration would be invalid and the agreement would not be binding.

9-2 TYPES OF CONSIDERATION

Generally, consideration takes the form of money, property, or services. In certain special kinds of agreements and promises, however, the benefits and sacrifices are in some manner unique. Significant among these agreements are promises not to sue and charitable pledges.

Money as Consideration

Money is the usual consideration offered by parties seeking another's promise or performance. The parties are free to negotiate privately the amount of money to be paid except when price structures have been established through administrative rulings or legislation. Historically, rent, fuel, oil, natural gas, and other goods have been the subject of price controls. Likewise, employers engaged in interstate commerce may not bargain with qualified employees for a wage rate less than that guaranteed by the federal Fair Labor Standards Act.

Property and Services as Consideration

Before money was accepted as a medium of exchange, consideration consisted of property and services. In modern times, especially during recessionary or inflationary cycles, parties have sometimes found it more beneficial to enter into barter agreements than to base their promises on cash payments. The courts have held that barter agreements do contain valid consideration. For example, the exchange of services in return for the use of another's car or a promise to trade a watch for a typewriter represent benefits and sacrifices that constitute valid consideration to support a legally binding contract.

Promises Not to Sue

A promise not to sue, when there is the right to sue, is enforceable when supported by consideration. Promising not to sue is a forbearance. A promise not to sue, in exchange for an amount of money is a customary way to settle a pending lawsuit. Settlements of this type are often preferred to expensive and time-consuming litigation.

Nguyen was injured on an interstate highway when a truck owned and operated by Transcontinental Shipping, Inc., went out of control, crossed the median, and hit Nguyen's car. Nguyen discussed his legal rights with an attorney who suggested that he might receive compensation from Transcontinental if he brought suit against the company. Transcontinental offered Nguyen $200,000 if he would agree not to bring suit against the company. Nguyen agreed to these terms. A court would uphold this agreement based on the promise between the parties.

Acceptance of an agreement not to sue, supported by consideration, terminates one's right to continue any action, presently or in the future, on grounds described in the agreement. A promise not to sue is commonly called a **release.** Agreements of this kind are frequently negotiated between attorneys even after a lawsuit has been filed and a trial begun. In such an event, the settlement is arranged in cooperation with the court and presiding judge.

Charitable Pledges

The dependence of charitable institutions and nonprofit organizations upon the solicitation of contributions has encouraged the courts to enforce charitable pledges as though they were contractual obligations. When pledges are made to fund a specific project, the pledgee's sacrifice is the carrying out of that project. Pledges, in this sense, are considered unilateral agreements, enforceable only when accepted by commencement of the proposed project.

Minnifield University began a campaign to fund expansion of the university's learning resource center. Three million dollars was pledged by alumni and friends of the university. Relying on these pledges, Minnifield started work on the expansion. Each of the pledges, however small, became an enforceable agreement at that point. Carrying out the proposed plan as explained to the pledgors was valid consideration supporting their pledges.

At times pledges are used for the general operation and maintenance of a charitable or nonprofit organization. When there is no promise to carry out a specific project, the courts have held that each pledge made is supported by the pledges of all others who have made similar pledges. This concept of consideration is used in support of all promises of money for undefined causes.

9-3 PROBLEMS WITH CONSIDERATION

Problems sometimes arise when the consideration involved in a contract is money and the parties disagree as to the amount of money that the debtor owes the creditor. How such problems are resolved depends upon whether the transaction involves a genuine dispute as to the amount owed. One way such disputes can be settled is by an agreement known as accord and satisfaction.

Disputed Amounts

A **disputed amount** is one on which the parties never reached mutual agreement. Final settlement of disputed claims may lead to misunderstanding, dispute, and lengthy negotiation. If a creditor accepts as full payment an amount that is less than the amount due, then the dispute has been settled by an **accord and satisfaction.** **Accord** is the implied or expressed acceptance of less than what has been billed the debtor. **Satisfaction** is the agreed-to settlement as contained in the accord. Only if the dispute is honest, made in good faith, and not superficial or trivial will the courts entertain arguments based on accord and satisfaction.

Durslay called in a repair team from Annenberg Equipment Maintenance to work on the company's duplicating equipment. No agreement was made as to charges to be made for the work to be performed. When Annenberg completed the work, they sent a bill to Durslay for $1,196. Durslay thought this amount was excessive. Consequently, he sent a check to Annenberg for $800, writing on the check "in full payment for all services and parts used to repair our duplicating equipment." Annenberg cashed the check and later sued Durslay's company for the $396 balance. Annenberg would not succeed in this lawsuit because they had already accepted a lesser amount which had been offered by Durslay in good faith, in full payment of the amount in dispute.

Undisputed Amounts

An **undisputed amount** is one on which the parties have mutually agreed. Although a party may have second thoughts about the amount promised for goods or services rendered, the amount that was agreed to by the parties when they made their contract remains an undisputed amount. A part payment in lieu of full payment when accepted by a creditor will not cancel an undisputed debt.

Provenza had new carpet laid in her family room, agreeing to pay the O'Shea Department Store $375 for the carpet and the labor charge for installation. A week later, before paying the $375, Provenza saw the same carpet in another department store. She talked to the salesperson who told her he would have been able to sell her the carpet and have it installed for only $261. Provenza sent a check to O'Shea for $261 with the notation "In full payment for the carpet laid in my family room." O'Shea deposited the check and demanded payment of the balance of $114. Provenza would still be obligated to pay that balance.

In this situation, there was no good faith dispute over what Provenza owed to O'Shea for the carpet and its installation. The buyer was simply trying to get the carpet at the lower price that she could have paid the other department store. The sum of $375 was an undisputed amount, and the balance is still owed to O'Shea.

9-4 AGREEMENTS WITHOUT CONSIDERATION

As a general rule, a contract is not enforceable if it lacks consideration. However, some states eliminate the requirement of consideration in specific types of agreements. In contrast, there are certain promises which the courts always refuse to enforce because they lack even the rudimentary qualities of valid consideration, even though on the surface they may appear to offer that much needed element.

Enforceable Agreements

As noted above, some states have chosen to eliminate the element of consideration in a few specifically named contracts. Unfortunately, as is frequently the case in such matters, there is no uniformity among states as to the types of agreements subject to such laws. Nevertheless, typical agreements falling into this category include: promises bearing a seal, promises after discharge in bankruptcy, debts barred by the statute of limitations, promises enforced by promissory estoppel, and options governed by the UCC.

Promises Bearing a Seal Where state law requires that contracts bear a seal, the seal retains its historical significance. As previously defined in Chapter 5, a **seal** is a mark or an impression placed on a written contract indicating that the instrument was executed and accepted in a formal manner. Today a seal is usually indicated by the addition of the word seal or the letters L.S. (**locus sigilli,** meaning "place of the seal") following a party's signature. In some states, the seal takes the place of consideration. In others, the seal gives a written contract the presumption of consideration which can be rebutted by evidence that there really was none. The UCC has eliminated the use of the seal in contracts for the sale of goods. However, statutes in some states still require the use of the seal in real property and certain other types of transactions. Since there is no uniformity in this regard, it is advisable to research and consult individual state requirements.

UCC 2-203
(see p.616)

Promises After Discharge in Bankruptcy Persons discharged from indebtedness through bankruptcy may reaffirm and resume their obligations, prompted perhaps by moral compulsion. In the past, reaffirmation has been the subject of abuse by creditors who used pressure against those whose debts have been excused. Under the new and far-reaching Bankruptcy Reform Act of 1978, Congress included measures that make it more difficult for creditors to extract such promises. The bankruptcy court now must hold a hearing when a reaffirmation is intended, informing the debtor that reaffirmation is optional, not required, and of the legal consequences of reactivating a debt. State laws, in most cases, provide that no new consideration need be provided in support of reaffirmation. Most states require that a reaffirmation be supported by contractual intent. Some states require the new promise to be in writing. However, when there is no such provision, an oral promise or reaffirmation is usually sufficient.

Debts Barred by Statutes of Limitations State laws known as **statutes of limitations** limit the time within which a party is allowed to bring suit. The time allowed for the collection of a debt varies from state to state, usually from 3 to 10 years. Some states allow more time for collection when the document of indebtedness is under seal, as in the case of a promissory note containing the seal of the maker. Debtors may revive and reaffirm debts barred by the statutes of limitations without the necessity of new consideration. Affirmation will result from the part payment of the debt. When a debt is revived, the creditor again is permitted the full term, as provided by the statute, to make collection.

Promises Enforced by Promissory Estoppel The doctrine of **estoppel** denies rights to complaining parties that are shown to be the cause of their own injury. **Promissory estoppel,** then, is the legal doctrine that restricts an offeror from revoking an offer, under certain conditions, even though consideration has not been promised to bind an agreement. To be effective, promissory estoppel requires that the offeror know, or be presumed to know, that the offeree might otherwise make a definite and decided change of position in contemplation of promises contained in the offer. Courts, in reaching this doctrine, have accepted the principles of justice and fairness in protecting the offeree from otherwise unrecoverable losses.

Curtiss was arrested for a crime she did not commit. Michaelson, her employer, told her that he had to suspend her. However, he also told her that if she were later found not guilty and released, she would have her old job with back pay for all the time she was suspended. Three months later, the charges were dropped and Curtiss tried to get her job back. Michaelson refused to let her work or to pay her any back pay. In a suit brought by Curtiss against Michaelson to recover her back pay, the court ruled in her favor. Michaelson was stopped from denying the promise he'd made to Curtiss despite the absence of consideration from her because she had relied on that promise and had not looked for other work while suspended.

Although Michaelson had received no consideration supporting the promise to hold open Curtiss's job and pay her while she was suspended, Curtiss had accepted the promise and had placed herself in a very different and difficult position through her reliance upon the promise. Had Michaelson not made such a promise, Curtiss would no doubt have looked for another job after Michaelson had suspended her.

Options An **option** is the giving of consideration to support an offeror's promise to hold open an offer for a stated or reasonable length of time. The UCC has made an exception to the rule requiring consideration when the offer is made by a merchant; in such cases, an offer in writing by a merchant, stating the time period over which the offer will remain open, is enforceable without consideration. The offer, which is called a firm offer, or an irrevocable offer, must be signed by the offeror, and the time allowed for acceptance may not exceed three months. When the time allowed is more than three months, firm offers by merchants must be supported by consideration to be enforceable.

UCC 2-205
(see p. 616)

Unenforceable Agreements

The promises just described are exceptions to the general rule that consideration must support an enforceable contract. The exceptions are allowed by state statute or because the courts, in the interest of fairness or justice, find it inappropriate to require consideration. There are certain promises, however, which the courts will not enforce because they lack even the rudimentary qualities of valid consideration. Included in this category are illusory promises, promises of future gifts, promises of legacies, promises based on past consideration, and promises based on preexisting duties.

Table 9-1 AGREEMENTS WITHOUT CONSIDERATION

Agreement	*Legal Status*
Promises under seal	Enforceable in some states for contracts not involving personal property; unenforceable under the UCC for contracts involving personal property
Promises after discharge in bankruptcy	Enforceable in most states
Promise to pay debts barred by statute of limitations	Enforceable
Promises enforced by promissory estoppel	Enforceable only if offeror knew that offeree would rely on the promise and offeree places himself or herself in a different and difficult position as a result of that promise
Option	Enforceable under the UCC if made between merchants, in writing, stating the time period over which the offer will remain open
Illusory promises	Unenforceable
Promise of a gift	Unenforceable
Past considerations	Unenforceable
Preexisting duties	Unenforceable as consideration in a new contract

Illusory Promises An **illusory promise** is one that does not obligate the promissor to anything. A party who makes an illusory promise is the only one with any right to determine whether the other party will be benefitted in any way. Illusory promises fail to provide the mutuality of promises required in establishing consideration.

Sinaiko Industries agreed to buy such fuel oil as it "might desire" for one heating season from the Orazio Oil Company. In return for this promise, Orazio negotiated terms whereby it would give Sinaiko a special schedule of discounts for the oil. The promise to buy as much as it "might desire" had actually obligated Sinaiko to do nothing. Its promise was illusory because Sinaiko might desire absolutely no fuel oil and still keep its promise. The benefits that Sinaiko was to derive from the schedule of discounts were not supported by a real or enforceable promise on Sinaiko's part. A suit brought by either party to enforce this agreement would fail for want of consideration.

Gifts The promise of a gift to be given at some future time or in a will is not enforceable if no consideration is given for the promise. Included here are promises to provide gratuitous services or to lend one's property without expectation of any benefits in return.

Past Consideration A promise to give another something of value in return for goods or services rendered and delivered in the past, without expectation or reward, is **past consideration.** Only when goods or services are provided as the result of bargained-for present or future promises is an agreement enforceable.

Matolini, without any mention of payment, helped her friend, Hillerman, move from Shelby to Loudonville. The entire move took 18 hours to complete. At the end of the day, after Hillerman was in his new apartment, he told Matolini that he'd give her $200 for helping him move. Hillerman's promise to Matolini is not enforceable because Matolini has already completed the work. Her consideration is, therefore, in the past.

Pre-Existing Duties A promise to do something that one is already obligated to do by law or by some other promise or agreement cannot be made consideration in a new contract. Such obligations are called **pre-existing duties.**

Carqueville Electronics has contracted with Hiroshiqe Laserphototronics, Inc., to supply Hiroshiqe with 4,000 component parts for a project which Hiroshiqe has agreed to deliver to the U.S. Navy by October 31. After delivering 2,000 of the parts, Carqueville tells Hiroshiqe that it wants twice the amount agreed upon to deliver the remaining 2,000 parts. Since Carqueville is already under a contractual obligation to deliver those 2,000 parts, it cannot make that action consideration in a new agreement with Hiroshiqe.

The same rule applies to police officers, fire fighters, and other public servants and officials who may promise some special service for monetary or other reward for doing what is actually their job. Suppose, for example, a police officer promises to provide a store owner additional protection against crime by making additional rounds of the store in return for some money. Neither the police officer nor the store owner could enforce such an agreement in a court. It is based on the officer's empty promise to do what the law already requires.

SUMMARY

9-1. The fifth element necessary to any valid contract is consideration. Consideration is the mutual exchange or promise to exchange benefits and sacrifices between contracting parties. Consideration has three requirements: (1) promises made during bargaining are dependent on the consideration to be received; (2) the consideration must involve something of value; (3) the benefits and detriments promised must be legal.

9-2. Generally, consideration takes the form of money, property, or services. There are, certain special kinds of agreements and promises where the benefits and sacrifices are unique. Among these are promises not to sue and charitable pledges.

9-3. Problems sometimes arise when the consideration involved in a contract is money and the parties do not agree on the amount of money owed. If there is a genuine dispute, a creditor can accept an amount as full payment even though it is less than the amount claimed. Once the creditor has accepted the lesser amount, the dispute is settled by an act of accord and satisfaction. If the dispute is not genuine, accord and satisfaction do not apply.

9-4. As a general rule, contracts are not enforceable without consideration. However, some states eliminate the need for consideration in some agreements. These agreements include promises bearing a seal, promises after discharge in bankruptcy, debts barred by the statute of limitations, promises enforced by promissory estoppel, and options governed by the UCC. There are other agreements which seem to involve consideration but which the courts will not enforce. These agreements involve illusory promises, gifts, past consideration, and pre-existing duties.

Understanding Key Legal Terms

accord (p. 106)
accord and satisfaction (p. 106)
bargained-for exchange (p. 103)
consideration (p. 103)
detriment (p. 103)
disputed amount (p. 106)
estoppel (p. 108)
forbearance (p. 103)
illusory promise (p. 110)
locus sigilli (p. 108)
option (p. 109)
past consideration (p. 110)
pre-existing duties (p. 111)
promissory estoppel (p. 109)
release (p. 106)
satisfaction (p. 106)
statutes of limitations (p. 107)
unconscionable (p. 104)
undisputed amount (p. 106)

Questions for Review and Discussion

1. Explain what is meant by this statement: "Where consideration is concerned, one contracting party's benefits are the other party's sacrifices and vice versa."
2. List the three characteristics that are necessary for valid consideration to exist in an agreement.
3. Discuss the meaning of bargained-for exchange as it applies to valid consideration.
4. Describe the court's position in relation to questions involving the adequacy of consideration. Identify exceptions to this position.
5. What types of consideration are usually used in commercial and consumer transactions?
6. Explain the court's position on whether promises not to sue and charitable pledges can be consideration.
7. How does an accord and satisfaction operate to eliminate debts where there is a disputed amount? Does it serve to eliminate a debt where there is an undisputed amount? Explain.
8. What are the most common agreements that are enforceable without proof of consideration?
9. Illustrate by example what is meant by an illusory promise.
10. Why will the courts refuse to enforce agreements supported by promised gifts, past consideration, or preexisting duties?

Analyzing Cases

1. Seier agreed to pay $10,000 to Peek in exchange for all the stock in a corporation. The agreement was placed in writing. Nevertheless, when the time came for payment, Seier refused to live up to his end of the deal. His argument was that the stock was

not worth the $10,000 that he had agreed to pay for it. Will the court listen to Seier's argument and attempt to determine the value of the consideration? Explain. *Seier v. Peek,* 456 So.2d 1079 (Alabama).

2. N.B. West Contracting Co., Inc., agreed to repave Koedding's parking lot. When the repaving work was done, Koedding found that he was not at all satisfied with the quality of the work. Consequently, he informed West of his intention to bring suit. West told Koedding that the lot would be resealed and that the job would be guaranteed for 2 years if Koedding agreed not to pursue the lawsuit, which had already commenced. Koedding agreed. After the repaving was completed a second time, Koedding was still not satisfied. This time he followed through on the lawsuit. Does the agreement not to sue operate to stop Koedding's lawsuit? Explain. *Koedding v. N.B. West Contracting Co., Inc.,* 596 S.W.2d 744 (Missouri).

3. Evans used his credit card to run up a $98.75 bill with the Rosen Department Store. When Rosen tried to collect, Evans wrote out a check for $79.00. He wrote on the check that he meant it to be "full payment of all accounts to date." He then sent the check to Rosen. When Rosen received the check, they cashed it. When Evans was sued by Rosen for the rest of the money he owed to them, Evans argued that under accord and satisfaction, the fact that Rosen cashed the $79.00 check meant that they had accepted that amount as full payment. Is Evans correct? Explain.

4. Dwyer told Erlick that he would hire her to work on an architectural job. He gave her a date to show up for work and told her to leave her present job. Relying on Dwyer's statements, Erlick left her job. Dwyer never did let Erlick begin work, and as a result, she was out of work for 4 months. Erlick sued Dwyer for the wages she lost during those 4 months. Dwyer argued that since they'd never decided on the final terms of employment, no contract ever existed between the two of them. Erlick argued that the principle of promissory estoppel should apply here. Is Erlick correct? Explain.

5. Tim W. Koerner and Associates, Inc., was a distributor for electrosurgical products for Aspen Labs, Inc. Zimmer U.S.A., Inc., purchased Aspen and replaced Aspen's distribution system with its own. Aspen remained in business as a subsidiary. Koerner sued Aspen and Zimmer, joined as defendants, trying to force them to honor a contract that Aspen and Zimmer had made that had been designed to compensate old Aspen dealers for their past efforts. Zimmer refused to honor the agreement. Judgment for whom and why? *Tim W. Koerner & Assocs., Inc. v. Aspen Labs, Inc.,* 492 F. Supp. 294 (D. Texas).

6. Trisko purchased a loveseat from the Vignola Furniture Company. The loveseat arrived at Trisko's home in a damaged condition. Vignola agreed to repair the loveseat if Trisko agreed not to sue. Trisko agreed, but then later brought suit. Vignola argued that Trisko could not bring suit because he had promised not to sue them in exchange for the repair of the loveseat. Trisko argued that Vignola already had a preexisting duty to deliver an undamaged loveseat. This preexisting duty could not, therefore, be valid consideration in a new agreement. Is Trisko correct? Explain. *Trisko v. Vignola Furniture Company,* 299 N.E.2d 421 (Illinois).

CHAPTER 10
Legality

OUTLINE

10-1 Agreements to Engage in Unlawful Activity
- Agreements to Engage in Criminal Activity
- Agreements to Engage in Tortious Activity

10-2 Agreements Made Illegal Under Statutory Law
- Usurious Agreements
- Wagering Agreements
- Unlicensed Agreements
- Unconscionable Agreements
- Sunday Agreements

10-3 Agreements Contrary to Public Policy
- Agreements to Obstruct Justice
- Agreements Interfering with Public Service
- Agreements to Defraud Creditors
- Agreements to Escape Liability
- Agreements in Restraint of Trade

10-4 Consequences of Illegality
- Illegality in Entire Agreements
- *In Pari Delicto* and Divisible Contracts

COMMENTARY

Angelitis was a loan officer for the Hawthorne Savings and Loan Association. Hawthorne is a relatively small savings and loan association operating exclusively out of three branches which cater to the three major Lithuanian neighborhoods in Cleveland. Angelitis, who spoke Lithuanian, built up a sizable clientele among the Lithuanian residents of the neighborhood located in the area of East 185th Street. As part of his employment contract, Angelitis agreed that, should he leave Hawthorne, he would not work in any capacity for any other financial institution anywhere in Cleveland. The restriction was supposed to last 12 years. However, 6 months after leaving Hawthorne, Angelitis became branch officer of the Excaliber Savings and Loan Association which was located at St. Clair and Norwood Avenue, in the heart of one of the other two Lithuanian neighborhoods in Cleveland. Angelitis claims that Hawthorne cannot enforce the restriction on his employment because it is an illegal restraint of trade. Hawthorne argues that the restriction is not unreasonable and is, therefore, perfectly legal. Can Hawthorne actually prevent Angelitis from working for another savings and loan, or would such an agreement be illegal? Chapter 10 on legality in contract law attempts to answer this and other questions.

OBJECTIVES

1. Justify the refusal of the courts to enforce agreements that violate the law.
2. Explain why most states have usury laws to regulate the interest rate and the maximum rate of interest which is permissible in a consumer transaction.

3. Determine what wagering agreements states may make exceptions for.
4. Distinguish between licenses designed to raise revenue and those designed to provide supervision and regulation of a business or profession, and determine the legal effect of a contract made by parties who are not licensed in a particular business or profession.
5. Describe when an agreement might be considered unconscionable by the courts, and indicate how a party might defeat a claim of unconscionability.
6. Account for the differing attitudes of the states regarding Sunday blue laws, and outline the general rules which apply to the making of Sunday contracts where such contracts are permitted.
7. Explain the legal principle of public policy, and note how the courts usually treat agreements found contrary to public policy.
8. Enumerate the types of contracts that have been found by various courts to involve violations of public policy.
9. Justify the tendency of the courts to closely scrutinize contracts which limit competition or restrain trade in some other way.
10. Distinguish between the application and effect of the rule of *in pari delicto* when an illegal contract is (*a*) entire and indivisible or (*b*) divisible.

10-1 AGREEMENTS TO ENGAGE IN UNLAWFUL ACTIVITY

The sixth requirement of a complete contract is legality. An agreement may involve a valid offer, an effective acceptance, mutual assent, competent parties, and valid consideration and yet still be void because of illegality. Parties cannot be allowed to enforce agreements that are contrary to the law. If the courts enforced illegal contracts, those contracts would have more power than the law itself. If such logic were the rule, then anyone could avoid the law simply by entering into a contract. The most obvious type of illegal contract is the one in which parties agree to perform some sort of unlawful activity. This activity could be a crime or a tort, depending upon the circumstances.

Agreements to Engage in Criminal Activity

Clearly, the law cannot honor any agreement if the objective of the agreement is to commit a crime. If, for example, a storekeeper would pay a known criminal to vandalize the shop of a competitor, that storekeeper would not be able to sue the criminal for breach of contract should his criminal friend decide to take the money and run. Although the shopkeeper in this case would be victimized by his criminal cohort, the law gives him no remedy since he should not have entered into the illegal agreement in the first place.

Agreements to Engage in Tortious Activity

Similarly, the law will not uphold any contract that involves a promise to commit a tort. For example, a newspaper reporter who agrees to libel several politicians in return for a job as their opponent's press secretary would find no remedy in the law should his benefactor fail to follow through after the election. His agreement to commit a tort would be void in the eyes of the law.

10-2 AGREEMENTS MADE ILLEGAL UNDER STATUTORY LAW

Some activities that are neither crimes nor torts have been made illegal by specific statutory enactments. Chief among these special situations are usurious agreements, wagering agreements, unlicensed agreements, unconscionable agreements, and Sunday agreements.

Usurious Agreements

The practice of charging more than the amount of interest allowed by law is called **usury** and is illegal. To protect borrowers from excessive interest charges, each state has passed laws which specify the rate of interest that may be charged in lending money. These interest rates vary from state to state. Agreements to charge more than is allowed by law are void. Special statutes allow small loan companies, pawn shops, and other lending agencies accepting high-risk applicants for credit to charge a higher rate of interest. Many states provide for a different maximum interest rate when the loan goes to a business or when it involves a mortgage (see Chapter 29). Most states also have special usury statutes to monitor the interest charges by retailers and others when the contract involves an installment loan. Such statutes are often referred to as retail installment sales acts. Some transactions involve charges which, although they appear to be interest, are actually legitimate expenses that can be collected without violating usury laws. The fee for a title search, an appraisal of land, or a credit report would fall into this category. Such fees must be genuine; any attempt to disguise usury as a special fee will not be tolerated by the courts.

Patchenko decided to replace the windows on his porch. To do so he went to the Bonn-Eastern Financial Bank and applied for a loan. Faliero, the loan manager of Bonn-Eastern, told Patchenko that they would need $500 up front to process the loan. This processing, she told Patchenko, would involve a credit check, an appraisal of the value of the house, and a title search. In fact, these things were not done, and the $500 fee was simply a way to charge extra interest above the maximum rate. Such a scheme is illegal.

Wagering Agreements

Any agreement or promise concerning gambling or a wager is invalid and may not be enforced. States make exceptions when bets are placed in accordance with laws that permit horse racing, lotteries, church-related or charitable games of bingo, and gambling casinos regulated by state authority.

Unlicensed Agreements

Certain businesses and professions must be licensed before they are allowed to operate legally. One reason for requiring a license is to provide a source of revenue, part of which is used to supervise the business or profession being licensed. A city ordinance requiring all door-to-door salespeople to be licensed would fall into this category. Another objective of licensing is to provide supervision and regulation of businesses and professions that might inflict harm on the public if allowed to operate without such controls. Physicians, nurses, dentists, attorneys, engineers, architects, and others in public service must be closely supervised for the protection of the public. Courts distinguish between licenses purely for revenue and licenses for protection of the public. If a license is required simply to raise revenue, the lack of a license will not necessarily make a contract void. In contrast, if a licensing requirement is designed to protect the public, it is likely that unlicensed people will not be able to enforce their contracts.

Califano was hired by the Rowan-Gain Steel Corporation in Oregon to work on certain industrial engineering projects. Unfortunately, Califano had never taken the time to obtain a license and become a registered engineer. An Oregon statute prohibits people from performing engineering services without having the appropriate license. When Rowan-Gain refused to pay Califano for a job they felt was poorly done, he sued them for breach of contract. The court found in favor of the steel company. The court felt that public welfare allowed the state to regulate and license engineers in order to provide for public safety.

Unconscionable Agreements

UCC 2-302 (see p. 618)

The courts are not required to enforce a contract or any part of a contract that the court feels is unconscionable. An agreement is considered unconscionable if its terms are so grossly unfair that they shock the court's conscience. If the court so desires, it can also limit how the unconscionable clause in an agreement is carried out if it can do so to avoid the unfair consequences.

A door-to-door salesperson for the St. George Kitchen Supply Company convinced Hideakis, an 80-year-old widow who lived alone, to purchase a set of pots and pans for $5,000. The actual value of the set was about $500. When Hideakis's nephew found out that the salesperson had pressured his aunt into this grossly unfair agreement, he told her not to pay the outrageous amount. When she failed to pay her bill and demanded that St. George take the pots and pans back, the company sued her. Because of the difference in bargaining power and the incredibly unfair price, it is likely that the court would refuse to enforce the contract.

Naturally, the party seeking to uphold the contract is allowed to present evidence that would show that the agreement is not as unfair as it may, at first, appear. The court would look at the commercial setting as well as the purpose and the effect of the agreement to determine its overall fairness.

Sunday Agreements

State statutes and local ordinances regulate the making and performing of contracts on Sunday. These laws are usually called **blue laws** because one of the first laws banning Sunday contracts was written on blue paper. Varying application and enforcement of restrictive blue laws in different geographical areas have materially changed the status of Sunday agreements in recent years. Certain states have eliminated uniform statewide laws regulating Sunday activities, but permit their separate counties and incorporated cities, towns, and villages to adopt their own special ordinances under a concept known as **local option.** Thus, adjoining counties may have opposing laws, with one opting, by popular referendum, to permit Sunday sales and the other opting to make such sales illegal.

Where laws do restrict Sunday business, two rules are usually observed. First, agreements made on Sunday or any other day requiring performance on Sunday may be ruled invalid. Exceptions to this rule are those agreements necessary to the health, welfare, and safety of the community and its residents. Second, agreements made on Sunday for work to be done or goods to be delivered on a business day are valid and enforceable. However, some states still require that there be an affirmation of such agreements on a day other than Sunday if such agreements are to be enforceable.

The enforcement of blue laws varies widely from state to state, county to county, and village to village. Some localities have restrictive laws but prefer not to enforce them, permitting all types of commercial activity without interference. Religious influences have been of major importance where enforcement is strict. The highly populated urban areas have almost entirely succumbed to the pressures of commercialism and have removed the Sunday blue laws from the books.

10-3 AGREEMENTS CONTRARY TO PUBLIC POLICY

The government has the power to regulate the health, safety, welfare, and morals of the public. This power is granted to the states simply because of their status as governing bodies. It has also become a part of the federal government's power under various interpretations of the U.S. Constitution. Any action that tends to harm the health, safety, welfare, or morals of the people is said to violate public policy. **Public policy** is that general legal principle that says no one should be allowed to do anything that tends to injure the public at large. Agreements most commonly invalidated as contrary to public policy are agreements to obstruct justice, agreements interfering with public service, agreements to defraud creditors, agreements to escape liability, and agreements in restraint of trade.

Agreements to Obstruct Justice

Agreements to obstruct justice include agreements to protect someone from arrest, to suppress evidence, to encourage lawsuits, to give false testimony, and to bribe a juror. The category also includes a promise not to prosecute someone or not to serve as a witness in a trial. Any agreement promising to perform any of these activities would be void.

Sanchez was walking down the street minding his own business when he was struck by a window panel dislodged from the fifth floor of the Risatti Building in downtown Wausau. Barbiero, who witnessed the entire incident, was paid $200 by the owners of the Risatti Building to forget everything she'd seen. Barbiero later changed her mind and testified truthfully about the facts concerning the incident. The agreement made with the owners of the Risatti Building is void because it is considered against public policy. Any effort to hold her to it will be unsuccessful.

Agreements Interfering with Public Service

Agreements interfering with public service are illegal and void. Contracts in this group include agreements to bribe or interfere with public officials, to obtain political preference in appointments to office, to pay an officer for signing a pardon, or to illegally influence a legislature for personal gain.

Carlyle entered into an agreement with the state highway engineer in which the engineer agreed to use his influence to have the new state highway run adjacent to Carlyle's motel. Carlyle paid the engineer $5,000 for his promise to attempt to grant this request. This agreement is void and may not be enforced. The failure of the engineer to exert his influence would give Carlyle no rights in seeking the return of the $5,000 paid.

Agreements to Defraud Creditors

Agreements to defraud creditors, that is, those that tend to remove or weaken the rights of creditors are void as contrary to public policy. Thus a debtor's agreement to sell and transfer personal and real property to a friend or relative for far less than actual value would be void if done for the purpose of hiding the debtor's assets from creditors with a legal claim to them.

Claremont's financial condition had deteriorated rapidly after the second great Stock Market Crash. Eventually, he was forced to declare bankruptcy. However, before doing so he sold his car and his van to his sister for $1,000 each. His objective was to protect these assets from the bankruptcy process so that they would not be sold to pay off debts owed to creditors. When the bankruptcy proceedings were over, he intended to buy back the van and the car for the same $2,000. Since the entire transaction was designed to defraud Claremont's creditors, it would be void.

Agreements to Escape Liability

A basic policy of the law is that all parties should be liable for their own wrongdoing. Consequently, the law looks with disfavor on any agreement which allows a party to escape this responsibility. One device frequently used in the attempt to escape legal responsibility is the exculpatory agreement. An **exculpatory agreement** is usually found as a clause in a longer, more complex contract or on the back of tickets and parking stubs. The exculpatory clause will state that one of the parties, generally the one who wrote the contract, will not be liable for any economic loss or physical injury even if that party caused the loss or injury.

Jacobson Communications Enterprises sold a fusion splicing machine to National Telephone, Inc., for their fiber optics work. The bill of sale contained a clause which said that Jacobson would not be liable for any harm caused by a malfunction of the machine. The clause also exempted Jacobson from liability for any injuries caused by a defect in the machine, whether or not the defect was caused by the manufacturing process or a flaw inherent in the design. This is the type of exculpatory clause which the courts have found to be a violation of public policy.

Agreements in Restraint of Trade

The law tries to be a constant protector of the rights of persons to make a living and to do business freely in a competitive market. If persons enter into contracts that take away these rights, the law will restore the rights to them by declaring such contracts void. A **restraint trade** is a limitation on the full exercise of doing business with others. Agreements which have the effect of removing competition or denying to the public services they would otherwise have or which result in higher prices and resulting hardship are **agreements in restraint of trade** and can be declared void.

Agreements to Suppress Competition Any agreement made with the intent of suppressing competition, fixing prices, and the like is void as an illegal restraint of trade. Such agreements are unenforceable because they deprive the public of the advantages guaranteed in an economy based on freedom to contract, laws of supply and demand, and fair and honest business dealing. Agreements of this type may be legal and enforceable, however, if they do not violate the so-called rule of reason that is usually applied by the courts. The rule of reason is that such agreements are enforceable when they do not unreasonably restrict businesses from competing with one another. (See the discussion of restraint of trade in Chapter 38.)

Sale of Business When a business is sold, it is common practice for the agreement to contain covenants which restrict the seller from entering the same type of business. Such **restrictive covenants** in a contract for the sale of a business will be upheld by the court if they are reasonable in time and geographical area. What is reasonable is determined by a careful examination of the business being sold. For example, an agreement by the seller of a barbershop not to open a similar shop in the same community for the next three years would undoubtedly be reasonable. In contrast, a wider geographical area or longer period of time might not be allowed by the court.

Vladeck owned a neighborhood printing business in Buffalo which he sold to Mazaroff. A condition to the sale was a clause in the contract which prohibited Vladeck from opening another printing plant anywhere east of the Mississippi for a period of 20 years. Vladeck sought to have this condition invalidated as contrary to public policy. The court ruled that the provision covered such a vast geographical area and such an extensive period of time that it was unreasonable. The agreement was declared void as a violation of public policy.

RESTRICTIVE EMPLOYMENT COVENANT

FOR GOOD CONSIDERATION, and in consideration of my being employed by Hawthorne Savings and Loan, I, Vytataus Angelitis, the undersigned, hereby agree that when I leave the employment of Hawthorne, regardless of the reason I leave, I will not compete with Hawthorne, or its assigns or successors.

The phrase "NOT COMPETE" stated above, means that I will not directly or indirectly work as a loan officer for a savings and loan association or any other financial institution which is in competition with Hawthorne.

This restrictive employment covenant will extend for a radius of five miles from the present location of Hawthorne at 6802 East 185th Street, Cleveland, Ohio. This covemant will be in effect for six months, beginning on the date of the termination of employment.

Signed this second day of March, 19--.

Vytataus Angelitis
Employee

Figure 10-1 Unlike the restrictive employment covenant in the opening commentary, this version of the agreement would be upheld by the court. Note that the agreement is reasonable as to the type of work Angelitis is allowed to do (loan officer), the length of time involved (six months), and the geographical area covered by the prohibition (a 5-mile radius from Hawthorne's East 185th Street location).

Restrictive Employment Covenants A restrictive employment covenant in an employment contract limits a worker's employment options after leaving her or his present job. The objective of such a clause is to protect the present employer from an employee who might take trade secrets, customer lists, or other confidential material to a competitor. In a typical restrictive employment covenant, an employee promises not to work for a competitor in the same field for a specified time period and within a specified geographical area after leaving the current job. (See Figure 10-1.) Agreements like this are not favored by the law because they could deprive people of their livelihood and they could severely limit competition. Consequently, restrictive employment covenants must be reasonable in the type of work they prohibit, the length of time involved in the prohibition, and the geographical area covered by the prohibition. Naturally, reasonableness as to work, time, and geography will vary from case to case, depending upon the nature of the job involved in the prohibition.

In the opening commentary, Hawthorne Savings and Loan Association attempted to prevent Angelitis from working for any other savings and loan association anywhere in Cleveland in any capacity for 12 years. Six months after leaving Hawthorne, Angelitis took a job at Excaliber Savings and Loan as a branch manager. Excaliber is located on St. Clair Avenue at Norwood Avenue in the heart of one of the other two Lithuanian neighborhoods in Cleveland. Hawthorne tried to stop Angelitis claiming his knowledge of their customer lists would hurt their business. Hawthorne pointed to the restrictive employment covenant prohibiting Angelitis from taking such a job anywhere in Cleveland for 12 years. The court held that the time restriction was too long and was, therefore, unreasonable. Also, since Angelitis had worked only at the East 185th Street branch, it was unreasonable to stop him from working in another Cleveland neighborhood. Angelitis kept his job at Excaliber.

10-4 CONSEQUENCES OF ILLEGALITY

Illegality of contract, as in promises to commit criminal acts, not only serves to void existing agreements but may lead to indictment and prosecution when sufficient evidence warrants such an action. Persons who agree to commit criminal acts for a promised consideration are involved in what criminal law defines as a **conspiracy.** Agreements that do not violate criminal laws may still be invalid. Thus, many agreements considered contrary to public policy have been declared invalid as against the public good, but not illegal in terms of criminal liability. Both types of agreements fail to have the characteristics that permit legal enforcement.

Illegality in Entire Agreements

In cases where the entire agreement is tainted with illegality, no valid contract will result. Even though specific sections of the agreement, if standing alone, may have been legally enforceable, illegality of any part of the entire contract will render it void.

In Pari Delicto and Divisible Contracts

When an agreement is divisible and the illegal promises and acts are completely segregated from other promises and acts that are not tainted by illegality, courts may enforce those parts that are legal and rescind those parts ruled illegal and invalid. Enforcement of that part determined to be valid and enforceable, of course, is tempered by the extent of illegality of the other divisible parts.

Harkness, a truck driver, agreed to drive a sixteen wheeler from the orange groves of Florida into Boston. Interstate Commerce Commission rules prohibit drivers from driving more than 8 hours without layover and rest. Harkness's straight-through trip required longer than the ICC 8-hour limit. Harkness would still be able to sue for the wages promised, separating the illegal driving time from the main purpose of the agreement. However, suppose Harkness had agreed to drive the rig knowing that bales of marijuana were to be secreted among the crates of oranges. The courts would then declare the agreement to be illegal in its entirety and would deny Harkness any rights whatsoever under the contract.

When both parties to an illegal agreement are equally wrong in the knowledge of the operation and effect of their contract, they are said to be ***in pari delicto*** (in equal fault). In such cases no aid will be given to either party in an action against the other, and the court will award no damages to either.

When the parties are not *in pari delicto,* relief will often be allowed if sought by the more innocent of the two. Although this rule is not applicable where one may be less guilty of premeditation (plotting or planning an illegal act) and intent to achieve a gain through known illegal acts, it may be applied when one party is not aware that a law is being broken and where there is no intent to do a wrong.

Haines agreed to remodel Kronski's house so that it might be used as a public restaurant. Haines accepted $5,000 with Kronski's promise to pay an additional $12,000 when the job was done. Haines was aware that zoning laws would not permit commercial use of any property in the area. Kronski was not aware of this fact, and in an action against Haines, the court would rule that Kronski might recover his $5,000 as the parties were not *in pari delicto.*

SUMMARY

10-1. An agreement might have offer, acceptance, mutual assent, competent parties, and consideration and still be invalid if the objective of the agreement is to do something that is illegal. One type of contract that fails for illegality is the one in which the parties agree to do some otherwise illegal act. This illegal act could be a crime or a tort.

10-2. Some agreements are made illegal by statute even though the activities themselves are neither crimes nor torts. These agreements include usurious agreements, wagering agreements, unlicensed agreements, unconscionable agreements, and Sunday agreements.

10-3. Public policy is a general legal principle that says no one should be allowed to do anything that tends to hurt the public at large. Agreements found void for a violation of public policy include agreements to obstruct justice, agreements interfering with public service, agreements to defraud creditors, exculpatory agreements, and agreements in restraint of trade.

10-4. Contracts that involve illegal agreements are invalid. Moreover, promises to commit illegal acts may also lead to indictment and prosecution. If an entire agreement is illegal, no binding contract results. If only part of an agreement is illegal, the court may rescind only those parts found to be illegal. When both parties are equally at fault in creating an illegal agreement, the court will award no damages to either. When the parties are not in equal fault, relief will often be granted if sought by the innocent party.

Understanding Key Legal Terms

agreements in restraint of trade (p. 120)
blue laws (p. 117)
conspiracy (p. 122)
exculpatory agreement (p. 119)
in pari delicto (p. 123)
local option (p. 118)
public policy (p. 118)
restraint of trade (p. 120)
usury (p. 116)

Questions for Review and Discussion

1. What is the underlying rationale of the courts in voiding agreements that are contrary to the law?
2. Why do most states have usury laws to regulate the interest rate that may be charged in consumer transactions?
3. What wagering agreements might states make exceptions for?
4. What is the legal effect of a transaction entered into by a party who should have a license but does not?
5. When is an agreement considered by the courts to be unconscionable? How can a claim of unconscionability be defeated?
6. Why do states differ in their attitude toward and enforcement of Sunday blue laws? What usually determines whether Sunday contracts will be enforced in a particular state or location?
7. What is meant by the term public policy in relation to the enforcement of contracts? How do the courts normally treat agreements found to be contrary to public policy?
8. Identify those types of contracts generally held to be a violation of public policy.
9. Explain why the courts will closely scrutinize contracts that appear to limit competition or to restrain trade.
10. Two types of contracts, one a divisible contract and the other an entire contract, are before a court for consideration as to their legality and enforceability at law. Each agreement contains clauses which are partly legal and partly illegal. How is the court likely to treat the enforcement and disposition of these two types of contracts?

Analyzing Cases

1. A group of men known as the "last man's club" bought a hunting lodge in upstate New York to be used as their headquarters. The men agreed that the land would belong to the last surviving club member. The lastsurviving member turned out to be Crawford, who claimed exclusive title to the land. Crawford's claim was challenged by Quinn, the daughter of a member of the group who had predeceased Crawford. Quinn argued that the agreement made by the members of the "last man's club" was actually a wagering agreement and, therefore, invalid. Is Quinn's claim correct? *Quinn v. Stuart Lakes Club, Inc.*, 439 N.Y.S.2d 30 (New York).

2. West was hired by the data processing department of the Alberto-Culver Company as a senior programmer. Since West had ob-

tained the job through an employment agency, Alberto-Culver was supposed to pay the agency fee. However, Alberto-Culver found out that the employment agency was not licensed, as was required by Illinois law. Since the employment agency was not licensed, Alberto-Culver claims it does not have any duty to pay the agency fee. Is Alberto correct? Explain. *T.E.C. and Associates v. Alberto-Culver Company,* 476 N.E.2d 1212 (Illinois).

3. Williams was a regular customer at Walker-Thomas Furniture. On a fairly regular basis, he would buy household goods on time payments. A clause in each installment contract indicated that an unpaid balance would affect all items he had ever purchased. In effect, this meant that if Williams missed even one monthly installment, Walker could repossess every item Williams had ever obtained from Walker regardless of how long ago they had been purchased. Williams missed a single monthly installment and Walker tried to take back everything Williams had purchased over the last 5 years. Williams claims the default clause is unconscionable. Is Williams correct? Explain. *Williams v. Walker-Thomas Furniture Company,* 350 F.2d 445 (D.C. Cir. Ct.).

4. Peeples fell from a scaffold set up by Donar Systems, his employer. As a result of the fall, Peeples sustained serious injuries. At the time of the fall, the work was being done for the city of Detroit. The city claimed it was not liable because Donar's employment contract contained a clause which absolved the city of any liability for negligence regardless of who was at fault. Peeples claims that this is an illegal exculpatory clause and asks the court not to uphold it. Will the court comply with Peeples' request? Explain. *Peeples v. City of Detroit,* 297 N.W.2d 839 (Michigan).

5. The Topps Chewing Gum Company and the Major League Baseball Players Association entered into exclusive 5-year contracts for the services of baseball players. For the 5-year period covered by the agreements, photographs of major league baseball players were to appear exclusively on baseball cards distributed by Topps with the sale of its chewing gum. The Fleer Corporation, a rival of Topps, brought suit for $16 million, alleging that the exclusive contracts were an effort to freeze out competition in this area and thus constituted "an illegal restraint on trade." Topps argued that Fleer could compete with Topps by seeking the agreements with players still in the minor leagues. Thus, Topps concluded that their competitive efforts were not unreasonable. Is Topps correct? Explain. *Fleer Corporation v. Topps Chewing Gum, Inc.,* 501 F. Supp. 485 (E.D. Pennsylvania).

6. Trecher worked for Columbia Ribbon and Carbon Manufacturing Co., Inc., as a salesperson for several years. His employment agreement included a restrictive employment covenant that said he could not obtain a similar job anywhere in the U.S. for 2 years after he left Columbia. Trecher left Columbia and was hired as a salesperson by A-1-A Corporation, one of Columbia's competitors. Columbia filed suit to stop Trecher from working for A-1-A based on the restrictive employment covenant. Will the court stop Trecher from working for A-1-A? Explain. *Columbia Ribbon and Carbon Manufacturing v. A-1-A Corporation,* 369 N.E.2d 4 (New York).

CHAPTER 11
Form of the Agreement

OUTLINE

11-1 The Statute of Frauds
- Historical Context
- Contracts Requiring Written Form
- Definition of a Writing

11-2 Special Rules Involving Written Contracts
- The Parol Evidence Rule
- The Equal Dignities Rule

11-3 Formalities of Contract Construction
- Signatures
- Witnesses and Acknowledgments
- Seal
- Recording for Protection of the Parties

COMMENTARY

Mihalic wanted to purchase a personal computer. Unfortunately, he did not have the ready cash. Also, since he was only 22 years old, he did not have any established credit history, and as a result, the Brennan Brothers Department Store would not sell him the personal computer under an installment plan. Mihalic went to his brother-in-law, Rosebrock, and asked for his help. Rosebrock went to Brennan Brothers with Mihalic. He told the manager that he would pay for the personal computer if Mihalic defaulted on any of his installment payments. Under these circumstances, the manager agreed to sell the personal computer to Mihalic. On the same day, Rosebrock took his daughter, Julianne, to a clothing store. He told the clerk to help his daughter pick out a summer wardrobe. He also told the clerk to send him the bill. The clerk at the store agreed to this arrangement. While these two situations appear to be similar, they are actually very different. One of them requires a written agreement for enforceability, the other does not. Which of the two must be in writing? Questions like this are addressed in this chapter.

OBJECTIVES

1. Discuss the historical development of the Statute of Frauds, and indicate what abuses the statute was designed to eliminate.
2. Identify the six types of agreements that must be in writing under the Statute of Frauds.
3. List the essential information that should be included in a memorandum under the Statute.
4. Outline what is meant by the parol evidence rule as it applies to written contracts.
5. Indicate the situations in which the law will allow the introduction of oral evidence to interpret or explain a written contract.
6. Describe what is meant by the equal dignities rule, and explain how it can be a factor in determining the form a contract should take.

7. Illustrate the methods by which the physically handicapped and the illiterate may sign a contract.
8. Enumerate the duties and obligations of a notary public regarding the acknowledgment of a signature on a contract.
9. Indicate how the role and the use of the seal in contract law has evolved over the years.
10. Explain why the law requires some written contracts to be recorded in a public office.

11-1 THE STATUTE OF FRAUDS

In discussing the six requirements of a valid contract, we have examined many contract situations. Some of the agreements were written, some oral, and some only implied. The validity of the contracts did not always depend on their being written. You might have concluded, therefore, that a valid contract does not need to be written. It is, of course, sometimes desirable to have a contract in writing if it is not to be performed at the time it is entered into or if the agreement is very complicated. Most contracts, however, do not have to be in writing to be enforceable. The exceptions to this general rule are found in the Statute of Frauds.

Historical Context

Early English law permitted the enforcement of all oral contracts when they could be proved through testimony of witnesses. Witnesses were required to prove or disprove the existence of an oral agreement, the parties themselves being barred from testifying on their own behalf. Perjury was not uncommon at the time, opening the door to enforcement of numerous alleged contracts that a defendant was unable to disclaim. To correct this matter, the English Parliament in 1677 passed the Act for the Prevention of Fraud and Perjuries, later shortened to **Statute of Frauds.** The provisions of the English Statute of Frauds were adopted into practice in the courts of the states after the colonies separated from England. Each state now has its own statute of frauds. One type of agreement mentioned in the original act has found its way into the UCC.

Contracts Requiring Written Form

According to the modern Statute of Frauds applicable in most states today, six types of executory contracts must be in writing to be enforceable: contracts not to be completed within one year, contracts for the sale of real property, contracts for the sale of personal property worth $500 or more, contracts of executors and administrators, a guaranty of debts or wrongdoing of another, and contracts in consideration of marriage.

Contracts Not to Be Completed Within One Year If the terms of an executory agreement make it impossible to complete the agreement within one year of the date of the agreement, the contract must be in writing.

Chernoff was offered a job as a traveling public relations representative for Scioto-Auglaize Airlines. Chernoff's job will require her to make a worldwide tour during which she will visit all 30 foreign offices of S-A Airlines. The plan is for her to make a two-week stay at each office as she works on their publicity campaigns. When Chernoff reports to work, the human resources director tells her that the position is no longer open, even though she had accepted. Any action by Chernoff against S-A Airlines would fail because the contract could not be completed within a year and it was not in writing.

In situations where an agreement could extend beyond one year, but where performance need not require more than a year, an oral agreement is sufficient.

Suppose in the previous case S-A Airlines had simply told Chernoff that she was to complete her world tour within 60 weeks. The contract would not have to be in writing since 60 weeks is merely the time period during which the job must be completed. Chernoff could complete the work in 52 weeks or even less. There is no requirement that she take the full 60 weeks.

It is generally held that contracts of employment intended to be for the life of the employee need not be in writing. There is no certainty that the employee might live beyond the one-year limitation of the statute. To clarify claims of this kind, some states have enacted statutes which require lifetime agreements to be in writing, thereby following the different concept that both employer and employee intended the agreement to continue for more than one year. Under the Statute of Frauds, the time period commences on the date a contract is made, not on the date when performance is to begin. An agreement entered into on Wednesday in which a person agrees to start working the following Monday for one year would therefore have to be in writing.

Contracts for the Sale of Real Property All contracts for the transfer or sale of any interest in real property must be in writing. In some states in which the seal is still in use, these contracts must be under seal. Real property transactions are formal and of a most serious nature because of the finality of transfer of irreplaceable rights by the owner.

A lease for the renting of another's real property must be in writing unless it is for a period of less than one year.

UCC 2-201 **(see p. 616)**

Contracts for Sale of Personal Property Worth $500 or More Contracts for the sale of goods of $500 or more must be in writing to be enforceable. Oral agreements over that amount not evidenced by a written memorandum are not enforceable. (There are, however, four exceptions to this rule. These are discussed in Chapter 14.) It has been held that the buyer's check given in partial payment may provide sufficient evidence to prove a contract of sale in an action where a written memorandum is required by the UCC Statute of Frauds. In addition to the parties and the price, both of which are on a check as a matter of course, a description of the subject matter, including the quantity desired, would have to appear somewhere on the check.

Caldwell offered to sell his regulation-size pool table to Hasenzahl for $850. Hasenzahl gave Caldwell a check for $600. Hasenzahl wrote on the check that it was a deposit on Caldwell's pool table as part of the purchase price of $850. In a subsequent dispute, Hasenzahl did not deny the oral agreement but stated that the contract was not enforceable because the price was more than the $500 set forth in the UCC Statute of Frauds. The court said that the check itself was evidence of a contract by the one obligated to make the purchase because it described the subject matter and the price to be paid.

Contracts of Executors and Administrators. Agreements by an executor or an administrator to pay the debts of a deceased person out of his or her own personal funds must be committed to writing. An **executor** may be either a person or a corporation named in a will to oversee the distribution of the deceased's estate according to the provisions contained in a will. An **administrator** is one named by a court to do the work of an executor if none is named in the will or if the executor either refuses to perform or is incapable of performing the duties. Persons having the responsibility of executor or administrator often make promises under emotional stress for the protection of the survivors. Such promises must be in writing to be enforceable, thus removing the possibility of enforcing unintentional or ill-advised oral statements.

Jolas was named as the executor of his sister's estate. One of his sister's creditors, the Nocenti Department Store, demands the immediate payment of a $750 debt owed by the deceased. To protect both his sister's good name he promises Nocenti that he will pay the bill himself. Nocenti refuses to go along with this plan unless Jolas places the promise in written form. Jolas agrees. After things have become a bit calmer, Nocenti attempts to collect the money. Jolas refuses to pay. Nocenti will be able to enforce the promise because the store has written evidence of Jolas's agreement to pay the debt.

Guaranty of Debts or Wrongdoing of Third Parties A promise to pay another's bills or to settle for any of another's wrongful acts, if that party does not settle them personally, is an obligation that must be in writing if it is to be valid and enforceable. This is a **guaranty of payment.**

In the opening commentary, Rosebrock promised to pay the Brennan Brothers Department Store should his brother-in-law, Mihalic, default on his installment payments for the home computer. Rosebrock also agreed to pay for his daughter's summer wardrobe. In the first situation, Rosebrock is guaranteeing his brother-in-law's obligation by promising to pay the bill if Mihalic does not. This type of agreement requires a writing to be enforceable. In the second instance, Rosebrock's promise is not one of guaranty, but one in which he made himself directly and primarily responsible for the amount of credit extended. Thus, he was not guaranteeing another's obligations. Rather, he was creating one of his own. This one would not require a writing unless his daughter spent more than $500.

CONTRACT FOR SALE OF PERSONAL PROPERTY

AGREEMENT made by and between Ozzie Caldwell (Seller), and Geordi Hasenzahl (Buyer).

For good consideration, it has been agreed between the two parties that:

1. Seller agrees to sell, and Buyer agrees to buy the following described property: one regulation size pool table now located at the residence of Ozzie Caldwell, RD #1, Box 118, Ashberry, Kentucky.
2. Buyer agrees to pay to Seller the total price of $850.00; payable as follows:
   $600.00 deposit herewith
   $250.00 balance by cash or certified check at time of transfer
3. Seller warrants he has full legal title to said property, authority to sell said property, and that said property shall be sold free and clear of all claims by other parties.
4. Said property is sold in "as is" condition. Seller does not guarantee the property except that it is sold in its present condition.
5. Parties agree to transfer title on February 7, 19--, at RD #1, Box 118, Ashberry, Kentucky, the address of the Seller.
6. This agreement shall be binding on the parties, their successors, assigns, and personal representatives.
7. This writing is intended to represent the entire agreement between the parties.

Signed under seal this nineteenth day of January, 19--.

Geordi Hasenzahl — Buyer

Ozzie Caldwell — Seller

Figure 11-1 The court in the Hasenzahl-Caldwell case discussed on page 129 held that Hasenzahl's $600 check was sufficient to satisfy the Statute of Frauds requirement of a writing for contract involving personal property valued at $500 or more. If Hasenzahl and Caldwell would have used the above agreement, none of the subsequent problems would have arisen.

Contracts in Consideration of Marriage Agreements made in consideration of marriage must be in writing. This section does not relate to the marriage contract itself, which in almost all cases is oral. It refers to those promises made by parties prior to marriage in which they accept additional obligations not ordinarily included in the implied obligations of marriage itself. Included in this category are **prenuptial agreements,** sometimes called **premarital agreements** or **antenuptial agreements,** in which two people planning marriage agree to change the property rights that usually arise in marriage. Such promises are enforceable only if they are in writing and are agreed upon prior to the marriage.

Tony DelCampo was engaged to Lynette Adams for many years. In November, DelCampo and Adams entered into a prenuptial agreement. In this agreement Adams promised that she would have no claim on DelCampo's property or business should they become divorced. DelCampo agreed to give Adams $30,000 over a 5-year period in the event of their divorce. This contract would be enforceable only if written evidence were available to prove their agreement.

Other Contracts Each state has enacted special statutes outlining other agreements that must be in writing. Other contracts usually required by special statutes to be in writing include the release of a party from debt (general release) and the resumption of obligations after a bankruptcy. However, the diversity of these special statutes makes it impractical to list them here.

Definition of a Writing

Just what is meant when the statute states that "the agreement must be in writing?" The statute requires only that the agreement be in writing—nothing more! A pen, pencil, a typewriter, or any other mechanical device comes within this definition. The writing should be intelligible. It may be embodied in letters, memos, telegrams, invoices, and purchase orders sent between the parties; it may be written on any surface suitable for the purpose of recording the intention of the parties as long as all the required elements are present.

Elements of a Writing To be absolutely complete, the written agreement, or **memorandum,** as it is often called, should contain the following elements: (1) terms of the agreement, (2) identification of the subject matter, (3) statement of the consideration promised, (4) names and identities of the persons to be obligated, and (5) the signatures of the parties to the contract. Actually, the only signature needed on the memorandum is the signature of the party sought to be bound to the agreement.

Storms contracted to rent pasture land from Weaver for grazing her horses. The agreement was for two years, and the state statute of frauds required that it be in writing to be enforceable. Storms noted the conditions and terms of the agreement on the back of an envelope and handed it to Weaver, who then approved what had been written and signed it. Storms returned the envelope to her briefcase without adding her signature. The information contained in the memorandum would satisfy the statute. However, Weaver alone could be held liable, because Storms had never added her signature to the agreement.

Missing, Vague, or Incorrect Terms While the elements noted above are preferred to ensure clarity in the event of a lawsuit, the writing may be acceptable even though it omits or does not correctly state some term agreed upon by the contracting parties. Such written agreements may be enforced even though material terms are omitted. The court may supply omitted terms, including the price, terms and place of payment; terms of delivery, and other factors. To be enforceable, only the following must be shown in the writing: proof of the contract intent, quantity ordered, names of parties, and the signature of the party against whom enforcement is sought.

11-2 SPECIAL RULES INVOLVING WRITTEN CONTRACTS

Throughout the years, the courts have developed certain rules which make the interpretation and enforcement of written contracts consistent and predictable. The two most important rules in this regard are the parol evidence rule and the equal dignities rule. The parol evidence rule involves the interpretation of written contracts, while the equal dignities rule involves their enforcement.

The Parol Evidence Rule

The **parol evidence rule** says that evidence of oral statements made before signing a written agreement is usually not admissible in court to change or to contradict the terms of a written agreement. Following oral discussion and negotiation, it is customary for parties to reduce their agreements to some written form. Of the terms, conditions, and promises discussed, only those included in the writing will be enforced. Exceptions to the general rule are discussed in this section.

Eldridge purchased a $600 microwave oven from the Lewisohn Sisters Department Store. After all the sales documents had been signed, the salesperson stated that if Eldridge had any trouble with the oven that the Lewisohn Sisters would take care of it. The present action resulted from the department store's refusal to take care of numerous problems that Eldridge claimed should be taken care of under the salesperson's express warranty. The court ruled that the salesperson's oral statements were not admissable in court because they were not contained, with other conditions, in the written sales agreement.

Under the **best evidence rule,** the courts generally will accept into evidence only the original of a writing, not a copy. Under this rule, a written instrument is regarded as the primary or best possible evidence. Thus the best evidence rule concurs with and supports the parol evidence rule.

The parol evidence rule will not apply when unfair and unjust decisions might result from its application. While many unjust situations can occur, they generally fall into one of five categories: (1) incomplete, ambiguous, or erroneous agreements, (2) void and voidable agreements, (3) agreements based on a condition precedent, (4) modified or rescinded agreements, or (5) agreements involving past or usual commercial practice.

In those cases where the written agreement is incomplete, oral evidence may be used to supply the missing terms. Ordinarily what the court will conclude in such a case is that the parties never intended the writing to be the entire agreement. Similarly, when a written contract is obscure or indistinct in certain of its terms, oral evidence may be used to clarify those terms. Also, if the written agreement contains a typographical or clerical error of some sort, the court will allow oral evidence as to the true intent of the parties.

Luoc, a professional freelance writer, contracted with the Calgary Press to ghostwrite the memoirs of a famous Hollywood movie star. The written agreement contained a typographical error indicating that Luoc was to receive $200 per chapter. Actually the amount was supposed to be $2,000. The court would allow oral evidence to clear up this obvious typographical error.

In general, the courts will allow a party to a written agreement to introduce oral testimony to show that the contract is void or voidable due to a lack of mutual assent or contractual capacity. The courts are willing to allow such testimony because it does not affect the terms of the agreement. Rather, it seeks to discredit the entire transaction. Thus, it is permissible to introduce oral evidence as to fraud, duress, misrepresentation, mistake, and undue influence. Similarly, it is appropriate to offer oral testimony as to a party's minority or mental incompetence.

Baraka, a minor, entered a written agreement with Oswald of Oswald Motors, Inc., for the purchase of a motorcycle. Two days later, Baraka chose to rescind the contract. When Oswald refused to do so, Baraka took him to court. Oswald argued that Baraka could introduce no oral testimony about the contract under the parol evidence rule because the written agreement was intended to be the entire agreement and because no part of it was erroneous, ambiguous, or incomplete. The court disagreed and allowed Baraka's oral testimony as to his age because the issue before the court did not affect the terms of the agreement. Rather, it affected the capacities of the party to agree to those terms in the first place.

If a written agreement is dependent upon some event before it becomes enforceable, then oral evidence may be offered concerning that condition precedent. A **condition precedent** is an act or promise that must take place or be fulfilled before the other party is obligated to perform his or her part of the agreement. The courts allow this type of oral evidence because, like the oral evidence involving assent and capacity, it does not impact upon the terms of the agreement but on the enforceability of the entire contract.

Morrison entered an agreement under which he agreed to purchase Kinnebrew's Florida condominium. The terms of the purchase were laid out quite specifically in a lengthy, detailed written contract. However, as a condition precedent, Morrison had to have his credit checked by Kinnebrew's real estate agent and that credit record had to be flawless. When several credit problems showed up in the report, Kinnebrew refused to go through with the deal. Morrison sued to force Kinnebrew to perform according to the written agreement. Kinnebrew could offer oral testimony that a clean credit report on Morrison was a condition precedent to performance of the written terms.

Oral evidence may be used to prove that the parties, after entering into a written contract, orally agreed to rescind or modify its terms. The courts allow such testimony because the written contract is seen as representing the parties' negotiations and agreements up to the time the contract is reduced to writing. Subsequent negotiations to change or rescind the agreement are permitted, and evidence to that effect does not undermine the spirit of the parol evidence rule. However, if the change in the contract involves an agreement that would have to be in writing under the Statute of Frauds, then a writing would be required. Similarly, if the original written contract requires later modifications to be in writing, then that written requirement will rule.

Slaughter entered into a temporary employment agreement with Larchmore Industries. Under terms of his temporary employment, Slaughter was to work as an efficiency expert for six months. A clause in the written agreement said it could only be altered by an appropriately drawn written modification. Guilfoyle, Slaughter's supervisor, orally told Slaughter that he had become a full-time employee and that his contract would run for three years. At the end of his original six-month contract, Slaughter was told his services were no longer required. Slaughter's oral agreement with Guilfoyle would have no effect for two reasons. First, the agreement was to last longer than one year and should, therefore, have been in writing under the Statute of Frauds. Second, the original written contract limited all changes to written modifications.

UCC 1-205, 2-202, 2-208 **(see pp. 613, 616, 617)**

As a final exception to the parol evidence rule, the UCC allows oral testimony about how the parties have done business together over a long time period. The UCC makes allowance for this type of testimony because from a practical point of view, parties often get so used to dealing with each other in a particular way, that they neglect to include certain terms in their written agreements. Similarly, some practices are so universal in a particular trade, business, or industry, that the parties will feel no need to include such universal practices in their written contracts. Accordingly, the UCC allows oral testimony to supplement a written agreement as to these practices.

Superior Printing, Inc., and the Tuscawaras Chemical Company have been doing business together for 10 years. Superior prints all labels, business cards, letterheads, invoices, and purchase orders for Tuscawaras. During their long tenure together, Superior has always delivered orders to Tuscawaras. When a new manager took over Superior's bindery and delivery operation, he forbade deliveries to any customers outside a seven-mile radius of Superior's plant. As a result, Tuscawaras did not receive an important shipment of labels and lost several big orders. When Tuscawaras sued Superior for breach of contract, Superior pointed to the written agreement which mentioned nothing about Superior's delivery responsibilities. However, because of their 10-year history of consistently dealing with one another in the same way, the court, citing the UCC, allowed oral testimony to supplement the written contract.

The Equal Dignities Rule

Not in State of Washington. Since 1907.

The **equal dignities rule** provides that when a party appoints an agent to negotiate an agreement which itself must be in writing, the appointment and authorization of the agent must also be in writing. In contrast, the appointment of an agent to negotiate an agreement that the law does not require to be in writing may be accomplished through an oral agreement.

A state statute required that all agreements for the sale of real property must be in writing, signed, and under seal. Layton orally agreed to sell Williams's house and lot on promise of a 10 percent commission and the exclusive right to represent Williams for 90 days. Layton did secure a buyer and delivered a purchase agreement to Williams, signed and sealed by the prospective buyer. By application of the equal dignities rule, the contract of sale is voidable by Williams due to Layton's failure to secure a signed and sealed authorization to sell the property.

11-3 FORMALITIES OF CONTRACT CONSTRUCTION

Certain formalities are usually followed in the formation of other than the simplest kinds of written agreements. While the Statute of Frauds may necessitate nothing more than the briefest written disclosure of promises, conditions, and terms, plus the signature(s) of the obligated party or parties, usually contracts in general commercial and consumer use are carefully written, researched for legal compliance, signed, and often sealed, acknowledged, and recorded. In addition, leases and contracts for the sale of real property may have additional requirements of content and formality extending beyond even these formalities.

Signatures

Written agreements should be signed by both parties, but they need not be. If signed by only one party, any obligation on the agreement would be limited to that party alone. Parties should use their usual signatures, that is, the signatures used in other matters in the regular course of business. However, any mark which the signer intends to be a signature will be the legal signature of that person. Although it is unusual, one may adopt any name desired in creating a contractual obligation as long as the party intends to be bound by that signature. Thus, a well-known actress may sign a hotel register using a name other than her real name as a means of protecting her privacy. A signature may be the full name or initials, and it may be printed, typewritten, or stamped, as with a rubber stamp. However made, it must be made with the intent to be bound thereby.

In cases where a party cannot sign the written agreement due to illness, physical handicap, or some other physical reason, another person may sign for that person. The signature should be followed by a statement indicating that the contracting party was physically unable to sign the document and that a signature was placed on the document by another person in the contracting party's presence and at the request of the contracting party. The person who has signed for the contracting party then signs the document (see Figure 11-2). Persons who lack the ability to read or write are often obliged to sign contracts. In such situations, the law accepts the person's mark, usually an "X," properly witnessed, as a valid signature (see Figure 11-3).

Witnesses and Acknowledgments

Witnesses are required in the signing of a will, but in most other documents their signatures are at the option of the contracting parties. To ensure that no misunderstanding will arise as to the acceptance and signing of a written agreement, the use of witnesses is advised. Certain official documents, such as a certificate of title to a motor vehicle, require the owner's signature and an **acknowledgment** by a notary public, when transferring ownership. The notary witnesses the signing of the document and then acknowledges this act by signing the document and adding the official seal to it. A notary is not authorized to read the document being signed and may be prevented from doing so. The notary's legal authority includes the act of acknowledging another's signature to be the result of this person's own free act and deed before the notary.

Seal

Some states still require the use of one's seal when signing a formal contract. Contracts for the sale and transfer of real estate sometimes come within this category. Historically, the seal was a carefully designed coat of arms or other suitable design, mounted in a ring and used to impress markings in melted sealing wax placed on the document. As noted in Chapter 9, modern practice has dispensed with this custom, and today's seal is usually nothing more than the word *seal* or the *L.S.* (*locus sigilli,* meaning "place of the seal") printed or written next to the signature.

signature: Daniel Colletti

WITNESS: I hereby attest that Daniel Colletti was physically unable to sign his name and that his name was signed by me in his presence and at his request.

Jonas Abraham

Figure 11-2 Signature for an incapacitated person.

Her

Samantha X Cunningham

Mark

WITNESS: I hereby attest that Samantha Cunningham made her mark as her signature and that, at her request, I added her name to her mark.

Lindsay Quartermain

Figure 11-3 Signature of a person who does not know how to write.

Recording for Protection of the Parties As a protection to lenders, persons selling goods through installment contracts, and the like, the law provides that certain documents be recorded in a public office for inspection by anyone wishing to know about them. For example, when money is loaned on a motor vehicle, the lender may record that transaction in the appropriate public office to protect his or her interest in the vehicle. The recording requirement is discussed in detail in Chapter 29.

SUMMARY

11-1. While most contracts do not have to be in writing to be enforceable, those which must be in written form are outlined in the Statute of Frauds. The six types of executory contracts that must be in writing include contracts not to be completed within one year, contracts for the sale of real property, contracts for the sale of personal property for $500 or more, contracts of executors and administrators, a guaranty of debts or wrongdoings of third parties, and contracts in consideration of marriage. To be absolutely complete, the written agreement must contain the terms of the agreement, the subject matter, the consideration, and the names and signatures of the parties.

11-2. Two important rules which aid in the interpretation and enforcement of written contracts are the parol evidence rule and the equal dignities rule. The parol evidence rule restricts the use of oral evidence to change, delete, or add to the terms of a written contract. Exceptions to this rule involve incomplete, ambiguous, or erroneous agreements, void and voidable agreements, agreements based on conditions precedent, modified or rescinded agreements, and agreements involving past or usual commercial practice. The equal dignities rule provides that when one appoints an agent to negotiate an agreement which itself must be in writing, the appointment and authorization of the agent must also be in writing.

11-3. Certain formalities are usually followed in the formation of many written agreements. Written agreements need not be signed by both parties. However, any agreement signed by only one party would obligate only that party. When a person is incapable physically of signing a written contract, another person may sign it for him or her. Persons who are illiterate usually sign written contracts with an "X." Such signatures should be witnessed. Witnesses are not required when parties enter written agreements. However, to avoid misunderstanding, the use of witnesses is advisable. Some states still require the use of one's seal when signing a contract. Most, however, have dispensed with this custom. The law provides that some documents be recorded in a public office for inspection by those who have a legitimate right to seek the recorded information.

Understanding Key Legal Terms

acknowledgment (p. 136)
administrator (p. 129)
best evidence rule (p. 132)
condition precedent (p. 133)
equal dignities rule (p. 135)
executor (p. 129)
guaranty of payment (p. 129)
memorandum (p. 131)
parol evidence rule (p. 132)
Statute of Frauds (p. 127)

Questions for Review and Discussion

1. Trace the historical development of the Statute of Frauds from England to the United States, and indicate what abuses the Statute of Frauds was designed to correct.
2. Name the types of contracts that must be in writing under the Statute of Frauds.
3. According to the Statute of Frauds, what essential information should a written memorandum usually contain?
4. How does the parol evidence rule operate if a party seeks to include, by oral statement and proof, additional terms and conditions not previously mentioned in a written contract?
5. When will the courts allow the introduction and use of oral evidence?
6. How does the equal dignities rule apply to the appointment of contracting agents?
7. How may a person who is physically handicapped sign a contract? How may an illiterate sign?
8. What are the duties and obligations of a notary public regarding the acknowledgment of a signature on a contract?
9. How has the use of the seal in formal written contracts changed in recent years?
10. Why does the law require that certain written contracts be recorded in a public office?

Analyzing Cases

1. Lawson hired Konves to conduct extensive audits of her 87 Boutiques, located throughout the United States. As part of the agreement, Lawson required Konves to spend one week at each boutique. Konves demanded a written agreement before she would agree to Lawson's terms. Why was Konves correct in making this demand?

2. Kowal, an attorney, and Webster, a physician, orally agreed that Kowal would pay off Soule's medical bills if Webster would testify on Soule's behalf at an upcoming civil trial. The medical bills were to be paid out of any money recovered if Soule won his civil suit. Kowal claims the agreement should have been in writing. Since it was not placed in writing, he claims the agreement is unenforceable. Webster sued Kowal to force him to pay Soule's bill. Will Kowal win the case? Explain. *Webster v. Kowal,* 476 N.E.2d 205 (Massachusetts).

3. Johnson's lease agreement contained a clause which allowed her to purchase certain property if she later decided to do so. When she decided to exercise this option, she informed the owner. The owner agreed to allow Johnson to purchase the property, and a closing date was set up. The agreement, however, was not placed in writing. Later, the owner told Johnson that the property was going to be sold to someone else. Johnson sued the owner asking the court to compel the owner to go through with their original agreement. The owner holds that the oral agreement to sell the property to Johnson is not enforceable. Is the owner correct? Why or why not? *Johnson v. Bourchier,* 263 S.E.2d 157 (Georgia).

4. Butler and Wheeler agreed that Butler would lease a certain piece of property with the option to purchase that property at a later date. The agreement was handwritten and consisted of two separate documents, each document listing part of the transaction. Butler later attempted to purchase the property according to their earlier agreement. Wheeler refused to honor the agreement, claiming that it was unenforceable under the Statute of Frauds. Wheeler argued that since the agreement was contained in two documents, the intent of the statute had not been followed. Is Wheeler correct? Explain. *Butler v. Lovoll,* 620 P.2d 1251 (Nevada).

5. Ray's Motor Sales sold a mobile home to Hathaway. Before the written contract was signed, the seller told Hathaway that Ray's would take care of any problems that Hathaway might have with the mobile home. This promise was not included in the written document. When Hathaway had problems with the mobile home, he asked Ray's to take care of them. Ray's refused to be of any assistance. Hathaway sued Ray's to compel the enforcement of the promise. Ray's argues that under the parol evidence rule, no oral evidence can be introduced as to this separate oral agreement. Is Ray's correct? Explain. *Hathaway v. Ray's Motor Sales,* 247 A.2d 512 (Vermont).

6. Madden sued the president and board of directors of Georgetown College on a number of different issues involving breach of contract and negligence. One question before the court was whether the contract was under seal. The question was crucial because it affected the statute of limitations. In this case, the word *seal* was printed on the page. However, it was not next to the signatures but an inch above and to the left, over the word *attest.* Was this a sealed contract? Explain. *President of Georgetown College v. Madden,* 505 F. Supp. 557 (D. Maryland).

CHAPTER 12
Third Parties in Contract Law

OUTLINE

COMMENTARY

Sjögren, an award-winning artist with a worldwide reputation, agreed to paint a portrait of Kosaka's wife and daughter. When the time came for the portrait work to be done, Sjögren found that he was also committed to doing some portrait work for VonSchmidt. Since he could not be in two places at once, Sjögren delegated the Kosaka job to Liebow. When Liebow showed up to paint the portrait, Kosaka refused to honor the change in the agreement. Kosaka claimed he had hired Sjögren, not Liebow, and he wanted Sjögren or no one. Liebow argued that Sjögren had the right to delegate the portrait work to him and that Kosaka could do nothing about it. Who is correct here? Kosaka, the disgruntled art patron? Or Liebow, the frustrated portrait painter? Answers to questions like these involve the rights of third parties who are not part of an original contractual situation.

OBJECTIVES

1. Explain the legal rights of third parties who are designated creditor beneficiaries and the rights of those designated donee beneficiaries.
2. Indicate whether an insurance beneficiary is a creditor beneficiary or a donee beneficiary.
3. Differentiate between the legal rights accorded intended beneficiaries and those accorded to incidental beneficiaries to a contract.
4. Contrast assignment with delegation, and explain the difference between the two concepts.
5. Identify the three parties that are associated with any contractual assignment.

6. Explain how the equal dignities rule is applicable to an assignment.
7. Indicate who is responsible for giving notice of an assignment and explain the legal consequences of failing to give proper notice.
8. Explain the obligations of the assignor, the assignee, and the obligor after an assignment has been made.
9. Identify those contracts that cannot be assigned by the parties involved.
10. Distinguish between a novation and an assignment in contract law.

12-1 THIRD PARTIES AND OPERATION OF CONTRACTS

A **third party** is a person who may, in some way, be affected by a contract but who is not one of the contracting parties. A third party, also known as an **outside party,** is at times given benefits from a contract made between two other parties. A third party receiving benefits from a contract made by others is known as a **beneficiary.** Although not obligated by the agreement made between those in privity, third parties may have the legal right to enforce the benefits given them by such agreements.

Intended Beneficiaries

A beneficiary in whose favor a contract is made is an **intended beneficiary.** Those who are most frequently recognized to be intended beneficiaries, with the right to demand and enforce the benefits promised, are (1) creditor beneficiaries, (2) donee beneficiaries, and (3) insurance beneficiaries.

Creditor Beneficiaries A **creditor beneficiary** is an outside third party to whom one or both contracting parties owe a continuing debt of obligation arising from a contract. Frequently the obligation results from the failure of the contracting party or parties to pay for goods delivered or services rendered by the third party at some time in the past.

Morehead owed Hayakawa a balance of $825 for Hayakawa's work in the installation of Morehead's pool. On another contract, Morehead figured out Carnevali's income tax return on the condition that Morehead's $200 fee would be given to Hayakawa toward payment of the $825 debt. Hayakawa has become a creditor beneficiary with the right to demand payment from Carnevali if the $200 is not paid.

Donee Beneficiaries A third party who does not provide any consideration for the benefits received and who owes the contracting parties no legal duty is known as a **donee beneficiary.** However, the contracting parties owe the donee beneficiary the act promised, and if it is not forthcoming, the donee beneficiary may bring suit. The consideration that supports this type of agreement is the consideration exchanged by the parties in privity to the contract.

Clancy agreed to cut down a dead tree on Schottenheimer's property for $500. Clancy, however, wanted Schottenheimer to pay the $500 fee to Clancy's son. The son would be the donee beneficiary. If Schottenheimer failed to pay him the $500, Clancy's son would have the right to bring suit to collect the money.

Insurance Beneficiaries An individual named as the beneficiary of an insurance policy is usually considered a donee beneficiary. The beneficiary does not have to furnish the insured with consideration to enforce payment of the policy. In some cases an insurance beneficiary may also be a creditor beneficiary. This occurs when in consumer or mortgage loans the creditor requires the debtor to furnish a life term insurance policy naming the creditor as the beneficiary. The policy will pay the debt if the debtor dies before the loan has been repaid. (See Chapter 28.)

Incidental Beneficiaries

An **incidental beneficiary** is an outside party for whose benefit a contract was not made but who would substantially benefit if the agreement were performed according to its terms and conditions. Through interpretation of facts, a court might be called upon to determine whether in any particular case a third party was an intended or an incidental beneficiary. Incidental beneficiaries, as opposed to intended beneficiaries, have no legal grounds for enforcing the contract made by those in privity of contract.

Francona owned a major restaurant in downtown Milwaukee. The National Organization of Chemical Research Scientists had a contract with the city of Milwaukee for the use of the Municipal Convention Center for their annual convention. Two weeks before the convention, the organization announced plans to move the convention to St. Louis. The move was in direct violation of the organization's contract with Milwaukee. Francona brought suit against the organization for damages caused by a loss of business because the convention had moved to St. Louis. The court held that Francona was nothing more than an incidental beneficiary to the contract between the organization and Milwaukee. As such, he had no rights as would have been allowed a creditor or donee beneficiary.

12-2 ASSIGNMENT OF CONTRACTS

Contracts represent intangible property rights which a party in privity may wish to sell or transfer to another. Transfer of such a right to a third party may be accomplished through an **assignment.** In its simplest terms, an assignment is a transfer of a contract right; a **delegation** is a transfer of contract duty.

Cordwainer International held an option to purchase an offshore drilling platform owned by Isis-Zender Petroleum. One week before termination of the option, Kendall & Morrison Oil approached Cordwainer and offered to buy the option at a price that gave Cordwainer an enormous profit. Cordwainer assigned the option to Kendall & Morrison, which exercised the option and bought the platform as assignee of Cordwainer's rights to the property.

Assignment and Delegation Distinguished

Generally, rights are *assigned* and duties are *delegated.* In most cases, both are governed by the same rules. If A is owed money by B, A may assign to C the right to collect the money. On the other hand, if A has agreed to pay B to harvest 200 acres of wheat for a price, B may delegate the duty of harvesting to C. There are restrictions against the delegation of duties that will be presented later in this chapter.

Weigel agreed to lay a cement driveway for Langhorne for $2,000. Plans and specifications were provided by Langhorne. Weigel would have the right to delegate to another contractor the duties involved in laying the concrete driveway. Similarly, the new party might assign to another the right to collect the $2,000 from Langhorne after the job was completed.

Parties to Assignment

Three parties are associated with any assignment. Two of the parties are the ones who entered the original agreement. The party who assigns rights or delegates duties is the **assignor.** The outside third party to whom the assignment is made is the **assignee.** The remaining party to the original agreement is the **obligor.**

Immendorf owed Koberling $250 for some photography work that Koberling had done for her. Koberling, who owed Walker $250, authorized Walker to collect the $250 that Immendorf owed to Koberling. In this situation, Koberling is the assignor, Walker the assignee, and Immendorf the obligor.

Consideration in Assignment

Consideration is not required in the creation of an assignment. When there is no supporting consideration, however, the assignor may repudiate the assignment at any time prior to its execution. In the previous example there was consideration supporting Koberling's assignment. In consideration of the right to make the collection from Immendorf, Walker sacrificed the right to collect money owed by Koberling. If the assignment had been a gift of the $250, it could have been rescinded.

Method of Assignment

To be valid, an assignment must follow certain accepted procedures designed to protect all the parties. Form of assignment, notice of assignment, and the rights of parties in successive or subsequent assignments must conform to practices established by case law and state statutes.

Assignment

For value received, I, Francois Joliet, of 4444 Flowers Road, Lewiston, Maine, hereby assign, transfer, and set over to Daniel Parenti, of 2441 Kenwood Circle, Bainesville, Maine, all my rights and interest in and to a contract with Alexis Amenott, dated March 2 of this year, a copy of which is attached hereto, subject to all terms and conditions thereof. In witness whereof, I have executed this assignment at 97 Erieview Plaza, Mercedes, Maine, on May 4, 19--.

F. Joliet
Francis Joliet, Assignor

Acceptance of Assignment

Daniel Parenti hereby accepts the foregoing assignment, subject to all terms and conditions thereof.

May 4, 19-- Daniel Parenti
Daniel Parenti, Assignee

Figure 12-1 This is the type of assignment that Joliet should have made to Parenti in the case below.

Form of Assignment Assignment may be accomplished through written, oral, or implied agreements between the assignor and the assignee. Parties to an assignment must observe the requirement provided by the equal dignities rule. If the law requires that the agreement by the original parties be in writing, the assignment, too, must be in writing.

Amenoff agreed in writing to sell his collection of antique glassware to Joliet for $1,600. The written agreement was properly executed following the requirements of the Statute of Frauds. Joliet later made an oral assignment of the contract to Parenti. Still later, Joliet changed his mind and refused to honor the assignment. When Parenti sued to enforce the assignment, he discovered that since the assignment was not in writing, the court could not enforce it.

Notice of Assignment An assignment is valid at the time it is made. As a measure of protection against subsequent assignments, the assignee should give notice of the assignment to the obligor. This is an obligation of the assignee, not the assignor. If notice is not given, it would be normal practice for the obligor to render performance to the other original contracting party, the assignor in this case. If, after due notice has been given, the obligor makes payment to the assignor, the obligor is not excused from making payment to the assignee.

Czapnik & Bryant, Inc., was assigned a debt owed by Newfield to Pendleton for architectural work done by Pendleton for Newfield. Czapnik & Bryant gave notice of the assignment and a demand for payment to Newfield. Newfield disregarded the notice and the demand, and paid Pendleton instead. In a suit against Newfield, the court held that Newfield was liable to Czapnik & Bryant since notice and demand had been made prior to his decision to pay Pendleton.

Subsequent Assignments Should the assignor make a subsequent assignment of the same right, the courts must decide which of the two assignees has a superior right and claim against the obligor. A majority of the states hold that the first assignee has a superior right even if a later assignee was the first to give notice of the assignment to the obligor. A minority of courts hold that whichever assignee gives notice of assignment first has a superior right and claim to any assigned benefits.

Rights and Duties of the Assignee

The rights and duties of the assignee are the same as those previously held by the assignor under the original contract. It is fair to say that the assignee "steps into the shoes" of the assignor. Claims the assignor may have had against the obligor now belong to the assignee. Defenses the obligor may have had against the assignor's claims may now be used against the assignee.

Shapolsky and Sons contracted to build a two-car garage for Levine. When several other job opportunities opened up for Shapolsky, he assigned the contract with Levine to the Romita Brothers. By this assignment the Romita Brothers stepped into the shoes of Shapolsky and Sons. Any rights or claims that previously existed between Shapolsky and Levine have been shifted over to the Romita Brothers. The Romita Brothers have the rights and obligations descending from Shapolsky's contract. Similarly, Levine may now hold the Romita Brothers liable for all terms and conditions in the agreement made with Shapolsky.

The assignee's duty in an assignment is to give notice of the assignment to the obligor. The obligor is allowed a reasonable time to seek assurance that an assignment has been truly made. Making the assignment in writing reduces the possibility of one's fraudulent representation as an assignee.

Czapnik & Bryant, Inc.
6225 St. Clair Avenue
Cleveland, Ohio 44103

June 15, 19--

Mr. Carl Newfield
750 Maple Street, Apt. 4-C
Lakewood, Ohio 44117

Dear Mr. Newfield:

You are hereby notified that Pendleton Architects Limited of Euclid, Ohio, has assigned to Czapnik & Bryant, Inc., all rights to its claim against you in the amount of $750.

You are further notified to direct all payments to Czapnik & Bryant, Inc. at the above address to insure credit for payment.

Sincerely yours,

Norbert Bryant

Norbert Bryant
Vice President

Figure 12-2 This was the format used by Czapnik & Bryant, Inc. in the case on page 145 to notify Newfield of the assignment from Pendleton.

Quitter appeared at the payroll department of the Meadville Delivery Company and told the paymaster that one of Meadville's drivers, Stralka, had made an assignment of part of his paycheck to her. Under terms of the assignment, Quitter was to receive $150 of the money that Meadville owed to Stralka. Meadville, the obligor, need not pay Quitter the $150 until the paymaster has had a reasonable amount of time to verify the assignment.

Liabilities and Warranties of the Assignor

The assignor is obligated to any express and implied warranties that serve to protect either the assignee or the obligor. A **warranty** is a promise, statement, or other representation that a thing has certain qualities.

Warranties to the Assignee The assignor is bound by an implied warranty that the obligor will respect the assignment and make performance as required by the original agreement between the assignor and the obligor.

Suppose in the Quitter-Stralka assignment that the Meadville Trucking Company had been either unwilling or unable to pay Quitter the $150. Stralka would be bound by an implied warranty to Quitter that the $150 would be paid. If the assignment were a gift to Quitter, there would be no enforceable warranty in the absence of consideration between the assignor and the assignee.

Warranties to the Obligor If through an assignment the assignor delegates to an assignee duties owed the obligor, there is an implied warranty that the duties delegated will be carried out in a complete and satisfactory manner.

Heinecken assigned a contract for the remodeling of Donohue's kitchen to Edberg. Edberg's work was unsatisfactory. In fact, after careful investigation, Donohue discovered that the work done by Edberg was far below what was considered satisfactory in the home remodeling profession. Donohue sued Heinecken for the amount of money Donohue spent to have the kitchen done properly. The court awarded that money to Donohue stating that Heinecken had breached the implied warranty that duties delegated will be carried out in a complete and satisfactory manner.

Restrictions on Assignments

While most contracts may be assigned, those for personal and professional services may not be. The right of assignment may also be restricted by agreement of the parties in privity and in certain cases by law.

Restrictions on Personal and Professional Service Contracts A party may not delegate duties that are of a personal or professional nature. *Personal,* in this context, means "other than routine." A musician or artist, for example, could not delegate their services to someone else. They were chosen for their ability or artistic talent. Professional services are those rendered by physicians, lawyers, certified public accountants, ministers, and others. People in these occupations are selected because of their special abilities, and their services could not be delegated to someone else. In contrast, routine services may usually be delegated. They are those services performed by electricians, mechanics, woodworkers, plumbers, waitresses, bankers, publishers, and others whose skills and abilities are judged according to the usual custom and standards of the marketplace.

In the opening commentary, Kosaka contracted with the world-famous artist, Sjögren, to have a portrait painted of his wife and daughter. Sjögren, however, delegated the portrait work to Liebow, Kosaka refused to submit to the altered agreement. Kosaka had to abide by Sjögren's decision to delegate. In a suit to compel Kosaka's compliance, Kosaka would win because Kosaka had hired Sjögren because for his unique artistic abilities. In contrast, Liebow was a relative unknown. Since Sjögren's special abilities and skills are not of a routine nature but are unique, Kosaka's refusal would be upheld by the courts.

Restrictions Imposed by Original Contract Parties to a contract may include a condition that will not allow its assignment. Some courts have held that a restriction against assignment of a debt owed by the obligor robs the assignor of a property right guaranteed by law, and would be contrary to public policy. Other courts have permitted this restrictive condition. If, in the Heinecken kitchen remodeling case on page 147, Donohue had included a condition against assignment, the assignment to Edberg would have been void.

Restrictions Imposed by Law Assignment, in special situations, may be restricted by law or declared void because it is contrary to public policy. Thus, members of the armed services may not assign any part of their pay, except to a spouse or family member. Police officers, persons elected or appointed to public office, and others are likewise restricted from making assignment of their pay or of duties which they have been especially chosen to perform.

12-3 NOVATIONS

When two contracting parties agree to replace one of the original parties to the contract with a new party, this replacement creates what is known as a **novation.** A novation is actually a new contract, based upon a former one but containing one or more significant changes.

Novation Requirements

To be valid, a novation must involve three basic requirements. First, the original parties to the contract must agree to eliminate that contract. Secondly, one of the original parties to the contract is replaced by a new party. Finally, a new contract supported by valid consideration must arise. This new contract is the actual novation.

While forming the new corporation, Neruda International, Lanuza entered a contractual agreement with Asturias Properties. Under terms of the contract, Lanuza leased office space for Neruda. Since the corporation was not yet officially formed, the original contract was between Lanuza and Asturias. After the corporation was formed, the new president of Neruda International and representatives from Asturias sat down with Lanuza. The parties agreed to discharge the original agreement which named Lanuza as the one responsible to Asturias for the lease. They then agreed to substitute Neruda International as the responsible party. Neruda agreed to pay all rent to Asturias. The new contract is the novation.

Novation and Assignment Distinguished Novations differ from assignments in three ways. First, assignments can be made without the mutual consent of both contracting parties. Novations, on the other hand, require the assent of all the parties involved. Second, assignments may not release assignors of their obligations. In contrast, novations transfer all rights and obligations, giving the replaced party complete freedom from the original contract. Third, in an assignment the assignee "steps into the shoes" of the assignor. This is not necessarily true in a novation. This new agreement may or may not have terms different from the original contract.

SUMMARY

12-1. Third parties are at times given benefits through a contract made between two other parties. Some contracts are made specifically to benefit a third party. Such a third party is known as an intended beneficiary. Three types of intended beneficiaries include creditor beneficiaries, donee beneficiaries, and insurance beneficiaries. Some third parties benefit from a contract even though the contract was not made for their benefit. Such beneficiaries are known as incidental beneficiaries.

12-2. The transfer of a contract right to a third party outside the original agreement is an assignment. Generally, rights are assigned while duties are delegated. However, both are governed by rules applicable to assignment. The party who assigns rights or delegates duties is the assignor. The outside third party to whom the assignment is made is the assignee. The remaining party to the original agreement is the obligor. Consideration is not required in an assignment. The assignee must give notice of the assignment to the obligor. The rights and duties of the assignee are the same as those held by the assignor under the original agreement. Contracts for personal and professional services cannot be assigned. Assignments can also be limited by agreement.

12-3. A novation occurs when two contracting parties agree to replace one of the original parties to the contract. A novation requires that (1) the parties to the original contract eliminate the original contract, (2) one of the original parties to the contract is replaced by a new party, and (3) a new contract is entered into. A novation is not an assignment because it requires the mutual consent of both parties. It also differs from an assignment because a novation may release one of the parties from an obligation. Assignments do not release assignors from their obligations. Finally, a novation differs from an assignment because in an assignment the assignee "steps into the shoes" of the assignor.

Understanding Key Legal Terms

assignee (p. 143)
assignment (p. 142)
assignor (p. 143)
beneficiary (p. 141)
creditor beneficiary (p. 141)
delegation (p. 142)
donee beneficiary (p. 141)
incidental beneficiary (p. 142)
intended beneficiary (p. 141)
novation (p. 148)
obligor (p. 143)
outside party (p. 141)
third party (p. 141)
warranty (p. 146)

Questions for Review and Discussion

1. What are the legal rights of a creditor beneficiary? What are the legal rights of a donee beneficiary?
2. Is an insurance beneficiary a creditor beneficiary or a donee beneficiary? Explain your response.
3. How do the legal rights of an intended beneficiary differ from the legal rights of an incidental beneficiary?
4. What is the difference between an assignment and a delegation? Give an example of each.
5. Identify and explain the three parties associated with any assignment.
6. In what way is the equal dignities rule applicable to an assignment?
7. Which party is responsible for giving notice of an assignment? What are the legal consequences of failure to give notice? What are the legal consequences if the obligor, after receiving due notice, makes payment to the assignor?
8. After an assignment has been made, what are the obligations of (*a*) the assignor, (*b*) the assignee, and (*c*) the obligor?
9. List the kinds of contracts that may not be assigned.
10. In what way does a novation differ from an assignment?

Analyzing Cases

1. Powder Power Tool Corporation negotiated a collective bargaining agreement with the International Association of Machinists. The agreement went into effect on August 24. Employees, however, were to receive a wage increase retroactive to April 1. Several workers who had been employed on April 1 at the old wage scale were not working on August 24. These workers assigned their rights to the retroactive wage increase to Springer. When the corporation refused to pay Springer, he brought suit. The corporation argued that the former employees were not parties to the contract and as incidental beneficiaries could not bring suit to enforce the contract. Since they could not bring suit, Springer, as their assignee cannot bring suit either. Springer argued that the employees were intended beneficiaries and had the right to bring suit against the corporation to enforce the agreement. Therefore, as their assignee, Springer can bring suit. Is Springer correct? Explain. *Springer v. Powder Power Tool Corporation,* 348 P.2d 1112 (Oregon).

2. The Chicago Tribune Syndicate and Press Service, Inc., had a contract to furnish the old Washington Post Company with four comic strips. These strips included *The Gumps, Gasoline Alley, Winnie Winkle,* and *Dick Tracy.* The *Washington Post* went bankrupt, and the bankruptcy trustee assigned the right to receive these comic strips to the reorganized company owned by Meyer. The Tribune Syndicate claimed the contract could not be assigned. Accordingly, they canceled it and sold the rights to those strips to the *Washington Times.* Was the contract to furnish the comics assignable? Explain. *Meyers v. Washington Times Co.,* 76 F.2d 988 (D.C. Cir. Ct.).

3. Van Waters and Rogers, Inc., were assigned a debt that was owed by Interchange Resources to a construction company. Van Waters and Rogers, Inc., made a timely notice to Interchange indicating that payments of the construction debt were to be made to them. Interchange ignored the notice and paid the construction company in-

stead. Van Waters and Rogers brought suit to compel Interchange to pay them the amount due under the original construction agreement. Will Van Waters and Rogers succeed in their suit? Explain. *Van Waters and Rogers, Inc. v. Interchange Resources, Inc.* 484 P.2d 26 (Arizona).

4. Copeland contracted with McDonald's Systems, Inc., for a franchise fast-food outlet. Copeland was granted the fast-food outlet franchise for Omaha. McDonald's also gave Copeland first refusal rights for any plans to open other franchise outlets in Omaha. Copeland exercised the right several times, opening several additional outlets. He then sold the franchise to Schupack and assigned to Schupack the right to open new McDonald's outlets in Omaha. When Schupack tried to exercise the first refusal right, McDonald's argued that the assignment was invalid. McDonald's claimed its relationship with Copeland developed through a special confidence in Copeland's ability in managing and promoting its new franchise outlets. Schupack argued that such services should be considered routine by the court. Is Schupack correct? Explain. *Schupack v. McDonald's Systems, Inc.*, 264 N.W.2d 827 (Nebraska).

5. Timbercrest built a house for the Murphys. After occupying the house for a while, the Murphys complained of several problems. Timbercrest fixed the problems, and the Murphys had no further complaints. The Litwins bought the house from the Murphys 3 years later. When the house was sold, neither the Litwins nor the Murphys were aware of any problems. After living in the house for 2 years, the Litwins became aware of several problems. The Litwins then contacted the Murphys and had the Murphys assign them their rights under the original construction agreement with Timbercrest. The Litwins then sued Timbercrest, claiming Timbercrest had breached its contract with the Murphys by not providing them with a house free of defects. Timbercrest claimed that the Murphys had had no claim against them at the time of the sale to the Litwins or at the time of the assignment. Since the Murphys had no claim, the Litwins have no claim since all they did was "step into the shoes" of the assignors. Is Timbercrest correct? *Litwin v. Timbercrest Estates, Inc.*, 347 N.E.2d 378 (Illinois).

6. Nolan wrote the song "Tumbling Tumbleweeds" and in an agreement with Sam Fox Publishing Company transferred all rights to the song to the company. In return, Nolan was to receive royalties according to terms laid out in the agreement. Sam Fox later assigned all rights and interests in "Tumbling Tumbleweeds" to Williamson Music, Inc. Nolan objected to the assignment and rescinded his original transfer to Sam Fox Publishing. Nolan claimed the assignment to Williamson was invalid because the agreement between Fox and Nolan involved Nolan's personal trust and confidence in Fox. Because Fox's duties were of a personal nature, Nolan says Fox could not assign the contract without getting his consent first. Was it necessary for Sam Fox to obtain Nolan's consent before making the assignment to Williamson? Explain. *Nolan v. Williamson Music, Inc.*, 300 F. Supp. 1311 (S.D.N.Y.).

CHAPTER 13
Discharge and Remedies

OUTLINE

13-1 Discharge by Performance
- Complete and Substantial Performance
- Satisfactory Performance
- Time of Performance
- Contractual Conditions and Terms
- Conditions Concurrent

13-2 Discharge by Nonperformance
- Discharge by Agreement
- Discharge by Operation of Law
- Discharge by Breach of Contract

13-3 Remedies
- Damages
- Mitigation of Damages
- Equitable Remedies

COMMENTARY

Krantz was hired by Yood as a computer information specialist for Scheele Enterprises. The job was supposed to begin on October 15. Krantz had to move from Illinois to Oklahoma. On September 9, Yood told Krantz she would not be needed at Scheele. In reliance on the contract with Scheele, Krantz made several changes in her life. She had moved from Illinois to Oklahoma. She had sold her home in Illinois and obligated herself to a one-year lease in Oklahoma. She had also entered into contracts with the telephone company, the gas company, the electric company, and the city's sanitation and sewer departments. Does Krantz have any legal recourse against Scheele? If so, can she bring suit immediately or must she wait until October 15 to see whether Yood and Scheele will reconsider and hire her as promised? If she elects to sue, what remedies, if any, are available to her? These questions and many others like them are addressed in this final chapter on contract law.

OBJECTIVES

1. Explain performance, and differentiate complete performance from substantial performance and satisfactory performance.
2. Indicate when and how the discharge of a contract occurs if satisfactory performance is to be determined by the personal taste of one of the contracting parties or by factors other than personal taste.
3. Explain when a court will permit nonperformance of a contract containing the phrase *time is of the essence.*
4. Indicate when performance occurs if there are conditions precedent, conditions concurrent, or conditions subsequent in a contract.
5. Relate how contractual obligations may be discharged (*a*) in accordance with the terms of the contract itself, (*b*) by mutual rescission, waiver, or novation, (*c*) by an accord and satisfaction, or (*d*) by general release.
6. Outline and explain the four circumstances that result in a discharge of a contract by operation of law.

7. Enumerate the conditions that excuse performance on grounds of impossibility.
8. Judge in particular situations whether a breach of contract resulted from (*a*) deliberate wrongful performance or nonperformance, (*b*) an anticipatory breach, or (*c*) the abandonment of contractual obligations.
9. Identify the types of damages that can be awarded to a party in a breach of contract suit, and explain the mitigation of damages.
10. Outline the conditions that must be present for a court to grant a request for equitable relief, and list the equitable remedies available.

13-1 DISCHARGE BY PERFORMANCE

Most contracts are discharged through performance. **Discharge** is an act by which a person is freed from performing a legal obligation. **Performance** means that the parties to the contract have done that which they agreed to do. Performance, then, is directly related to the conditions and terms of the contract and to the fact that these conditions and terms have or have not been satisfactorily carried out by each party. The possibility of nonperformance should be anticipated when drawing up contract terms and conditions. Terms should be sufficiently clear so that no misunderstanding or dispute might develop before, during, or subsequent to performance. Too often a failure by the parties to define their respective obligations adequately means that the courts must step in to sort the matter out for them, sometimes with unforeseen outcomes for the parties.

Complete and Substantial Performance

Complete performance occurs when both parties fully accomplish every term, condition, and promise to which they agreed. **Substantial performance** results when a party, in good faith, executes all promised terms and conditions with the exception of minor details that do not affect the real intent of their agreement. Complete performance terminates an agreement, discharging the parties of any further obligation to one another. Ordinarily, substantial performance also serves to discharge the agreement, but with a difference. A party who complains that performance has been substantial, but not complete, has the right to demand reimbursement from the offending party to correct those details that prevented complete performance.

Mueller went on a cruise arranged through an agent of Mediterranean Tours, Inc. The agent explained that the cruise would last seven days and six nights and would make stops at four different ports of call. Due to unforeseen problems on shore at one port of call, that stop was canceled. The rest of the scheduled stops were made and the cruise did last the full seven days. Mueller demanded a return of his entire $2,000 paid to Mediterranean Tours, claiming that there had been less than complete performance of the contract. A court would hold that there had been substantial performance, allowing a refund to Mueller only in the amount Mediterranean had saved by canceling one stop.

Satisfactory Performance

Satisfactory performance exists when either personal taste or objective standards have determined that the contracting parties have performed their contractual duties according to the agreement. Satisfactory performance is either an express or implied condition of every contract. Sales agreements for consumer goods often express this condition by including the words "money back if not entirely satisfied." In other contracts satisfaction may be carefully defined according to the expectations of the parties. When there is no express agreement, the law implies that work will be done in a skillful manner and that the materials or goods will be free of defects. Ordinarily the parties may be discharged from a contract only if there has been satisfactory performance. What is satisfactory performance, however, is something that is not always easy to ascertain. Therefore, the courts are often called upon to determine whether there has been a breach of the guarantee of satisfactory performance.

Sometimes one person will agree to do something to another person's satisfaction. Services rendered in a beauty salon or barbershop, photographs taken at a studio, and portraits painted by an artist are in this classification. Regardless of the skill and application of the person doing the work, customers may, on the basis of their personal judgment and satisfaction, refuse payment.

Haugen commissioned Farelli to paint his portrait. Under the terms of the agreement, Farelli told Haugen that unless he were satisfied with the portrait, he would not have to pay for her services. Haugen's personal taste and judgment alone would be the determining factor as to satisfaction in this situation. If Haugen should not like the portrait, he would not have to pay Farelli for her services. Farelli would not be discharged from the obligations or freed from her liability until she performed satisfactorily according to Haugen's personal taste and preferences.

Satisfactory performance of contracts not involving personal taste will be determined by objective standards. Contracts for the sale of mechanical devices and services offered by tradespeople are of this type. Both parties may introduce expert witnesses in determining whether satisfaction has been achieved. A jury is often required to make the final decision after sifting the opinions offered on both sides of a case. The jury's decision would also determine whether a discharge is permissible.

Hammerlund Construction, Inc., contracted with the city of Baytown to build a new ice hockey arena for the Baytown Bombers. Due to a serious defect in the construction plans, the icing machine failed to work properly. As a result, the entire skating rink was never totally frozen at one time. This defect made it impossible for the Bombers to use the rink. Consequently, they had to remain in their old arena. When Baytown refused to pay Hammerlund, the construction firm sued. The city won the case because the question of whether an ice hockey arena can or cannot be used for ice hockey is not a matter of personal taste.

Time of Performance

The time within which a contract is to be completed may or may not be essential to the obligation of performance. Whether performance is so dependent upon a time limit that time becomes a materially important condition of the contract must be determined from the facts surrounding the agreement.

Often agreements stipulate a time limit for delivery of goods and services when the passing of such a time limit, in fact, has little or no real consequence. In such cases, where time is of secondary importance, the courts may disregard the time stipulations and allow additional time to perform.

Leinster Development Inc. contracted with Langehorne Printing for the design and printing of a new letterhead for the development firm. The letterheads were to be delivered 60 days after the agreement was entered. Langehorne was four days late in its delivery of the letterheads. Leinster sued to rescind the entire agreement, claiming that time was of the essence. The court ruled that time was not of the essence and had not been clearly established as essential to satisfactory performance. Leinster was held to the contract.

The phrase *time is of the essence* may be included among the terms of a contract. This phrase implies that the time element is of the utmost importance to the parties. When time is of the essence in a contract, the court will enforce the time period stated in the contract.

Leflar contracted with Connover Motors for a van to be used by Leflar in his annual hunting trip to New Mexico. The trip was to start on August 25. Connover agreed to deliver the van to Leflar on August 20 so that he could prepare and pack the van in time for the August 25 starting date. The van was not delivered on August 20. When Leflar contacted Connover, the manager told him that they could not get the van to him until August 26. Leflar told Connover the deal was off. He then purchased a similar van from Amesberry Motors. Under these circumstances, since time was of the essence, Leflar's rescission would be upheld.

Contractual Conditions and Terms

Some contracts have conditions or terms which will determine the rights and duties of the parties prior to performance, during performance, and following performance. Conditions may be classified as (1) conditions precedent, (2) conditions concurrent, or (3) conditions subsequent (see Table 13-1).

Conditions Precedent A **condition precedent** is a condition that requires performance of certain acts or promises before the other party is obligated to pay money or give other consideration agreed to. In a unilateral contract, the performance of a condition precedent serves as the offeree's acceptance of the offer. In a bilateral contract, it is a promise which if not performed leads either to rescission or to termination of the entire agreement.

Ponzini, a third-year law student, signed an agreement to accept a position with the law firm of Flovin, Carter, and Curtis. The members of the firm agreed to hire Ponzini on condition that she receive her law degree and pass the bar examination in their state. Earning the law degree and passing the bar examination are conditions precedent to the performance of the obligation of Flovin, Carter, and Curtis in giving Ponzini the position in their firm.

Conditions Concurrent

A condition which requires both parties to perform at the same time is a **condition concurrent.** A promise to deliver goods supported by the buyer's promise to pay on delivery is a very common condition concurrent. Real estate sales agreements, by custom, usually state that the owner-seller will deliver a good and complete deed to the real property on the buyer's presentation of either cash or a certified check for the amount of the purchase price. Failure of either to do as promised concurrently would be a breach of the express contract condition.

McClanahan agreed to purchase a condominium in the Knollwood Riverview Estates project. Wycke, the present owner, agreed to deliver the deed for the condominium to McClanahan on October 31. McClanahan agreed to give Wycke a certified check for $67,000 in exchange for the deed on the same date. The simultaneous presentations of the certified check and the deed for the condominium are conditions concurrent in this transaction.

Conditions Subsequent A **condition subsequent** is one in which the parties agree that the contract will be terminated on a prescribed event occurring or not occurring. A contract between a builder and a client stating that contract performance would terminate if a required building permit were not obtained from the issuing public authority within 60 days after the signing of the agreement is a condition subsequent. Some warranties included in contracts are also illustrative of such conditions.

Marceau agreed to remodel a loft apartment for Gastineau for $12,000. Both parties signed the written agreement. One clause in the contract stated that Marceau would guarantee that the improvements were free from defects for 12 months after having completed the work. Gastineau agreed to pay for the improvements upon completion. Marceau's guarantee constituted a condition subsequent, a con-

Table 13-1 CONTRACTUAL CONDITIONS

Condition	*Explanation*
Condition precedent	A condition that requires the performance of certain acts or promises before the other party is obligated to pay money or give other consideration
Condition concurrent	A condition that requires both parties to perform at the same time
Condition subsequent	A condition in which the parties agree that the contract will be terminated if a prescribed event occurs or does not occur

dition that applies after both parties have performed their primary obligations to the contract.

Another common condition of this kind is the one contained in a fire insurance policy. The insured typically agrees in the policy that the report of a fire loss must be made within 30 days of the loss or the insurer will be free of obligation to reimburse for loss.

13-2 DISCHARGE BY NONPERFORMANCE

Nonperformance may be defined as failing to fulfill or accomplish a contract according to its terms. Sometimes the failure to perform opens a party to legal action. However, not every instance of nonperformance results in a legal action. Sometimes nonperformance results from mutual agreement between the parties. At other times nonperformance is excused by operation of law. Nevertheless, under certain circumstances nonperformance will result in a breach of contract. All three situations, discharge by agreement, discharge by operation of law, and discharge by breach of contract, are explained here.

Discharge by Agreement

Parties to a contract may stipulate the time and conditions for termination and discharge as part of their agreement. Instead, they may subsequently agree not to do what they had originally promised to do. The latter is the case when there is a mutual rescission of the contract, a waiver of performance by one or more of the parties, a novation, or an accord and satisfaction to liquidate an outstanding debt or obligation.

Termination by Terms of the Contract Parties, during contract negotiation, may agree to certain terms that provide for automatic termination upon the occurrence or nonoccurrence of stated events. These terms are labeled as conditions subsequent. For example, a professional athlete may contract with management that their agreement will be terminated if for any reason the player becomes either physically or mentally incapable of rendering full performance. Such an agreement may also spell out management's obligations should there be a termination of the agreement before full performance has been made. In other situations the clause providing for automatic termination may be related to a promisor's success in acquiring the raw materials or other supplies upon which performance will depend.

The Chapman Nuclear Power Supply Company agreed to furnish plutonium to the Lambarene Consolidated Electric Power Corporation for use in its new nuclear power plant. Chapman and Lambarene agreed that if Chapman could not obtain the plutonium through its suppliers, the contract would be terminated. In this case, the two corporations had mutually agreed to a condition subsequent that would free both parties of continuing obligations should the predetermined eventuality, the failure to obtain plutonium, occur.

Mutual Rescission Contracting parties may, either before or after performance commences, rescind their contract as a result of further negotiation and by their mutual assent. **Mutual rescission,** in the majority of cases, requires both parties to return to the other any consideration already received or to pay for any services or materials already entered. Mutual rescission may be created through an oral or written agreement. Following the requirement of the equal dignities rule, if the original agreement required a contract in writing, the rescission agreement must also be written.

Bohn worked as assistant director of the Svedberg-Moran Art Gallery. He had a five-year written contract that outlined his duties and responsibilities as well as his salary and other benefits. Bohn became disenchanted with the administration and decided to seek a job in education. When he was offered a job at the Puzzuoli Institute of Creative and Performing Arts, he went to the owners of the Svedberg-Moran Art Gallery and asked to be released from his contract. After some discussion, the owners agreed to the release. This mutual release would have to be in writing under the equal dignities rule.

Termination by Waiver **Termination by waiver** occurs when a party with the right to complain of the other party's unsatisfactory performance or nonperformance fails to complain. It is a voluntary relinquishing (waiver) of one's rights to demand performance. A waiver differs from a discharge by mutual rescission in that a waiver entails no obligation by the parties to return any consideration that may have been exchanged up to the moment of rescission. Discharge by waiver, when made, is complete in itself.

Eckart was hired as a foreign correspondent for the Tri-Cities Consolidated News Service. Six weeks after starting her job as correspondent, Eckart failed to show up for work. Tri-Cities made no attempt to find Eckart to fulfill the terms of her employment. Further, Tri-Cities did not file suit against Eckart. Instead, Tri-Cities simply dropped the issue entirely. This action would terminate the contract by waiver. Tri-Cities has voluntarily relinquished its rights, thereby discharging both parties from future obligations.

Novation By a novation the parties to a contract mutually agree to the termination of an existing contract, replacing it with a new one. Through a novation all parties are discharged from further obligation to the former agreement. Novation is discussed in detail in Chapter 12.

Accord and Satisfaction An accord and satisfaction is a resulting new agreement arising from a bona fide dispute between the parties as to the terms of their original agreement. The mutual agreement to the new terms is the accord; performance of the accord is the satisfaction—thus, accord and satisfaction. The accord, although agreed to, is not a binding agreement until the satisfaction has been made. The original agreement is not discharged, therefore, until the performance or satisfaction has been provided as promised. Accord and satisfaction is discussed in Chapter 8 on consideration.

General Release A **general release** is a document expressing the intent of a creditor to release a debtor from obligations on an existing and valid debt. A general release terminates a debt and excuses the debtor of any future payment without the usual requirement that consideration be given in return.

Discharge by Operation of Law

Performance of a promised act may be discharged automatically by operation of law. Generally this occurs because conditions make performance impossible. However, bankruptcy and the statute of limitations can also discharge a contract by operation of law.

Conditions Making Performance Impossible Fulfilling contractual obligations may become impossible because of some condition existing at the time the contract was made. Such impossibility will render the contract void.

While working in Portland, Oregon, Merriweather agreed to buy a warehouse in Florida belonging to Steinmetz for $67,000. The contract was drawn up and signed and Merriweather gave Steinmetz a certified check. Neither party knew at the time that a hurricane had destroyed the warehouse the night before at its Florida location. At the time they'd made their contract, performance was already impossible. Both parties are discharged of any promise of performance and Steinmetz must return the $67,000 check.

Conditions that arise subsequent to the making of a contract may either void the agreement or make it voidable by one of the parties. Discharge through impossibility of performance may, in some situations, be allowed only if the specific and anticipated impossibility has been made a condition to the agreement.

An **act of God,** in contract law, is any natural disaster that is not reasonably foreseeable. This includes floods, cyclones, hurricanes, lightning, earthquakes, and volcanic eruptions. Courts will not excuse a party from performance based on an act of God unless there was an act of God clause in the contract excusing performance in the event the unforeseeable natural disaster or unless the act of God was, in fact, not reasonably foreseeable. The courts will also not excuse a party whose own negligence contributed to its loss. Statutes in most states now provide interpretation of termination through acts of God. Courts in those states have repeatedly held that, when substantial performance of a contract is possible, the impossibility of precise performance due to an act of God does not excuse either party to the contract.

When the subject matter of an executory contract has been selected by the parties and later is destroyed, the performance obligation is discharged. When the contract is not specific in the description or the location of the subject matter, a promisor is not discharged if the subject matter intended for delivery is destroyed. In this case the promisor is obligated to locate and deliver subject matter of the same kind and quantity that could be secured elsewhere. Any financial losses due to the misfortune must be borne by the promisor. If, however, the subject matter of the contract is specific as to location and description, the obligor may be excused from performance when that subject matter is destroyed.

When the performance of a contract promise requires execution of acts declared illegal because of existing common law, statute, or public policy, the contract is unenforceable from its inception. When the performance of a contract is made illegal through the passing of laws subsequent to the formation of the contract, the contract is likewise declared unenforceable.

Death, insanity, or disability of a party obligated to the performance of a promise that requires a special talent or skill terminates and discharges an agreement. Musicians, artists, writers, and certain professionals are included here. When promised services are to be performed for the personal benefit of a promisee, the death of the promisee will also terminate the agreement. When contract promises relate to services that may be performed by others and do not demand the personal services of the contracting party, performance is not excused through death, insanity, or disability. The guardian of the party involved or the estate of the deceased may be held liable for performance.

Effect of Frustration-of-Purpose Doctrine The **frustration-of-purpose doctrine** releases a party from a contractual obligation when performing the obligations would be thoroughly impractical and senseless. The doctrine is applied only in those cases where a party recognizes and understands possible risks and accepts them in contemplation of performance.

Pappagallo contracted to act as a sports reporter for the *Biloxi News Herald,* a newly formed newspaper with dubious financial backing. The *Biloxi News Herald* had been formed to compete with two other well-established newspapers in town. At the time he signed his contract, Pappagallo was aware, as was everyone else in town, of the paper's instability and uncertain future. Before the first issue was printed, the paper folded. Pappagallo's claim under the contract was dismissed and the contract discharged. Applying the frustration-of-purpose doctrine, the court held that demanding performance would be impractical, unfair, and unjust to the *Biloxi News Herald.*

Bankruptcy of a Contracting Party Through the provisions of the Bankruptcy Reform Act (see Chapter 30), a discharge in bankruptcy from a court will be allowed as a defense against the collection of most, but not all, debts of the bankrupt.

Release Through Statute of Limitations State statutes providing time limits within which suits may be brought are known as statutes of limitations. Each state sets its own time limits. Generally, actions for collection of open accounts (charge accounts) must be brought within three to five years, written agreements usually within ten years, and judgments from ten to twenty years. Those states requiring the seal on certain contracts have still other limitations and requirements that are much broader than those applied to simple contracts. The statute of limitations does not technically void the debt, but it gives the debtor a defense against any demand for collection.

Discharge by Breach of Contract

When contractual obligations terminate by agreement or by operation of law, no liability falls to either party. When one of the parties fails to carry out the terms of a contract, a breach of contract occurs and liability falls to the party who has not done what was promised. Breach of contract comes from negligent or intentionally wrongful performance, expressed repudiation of contractual obligations, or an abandonment of performance sometime after performance has begun. When there is a breach of contract, the injured party has the right to a remedy in court.

Deliberate Breach of Contract A breach of contract results when one of the parties fails to do what was agreed to under the terms of the contract within a reasonable time. When time is of the essence, there is a breach if performance is not completed within the time limits agreed to by the parties. A breach also results if the performance has been negligent or unskillful. The services rendered must adhere to the standards of skill as determined by the custom of the marketplace. Wrongful performance or nonperformance discharges the other party from further obligation and permits that party to bring suit to rescind the contract or to recover money to compensate that party for any loss sustained. Such compensation is known as *damages.*

Balanchine, a world famous modern artist, agreed to have her artwork displayed in a special one-woman show at the Darayni-Correcano Gallery. The gallery had posters, brochures, and invitations printed up. It advertised in the newspapers, art magazines, and on the radio. On the day the show was supposed to open, Balanchine informed the gallery that she was not going to allow her work to be put on display. Through Balanchine's nonperformance, the contract between her and the gallery has been discharged. Darayni-Correcano can now seek damages from Balanchine on grounds of breach of a valid contract.

Repudiation and Anticipatory Breach An **anticipatory breach** occurs when a party to a contract either expresses or clearly implies an intention not to perform the contract even before being required to act. The repudiation must be clear and absolute. It must also indicate a deliberate and complete refusal to perform according to the terms of the contract. Breaches of this kind are also called **constructive breaches.** Injured parties may seek damages by showing that in reliance on the contract they have changed their position in a very critical manner. The injured party may either commence suit at the time of the anticipatory breach or await the date agreed to for performance, thus giving the breaching party time to reconsider and begin performance.

In the opening commentary, Krantz was hired by Scheele as a computer information specialist. The job was to begin on October 15. Before that time, she moved from Illinois to Oklahoma. She sold her home in Illinois and entered a lease in Oklahoma. She also entered into several other contractual arrangements. Then on September 9, Scheele told her they would not require her services after all. Krantz may either bring suit and seek damages immediately or wait until October 15 to see if Yood and Scheele will reconsider and hire her as promised.

Abandonment of Contract Obligations Stopping performance once it has begun is called **abandonment of contract obligations.** Leaving or deserting a party's obligations discharges the other party from any promises made and permits a suit for damages. A temporary, or short-lived, interruption of performance is not deemed to be abandonment. To constitute abandonment, the promisor must have inexcusably interrupted performance with the obvious intention of not returning to complete the obligations promised.

Perkowetz hired Sydorak to dig a new well on his property. Sydorak began the project on July 20 as agreed in the written agreement. After digging a hole approximately 10-feet deep, Sydorak was called away to another job. He told Perkowetz that he would return in three days. Two weeks went by before Perkowetz heard anything from Sydorak despite many attempts to contact him. When Sydorak finally called Perkowetz, he told him he had no idea when he'd get back to digging the well. At this point it was clear to Perkowetz that Sydorak had no intention of completing the well. Perkowetz is thereby discharged of any obligation to Sydorak. He has the right to seek any damages resulting from Sydorak's breach.

13-3 REMEDIES

A breach of contract releases the injured party from any obligations under the contract and gives that party the right to ask a court of law for a remedy. The usual remedy for breach of contract is the payment of damages in the form of money. At times, however, the payment of money damages is not enough to satisfy the injured party. In such situations, the injured party will ask the court for rescission, specific performance, or an injunction. An injunction is a court order preventing someone from performing a particular act.

Damages

Damages is a term that describes money awarded to parties who have been victimized or have suffered injury to their legal rights by others. Damages are of different kinds, and the nature of a claim usually determines what type of damages will apply. In some states, by statute or judicial rule, juries are charged with two decisions: (1) They must decide which party is to be given favorable judgment and (2) how much damages are to be awarded. Appeals to a higher court are allowed when the amount of damages awarded appears to be unreasonably low or excessively high.

Actual or Compensatory Damages **Actual damages** are a sum of money equal to the real financial loss suffered by the injured party. Since they are intended to compensate the injured party, actual damages are also called **compensatory damages.** Thus, damages awarded for nondelivery of promised goods or services would be an amount equal to the difference between the price stated in the contract and what the promisee would have to pay elsewhere. Should the same goods or services be conveniently available elsewhere at the same or at a lower price, no actual loss could be claimed.

Sujecki agreed to give Tallocini's 1957 Chevy Impala a customized paint job for $550. When the time came to start the job, Sujecki refused to go through with the contract, arguing that inflationary costs of materials made it impossible for him to paint the Chevy for the agreed price without suffering great financial loss. Tallocini took his car to Wersfeld who did the job for $700. Should Tallocini sue Sujecki for breach of contract, actual damages would be $150, the difference between the $550 agreed to by Sujecki and the $700 that Tallocini was charged by another equally competent and reputable painter.

Incidental and Consequential Damages Incidental damages and consequential damages are awarded for losses indirectly but closely attributable to a breach. **Incidental damages** cover any expenses paid out by the innocent party to prevent further loss. **Consequential damages** result indirectly from the breach because of special circumstances that exist with a particular contract. To recover consequential damages, the injured party must show that such losses were foreseeable when the contract was first made.

Tamura contracted to buy a pickup truck from Collymore Motors, Inc. Collymore knew that Tamura intended to use the pickup truck to take his crops to market. Collymore also knew that Tamura's livelihood depended on delivering those crops to market on time. Nevertheless, the day the truck was to be picked up by Tamura, Collymore told him that the truck would not be available as agreed. As a result, Tamura had to rent a truck to take his crops to market. In addition, because the crops arrived at the market late, their quality had dropped and Tamura could no longer get top dollar. As a result, he lost certain profits he could have made had the truck been delivered on time. In a suit against Collymore, Tamura could ask the court to compel the car dealer to reimburse him for all rental charges on the replacement truck. Such out-of-pocket expenses are labeled incidental damages. He could also ask to be reimbursed for the lost profits. Such foreseeable losses are called consequential damages.

Punitive or Exemplary Damages **Punitive damages,** also called **exemplary damages,** are damages awarded in excess of actual, incidental, or inconsequential damages where it is shown that the wrongful party acted with malicious intent and willful disregard for the rights of the injured party. They are in the nature of court-ordered punishment rather than compensation for a known loss. They are usually awarded in cases involving torts rather than contracts. However, they have been awarded when a defendant in a contract action is found to be guilty of abusive and dishonest practices in consumer transactions that are unconscionable and contrary to the public good.

Nominal Damages **Nominal damages** are only token damages awarded to parties who have experienced an injury to their legal rights but no actual loss.

The common law usually awarded six cents to the successful plaintiff when no actual losses were shown. In today's practice the award is usually $1.

> The United States Football League (USFL) sued the National Football League (NFL) alleging that the NFL had engaged in unfair competitive practices which violated federal statutory law. The USFL also claimed that the NFL had intentionally interfered with certain contractual relationships that the USFL had and even with some potential contracts. The jury decided that the NFL had been involved in some unfair competitive practices but that this had not hurt the USFL. As a result, the USFL was awarded $1 in nominal damages. This figure was raised to $3 since the statute that was violated allowed for three times the damages awarded.

Present and Future Damages Damages may be awarded for present injuries and for others that might reasonably be anticipated in the future. Thus, a party charged with fraud in the sale of a building infested with termites may be held liable for all damages revealed at the time of the suit and for damages that would reasonably be forthcoming as the result of the undisclosed and concealed infestation of the property.

Speculative Damages Courts do not allow **speculative damages.** These are damages computed on losses which have not actually been suffered and which cannot be proved; they are damages based entirely on an expectation of losses that might be suffered from a breach. They differ from future damages in that speculative damages are not founded on fact but only on hope or expectation. Their basis is nothing more than a calculated guess as to the gains one might have received had there not been a breach.

Damages Under *Quantum Meruit* The doctrine of ***quantum meruit*** ("as much as one had earned") is important in the assessing of damages in cases founded on contracts implied-in-law, or quasi contracts. Thus, where there has been no express or implied mutual agreement, a court will at times impose an obligation against a party who has been unjustly rewarded at the innocent expense of another. Damages awarded will be in an amount considered reasonable in return for the benefits that the one party derived through the quasi-contract relationship.

Liquidated Damages Parties may stipulate (agree) as a condition of their contract the amount of damages that might be assessed if there is a breach. Damages agreed to in the initial contract are called **liquidated damages.** Liquidated damages must be realistic and in proportion to the losses that might be reasonably anticipated should there be a breach. When liquidated damages are found to be excessive or unfair; a court will disregard them and leave the matter of setting damages to the discretion of a jury.

Mitigation of Damages

The injured party has an obligation to do what is reasonably possible to **mitigate the damages,** that is, to keep damages to a minimum. A party who has been wronged by another's breach must exercise reasonable precautions to prevent the damages from becoming unfairly and unreasonably burdensome to the other party.

Hakanoglu was hired by the Fort LaForge International Airport to repave all the airport's runways. Two weeks after the job was completed, one of the runways began to buckle and crack. A week later a second runway buckled and cracked. With two runways shut down, Fort LaForge was having serious air traffic control problems. Hakanoglu offered to provide the needed repair work to correct the original errors. Fort LaForge refused to allow Hakanoglu to do the work. In a lawsuit by Fort LaForge against Hakanoglu for damages caused by the faulty work, the court ruled that Fort LaForge had failed to mitigate the mounting damages by refusing Hakanoglu's offer to correct the defects.

Had Hakanoglu been allowed to provide the engineering services offered, the damages sought by Fort LaForge would have been considerably less than the airport claimed as actual damage.

Equitable Remedies

When money in the form of damages will not be enough to provide a fair and just award to the injured party, the court may grant one of the equitable remedies. Rather than simply order the breaching party to pay damages, a court issuing an **equitable remedy** compels the breaching party to perform an act or to refrain from performing an act. Equitable remedies are based upon principles of fairness and justice rather than the dictates of common law. The two most common equitable remedies are specific performance and injunctive relief.

Specific Performance A decree of **specific performance** is a court order calling for the breaching party to do what he or she promised to do under the original contract. Historically, the courts would order specific performance only when the subject matter of the contract was unique. The classic example of unique subject matter calling for specific performance is a contract for the sale and transfer of title to land since each piece of land is unique. However, unique subject matter could also include unique goods such as antiques, family heirlooms, original works of art, and certain special animals, such as a particular race horse. Obviously an award of money damages would not provide the injured party satisfaction in any of these situations.

Contracts for personal services are rarely enforced through specific performance. Demanding that an unwilling party perform promised personal services would be contrary to Amendment 13 of the U.S. Constitution, which prohibits human servitude. A remedy in cases of this kind, however, may be found through injunctive relief.

Injunctive Relief An **injunction** is an order issued by a court directing that a party do or refrain from doing something. An injunction may be either temporary or permanent. A temporary injunction is issued as a means of delaying further activity in any contested matter until the court determines whether a permanent injunction should be entered or the injunction removed entirely. One who disobeys an injunction does so under penalty of contempt of court.

SUMMARY

13-1. A contract can be discharged by performance. Performance is the fulfillment of a promise, contract, or other obligation according to its terms. Types of performance include complete performance, substantial performance, and satisfactory performance. To determine whether the time of performance is "of the essence," the court will look at the circumstances surrounding the making of the contract and the intent of the parties to the contract. Conditions determine the rights and duties of the parties prior to performance, during performance, and following performance. Conditions can be classified as conditions precedent, conditions concurrent, or conditions subsequent.

13-2. Nonperformance can also discharge contractual obligations. Nonperformance is the failure to fulfill or accomplish a promise, contract, or obligation according to its terms. Not every instance of nonperformance results in a breach of contract. Parties can agree to discharge a contractual obligation by terms in the contract, by mutual rescission, by waiver, by novation, by accord and satisfaction, and by general release. Contractual obligations can also be discharged by operation of law under principles of impossibility, bankruptcy, and the statute of limitations. When contractual obligations terminate by agreement or by operation of law, no liability falls to either party. However, when breach of contract comes from a deliberate breach, a repudiation of contractual obligation, or an abandonment of performance, liability will result.

13-3. A breach of contract relieves the injured party from any obligation under the contract. Breach of contract also gives the injured party the right to ask a court of law for a remedy. The usual remedy in contract law is the payment of money in the form of damages. The different types of damages include actual or compensatory damages, incidental and consequential damages, punitive or exemplary damages, nominal damages, present and future damages, speculative damages, damages under *quantum meruit,* and liquidated damages. Injured parties are also required to mitigate their damages. When money will not be sufficient relief, the injured party may ask for specific performance or for injunctive relief.

Understanding Key Legal Terms

abandonment of contractual obligations (p. 162)
actual damages (p. 162)
anticipatory breach (p. 161)
compensatory damages (p. 162)
complete performance (p. 153)
condition concurrent (p. 156)
condition precedent (p. 156)
condition subsequent (p. 156)
consequential damages (p. 161)
discharge (p. 153)
frustration-of-purpose doctrine (p. 160)
general release (p. 159)
incidental damages (p. 163)
injunction (p. 165)
liquidated damages (p. 164)
mutual rescission (p. 158)
nominal damages (p. 163)
performance (p. 153)
punitive damages (p. 163)
satisfactory performance (p. 154)
specific performance (p. 165)
substantial performance (p. 153)
speculative damages (p. 164)
termination by waiver (p. 158)

Questions for Review and Discussion

1. Distinguish among complete performance, substantial performance, and satisfactory performance of one's contractual obligations.
2. Contrast the discharge of contractual obligations by satisfactory performance as determined by personal taste, and by satisfaction unrelated to personal taste.
3. In a written contract what is the legal significance of the phrase *time is of the essence?*
4. Give examples of conditions (*a*) precedent, (*b*) concurrent, and (*c*) subsequent in the performance of a contract.
5. Explain how contractual obligations can be discharged (*a*) in accordance with terms of the contract itself, (*b*) by mutual rescission, waiver, or novation, (*c*) by an accord and satisfaction, or (*d*) by general release.
6. List the four situations that would discharge contractual obligations by operation of law.
7. What are the four types of impossibility of performance recognized by the law?
8. Explain what is meant by deliberate breach of contract. When may a victim of an anticipatory breach commence legal action against the other party? Under what circumstances may a party declare a breach of contract under the doctrine of abandonment?
9. What types of damages are available to an injured party in a breach of contract suit? Explain mitigation of damages.
10. Under what condition does a party seek equitable relief and what equitable remedies are available?

Analyzing Cases

1. The Congress-Kenilworth Corporation hired Erickson Construction to build its new concrete water slide, Thunder Mountain Rapids. The project was completed and was opened to the public. When Congress-Kenilworth discovered extensive cracking of the concrete flumes within the water slide, the corporation refused to pay the amount due under the contract. The operation of the structure as a water slide was not affected by the cracking. Erickson sued to recover the amount due under the contract. Erickson claimed that under the doctrine of substantial performance, Congress-Kenilworth should pay for the amount due under the contract, less an amount needed to offset the defects. Is Erickson correct? Explain. *W. E. Erickson Construction Inc. v. Congress-Kenilworth Corporation,* 477 N.E.2d513 (Illinois).
2. Baldwin agreed to sell some land to Kenison. Under the terms of the agreement, Baldwin was to personally execute the new deed for Kenison. When the time came for the closing of the deal, Baldwin did not execute the deed as agreed. The deed was, instead, executed by a third person. Kenison, however, willingly accepted the deed as executed. Kenison later claimed that the contract was void because Baldwin did not personally execute the deed. Baldwin argued that when Kenison accepted the deed from the third party, he waived his rights to complain at a later time and sue for nonperformance. Is Baldwin correct? Why or why not? *Kenison v. Baldwin,* 351 P.2d 307 (Oklahoma).
3. Arthur Murray, Inc., and Parker entered a series of contracts under which Arthur Murray agreed to teach Parker how to dance. Under the terms of each agreement, refunds were impossible and the lessons could not be canceled. After the contracts were entered, Parker suffered a permanent

disability which made it physically impossible for him to dance. When Arthur Murray refused to refund any part of Parker's money, he sued to rescind the contracts on grounds of impossibility. Arthur Murray claimed that the nonrefund clause must be upheld by the court. Is Arthur Murray correct? Explain. *Parker v. Arthur Murray, Inc.*, 295 N.E.2d 487 (Illinois).

4. Shaw leased a service station from Mobil Oil. Shaw's monthly rent was based on his purchase of gasoline from Mobil. He was to pay 1.4 cents per gallon or a $470 minimum monthly rent. Each month Shaw would have to purchase 33,572 gallons to meet this minimum. In July, Shaw ordered 34,000 gallons. This would have allowed him to meet more than the minimum rent. Mobil, however, could deliver only 25,678 gallons. Nevertheless, Mobil attempted to collect the $470 minimum monthly rent. Shaw brought suit against Mobil, claiming that his payment of the $470 minimum and Mobil's delivery of at least 33,572 gallons were conditions concurrent. Shaw argued that since Mobil had not met its part of the bargain, he was not obligated to meet his because Mobil's failure was a breach of contract. Is Shaw correct? Explain. *Shaw v. Mobil Oil Corporation,* 535 P.2d 756 (Oregon).

5. Bob Pagan Ford, Inc., hired Smith to work as a car salesperson in Galveston County. As part of his contract, Smith agreed not to work as an auto salesperson in Galveston County for three years after leaving his employment with Bob Pagan Ford. Smith worked for Bob Pagan for only a few months. He then left and took a sales job with another dealership in Galveston County. Is injunctive relief an appropriate remedy in this case? Explain. *Bob Pagan Ford, Inc. v. Smith,* 638 S.W.2d 176 (Texas).

6. Kucha sold a house to Pilder for $75,293. The agreement was in writing as required by the statute of frauds. As part of the contract, Kucha agreed to pay for the remodeling of the sunporch. However, when Kucha found out that it would cost $12,728 to do the remodeling, he refused to sell the property. Pilder sued to compel Kucha to go through with the deal. Kucha argues that under the circumstances, the court cannot force him to sell under any equitable remedy. Is Kucha correct? Why or why not?

PART 2
Case Study
Shepherd Realty Company v. Winn-Dixie Montgomery

Supreme Court of Alabama
418 So.2d 871

SUMMARY

Winn-Dixie Montgomery, Inc., entered a lease with the Eugene Wylie Corporation. The 20-year lease allowed Winn-Dixie to operate a supermarket in the Brookwood Village Convenience Center. Eugene Wylie Corporation later assigned its rights as landlord and leasor to Shepherd Realty. Paragraph 42 of the lease required Winn-Dixie to follow all regulations established by the landlord of Brookwood Village. Shepherd Realty argued that this clause required Winn-Dixie to be a member of the Brookwood Village Merchants Association and to pay the required dues to the association. Winn-Dixie argued that the clause required nothing of the sort. Nevertheless, Winn-Dixie did pay dues to the merchants association until those dues were increased from 20 cents to 28 cents per square foot. Although Winn-Dixie did eventually pay the increased dues, it did so under protest. Shepherd Realty sued Winn-Dixie for breach of contract. Shepherd later amended the complaint to include a claim of fraud against Winn-Dixie. The dispute centered on whether Paragraph 42 required Winn-Dixie to be a member of the Brookwood Village Merchants Association. The court held that the clause, as written, did not require the supermarket to become a member of the association.

THE COURT'S OPINION: JUSTICE EMBRY

On 11 May, 1971, the Eugene Wylie Corporation and Winn-Dixie Montgomery entered into a twenty-year lease for occupancy by Winn-Dixie of 30,000 square feet of premises for the operation of a supermarket in a development known as Brookwood Village Convenience Center immediately adjacent to the then proposed Brookwood Mall. Winn-Dixie Stores was the guarantor of the obligations of Winn-Dixie Montgomery under the terms of that lease. Shepherd Realty is the current owner of the premises and the assignee of the rights of the landlord-lessor party to the 1971 lease to Winn-Dixie.

The 1971 lease was the result of arm's-length negotiations that took place in the usual course of business....

Winn-Dixie prepared a draft of the lease and it was reviewed, discussed, and modified, by both parties until agreement was reached regarding terms of the lease, which were then reduced to writing. There was no specific reference requiring membership in the BrookwoodVillage Merchants Association contained in the lease. There was, however, paragraph 42, entitled "Rules and Regulations," that stated:

"42. Tenant agrees to abide by all reasonable rules and regulations promulgated by Landlord from time to time, the purpose of which rules and regulations is to promote the best interests of the shopping center and its customers.

Shepherd Realty contends that paragraph 42 was intended to require Winn-Dixie to join the merchants association and to remain a member....

Winn-Dixie paid monthly dues from the time the merchants association was organized in 1974 until the dues were increased to twenty-eight cents per square foot in August 1979. It initially refused to pay the increased dues; later it sought to discontinue paying any dues. Shepherd Realty threatened to declare Winn-Dixie's lease in default for nonpayment of dues, whereupon Winn-Dixie agreed to pay the increased dues under protest.

Shepherd Realty filed a complaint against Winn-Dixie on 9 May 1979 for breach of contract based upon Winn-Dixie's refusal and protest of payment of the increased dues. Winn-Dixie answered the complaint by generally denying that it was *required* to be a member of the merchants association. Also, it specifically denied that paragraph 42 of the lease required membership in the association.

Shepherd Realty amended its complaint to allege fraud by Winn-Dixie in misrepresenting that it would become a mandatory member of the merchants association and sought one million dollars in punitive damages.

On 29 December 1980 this case was heard by the trial court without a jury. Judgment was entered, and a memorandum opinion filed on 17 April 1981, in favor of Winn-Dixie....

There was no error in the trial court's ruling that Winn-Dixie was not required to be a member of the Brookwood Village Merchants Association. There is no specific language in the lease requiring Winn-Dixie to join the merchants association. Furthermore, the record reflects that specific language requiring such membership was found in the leases of other tenants of Brookwood Village but not in the Winn-Dixie lease.

The trial court was correct in refusing to admit parol evidence to show the "true intent" of the parties. It is fundamental that the parol evidence rule prohibits the contradiction of a written agreement by evidence of a prior oral agreement. The rule provides, generally, that when the parties reduce a contract to writing, intended to be a complete contract regarding the subject covered by that contract, no extrinsic evidence of prior or contemporaneous agreements will be admissible to change, alter or contradict such writing.

There is no evidence in the record to support Shepherd Realty's contention that fraud was committed upon it by Winn-Dixie. Fraud, which is never presumed, must be clearly and satisfactorily proved by the party seeking relief upon that basis...we conclude the trial court did not err in its findings or entry of judgment. The judgment below is due to be and is hereby affirmed. AFFIRMED.

QUESTIONS FOR ANALYSIS

1. The Eugene Wylie Corporation assigned Winn-Dixie's lease to Shepherd Realty. What rights and duties accompany an assignment?
2. What characteristic(s) does this contract possess that requires it to be in writing under the Statute of Frauds?
3. What is the parol evidence rule the court talks about in this case?
4. How is the parol evidence rule applied here to the benefit of Winn-Dixie?
5. In addition to breach of contract, Shepherd Realty sued Winn-Dixie for fraud. What are the elements of fraud?
6. In this case, Shepherd Realty sued Winn-Dixie for breach of contract. Could Winn-Dixie have brought suit against Shepherd Realty for economic duress?

PART 3
Sales and Consumer Protection

CHAPTER 14
The Sales Contract

OUTLINE

COMMENTARY

Amy Holt, a college student, agreed to buy a secondhand car from Tim Rice, another student. That same day, Amy's parents accepted an offer to sell the house that Amy grew up in. Real property law and the law of contracts will apply to the sale of the house. A different law, known as the law of sales, will govern the purchase of the car. Contained in Article 2 of the Uniform Commercial Code (UCC), the law of sales was developed to meet people's needs as they buy and sell goods in today's society. In some ways, the law of sales is more flexible than the law of contracts. In addition, by being part of the UCC, the law of sales is uniform, with some exceptions, throughout the country.

OBJECTIVES

1. Determine when to apply the law of sales under the UCC.
2. Define the term *goods,* and name several different goods.
3. Differentiate between a sale and a contract to sell.
4. Describe the special rules for sales contracts.
5. Explain the four exceptions to the rule requiring contracts for the sale of goods costing $500 or more to be in writing.
6. Judge, in a given situation, whether a writing satisfies the requirements of the UCC.
7. Contrast an auction with reserve with an auction without reserve.
8. Determine, in the case of a bulk transfer, whether the four requirements of the UCC have been met.

14-1 THE LAW OF SALES

The law of sales began in England when the customs and practices of merchants developed into what was known as the **law merchant;** this was the commercial law developed by merchants who needed a set of rules to govern their business transactions. As time went on, the law merchant was combined with the English common law and put into a code called the English Sale of Goods Act. Following the English lead, the Uniform Sales Act was written in the United States and adopted by 35 states. Today, the Uniform Commercial Code (UCC) has replaced the Uniform Sales Act and has been adopted, either in whole or in part, by every state in the United States. (Louisiana has adopted Articles 1, 3, 4, and 5 of the UCC.)

14-2 WHEN THE LAW OF SALES APPLIES

UCC Article 2 **(see pp. 614–637)**

Article 2 of the UCC, which contains the law of sales, applies whenever people buy or sell goods. This law applies to transactions between private parties as well as to transactions by business people or merchants. To determine whether the UCC applies, simply ask, "Is this a contract for the sale of goods?" If the answer is yes, apply the law under the UCC. If the answer is no, apply the common law of contracts discussed in Chapters 5 to 13 (see Table 14-1).

Whenever anyone buys food in a supermarket, gasoline at a gas station, clothing at a shopping mall, a meal at a restaurant, or even a daily newspaper, a sale of goods occurs. In fact, several sales contracts usually occur for a particular item before the item reaches the consumer and sometimes even after it reaches the consumer.

The Matthew Allen Corporation manufactures lawn mowers. The company enters into sales contracts with its suppliers every time it purchases parts and materials to make the mowers. In addition, the company enters into sales contracts with wholesalers when it sells the mowers. Similarly, wholesalers enter into sales

Table 14-1 DIFFERENT LAWS APPLY TO DIFFERENT TRANSACTIONS

Transaction	*Applicable Law*
Contract for the sale of real estate	General contract law (sometimes referred to as common law) and real property law
Contract for employment	General contract law
Sale of goods between two private parties	Uniform Commercial Code (Article 2)
Sale of goods by a merchant to a consumer	Uniform Commercial Code (Article 2) and state consumer protection laws
Sale of goods between two merchants	Uniform Commercial Code (Article 2)
Contract for a mixture of goods and services—consisting mostly of goods	Uniform Commercial Code (Article 2)
Contract for a mixture of goods and services—consisting mostly of services	General contract law
Sale of stock on the stock market	Uniform Commercial Code (Article 8)
The writing of a check, promissory note, or draft	Uniform Commercial Code (Article 3)

contracts when they sell the mowers to retailers. In the same manner, retailers enter into sales contracts when they sell the mowers to consumers. Going even further, consumers enter into sales contracts when they sell their secondhand lawn mowers to other private parties.

UCC 2-105(1) **(see p. 615)**

UCC 2-107(1) **(see p. 615)**

Goods are defined as all things (other than money, stocks, and bonds) that are movable. They include the unborn young of animals, growing crops, timber, and minerals if they are to be sold separately from the real property. Office furniture, mobile homes, human blood, milk, numismatic coins, wedding pictures, electricity, waste paper, kerosene, Christmas trees, ships, airplanes, horses, soybeans, polyethylene film, a printing press, and a book of recipes have all been held to be goods by the courts.

UCC 2-105(2) **(see p. 615)**

Goods that are not yet in existence or not yet under the control of people are called **future goods.** They include fish in the sea, minerals in the ground, goods not yet manufactured, and commodities futures.

A.G. Estes, Inc., contracted to sell its cotton crop to Cone Mills Corp. before the crop has been planted. This was a legally enforceable agreement to sell a commodity at a certain time in the future for a certain price.

When a contract includes both goods and services, the dominant element of the contract determines whether it is a sales contract or a services contract. If the sale of goods is dominant, as when someone purchases a furnace and has it installed, the law of sales applies. In contrast, if the performance of services is dominant, as when someone has a furnace repaired and a few new parts are installed, the common law of contracts applies instead of the law of sales.

14-3 THE SALES CONTRACT

UCC 2-106(1) (see p. 615)

A sales contract may be either a sale or a contract to sell. A **sale** is defined as the passing of title (ownership) from the seller to the buyer for a price. Thus, every time anyone buys goods, either for cash or on credit, and receives title to them, a sale occurs. (Title is explained in Chapter 15.)

Calloway traded horses with Manion, a horse trader. Later, when a dispute arose, it was argued that the UCC did not apply to the transaction. The court, in holding that the UCC did apply, said that "a sale is defined as the passing of title from the seller to the buyer for a price, and the price may be payable in goods or otherwise."

If title is to pass at some future time, the agreement is a **contract to sell** rather than a sale.

Ryan signed a contract to buy a boat from Seaside Boat Sales. The boat was to be ordered from the manufacturer and would be delivered in about eight weeks. This was a contract to sell because title was to pass at a future time. Since the boat was not yet built, it was a future good and could not yet be the subject matter of a sale.

A gift is not considered a sale because, although title passes, it is not given for a price. Similarly, a bailment (as when a car is left at a garage for repair) does not meet the definition of a sale because title does not pass between the parties.

14-4 SPECIAL RULES FOR SALES CONTRACTS

One of the purposes of the UCC is to simplify, clarify, and modernize the law governing commercial transactions. With that in mind, the authors of the UCC used the fundamental rules of contract law as a base but made them less rigid. For example, sales contracts may be formed by any manner of expression—oral, written, or otherwise. Strict rules regarding the method of communication of offers and acceptances are relaxed. A merchant's written promise to keep an offer open is binding without consideration. The price may be omitted from a sales contract, and the amount of goods to be sold need not always be definite. Additional terms may sometimes be added by an offeree when accepting an offer. No consideration is necessary to modify a contract for the sale of goods. These special rules relating to sales contracts are discussed in more detail below.

Good Faith
UCC 1-203
(see p. 613)

Under the UCC, every contract or duty imposes an obligation of good faith. This means that the parties to a sales contract must act and deal fairly with each other.

Course of Dealings and Usage of Trade
UCC 1-205
(see p. 613)

When the parties have dealt with each other before, their prior dealings give special meaning to sales contracts. Similarly, any **usage of trade,** that is, any method of dealing that is commonly used in the particular field, is given special meaning. Unless the parties express otherwise, a course of dealings or usage of trade may be used to supplement or qualify the terms of a sales contract.

Formation of a Sales Contract
UCC 2-204(1)(2)
(see p. 613)

A contract may be made in any manner that shows that the parties reached an agreement. It may be oral (with some exceptions) or in writing, or it may be established by the conduct of the parties. An enforceable sales contract may come about even though the exact moment of its making cannot be determined and even though some terms are not completely agreed upon.

Cargill, Inc., entered into a written contract with Fickbohm for the purchase of a certain amount of corn at $1.26 a bushel. The parties had orally agreed that the corn would be delivered sometime between June 1 and July 31, but the delivery date was omitted from the writing. Fickbohm failed to deliver the corn and argued that the contract was unenforceable because the delivery date had been omitted from the writing. The court disagreed, saying that the contract was enforceable even though all the terms were not set forth in the writing.

Offer and Acceptance
UCC 2-206(1)(a)
(see pp. 616–617)

As explained in Chapter 6, it is a general rule of contract law that if the offeror sends an offer by one method of communication (such as by mail) and the offeree accepts by the same method (mail), the contract comes into existence when the acceptance is sent. On the other hand, under contract law still followed in some states, if the offeree accepts by a different method (such as by telegram in the above example), the contract comes into existence when the acceptance is received by the offeror rather than when it was sent by the offeree. The UCC does away with this distinction. To establish a contract for the sale of goods, unless otherwise indicated by the offeror or the circumstances, the offeree may accept the offer in any manner and by any medium that is reasonable. A contract for the sale of goods comes into existence when the acceptance is sent, so long as the method used to send it is reasonable.

Goodwin sent a letter to Callaghan offering to buy ten file cabinets for $700 if Callaghan would ship them promptly. Callaghan accepted the offer by telegram. The contract came into existence when the telegram was sent.

UCC 2-206(1)(b)
(see p. 617)

Unless the buyer indicates otherwise, an order or other offer to buy goods for prompt shipment may be accepted by either a prompt shipment or a prompt promise to ship. In the example given above, Callaghan could have accepted the offer by promptly shipping the file cabinets instead of by promising to ship

UCC 2-106(2) (see p. 615)

them. Under this rule, the goods that are shipped may be either conforming or nonconforming goods. **Conforming goods** are those which are in accordance with the obligations under the contract. **Nonconforming goods** are those which are not the same as those called for under the contract or which are in some way defective.

Firm Offer

UCC 2-104(1) (see p. 614)

The UCC holds merchants to a higher standard than nonmerchants. A **merchant** is a person who deals in goods of the kind sold in the ordinary course of business or who otherwise claims to have knowledge or skills peculiar to those goods. Although most rules under the UCC apply to both merchants and nonmerchants alike, some rules apply only to merchants. One such rule involves a firm offer.

UCC 2-205 (see p. 616)

No consideration is necessary when a merchant promises in writing to hold an offer open for the sale of goods. Known as a **firm offer,** the writing must be signed by the merchant, and the time period for holding the offer open may not exceed three months. This differs from the general rule of contract law (discussed in Chapter 6), which requires consideration in an option contract.

Sunrise Supply Co. offered to sell Jones a pool filter for $150. This was an especially good price for that product. Although he wanted the filter, Jones thought that he might be transferred to another location. He needed four weeks to decide whether to buy the filter. Sunrise Supply Co. agreed in writing to hold the offer open to Jones for four weeks. Although Jones provided no consideration for holding the offer open, it was a firm offer and could not be revoked by Sunrise Supply Co. Sunrise's firm offer also came within the UCC's three-month limit.

Open Price Terms

UCC 2-305(1) (see p. 618)

Another change that the UCC has made is that a contract for the sale of goods may be made even though the price is not settled. Such **open-price terms** may occur when the parties intend to be bound by a contract but fail to mention the price or decide to set the price later. Under the non-UCC law, no contract would come about because the terms are not definite. The UCC allows such a contract to come into existence. If the parties cannot agree on the price at the later date, the price will be a reasonable price at the time for delivery of the goods.

Ayers contracted to buy chicken feed from Sparton Grain & Mill Co. As part of the contract, Sparton agreed to buy and market all Ayer's eggs. The price that Ayers was to pay for the feed was not mentioned. The court held that the UCC requires the price to be a reasonable one when no price is quoted.

Output and Requirements Terms

Sometimes a seller will agree to sell "all the goods we manufacture" or "all the crops we produce" to a particular buyer. This is known as an **output contract.** At other times a buyer will agree to buy "all the oil we need to heat our building" (or some similar requirement) from a particular seller. This is called a **requirements contract.** Such contracts were often not allowed at common

UCC 2-306
(see pp. 618–619)

law because the quantity of the goods to be bought or sold is not definite. The UCC allows output and requirements contracts for the sale of goods as long as the parties deal in good faith and according to reasonable expectations.

Spencer Oil Co. agreed to sell to Lopaz Manufacturing Co. all the heating oil Lopaz would need during the next year. Spencer knew that Lopaz used about 5,000 gallons of oil each year. Over the summer, Lopaz enlarged its building to an extent that it would require 25,000 gallons of heating oil during the next year. Spencer would not be bound to supply that amount of oil to Lopaz because it was far beyond the amount it expected to supply.

Additional Terms in Acceptance

UCC 2-207
(see p. 617)

Under the general rules of contract law, an acceptance of an offer must be an absolute, unqualified, unconditional assent to the offer. If the acceptance differs in the slightest from the offer, it operates as a rejection. The UCC changes this rule somewhat. A contract for the sale of goods comes into existence even though the acceptance states terms additional to or different from those offered or agreed upon (unless acceptance is made conditional on assent to the additional terms). The additional terms are treated as proposals for additions to the contract if the parties are not both merchants. If both parties are merchants, the additional terms become part of the contract unless they materially alter it, or the other party objects within a reasonable time, or the offer limits acceptance to its terms.

This rule is intended to deal with two typical situations. The first is where an agreement has been reached either orally or by informal correspondence between the parties and is followed by one or both of the parties sending formal acknowledgments or memos which contain additional terms not discussed earlier.

The Gateway Co. reached an oral agreement with Charlotte Theatres, Inc., for the sale of an air-conditioning system. Later, Gateway put the agreement in writing, signed it, and sent it to Charlotte for its signature. Charlotte signed the writing but added additional terms relative to the date of completion of the contract. Since both parties were merchants, the additional terms would become part of the contract unless Gateway objected to them within a reasonable time. Had one of them not been a merchant, a contract would have to come into existence without the additional terms, and the added terms would have been treated as proposals for additions to the contract.

The second situation in which this rule applies is one in which a telegram or letter which is intended to be the closing or confirmation of an agreement adds further minor suggestions or proposals such as "ship by Thursday" or "rush."

Cal-Cut Pipe and Supply, Inc., offered in writing to sell used pipe to Southern Idaho Pipe and Steel Co., specifying a delivery date. Southern Idaho accepted by sending a check but changed the delivery date. Cal-Cut mailed a confirmation containing the original delivery date with the postscript, "We will work it out." The court held that there was a binding contract between them despite the conflicting delivery terms.

Modification

UCC 2-209(1) (see p. 617)

UCC 2-209(2) (see p. 617)

Under the general rules of contract law, if the parties have already entered into a binding contract, a later agreement to change that contract needs consideration to be binding. The UCC has done away with this rule in contracts for the sale of goods. An agreement modifying a contract for the sale of goods needs no consideration to be binding. Any such modification may be oral unless the original agreement is in writing and provides that it may not be modified except by a signed writing. Any such clause in a form supplied by a merchant to a nonmerchant, however, must be separately signed by the nonmerchant to be effective.

14-5 FORM OF SALES CONTRACTS

Many sales contracts are oral rather than written. They are often made by telephone; or at a store counter; or face to face between private parties or business people, or both. So long as the price is under $500, an oral contract for the sale of goods is enforceable. Millions of such contracts are made daily by people in our society.

UCC 2-201(1) (see p. 616)

If the price is $500 or more, a sales contract must be in writing to be enforceable. This rule, however, has four exceptions.

David Ruffo agreed to buy a car from Marcia Woodly for $850. The agreement was oral and called for payment of the full amount in cash upon delivery of the car the next day. Unless one of the exceptions in the discussion to follow applies, the oral contract cannot be enforced by either party because it was not evidenced by a writing of any kind.

Exceptions to the General Rule

There are four exceptions to the requirement that contracts for the sale of goods for $500 or more must be in writing to be enforceable. These involve (1) oral contracts between merchants in which a confirmation has been received by one party and not objected to by the other party, (2) specially manufactured goods, (3) admissions in court, and (4) executed contracts.

UCC 2-201(2) (see p. 616)

Oral Contracts Between Merchants An exception to the general rule occurs in certain cases when there is an oral contract between two merchants. If either merchant receives a written confirmation of the oral contract from the other merchant within a reasonable time and does not object to it in writing within ten days, the oral contract is enforceable.

Pamela Brown, the owner of Londonderry Frameworks, telephoned Northeast Frame Co. and placed an order for $760 worth of stock. Later that day, she mailed a written confirmation of the order. Northeast Frame Co. received the confirmation and made no objection to it, making the oral contract enforceable.

UCC 2-201(3) (see p. 616)

Specially Manufactured Goods Another exception occurs when goods are to be specially manufactured for the buyer and are not suitable for sale to others in the ordinary course of the seller's business. If the seller has made either a substantial beginning in manufacturing the goods or has made commitments to buy them, the oral agreement will be enforceable.

Lifetime Aluminum Co. entered into an oral agreement to manufacture 15 oversized aluminum windows for Harold Cohen for the price of $1,500. The windows were such an odd shape that no one else would have a need for them. When the windows were manufactured, Cohen refused to take them on the ground that the oral contract was unenforceable. The court held against Cohen, however, and enforced the oral agreement. The windows were specially manufactured and were not suitable for sale to others.

UCC 2-201(3)(c) (see p. 616)

Admissions in Court If the party against whom enforcement is sought admits in court that an oral contract for the sale of goods was made, the contract will be enforceable. The contract is not enforceable under this exception, however, beyond the quantity of goods admitted.

Anderson admitted in court that he orally agreed to sell 18,000 bushels of durum wheat to Farmer's Elevator Co. Because of the admission, the oral contract was enforceable.

Executed Agreements When the parties carry out their agreement in a satisfactory manner, the law will not render the transaction unenforceable for want of an agreement in writing. Executed contracts need not be in writing; the writing requirements apply only to contracts which are *executory*, that is, not yet performed. This means that contracts for goods which have been received and accepted need not be in writing.

UCC 2-201(3)(c) (see p. 616)

If there has been a part payment or a part delivery, the court will enforce only that portion of the agreement that has been performed.

Gilmore orally agreed to sell Nash three electric guitars and a powerful amplification system for $900. Delivery was to be made in ten days, at which time Nash agreed to have the money ready for payment. If Gilmore had delivered one of the three guitars to Nash, the court would enforce payment for that one instrument.

Requirements of Writing

UCC 2-201(1) (see p. 616)

The writing that is required to satisfy the UCC must indicate that a contract for sale has been made between the parties and must mention the quantity of goods being sold. It must also be signed by the party against whom enforcement is sought (the defendant). A writing is acceptable even though it omits or incorrectly states a term agreed upon. However, a contract will not be enforceable beyond the quantity of goods shown in such writing. For that reason, it is necessary to put the quantity of goods to be bought and sold in the written agreement. An informal note, memorandum, or sales slip will satisfy the writing requirements.

Had Gilmore, in the previous case, noted the terms of the agreement on the back of an envelope and had Nash signed it, the requirements of a written agreement would have been met, thereby obligating Nash to the sales contract. Only the defendant in a lawsuit must have signed the writing.

14-6 AUCTION SALES

In *auction sales* the auctioneer presents goods for sale and invites the audience to make offers which are know as bids. This is similar to an invitation to trade. Bidders in the crowd respond with their offers. The highest bid (offer) is accepted by the auctioneer, usually by the drop of the hammer together with the auctioneer's calling out "Sold."

UCC 2-328(2) (see p. 624)

A sale by auction is complete when the auctioneer so announces by the fall of the hammer or in some other customary manner. If, while the hammer is falling, a higher bid comes from those in the crowd, the auctioneer has two options: to declare the goods sold or to reopen the bidding.

UCC 2-328(3) (see p. 624)

Such a sale is "with reserve" unless the goods are expressly put up for bid. In an **auction with reserve** the auctioneer may withdraw the goods at any time before announcing completion of the sale. In an **auction without reserve,** after the auctioneer calls for bids on an article or lot, that article or lot cannot be withdrawn unless no bid is made within a reasonable time. In either case, a bidder may retract a bid until the auctioneer's announcement of completion of the sale. A bidder's retraction does not revive any previous bid.

Swenson, an auctioneer, was silent as to whether a sale would be with or without reserve. Durocher bid $1,500 on an Oriental vase. She was the highest bidder. Swenson refused to sell the vase at that price. Durocher demanded that the $1,500 bid be accepted. Swenson was justified in withdrawing the vase from the auction because the terms were not announced, making it a sale with reserve.

UCC 2-328(4) (see p. 624)

The practice of planting persons in the crowd for the purpose of raising bids by innocent purchasers is not allowed. Except in a forced sale, such as by a sheriff, if a seller (or the seller's agent) makes a bid at an auction without notifying other bidders, a buyer has two options. Under the UCC, a buyer may either avoid the sale or take the goods at the price of the last good faith bid prior to the completion of the sale.

In the preceding example, if the owner of the Oriental vase had bid against Durocher, Durocher could have purchased the vase for the price of the last bid other than the owner's that had been made before her final bid.

14-7 BULK TRANSFERS

UCC 6-102(1) Over the years, bulk transfers have caused special problems for business people. Merchants, owing debts, would sometimes sell out their entire stock in trade for less than what it was worth. This practice left creditors with no way of reaching and selling the goods to obtain the money owed them. Article 6 of the UCC protects creditors from this practice. It is called the Bulk Transfer Article of the UCC. A **bulk transfer** is any transfer of a major part of the materials, supplies, merchandise, or other inventory of an enterprise which is not in the ordinary course of the transferor's business.

UCC 6-104(1) The UCC lists four requirements that must be followed whenever a bulk transfer is made. If the four requirements are not met, any transferee of the goods (such as a buyer) can lose all ownership rights to them. Creditors who have suffered damages may demand the return of all goods bought, with no obligation to reimburse the transferee. The four requirements of the bulk transfer law are as follows:

UCC 6-105

1. The transferee must require the transferor to furnish a list of any existing creditors with their addresses and amounts due.
2. The parties must prepare a schedule of the property being transferred so that it can be identified.
3. The transferee must preserve the list and schedule for six months following the transfer and make it available for inspection.
4. The transferee must give notice of the transfer to all the creditors at least ten days before taking possession of the goods or paying for them, whichever happens first.

After observing these four requisites, the transferee may pay for and take title and possession of the inventory. Creditors who have not, to that time, taken any action to interrupt the transfer have lost their right to do so.

The bulk transfer law is applicable to businesses whose principal activity is to sell merchandise from stock. It also includes firms which manufacture the goods they sell.

UCC 6-108 If the bulk transfer is an auction, the auctioneer must meet the obligations of the transferee that are listed above. An auctioneer who knows that the auction is a bulk transfer and fails to meet the requirements will be liable to the creditors up to the amount of the net proceeds of the auction.

SUMMARY

14-1. The Uniform Commercial Code, (UCC), which contains the law of sales, has been adopted, either in whole or in part, by every state in the United States.

14-2. Article 2 of the Uniform Commercial Code applies whenever people buy or sell goods. It applies to transactions between private parties as well as to transactions by business people or merchants.

14-3. A sales contract may be either a sale or a contract to sell.

14-4. Special rules, which are different from general contract law, apply to sales contracts:

- **a.** Prior dealings and usage of trade may be used to supplement or qualify the terms of a sales contract.
- **b.** A sales contract may be made in any manner that shows that the parties reached an agreement.
- **c.** A contract may come about even though some terms are not agreed upon.
- **d.** Unless otherwise specified, an offeree may accept an offer in any way that is reasonable, including a prompt shipment of the goods.
- **e.** A written promise by a merchant to hold an offer open needs no consideration to be binding.
- **f.** A sales contract may be made even though the price is not settled. If the parties cannot agree on a price, it will be a reasonable price at the time of delivery.
- **g.** Output and requirements contracts are allowed in sales contracts as long as the parties deal in good faith and according to reasonable expectations.
- **h.** A sales contract may result even when an offeree adds different or additional terms from those offered or agreed upon. The different terms do not become part of the contract unless the parties are both merchants and no objection is made to them within a reasonable time.
- **i.** No consideration is necessary to modify a contract for the sale of goods.

14-5. With four exceptions, a contract for the sale of goods for $500 or more must be in writing. The exceptions are:

- **a.** oral contracts between merchants in which a confirmation has been received by one party and not objected to by the other party,
- **b.** specially manufactured goods,
- **c.** admissions in court,
- **d.** executed contracts.

14-6. In an auction sale, offers are made by the people in the audience. The acceptance takes place when the auctioneer bangs the hammer. In an auction *with reserve* the auctioneer need not accept the highest bid. In an auction *without reserve* the auctioneer must accept the highest bid.

14-7. To protect creditors from losing access to goods, creditors must be notified at least ten days before a bulk transfer takes place.

Understanding Key Legal Terms

auction with reserve (p. 180)
auction without reserve (p. 180)
bulk transfer (p. 181)
conforming goods (p. 176)
contract to sell (p. 174)
firm offer (p. 176)
future goods (p. 173)
goods (p. 173)
law merchant (p. 172)
merchant (p. 176)
nonconforming goods (p. 176)
open-price terms (p. 176)
output contract (p. 176)
requirements contract (p. 176)
sale (p. 174)
usage of trade (p. 175)

Questions for Review and Discussion

1. The law of sales applies to what types of contracts?
2. Name three items that are goods and one item that is a future good.
3. Explain in what way a sale is different from a contract to sell.
4. Describe three special rules that apply to sales contracts.
5. Compare an option contract with a firm offer. How do they differ?
6. When must a sales contract be in writing?
7. What four exceptions apply to Question 6?
8. What are the requirements of a writing, when one is required, under the UCC?
9. Compare an auction with reserve with an auction without reserve and explain when each comes about.
10. Discuss the reason for the bulk transfer provisions of the UCC. What does this law require?

Analyzing Cases

1. Data Processing Services, Inc. entered into a contract with L.H. Smith Oil Corporation to develop and implement a data processing accounting system for Smith's new IBM System-34 computer. In a lawsuit that followed, the lower court held that this was a contract for the sale of goods and applied the UCC to the transaction. Data Processing Services, Inc. argued that this was a contract for services, not goods, and that the UCC should not be applied. How would you decide? *Data Processing v. L.H. Smith Oil Corp.*, 492 N.E.2d 314 (Indiana).
2. Curry entered into a contract to sell four wheel bearings to Litman for $300. Before the contract was carried out, Curry told Litman that the cost of bearings had increased and that he would have to change the price to $400. Litman agreed to pay $400 for the bearings. Later, Litman refused to pay the additional $100, claiming that Curry gave no consideration for Litman's promise to pay the extra money. Is Litman correct? Why or why not?
3. Coleman bid $2,050 for a D-7 tractor at a public auction. Nothing was stated that the auction was with reserve. The auctioneer yelled "Sold," accepting Coleman's bid. Later, the owner of the tractor refused to sell it for $2,050, saying that the auction was with reserve and that therefore he could refuse to accept the bid. Must the owner sell the tractor to Coleman for $2,050? Why or why not? *Coleman v. Duncan*, 540 S.W.2d 935 (Missouri).

4. Ireland, who owed money to West Denver Feed Company, sold his entire business to Hall. Ireland did not comply with the Bulk Transfer Act. Two years later, Hall filed for bankruptcy. The West Denver Feed Co. brought suit against Ireland for the money owed. May it recover under the Bulk Transfer Act from Ireland? Explain. *West Denver Feed Co. v. Ireland,* 551 P.2d 1091 (Colorado).

5. Ferguson agreed to sell to R.L. Kimsey Cotton Co., Inc., all the cotton produced by Ferguson on a specified parcel of land at an agreed price. The agreement was in writing and contained other terms. Later, Ferguson argued that the agreement was invalid because the quantity and subject matter were vague and indefinite. Is Ferguson correct? Why or why not? *R.L. Kimsey Cotton Co., Inc. v. Ferguson,* 214 S.E.2d 360 (Georgia).

6. Carolina Transformer Co., Inc., brought suit against Anderson for several thousand dollars owed them for the purchase of transformers. Anderson testified in court that he had orally negotiated the contract and had reached a final agreement with Carolina for the purchase of the transformers. Anderson argued, however, that he was not responsible because under the UCC a contract for the sale of goods of $500 or more is not enforceable unless it is in writing. Do you agree with Anderson? *Carolina Transformer Co. v. Anderson,* 341 So.2d 1327 (Mississippi).

7. O'Brien placed a telephone order for 20 shipments of lettuce from Soroka Farms. Soroka Farms shipped the lettuce to a cooler, where it was held under cold storage. It was later shipped on O'Brien's orders directly to O'Brien's customers. O'Brien refused to pay for the lettuce, arguing that the contract was not enforceable because it was over $500 and was not in writing. Do you believe that the oral contract was enforceable in this case? Why? See also *O'Day v. George Arakelian Farms, Inc.,* 540 P.2d 197 (Arizona).

8. Representatives of a fish marketing association (AIFMA) and a fish company (NEFCO) met at Bristol Bay, Alaska, to negotiate a marketing agreement for the forthcoming fishing season. At this meeting, NEFCO's agent, Gage, signed an agreement that contained the price that was to be paid for the fish and other details about the transaction. It omitted the quantity of fish that was to be purchased. Later, when suit was brought on the agreement, NEFCO argued that it was unenforceable because the written agreement failed to mention the quantity. Do you agree with NEFCO? Explain. *Alaska Ind. Fish Mktg. Ass'n v. New England Fish Co.,* 548 P.2d 348 (Washington).

CHAPTER 15
Title and Risk of Loss

OUTLINE

COMMENTARY

Katherine Cronin, a boat dealer, sold her car to Anthony Anzalone, who agreed to pick it up the next day. That night, the car was stolen. Two days later, Cronin contracted to sell a yacht to Kevin Daly, a private party. After the contract was signed, but before Daly received the yacht, it sank when a tornado struck the area. The same tornado destroyed a railroad car containing boating supplies being shipped to Cronin's dealership. In some of these situations, it is necessary to determine who must bear the risk of loss, the buyer or the seller. In others, it is important to determine who has title to the goods. These subjects are addressed in this chapter.

OBJECTIVES

1. Contrast voidable title with void title.
2. Discuss the rights of the parties when goods that are entrusted to merchants are sold to others in the ordinary course of business.
3. Determine, in a given case, when title to goods passes from the seller to the buyer.
4. Decide, in different situations, whether the buyer or the seller of goods must bear the risk of loss.
5. Compare a sale on approval with a sale or return.
6. Describe when buyers and sellers of goods have insurable interests in those goods.

15-1 VOID AND VOIDABLE TITLE

Title is the right of ownership to goods. People who own goods have title to them. Sellers sometimes give a bill of sale to a buyer as evidence that the sale took place. A **bill of sale** is a written statement evidencing the transfer of personal property from one person to another. It does not prove, however, that the seller had perfect title to the goods. The goods may have been stolen, obtained by fraud, purchased from a minor or incompetent, or entrusted with the seller by the true owner and sold by mistake. The question that arises in such cases is whether an innocent purchaser for value receives good title to the goods. The answer to this question depends on whether the seller's title to the goods was void or voidable and whether the goods had been entrusted to a merchant.

Void Title

With the exception of voidable title, discussed below, buyers of goods acquire whatever title their sellers had to the property. If a seller has **void title** (no title at all), as does a seller of stolen goods, a buyer of the goods obtains no title to them either.

A thief entered Alton's apartment and stole her brand-new 21-inch color television set, which had just been purchased that day and had not yet been removed from its original carton. The thief sold the set to Guthrie, an innocent purchaser, who believed that the thief was the real owner of the set. Alton would have the legal right to the return of the television set from Guthrie if its whereabouts were located. Guthrie's only right of recourse would be against the thief for the money paid for the set. Anyone who buys stolen goods receives no title to them.

The continued sale of the stolen property through several innocent buyers would not in any way defeat the real owner's right in the property. The rights of possession and title of successive buyers of stolen property can never be any better than the rights of the thief, who had no title to them.

Innocent purchasers may bring suit against the person from whom stolen goods were purchased for breach of warranty of title. This is explained in Chapter 16.

Voidable Title

Anyone who obtains property as a result of another's fraud, misrepresentation, mutual mistake, undue influence, or duress holds only voidable title to the goods. This kind of title is also received when goods are bought from a minor or person who is mentally ill. **Voidable title** means title that may be voided if one of the parties elects to do so. Some people refer to voidable title as title which is valid until voided.

UCC 2-403(1) **(see p. 625)**

Anyone with voidable title to goods is able to transfer good title to others. The UCC provides, "A person with voidable title has power to transfer a good title to a good faith purchaser for value."

Reed bought an expensive television set from Merchandise Mart on a 30-day charge account. In making the purchase, Reed made several fraudulent statements to the store's credit department. Although the set was bought by fraudulent means, a resale by Reed to an innocent purchaser for value would cut off the right of Merchandise Mart to demand the return of its former property.

Although the store cannot recover the goods, it may bring an action against Reed for any loss suffered due to the fraud or other wrongdoing.

Entrusting Goods to a Merchant

UCC 2-403(2) (see p. 625)

People often entrust goods which belong to them to merchants. For example, they leave their watches with jewelers and their television sets with stores to be repaired. When this occurs, if the merchant sells the goods in the ordinary course of business to a third party who has no knowledge of the real owner's rights, the third party receives good title to them. The original owner who entrusted them to the merchant loses title to the goods altogether, but may bring an action against the merchant for money damages caused by the loss.

> Enright brought his diamond ring to a jeweler for a new setting. He was told that he would be able to pick up the ring at around five o'clock that afternoon. The jewelry store sold used rings as part of its regular business. By mistake, a salesperson who worked at the store sold Enright's ring to Reilly, who was unaware that the ring belonged to Enright. Reilly will receive good title to the ring. Enright's cause of action will be against the jewelry store for the conversion of his diamond ring.

The reason for this rule of law is to give confidence to people who buy in the marketplace. People can be assured that they will receive good title to property (except stolen property) which they buy from a merchant who deals in goods of that kind in the ordinary course of business.

15-2 THE PASSAGE OF TITLE AND RISK OF LOSS

It is not unusual for goods to be stolen, damaged, or destroyed while awaiting shipment, while being shipped, or while awaiting pickup after a sales contract has been entered into. When this occurs, it becomes necessary to determine who must suffer the loss, the seller or the buyer. The rules for determining risk of loss are contained in the UCC. Except when goods are to be picked up by the buyer and in a few other cases, whoever has title to the goods bears the risk of loss.

UCC 2-509 (see p. 625)

Goods must be **identified** to the contract before title can be transferred to the buyer. This means that specific goods have to be selected as the subject matter of the contract. Once goods are identified, title passes to the buyer when the seller does whatever is required, under the contract, to deliver the goods. Contracts calling for the seller to deliver the goods are either shipment contracts or destination contracts.

UCC 2-501(1) (see p. 627)

Shipment Contracts

A **shipment contract** is one in which the seller turns the goods over to a carrier for delivery to the buyer, without the responsibility for seeing that they

UCC 2-401(2) (see p. 624)

reach their destination. In a shipment contract, both title and risk of loss pass to the buyer when the goods are given to the carrier.

Underwood was employed by Kentucky Cardinal Dairies to pick up milk from various farmers and deliver it, in the farmers' cans, to the dairy. When no one was looking, he poured some of the milk from the farmers' cans into his own cans and sold it to another dairy. He was charged with the unlawful conversion of milk "which was the property of Kentucky Cardinal Dairies." In his defense, he argued that the milk was still the property of the farmers because it had not yet reached the dairy. The court disagreed, holding that title to the milk passed to the dairy the moment it was picked up by Underwood because that was the time and place of shipment.

UCC 2-319 (see p. 621)

Shipment contracts are often designated by the term *f.o.b. the place of shipment* (such as f.o.b. Chicago). The abbreviation **f.o.b.** means "free on board." When goods are sent **f.o.b. the place of shipment,** they will be delivered free to the place of shipment. The buyer must pay all shipping charges from there to the place of destination. More important to this study, the terms indicate that title to the goods and the risk of loss passes at the point of origin. Delivery to the carrier by the seller and acceptance by the carrier complete the transfer of both title and risk of loss. Thus the buyer accepts full responsibility during the transit of the goods.

Marcus Manufacturing of Boston, Massachusetts, shipped goods to Harlan, Inc., in Memphis, Tennessee. Terms of the shipment were f.o.b. Boston, Massachusetts. During shipment the goods were destroyed by fire. Harlan, not Marcus, would suffer the loss. Undoubtedly, Harlan would place a claim against the carrier in its obligation as insurer of goods accepted for shipment.

Destination Contracts

UCC 2-401(2) (see p. 624)

If the contract requires the seller to deliver goods to a destination, it is called a **destination contract.** Both title and risk of loss pass to the buyer when the seller tenders the goods at the place of destination. **Tender** means to offer to turn the goods over to the buyer.

UCC 2-319 (see p. 621)

Destination contracts are often designated by the terms **f.o.b. the place of destination;** goods shipped under such terms belong to the seller until they have been delivered to the destination shown on the contract. Similarly, the risk of loss remains with the seller until the goods are tendered at destination. Tender at destination requires that (*a*) the goods arrive at the place named in the contract, (*b*) the buyer is given notice of their arrival, and (*c*) a reasonable time is allowed for the buyer to pick up the goods from the carrier.

Suppose, in the previous example, the shipment to Harlan, Inc., had been made under terms of f.o.b. Memphis, Tennessee. Title and risk would not have passed at the shipping point. The seller would have had to suffer the loss, and Harlan would have had no obligation for payment.

When terms of shipment do not specify shipping point or destination, it is assumed to be f.o.b. the place of shipment. Adding the term **c.o.d.** (cash on delivery) instructs the carrier to retain possession until the carrier has collected the cost of the goods.

UCC 2-320 **(see p. 622)**

The term **c.i.f.** (cost, insurance, and freight) instructs the carrier to collect all charges and fees in one lump sum. This includes the cost of goods shipped, insurance, and freight charges to the point of destination. The term **c.f.** means that insurance is not included.

UCC 2-319(2) **(see p. 621)**

The term **f.a.s. vessel** (free alongside vessel) at a named port requires sellers to deliver the goods at their own risk alongside the vessel or at a dock designated by the buyer.

No Delivery Required

UCC 2-401(3)(b) **(see p. 625)**

UCC 2-509(3) **(see p. 627)**

When the contract calls for the buyer to pick up the goods, title passes to the buyer when the contract is made. Risk of loss, on the other hand, passes at different times depending on whether the seller is a merchant. If the seller is a merchant, the risk of loss passes when the buyer receives the goods. If the seller is not a merchant, the risk of loss passes to the buyer when the seller tenders the goods to the buyer (see Table 15-1).

Rivera agreed to sell her boat to Gray for $2,500. Gray paid for the boat and said that he would pick it up from Rivera's front yard the next evening. Gray was called out of town, however, and did not pick up the boat, which had been made ready for him. The boat was stolen a week later from Rivera's front yard. Gray must suffer the loss because the boat had been tendered to him. Had Rivera been a merchant, she would have had to assume the loss because Gray had not yet received possession of the boat.

Fungible Goods

Fungible goods are "goods of which any unit is, by nature or usage of trade, the equivalent of any like unit." Wheat, flour, sugar, and liquids of various kinds are examples of fungible goods. They are usually sold by weight or measure. Title to fungible goods may pass without the necessity of separating goods sold from the bulk. Under the UCC, "an undivided share of an identified bulk of fungible goods is sufficiently identified to be sold although the quantity of the bulk is not determined."

UCC 2-105(4) **(see p. 615)**

Logan Trucking Co. owned a large fuel storage tank which was partially filled with diesel fuel. The exact quantity of fuel in the tank was not known. The company was going out of business. Interstate Trucking Co. contracted to buy half the fuel in the tank, and Union Trucking Co. contracted to buy the other half. Both buyers agreed to send their own trucks to pick up the fuel. Title passed to the buyers when the contract was made even though the exact quantity of each sale was unknown and neither buyer had taken a share of the fuel from the entire lot.

Table 15-1 PASSAGE OF TITLE AND RISK OF LOSS

Terms of Contract	*Title Passes*	*Risk of Loss Passes*
Shipment contract	When goods are delivered to carrier	When goods are delivered to carrier
Destination contract	When goods are tendered at destination	When goods are tendered at destination
No delivery required	When contract is made	*Merchant Seller:* When buyer receives goods; *Nonmerchant Seller:* When seller tenders goods to buyer
Document of title	When document of title is given to buyer	When document of title is given to buyer
Agreement of the parties	At time and place agreed upon	At time and place agreed upon

Documents of Title

Sometimes when people buy goods, they receive a document of title to the goods rather than the goods themselves. They then give the document of title to the warehouse or carrier that is holding the goods and receive possession of them. A **document of title** is a paper giving the person who possesses it the right to receive the goods named in the document. Bills of lading and warehouse receipts, explained in Chapter 20, are examples of documents of title. An automobile title certificate has not been given the legal status of a document of title as the term is used in the UCC.

UCC 2-401(3)(a) **(see p. 624)**

When a document of title is used in a sales transaction, both title and risk of loss pass to the buyer when the document is delivered to the buyer.

Sanchez stored a large quantity of wheat in a grain elevator and, in return, was given a warehouse receipt. Later, Sanchez sold the wheat to Cain. Upon receipt of the money for the wheat, Sanchez signed and delivered the warehouse receipt to Cain. Cain received title to the wheat when the document was delivered to her.

Agreement of the Parties

The parties may, if they wish, enter into an agreement setting forth the time that title and risk of loss passes from the seller to the buyer. With one exception, title and risk of loss will pass at the time and place agreed upon. If the agreement allows the seller to retain title after the goods are shipped, title will pass at the time of shipment regardless of the agreement and the seller will have a security interest in the goods. A security interest (see Chapter 30) gives the seller a right to have the property sold in the event the buyer fails to pay money owed to the seller.

UCC 2-401(1) **(see p. 624)**

Raymond agreed to sell Glover her Datsun 280Z for $4,000. The agreement called for Glover to pay $2,000 down and the balance in monthly installments for two years. Under the agreement, title to the vehicle would not pass to Glover until the $4,000 was paid in full. Since Raymond delivered the car to Glover on the day the agreement was signed, title passed to Glover at that time regardless of the terms to the contract. The effect of those terms was to give Raymond a security interest in the vehicle for the balance of the money owed to her.

Revesting of Title in Seller

UCC 2-401(4) (see pp. 624–625)

Buyers, after entering into sales contracts, sometimes refuse to accept the goods that are delivered or are otherwise made available to them. In all such cases, title to the goods returns to the seller. This is true whether or not the buyer's rejection of the goods was justified. Similarly, title to goods returns to the seller when the buyer accepts the goods and then, for a justifiable reason, decides to revoke the acceptance. A justifiable reason for revoking an acceptance would be the discovery of a defect in the goods after having inspected them.

UCC 2-510 (see pp. 627–628)

When the seller sends goods to the buyer which do not meet the contract requirements and are, therefore, unacceptable, the risk of loss remains with the seller. In situations where the buyer accepts the goods but later discovers some defect and rightfully revokes the acceptance, the passage of risk of loss depends upon whether the buyer is insured. If the buyer has insurance, that insurance will cover the loss. To the extent that there is no insurance, the risk of loss remains with the seller from the beginning.

UCC 2-510(3) (see pp. 627–628)

When the buyer breaches the contract as to goods which have been identified to the contract, the seller may, to the extent of having no insurance coverage, treat the risk of loss as resting with the buyer.

15-3 SALES WITH RIGHT OF RETURN

Because of competition and a desire to give satisfaction, goods are sometimes sold with the understanding that they may be returned even though they conform to the contract. Determination of ownership and risk of loss while such goods are in the buyer's possession is sometimes necessary. Sales with the right of return are of two kinds.

Sale on Approval

UCC 2-326 (see p. 623)

A sale which allows goods to be returned even though they conform to the contract is called a **sale on approval** when the goods are primarily for the buyer's use. When goods are sold on approval, they remain the property of the seller until the buyer's approval has been expressed. The approval may be indicated by the oral or written consent of the buyer or by the buyer's act of retaining the goods for more than a reasonable time. Using the goods in a reasonable and expected manner on a trial basis will not imply an acceptance. Grossly careless use and a failure to inform the seller of the buyer's intent to return, however, could constitute an acceptance.

UCC 2-327 (see pp. 623–624)

Goods held by the buyer on approval are not subject to the claims of the buyer's creditors until the buyer decides to accept them. In addition, the risk of loss remains with the seller until the buyer has accepted the goods.

Sale or Return

UCC 2-326 (see p. 623)

A sale that allows goods to be returned even though they conform to the contract is called a **sale or return** when the goods are delivered primarily for resale. When such a sale occurs, the buyer takes title to the goods with the right to revest title in the seller after a specified period or reasonable time. In such cases, the buyer must accept all the obligations of ownership while retaining possession of the goods. Goods held on sale or return are subject to the claims of the buyer's creditors.

While in the buyer's possession, the goods must be cared for and used in a reasonable manner, anticipating their possible return in the same condition as when received, after making allowance for ordinary wear and tear. Also, the goods must be returned at the buyer's risk and expense.

Butcher owned a gift shop in which she sold other people's goods on consignment. Hanson delivered a dozen handmade braided rugs to Butcher with the understanding that she would be paid for any that were sold. Any rugs that did not sell after three months would be returned to Hanson. This was a sale or return because the rugs were delivered primarily for resale. Butcher would be required to pay Hanson for any rugs that were damaged, lost, or stolen while in Butcher's possession.

15-4 INSURABLE INTEREST

UCC 2-501(1) **(see p. 625)**

People must have an insurable interest in property to be able to place insurance on it. An **insurable interest** is the financial interest that an insured party has in the insured property. Buyers may place insurance on goods the moment a contract is made and the goods are identified to the contract. It is then that buyers receive an insurable interest in the goods they buy. They obtain an insurable interest even though they later reject or return the goods to the seller. Notwithstanding the buyer's right to insure the goods, sellers retain an insurable interest in goods so long as they still have title to them.

While shopping on vacation in an antique store in Connecticut, Maniff, who lived in Nevada, came upon a dining room set that she liked. She decided to buy the set on the condition that the antique dealer would ship the goods f.o.b. Winnemucca, Nevada. The dealer agreed. Maniff received an insurable interest in the goods when they were identified to the contract. At the same time, the dealer retained an insurable interest in the goods until they were tendered at their destination in Winnemucca. Both Maniff and the antique dealer could insure the goods.

SUMMARY

15-1. Anyone with void title to goods, such as a thief, can never give good title to another person. Anyone with voidable title, such as someone who buys goods from a minor, may transfer good title to a good faith purchaser for value. When goods are entrusted to a merchant who sells them without authority to someone in the ordinary course of business, the purchaser obtains good title.

15-2. With few exceptions, such as when goods are to be picked up by the buyer, whoever has title to the goods bears the risk of loss. Goods must be identified to the contract before title can be transferred to the buyer. Once goods are identified, title passes to the buyer when the seller does whatever is required, under the contract, to deliver the goods.

In a shipment contract, both title and risk of loss pass to the buyer when the goods are given to the carrier. In a destination contract, both title and risk of loss pass to the buyer when the seller tenders the goods at the place of destination.

When the contract calls for the buyer to pick up the goods, title passes to the buyer when the contract is made. If the seller is a merchant, the risk of loss passes when the buyer receives the goods. If the seller is not a merchant, the risk of loss passes when the seller tenders the goods to the buyer.

Title to fungible goods may pass without the necessity of separating goods sold from the bulk.

When a document of title is used, both title and risk of loss pass to the buyer when the document is delivered to the buyer.

In general, the parties may establish by agreement the time and place for the passage of both title and risk of loss.

Title returns to in the seller when the buyer refuses to accept the goods. Similarly, the risk of loss remains in the seller when the goods that are shipped do not meet the contract requirements.

15-3. Goods sold on approval remain the property of the seller until the buyer's approval is expressed. In addition, the seller retains the risk of loss. In contrast, in a sale or return, the buyer takes title to the goods but is given the right to return the goods to the seller at a later time. The buyer must care for the goods in a reasonable manner and suffer the risk of loss.

15-4. Buyers have an insurable interest in goods the moment a contract is made and the goods are identified to the contract. In addition, sellers retain an insurable interest in goods so long as they still have title to them.

Understanding Key Legal Terms

c.f. (p. 189)
c.i.f. (p. 189)
c.o.d. (p. 189)
destination contract (p. 188)
document of title (p. 190)
f.a.s. vessel (p. 189)
f.o.b. (p. 188)
f.o.b. the place of destination (p. 188)
f.o.b. the place of shipment (p. 188)
fungible goods (p. 189)
identified (p. 187)
insurable interest (p. 192)
sale on approval (p. 191)
sale or return (p. 191)
shipment contract (p. 187)
tender (p. 188)
title (p. 185)
void title (p. 186)
voidable title (p. 186)

Questions for Review and Discussion

1. Explain the difference between void and voidable title.
2. What are the rights of an innocent purchaser of stolen goods?

3. Give an example of someone who has voidable title to goods.
4. What are the rights of the owner of goods who entrusts the goods to a merchant who sells them in the ordinary course of business?
5. When do title and risk of loss pass to the buyer in a shipment contract?
6. When do title and risk of loss pass to the buyer in a destination contract?
7. When do title and risk of loss pass to the buyer when the contract calls for the buyer to pick up the goods?
8. When do title and risk of loss pass to the buyer when a document of title is used?
9. What is the difference between a sale on approval and a sale or return?
10. When may buyers place insurance on goods they purchase?

Analyzing Cases

1. Estes purchased a late-model Chevrolet Caprice sports coupe from Howard, an automobile dealer in Mississippi. Later, it was discovered that the vehicle had been stolen from a Chevrolet dealership in Florida and, after a circuitous route, eventually had come to rest in Mississippi. The bill of sale to the vehicle had been forged. Estes contends that he has good title to the vehicle because he bought the auto from a dealer. Is Estes correct? *Allstate Ins. Co. v. Estes,* 345 So.2d 265 (Mississippi).
2. Brown, who operated Jack's Skelly Service Station, was sued by his former wife for child support payments. During the trial, the question arose as to who owned the gasoline in the service station tanks, Brown or Brown's supplier, Martin. Brown had entered into a "special Keep-Full motor fuel sales agreement" under which Martin agreed to deliver to Brown's place of business Skelly motor fuel. The agreement stated that title to the fuel "shall be and remain in Martin until removed from the tanks through and by means of computing pumps." Who owned the gas in the tanks, Brown or Martin? Why? *Stewart v. Brown,* 546 S.W.2d 204 (Missouri).
3. Harold Marcus entered into a contract with Corrigan's Yacht Yard & Marine Sales, Inc., to trade in his 34-foot Silverton power boat toward a later-model Mainship boat. He delivered his Silverton boat to the yacht yard at the time of the contract in November. The new boat was not to be delivered until the following April. The yacht yard sold the Silverton boat to William Heiselman soon after receiving it. When the yacht yard was unable to deliver the Mainship boat to Marcus in April, Marcus took back his Silverton boat. Who has title to the boat, Marcus or Heiselman? Explain. *Heiselman v. Marcus,* 488 N.Y.S.2d 571 (New York).
4. Gallo entered into a contract in October to deliver 3,500 heifers to Weisbart's ranch between May 1 and October 1 of the next year. Gallo experienced difficulty in raising the heifers due to rising costs and a severe winter, and his bank foreclosed on the cattle before they could be delivered to Weisbart. Weisbart claims that sale of the cattle occurred in October when the contract was made and that title passed to him at that time. Do you agree with Weisbart? Why or why not? *Weisbart & Co. v. First Nat. Bank,* 568 F.2d 391 (5th Cir. Ct.).
5. Mann bought a Lincoln Continental Mark IV automobile from Kilbourn American Leasing, Inc., for $6,500 cash. He received by mistake from Kilbourn a title certificate for a similar but different vehicle. Kilbourn later borrowed money from a bank and gave the correct title certificate for Mann's

car to the bank as security for the loan. The bank claims that Mann does not have title to the car because he did not receive the title certificate. Is the bank correct? Why or why not? *National Exch. Bank v. Mann,* 260 N.W.2d 716 (Wisconsin).

6. Martin Silver ordered two rooms of custom-made furniture from Wycombe, Meyer & Co., Inc. The price was $7,053 plus delivery, and all invoices provided for shipment to Silver's home "Truck prepaid." Wycombe notified Silver when the furniture was ready to be delivered. Silver paid for the furniture in full and directed Wycombe to ship one room of the furniture but to hold the other until instructed further. Wycombe did as directed. Before any instructions were received regarding the second room of furniture, the furniture was destroyed by fire. Who must suffer the loss, Silver or Wycombe? Explain. *Silver v. Wycombe, Meyer & Co., Inc.,* 477 N.Y.S.2d 288 (New York).

7. Eberhard Manufacturing Company sold goods to Brown Industrial Sales Company without agreeing on who would bear the risk of loss. The contract contained no f.o.b. terms. Eberhard placed the goods on board a common carrier with instructions to deliver them to Brown. The goods were lost in transit. Who will suffer the loss, Eberhard or Brown? Why? *Eberhard Mfg. Co. v. Brown,* 232 N.W.2d 378 (Michigan).

8. Henry Heide, Incorporated, received a warehouse receipt for 3,200 100-pound bags of sugar which it bought from Olavarria. The corporation withdrew 800 bags of the sugar from the warehouse (which had thousands of pounds stored there), but when it returned for the balance, it discovered that the warehouse was padlocked and empty. Some 200,000 pounds of sugar had mysteriously disappeared from it. Henry Heide, Incorporated, carried insurance for such a loss, but its insurance company refused to pay, claiming that the corporation had no insurable interest in the sugar. Do you agree with the insurance company? Why or why not? *Henry Heide, Inc. v. Atlantic Mut. Ins. Co.,* 363 N.Y.S.2d 515 (New York).

CHAPTER 16
Warranties and Product Liability

OUTLINE

16-1 Express Warranties
- Statement of Fact or Promise
- Description of the Goods
- Sample or Model
- Magnuson-Moss Warranty Act

16-2 Implied Warranties
- Merchantability
- Fitness for a Particular Purpose
- Usage of Trade

16-3 Warranty of Title

16-4 Exclusion of Warranties

16-5 Duty to Notify Seller of Defective Product

16-6 Privity Not Required

16-7 Product Liability
- Negligence
- Strict Liability

COMMENTARY

Have you ever bought from a store or other business establishment something that did not work or that broke the first time you used it? Have you ever relied on a salesperson's promise that did not come true? Have you ever purchased food that was inedible or clothing that was defective? Have you ever purchased something that turned out to be different from the sample or model shown to you earlier? Have you ever been injured by a dangerous product? In each of these situations, you were protected by either the law of warranties or the law of product liability.

Warranty and product liability laws are important for everyone involved in the marketing process. Manufacturers, for example, guarantee their products to retailers, who, in turn, guarantee them to consumers. In this way, all parties connected with the sale of a product are given protection. Sometimes, manufacturers guarantee their products directly to consumers as an incentive to buy their product. The guarantees are known as warranties. Product liability laws place responsibility on manufacturers and sellers when products they make or sell are unreasonably dangerous.

OBJECTIVES

1. Describe the three ways in which an express warranty may be created.
2. State the requirements of the Magnuson-Moss Warranty Act.
3. Compare the meaning of a "limited" warranty with the meaning of a "full" warranty.
4. Differentiate between the implied warranty of fitness for a particular purpose and the implied warranty of merchantability.
5. Explain the warranty of title.
6. Recognize the ways in which warranties may be excluded.

7. Describe the duty to notify sellers of a defective product.
8. Determine the persons to whom warranties are made under the law of your state.
9. State why it is often difficult for a consumer to win a product liability case on the theory of negligence.
10. Explain what an injured party must prove to recover from the manufacturer of a dangerous and defective product.

16-1 EXPRESS WARRANTIES

UCC 2-313
(see p. 620)

A warranty is another name for a guarantee. An **express warranty** is an oral or written statement, promise, or other representation about the quality of a product. Express warranties arise in three different ways: by a statement of fact or promise, by a description of the goods, and by a sample or model.

Statement of Fact or Promise

UCC 2-313(1)(2)
(see p. 620)

Whenever a seller of goods makes a statement of fact about the goods to a buyer as part of the transaction, an express warranty is created. The seller's statement is treated legally as a guarantee that the goods will be as they were stated to be. This is true whether the seller is a merchant or not. If the goods are not as they were stated to be, the seller has breached an express warranty.

Candella went into a furniture store and told the clerk that he wanted a mahogany table. The clerk showed Candella a table and said that it was made of solid mahogany. Soon after buying it, Candella learned that the table was made of pressed wood covered by a mahogany veneer. The statement by the clerk was an express warranty that the table was made of solid mahogany. Candella would be able to sue the store for breach of the express warranty if the store refused to remedy the situation.

An express warranty also occurs when a seller makes a promise about the goods to the buyer. The promise must relate to the goods and be part of the transaction.

Boehm, a farmer, purchased 50 pounds of feed additive called Proto-Tone 316 Medicated from Triple F Feeds. The salesperson from Triple F had told Boehm that the additive would not hurt the dairy cattle and that milk production would increase by 25 percent. In fact, the additive caused milk production to decline, and the cattle refused to eat. The cows had to be sold at half their value. The court held that the promises made by the salesperson were express warranties, which were breached when they failed to come true.

Manufacturers often include express warranties with the products they sell. They are usually found inside the package containing the product and are sometimes referred to as guarantees.

Fields bought a microwave oven for her mother as a birthday gift. In the package with the oven was a card that said, "Full one-year warranty. If, within one year from the date of purchase, this microwave oven fails due to a defect in material or workmanship, this company will repair or replace it, free of charge." This promise by the company was an express warranty.

Formal words such as *warrant* or *guarantee* do not have to be used to create an express warranty. A seller may not intend to make a warranty, but if the language used by the seller is a statement of fact or a promise about the goods and is part of the transaction, an express warranty is created. Advertisements often contain statements and promises about goods which are express warranties.

Twentieth Century Auto Polish was advertised as a safe, noncorrosive polish, manufactured to the highest standards required of finishes. Rankin bought a can of the polish, and it ruined the finish of her new car. Rankin could seek damages against the manufacturer, claiming that the advertised statements were warranties made to any prospective purchaser.

Warranties are based on statements of fact. Opinions of salespersons, exaggerated and persuasive statements, and the like are not included. Courts have long recognized the temptation of salespersons to indulge in "sales puffery," or extolling their wares beyond the point of fact. Buyers must use good judgment in separating a seller's statements of fact from those statements that are only opinion, or puffing. Such statements as "this is the best television set on the market," or "this VCR is a good buy," are examples of sales talk, or puffing. They are not express warranties.

Description of the Goods

UCC 2-313(1)(b) **(see p. 620)**

Any description of the goods that is made part of the basis of the bargain creates an express warranty that the goods will be as described.

Kincaid ordered a gas grill from a catalog. The catalog description said that the grill contained a swing-away warming rack. The grill that was delivered, however, had a fixed warming rack. Kincaid would have a cause of action against the seller for breach of express warranty in the event that the seller refused to remedy the situation.

Sample or Model

It is a common practice of salespeople to show samples of their products to prospective buyers. When this is done, and a sample or model becomes part of the

UCC 2-313(1)(c) (see p. 620)

basis of the bargain, an express warranty is created. The seller warrants that the goods which are delivered will be the same as the sample or model.

A company that manufactured sausage-stuffing machines contracted to buy various castings from a foundry. The castings were to conform to samples that the foundry had made according to plans submitted by the manufacturing company. When the castings were delivered, the company rejected them because they were not the same as the samples. The foundry had breached its express warranty, giving the company the right to rescind the contract.

Magnuson-Moss Warranty Act

The Magnuson-Moss Warranty Act was passed in 1975 to prevent deceptive warranty practices and to provide consumers with more information about warranties that are made on products they buy. The act applies only when written warranties are made voluntarily on **consumer products.** These are defined as tangible personal property normally used for personal, family, or household purposes. Because it is a federal law, the act affects only warranties on products that are sold in interstate commerce.

Under the act, when a written warranty is given to a consumer on goods costing more than $10, all the following must be done:

1. The written warranty must be made available before the consumer decides to buy the product.
2. The writing must express the terms and conditions of the warranty in simple and readily understood language.
3. The warranty must disclose whether it is a full or a limited warranty.

A **full warranty** is one in which a defective product will be repaired without charge within a reasonable time after a complaint has been made about it. If it cannot be repaired within a reasonable time, the consumer may have either a replacement of the product or a refund of the purchase price. The consumer will not have to do anything unreasonable to get warranty service, such as ship a heavy product to the factory. A full warranty applies to anyone who owns the product during the warranty period, not only the original buyer. A full warranty must also state its duration, as, for example, a "full one-year warranty."

Kienitz bought an electric range manufactured by a well-known firm. Attached to the box containing the range were several papers, one of which read: "Full one-year warranty. If your range fails because of a manufacturing defect within one year from the date of original purchase, we will repair the product without charge to you. Parts and service labor are included. Service will be provided in your home in the forty-eight contiguous states, the state of Hawaii, or in the District of Columbia." This was a full warranty. The range would be repaired or replaced at no cost to the consumer if it turned out to be defective.

Limited Twelve Month Warranty

This **Beauty Plus** appliance is warranted against defect in material or workmanship for twelve months from the date of purchase. Any problems arising from misuse, dropping, or extreme wear are not covered by this warranty.

The store where this item was purchased is authorized to make an exchange only if the return is made within 30 days of purchase. Returns after 30 days must be made to the **Beauty Plus Service Center,** P.O. Box 608, Middletown, Ohio 44900. Send it postage paid along with proof of purchase, a note explaining reason for return, and $4.00 to cover handling, insurance, and return postage costs.

Any product returned for repair not under the warranty will be repaired and/or returned, all charges C.O.D.

© 1987 Beauty Plus, Appliance Div.

Figure 16-1 This is a limited warranty because the return must be made within 30 days of purchase.

A **limited warranty** is any written warranty that does not meet all the requirements for a full warranty. The consumer is not given the absolute, free-of-charge repair or replacement of a defective product as is given in the full warranty. Something less than a complete remedy is given to a consumer.

Farver, who lived in Alaska, bought an electric range similar to the one bought by Kienitz in the above example. Attached to the box containing the range was a paper which read: "Limited warranty applicable to the state of Alaska. In the state of Alaska free service, including parts, will be provided to correct manufacturing defects at our nearest service shop location or in your home, but we do not cover the cost of transportation of the product to the shop or the travel costs of a technician to your home. You are responsible for these costs. All other provisions of this limited warranty are the same as those stated in the above warranties [referring to full warranties]." This was a limited warranty because it included a charge to the consumer.

Other examples of limited warranties are those which (*a*) cover only parts, not labor (*b*) allow only a *pro-rata* refund or credit in the case of a defect rather than a full refund, (*c*) require the buyer to return a heavy product to the store for service, or (*d*) cover only the first purchaser.

16-2 IMPLIED WARRANTIES

An **implied warranty** is a warranty imposed by law rather than by statements, descriptions, or samples given by the seller. It arises independently and outside the contract. The law annexes it or writes it, by implication, into the contract that the parties have made. Implied warranties are designed to promote high standards in business and to discourage harsh dealings. There are three types of implied warranties: the implied warranty of merchantability, the implied warranty of fitness for a particular purpose, and the implied warranty which is derived from a course of dealing or usage of trades.

Merchantability

UCC 2-314(1) **(see p. 620)**

One of the most beneficial warranties, from the point of view of a buyer, is the implied **warranty of merchantability.** The warranty is this: Unless excluded in one of the ways discussed below, whenever a merchant sells goods, the merchant warrants that the goods are merchantable. This warranty is given when the seller is a merchant with respect to goods of that kind. It is given by manufacturers, wholesalers, and retailers whenever they sell goods to give assurance that products sold by them are fit for the purpose for which the goods are to be used. The warranty of merchantability is not given by someone who is not a merchant.

Perez bought a secondhand car for $3,500 from Osgood, a private party. Perez drove the car home, parked it in her driveway, and turned off the engine. The next morning, the car would not start. The automobile mechanic who was called to try to start the car informed Perez that it would cost $1,200 to repair the car so that it would start properly. Perez cannot sue Osgood for breach of warranty of merchantability because Osgood was not a merchant.

UCC 2-314(2) **(see p. 620)**

To be merchantable, goods must at least (1) pass without objection in the trade under the contract description; (2) if fungible goods, be of fair average quality; (3) be fit for the ordinary purposes for which such goods are used; (4) be of the same kind, quality, and quantity; (5) be adequately contained, packaged, and labeled as the agreement may require; and (6) conform to any promises or statements of fact made on the container or label.

If Osgood had been a merchant, in the preceding case, Perez could have sued him for breach of warranty of merchantability. An automobile that will not start is not fit for the ordinary purposes for which automobiles are used.

A claim for breach of warranty of merchantability can be made only when a defect exists at the time the goods are purchased.

Haven Hills Farm purchased a truck tire from Sears, Roebuck. On a trip from Mississippi to Alabama the tire blew out, causing the truck to turn on its side, destroying 11,862 dozen eggs. At the time of the blowout, the tire was 4½ months old and had been driven 30,000 miles. Haven Hills claimed that Sears was liable for breach of the implied warranty of merchantability. It argued that Sears sold the tire in a defective condition. In finding in favor of Sears, Roebuck, the court held that there was no evidence of a defect in the tire at the time it left the control of the manufacturer or seller.

The courts have held the following to be nonmerchantable: day-old chickens with bird cancer; contaminated blood received in a blood transfusion; applesauce that was inedible because of poor taste and smell; contaminated cheese; and food containing impurities, such as bits of wood, metal, or glass.

Fitness for a Particular Purpose

UCC 2-315
(see p. 620)

Sometimes, buyers will have the seller select goods for them rather than select them themselves. They rely on the seller's knowledge and experience to choose the product after telling the seller of the particular use they have for the goods. This creates the implied **warranty of fitness for a particular purpose.** When the buyer relies on the seller's skill and judgment to select the goods, the seller impliedly warrants that the goods will be fit for the purpose for which they are to be used.

McGuire purchased a television set in a store that had a sign on the wall declaring, "No refunds! All sales final!" McGuire told the clerk that she needed a cable to connect the new set to her VCR. The clerk went to the shelf, selected a cable, and told McGuire that the cable would do the job. That evening, McGuire discovered that the cable would not fit the VCR. Even though the sign said that all sales were final, McGuire would be able to return the cable. McGuire relied on the store clerk's judgment in selecting the cable, creating a warranty that the cable would connect to the VCR.

Usage of Trade

UCC 2-314(3)
(see p. 620)

Other implied warranties may arise from ways in which the parties have dealt in the past or by usage of trade. For example, when a person sells a pedigreed dog, there is an implied warranty that the seller will provide pedigree papers to evidence conformity of the animal to the contract. The reason this implied warranty arises is that providing such papers has become a well-established custom or practice of the trade.

16-3 WARRANTY OF TITLE

UCC 2-312(1)
(see pp. 619–620)

Whenever goods are sold, either by a merchant or a private party, the seller warrants that the title being conveyed is good and that the transfer is rightful. This warranty is known as the **warranty of title.** It includes an implied promise that the goods will be delivered free from any liens (claims of others) about which the buyer has no knowledge. When anyone buys goods that turn out to be stolen, the rightful owner will be entitled to the return of the goods. The innocent purchaser may sue the seller for breach of warranty of title.

Lopez bought a racing bicycle from Perkins at a yard sale for $125. Shortly thereafter, Lopez learned that the bicycle had been stolen from Garcia. Garcia, the true owner, would be entitled to the return of the bicycle. Lopez's rights would be against Perkins for breach of warranty of title.

When the buyer is aware that the person selling the goods does not personally claim title to them, the warranty of title is not made by the seller. This is the case in such sales as sheriff's sales and sales by personal representatives of estates.

16-4 EXCLUSION OF WARRANTIES

UCC 2-316(2)
(see p. 620)

Except when express warranties are made under the Magnuson-Moss Warranty Act, sellers may exclude or modify implied warranties by stating that no warranties are given when a contract for sale is made. Special rules, however, must be followed. To exclude the implied warranty of merchantability, the word *merchantability* must be used in the disclaimer. If the exclusion is in writing, it must be in large, bold type so that it is conspicuous. To exclude the implied warranty of fitness for a particular purpose, the exclusion must be in writing and also be conspicuous.

Valdez bought a used car from Kinkaid Motors, Inc., for $2,095. Printed on the sales slip, which Valdez signed, were the following words in large, bold capital letters: "THE SELLER HEREBY EXCLUDES THE WARRANTY OF MERCHANTABILITY AND FITNESS FOR A PARTICULAR PURPOSE." Two days later, when the car broke down, Valdez had no recourse against the car dealer for breach of either of the implied warranties.

UCC 2-316(3)(a)
(see pp. 620–621)

A common practice in the sale of used cars, lawnmowers, electrical appliances, and similar merchandise is for the seller to stipulate that the goods are being sold as is. The use of such expressions as *as is, with all faults,* and others is another way to exclude implied warranties. However, those words do not exclude the warranty of title.

UCC 2-316(3)(b) **(see p. 621)**

Implied warranties may also be excluded under the UCC by having buyers examine the goods. When buyers have examined the goods or the sample or model as fully as they desire (or have refused to examine them when given the opportunity), there is no implied warranty as to defects that an examination would have revealed.

Under the Magnuson-Moss Warranty Act, any clause purporting to exclude or limit consequential damages for breach of warranty must appear conspicuously on the face of the warranty. **Consequential damages** are losses which do not flow directly and immediately from an act but only from some of the consequences or results of the act.

Souci bought a freezer made by a reputable manufacturer, carrying a full one-year warranty. The following sentence appeared in boldface type on the face of the warranty: "In no event shall this company be liable for consequential damages." Shortly after buying the freezer, Souci filled it with $1,500 worth of meat. Several days later, the freezer stopped working owing to a defect in its manufacture. Under the warranty, the company will have to either repair or replace the freezer, but it is not responsible for the loss of the meat. This loss is considered to be a consequential damage, which the company had effectively disclaimed.

The Magnuson-Moss Warranty Act places limits on the exclusion of implied warranties to consumers. Under the act, if either a full or limited express warranty is made to a consumer, the implied warranties of merchantability and fitness for a particular purpose may not be excluded during the warranty period. This law also applies if the seller gives the buyer a service contract.

16-5 DUTY TO NOTIFY SELLER OF DEFECTIVE PRODUCT

UCC 2-607(3)(a) **(see p. 630)**

In order to recover money damages for breach of warranty, buyers of defective goods must notify the seller of the defect within a reasonable time after the discovery or within a reasonable time after the defect should have been discovered. Failure to do so will prevent them from recovering damages for breach of warranty.

Shortly after buying an electric stove from an appliance store, Schloss discovered that the self-cleaning unit of the stove did not work. She did not get around to notifying the store of the defect until seven months later. Because of the delay in notifying the store of the defect, Schloss lost the right to recover from the store for breach of the implied warranty of merchantability.

16-6 PRIVITY NOT REQUIRED

UCC 2-318 (see p. 621)

Under earlier law, warranties extended only to the actual buyer of the product, that is, the one with whom the seller had dealt or was in privity of contract. People who were injured by defective products had no remedy against the seller for breach of warranty unless they themselves had purchased the goods. Thus, if children were injured by foreign objects in food that had been bought by their parents, the children could not recover for injuries because they had not purchased the goods. The UCC has abolished the requirement of privity. Instead, it provides three alternatives from which a state may choose. In all of the alternatives, warranties extend to people who would normally be expected to use the goods as well as to those who actually buy them.

Alternative A A seller's warranty whether express or implied extends to any natural person who is in the family or household of his buyer or who is a guest in his home if it is reasonable to expect that such person may use, consume or be affected by the goods and who is injured in person by breach of the warranty. A seller may not exclude or limit the operation of this section.

Alternative B A seller's warranty whether express or implied extends to any natural person who may reasonably be expected to use, consume or be affected by

Table 16-1 UCC ALTERNATIVES TO PRIVITY*

State	Alternative	State	Alternative
Alabama	B	Montana	A
Alaska	A	Nebraska	A
Arizona	A	Nevada	A
Arkansas	A	New Hampshire	Own version
California	None adopted	New Jersey	A
Colorado	B	New Mexico	A
Connecticut	A	New York	Own version
Delaware	B	North Carolina	A
District of Columbia	A	North Dakota	C
Florida	A	Ohio	A
Georgia	A	Oklahoma	A
Hawaii	C	Oregon	A
Idaho	A	Pennsylvania	A
Illinois	A	Rhode Island	Own version
Indiana	A	South Carolina	A
Iowa	C	South Dakota	B
Kansas	B	Tennessee	A
Kentucky	A	Texas	Own version
Louisiana	None adopted	Utah	C
Maine	Own version	Vermont	B
Maryland	A	Virginia	Own version
Massachusetts	Own version	Washington	A
Michigan	A	West Virginia	A
Minnesota	C	Wisconsin	A
Mississippi	A	Wyoming	B
Missouri	A		

*See page 607.

the goods and who is injured in person by breach of the warranty. A seller may not exclude or limit the operation of this section.

Alternative C A seller's warranty whether express or implied extends to any person who may reasonably be expected to use, consume or be affected by the goods and who is injured by breach of the warranty. A seller may not exclude or limit the operation of this section with respect to injury to the person of an individual to whom the warranty extends.

Most states have adopted one of the alternatives provided in the UCC. A few states, however, have written their own version of the law. Table 16-1 indicates the alternative that has been adopted by each state.

16-7 PRODUCT LIABILITY

One of the most important areas of law for consumers today is known as **product liability**. Under this law, which is a tort rather than a breach of contract, a buyer or user of a product who is injured because of the product's unsafe or defective condition may recover damages from the manufacturer, the seller, or the supplier of the goods. Injuries to persons or damage to property caused by defects in design and manufacture give consumers a right to seek recovery under the law of product liability.

Product liability suits are usually based on either of two legal theories, negligence or strict liability—both of which are tort actions.

Negligence

One legal theory that is available to people who are injured by faulty products is negligence. This tort, which is explained more fully in Chapter 4, may be defined as the failure to exercise that degree of care which a reasonably prudent person would have exercised under the same circumstances and conditions. In order to recover for negligence in a product liability case, it is necessary to prove all of the following:

1. That there was a negligent act on the part of the manufacturer or supplier of the goods
2. That injuries were suffered by someone who used the goods
3. That the injuries were caused by the negligent act

It is not easy for an injured consumer to win a case on the theory of negligence. This is because injured parties usually have no evidence of a negligent act by the manufacturer. They were not present when the goods were made and normally have very little information about the manufacturing process. Injured parties are often more successful in bringing suit for breach of warranty of merchantability rather than negligence.

Valez was driving on an interstate highway in a brand-new automobile she had purchased a week earlier. She was traveling at the speed limit of 55 miles per hour. Suddenly she heard something snap. The car veered off the highway and smashed into a tree. Valez was thrown out of the car and received back, leg, and neck injuries. A mechanic who inspected the vehicle after the accident discovered that there was no fluid in the car's steering mechanism and that there was a strong burning odor. There was no evidence, however, as to why the fluid was missing. Valez could not recover on the theory of negligence because she was unable to prove a negligent act on the part of the manufacturer or seller of the automobile. She would be able to recover for breach of warranty because an automobile with a defective steering mechanism is not merchantable.

Strict Liability

Under the doctrine of strict liability, it is not necessary to prove a negligent act on the part of the manufacturer or seller when someone is injured by a defective product. **Strict liability** is a legal theory, adopted by two-thirds of the states, which imposes liability on manufacturers or suppliers for selling goods which are unreasonably dangerous, without regard to fault or negligence. The principal consideration under the doctrine of strict liability is the safety of the product, not the conduct of the manufacturer or supplier of the goods. Under this rule of law, manufacturers have the duty to design reasonably safe products. They must also give proper instructions for the product's use and provide warnings of possible danger.

It is difficult to recover damages under the strict liability doctrine. People who are injured or who suffer property damage from a defective product may recover from the manufacturer or seller only if they can prove all of the following:

1. The manufacturer or seller sold the product in a defective condition.
2. The manufacturer or seller was engaged in the business of selling the product.
3. The product was unreasonably dangerous to the user or consumer.
4. The defective condition was the proximate cause of the injury or damage.
5. The defective condition existed at the time it left the hands of the manufacturer or seller.
6. The consumer sustained physical harm or property damage by use or consumption of the product.

The defective condition may arise through faulty product design, faulty manufacturing, inadequate warning of danger, or improper instructions for the product's use.

Stewart stood on the lifting platform of a forklift and caused it to raise him to a rack 16 feet above the floor level so that he could inventory some ball bearings. Suddenly, the lift apparatus failed. The platform fell to the floor, and Stewart was seriously injured. The cause of the failure was attributed to negligent repair work performed a few days earlier by Scott-Kitz Miller Co., a company responsible for maintenance of the equipment. Scott employees had removed some bolts holding the lift guide and reinserted them backward. In this position, the bolts protruded in such a way that when an attempt was made to lower the raised platform, the lift assembly would hang at the top of the mast, then fall to the floor.

The court held that the forklift was defectively designed. It would have required very little effort or expense to design the bolts so that they could not accidentally be inserted backward.

The manufacturer's and seller's liability extends to all persons who may be injured by the product. Injured bystanders, guests, or others who have no relationship with the product, the seller, or the manufacturer may seek damages caused by defects in the offending product.

Ryder Truck Rental rented a truck to Jackson. While Jackson was waiting for a light to change, the truck moved forward owing to a faulty brake system. Martin, in another car, was injured when the truck hit her car. The Delaware Supreme Court ruled, on appeal, that Ryder could be held liable even without proof of its negligence. It was only necessary for the injured party to prove that the truck had an unreasonably dangerous product design that caused personal injury or property damage to the plaintiffs.

Duty to Warn Sometimes a duty is placed upon manufacturers to warn consumers that harm may result from a product. Unavoidably unsafe products may require a warning to inform the consumer of possible harm. If the warning is adequate, consumers may be required to use the product at their own risk. A warning must specify the risk presented by the product and give a reason for the warning.

Palmer, an 11-year-old boy, received injuries necessitating the amputation of his leg well above the knee when his left leg got caught in the agitator of the fertilizer spreader on which he was riding. The following warning was placed by the manufacturer in front of the spreader near the operator's controls:

Figure 16-2

The court held that this warning was inadequate because it did not specify the danger presented by the agitator. It was too general. It did not detail the extent of the risk it posed to life and limb.

Punitive Damages In addition to recovering damages to compensate them for their losses, injured parties in strict liability cases sometimes recover punitive damages. These are a monetary penalty imposed as a punishment for a wrongdoing.

Four-year-old Lee Ann Gryc was clothed in pajamas made from a cotton material manufactured by Riegel Textile Corporation. The material was commercially known as flannelette. It was not treated and did not meet the minimum federal standards of flammability. Lee Ann reached across the electric stove in her home to shut off a timer. Her pajamas were instantly ignited, and she received severe burns over her upper body. The jury found Riegel Textile Corporation liable for these injuries and awarded Lee Ann $750,000 in compensatory damages and $1,000,000 in punitive damages.

SUMMARY

16-1. Express warranties arise by a statement of fact or promise, by a description of the goods, and by a sample or model. Federal law requires that written warranties on consumer products be labeled as either "full" or "limited" warranties.

16-2. When merchants sell goods, they warrant that the goods are merchantable. In addition, when a buyer relies on the seller's skill and judgment in selecting the goods, the seller warrants that the goods will be fit for the purpose for which they are to be used. Other warranties may arise from ways in which parties have dealt in the past.

16-3. When goods are sold, either by a merchant or a private party, the seller warrants that the title is good and that there are no liens on the goods.

16-4. Except when express warranties are made, sellers may exclude the warranties of merchantability and fitness for a particular purpose. Such an exclusion must be in writing and conspicuous. The words *as is* and *with all faults* serve to disclaim implied warranties but not the warranty of title.

16-5. To be able to sue for breach of warranty, a buyer of defective goods must notify the seller of the defect within a reasonable time after discovering the defect.

16-6. Warranties extend to people who would normally be expected to use the goods as well as to those who actually buy them.

16-7. Buyers who are injured from unsafe or defective products may sometimes recover damages from the manufacturer, seller, or supplier of the goods under product liability laws. Lawsuits are brought under either of two theories, negligence or strict liability.

Understanding Key Legal Terms

consequential damages (p. 204)
consumer products (p. 199)
express warranty (p. 197)
full warranty (p. 199)
implied warranty (p. 201)
limited warranty (p. 200)
product liability (p. 206)
strict liability (p. 207)
warranty of fitness for a particular purpose (p. 202)
warranty of merchantability (p. 201)
warranty of title (p. 203)

Questions for Review and Discussion

1. In what three ways may express warranties by created?
2. Under the Magnuson-Moss Warranty Act, what must be done when a written warranty is given to a consumer?
3. What is the difference between a full warranty and a limited warranty?
4. When does the implied warranty of fitness for a particular purpose arise? When and by whom is the warranty of merchantability given?
5. Describe the warranty of title that is made by a seller of goods.
6. What special rules must be followed to exclude the warranties of merchantability and fitness for a particular purpose? In what other ways may warranties be excluded?
7. Describe the buyer's duty to notify the seller of a breach of warranty when a buyer seeks to recover damages for the breach.
8. What provision does the UCC make relative to privity of contract under the law of warranties?
9. Why is it often difficult for a consumer to win a product liability case on the theory of negligence?
10. What must an injured party prove to recover from a manufacturer for strict liability?

Analyzing Cases

1. Shaffer ordered a glass of rosé wine at the Victoria Station Restaurant. As he took his first sip of wine, the glass broke in his hand, causing permanent injuries. Shaffer brought suit against the restaurant for breach of warranty of merchantability. The restaurant's position was that since it did not sell the wineglass to Shaffer (only its contents), it was not a merchant with respect to the glass, and therefore made no warranty. Do you agree with the restaurant? Why or why not? *Shaffer v. Victoria Station, Inc.*, 588 P.2d 233 (Washington).

2. McCoy bought an antique pistol from the Old Fort Trading Post for $1,000. Later, the gun was taken from McCoy by the police when they learned that it was stolen property. The police turned the gun over to the rightful owner. McCoy notified the Old Fort Trading Post of what had happened and asked for the return of his money, but the

owner of the business refused to give him a refund. What remedy, if any, does McCoy have against the owner of the trading post? Explain. *Trial v. McCoy,* 553 S.W.2d 199 (Texas).

3. Werner purchased a sloop from Montana for $13,250. During the negotiations before the sale, Montana had told Werner that the sloop would "make up" when placed in the water and become watertight. Werner placed the sloop in the water and allowed sufficient time for the planking to swell, or "make up," to form a watertight hull, but it still leaked and could not be sailed. He then discovered extensive dry rot in the hull and learned that the cost of repairs would be substantial. Montana refused to take the sloop back and refund Werner's purchase price. Does Werner have a cause of action against Montana? If so, on what grounds? Explain. *Werner v. Montana,* 378 A.2d 1130 (New Hampshire).

4. Romedy bought a car from Willett Lincoln-Mercury, Inc. He did not inspect it until 4 or 5 days after it was delivered to him. Three weeks later, he notified the dealer that the car did not contain the equipment that the dealer had said it would contain. He did, however, continue to make payments on the car. Later, he brought suit against the dealer for breach of warranty. Will he recover? Explain. *Romedy v. Willett Lincoln-Mercury, Inc.,* 220 S.E.2d 74 (Georgia).

5. Mr. and Mrs. Benfer bought a mobile home from Thomas, a mobile home retailer. Prior to the purchase, Thomas had told them that the type of mobile home he carried had a ¼-inch sheathing on the siding that made it better than cheaper units. Thomas showed them a model of the mobile home that he carried and pointed out to them the grade of plywood sheathing that was on the model. When the mobile home was delivered to them, they were given several written warranties signed by the manufacturer, Town & Country Mobile Homes, Inc., including one which specifically warranted that the mobile home was sheathed with ¼-inch plywood beneath the prefinished aluminum exterior wall surface. Later, the Benfers discovered that their mobile home did not contain this sheathing. Do they have a cause of action against the retailer, Thomas? Why or why not? *Town & Country Mobile Homes, Inc., v. Benfer,* 527 S.W.2d 523 (Texas).

6. Hensley bought a used Plymouth automobile from Colonial Dodge, Inc. The following language was written in small print on the back of the purchase agreement: "No warranties, expressed or implied, are made by the dealer with respect to used motor vehicles or motor vehicle chassis furnished hereunder except as may be expressed in writing by the dealer." After driving only three or four blocks, Hensley noticed that the windshield wipers and the brake lights were not working properly. He returned the car to the dealer to correct the problems. When he next received the car, it started to lose compression and slowed down to 20 or 25 miles per hour before he got halfway home. The engine sounded as if it were "missing quite badly." After arriving home, which was about six miles from the dealer's place of business, Hensley was unable to get the car started again. An investigation revealed that the car needed a new engine, which the dealer refused to provide. May Hensley recover from the dealer for breach of warranty? Why or why not? *Hensley v. Colonial Dodge, Inc.,* 245 N.W.2d 142 (Michigan).

7. Paul and Cynthia Vance invited Carl and Jeanne Leichtamer to go for a ride in the Vances' four-wheel drive jeep at an "off the road" recreation facility called the Hall of Fame Four-Wheel Club. The club had been organized by a jeep dealer who showed films to club members of jeeps traveling in hilly country. This activity was coupled

with a national advertising program of American Motor Sales Corporation encouraging people to buy jeeps that could drive up and down steep hills. As the jeep went up a 33-degree sloped, double-terraced hill, it pitched over from front to back and landed upside down. The Vances were killed, and the Leichtamers were severely injured. The jeep was equipped with a factory-installed roll bar attached to the sheet metal that housed the rear wheels. When the vehicle landed upside down, the flat sheet metal gave way, causing the roll bar to move forward and downward 14 inches. The Leichtamers argue that the weakness of the sheet metal housing upon which the roll bar had been attached was the cause of their injuries. The manufacturer claims that the roll bar was provided solely for side-roll protection, not pitchover, as occurred in this case. Can the Leichtamers recover against the manufacturer on a theory of strict liability? Why or why not? *Leichtamer v. American Motors Corp.*, 424 N.E.2d 568 (Ohio).

8. Michael P. Babine was injured when he was thrown from an "El Toro" mechanical bull that he rode at a nightclub. The club had placed mattresses around the bull to cushion the fall of riders, but the mattresses were not adequately pushed together. Babine was thrown off during his ride, and hit his head on the floor at a place where there was a gap between the mattresses. Before riding the bull, Babine had signed a form releasing the nightclub from liability for injuries sustained from the activity. The mechanical bull had been manufactured for the purpose of being a training device for rodeo cowboys and was purchased secondhand by the nightclub. Babine seeks to recover damages from the manufacturer under the theory of product liability? Will he succeed? Why or why not? *Babine v. Gilley's Bronco Shop, Inc.*, 488 So.2d 176 (Florida).

CHAPTER 17
Performance and Breach of the Sales Contract

OUTLINE

COMMENTARY

Most contracts are completed by performance; that is, the parties do what they agreed to do. Usually, this means that the seller delivers the goods without any defects and the buyer pays for them. At this point, their obligations come to an end. Occasionally, however, one or both of the parties fail to abide by the agreement. The seller delivers faulty goods or no goods at all. The buyer refuses to accept the goods or fails to pay for them. The UCC has special rules to address these various situations.

OBJECTIVES

1. Discuss, generally, the obligations of the parties to a sales contract.
2. Determine whether the requirements for tender of delivery and tender of payment have been met in given cases.
3. Explain the buyer's right to inspect goods.
4. Describe the buyer's rights and duties when improper goods are delivered.
5. Judge, in given cases, whether the seller has the right to correct an improper tender of delivery.
6. Compare the remedies that are available to the seller with those available to the buyer when sales contracts are breached.

17-1 OBLIGATIONS OF THE PARTIES

UCC 1-203 **(see p. 613)**

The obligations of the parties to a sales contract are simple and straightforward. The seller is obligated to turn the goods over to the buyer, and the buyer is obligated to accept and pay for them, both acting in accordance with the terms of the contract. In addition, all parties must act in **good faith**. This means that they must act honestly.

UCC 2-302 **(see p. 618)**

The court need not enforce a contract or part of a contract that it finds to be unconscionable. An **unconscionable contract** is one that is so one-sided that it is oppressive and gives unfair advantage to one of the parties. Unequal bargaining power, the absence of a meaningful choice by one party, and unreasonably one-sided terms, when put together, are indications of unconscionability.

UCC 1-205 **(see p. 613)**

When disputes arise between parties who have dealt together in the past, the court often looks to their past dealings to give meaning to the disputed transaction. When interpreting the meaning of contracts, the court may also consider any usage of trade, that is, any particular methods of doing business, that are commonly used in that field. Although terms which are expressly stated in a contract will usually control the contract's meaning, the parties' past dealings and usage of trade are often looked at to supplement or qualify the express terms.

Associated Hardware Supply Co. negotiated with Big Wheel Distributing Company for the purchase of merchandise. The parties could not agree on pricing the goods. Associated Hardware wanted to pay cost plus 10 percent, while Big Wheel insisted on dealer-catalog less 11 percent. Although the parties exchanged letters, there was never any formal agreement on pricing. Over a two-year period, Associated Hardware ordered goods from Big Wheel amounting to more than $850,000, paying for them on a dealer-catalog-less-11-percent basis. Later, when an additional $40,000 was owed for merchandise purchased, Associated Hardware refused to pay, claiming that no agreement had been reached as to the pricing of the goods. Finding in favor of Big Wheel, the court attached great weight to the way the parties had dealt in the past. It held that the parties' course of dealing for the two-year period governed the sale of the remaining merchandise.

17-2 TENDER OF PERFORMANCE

Tender of performance occurs when the seller offers to turn the goods over to the buyer and when the buyer offers to pay for them. It is the offering by the parties to do what they have agreed to do under the terms of the contract. Tender is necessary in order to test the other party's ability and willingness to perform his or her part of the bargain. The seller must make tender of delivery, and the buyer must make tender of payment. If either party fails to do this and the other breaches the contract, the one not making tender cannot bring suit.

Tender of Delivery by Seller

To be in a position to bring suit on a sales contract, the seller of goods must make **tender of delivery,** that is, offer to turn the goods over to the buyer. Failure to do this is an excuse for buyers not to perform their part of the bargain.

UCC 2-507 (see p. 627)

Manner of Seller's Tender To make proper tender, the seller must put and hold conforming goods at the buyer's disposition during a reasonable hour of the day.

Gipsum Canning Co. agreed to sell 1,000 cases of canned beets to Green Grocers for $8.40 a case. Before shipping the goods, however, Gipsum was offered $9.60 a case from another company. Gipsum delivered the 1,000 cases of beets to Green Grocers' loading platform at 3 o'clock in the morning. Finding no one there, Gipsum took the goods and sold them to the other company at the higher price. When sued, Gipsum claimed that Green Grocers had breached the contract by not accepting the goods when they were tendered at the loading platform. The court disagreed, saying that Gipsum did not put and hold the goods at the buyer's disposition during a reasonable hour of the day.

UCC 2-503(1)(b) (see p. 626)

In addition, the seller must notify the buyer that the goods are being tendered. It is the responsibility of the buyer, on the other hand, to furnish facilities that are suitable for receiving the goods.

UCC 2-504 (see p. 626)

Shipment Contract In a shipment contract, the seller must put the goods in the possession of a carrier and contract with that carrier for their transportation. Any necessary documents must be sent to the buyer, who must be promptly notified of the shipment.

UCC 2-503(4) (see p. 626)

Goods in Possession of Warehouse Sometimes goods are in the possession of a warehouse and are to be turned over to the buyer without being moved. When this occurs, tender requires that the seller either tender a document of title covering the goods or obtain an acknowledgment by the warehouse of the buyer's right to their possession.

Spiegel purchased 5,000 cases of canned onions from Ingalls at a price that was much lower than the wholesale market price of the same product. The cases of onions had been stored by Ingalls at the East Side Storage Warehouse. Spiegel wished to continue storing the onions at the same warehouse, as she had no immediate use for them. Ingalls notified East Side Storage Warehouse that the onions had been sold to Spiegel. Tender occurred when the warehouse acknowledged to Spiegel that it was now holding the cases of onions for her instead of for Ingalls.

Tender of Payment by Buyer

UCC 2-511(1) (see p. 628)

Although the seller is obligated to deliver the goods to the buyer, this obligation stands on the condition that the buyer make tender of payment unless otherwise agreed. **Tender of payment** means offering to turn the money over to the seller. Such tender may be made by any means or in any manner that is commonly used in the ordinary course of business. The seller has the right to demand payment in legal tender but must give the buyer a reasonable time to obtain it. **Legal tender** is money that may be offered legally in satisfaction of a debt and that must be accepted by a creditor when offered.

Thompson Computer Sales agreed to sell a computer to Rubin for $6,000 on c.o.d. terms. When the equipment was delivered, Rubin offered to pay Thompson with a check. This was a sufficient tender of payment because checks are commonly used in the ordinary course of business. Thompson did not have to accept Rubin's check if it did not wish to do so. If the company refused to take the check, however, it would have to give Rubin a reasonable time to obtain legal tender.

UCC 2-511(3) (see p. 628)

Payment by check is conditional under the UCC. If the check clears, the debt is discharged. If the check is dishonored, the debt is revived.

UCC 2-512 (see p. 628)

When a contract requires payment before inspection, as when goods are shipped c.o.d., the buyer must pay for them first, even if they turn out to be defective when they are inspected. Of course, if the defect is obvious, the buyer would not have to accept or pay for the goods. Payment by the buyer before inspecting the goods does not constitute an acceptance of them. Upon discovering a defect, the buyer may use any of the remedies that are mentioned later in this chapter against the seller for breach of contract.

17-3 BUYER'S RIGHT TO INSPECT GOODS

UCC 2-513 (see p. 628)

Except when goods are shipped c.o.d. or when the contract provides for payment against a document of title, the buyer has the right to inspect the goods before accepting them or paying for them. The inspection may take place after the goods arrive at their destination. Expenses of inspection must be borne by the buyer but may be recovered from the seller if the goods do not conform to the contract and are rejected by the buyer.

Vargas ordered a glass-topped coffee table from a furniture store. The table was packed in a sealed box when it was delivered. Vargas had the right to open the box and inspect the table before accepting delivery of the goods. Had the table been shipped c.o.d., however, Vargas would have had no right to open the box before paying for the table. She could do so only after paying for the goods.

17-4 BUYER'S RIGHTS AND DUTIES UPON DELIVERY OF IMPROPER GOODS

UCC 2-601 (see p. 628)

When defective goods or goods not of the kind specified in the contract are delivered, the buyer may elect to reject them all, accept them all, or accept any commercial unit or units and reject the rest. A **commercial unit** is a single whole for the purpose of sale, the division of which impairs its character or value on the market. For example, a commercial unit may be a single article (as a machine) or a set of articles (as a suite of furniture or an assortment of sizes). It may be a quantity (as a bale, gross, or carload) or any other unit treated in the marketplace as a single whole item.

Rejection

UCC 2-605 (see p. 629)

UCC 2-602(2)(b) (see p. 629)

A rejection occurs when a buyer refuses to accept delivery of goods tendered. A rejection must be done within a reasonable time after delivery or tender to the buyer. After a rejection, the buyer may not claim ownership of the goods. In addition, the buyer must notify the seller of the particular defect in the goods so as to give the seller an opportunity to correct the defect. If the goods are in the buyer's possession, the buyer must hold them with reasonable care long enough for the seller to remove them. A buyer who is not a merchant has no other obligation as to goods that are rightfully rejected.

UCC 2-604 (see p. 629)

Buyer's Duties Generally If the seller gives no instructions within a reasonable time after being notified of the rejection, the buyer may store the goods for the seller, reship them to the seller, or resell them for the seller. In all cases, the buyer is entitled to be reimbursed for expenses.

Cleary ordered a case of grapefruit to be shipped to her from a Florida-based fruit company. When she opened the package soon after it arrived, she discovered that it contained oranges rather than grapefruit. Cleary is obligated to notify the company of its error and hold the oranges with reasonable care long enough for the seller to remove them from her possession. If Cleary receives no instructions from the fruit company and it does not remove them, she may take any of the three actions mentioned above and be reimbursed for her expenses.

UCC 2-603(1) (see p. 629)

Merchant Buyer's Duties A special duty comes into existence when a buyer who is a merchant rejects goods. Merchant buyers have a duty after the rejection of goods in their possession or control to follow any reasonable instructions received from the seller with respect to the goods. If there are no such instructions, they must make reasonable efforts to sell the goods for the seller if they are perishable or threaten to speedily decline in value.

UCC 2-603(2) (see p. 629)

Merchants who sell rejected goods are entitled to be reimbursed either by the seller or from the proceeds of the sale for reasonable expenses of caring for and selling the goods. They are also entitled to such commission as is usual in the trade or, if none, to a reasonable sum not exceeding 10 percent of the proceeds of the sale.

If Cleary had been a merchant, in the above case, and unless she had been notified to do something else by the seller, she would have had a duty to try to resell the oranges. Any proceeds from the sale, less expenses and a sales commission, would have to be turned over to the fruit company.

Acceptance

UCC 2-606
(see p. 629)

Acceptance of goods takes place when the buyer, after a reasonable opportunity to inspect them, does any of the following.

1. Signifies to the seller that the goods are **conforming,** that is, that they are in accordance with the obligations under the contract
2. Signifies to the seller a willingness to take them even though they are not conforming
3. Fails to reject them
4. Does any act that is inconsistent with the seller's ownership

---

Kandy Corp. bought concrete-forming equipment from Economy Forms Corp. Kandy used the equipment for six months before notifying Economy that it was inadequate. The court held that the use of the forms in construction was an act inconsistent with the seller's ownership and constituted an acceptance of the goods by Kandy Corp.

Once goods have been accepted, they cannot be rejected. A buyer who accepts goods with knowledge of something wrong with them cannot revoke the acceptance unless the acceptance was on the assumption that the nonconformity would be corrected.

Revocation of Acceptance

UCC 2-608
(see p. 630)

If a buyer has accepted goods on the assumption that their nonconformity would be corrected by the seller and the seller does not do so, the buyer may revoke the acceptance. This may also be done in cases in which the nonconformity is difficult to detect. The revocation must be made within a reasonable time after the buyer discovers the nonconformity. A revocation of an acceptance is not effective until the buyer notifies the seller of it. Buyers who revoke an acceptance have the same rights and duties with regard to the goods involved as if they had rejected them.

17-5 SELLER'S RIGHT TO CURE IMPROPER TENDER

UCC 2-508(1)
(see p. 627)

UCC 2-508(2)
(see p. 627)

Sellers may sometimes **cure** an improper tender or delivery of goods; that is, they may correct the defect which caused the goods to be rejected by the buyer. When the time for performance has not yet expired, the seller has the right to cure the defect and make a proper tender within the contract time. In cases where the time for performance has expired, the seller is allowed to have an additional amount of time to substitute a conforming tender if the seller had reasonable grounds to believe that the goods which were delivered were acceptable. In all cases, sellers must notify buyers that they are going to cure the improper tender or delivery.

Caravan Motel ordered ten dozen bath towels from samples shown by Fleming Towel Company's representative. The representative made a mistake in writing up the order. As a result, the towels that were delivered were inferior to those shown to Caravan at the time the order was given. Caravan rejected them. Because the Fleming Towel Company had reasonable grounds to believe that Caravan Motel would accept the towels that were delivered, it would have additional time to substitute correct towels for the ones that were delivered. When it learned of the rejection, Fleming Towel Company would be required to notify the motel that it intended to cure the nonconforming delivery.

The seller does not have the right to cure improper tender when a buyer accepts nonconforming goods, even though the buyer later sues the seller for breach of contract. The seller has the right only when the buyer either rejects the goods tendered or revokes an acceptance of the goods.

17-6 BREACH OF CONTRACT

Breach of contract occurs when one of the parties fails to do what was agreed upon in the contract. When this happens, the other party to the contract has specific remedies available under the UCC.

Anticipatory Breach

UCC 2-610 **(see p. 630)**

Sometimes, one of the parties will notify the other party before the time for performance that he or she is not going to conform. This is known as *anticipatory breach.* (See Chapter 13, page 161.) It is a breach committed before there is a present duty to perform the contract. Under older contractual law, the injured party in such a case would have to wait until the actual time for performance before bringing suit or taking some other action. It was necessary to wait for the actual time for performance in order to know for sure that the other party was, indeed, not going to perform. Under the UCC, when either party repudiates the contract before the time for performance, the injured party may take action immediately if waiting would be unjust or cause a material inconvenience. Any of the remedies for breach of contract are available to the aggrieved party in addition to the right to suspend his or her own performance.

Baily ordered ten steel I beams to be made to order from Midwest Steel Co. for use in a building which Baily was going to begin building in 6 months. Midwest Steel agreed to deliver the I beams on or before that date. Two months before the delivery date, Midwest Steel notified Baily that it would not be able to fill the order. Baily could treat the contract as having been breached and use any of the buyer's remedies that are available to him under the UCC.

Seller's Remedies When Buyer Breaches

When a buyer breaches a sales contract, the seller may select from the following remedies.

UCC 2-703(a)
(see p. 632)

Withhold Delivery of Goods If the goods have not been delivered, the seller has a right to keep them upon learning of the buyer's breach.

Stop Delivery of the Goods If, after shipping the goods, the seller discovers that the buyer is **insolvent** (unable to pay debts), the seller may have the delivery stopped. This right is known as **stoppage in transit** and is permitted after goods have been shipped but before they have reached their destination. The seller must give information to the **carrier** (the transportation company) to satisfy the latter that the buyer is insolvent. In addition, the seller must accept responsibility for any damage suffered by the carrier for not completing the shipment. If the insolvency information is incorrect, both the seller and the carrier could be sued for damages.

UCC 2-705
(see pp. 632–633)

The seller may also stop delivery of a carload, truckload, or planeload, or of larger shipments of express or freight when the buyer repudiates or fails to make a payment that is due before delivery or otherwise breaches the contract. If the seller has issued a document of title, the seller can stop delivery only by surrendering the document to the carrier. If the buyer has received the document, delivery of the goods cannot be stopped in transit.

UCC 2-706(1)
(see p. 633)

Resell the Goods The seller may resell the goods or the undelivered balance of them. In the case of unfinished manufactured goods, a seller may either complete the manufacture and resell the finished goods or cease manufacture and resell the unfinished goods for scrap or salvage value. In such cases, the seller must use reasonable commercial judgment to avoid losses. After the sale, the injured party may sue the other for the difference between what the property brought on resale and the price the buyer had agreed to pay in the contract.

UCC 2-704(2)
(see p. 632)

Resale may be at public or private sale. If it is a private sale, the seller must give the buyer reasonable notice of intention to resell the goods. If it is a public sale, it must be made at a place that is normally used for public sales, if such a place is available. In addition, if the goods are perishable or threaten to decline in value speedily, the seller must give the buyer reasonable notice of the time and place of resale.

UCC 2-706(4)(b)
(see p. 633)

A purchaser who buys in good faith at a resale takes the goods free of any rights of the original buyer. Furthermore, the seller is not accountable to the buyer for any profit made on the resale. The seller who chooses to do so may buy the goods at the resale.

UCC 2-706(4)(d)
(see p. 633)

UCC 2-708
(see pp. 633–634)

Recover Damages The seller may retain the merchandise and sue the buyer for either (*a*) the difference between the contract price and the market price at the time the buyer breached the agreement or (*b*) the profit (including overhead) that the seller would have made had the contract been performed. In

Table 17-1 SELLER'S REMEDIES WHEN THE BUYER BREACHES

1. Withhold delivery of any goods not yet delivered.
2. If the buyer is insolvent, stop delivery of any goods that are still in the possession of a carrier.
3. Resell any goods that have been rightfully withheld, and then sue the buyer for the difference between the agreed price and the resale price.
4. If the goods cannot be resold, sue the buyer for the difference between the agreed price and the market price.
5. Sue the buyer for the price of any goods that were accepted by the buyer.
6. Cancel the contract.

UCC 2-710 (see p. 634)

either case, the seller is also entitled to *incidental damages*. These are reasonable expenses that indirectly result from the breach, such as expenses incurred in stopping delivery of goods, transporting goods, and caring for goods after the buyer's breach.

UCC 2-709(1) (see p. 634)

UCC 2-709(2) (see p. 634)

Sue for Price The seller may sue for the price of any goods which the buyer has accepted. Similarly, upon the buyer's breach, the seller may bring suit for the price of goods that cannot be resold at a reasonable price. In addition, the seller may sue the buyer for the price of any lost or damaged goods after the risk of their loss has passed to the buyer. The seller who sues the buyer for the price must hold for the buyer any goods that are under the seller's control. The goods may be sold, however, at any time resale is possible before the collection of a judgment in the case. The net proceeds of any resale must be credited to the buyer. Any goods that are not resold become the property of the buyer if the buyer pays for them as a result of a court judgment.

UCC 2-106 (see p. 615)

Cancel the Contract The seller can cancel the contract. This occurs when the seller puts an end to the contract because the other party breached. When this occurs, the seller may use any of the remedies mentioned above for breach of contract.

Buyer's Remedies When Seller Breaches

When the seller breaches the contract by failing to deliver goods or by delivering improper goods, the buyer may cancel the contract and recover any money paid out. The buyer may also choose any of the following remedies.

UCC 2-711 (see p. 634)

UCC 2-712 (see p. 634)

Cover the Sale The buyer may **cover** the sale, that is, buy similar goods from someone else. The buyer may then sue the seller for the difference between the agreed price and the cost of the purchase. Cover must be made without unreasonable delay.

Flamme Bros. contracted to deliver a specific quantity of corn to Farmers' Union Co-op Co., a cooperative grain elevator. When Flamme Bros. failed to deliver the corn, Farmers' Union bought corn from its members over a two-week period. The

Table 17-2 BUYER'S REMEDIES WHEN THE SELLER BREACHES

1. Cancel the contract.
2. Sue the seller for the return of any money that has been paid.
3. Cover the sale—that is, buy similar goods from someone else and sue the seller for the difference between the agreed price and the cost of the purchase.
4. Sue the seller for the difference between the agreed price and the market price at the time the buyer learned of the breach.
5. If nonconforming goods have been accepted, notify the seller that they do not conform to the contract. Then, if no adjustment is made, sue the seller either for breach of contract or for breach of warranty.
6. When goods are unique or rare, sue for specific performance.

court held that this was cover of the contract without unreasonable delay. Farmers' Union recovered the difference between the agreed price of the corn from Flamme Bros. and the price it paid to the farmers for the corn it bought.

UCC 2-713 (see pp. 634–635)

UCC 2-715 (see p. 635)

Sue for Breach When a seller breaches a contract by not delivering the goods, the buyer may sue for damages if any were suffered. The measure of damages is the difference between the price that the parties agreed upon and the price of the same goods in the marketplace on the date the buyer learned of the breach. In addition, the buyer may sue for incidental and consequential damages.

UCC 2-718(1) (see p. 635)

Damages for breach of contract may be *liquidated,* that is, agreed upon by the parties when they first enter into the contract. Liquidated damages will be allowed by the court if they are reasonable. These damages are discussed in more detail in Chapter 13.

UCC 2-714(2) (see p. 635)

Keep Goods and Seek Adjustment When improper goods are delivered, the buyer may keep them and ask the seller for an adjustment. If no adjustment is made, the buyer may sue the seller for either breach of contract or breach of warranty, whichever applies. The amount of the suit would be the difference between the value of the goods contracted for and the value of the goods received.

Bare Essentials, Inc., ordered 20 dozen swimsuits from a swimsuit manufacturer. The suits that were delivered were different from the samples shown to the store by the manufacturer's representative. Since the store needed the swimsuits for the spring trade, it decided to keep them. If no adjustment is made by the manufacturer, Bare Essentials, Inc., can sue the manufacturer for damages (including loss of profits) that were suffered because of the breach of the express warranty that the goods would be the same as the sample.

UCC 716(1) (see p. 635)

Sue for Specific Performance When the goods are unique or rare, the buyer may ask the court to order the seller to turn the goods over to the buyer under the contract terms. This is known as an action for *specific performance* of the contract. A decree of specific performance, if granted by the court, would require the seller to deliver to the buyer the goods described in the sales agreement. This type of action is permitted only when an award of money will not give the buyer sufficient relief. Contracts for *objets d'art,* rare gems, antiques, and goods described as one-of-a-kind come within the scope of this type of action. Under the UCC, the decree of specific performance may include the payment of the price, damages, or other relief as the court may deem just. Specific performance is discussed in more detail in Chapter 13.

UCC 2-716(3)
(see p. 635)

Buyers have a right of replevin for goods that have been identified to the contract if, after a reasonable effort, they are unable to buy the goods elsewhere. A **writ of replevin** is a court order that requires the seller to turn the goods over to the buyer.

Statute of Limitations

UCC 2-725
(see pp. 636–637)

Nearly all lawsuits have a time limit within which suit must be brought. If the time limit is exceeded, the action is forever barred. Generally, an action for breach of contract for sale must be commenced within four years after the date of the breach. The parties may, if they wish to do so, provide for a shorter time period, not less than one year, in their sales agreement. They may not, however, agree to a period longer than four years.

SUMMARY

17-1. Sellers and buyers must follow the terms of their contract and act in good faith.

17-2. Tender of performance is necessary in order to test the other party's ability and willingness to perform. Tender of delivery requires the seller to make conforming goods available to the buyer at a reasonable hour of the day. Tender of payment may be made by any means that is commonly used in the ordinary course of business. The seller, may demand legal tender if he or she gives the buyer a reasonable time to obtain it.

17-3. Except when goods are shipped c.o.d. or when the contract provides for payment against a document of title, the buyer has the right to inspect goods before accepting or paying for them.

17-4. When improper goods are delivered, the buyer may elect to (*a*) reject all of them, (*b*) accept all of them, or (*c*) accept any commercial unit or units and reject the rest. Rejection of goods must be done within a reasonable time, and the buyer must notify the seller of the reason for the rejection. Even after accepting goods, buyers may revoke an acceptance if the goods were accepted on the assumption that their nonconformity would be corrected or if the nonconformity could not be easily detected.

17-5. Sellers may correct defects or nonconformities that caused the goods to be rejected by the buyer.

17-6. When a buyer breaches a sales contract, the seller may

a. Withhold delivery of any goods not yet delivered
b. Under certain circumstances, stop goods that are in transit
c. Resell the goods or the undelivered balance of them
d. Retain the goods and bring suit for damages
e. Bring suit for the price of any goods that the buyer has accepted
f. Cancel the contract

When a seller breaches a sales contract, the buyer may

a. Buy similar goods from someone else and sue the seller for the difference in price
b. Deduct the cost of damages from any price still due
c. Sue the seller for damages for nondelivery
d. Sue for specific performance if the goods are rare or unique

Understanding Key Legal Terms

carrier (p. 220)
commercial unit (p. 216)
conforming goods (p. 218)
cover (p. 221)
cure (p. 218)
good faith (p. 214)
insolvent (p. 220)
legal tender (p. 215)
stoppage in transit (p. 220)
tender of delivery (p. 214)
tender of payment (p. 215)
tender of performance (p. 214)
unconscionable contract (p. 214)
writ of replevin (p. 223)

Questions for Review and Discussion

1. Describe in general terms the obligations of parties to a sales contract.
2. Why is tender of performance necessary?
3. What is required of the seller in making tender of delivery? What form of payment may be used by the buyer in making tender of payment? When may the seller demand legal tender?
4. Explain the right of the buyer to inspect goods that are received under a contract for sale.
5. What three choices does a buyer have when defective or nonconforming goods are delivered?
6. Describe the manner in which buyers must reject goods if they decide to do so. After a rejection, what may buyers do with goods in their possession? What special duty applies to a merchant buyer?
7. When can a seller correct an improper tender of delivery?
8. Compare older contractual law with the UCC as it applies to anticipatory breach.
9. Explain the remedies that are available to a seller when a buyer breaches a contract for sale.
10. Explain the remedies that are available to a buyer when a seller breaches a contract for sale.

Analyzing Cases

1. Brooklyn Union Gas Company contracted to sell a gas burner to Jimeniz, a landlord with limited knowledge of the English language. Instead of negotiating directly with Jimeniz, the company's agent used high-pressure tactics to induce Jimeniz's tenants to pressure him into signing the contract. When Jimeniz asked for an interpretation of the contract, one of the tenants instead told him to sign it. Jimeniz testified that

no one had ever explained the contract to him. The entire transaction took place at Jimeniz's apartment instead of at the company's sales office where an interpreter would have been available. Later, when the burner malfunctioned at a time when Jimeniz was behind in his payments, the gas company refused to repair it and sued Jimeniz for breach of contract. Jimeniz claimed that the contract was unconscionable and, therefore, void. Do you agree with Jimeniz? Explain. *Brooklyn Union Gas Company v. Jimeniz,* 371 N.Y.S.2d 289 (New York).

2. Herman Googe agreed to buy an automobile from Irene Schleimer. Later, Googe changed his mind and refused to buy the car. Schleimer, without making tender of delivery, brought suit against Googe for breach of contract. Will Schleimer recover? Explain. *Schleimer v. Googe,* 377 N.Y.S.2d 591 (New York).

3. Mr. and Mrs. Aldridge bought a motor home from Sportsman Travel Trailer Sales, located in Texas. Two years later, after traveling more than 14,000 miles on trips to Louisiana, Colorado, and California, they attempted to reject the motor home, claiming that it was defective. Can they return the vehicle and recover damages? Explain. *Explorer Motor Home Corp. v. Aldridge,* 541 S.W.2d 851 (Texas).

4. Dehahn agreed to sell and Innes agreed to buy for the price of $35,000 a 35-acre gravel pit, a back hoe, a bulldozer, a loader, two dump trucks, and a low-bed trailer. Since Dehahn had recently lost his bid for reelection as road commissioner in the town, he was required to remove the equipment from town property. He moved the equipment to a field owned by Innes across from the driveway to Innes's home and left the keys in the vehicles. Later, Innes canceled the contract and refused to make any payments. When sued, Innes argued that Dehahn failed to make tender of delivery of the equipment? Do you agree with Innes? State why or why not? *Dehahn v. Innes,* 356 A.2d 711 (Maine).

5. Formetal Engineering Co. placed an order with Presto Manufacturing Co., Inc., for 250,000 polyurethane pads to be used in making air-conditioning units. The pads were to be made according to samples and specifications supplied by Formetal. When the pads arrived, Formetal discovered that they did not conform to the sample and specifications in that there were incomplete cuts, color variances, and faulty adherence to the pads' paper backing. Formetal notified Presto of the defects and said that it was rejecting the goods and returning them to Presto. The goods, however, were never returned. Was the rejection proper? Explain. *Presto Mfg. Co. v. Formetal Eng'r Co.,* 360 N.E.2d 510 (Illinois).

6. City National Bank of Crete agreed to sell and deliver to Goosic Construction Company a set of concrete forms for the sum of $200, which Goosic paid. The forms had been repossessed at an earlier time by the bank and were stored at another location. When Goosic arrived at the storage location to pick up the forms, a Mr. Roberts claimed a storage lien and refused to allow Goosic to take possession of them. Goosic never received the forms, which had a fair market value of $1,500. Did the City National Bank make proper tender of delivery? If Goosic Construction Company wins the case, how much will it recover? Give reasons for your answers. *Goosic Const. Co. v. City Nat. Bank,* 241 N.W.2d 521 (Nebraska).

7. Sagebrush Sales Co. sold building materials to Pace, a retail lumber dealer. As the goods were unloaded at Pace's lumber yard, Pace noticed that two of the truckloads contained materials that he had not ordered. He nevertheless permitted the unordered goods to be unloaded without objection and wrote on his copy of the invoice "not ordered." Pace then telephoned Sagebrush's office and asked why they were sending

him extra lumber. The employee replied that he did not know but that he would have the salesperson call Pace. No further complaint was made by Pace to Sagebrush. The goods were placed into Pace's inventory and offered for sale to the public. Pace made a partial payment for the goods but refused to pay the full amount, claiming that he had not accepted the unordered goods. Do you agree with Pace? Why or why not? *Pace v. Sagebrush Sales Co.*, 560 P.2d 789 (Arizona).

8. Carolyn McQueen bought a new Fiat Spider from American Imports, Inc. The deal included a $500 trade-in allowance on McQueen's Oldsmobile, and McQueen borrowed the money to buy the car from a credit union. She paid for the Fiat by check and promised to deliver an Oldsmobile for trade-in the next week. Two days later, the Fiat overheated. McQueen had also discovered that neither the speedometer nor the odometer functioned properly. American Imports, Inc., towed the car to its garage, replaced a broken fan belt, and tightened a nut on the speedometer which also controlled the odometer. After the repairs were made, McQueen refused to take the car, saying that she wanted a new one. She stopped payment on the checks. When sued for the purchase price, McQueen claimed that she had revoked her acceptance of the Fiat and could, therefore, cancel the contract. Is McQueen within her rights? Why or why not? *American Imports, Inc. v. G.E. Emp. West. Region Fed. Credit Union*, 245 S.E.2d 798 (North Carolina).

CHAPTER 18
Consumer Protection

OUTLINE

18-1 Consumer Protection Laws

18-2 The Federal Trade Commission (FTC) Act
- Enforcing the FTC Act

18-3 The Federal Trade Commission Rules
- Used Car Rule
- Door-to-Door Sales Rule
- Mail Order Rule

18-4 Unfair or Deceptive Acts or Practices
- Unordered Merchandise
- Bait-and-Switch Schemes
- Odometer Tampering

18-5 Consumer Product Safety Act

18-6 Consumer Leasing Act

18-7 Consumer Credit Laws
- Truth-in-Lending
- Equal Credit Opportunity
- Unauthorized Use of Credit Cards
- Fair Credit Reporting
- Fair Credit Billing
- Fair Debt Collection Practices
- Credit Practices Rule

18-8 Food, Drug, and Cosmetic Act

18-9 Fair Packaging and Labeling Act

COMMENTARY

"Mustang convertible, $100 down $100 per month—low mileage, like-new condition!" The advertisement in the morning newspaper caught Kathleen Horack's attention. She needed a car and could afford that price. She went to the car lot immediately, arriving before the lot opened for the day. When the owner arrived, Horack was told that the car she saw advertised had been sold but that they had an even better one on the lot.

"This is a beauty," the car-lot owner said, showing her a car, "and look at that low mileage! You can have this for peanuts—just $150 a month! It's a steal!"

After buying the car and driving it home, Horack looked at the sales slip and saw for the first time the words, "As Is" written in the seller's handwriting. She also discovered that the rate of interest she had agreed to pay was much higher than she had realized and much higher than that charged by banks in the area. The same day, while cleaning the car, she found an old service slip showing the mileage to be 45,000, which was much greater than the present odometer reading of 30,000.

The car broke down three times during the first week that Horack owned it. The seller would do nothing for her, reminding her that she had bought the car as is.

Had this transaction happened in the past, Horack would have had little, if any, recourse against the seller. Today, both state and federal consumer protection laws would give her protection against the unfair and deceptive acts that occurred in her case.

OBJECTIVES

1. Identify the location, in general, of state consumer protection offices and discuss their purpose.
2. Discuss the main purpose of the FTC Act and explain how the act is enforced.
3. Identify three FTC rules designed to protect the consumer.
4. Describe three federal laws designed to prevent unfair or deceptive acts.
5. Recognize the purpose of the Consumer Product Safety Act.
6. Explain how consumers can benefit from the Consumer Leasing Act.
7. Identify and state the purpose of seven consumer credit laws.
8. Highlight the provisions of the Food, Drug, and Cosmetic Act.
9. Relate the main purpose of the Fair Packaging and Labeling Act.

18-1 CONSUMER PROTECTION LAWS

Consumer protection laws apply to transactions entered into between someone conducting a business activity and a consumer. A **consumer** is someone who buys or leases real estate, goods, or services for personal, family or household purposes. Thus, people who buy or rent things for personal use from a business are protected by consumer protection laws. On the other hand, if they buy the same things from another consumer or for business use, they are not, with some exceptions, protected by the consumer protection law.

Every state in the United States has some form of consumer protection law. Some state laws are patterned after the Federal Trade Commission Act discussed in this chapter. Others are slightly different. Most state consumer protection laws prohibit unfair or deceptive acts or practices in the conduct of any trade or business. State laws are designed to protect consumers against wrongful acts by businesses that operate within their state.

State consumer protection offices provide information to consumers about their own state laws. In addition, they help to enforce state consumer protection laws. In some cases, they will assist consumers with individual problems. Consumer protection offices are located in governors' offices, state attorney general's offices, various county offices, and even in the mayors' offices of some cities.

18-2 THE FEDERAL TRADE COMMISSION ACT

The Federal Trade Commission Act, passed by Congress in 1914 to prevent unfair methods of competition, has been updated and strengthened over the years. The act established the Federal Trade Commission (FTC), which reports to Congress on its actions. The commission is headed by five commissioners who are nominated by the President and confirmed by the Senate. Each commissioner serves a seven-year term. The Bureau of Consumer Protection is an important agency of the FTC. The Bureau's aim is to keep the marketplace free from unfair, deceptive, or fraudulent practices.

The FTC Act states that "unfair or deceptive acts or practices in or affecting commerce are hereby declared unlawful." The act defines **commerce** as "commerce among the several states or with foreign nations...or the District of Columbia." Thus, the act applies to businesses which sell real estate, goods, or services in interstate commerce or which somehow affect interstate commerce. **Interstate commerce** is business activity that touches more than one state. Purely local business activity, which has no out-of-state connections, called **intrastate commerce,** is not governed by the Federal Trade Commission Act.

Ortega owned a farm on which he grew a variety of vegetables. He sold the vegetables to a local store and also to consumers who stopped at his roadside stand. Since his business was purely local, it would not be governed by the Federal Trade Commission Act. Instead, his business would be regulated by the consumer protection laws, as well as other laws, of his own state.

Enforcing the FTC Act

The FTC is not authorized to resolve individual consumer complaints. However, it can act when it sees a pattern of possible violations develop. The FTC may begin an investigation in different ways. Letters from consumers or businesses, congressional inquiries, or articles on consumer or economic subjects often trigger FTC action. Investigations may be either public or nonpublic. Usually, an investigation of an entire industry is announced publicly. An exception is the investigation of an individual company. The investigation is nonpublic to protect both the investigation and the company.

If the FTC believes a violation of the law occurred, it may attempt to obtain voluntary compliance by entering into a consent order with the company. A **consent order** is an order under which the company agrees to stop the disputed practice without necessarily admitting that it violated the law. If a consent agreement cannot be reached, the FTC may issue a complaint. This begins a formal hearing before an administrative law judge. If a violation of law is found, a cease and desist order or other appropriate relief may be issued.

Jay Norris, Inc., made false claims about a number of products listed in its mail-order catalogs and advertisements. It described a "flame gun" that would dissolve the heaviest snowdrifts and whip through the thickest ice; the product did neither. A roach powder was described as completely safe to use and as never losing its killing power, even after years; the powder was neither safe to use nor very deadly to the roaches. Cars were listed as carefully maintained and thoroughly serviced; they were former New York taxicabs, many in poor condition. The FTC issued a cease and desist order prohibiting Jay Norris, Inc., from representing the safety or performance characteristics of any product unless such claims were fully and completely substantiated by competent and objective material available in written form.

18-3 FEDERAL TRADE COMMISSION RULES

To correct wrongdoings in the marketplace, the FTC has established rules which must be followed by companies that transact business in interstate commerce. Some of these rules are discussed here (see Table 18-1).

Used Car Rule

Many consumer complaints involve the purchase of a used car. To remedy this situation, the FTC, in 1985, established the **Used Car Rule.** The rule requires used-car dealers to place a window sticker, called a **Buyer's Guide,** in the window of each used car they offer for sale. The Buyer's Guide provides the following information:

1. A statement that the car is sold "As Is" if it is sold with no warranties. (Some states do not allow used cars to be sold "as is" by car dealers.)
2. A statement that the car is sold with implied warranties only if that is the case (see Chapter 16, pages 201–203).
3. A statement telling whether the warranty is "full" or "limited" (see pages 199–200 in Chapter 16) and citing the length of the warranty period if the car is sold with an express warranty. In addition, the guide must list the specific systems that are covered by the warranty and must state the percentage of the repair costs the buyer will be required to pay.
4. A statement that tells consumers not to rely on spoken promises.
5. A suggestion that consumers ask whether they may have the vehicle inspected by their own mechanic either on or off the premises.
6. A list of the 14 major systems of an automobile and some of the principal defects that may occur in these systems.

Dealers are required to post the Buyer's Guide on all used vehicles, including used automobiles, light-duty vans, and light-duty trucks. The guide becomes part of the sales contract and overrides any contrary provision that may be in the contract.

Door-to-Door Sales Rule

The FTC has established the **Door-to-Door Sales Rule** to give consumers an opportunity to change their minds after signing contracts with people who come to their houses. Under this rule, sales of consumer goods or services over $25 made away from the seller's regular place of business, such as at a customer's home, may be canceled within three business days after the sale occurs. This rule requires the seller to give the buyer two copies of a cancellation form, one of which the buyer may send to the seller any time before midnight of the third business day after the contract was signed, canceling the contract. The law also applies to consumer product parties given in private homes and to sales made in rented hotel rooms or restaurants.

Nesbit saw an advertisement in a local newspaper advertising Oriental rugs for sale at a local motel. She went to the motel, purchased an Oriental rug, and was given a sales slip saying that all sales were final. The company violated the FTC rule. It did not provide her with a cancellation form which she could use to cancel the contract within three days. Although the FTC cannot resolve individual complaints, it does want to know about them. Nesbit should notify her state consumer protection office and send a copy of her complaint to the Enforcement Division, Federal Trade Commission, Washington, D.C. 20580.

Under the laws of some states, such as New York, the three-day right to cancel does not begin until the seller gives the buyer a written notice of the right to cancel. Until such notice is given, the buyer may use any means to notify the seller of the cancellation of the contract.

The Door-to-Door Sales Rule does not apply to sales made at the seller's regular place of business, sales made totally by mail or phone, and sales under $25. In addition, it does not apply to sales for real estate, insurance, or securities, or to sales for emergency home repairs.

Mail Order Rule

The FTC has established a rule to protect consumers who order goods by mail. Under the rule, sellers must ship orders within the time promised in their advertisements. If no time period is promised, sellers must either ship the order within 30 days after they receive it or send the consumer an option notice. The option notice tells the consumer of a shipping delay and gives the consumer the option of agreeing to the delay or of canceling the order and receiving a prompt refund. Instructions on how to cancel the order must be included in

Table 18-1 FEDERAL TRADE COMMISSION RULES

Mail Order Rule	Requires companies to ship purchases made by mail when promised or to give consumers the option to cancel their order for a refund.
Care Labeling Rule	Requires textile clothing and fabrics used for home sewing to have a label giving care instructions.
Franchise and Business Opportunities Rule	Requires sellers of franchises and business opportunities to give prospective buyers a disclosure document containing specific information about the franchise and any earning claims.
R-value Rule	Requires sellers to disclose the thermal efficiency of home insulation.
Door-to-Door Sales Rule	Requires sellers to give consumers notice of their three-day cancellation rights for sales made at home.
Funeral Rule	Requires funeral directors to disclose price and other information about funeral goods and services.
Used Car Rule	Requires dealers to provide a "Buyers Guide" disclosing information about the warranty coverage offered, the meaning of an "as-is" sale, and a suggestion that consumers ask about obtaining an independent inspection before buying a car.
Negative Option Rule	Requires sellers who use negative option purchase plans, such as book and record clubs, to give members at least ten days to reject the monthly selection.
Appliance Labeling Rule	Requires the disclosure of energy costs of home appliances.
Octane Posting and Certification Rule	Requires the disclosure of the octane ratings of gasoline.

the notice. In addition, the seller must provide a free means for the consumer to reply.

18-4 UNFAIR OR DECEPTIVE ACTS OR PRACTICES

The FTC Act does not define the phrase "unfair or deceptive act or practice." Instead, it allows the Federal Trade Commission and the courts to determine what is unfair or deceptive. Among the considerations monitored by the FTC are the following:

1. Does the practice offend public policy?
2. Is the practice immoral, unethical, oppressive, or unscrupulous?
3. Does the practice cause substantial injury to consumers?

Such practices as false advertising (advertising that has the tendency to mislead); deceptive pricing; misrepresentations about the nature, quality, and use of a product; and the failure to disclose important facts about a product have all been held to be unfair or deceptive.

Unordered Merchandise

Except for (1) free samples clearly and conspicuously marked as such and (2) merchandise mailed by charitable organizations soliciting contributions, it is a violation of the postal law and the FTC Act to send merchandise through the mail to people who did not order it. Similarly, it is illegal to send a bill for such unordered merchandise or to send **dunning letters,** that is, letters requesting payments.

People who receive unordered merchandise through the mail may treat it as a gift. They may keep the merchandise or dispose of it in any manner they see fit without any obligation whatsoever to the sender. In addition, senders of unordered merchandise must attach a statement to the package informing recipients of their right to keep and use the goods.

Bait-and-Switch Schemes

A **bait-and-switch scheme** is an alluring but insincere offer to sell a product or service that the advertiser in truth does not intend or want to sell. Its purpose is to switch customers from buying the advertised merchandise in order to sell something else, usually at a higher price or on a basis more advantageous to the advertiser. The primary aim of a bait advertisement is to obtain leads as to persons interested in buying merchandise of the type so advertised.

The FTC rule prohibiting bait-and-switch activity states: "No advertisement containing an offer to sell a product shall be made when the offer is not a *bona fide* effort to sell the advertised product."

Any of the following activities could indicate a bait-and-switch scheme:

1. The refusal to show, demonstrate, or sell the product offered in accordance with the terms of the offer
2. The "put down" of the product by acts or words of the seller

3. The failure to have available at all outlets listed in the advertisement a sufficient quantity of the advertised product to meet reasonably anticipated demands
4. The refusal to take orders for the advertised product to be delivered within a reasonable period of time
5. The showing of a product that is defective, unusable, or impractical for the purpose represented in the advertisement

Odometer Tampering

The Federal Odometer Law prohibits people from disconnecting, resetting, or altering the odometer of a motor vehicle to register any mileage other than the true mileage driven. Anyone who sells a car or even gives it away, unless it is over 25 years old, must provide the new owner with a written statement disclosing the odometer reading at the time of the transfer. If the seller has reason to believe that the mileage reading on the odometer is incorrect, the disclosure statement must indicate that the actual mileage traveled is unknown.

An odometer must be set at zero if it is repaired and cannot be adjusted to show the true mileage. In addition, the car owner must attach to the left-door frame a written notice showing the true mileage before the repair or replacement and the date that the odometer was set at zero. It is illegal for anyone to alter or remove any such notice attached to the door frame of a car.

18-5 CONSUMER PRODUCT SAFETY ACT

To protect consumers from dangerous products, Congress passed the Consumer Product Safety Act. The act established the Consumer Product Safety Commission (CPSC) to protect consumers from unreasonable risk or injury from hazardous products. The act covers products or component parts, American-made or imported, which are manufactured or distributed for sale to a consumer for personal use, consumption, or enjoyment.

Hundreds of people were being killed and thousands injured while riding on three-wheel, all-terrain vehicles (ATVs). The vehicles have large, soft tires and are designed for off-road use. Because of so many deaths and injuries, the Commission banned the sale of new three-wheel ATVs in the United States in 1987. In addition, the Commission required manufacturers of ATVs to spend over $8 million advertising to the public the safety problems associated with the three-wheel vehicles.

The Commission has the authority to establish and issue safety and performance standards. The standards generally consist of requirements as to performance, composition, contents, design, construction, finish, or packaging of a consumer product. Standards may also include requirements that a product be marked or accompanied by clear and adequate warnings or instructions.

The Commission can order the recall of products found to be inherently unsafe and dangerous. It has the authority to impose civil fines for violations of its standards and cease and desist orders. Private citizens, acting in their own behalf, may bring suit to establish or enforce a safety rule if the Commission fails to act. Commission findings must be supported by substantial evidence in the record as a whole. Rules and findings issued by the Commission are subject to judicial review.

18-6 CONSUMER LEASING ACT

The Consumer Leasing Act is a federal law requiring leasing companies to inform consumers of all the terms of a lease of personal property. Consumers can use the information to compare one lease with another or to compare the cost of leasing with the cost of buying the same property.

The law applies only to personal property leased by an individual for a period of more than four months for personal, family, or household use. It does not cover daily or weekly rentals, leases for apartments or houses, or leases to anyone for business purposes.

Wagner decided that her business could be managed much more efficiently if it had a computer. The cost of buying a computer, however, was more than Wagner could afford. She considered leasing one. The Consumer Leasing Act would not apply to Wagner's lease, because the computer was for business rather than personal use. She would be able to make a better decision, however, if she asked the leasing company for the same information the company would be required to provide to a consumer.

The law requires that consumers be given a written statement informing them of the full cost of the lease including the cost of any necessary licenses, taxes, or other fees. Consumers must be informed of any insurance requirements, and of any penalties for late payment. They must also be told who is responsible for maintaining and servicing the property. In addition, they must be told whether or not they can buy the property, and if so, when and at what price. The law also places a limit on the amount of a **balloon payment** (a very large final payment) to no more than three times the average monthly payments.

Advertisements of leases are also regulated by law. If an advertisement mentions the amount or number of payments or specifies a particular down payment or that no down payment is required, it must also disclose the total of regular payments, the consumer's responsibility at the end of the lease, and whether the consumer may purchase the property.

18-7 CONSUMER CREDIT LAWS

People buy more on credit today than ever before. They borrow money from banks, credit unions, finance companies, and automobile manufacturers. They have charge accounts with stores, restaurants, and major oil companies. They often have more than one nationally recognized credit card. Due to this extensive use of credit, Congress has found it necessary to pass federal laws to protect the consumer. Some of these laws are discussed here.

Truth in Lending

Because lending institutions and businesses charge different rates of interest to consumers, it often pays to shop around before borrowing money or buying on credit. To help consumers know the truth about the cost of borrowing money, Congress passed the Truth-in-Lending Act. Under this act, lenders must disclose two important things to borrowers: (1) the **finance charge** (the actual cost of the loan in dollars and cents) and (2) the **annual percentage rate (APR)** (the true rate of interest of the loan). With this information, consumers can compare the cost of a loan from different lenders before deciding where to borrow. Surprisingly, the APR sometimes turns out to be greater than would appear at first glance.

Whitehead borrowed $100 for one year and agreed to pay a finance charge of $10. If she kept the $100 for the year, and at the end of the year paid the full amount back together with the $10 finance charge, the APR would be 10 percent. If, on the other hand, she paid the $110 in 12 monthly installments of $9.17 each, the APR would be 18 percent. This is because during the course of the year she would have the use, on the average, of only about half of the $100.

The APR is computed by the use of a complicated mathematical formula. Tables provided by the Federal Reserve Banks are helpful in determining the exact APR on any loan.

The Truth-in-Lending Act applies to transactions involving the borrowing of money as well as to the purchasing of goods and services on credit. Under the act, there are two kinds of credit, open-end credit and closed-end credit. **Open-end credit** is credit that can be increased by the debtor, up to a limit set by the creditor, by continuing to purchase goods on credit. Credit cards and charge accounts are examples of open-end credit. **Closed-end credit** is credit which is extended only for a specific amount of money, such as for the purchase of a car or other expensive item.

The Truth-in-Lending Act also regulates the advertising of credit terms. If an advertisement mentions one feature of credit, such as the amount of a down payment, it must also mention all other important terms, such as the terms of repaying the loan. Whenever an advertisement mentions a finance rate, it must be stated as an annual percentage rate (APR), and that term must be used.

Equal Credit Opportunity

The Equal Credit Opportunity Act was passed by Congress to ensure that all consumers are given an equal chance to receive credit. The law makes it illegal for banks and businesses to discriminate against credit applicants because of their sex, race, marital status, national origin, religion, or age or because they get public assistance income. The law must be followed by anyone who regularly extends credit, including banks, credit unions, finance companies, credit card issuers, and retail stores. Some of the rights to consumers under the act are as follows:

1. People who apply for credit may not be asked to reveal:
   a. Their sex, race, national origin, or religion
   b. Whether they are divorced or widowed
   c. Their marital status, unless they are applying for a joint account or a secured loan [Marital status may, however, be asked in the states of Arizona, California, Idaho, Louisiana, Nevada, New Mexico, Texas, and Washington—all of which are community property states (see Chapter 21)]
   d. Information about their spouse, except in community property states, unless the spouse is also applying for credit or will use the account
   e. Their plans for having or raising children
   f. Whether they receive alimony, child support, or separate maintenance payments if they will not be relying on that income
2. When deciding to extend credit, creditors may not
   a. Consider the applicant's sex, marital status, race, national origin, or religion
   b. Consider the applicant's age unless the applicant is a minor or is considered favorably for being over 62
   c. Refuse to consider public assistance income in the same manner as other income
   d. Refuse to consider income from part-time employment, pensions, or retirement programs
3. Applicants may apply for credit under the name given to them at birth or their married name, or under a combination of both names. They may receive credit without a consignor if they meet the creditor's standards. In addition, applicants have a right to know within 30 days whether their application for credit has been accepted or rejected. If rejected, they have a right to know the reasons for the rejection within 60 days.
4. People may bring suit in a federal district court either individually or with others against creditors who violate this law. If they win, they may be awarded their actual losses plus attorney's fees, court costs, and punitive damages (damages designed to punish the wrongdoer).

Unauthorized Use of Credit Cards

Sometimes credit cards are lost, stolen, or used by people who have no authority to use them. Under the Truth-in-Lending Act, credit cardholders are not responsible for any unauthorized charges made after the card issuer has been notified of the loss, theft, or possible unauthorized use of the card. Such notice may be given to the card issuer by telephone, letter, or any other means. Even then, credit cardholders are responsible only for the first $50 of any unauthorized charges.

O'Brien's wallet, containing her VISA credit card, was stolen. She immediately notified VISA by mail that the card had been lost. In spite of her prompt notice, the thief was able to charge purchases totaling $860. If the charges occurred before VISA received notice of the theft, O'Brien would be liable for $50 of the unauthorized charges. If the charges occurred after VISA had received notice, O'Brien would have no liability.

The credit card holder can avoid the $50 liability if the credit card issuer has not included on the card a method to identify the user of the card, such as a signature, a photograph, or other means of identification. Card issuers must notify cardholders in advance of the potential $50 liability.

Under the Truth-in-Lending Act, credit card issuers are not allowed to send out unsolicited credit cards unless they are a renewal or substitute for a card already in use.

Fair Credit Reporting

The Fair Credit Reporting Act was passed by Congress to ensure that consumers are treated fairly by credit bureaus and consumer reporting agencies. Under the act, a consumer has the right to know all information (other than medical information) that is in its files about that consumer. A consumer also has the right to know, in most cases, the source of the information that is on file. In addition, a consumer the right to be told the name of anyone who received a credit report in the past six months (two years if the credit report relates to a job application).

Consumers who wish to know what information a credit bureau has on file about them must first establish their identity. Then they can arrange either a personal interview at the bureau's office or an interview by telephone. If errors are found, credit bureaus must investigate and then correct or delete information that is inaccurate, incomplete, or obsolete. If the credit bureau retains information that the consumer believes to be incorrect, the consumer's version of the facts must be inserted in the file.

Also, under the act, creditors are required to tell consumers the specific reasons for the denial of credit. With this information, consumers can determine whether inaccuracies exist. Credit bureaus must adhere to specific rules as to the length of time they can keep credit reports and as to who may ask for credit information.

Fair Credit Billing

Errors are sometimes made in bills sent out by retail stores, credit card companies, and other businesses that extend credit. To make it easier for billing errors to be corrected, Congress has passed the Fair Credit Billing Act (FCBA). The law establishes a procedure for the prompt handling of billing disputes in the case of open-end and revolving charge accounts. A **revolving charge account** is one with an outstanding balance at all times.

Under the act, when consumers believe an error has been made in a bill, they must notify the creditor within 60 days after the bill was mailed. The notice must identify the consumer, give the account number, the suspected amount of error, and an explanation of why the consumer believes there is an error. The creditor must acknowledge the consumer's notice within 30 days. Then, within 90 days, the creditor must conduct an investigation and either correct the mistake or explain why the bill is believed to be correct.

Another provision of the act gives consumers protection when they buy unsatisfactory goods or services with credit cards. If the purchase is over $50, consumers may withhold payment of the credit card bill and give the seller a chance to correct the problem. Then, if the problem is not corrected and suit is brought by the credit card issuer, the consumer may use as a defense the fact that unsatisfactory goods or services were received. For this law to apply, the initial transaction must have taken place in the consumer's state or within 100 miles of the consumer's mailing address. Creditors may not give cardholders a poor credit rating for exercising their rights under this act.

Fair Debt Collection Practices

To prevent the use of abusive, deceptive, and unfair debt collection practices, Congress has passed the Fair Debt Collection Practices Act. Under the act, specific rules must be followed by companies that are in the business of collecting debts for others. Some of these rules are as follows:

1. When trying to locate someone, a debt collector may not communicate by postcard or tell others that the consumer owes money.
2. When the debt collector knows that the consumer is represented by an attorney, the debt collector may communicate only with the attorney.
3. A debt collector may not communicate with the consumer at any unusual or inconvenient time or place. Unless there are circumstances to the contrary, the convenient time for communicating with a consumer is between the hours of 8 a.m. and 9 p.m.
4. A debt collector may not communicate with the consumer at the consumer's place of employment if the debt collector knows that the employer prohibits such communication.
5. A debt collector may not communicate, in connection with the collection of a debt, with any person other than the consumer, the consumer's attorney, the creditor's attorney, or a consumer reporting agency.
6. If a consumer notifies a debt collector in writing that the consumer refuses to pay the debt or wishes the debt collector to cease further communication, the debt collector must cease communication, except to notify the consumer of a specific action.
7. Debt collectors may not harass consumers or use abusive techniques to collect debts. The use or threatened use of violence or other criminal means to harm the person, property, or reputation of the consumers is not allowed. In addition, debt collectors may not use obscene or profane language or publish a list of those who allegedly refuse to pay debts. It is also illegal for a debt collector to cause a telephone to ring or to engage in repeated telephone conversations with the intent to annoy the consumer.

Debt collectors who violate this law may be sued for actual damages, punitive damages, and attorneys' fees.

Table 18-2 CONSUMER CREDIT LAWS

Equal Credit Opportunity Act	Prohibits any creditor from denying credit to a consumer on the basis of sex, marital status, color, race, religion, national origin, age, or receipt of public assistance
Fair Credit Reporting Act	Gives consumers the right to know what information consumer reporting agencies are reporting about them to creditors, insurance companies, and employers
Truth-in-Lending Act	Requires creditors to disclose in writing certain cost information, such as the annual percentage rate (APR), before consumers enter into credit transactions
Fair Credit Billing Act	Establishes procedures for resolving mistakes on credit card accounts
Electronic Fund Transfer (EFT) Act	Establishes procedures for resolving errors and provides other protection for EFT customers in connection with their savings and checking accounts, such as limitations on their liability and unauthorized transfers (see Chapter 27, page 373)
Consumer Leasing Act	Requires lessors to give consumers specific information on lease costs and terms
Fair Debt Collection Practices Act	Prohibits debt collectors from engaging in unfair, deceptive, or abusive practices, including overcharging, harassment, and disclosing consumers' debts to third parties
Holder-in-Due-Course Rule	Allows consumers who buy goods on credit to sue creditors, even if the debt paper is no longer held by the seller (see Chapter 26, page 361)
Credit Practices Rule	Prohibits, in consumer credit contracts, certain collection remedies, namely: confessions of judgment, wage assignments, waivers of exemption, and security interests in certain household goods; it also requires that specified notices be given to co-signers before they become obligated

Credit Practices Rule

The **Credit Practices Rule,** effective in 1985, prohibits creditors from including certain provisions in their consumer credit contracts.

Under the rule, credit contracts can no longer include provisions that

1. Require consumers to agree in advance, if they are sued for nonpayment of a debt, to give up their right to be notified of a court hearing. Clauses to this effect were used in credit contracts in some states and were called **confessions of judgment,** or **cognovits.**
2. Require consumers to give up their state law protection that allows them to keep certain personal belongings even though they are sued for nonpayment of a debt. These clauses were called **waiver of exemption clauses.**
3. Permit consumers to agree in advance to wage deductions that would pay the creditor directly if the consumer defaults on a debt, unless consumers can cancel that permission at any time. These clauses were called **wage assignments.** Wage or payroll deduction plans, under which consumers arrange to repay a loan, are still allowed under the rule.
4. Require consumers to use household and personal items as collateral for a loan. Such items include appliances, linens, china, crockery, kitchenware, wedding rings, family photographs, personal papers, the family Bible, and household

pets. These clauses were called **household goods security clauses.** This rule does not apply when consumers borrow money to buy personal and household items and use the purchased items as collateral for the loan.

Another provision of the rule is designed to inform people of their responsibility when they co-sign someone else's loan. Under the rule, co-signers must be given the following written notice:

> You are being asked to guarantee this debt. Think carefully before you do. If the borrower doesn't pay the debt, you will have to. Be sure you can afford to pay if you have to, and that you want to accept this responsibility.
>
> You may have to pay up to the full amount of the debt if the borrower does not pay. You may also have to pay late fees or collection costs, which increase this amount.
>
> The creditor can collect this debt from you without first trying to collect from the borrower.* The creditor can use the same collection methods against you that can be used against the borrower, such as suing you, garnishing your wages, etc. If this debt is ever in default, that fact may become a part of *your* credit record.
>
> This notice is not the contract that makes you liable for the debt.

18-8 FOOD, DRUG, AND COSMETIC ACT

The Food and Drug Act of 1906 gave the federal government regulatory control over foods and drugs. The act prohibited interstate commerce in misbranded and adulterated foods, drinks, and drugs. The 1938 federal Food, Drug, and Cosmetic Act broadened the original legislation by extending the regulatory power of the Food and Drug Administration (FDA) to cosmetics and medical devices. Predistribution approval of new drugs was also required. A new drug, as defined in the act, includes "any drug...not generally recognized...as safe and effective for use under conditions prescribed, recommended, or suggested in the labeling." Exceptions to this requirement include experimental drugs under limited investigational use. The 1958 Delaney amendment to the act forbids the use of new food additives until they are proved safe for public consumption. The amendment further provides that any food containing a substance shown to cause cancer in humans or animals must be removed from the market, no matter how small the risk. Subsequent to 1962, drug amendments required that all drugs be proved effective as well as safe before they are marketed. The FDA was also given responsibility to regulate prescription drug advertising.

18-9 FAIR PACKAGING AND LABELING ACT

The Fair Packaging and Labeling Act of 1966 gave the FDA power to require that labels on packages of food, drugs, cosmetics, and medical devices be uni-

*If state law forbids a creditor from collecting from a co-signer without first trying to collect from the primary debtor, this sentence may be crossed out or omitted from the co-signer notice.

form and accurate. The act's major purpose is to make possible value comparisons among similar products. To this end, labels must indicate (1) who made the product, (2) what is in the package, (3) how much the package contains, and (4) the net quantity of one serving, if the number of servings is given. The use of qualifying words such as *jumbo* or *super* in statements of net quantity of contents is prohibited.

Econ Home Products, Inc., included on the label of its detergent the statement "12 jumbo ounces of detergent." Under the provisions of the Fair Packaging and Labeling Act, the FDA should issue cease and desist orders to Econ Home Products for noncompliance with the prohibition of the addition of qualifying words or phrases to the net-content statement. Had the label read "12 ounces of fast-acting detergent," it would have been allowed.

The FDA monitors compliance through its administration bureaus. Violations of the law can lead to a recall to remove defective products from the marketplace. If a voluntary recall is ineffective, the FDA may begin a civil action to stop the continued manufacture or distribution of a defective product. The FDA can carry out a seizure of the defective product by filing a complaint with the appropriate district court.

One evening the Cochrans had vichyssoise, a cold potato soup made by Bon Vivant, Inc. The couple did not eat much because the soup tasted spoiled. The next morning Mr. Cochran felt ill. He began seeing double and had difficulty speaking. He was admitted to the hospital and by evening was dead. Mrs. Cochran was later admitted to the same hospital, totally paralyzed. Investigation soon revealed that the Cochrans were victims of botulism—deadly botulin toxin. As a result, the Food and Drug Administration went to court to obtain orders to seize and hold all Bon Vivant products. Bon Vivant also went to court—to file for bankruptcy.

SUMMARY

18-1. State consumer protection laws are patterned after the Federal Trade Commission Act. Consumer protection offices help to enforce state consumer protection laws and, in some cases, will assist consumers with individual problems.

18-2. The Federal Trade Commission Act makes unfair or deceptive acts or practices in or affecting commerce unlawful. The law applies to businesses that deal in interstate commerce or that affect interstate commerce. The FTC does not resolve individual consumer complaints. Instead, it takes action when it sees a pattern of violations develop.

18-3. The FTC has established rules to help correct wrongdoings in the marketplace. The Used Car Rule requires dealers to inform buyers of the warranties that go with the car by placing a "Buyer's Guide" in the window of each used car offered for sale. The Door-to-Door Sales Rule gives consumers three days to change their minds when they enter into contracts away from the place of business of the seller. The Mail Order

Rule requires sellers to ship orders within the time promised in their advertisements. If no time period is promised, they must ship orders within 30 days. If they cannot do so, they must give consumers the option to cancel the order and receive a refund.

18-4. The FTC has determined that certain acts are unfair and deceptive. Only free samples and items sent by charities may be mailed to people who did not request them. People who receive unordered merchandise through the mail may treat the merchandise as a gift. Bait-and-switch schemes are prohibited. True odometer readings on cars must be disclosed to buyers.

18-5. The Consumer Product Safety Commission establishes safety standards for consumer products. The commission has the power to recall unsafe products and to impose fines on violators.

18-6. The Consumer Leasing Act requires companies that lease personal property to consumers for longer than four-month periods to disclose the full cost of the lease as well as other details of the transaction.

18-7. Many laws protect consumers who apply for or obtain credit. Lenders must make certain disclosures before lending money. It is illegal for creditors to discriminate against credit applicants because of their sex, race, marital status, national origin, religion, or age or because they get public assistance income. Credit cardholders are not responsible for any unauthorized charges made after the card issuer has been notified of the loss, theft, or possible unauthorized use of the card. Even then, cardholders are responsible only for the first $50 of any unauthorized charges. Consumers have the right to know all information about them (other than medical information) that is on file with a credit bureau. They also have a right to know the name of anyone who received a credit report in the past six months. A procedure has been established for the prompt handling of billing disputes dealing with charge accounts. Debt collectors are prohibited from harassing or abusing debtors when they attempt to collect debts. Confessions of judgment, wage assignments, waivers of exemption, and security interests in certain household goods can no longer be used in consumer credit contracts.

18-8. The Food, Drug, and Cosmetic Act safeguards against the use of misbranded and adulterated foods, drugs, cosmetics, and medical devices in the marketplace. New drugs must be approved by the FDA before they can be placed on the market.

18-9. Under the Fair Packaging and Labeling Act, labels on packages of food, drugs, cosmetics, and medical devices must indicate who made the product, what is in the package, how much the package contains, and in the sale of food, the net quantity of one serving if the number of servings is given.

Understanding Key Legal Terms

annual percentage rate (APR) (p. 235)
bait-and-switch scheme (p. 242)
balloon payment (p. 234)
Buyer's Guide (p. 230)
closed-end credit (p. 235)
cognovits (p. 239)
commerce (p. 229)
confessions of judgment (p. 239)
consent order (p. 229)
consumer (p. 228)

Credit Practices Rule (p. 239)
Door-to-Door Sales Rule (p. 230)
dunning letters (p. 232)
finance charge (p. 235)
household goods security clauses (p. 239)
interstate commerce (p. 229)
intrastate commerce (p. 229)
open-end credit (p. 235)
revolving charge account (p. 237)
Used Car Rule (p. 230)
wage assignments (p. 239)
waiver of exemption clauses (p. 239)

Questions for Review and Discussion

1. What services do state consumer protection offices provide? Generally speaking, where are they located?
2. What is the main purpose of the FTC Act? How is the act enforced?
3. Name and describe three FTC rules.
4. Discuss three federal laws that are designed to prevent unfair or deceptive acts.
5. Describe the scope of the Consumer Product Safety Act and the powers of the Consumer Product Safety Commission.
6. What benefits do consumers receive from the Consumer Leasing Act?
7. Name and give the purpose of seven consumer credit laws.
8. What protections are given to consumers by the Food, Drug, and Cosmetic Act?
9. Identify the information that the Fair Packaging and Labeling Act requires to be displayed on packages of food, drugs, cosmetics, and medical devices.

Analyzing Cases

1. Barrett owned some apartment buildings which he operated for business purposes. He did not live in any of the apartments. The Adirondack Bottled Gas Corp. supplied the apartment buildings with a propane-tank storage system. A dispute arose, and in a suit against Adirondack, Barrett claimed that the consumer protection law applied to the transaction. Do you agree with Barrett? Why or why not? *Barrett v. Adirondack Bottled Gas Corp.*, 487 A.2d 1074 (Vermont).
2. Harriet Glantz lost her job. She was unable to find work for several months and fell behind in the payment of her debts. A debt collector telephoned her at 11:45 p.m., used profanity, and threatened to "take care of her" if she didn't pay the amount owed. Were Glantz's rights violated? Explain.
3. Ingram went to a used-car lot in a large city and bought a used car. On his way home from the lot, the car that he had purchased broke down. The engine stopped running altogether. The used-car lot refused to fix the car because the salesperson had written "as is" on the sales slip. Ingram had not been informed that the car was sold to him as is. Has a consumer protection law been violated? Explain.
4. Prior to his marriage, Edward Garber had been in financial difficulty and had a poor credit rating. His wife, Natalie, applied for a credit card in her maiden name, fearing that she would be turned down if she used her married name of Garber. She was told that she must use her married name on a credit application. May Natalie use her maiden name when applying for credit? Explain.

5. In the opening commentary, Horack bought a used mustang from a used-car lot. The odometer showed that the car had been driven only 30,000 miles. Later, while cleaning her car, Andrews found a service receipt showing that the actual mileage on the car a year earlier was 45,000 miles. Has a law been violated? Explain.
6. Carboni's MasterCard bill contained several charges that she had not made. Upon investigation, she discovered that her credit card was missing from her wallet. She immediately notified the bank of the lost credit card. The unauthorized charges on the bill that she received amounted to $375. Must Carboni pay the full amount of the bill? Explain.
7. Delores Bierlein paid a $200 deposit toward the rental of the Silver Room at Alex's Continental Inn for her wedding reception. Later, Delores canceled the reception because her fiance was transferred from Ohio to New York. The inn refused to refund Delores's deposit. The consumer protection law of that state requires suppliers to furnish receipts when they receive deposits. Delores was not given a receipt for her $200 deposit. When she sued for the return of the $200 deposit, the question arose as to whether this transaction fell within the consumer protection law. Do you think it does? Explain. *Bierlein v. Alex's Continental Inn, Inc.*, 475 N.E.2d 1273 (Ohio).
8. In response to a radio advertisement, Mr. and Mrs. Lancet telephoned Hollywood Decorators, Inc., and arranged for Mr. Wolff, a company representative, to visit their home. During Wolff's visit, the Lancets signed a contract for interior decoration and paid a $1,000 deposit. Two days later, the Lancets canceled the contract by telephone and asked for the return of their deposit. Twelve days after that, the Lancets' attorney wrote a letter to the company renewing the cancellation. Are they bound by the contract they signed? Why or why not? *Hollywood Decorators, Inc. v. Lancet*, 461 N.Y.S.2d 955 (New York).

PART 3
CASE STUDY
Conway v. Larsen Jewelers, Inc.

Civil Court of the City of New York
Kings County, Small Claims Part
429 N.Y.S.2d 378

SUMMARY

Mrs. Conway purchased a gold necklace for $450 from Larsen Jewelers, Inc., on a layaway plan. She paid some money down and made additional payments from time to time. Under the arrangement, the jewelry store kept the necklace aside, or "laid away," until the purchase price was paid. At the point where Mrs. Conway had paid $265 toward the necklace, the jewelry store was burglarized and the necklace stolen. To gain access to the jewelry, the burglars had to disconnect or bypass two separate burglar alarm systems, rip open a locked iron gate, and tear apart a locked safe. Mrs. Conway brought suit in the small claims court, asking for either a duplicate necklace or its market value at the time of the theft.

THE COURT'S OPINION: JEROME L. STEINBERG, JUDGE

There are two problems presented for consideration of the Court:

First, absent a finding of negligence on the part of defendant, who bears the risk of loss under these circumstances? If the risk is upon the buyer, then under the Uniform Commercial Code, claimant would be denied any recovery, in the absence of negligence on the part of the seller; if the risk was seller's, we reach a second question, to wit: the nature or amount of recovery owed to claimant...

U.C.C. 2-509 is entitled *"Risk of Loss in the Absence of Breach."*...

Sub. 3 states as follows: *"In any case not within Subsections (1) and (2), the risk of loss passes to the buyer on his receipt of the goods, if seller is a merchant; otherwise the risk [of loss] passes to buyer on tender of delivery."*

Here, the claimant never received possession of the necklace. There was no written contract of sale between the parties. All claimant has is a receipt given to her by defendant. Claimant did not have the right to use or possession of the necklace until some time in the future, when the balance of the purchase price was paid. There was no delivery. Defendant is clearly a merchant under the U.C.C. 2-104 sub. (1), which defines merchant as *"a person who deals in goods of the kind or otherwise by his occupation holds himself out as having knowledge or skill peculiar to the practice or goods involved in the transaction."* Even had payment been made in full, the risk of loss would remain with defendant until actual receipt by buyer or tender of delivery by seller. The underlying theory is that since a merchant, who is to make physical delivery at his own place of business, has complete control of the goods, he is expected to ensure his interest in them. *Ramos v. Wheel Sports Center,* 96 Misc.2d 646, 409 N.Y.S.2d 505 (N.Y. Civil Ct., Bronx Co., 1978).

Having reached a conclusion on the question of liability, we turn to the second question; that of damages. The article in question was a necklace of gold filigree beads, uniformly interspersed with pearls and coral beads. The agreed price was $450, upon which claimant had made payments to the date of theft of $265. The value of the necklace has appreciated substantially between the time the "lay away" began, and the time of its theft; and therein lies the principal bone of contention between the parties.

Claimant asserts that the recovery should be with a duplicate necklace or the value thereof in the market at the time of its theft. She has offered to accept a similar necklace. Defendant argues that its maximum liability should be the $265 in payments made by claimant.

Clearly, the Court cannot direct the award of a similar necklace. Specific performance is not a remedy available in Small Claims Court. It appears from the testimony that the necklace was a unique item. While others may have been manufactured at one time, defendant had only one such necklace in his store, and his testimony that the necklace is no longer available is uncontradicted. Claimant has come forth with no evidence that such a necklace is readily available (although afforded an opportunity to do so) nor even that a substantially similar necklace is to be found. On the contrary, her own statements indicate that it was unique in its beauty and was similar to no other necklace she had seen.

When the subject matter of a contract is destroyed (or, as in this case, stolen) through no fault of the seller, the contract is deemed avoided. U.C.C. 2-613(a). If the chattel was identified and was unique it would come under this section of the U.C.C. *Valley Forge Flag Co., Inc. v. New York Dowel and Moulding Import Co., Inc.,* 90 Misc.2d 414, 415, 395 N.Y.S.2d 138 (Civil Court, N.Y. County, 1977). This would also be the case under long standing contract principles of impossibility of performance.

The defendant's only obligation is to return what has already been paid to him. Claimant would not be entitled to the market value of the necklace at the time of its theft. There was no testimony as to the value of the necklace at that time, and the Court is not invested with jurisdiction to speculate on values of jewelry or gold necklaces. Had there been such testimony as to "current value," many other interesting questions as to measure of damages and windfall profit would have had to be considered. However, since such is not the case, the Court declines to issue such dicta in this Small Claims action.

The contract between claimant and defendant is deemed avoided under U.C.C. § 2-613(a) and defendant shall refund claimant her $265.00.

QUESTIONS FOR ANALYSIS

1. For what legal reasons did the court say that the risk of loss would remain with the jewelry store?
2. What is the cause of the principal bone of contention between the parties?
3. Can this court order the jewelry store to give Mrs. Conway a similar necklace? Why or why not?
4. What is the legal status of a contract when its unique subject matter is destroyed through no fault of the seller?
5. What did Mrs. Conway win in this case?

PART 4
Property

CHAPTER 19
Personal Property and Bailments

OUTLINE

COMMENTARY

Dan Granit borrowed a friend's car, promising to take it only to a local restaurant. Instead, Dan and his friend, Carmela, drove the car to a distant city. They parked the car in a parking garage and walked to a nearby restaurant. After leaving the restaurant, Carmela realized that she had left her purse at the table where they had eaten. Later, she learned from the restaurant manager that another party had found it and was supposed to have returned it to her. To make things worse, the borrowed car was stolen from the parking garage. Who is responsible for the loss of the car? What duty did Dan owe to the friend whose car he had borrowed? What duty did the restaurant owe to Carmela with regard to her purse? The answer to these and other questions are found in the law of personal property and bailments.

OBJECTIVES

1. Explain the law that applies to lost and stolen property and gifts of personal property.
2. Judge whether a patent, copyright, or trademark is needed in a particular situation.
3. Determine when a bailment occurs.
4. Name and describe the principal types of bailments.
5. Give examples of two bailments that are imposed by law.
6. Explain the duties of bailors and bailees in various situations.
7. Describe four types of tortious bailees.

19-1 PERSONAL PROPERTY

Personal property, broadly defined, is everything that can be owned other than real estate. It is divided into two kinds, tangible and intangible.

Tangible personal property is property that has substance and that can be touched, such as a book, a pair of jeans, or a television set. Also called *goods,* or **chattels,** tangible personal property is movable and includes animals and growing crops.

Intangible personal property, on the other hand, is property that is not perceptible to the senses and cannot be touched. Such things as accounts receivables and stock certificates are examples of intangible personal property. Another name for this type of property is **chose in action,** which means evidence of the right to property but not the property itself. In addition to the items mentioned above, choses in action include money due on a note or contract, damages due for breach of contract or tort, and rights under insurance policies.

Lost Property

The finder of lost property has a legal responsibility, usually fixed by statute, to make an effort to learn the identity of the owner and return the property to that person. Advertising the property in a general-circulation newspaper is usually evidence of the finder's honest effort to locate the owner. Statutes in many states provide that if the finder of lost property has made an effort to locate the owner and has not been successful within a period specified by law, the property then belongs to the finder.

If lost property is found on the counter of a store, on a table in a restaurant or hotel, on a chair in a washroom, or in some similar public or semipublic place, it is considered not to be *lost* but to have been *misplaced.* It is reasonable to suppose that the owner will remember leaving it there and return for it. For this reason, the finder may not keep possession of the article but must leave it with the proprietor or manager to hold for the owner. If the property is found on the floor or in the corridor or any other place that would indicate it was not placed there intentionally, the finder may retain possession of the article while looking for the true owner. In this case, it is not likely that the owner would recall where it was lost.

While walking along a beach one morning, Carlow noticed a plastic bag near the edge of the water. She opened the bag and discovered that it contained a large sum of money. In the bag with the money was a bank deposit slip made out in the name of a nearby seafood restaurant. Carlow has a legal duty to return the money to the restaurant.

Suppose the bank deposit slip had not been in the bag and Carlow was unsuccessful in an attempt to find the rightful owner. After making a sincere effort to locate the real owner, and after a period of time set by state statute, Carlow would become the owner of the money.

When property is found and turned over to officials of a state, without any claim registered by the finder, the property becomes the property of the state after a period of time set by statute. The same rule applies to bank deposits and other claims which have been abandoned by persons in whose names such claims were registered. In these latter instances, a period of up to 20 years is usually required to establish the right of the state to take title. When property reverts to the state, it is said to **escheat.**

Gifts of Personal Property

People often make gifts of personal property. There are three requirements for a gift to be completed: (1) the **donor** (the one giving the gift) must intend to make a gift, (2) the gift must be delivered to the **donee** (the one receiving it), and (3) the donee must accept the gift. Once all three requirements are met, the gift cannot be taken back by the donor. It is known as an absolute gift, or gift ***inter vivos*** (between the living).

The gift of an engagement ring is a conditional gift, given in contemplation of marriage. Most courts hold that the donor of an engagement ring is entitled to its return if the engagement is broken by mutual agreement or by the donee. A few courts allow the return of the ring even when the donor breaks the engagement. These courts theorize that it is better to break the engagement without penalty than to have an unhappy marriage.

Uniform Gifts to Minors Act Problems can easily arise when gifts are given to minors. Sometimes parents or guardians use such gifts for themselves rather than for the minor. At other times, donors make gifts to minors and then change their minds and take the gifts back. In some circumstances, the Internal Revenue Service may not recognize a gift given to a minor who is over the age of 14. Instead it may tax the income from the gift to the donor, who is usually taxed at a higher rate than the minor. Under the Tax Reform Act of 1986, income from unearned income, such as interest and dividends, received by children under 14 years of age is taxable to the child's parents in any event.

To prevent these problems, most states have made the Uniform Gifts to Minors Act part of their state law. The act establishes a procedure for gifts to be made to minors. Under the procedure, minors are assured that gifts to them will either be used for their benefit or made available to them when they become adults. In addition, the income from gifts that are given to minors over the age of 14 is taxable to the minor rather than to the person who made the gift.

Planchard placed $10,000 in a joint certificate of deposit with his 15-year-old daughter, Danielle. He claimed that the money was a gift to his daughter and that the interest from the certificate should be taxable to her rather than to him. The Internal Revenue Service required Planchard to declare the interest from the joint certificate of deposit on his tax return as part of his gross income. Planchard would have avoided taxation by following the provisions of the Uniform Gifts to Minors Act.

Gifts *in Causa Mortis* A gift given during one's lifetime, in contemplation of death from a known cause, is a **gift *in causa mortis*.** Gifts *in causa mortis* are conditional. A gift *in causa mortis* is ineffective if the donor does not die as expected or if death is caused by circumstances other than those feared.

Rossano was seriously ill following an abdominal operation. Realizing that death might be near, Rossano signed over a savings account to Hall, giving Hall the savings book with necessary notations of assignment. Rossano did die three weeks later, not because of the surgery but because of pneumonia. Rossano's executor may declare the gift *in causa mortis* void and demand the return of Rossano's savings for benefit of the estate.

Stolen Personal Property

Although a presumption of title to goods usually follows possession of them, it is possible for a person to have possession of goods without having title, just as it is possible for a person to have title without having possession. Thus, a thief acquires no title to goods that are stolen and, therefore, cannot convey a good title. The true owner never relinquished title to the goods, and even an innocent purchaser, who acquired the goods in good faith and for value, would be obliged to return the goods to the owner. Title to stolen goods never left the true owner, and possession can always be regained by that owner if the goods can be found, no matter in whose possession they may be at the time.

Long bought a moped from Garrison, paying a fair price for it. Later, it was discovered that the moped had been stolen from Hinkley. Hinkley will be entitled to the return of the moped because she is the true owner and still has title to it. Long can recover his loss from Garrison, the person from whom he bought the moped, for breach of warranty of title (see Chapter 16).

19-2 PATENTS, COPYRIGHTS, TRADEMARKS

To encourage innovation and creativity, the government has enacted patent, copyright, and trademark laws. These laws give property rights to their owners.

Patents

A **patent** is an official document that gives the owner the exclusive right to make, use, or sell an invention for a term of 17 years. To be patentable, a device must consist of some new idea or principle not known before. It must be a discovery as distinguished from mere mechanical skill or knowledge. The device may be a process, an article of manufacture, or a composition of matter.

A microbiologist invented a bacterium capable of breaking down crude oil. The U.S. Patent and Trademark Office denied a patent on the bacterium, claiming that it was alive and therefore not patentable. On appeal, the U.S. Supreme Court held that the live, human-made bacterium is patentable. The court said that such a microorganism is a "manufacture" or "composition of matter" within the meaning of the patent law.

A patent may not be obtained if the subject matter of the patent would be obvious to a person having ordinary skill in the field.

In the past, organizations which had been awarded federal contracts for research sometimes had difficulty obtaining patents on their discoveries. Some agencies of the federal government granted patent rights; others did not. Consequently, every government agency supporting private research had its own patent policy. There was no uniformity among agencies. Many worthwhile inventions were never marketed because the government retained title to them. In 1980, Congress amended the patent law, allowing federal contractors greater control over the results of their research. The amendment permits universities, small companies, and nonprofit organizations to retain ownership of patents gained as a result of federal grants and contracts. Large corporations are excluded from the provisions of the amendment. It is expected that this amendment to the patent law will have far-reaching effects in the marketplace.

Another amendment, passed in 1984, allows the 17-year term of a patent to be extended in certain cases. The amendment applies to new products, such as drugs, which must go through a governmental review period before they can be marketed. Under the amendment, the review period during which the product cannot be sold is not counted as part of the 17-year term of the patent.

Copyrights

Copyrights are intangible property rights granted by statute to authors or originators of literary, musical, or artistic productions. They give to their owners the exclusive legal right to reproduce, publish, and sell their work for a specific time period. Works created after January 1, 1978, when the present copyright law came into effect, are protected for the life of the author plus 50 years. The law allows some copying to be done without permission under the **fair use doctrine.** This doctrine provides that copyrighted material may be reproduced without permission if the use of the material is reasonable and not harmful to the rights of the copyright owner. Copying items for such purposes as criticism, comment, news reporting, teaching, scholarship, and research is permissible. In addition, libraries and archives may reproduce single copies of certain copyrighted materials for noncommercial purposes without obtaining permission of the copyright owner.

Universal City Studios, Inc., and Walt Disney Productions, Inc., brought suit against Sony Corporation of America, manufacturers of Betamax. Universal and Disney claimed that Sony infringed on their copyrights by manufacturing and selling Betamax video tape recorders, allowing people to tape-record their copyrighted films at home. The U.S. Supreme court held in favor of Sony. The court said that noncommercial recording of material broadcast over the public airwaves that is intended for home use only is a fair use of copyrighted works and does not constitute copyright infringement.

Trademarks

A **trademark** is any word, name, symbol, or device adopted and used by a manufacturer or merchant to identify the goods and distinguish them from those manufactured or sold by others. It is different from a patent in that it does not apply to an invention or manufacturing process. Rather, it applies to the name or mark used to identify a product. The function of a trademark is to identify the source of a product, that is, the one who makes it. Coke, for example, is made only by the Coca-Cola Company, and Wheaties are made only by General Mills. Owners of trademarks have the exclusive right to use the particular word, name, or symbol that they have adopted as their trademark. Trademarks can be established in three different ways: under the common law, under a state statute, or under the Federal Trademark Act of 1946.

Common Law Trademarks Under the common law, trademarks may be established by usage rather than by registration with the state or federal government. To claim such a mark, the party must demonstrate that use of the mark has been of such quality and for such a duration that it has come to identify goods bearing it as originating from that party. The mark must have developed a secondary meaning—not merely identification of the product, but rather identification of its producer.

Powers, who published a small newspaper, decided to name the paper the *Daily Planet*. D.C. Comics, Inc., publishers of the Superman comic book, brought suit to stop Powers from using that name. Evidence was introduced to show that the *Daily Planet* first appeared in the Superman story in 1940. Since then it has played a key role, not only in the Superman story, but also in the development of the Superman character. In addition, D.C. Comics, Inc., has utilized the Superman character in connection with many products born of the Superman story. These products have included school supplies, toys, costumes, games, and clothes. The court enjoined Powers from using the name *Daily Planet*. It held that D.C. Comics, Inc., had demonstrated an association of such duration and consistency with the *Daily Planet* that it had established a common law trademark in that name. The *Daily Planet* has over the years become inextricably woven into the fabric of the Superman story.

State Trademark Statutes Although the U.S. Constitution gives exclusive control to the federal government over patents and copyrights, it is silent about trademarks. Therefore, federal laws apply only to trademarks that are used in interstate commerce. Each of the 50 states has statutes that regulate the use of trademarks in intrastate commerce, that is, within the boundaries of the state. Although there has been an attempt to make the trademark laws of each state uniform, they differ substantially.

The Federal Trademark Act of 1946 The Federal Trademark Act of 1946, called the Lanham Act, provides for registration of trademarks with the U.S. Patent and Trademark Office. To be eligible for registration, the goods or services must be sold or used in more than one state or in this and a foreign country. A trademark cannot be registered if it consists of

1. Immoral, deceptive, or scandalous matter
2. Matter which may disparage or falsely suggest a connection with persons, living or dead, institutions, beliefs, or national symbols, or which may bring them into contempt, or disrepute
3. The flag or coat of arms or other insignia of the United States, or of any state or municipality, or of any foreign nation, or any simulation thereof
4. The name, signature, or portrait of any living individual, except with that person's written consent
5. The name, signature, or portrait of a deceased President of the United States during the life of a surviving spouse, if any, except by the written consent of the spouse
6. A mark that so resembles a mark registered in the Patent and Trademark Office or a mark or trade name previously used in the United States by another and not abandoned, as to be likely, when applied to the goods of the applicant, to cause confusion, or to cause mistake, or to deceive

---

Spangler Candy Co., makers of Dum Dums lollipops, claimed that its competitor, Crystal Pure Candy Co., copied its trademark. Crystal Pure produced a candy called Pop Pops. The makers of Dum Dums claimed that the makers of Pop Pops copied precisely the type of font and logo of its trademark (see Figure 19-1). The court allowed Pop Pops mark, holding that it does not resemble the Dum Dums mark so as to be likely to confuse or to deceive purchasers.

Spangler Mark

Crystal Pure Candy Mark

Figure 19-1 Marks at issue in the Spangler case.

Anyone who registers a trademark may give notice that the mark is registered by displaying with the mark the words "Registered in U.S. Patent and Trademark Office" or "Reg. U.S. Pat. & Tm. Off." or the letter R enclosed within a circle, thus: ®.

A trademark registration remains in force for 20 years and may be renewed for additional 20-year periods, unless it is canceled or surrendered.

19-3 BAILMENTS OF PERSONAL PROPERTY

A person rents a movie from a video shop. An early-morning jogger finds someone's lost wallet. A neighbor borrows a friend's picnic table. In each of these situations, possession of tangible personal property has been given to someone other than the owner, but in no case was there an intent to give title. Each situation illustrates a transaction known as a bailment.

A **bailment** is the transfer of possession and control of personal property to another with the intent that the same property will be returned later. The person who transfers the property is the **bailor.** The person to whom the property is transferred is the **bailee.** In a bailment, neither the bailor nor the bailee intends that title to the property should pass. The bailee has an obligation to return the same property to the bailor, or to someone the bailor designates, at a later time.

When an individual loans goods to another with the intention that the goods may be used and later replaced with an equal amount of different goods, it is not a bailment. Instead, it is known as a ***mutuum.***

Matthew McCarthy borrowed a cup of sugar from his neighbor. He used the sugar in a pie he made that evening. He returned a cup of sugar to his neighbor the next day after shopping at a grocery store. The loan of the sugar was a *mutuum* rather than a bailment because the parties did not intend that the identical particles of sugar that were borrowed would be returned.

19-4 PRINCIPAL TYPES OF BAILMENTS

There are three principal types of bailments: bailments for the sole benefit of the bailor, bailments for the sole benefit of the bailee, and mutual-benefit bailments. The first two types are called gratuitous bailments. In **gratuitous bailments,** property is transferred to another person without either party's giving or asking for payment of any kind. Such bailments lack consideration; therefore, they may be rescinded at any time by either party. Parties to such agreements usually consider them only as favors. In reality, however, definite legal responsibilities are placed upon both the bailor and the bailee.

Bailments for Sole Benefit of Bailor

When possession of personal property is transferred to another for purposes that will benefit only the bailor, a **bailment for the sole benefit of the bailor** results.

Conte agreed to deliver Higgins's watch to a jewelry shop, which she would pass on the way to work. Higgins gave her the watch, and she placed it in a briefcase with other valuables. Conte was promised no reward for this act. It was a favor. It was also a bailment for the sole benefit of the bailor.

Bailments for Sole Benefit of Bailee

Transactions in which the possession of personal property is transferred for purposes that will benefit only the bailee are gratuitous **bailments for the sole benefit of the bailee.**

Martin asked Kahn if she might use the latter's car for a trip she planned to make to Kansas City. Kahn agreed to lend the car, asking nothing in return for this favor. The bailment was created for the sole benefit of the bailee, Martin.

Mutual-Benefit Bailments

When personal property is transferred to a bailee with the intent that both parties will benefit, a **mutual-benefit bailment** results. The ordinary bailments involving business transactions are usually mutual-benefit bailments in which the business person is a **compensated bailee,** that is, one who is paid for the services.

In preparing for a trip to Detroit, Cassidy left a suit at the Valet Shop to be cleaned and pressed. The agreed-upon price for these services was $8. Both Cassidy and the Valet Shop will benefit from the transaction. This is a mutual-benefit bailment. The Valet Shop is a compensated bailee.

Four basic kinds of mutual-benefit bailments exist. These are (1) a pledge, or pawn; (2) a contract for use of goods; (3) a contract for custody of goods; and (4) a contract for work or service on goods. In addition, a bailment by necessity, also described below, may be implied by law.

Pledge, or Pawn A person wishing to borrow money must often give the lender possession of personal property as security for repayment of the debt. The property thus left as security is called the **pledge,** or **pawn.** The borrower, or debtor, is the **pledgor,** or bailor. The lender, or creditor, is the **pledgee,** or bailee. The pledgee may be a bank, a loan company, a credit union, a pawnbroker, or another person.

Cohen borrowed $7,400 from the American Arlington Bank. As security for the loan, the parties signed a bailment agreement making the bank the bailee of

Cohen's valuable painting of King George III of England, allegedly one of three portraits of the king by the eighteenth-century painter George Ramsey. The painting was hung in the office of the bank's vice president. This was a pledge because the bank had possession and complete control over the painting while the loan was outstanding.

UCC 9-207

The UCC sets out the rights and duties of pledgors and pledgees. These rights and duties are explained in detail in Chapter 30.

Contracts for Use of Goods A mutual-benefit bailment results when an agreement is made for renting goods for a fixed sum or at a definite rate. Examples are renting a tool from a rental store or hiring a horse from a riding academy or an automobile from a drive-it-yourself firm.

The bailee has the right to the exclusive possession and use of the article during the period of the contract. The bailee must exercise reasonable care in the use and protection of the property. **Reasonable care** means that degree of care which a reasonably prudent person would use under the same circumstances and conditions. Damages resulting from causes outside the bailee's control will not make the bailee liable. However, damage or destruction caused by the bailee's use of the article in a way different from that agreed upon makes a bailee absolutely liable to the bailor.

Contracts for Custody of Goods Contracts for the storage of property are mutual-benefit bailments when a fee is charged. Garages, warehouses, grain elevators, and similar businesses are engaged in bailments of this kind.

The bailee, except by special agreement, is not an insurer. (See Figure 19-2.) The bailee must exercise reasonable care and has no implied authority to use the bailed property unless use is necessary to maintain the property's value.

Courts have held it to be a bailment when someone parks a car in a garage or lot which has an attendant present at all times to check cars going in and out.

Richard drove his car to the entrance of the public parking garage at Logan International Airport in Boston. He entered the garage through a gate by taking a ticket from a machine, drove into the garage, parked and locked his car and took the keys with him. The exit from the garage was attended at all times. When Richard returned four days later, he discovered that his car had been stolen. The court held that this was a bailment because the parking garage had possession and control of the vehicle. Richard recovered the value of the car from the parking garage because the garage could not prove that it had used reasonable care to prevent the theft of the car.

It is not a bailment, however, when someone parks a car in an unattended parking area.

906-540

THIS IS A SELF-PARKING FACILITY CLAIM CHECK. PLEASE BE CAREFUL in parking your car so that you do not damage your own car or those of your fellow parkers. PARK AT YOUR OWN RISK. THIS IS NOT A BAILMENT. EMPLOYEES NOT AUTHORIZED TO ACCEPT DELIVERY OF YOUR CAR.

This check is a Contract of Lease between Middletown Parking Authority, Lessor, and you as Tenant, for a parking space. By renting the space, you agree that there is no Bailor-Bailee relation between you and Lessor. Term of lease from hour to hour, rental as payable.

1. **Lessor is not responsible for personal property; and Lessor assumes no liability for fire, theft or casualty except from its own negligence.**
2. **Any suits or actions against Lessor for any claim arising out of this lease shall be filed within ninety (90) days of date of occupancy of the leased premises.**

MIDDLETOWN PARKING AUTHORITY
FIRST & MAIN STREETS

PLEASE PAY CASHIER
BEFORE GETTING YOUR CAR

Figure 19-2 The small print on this parking-garage ticket states that it is not a bailment.

Sewall parked his car in a parking lot where he parked each day. He paid the attendant, locked the car, and took the keys with him. The attendant remained on duty only in the morning and left the lot unattended for the rest of the day. There were several entrances and exits to the lot. When Sewall returned for his car, he discovered that it had been stolen. The court held that this was not a bailment. The attendant had exercised no control over the vehicle whatsoever. Instead, it was simply a rental of a parking space. Sewall lost the case against the parking garage because he could not prove that garage employees had committed a negligent act.

It is important to note the difference in the burden of proof in the above two cases. Modern bailment law requires the bailee to prove that reasonable care was used. This is because the bailee held the goods and thus is the one who can best prove what happened. Since the Richard case involved a bailment, the burden was on the bailee to prove that it was not negligent. In the Sewall case, which was not a bailment, the burden was on Sewall to prove that the parking lot owner was negligent.

The courts have held that the surrender of car keys to a parking lot or garage attendant is a sufficient delivery of possession and control to create a bailment. Factors that have been considered to be important in determining a bailment relationship are whether there are attendants at the entrance and exits of the lot, whether the car owner receives a claim check that must be surrendered before the car can be removed, and whether the parking lot is enclosed.

A bank operating a safe-deposit-box service has the possession of the property placed in the box by the customer. The legal relationship created by this transaction, under the prevailing view, is that of bailor and bailee.* The fact that the bank does not know the character and description of the property that the customer places in the safe-deposit box does not change that relationship. It has been argued that a bailment cannot exist because the bank does not have exclusive possession of the property that is left in the safe deposit box. Most courts, however, have rejected this argument, saying that the bank has exclusive access to the property. The depositor cannot gain access to the safe-deposit box without the consent and active participation of the bank.

Contracts for Work or Service on Goods Agreements in which property is transferred to another for work, repairs, or other service—for which the owner agrees to pay a fee—are mutual-benefit bailments. Cleaners, repair shops, and persons developing photographic film, for example, are engaged in bailment transactions of this kind. The bailee is not an insurer, but must exercise reasonable care. Losses by fire, theft, or other causes beyond the control of the bailee do not excuse the bailor from paying for the bailee's services if the work is completed prior to the time of loss and if the bailor is notified that the property is ready for delivery.

> Ricotta left a car at Modern Paint Shop for a new paint job. When the car was ready to be picked up, she was notified. Two days later, before she took delivery of the car, the shop was burned out, together with the newly painted car. The fire resulted when burglars entered an adjoining building, where they started a fire. Modern Paint Shop has no obligation to compensate Ricotta for the loss. This was a bailment requiring ordinary care. The loss did not result from negligence or lack of care on the part of Modern Paint Shop.

Bailments by Necessity A common type of mutual-benefit bailment, implied by law, is the **bailment by necessity.** This arises when one purchases a suit or dress and is required to give up possession of one's own property while being fitted; when one receives services in a barber or beauty shop, where one must give up possession of a hat or other articles of apparel; and in other similar situations which require a customer to give up possession of property for

*Courts in a few states, such as Delaware, have held that the safe-deposit-box holder is a renter of space and that therefore the lessor-lessee relationship applies.

the benefit of both parties. In such cases the bailee is required to accept the other's property and to exercise reasonable care in its protection.

Cook had an appointment at a hairdresser's. The day was cold and rainy, and she wore a heavy coat, overshoes, and a storm hat. The operator asked Cook to put her things on a rack outside the booth, which was out of sight. There was no other place to leave them.

This is a typical bailment by necessity. It would have been inconvenient, improper, and perhaps impossible for Cook to have remained clothed in her rainwear while being served by the shop. Even though the shop had placed a sign reading "Not Responsible for Articles Left Here" over the rack, it did not remove the shop's responsibility as a bailee of her things.

Restaurants are not always responsible for property left in a cloakroom.

Meisnere hung his coat in an unattended cloakroom at the request of a waitress after the coat had fallen from his chair. No claim check was given to Meisnere, and there was no charge for the service. A notice was posted in the cloakroom disclaiming any responsibility for lost belongings, but Meisnere did not see the notice. His coat was stolen. The court held in favor of the restaurant, saying that no bailment took place. There had been no delivery which resulted in a change of possession and control of the coat.

19-5 BAILMENTS IMPOSED BY LAW

The law recognizes two types of bailments where the obligation of the bailee is imposed by law rather than by mutual agreement of the parties. In these situations, the bailee must exercise the same degree of care as in other bailments for the sole benefit of the bailor. (See the earlier discussion in this chapter.)

Involuntary Bailments

In an **involuntary bailment,** personal property is delivered to a stranger through some agency beyond the control of either party, as by an act of God. The law implies delivery of the property to the one who comes into possession.

During a hurricane, personal property of many kinds was blown onto Vail's land. An involuntary bailment resulted, and Vail had the implied obligation to give some care, though slight, to the property until the real owners were located and the property returned.

Lost Property

By implication, the finder of lost property who takes possession of the goods becomes the bailee. The rights and duties of the finder are those of a bailee.

Thus, the finder of a purse or of any other property acquires an ownership that is second only to the real owner's right to the property. The finder is considered to be the bailee of the property, holding it for the true owner until that person can be located. The situation is the same when someone comes into possession of property by mistake.

19-6 DUTIES OF BAILOR AND BAILEE

As in other legal relationships, the law gives specific rights to and imposes specific duties on the parties to a bailment. Generally, the duties of the bailee are closely related to (and in a sense the opposite of) the rights of the bailor.

Duty of Bailor

The bailor must deliver safe goods to the bailee. If the goods are not safe and if the dangerous conditions are not apparent upon ordinary examination, the bailor has an obligation to call such facts to the bailee's attention.

Clark, a bus driver, volunteered to repair ceiling tiles at a church. Scaffolding was rented by a church employee from Rental Equipment Company, Inc., but guardrails were not selected by the employee to go with the scaffolding. Clark fell off the scaffolding and was seriously injured. An expert witness testified at the trial that scaffolding equipment is not safe without a guardrail. Clark recovered money damages from the rental company. The court said that the rental company owed a duty to warn the inexperienced volunteer that scaffolding without guardrails is inherently dangerous.

In a bailment for the sole benefit of the bailee, the bailor is not responsible for injuries to the bailee caused by defects in the bailed property unless the bailor had actual knowledge of the defect at the time of the bailment.

In a bailment for the sole benefit of the bailor, the bailor has a duty to reimburse the bailee for any expenses the bailee might have in the care of the property. The bailee has a corresponding duty to keep such expenses within a reasonable amount, depending upon the circumstances.

Duty of Bailee

Bailees must use care in handling a bailor's property.

Degrees of Care The bailee's duty of care has changed in recent years. Formerly, three degrees of care were generally recognized in the law of bailments: great care, ordinary care, and slight care. Some states still recognize these degrees of care as part of their bailment law.

In a bailment for the sole benefit of the bailee, the bailee was required to use *great care* because possession of the goods was solely for the bailee's benefit. The bailee was responsible for **slight negligence,** which is the failure to use that degree of care which persons of extraordinary prudence and foresight are accustomed to use.

Williamson borrowed her aunt's car and used it to drive 500 miles for a job interview. At no time during the entire trip did she check the oil in the engine. This resulted in damage to the motor. Since Williamson did not exercise great care, she will be responsible for any repairs resulting from her negligence.

In a mutual-benefit bailment, the bailee owed a duty to use *ordinary care.* The bailee was responsible for **ordinary negligence,** which is failing to use the care that a reasonable person would use under the same circumstances.

Levasseur stored his boat, motor, and trailer in Field's building for the winter for $10. Levasseur expressed some doubts about the soundness of the building, particularly concerning the structure of the roof. Field assured him that the building was safe. The roof collapsed after a winter snowstorm, damaging Levasseur's boat. In allowing Levasseur to recover from Field, the court said that the relationship imposed a duty on the bailee to use ordinary care, which he failed to do.

In a bailment for the sole benefit of the bailor, the bailee owed a duty to use only *slight care* since the bailee was receiving no benefit from the arrangement. The bailee was required only to refrain from **gross negligence.** This is very great negligence—much more serious than ordinary negligence.

The Martins asked two girls, Bell and Christian, to occupy their home during the Martins' vacation. The Martins did not pay the housesitters but left a few dollars for groceries. The contents of the house were badly damaged by fire when one of the girls left a pan of grease unattended on a range burner. This was a gratuitous bailment for the sole benefit of the bailor. Bell and Christian were not liable for damage to the Martins' property because they were not grossly negligent.

Modern Theory The modern theory, adopted by many courts and applied to bailees generally, is that there are no degrees of care or negligence. These courts hold that it is the duty of all bailees to exercise **reasonable care**, that is, the degree of care that a reasonably prudent person could have used.

Edwards took her Cadillac automobile to the Crestmont Cadillac garage to have a tire changed and the wheels aligned. When she returned later to pick up the car, she learned that it had been stolen from the garage. The court held Crestmont responsible. It had not used reasonable care in preventing the car from being stolen. The court said that a bailee is presumed to be negligentwhen it fails to redeliver the bailed property unless it can prove that it was not negligent.

Use of Bailor's Property In a bailment for the sole benefit of the bailee, the bailee has the right to use the property for the purposes for which the bailment was created. Use for other purposes or use over a longer period of time than provided for in the agreement will make the bailee responsible for any damages that may result to the property, regardless of the amount of care exercised.

Robbins used Castro's chain saw to cut up a small tree that fell during a storm. The cutting of the tree was all that Castro had agreed to allow Robbins to do with the saw. Robbins decided to cut up other timber awaiting the fireplace. Through no fault of Robinson, the saw's engine caught fire. Even though Robbins was in no way responsible for the fire, he is obligated to reimburse Castro for the damage because he used the saw for a purpose other than that which was agreed to.

Any *ordinary* and *expected expense* incurred in the use of another's property must be borne by the bailee. For example, gas and oil for the operation of the chainsaw in the above case should be paid for by Robbins. On the other hand, repairs and adjustments not caused by ordinary use or damages not attributed to the bailee's negligence become the responsibility of the bailor. The bailee is not obligated to replace parts which break down because of the gradual use and depreciation of the other's property over a long period. If the chainsaw in the above case had simply worn out through no fault of Robbins, he would not have been responsible.

Swanson, with Oberly's permission, took Oberly's motorcycle on a trial ride. Every precaution was taken to avoid damage. Nevertheless, on the way home, the front tire blew, and Swanson found it necessary to buy a new tire. The old tire had been badly worn in many places. The blowout was not caused by Swanson's negligent use. Oberly, the bailor, would be responsible for any *unusual* and *unexpected* expenses resulting from the tire blowout, including the obligation of reimbursing Swanson for the tire.

In a mutual-benefit bailment, the bailee must use the property only for the express purposes permitted by the bailor as provided for in the contract of bailment. The rental of a car, tools, or formal wear, for example, implies the right of reasonable use. Failing to use the property as agreed makes the bailee responsible for any damages that might result, regardless of the degree of care that was exercised.

Smith rented a tuxedo from the Valet Shop. While wearing it, he crawled under a friend's car to make an adjustment to the brakes. Smith was liable to the Valet Shop for the resulting damage to the suit. The bailed property had not been used for the purposes permitted by the bailor. A responsibly prudent person would know that one does not crawl under a car while wearing a rented tuxedo.

In a bailment for the sole benefit of the bailor, the bailee has no implied right to use the bailor's property. Use without permission is technically a tort of conversion on the part of the bailee; it would make the bailee fully liable for any damages that might result, even if the bailee had used great care and was not guilty of negligence. (Conversion is the civil wrong that arises when one unlawfully treats another's property as one's own.)

Lindstrom agreed to care for Holbart's car while Holbart was absent from the city. Although permission to use the car had not been given, Lindstrom drove the car many times to save having to walk.

Should Lindstrom become involved in an accident as a result of the unauthorized use of Holbart's car, he would be fully and indefensibly liable to Holbart for damages. In a case like this, it is not even necessary that the bailor prove lack of care by the bailee.

Some property, however, requires use or exercise to maintain its value. If the property is of a type that might depreciate from nonuse, the bailee would have an implied obligation to perform the services necessary to maintain the property in proper condition.

19-7 TORTIOUS BAILEES

Persons who have *wrongful possession* of another's property are said to be **tortious bailees.** There are four types of tortious bailees:

1. One in possession of stolen property
2. One wrongfully retaining possession of the lost property of another

---

Bradshaw found a wallet belonging to Compton. Intentionally and knowingly, she refused to either return the wallet or contact Compton about the matter. Bradshaw placed herself in a vulnerable position because of her failure to return Compton's property; she would be fully responsible for the wallet and contents, regardless of the circumstances under which Compton himself might have lost it. Such failure to act would also make her criminally liable on a complaint made to the police.

---

3. One using a bailed article for a purpose other than agreed upon
4. One refusing to return property at the termination of a bailment

Tortious bailees are responsible for any damage that results to property in their possession, regardless of the degree of care that they might exercise or the cause of the damage.

SUMMARY

19-1. Personal property is everything that can be owned except real estate. Anyone who finds lost property must make a reasonable effort to find the owner. Misplaced property must be turned over to the manager of the place where it is found. For a gift to be completed, the donor must intend to make a gift, it must be delivered to the donee, and the donee must accept the gift. A thief acquires no title to goods that are stolen and, therefore, cannot convey a good title to others.

19-2. A patent gives the owner the exclusive right to make, use, or sell an invention for a term of 17 years. Copyrights give their owners the exclusive right to publish their work for the life of the author plus 50 years. Trademarks, which protect product names and marks, may be established either by usage or by registration. Registered trademarks remain in force for 20 years and may be renewed.

19-3. A bailment occurs whenever someone transfers possession and control of personal property to another with the intent that the same property will be returned later.

19-4. The principal types of bailments are: (1) bailments for the sole benefit of the bailor, (2) bailments for the sole benefit of the bailee, and (3) mutual-benefit bailments. When goods are lost or damaged while in the possession of a bailee, the burden is on the bailee to prove that no negligence was involved; if this cannot be done, the bailee will be held responsible for the loss.

19-5. The law imposes a bailment when someone receives another's property through an act of God and when someone finds another's lost property.

19-6. Bailors owe a duty to deliver safe goods to bailees. Under modern law, bailees owe a duty to use reasonable care with the goods in their possession. Former law, still followed in some states, required the bailee to use great care in a bailment for the sole benefit of the bailee, slight care in a bailment for the sole benefit of the bailor, and ordinary care in a mutual-benefit bailment.

19-7. A tortious bailee is one who is wrongfully in possession of another's property. Tortious bailees are responsible for any damage that results to the property in their possession.

Understanding Key Legal Terms

bailee (p. 254)
bailment (p. 254)
bailment by necessity (p. 258)
bailment for the sole benefit of the bailee (p. 255)
bailment for the sole benefit of the bailor (p. 255)
bailor (p. 254)
chattels (p. 248)
chose in action (p. 248)
copyright (p. 251)
donee (p. 249)
donor (p. 249)
escheat (p. 249)
gift *in causa mortis* (p. 250)
gratuitous bailment (p. 254)
gross negligence (p. 261)
involuntary bailment (p. 259)
inter vivos gift (p. 249)
mutual-benefit bailment (p. 255)
mutuum (p. 254)
patent (p. 250)
pawn (p. 255)
personal property (p. 248)
pledge (p. 255)
pledgee (p. 255)
pledgor (p. 255)
reasonable care (p. 256)
slight negligence (p. 260)
tortious bailees (p. 263)
trademark (p. 252)

Questions for Review and Discussion

1. When may someone who finds lost property claim ownership of it?
2. Distinguish between an ordinary gift and a gift *in causa mortis*.
3. What assurances are minors and donors given by following the procedures of the Uniform Gift to Minors Act?
4. Describe the kind of title that is given by a thief who sells stolen goods to an innocent person.
5. What are protected by (*a*) patents, (*b*) copyrights, and (*c*) trademarks?
6. Describe the principal types of bailments, and give an example of each.
7. Give examples of two types of bailments that are imposed by law.
8. Explain the duty of the bailor.
9. How does the modern theory of care imposed on a bailee differ from the degrees of care recognized in former years?
10. Describe four types of tortious bailees.

Analyzing Cases

1. Vincent Hartwell, a college junior majoring in English, admired a valuable book collection on his uncle's bookshelf. To Hartwell's surprise, his uncle said that he planned to give the books to Hartwell as a gift and that he could have them at that moment. Hartwell replied that he was living in a dormitory and had no place to keep the collection. His uncle said, "Consider the books yours. I'll keep them here, and when you're ready for them, come and get them." Hartwell thanked his uncle and left for school. His uncle died a week later. Hartwell's cousin, Kathleen Lane, inherited the uncle's entire estate. She claimed that the valuable book collection belonged to her. Who is the legal owner of the book collection, Hartwell or Lane? Explain.

2. Grabert stored his Cessna 175A aircraft in Noel's hangar for $30 a month. The Cessna required a key to be started, and the key was left either in the plane's ignition or hung on a knob on the instrument panel. At night the hangar was locked. A key to the hangar door was left outside on the top of a meter box so that aircraft owners could get to their planes at any hour of the day or night. Cameron, a part-time employee of the airport, stole the plane one night when he was off duty. He did not have a pilot's license. The plane crashed, and Cameron was killed. Was the owner of the airport liable for the destruction of the plane? Explain. *Grabert v. James C. Noel Flying Service, Inc.* 360 So.2d 1363 (Louisiana).

3. Pollard found a valuable first edition that someone had dropped on the street. She took the book home, placing it with others in a collection of first editions. The owner's name could not be found in the lost book, and Pollard made no effort to locate the owner. Does she now have title to the book? Explain. See also *Doe v. Oceola,* 270 N.W.2d 254 (Michigan).

4. In his will, Gavegnano left all his tangible personal property to his daughter, Caroline. At the time of his death, he owned 19 thoroughbred horses. In addition, a cashier's check made payable to him for $33,000 was found among his belongings. The lower court judge held that the horses and the check were tangible personal property and should be given to Caroline under the terms of the will. Caroline's brothers appealed the decision, claiming that neither the horses nor the check were tangible per-

sonal property. Are Caroline's brothers correct? Explain. *Pagiarulo v. National Shawmut Bank,* 233 N.E.2d 213 (Massachusetts).

5. Rabinovitzch's husband delivered her motor vehicle to Sea Crest Cadillac-Pontiac, Inc., for service and repair. When he returned that evening to pick it up, the motor vehicle was missing from the garage. When suit was brought against Sea Crest to recover the value of the car, Sea Crest argued that Rabinovitzch had the burden of proving that Sea Crest had not exercised reasonable care to prevent the loss of the automobile. Who has the burden of proof in this case? *Rabinovitzch v. Sea Crest Cadillac-Pontiac, Inc.,* 335 N.E.2d 698 (Massachusetts).

6. In the course of writing a research paper for one of her classes, Kirby copied a number of pages from several books at the library. She took the copies home to continue her research in a more relaxed atmosphere. A friend in her law class told Kirby that she had violated the copyright laws by copying the pages from the various books. Was the friend correct? Why or why not?

7. Donovan, seventeen, was hired by Schlesner as a gas station attendant. This job included pumping gas, keeping the station clean, washing windows, and taking care of customers. Donovan was also required to keep the books to reflect the sale of such items as gas, milk, and candy. Schlesner deducted money from Donovan's pay each week for shortages that appeared from the books. In a suit which Donovan brought to recover the money so deducted, Schlesner claimed that Donovan was a bailee of the goods that were sold in the gas station. Do you agree with Schlesner? Why or why not? *Donovan v. Schlesner,* 240 N.W.2d 135 (Wisconsin).

8. F-M Potatoes, Inc., stored potatoes for Suda. The oral agreement provided for a storage rental price of 40 cents per hundredweight to February 1 and an additional 10 cents per hundredweight to April 1. F-M Potatoes, Inc., controlled the temperature and atmospheric conditions of the warehouse. Suda stored 13,000 hundredweight of potatoes in the warehouse. The potatoes spoiled because F-M Potatoes failed to maintain the proper temperature and atmospheric conditions. F-M Potatoes, Inc., argued that the arrangement was a lease rather than a bailment, and hence it was not liable for the spoilage. Do you agree? Explain. *F-M Potatoes, Inc. v. Suda,* 259 N.W.2d 487 (North Dakota).

CHAPTER 20
Innkeepers, Carriers, and Warehousers

OUTLINE

20-1 Innkeepers
- Obligation to Accept All Transients
- Innkeeper's Duty of Care
- Innkeeper's Lien

20-2 Carriers
- Contract Carriers
- Common Carriers of Goods
- Common Carriers of Passengers
- Deregulation of Carriers

20-3 Warehousers
- Classes of Warehousers
- Duties of Warehousers
- Rights of Warehousers
- Warehouser's Lien
- Warehouse Receipts

COMMENTARY

The Rosiers were guests at the Gainesville Holiday Inn. Before retiring for the night, they locked their outside door but did not secure the chain latch. At about 1:30 a.m., they awoke to find a ski-masked burglar in the room at the foot of their bed. Mr. Rosier jumped from the bed and tackled the intruder. A struggle ensued. Mr. Rosier was stabbed twice, and Mrs. Rosier was also injured. In a suit brought by the Rosiers against the inn, a security expert testified that the type of lock used in the door was a low-grade, residential lock. The expert said that the industrywide standard was a mortise lock, which when locked from the inside, would secure the door with a dead bolt and could not be opened by a maid's passkey or a duplicate room key. The lower court held that since the Rosiers failed to secure the chain latch to the outside door, the inn was not responsible. The court of appeals reversed the lower court's decision, holding that a jury should decide whether the motel used reasonable care in protecting its guests.

The law requiring innkeepers to protect their guests from harm is similar to the law governing carriers and warehousers. Like hotels, common carriers cannot turn away people who ask for their services. In addition, carriers, warehousers, and innkeepers involve special types of bailments. Carriers and warehousers carry and store other people's goods. Innkeepers often have possession of other people's goods that are brought onto their premises.

OBJECTIVES

1. Recognize the innkeeper's obligation to accept all transients.
2. Explain the innkeeper's duty of care to its guests.
3. Contrast contract carriers with common carriers.
4. Describe the liability imposed upon common carriers for damages to goods transported by them.

5. Discuss the duties and obligations of carriers toward passengers and their baggage.
6. Describe the deregulation that occurred between the mid-1970s and the mid-1980s in the transportation industry.
7. Identify the classes of warehouses and describe their rights and duties.
8. Explain the warehouser's lien.

20-1 INNKEEPERS

An **innkeeper** is the operator of a hotel, motel, or inn that holds itself out to the public as ready to entertain travelers, strangers, and transient guests. A **transient** is a guest whose length of stay is variable.

To assist travelers in obtaining accommodations, the common law imposed the duty upon innkeepers to accept all guests. In addition, innkeepers were considered to be insurers of their guests' property. With exceptions, this is still the law today.

Obligation to Accept All Transients

The innkeeper's obligation to accept all transients was established by common law to enable travelers to obtain a place to sleep wherever they went. At the time that this rule became law in England, it was extremely hazardous for travelers to be left on the highway after nightfall. The English law continued down through the years, and state laws today have statutes with similar requirements.

Section 7 of Chapter 140 of the Massachusetts General Law reads: "An innholder who, upon request, refuses to receive and make suitable provision for a stranger or traveler shall be punished by a fine of not more than fifty dollars."

The Civil Rights Act of 1964 prohibits discrimination in the selection of guests for reasons of race, creed, color, sex, or ethnic background.

People may be turned away when all rooms are occupied or reserved. In addition, innkeepers may refuse to accommodate people whose presence might imperil the health, welfare, or safety of other guests or the safety of the establishment itself.

Innkeeper's Duty of Care

Innkeepers must use reasonable care in protecting their guests from harm. They are responsible for injuries to their guests caused by the inn's negligence or the negligence of employees.

Innkeepers must respect their guests' right of privacy. Guests are guaranteed by law, exclusive and undisturbed privacy of rooms assigned by the hotel. Interruption of the guest's privacy through unpermitted entry by hotel employees or other guests, or through negligence, creates a liability in tort for *invasion of privacy*.

Dannenberg stopped at the Riverside Motel for the night. After taking a shower, she opened the bathroom door and discovered a couple bringing suitcases into her room. The motel clerk had assigned the room to another couple by mistake. Dannenberg may seek damages against the motel for invasion of privacy.

Innkeepers have a greater duty of care toward their guests' property than is imposed in the usual mutual-benefit bailment. With exceptions (noted below), innkeepers are held by law to be insurers of their guests' property. The insured property includes all personal property brought into the hotel for the convenience and purpose of the guest's stay. In the event of loss, the hotelkeeper may be held liable, regardless of the amount of care exercised in the protection of the guest's property.

Upon checking into the Concord Hotel, Mr. and Mrs. Modell placed two diamond rings in the hotel's safe-deposit vault. Later, Mrs. Modell withdrew the rings from the vault to wear that evening. When she went to return them later that night, she was told by the desk clerk that the vault was closed until the next morning. That night, the Modells' room was broken into, and the rings were stolen. The hotel was held liable for the loss of the rings because it did not provide a place for their safekeeping.

Innkeepers are not liable as insurers for the following:

1. Losses caused by a guest's own negligence.

Locks were installed on all sleeping rooms in the Mainline Hotel. Bellhops instructed guests in the use of the locks, and guests were advised to lock their doors whenever leaving their rooms. Hamlin left the hotel without locking the room door, and property was stolen from his room. The hotel is not liable for this loss.

---

2. Losses to the guest's property due to acts of God or from acts of the public enemy.
3. Losses of property due to accidental fire in which no negligence may be attributed to the hotelkeeper. This exception also includes fires caused by other guests staying at the hotel at the same time. Such persons, even though on other floors, are called *fellow guests*.
4. Losses arising out of characteristics of the property that cause its own deterioration.

In most states, innkeepers are further protected by laws limiting the amount of claim any guest may make for a single loss. The limit is usually $500 or less, depending upon the state in which a hotel is located. These laws also give the innkeeper the right to provide a safe or vault for the better protection of the guests' valuables. A guest who does not use the safe provided for valuables will be personally responsible for losses and may not seek recovery from the innkeeper. Hotels notify guests of the prevailing statutes by posting copies of the statutes in each room.

MacDonald, a professional photographer, was assigned to cover a national political convention. Many cameras, valuable lenses, and flash equipment were stored in his room. One evening a thief entered the room and removed cameras and lenses valued at $3,500. Under most state laws, the hotel is liable for no more than $500 of the loss reported.

A reasonable interpretation of the law permits a guest to keep in the room those valuables that one would ordinarily have on or about one's person at all times. These would include a watch, cufflinks, rings worn, and a reasonable amount of cash.

Innkeeper's Lien

Innkeepers have a lien on their guests' property. A **lien** is a claim that one has against the property of another. If a guest cannot pay the bill, the innkeeper is permitted to take possession of the guest's property as security for payment at some later date. Payment of the bill releases the property and terminates the right of lien.

When Isaksen completed her hotel stay, she discovered that she did not have sufficient cash to pay her bill at the Park Hotel. The hotel would not accept her check and took possession of her luggage as security until the bill was paid. After cash was wired to Isaksen, by her firm, she paid the bill. This terminated the hotel's right of lien on her property.

Some courts have held that before an innkeeper may make claim to a guest's luggage or property, the guest must have a hearing before a magistrate. In such cases, the magistrate reviews the available evidence. If it is warranted, the magistrate issues an order permitting the hotel to exercise its right of lien.

20-2 CARRIERS

Carriers are businesses that undertake to transport persons, goods, or both. If a carrier provides transportation for compensation only to those people with whom it desires to do business, it is called a **contract carrier.** If a carrier holds itself out to the general public to provide transportation for compensation, it is called a **common carrier.** Contract carriers and common carriers that operate in interstate commerce are regulated by the Interstate Commerce Commission (ICC). **Private carriers** are companies, not in the transportation business, which operate their own trucks and other vehicles to transport their own goods. Private carriers are not regulated by the ICC.

Safeway Stores owns its own fleet of trucks to transport groceries from its warehouses to its many different retail outlets. The company's primary business is selling groceries, not transportation. It is a private carrier, not regulated by the ICC.

Contract Carriers

Carriers that operate only within the border of a single state are called *intrastate carriers* and are not affected by ICC rules. They are regulated by their own state agencies. Contract carriers are permitted by law to select those with whom they want to do business. They are not required to operate on regular schedules. Their acceptance of merchandise creates a mutual-benefit bailment. They are required to exercise reasonable care, as in all other mutual-benefit bailments, and are responsible for any losses arising from their negligence. They are not considered to be insurers of the goods that they ship unless they contract to do so.

LaValley moved to a different state after the expiration of her lease. She called several moving companies and found that Easy Mover's Inc. offered the lowest price. The company agreed to move LaValley's furniture and belongings to the new location. Easy Mover's Inc. was regulated by the ICC; however, as a contract carrier, it could have refused to contract with LaValley if it wished to do so. As in other mutual-benefit bailments, Easy Mover's Inc. would not be an insurer of LaValley's household goods.

Common Carriers of Goods

Common carriers of goods are insurers of all goods accepted for shipment. They are liable as insurers regardless of whether they have or have not been negligent.

Whitehall Packing Co. engaged Amway Truck Lines to transport 40 barrels of fresh meat from its plant in Wisconsin to Howard Johnson's in New York. The federal government required plastic liners in the barrels, and Howard Johnson's would not allow dry ice in them. The refrigerator unit in Amway's truck operated properly. The truck experienced delays and took longer than its normal running time for the trip. When it arrived in New York, the meat in the barrels had an off or gassy odor and was not considered acceptable by the U.S. government inspector. An expert meat inspector testified that the barreled meat was smothered because of the use of the plastic liners and the absence of dry ice. Some hanging meat in the same truck was found to be in perfect condition. Although there was no evidence that Amway was negligent, the court held it responsible, saying that it was an insurer of the meat.

The Carmack Amendment to the Interstate Commerce Act, passed in 1978, codified this common law rule. It states that a carrier is liable for damage to goods transported by it unless there is proof that the damage comes within one of the following exceptions:

1. Acts of God (floods, tornadoes, cyclones, earthquakes, etc.)
2. Acts of the public enemy (wartime enemies, terrorists, and the like)
3. Acts of public authorities
4. Acts of the shipper
5. The inherent nature of the goods (perishable goods, evaporating and fermenting liquids, diseased animals, etc.)

This extraordinary duty of care is imposed upon common carriers, not contract carriers. Contract carriers are liable only for their negligent acts.

In addition to being insurers, common carriers of goods must accept *without discrimination* all goods offered to them for shipment. Under the Interstate Commerce Act, discrimination either through the selection of customers or through the use of preferential rates is illegal. Exceptions to the rule against discrimination are as follows:

1. A common carrier is not required to accept goods of a type it is not equipped to carry.
2. The carrier may refuse goods which are inherently dangerous and which would create hazards beyond the control of the carrier's usual safety facilities.
3. The common carrier may refuse goods that it does not represent itself as hauling.
4. The carrier may refuse goods that are improperly packed. Proper packaging is determined by the type of goods being shipped, the length of the haul, and the usual custom of the trade.
5. The carrier may refuse goods that are not delivered at the proper place and time.

Common carriers will not be excused from liability for losses due to strikes, mob violence, fire, and similar causes. Labor unions are required to give notice of impending strikes weeks in advance of the strike dates to allow carriers to reject shipments that might be damaged by delays caused by strikes.

The carrier is required to ship goods by the proper route, protect them during shipment, and deliver them to the proper person.

Bills of Lading A **bill of lading** is the written contract between a common carrier and a shipper. The shipper usually makes out the bill of lading on forms supplied by the carrier. When the goods are accepted by the carrier, its agent signs triplicate copies, giving evidence of receipt of the goods. One copy of the bill of lading is kept by the carrier. The other two are for the shipper and the person receiving the goods. A bill of lading may be used as a proof of ownership by the shipper or buyer, depending on the terms of the contract. One who has a bill of lading has the right to demand delivery of the goods from the carrier after the goods reach their destination.

The party shipping goods under a bill of lading is known as the **consignor;** the one to whom the goods are shipped is the **consignee.** When the bill of lading does not contain the words "to the order of," or "to bearer," it is called a **straight bill of lading** and is not negotiable. Conversely, when a bill of lading contains the words "to the order of" in front of the consignee's name or contains the words "to bearer," it is negotiable and is commonly called an **order bill of lading.**

If an employee of a common carrier issued a bill of lading without actually receiving the goods described in the bill, the carrier would be completely liable to any innocent third party who might have given value to someone for the bill of lading. The one giving value for the bill of lading has a right to depend upon the carrier's position in issuing a bill that would from all intents and appearances give the impression of being genuine.

Ace Appliances shipped eight freezers to Kaufman Stores over the Rio Grande and Eastern Railroad. The bill of lading called for ten freezers. The freight agent accepting the order signed the document without checking the number of crates. If the order bill of lading were sold to a buyer in the belief that there were ten freezers en route, the carrier would be liable for the two missing freezers.

Limitation of Liability in Bill of Lading Carriers may limit the amount of their liability to the value stated in the bill of lading.

Mrs. Bratton hired Allied Van Lines, Inc., to transport her household goods from Ohio to Florida. When the goods were picked up, Mrs. Bratton signed a bill of lading which contained a provision limiting the carrier's liability to $1.25 per pound (which amounted to $4,500) or the actual value of the goods as written on the bill of lading. There was a place on the bill of lading for Mrs. Bratton to fill in the actual value of the goods ($10,630). She failed to do this. The shipment was destroyed in transit. Mrs. Bratton argued that since she did not read the document and was unaware of any provision affecting the carrier's liability, she was not bound by the words in the bill of lading. The court held that a bill of lading containing a limitation of the carrier's liability is binding even though the shipper had not read the limitation and even though her attention had not been called to it by the carrier. She received only $4,500.

Rights of Common Carriers A common carrier has two rights which it may enforce against shippers of goods:

1. The right to the payment of fees agreed upon for the shipment of the goods.
2. A lien on all goods shipped for the amount of the shipping charges due. This lien is terminated when payment is received by the carrier. Should the shipper and the party receiving the goods fail to pay the charges, the carrier has the right to sell the goods at public sale, placing the receipts from the sale to the credit of the consignee.

Hanlon Book Company ordered paper from Maine Paper Company. The paper was shipped from Bangor, Maine, under terms that transferred title to the paper when delivered to the carrier. Hanlon Book Company refused to pay shipping costs when informed of the arrival of the shipment. Notice was finally given to both firms of the carrier's intention to sell the paper to recover shipping charges. At a public sale, the paper brought a high bid of $237. The carrier deducted shipping costs and turned over the balance to the Hanlon Book Company.

Connecting Carriers Common carriers often accept goods for shipment to points beyond the terminus of their own lines. The goods are then transferred to *connecting carriers* in order to complete delivery. Losses during shipment over the facilities of the connecting carriers will be determined according to the following rules:

1. The initial carrier will be responsible for damages while the goods are in the custody of connecting carriers if the shipment is an **interstate shipment**—one that goes beyond the borders of the state in which it originated.
2. The initial carrier is relieved of any liability for losses that may occur while the goods are in the possession of connecting carriers if the shipment is an **intrastate shipment**—one entirely within a single state.

Termination of Carrier's Liability as Insurer A common carrier ceases to be an insurer of goods after the goods have been delivered to their destination. The bill of lading, which is the carrier's contract, usually states that 48 hours after the goods have arrived at their destination and the consignee has been notified of their arrival, the carrier's status will be reduced to that of a mutual-benefit bailee. This change reduces the carrier's liability from that of an insurer to one required to exercise reasonable care. A delay by the consignee beyond the 48-hour limit also permits the carrier to charge additional fees for the storage of the goods still remaining in its possession. The fee is known as a **demurrage charge.**

Many carriers are willing to contract for what is called *door-to-door delivery.* Under these terms the carrier continues to be an insurer until the goods have been deposited at the street address or plant of the consignee.

Common Carriers of Passengers

A **passenger** is a person who enters the premises of a carrier with the intention of buying a ticket for a trip. One continues to be a passenger as long as one continues the trip. This relationship is terminated after one has reached the destination printed on the ticket and left the premises of the carrier.

A common carrier has an obligation to accept all persons who may seek passage over its lines. Carriers may not discriminate in the selection of passengers. There are, however, two exceptions to this general rule:

1. Common carriers may refuse passengers when all available space is occupied or reserved.
2. Passengers may be refused if they are disorderly, intoxicated, insane, or infected with a contagious disease. To accept such persons would be to endanger the health and welfare of the other passengers. If these persons were accepted for passage, the carrier would be liable for any resulting injuries to the other passengers.

A carrier must exercise reasonable care in the protection of passengers. Injuries which are reasonably foreseeable or preventable and result from the carrier's negligence give a passenger a right to sue for damages. However, if injuries are not reasonably foreseeable or preventable, the carrier is not responsible.

Three men who were intoxicated boarded a commuter train around midnight. They were talking loudly and making a lot of noise. A conductor saw them and told them not to bother passengers. At the next stop, while the conductor let passengers on and off the train, the men went to another car. There, they assaulted, hit, and kicked a passenger. As soon as the conductor reboarded the train, he sought out the three men, discovered what they had done, and had them arrested. In a suit brought by the injured passenger against the carrier, the court held in favor of the carrier. The court said that the incident occurred so quickly and unexpectedly that the conductor acting with the highest degree of care under the circumstances could not have averted it.

Bumped Airline Passengers When an airline flight is oversold, no one may be denied boarding against his or her will until airline personnel first ask for volunteers who will give up their reservation willingly, in exchange for a payment of the airline's choosing. If there are not enough volunteers, other passengers may be denied boarding involuntarily in accordance with the airline's priority rules. Airlines are required to establish and publish priority rules for determining which passengers holding confirmed reservation space will be denied boarding on an oversold flight.

Passengers who are denied boarding involuntarily, that is, "bumped," are entitled to a payment of *denied boarding compensation* from the airline unless: (1) They have not fully complied with the carrier's ticketing, check-in, or reconfirmation requirements or are not acceptable for transportation under the airline's usual rules and practices; or (2) they are denied boarding because the flight is canceled; or (3) they are denied boarding because a smaller capacity aircraft was substituted for safety or operational reasons; or (4) they are offered accommodations in a section of the aircraft other than specified in their ticket at no extra charge.

Passengers who are denied boarding involuntarily must be given a written statement explaining the rules about bumping and describing the airline's boarding priorities. Those who are eligible for denied boarding compensation must be offered, in addition to alternate transportation, a payment equal to the sum of the face value of their tickets, with a $200 maximum. In addition, if the airline cannot arrange alternative transportation for the passenger, the compensation is doubled with a $400 maximum. The alternate transportation must be scheduled to arrive at the passenger's destination or next stopover not later than two hours (four hours for international flights) after the planned arrival time of the originally scheduled flight. *Stopover* means a deliberate interruption of a journey by the passenger, scheduled to exceed four hours, at a point between the place of departure and the final destination. Instead of the cash payment mentioned above, airlines may offer free or reduced rate air transportation as long as its value equals or exceeds the cash payment requirement.

The airline must give each passenger who qualifies for denied boarding compensation a payment by cash or check for the amount specified above, on the day and place the involuntary denied boarding occurs. However, if the airline arranges alternate transportation for the passenger's convenience that departs before the payment can be made, the payment must be sent to the passenger within 24 hours. The air carrier may offer free tickets in place of the cash payment. The passenger may, however, insist on the cash payment, or refuse all compensation and bring private legal action.

The passenger's acceptance of the compensation relieves the airline from any further liability to that passenger by its failure to honor the confirmed reservation. However, the passenger may decline the payment and seek to recover damages in a court of law or in some other manner.

Passengers' Baggage In conjunction with the carrying of passengers, a carrier is obliged to accept a reasonable amount of baggage. Baggage includes those things necessary for the comfort of the passenger and for the purpose of the trip. Excess baggage may be shipped by a passenger on payment of additional fees. Personal luggage carried aboard an airline and kept at one's seat does not generally come within the weight limits permitted each passenger.

When a baggage car or baggage compartment is available for checking luggage, the carrier is considered an insurer of the luggage checked by the passengers and left in these places. Property kept by passengers at their seats or in overhead compartments places upon the carrier the obligation of exercising ordinary care for its safety.

The Carmack Amendment to the Interstate Commerce Act expressly permits the common carrier to limit its liability in connection with baggage carried in interstate commerce. Similarly, federal rules place limits on the liability of airlines for lost luggage. For travel wholly within the United States, the maximum liability of an airline for lost luggage is $1,250 per passenger. Excess valuation may be declared on certain types of articles. However, some carriers assume no liability for fragile, valuable, or perishable articles.

Deregulation of Carriers

The decade between the mid-1970s and the mid-1980s saw a revolutionary period of deregulation in the transportation industry. The Airline Deregulation Act of 1978 led to the end of the Civil Aeronautics Board (CAB). That board had previously controlled the airline industry's routes and fares.

The Motor Carrier Act of 1980 made significant changes in the regulation of truck transportation. The act enabled new businesses to enter the trucking industry more easily and allowed existing businesses to expand their operation with fewer restrictions. Carriers are able to set rates with less government interference. In addition, more truckers fall into the category of private carriers, which are not subject to government regulation.

The Staggers Rail Act of 1980 took strong steps toward deregulating the railroad industry. Railroads now have the freedom to charge different rates for their services as long as the rates fall within certain prescribed zones.

The Bus Regulatory Reform Act of 1982 brought reforms to the bus industry that were similar to those brought to the trucking industry by the Motor Carrier Act of 1980.

20-3 WAREHOUSERS

When goods are stored in a warehouse, the relation of bailor and bailee is created between the owner of the goods and the warehouser. The law discussed in Chapter 19 applies generally to such transactions. Some particular laws relating to warehousers is also found in Article 7 of the UCC. The UCC defines a **warehouser** as a person engaged in the business of storing goods for hire. A **warehouse** is a building or structure in which any goods, but particularly wares or merchandise, are stored. A **warehouse receipt** is a receipt issued by a person engaged in the business of storing goods for hire.

UCC 7-102(h)

UCC 1-201 **(see pp. 612–613)**

Although both common carriers and warehousers are mutual-benefit bailees, they perform different functions. Common carriers are engaged in moving goods. Warehousers keep goods in storage. At times, however, one or the other will perform both functions.

Classes of Warehousers

Warehousers may be classified as public and private warehousers. A **public warehouser** is one who owns a warehouse where any member of the public who is willing to pay the regular charge may store goods. Grain elevators in the Midwest, used to store farmers' grain, are sometimes established as public warehouses. A warehouser whose warehouse is not for general public use is a **private warehouser.** Most warehousers fall into this latter category.

Sometimes business people will borrow money using goods that they have stored in a warehouse as security for the loan. The one who lends the money is given the warehouse receipt. If the debt is not paid, the holder of the receipt may obtain possession of the goods that are in storage. This practice is called **field warehousing.**

Duties of Warehousers

UCC 7-204(1)

A warehouser must use that amount of care that a reasonably careful person would use under similar circumstances. Failure to use such care is negligence and makes the warehouser liable for losses or damages to the goods.

Bekins warehouse stored Keefe's household goods in its warehouse beneath some sprinkler system pipes. It did not inspect the area before placing the goods there. One of the pipes was unconnected, and water from the pipes leaked onto Keefe's goods, damaging them. Bekins's failure to inspect the area of storage was a negligent act which made Bekins responsible for the loss.

UCC 7-204(2)

The parties may limit the amount of liability of the warehouser by including terms to that effect in the storage agreement or warehouse receipt.

The warehouse receipt given by Bekins to Keefe in the above case limited Bekins's liability to 10 cents per pound per article. The limitation was enforceable even though it was not specifically called to Keefe's attention when the warehouse receipt was signed.

UCC 7-207(1)

Such a limitation is not effective, however, if a warehouse converts the goods to its own use. Unless the warehouse receipt provides otherwise, a warehouser must keep goods covered by each receipt separate from other goods. This is required so that the goods may be identified and delivered to the owner at any time. However, fungible goods may be **commingled** (mixed together). Fungible goods are goods of which any unit is, by nature, the equivalent of any other like unit.

UCC 7-20(2)

Fifty farmers stored their grain in the same grain elevator. The grain was mixed together. It was owned in common by all 50 owners. The warehouser was liable to each owner for that owner's share of the grain.

Rights of Warehousers

UCC 7-206

If, at the end of a storage period, goods are not removed from a warehouse, the warehouser may sell them. Before doing so, however, the warehouser must notify the owner that they are going to be sold and give that person the right to redeem them. If no time for storage is fixed in the agreement, the warehouser must give at least 30 days' notice to the owner before selling them. Goods may also be sold by the warehouser if they are hazardous to persons or to property and the warehouser had no knowledge of the hazard when the goods were placed in the warehouse. After warehouse charges are deducted, all proceeds from any such sale must be turned over to the person to whom the goods were to be delivered.

Warehouser's Lien

UCC 7-209

A warehouser has a lien on the goods that are in the warehouser's possession. A **warehouser's lien** is the right to retain possession of the goods until the satisfaction of the charges imposed on them. The lien is for the amount of money owed for storage charges, transportation charges, insurance, and expenses necessary for the preservation of the goods. The lien is a possessory one. It is lost when the warehouser voluntarily delivers the goods or unjustifiably refuses to deliver them. If the owner of the goods owes the warehouser money for the storage of other goods, the warehouser has a lien for the other debt only if it is so stated in the warehouse receipt.

UCC 7-210(1)

If the person who stored the goods is a merchant in the course of business, the warehouser's lien may be enforced by a public or private sale at any time or place and on any terms which are commercially reasonable. Notice must be given to all persons known to claim an interest in the goods. The notice must include a statement of the amount due, the nature of the proposed sale, and the time and place of any public sale. (See Figure 20-1.)

PUBLIC AUCTION
Warehouseman's Lien Sale
To be held at
The Carriage House
NORTH BROADWAY, ELMWOOD, N.H.

Wednesday, July 1 at 6:30 p.m.

Preview at 5 p.m.
We have moved for the convenience of the sale 12 containers with inventory of the following merchandise; living room sets, kitchen sets, bedroom sets, chests of drawers & more; Washer, dryers & refrigerators. Also, a large assort. of TV's, stereos, lamps, mirrors, shelves, glass, a lg. number of box lots, dishes, brick-a-brack & much, much more.
Terms: cash or check w/preapproval

E.B. MAPLE, Auctioneers N.H. Lic. 112
34 Main St., Elmwood, N.H. 555-1200

Figure 20-1 Before this Warehouser's Lien Sale is held, notice must be given to all persons known to have an interest in the goods.

UCC 7-210(2) If the person who stored the goods is not a merchant, more complicated rules must be followed to enforce the warehouser's lien. In addition to giving notice to all persons known to claim an interest in the goods, the nonmerchant must also advertise the pending sale in a local newspaper. Notices and advertisements must contain specific information set forth in the UCC. UCC 7-210(3) Date-of-sale requirements must also be followed. Anyone claiming a right to the goods may pay the money due before the sale and have the lien discharged.

Warehouse Receipts

UCC 7-201(1) A warehouse receipt may be issued by any warehouser. It need not be in any particular form, although it should include such essentials as the location of the warehouse, the date of issue, the rate of storage charges, and a description of the goods.

UCC 7-104 Such a receipt is negotiable, like a bill of lading, if by its terms the goods are to be delivered to *bearer* or to *the order of* a named person. A *negotiable warehouse receipt* may be transferred from one party to another by indorsement and delivery. When this is done, ownership of the goods which are stored in the warehouse is transferred to the transferee of the warehouse receipt.

SUMMARY

20-1. Innkeepers are required to accept all transients unless there are no vacancies. They must use reasonable care in protecting their guests from harm. In addition, they must respect their guests' right of privacy. With exceptions, innkeepers are insurers of their guests' property. In most states, however, they are protected by laws limiting their liability to a specific dollar amount. Innkeepers have a lien on guests' property for the amount of any unpaid bills.

20-2. Contract carriers are permitted by law to select those with whom they want to do business. They must use ordinary care in carrying out their duties. They are not considered to be insurers of the goods they ship. Common carriers of goods are liable as insurers regardless of whether they have or have not been negligent. They are not responsible for damages caused by: (*a*) acts of God, (*b*) acts of the public enemy, (*c*) acts of public authorities, (*d*) acts of the shipper, and (*e*) the inherent nature of the goods. With some exceptions, common carriers must accept all goods offered to them for shipment and all passengers seeking passage on their passenger lines. With some exceptions, bumped airline passengers are entitled to a payment of denied boarding compensation. In recent years, the government has deregulated the transportation industry. The Civil Aeronautics Board no longer exists, carriers can set rates with little government interference, and railroads and bus companies have fewer restrictions imposed upon them.

20-3. Public warehousers must accept goods for storage by any member of the public willing to pay for the service. Private warehousers are not for general public use. Warehousers must use reasonable care in storing goods. They have a lien on goods until storage charges are paid.

Understanding Key Legal Terms

bill of lading (p. 272)
carriers (p. 270)
commingled (p. 278)
common carrier (p. 270)
consignee (p. 272)
consignor (p. 272)
contract carrier (p. 270)
demurrage charge (p. 274)
field warehousing (p. 277)
innkeeper (p. 268)
interstate shipment (p. 274)
intrastate shipment (p. 274)
lien (p. 270)
order bill of lading (p. 273)
passenger (p. 274)
private carrier (p. 270)
private warehouser (p. 277)
public warehouser (p. 277)
straight bill of lading (p. 272)
transient (p. 268)
warehouse (p. 277)
warehouse receipt (p. 277)
warehouser (p. 277)
warehouser's lien (p. 278)

Questions for Review and Discussion

1. What obligation does an innkeeper have to accept guests?
2. What duty of care does an innkeeper owe to its guests?
3. Explain the difference between a common carrier and a contract carrier.
4. Describe a common carrier's liability for damage to goods they transport.
5. When may common carriers refuse to accept passengers?
6. What degree of care must a carrier use in protecting passengers from injury?
7. Describe changes in the transportation industry resulting from deregulation.
8. Name the two classes of warehousers, and explain their difference.
9. What duty of care is owed by a warehouser to the owner of stored goods?
10. Explain the warehouser's lien. What amount of money does it involve? When is it lost?

Analyzing Cases

1. W. J. Casey Trucking & Rigging Co. was engaged by General Electric Co. to transport a rotor from its North Bergen, New Jersey, plant to a generating station in Burlington, New Jersey. A crane was used by G.E.'s personnel to load the rotor onto Casey's truck. G.E.'s employees helped Casey's truck driver secure the rotor onto the truck. They directed the exact placement of the chains used to hold the rotor in place and rejected suggestions made by the truck driver. The rotor was damaged during transit when it shifted on the bed of the truck. Was the carrier responsible for the damage to the rotor? Give reasons for your answer. *W. J. Casey Trucking & Rigging Co. v. General Elec. Co.,* 376 A.2d 603 (New Jersey).

2. Poroznoff was living in a room at the YMCA on a week-to-week basis. It was his only residence. While there, he became drunk and disorderly and was arrested by the police. On his return to the YMCA, he found that his room was locked. He was told by the management not to reenter the building. Poroznoff argued that since the room at the YMCA was his only residence, he was not a transient guest. He claimed that he had rights of a tenant. Do you agree with Poroznoff? Why or why not? *Poroznoff v. Alberti,* 401 A.2d 1124 (New Jersey).

3. A state agency attempted to inspect Blair Academy's dormitories as hotels under the state's hotel and multiple-dwelling law. The law of that state defined a hotel as any building "which contains 10 or more units of dwelling space or has sleeping facilities for 25 or more persons and is kept, used, maintained, advertised as, or held out to be, a place where sleeping or dwelling accommodations are available to transient or permanent guests." Did Blair Academy's dormitories come within that state's definition of a hotel? Explain. *Blair Academy v. Sheehan,* 373 A.2d 418 (New Jersey).

4. Brewer was a guest at the Roosevelt Motor Lodge. It was a warm night, and although the room was air-conditioned, she left the bathroom window open to let out the steam after taking a bath. While she slept, an intruder removed the half screen and climbed through the open window. The intruder assaulted and raped Brewer and stole her diamond wristwatch. Was the motor lodge liable to Brewer? Why or why not? *Brewer v. Roosevelt,* 295 A.2d 647 (Maine).

5. A storage company stored Conrad's household furniture for $25 a month. Conrad made the first payment, left town, and paid nothing for five months. The storage company sold Conrad's furniture at an auction without notifying Conrad or advertising the sale in the newspaper. Conrad claims that his rights were violated by the storage company's sale of the goods. Do you agree with Conrad? Why or why not? See also *Poole v. Christian,* 411 N.E.2d 513 (Ohio).

6. The snow from a severe winter storm was still on the road when Mlynarchik, a 65-year-old woman, stepped off the bus on which she had been riding. A high snowbank was piled about 2½ to 4 feet from the side of the bus. Mlynarchik stepped back and faced the bus, waiting for it to go by so that she could cross the road. As the bus started up, it began to skid. The back of it moved toward Mlynarchik. She stepped back against the snowbank but slipped and fell down with her feet pointing out into the road. The bus continued to skid toward her, and although she moved her legs to the right against the snowbank, the right rear wheel rolled over her left leg. Was Mlynarchik still a passenger at the time of the accident? What duty of care was owed to her by the bus company? Was the bus company liable for her injuries? Explain. *Mlynarchik v. Massachusetts Bay Transp. Auth.,* 322 N.E.2d 433 (Massachusetts).

7. Fairbault Woolen Mill Co. shipped 120 bales of New Zealand "greasy wool" (uncleaned, freshly shorn wool) from New Zealand to its factory in Minnesota. The wool was shipped in a large metal ocean cargo container. The container left New Zealand aboard an ocean vessel which docked in Norfolk, Virginia. Wheels were attached and it was then hauled over the road to a railway terminal. The railroad's inspection reports stated that the outside of the container was in good condition at that time. A railroad flatcar took the container to its destination in Minnesota. When it was opened, an unpleasant odor and rotted condition of some bales announced that the cargo had been water-damaged. A hole 4 to 5 inches in diameter was discovered in the container's metal top, covered from the outside with tape. One side of the tape was loose, allowing a sliver of light to enter through the hole. Is the railroad responsible for the damaged cargo? Why or why not? *Fairbault Woolen Mill Co. v. Chicago, Rock Island and Pacific R.R.*, 289 N.W.2d 126 (Minnesota).

8. I.C.C. Metals, Inc., delivered three separate lots of an industrial metal called indium to the Municipal Warehouse Company for safekeeping. Municipal gave I.C.C. a warehouse receipt for each lot. Each receipt contained a clause limiting the warehouser's liability to $50 per lot. The metal was worth $100,000. Two years later, when I.C.C. requested the return of the metal, it was informed by Municipal that the metal could not be found. Although it could offer little evidence to support its position, Municipal suggested that the metal had been stolen through no fault of its own. Municipal claims that its responsibility is limited to $50 per lot. Do you agree? Explain. *I.C.C. Metals, Inc. v. Municipal Warehouse Co.*, 409 N.E.2d 849 (New York).

CHAPTER 21
Real Property

OUTLINE

COMMENTARY

Walter and Melonie Kahn were excited! They were about to make the largest purchase of their lives—their first home. It was a pretty house, beautifully landscaped with newly planted trees. Inside, the floors were covered with wall-to-wall carpeting, and the windows had new curtains. One side of the property formed the bank of a stream. Another side was bordered by a fence covered with roses. Many questions came to mind as they entered into this important transaction. Did the curtains and wall-to-wall carpeting go with the house? Were the rose bushes and newly planted trees included in the purchase? What rights would the Kahns have to the stream and the water flowing through it, and at what point in the stream was the property line. What kind of deed would they receive? Who would own the property if one of them died? This chapter examines these and other important questions that arise when people acquire title to real property.

OBJECTIVES

1. Explain what constitutes real property.
2. Identify three ways of creating an easement.
3. Differentiate between freehold and leasehold estates.
4. Describe the different types of co-ownership of real property.
5. Identify three methods of acquiring title to real property.
6. Give an example of a nonconforming use of real property, and discuss the granting of a variance.
7. Explain eminent domain.

21-1 THE NATURE OF REAL PROPERTY

Real property is the ground and everything permanently attached to it. It includes buildings, fences, and trees on the surface, earth, rocks, and minerals under the surface, and the airspace above the surface.

Trees and Vegetation

Trees, flowers, shrubs, vineyards, and field crops that grow each year without replanting *(perennials)* are considered to be real property. These plants have been planted and cultivated with the intention that they remain as a part of the real estate. Once planted and growing, such improvements to the land are called ***fructus naturales*** (fruit of nature).

The Paulsons really liked the small, quaint house that was shown to them by the real estate broker. It was surrounded by a well-groomed lawn and rose-covered picket fence. It would be ideal for their first home. They signed a contract to buy it. A month later, when they moved in, the Paulsons discovered that the former owners had dug up the roses and taken them. This was a violation of law. The roses were part of the real property that the Paulsons had purchased because they were perennial plants.

In contrast, crops or garden plantings that produce flowers, vegetables, or other harvest only for the year in which they are planted *(annuals)* are called ***fructus industriales*** (fruit of industry). These are treated as personal property rather than real property.

When the Freeman farm was sold early in the spring, the new owner was deeded "all the real property consisting of what is known as the Freeman Farm." A 25-acre section of winter wheat had been planted the fall prior to the sale and would be ready for harvest the following July. Unless the parties agreed otherwise, the wheat crop would not be part of the sale of the farm because it is an annual plant and is treated as personal property. The wheat crop would still belong to the person who planted it.

A tree belongs to the person on whose land the trunk is located. People who own adjoining land have the right to cut off trespassing tree branches in their airspace and trespassing roots at the boundary line of their property. Whenever property owners dig down at the very edge of their own property, however, they must provide support to their neighbor's land so that it does not cave in.

Air Rights

In early England, landowners owned the airspace above their property to "as high as the heavens." This law changed with the increased use of the airplane. Modern court decisions have held that landowners own the airspace above their land to as high as they can effectively possess or reasonably control. This is usually as high as the highest tree or structure on their property. It is a trespass for anyone to run wires through someone else's airspace or to use another's airspace in any way without permission. Electric and telephone companies must obtain easements (see pages 288–289) for the right to run wires through the airspace of property owners.

Congress has enacted legislation that gives the public the right of freedom of transit through the navigable airspace of the United States. The **navigable airspace** is the space above 1,000 feet over populated areas, and above 500 feet over water and unpopulated areas. In airport cases involving planes landing and taking off, the courts try to strike a balance between the landowners' rights to the exclusive possession of their airspace free from noise and exhaust fumes, and the public need for air travel.

Air rights are valuable and are often sold to interested buyers, particularly in land-depleted metropolitan areas. For example, in New York City, developers bought air rights over the access to the George Washington Bridge and constructed multistory buildings. Two privately owned buildings have been constructed in the airspace over the Massachusetts Turnpike near Boston. Use of air rights becomes important when land is no longer available for new buildings. The private use of airspace also becomes a tax source for otherwise untaxable land owned by a city or state government.

Subterranean Rights

The owner of land has exclusive title to material below the surface of the land. The right extends to a point determined to be the exact center of the earth. These **subterranean rights** (rights below the surface) are at times sold to corporations exploring for coal, oil, or other mineral deposits. Taking out oil or minerals from below the surface would constitute trespass if such rights were not obtained from their owners.

McGee's house and lot were adjacent to land on which a small industrial plant had been built. McGee discovered that the plant owners had driven drainage pipes underground from the plant into her land. She may charge the plant with trespass. She can also sell this right to the plant or demand that the practice be stopped and the pipes removed.

A landowner must not dig a cellar or other excavation so close to the boundary of a neighbor as to cause the neighbor's land to cave in or the neighbor's building to be damaged. A person excavating who fails to shore up the adjoining land is liable to the neighbor for damages.

Water Rights

People who own land along the bank of a river or stream are called **riparian owners.** They have certain rights and duties with respect to the water that flows, over, under, and beside their land. Owners of land through which a stream flows own the soil beneath the water. If a nonnavigable stream is a boundary line between two parcels of land, the owner on each side owns to the center of the stream. If the stream is navigable, however, each owner owns only to the bank of the stream, the bed being owned by the state. A **navigable**

stream in some states is defined as one that ebbs and flows with the tide. In other states, it is defined as a stream that is capable of being navigated by commercial vessels.

Although property owners may own the land under a stream, they do not own the water itself. Their right to the use of the water depends on the doctrine followed in their state. Most states east of the Mississippi River follow the **riparian rights doctrine.** Under this doctrine, owners of land bordering a stream have equal rights to use the water passing by or through their property. Each riparian owner may make reasonable use of the water for domestic purposes such as drinking, cooking, and bathing. In addition, they may use the water for irrigation purposes if it does not interfere unreasonably with the use being made by other riparian owners downstream. Owners may not sell the water from the stream to outside third parties.

Some states west of the Mississippi, where water is less plentiful, follow the **prior appropriation doctrine.** This doctrine follows a seniority system. The first person to make beneficial use of the water has the right to take all he or she is able to use before anyone else has any rights to it. If there is water left over, the next person in seniority may use all the water that can be put to beneficial use.

Lopez, who settled in Nevada, constructed an irrigation ditch from a nearby creek to his farm land. A year later, Griffin ran an irrigation ditch from the same creek to his farm land. Since Lopez was the first to make beneficial use of the water, he would always have priority over Griffin to as much of the water as he could put to beneficial use.

Other states west of the Mississippi follow a combination of the riparian rights doctrine and the prior appropriation doctrine.

In New England states, a **small pond** (under ten acres) is owned by the person who owns the ground underneath. In contrast, a **great pond** (10 acres or more) is owned by the state. Private abutters own the land only to the lower water mark. Great ponds are usually accessible to the public for swimming, boating, and fishing.

Percolating waters are waters that pass through the ground beneath the surface of the earth without any definite channel. They consist of rainwaters which slowly ooze and seep through the soil or waters which infiltrate the banks or bed of a stream. **Subterranean waters** are waters which lie wholly beneath the surface of the ground. They may be either percolating waters or waters that flow in underground channels or lie still in underground lakes. Common law gave property owners the absolute right to percolating waters below their land. Under modern statutes, however, property owners may draw only the water that is reasonably required to satisfy their needs. Other property owners damaged by unreasonable use may seek an injunction against such use in a court of equity.

Rainwater on the surface of the earth may not be artificially channeled to an abutter's property without permission of the abutter. Unless a drainage easement is obtained to drain water onto another's land, surface water must be left to its natural watercourse.

Fixtures

When personal property is attached to real property, it is known as a **fixture** and becomes part of the real property. Built-in stoves and dishwashers, kitchen cabinets, and ceiling light fixtures are examples of fixtures. Disagreements sometimes occur over whether an item is a fixture.

The Rodriguezes bought a house from the Smiths. After the closing, when they moved in, the Rodriguezes discovered that the Smiths had taken with them the wall-to-wall carpeting in the living room. The Rodriguezes had expected the carpeting to go with the sale of the house as part of the real property. The Smiths treated the carpeting as personal property and took it with them.

In deciding whether or not an item is a fixture, the courts ask the following:

1. Has there been a *temporary* or *permanent* installation of the personal property? Can it be removed without damaging the real property?

In the above example, if the carpeting were tightly nailed to the floor, there is a good chance that it would be held by the court to be a fixture. The same would be true if the carpeting covered plywood flooring. In both cases the carpeting would be considered part of the real property and belong to the new buyers.

---

2. Has the personal property been *adapted* (suited or fitted) to the intended use of the real property?

If, in the example referred to above, the living room were oddly shaped, and the carpeting were cut to fit that shape, it would be further evidence that the carpeting was a fixture. It had been adapted to be used in that odd-shaped room.

---

3. What was the *intent* of the party at the time the personal property was attached to the real property?

Franklin complained to her landlord that the kitchen in her apartment needed to be modernized. The landlord gave her permission to improve the kitchen as long as it could be done without cost to him. Franklin installed cabinets, a built-in stove, and an under-the-counter dishwasher. She also bought a new refrigerator. Even though Franklin paid for them, the cabinets, stove, and dishwasher would be fixtures and would belong to the landlord. The refrigerator, which was not built in, would remain the personal property of the tenant.

Trade fixtures are those items of personal property brought upon the premises by the tenant that are necessary to carry on the trade or business to which the premises will be devoted. Contrary to the general rule, trade fixtures remain the personal property of the tenant or occupier of the property and are removable at the expiration of the term of occupancy. Trade fixtures are not treated as part of the real property.

21-2 EASEMENTS

An **easement** (also called a **right of way**) is the right to use the land of another for a particular purpose. Easements are used to give people the right to pass over another's land, to run wires through another's airspace, to drain water onto another's property, and to run pipes underneath someone else's ground. The property to which the right or privilege of easement attaches is called the **dominant tenement.** In contrast, the property through which the easement is created or extends is known as the **servient tenement.**

An easement may be created in three ways: (1) by grant, (2) by reservation, and (3) by prescription. To create an easement by grant, the owner of the land signs a deed, giving the easement to the dominant tenement. To create an easement by reservation, the owner of the land grants to another person the entire parcel, except for the easement which he or she keeps. An **easement by prescription** is an easement that is obtained by passing over another's property without permission openly and continuously for a period of time set by state statute (20 years in many states). People claiming easements by prescription must show that they used (but did not possess) part of another's property openly, notoriously, and in a hostile manner for the prescribed period. This is similar to adverse possession, which is discussed later in this chapter.

Once an easement is created, it runs with the land. This means that future owners will have the right to use the easement unless one of them gives it up by a deed or by not using it for a long period of time.

By warranty deed in 1907, Jesse Horney conveyed the northern portion of his real estate to Wayne County Lumber Company. That deed included the following provision: "Said Jesse Horney hereby conveys to Wayne County Lumber Company the right of ingress and egress for teams and wagons in conducting their business through an open driveway along the South line to South Main Street." The property was conveyed to another lumber company in 1930 and to a third lumber company in 1943. Later, in a dispute over the easement, the court held that the easement ran with the land and belonged to the lumber company. In this case, Horney's property was the servient tenement. The lumber company's property was the dominant tenement.

Profits *à prendre* are a special type of easement with the added privilege of removing something of value from the servient property. For example, the right to enter another's property and remove sand, gravel, soil, or the like is a profit *á prendre*. A profit *á prendre* may be created by deed, will, or adverse use.

The Bates Company and Sawyer executed an agreement which provided that Bates could enter upon Sawyer's land and remove sand, gravel, and stone. Bates agreed to pay Sawyer a set rate per cubic yard or short ton for all the sand it removed. The agreement stated, "Sawyer will not grant to anyone else the privilege of removing sand and stone from said parcel during the period hereof...but Sawyer reserves to herself, her successors and assigns, the right during said period...to go on and use said tract of land for any purpose they may desire, but without unreasonable interference with the rights of said Bates." The court held that Bates possessed a profit *à prendre* under the agreement.

21-3 ESTATES IN REAL PROPERTY

An **estate** is the interest or right that a person has in land. A **leasehold estate** comes from a lease and is an interest in real estate. A **freehold estate** is an estate in which the holder owns the land for life or forever. Anyone having a freehold estate may transfer that interest to another by sale, gift, will, or by dying without a will. Freehold estates are either estates in fee simple or life estates.

Estates in Fee Simple

Anyone owning real property outright—that is, forever—is said to have an **estate in fee simple.** The estate descends, on the death of the owner, to the owners heirs. The owner of an estate in fee simple has *absolute ownership* in the real estate, with the right to use or to dispose of it as desired, so long as the use of it does not interfere with other's rights.

When the Gerlachs bought the land on which to build their house, they received an estate in fee simple from the former owners. They thus received full rights to the property. They may sell it, give it away, or use it as they wish. The only restrictions are those contained in the deed or required of them by law.

Life Estates

A person who owns real property for life or for the life of another owns an interest in real property called a **life estate.** Such an estate may be created by deed, by will, or by law. When the terms of a deed or will state that the property is to pass at the end of a life estate to someone other than the grantor or the grantor's heirs, the future interest is a **remainder estate.**

Rosengard deeded her farm to Kinkaid for life. She stated in the deed that uponKinkaid's death, the property was to pass to Arakelian in fee simple. Kinkaid owns a life estate in the farm. Arakelian owns a remainder estate.

The owner of a life estate may convey that interest to another. Thus, in the above example, if Kinkaid conveys his interest to Jenkins, Jenkins will own a life estate for the duration of Kinkaid's life, after which the property will belong to Arakelian. When the terms of a deed or a will state that property is to return to the grantor or to the grantor's heirs at the expiration of a life estate, the future interest is a **reversion estate.**

Life estates are sometimes created by operation of law. Dower and curtesy are examples. Years ago in England, **dower** was the right that a widow had to a life estate in one-third of the real property owned by the husband during the marriage. **Curtesy** was the right that a widower had, if children of the marriage were born alive, to a life estate in all real property owned by the wife during the marriage. The rights of dower and curtesy were in addition to rights given to spouses under the law of wills.

Before her marriage, Clark received title to an old house through a will left by her grandfather. While her husband had no rights in this property at the time of their marriage, such rights arose at the birth of their first child. Her husband thereafter had the right of curtesy should Clark die while she was still married to him.

Many states have either done away with common law dower and curtesy altogether or modified them to reflect modern-day needs.

21-4 CO-OWNERSHIP OF REAL PROPERTY

Real property may be owned individually or by two or more persons known as **cotenants.** The most common cotenant relationships are tenants in common, joint tenants, tenants by the entirety, and tenants in partnership.

Tenancy in Common

When two or more persons own real property as **tenants in common,** each person owns an undivided share and upon one cotenant's death, that person's share passes to the heirs of that cotenant. Each cotenant is entitled to possession of the entire premises. This is known as **unity of possession.** Tenants in common have the right to sell or deed away as a gift their share in the property without permission of the other cotenants. When this occurs, any new owner becomes a tenant in common with the remaining cotenants. One cotenant's interest is not necessarily the same as another cotenant's interest.

Ingalls and Carpenter owned a parcel of real property as tenants in common. When Ingalls died, his three children inherited his estate. The children became tenants in common (each owning a one-sixth interest) with Carpenter, who owned a one-half interest in the property.

Tenants in common may separate their interests in the property by petitioning the court for a *partition* of the property. If the court allows the petition, either it will divide the property into separate parcels so that each cotenant will own a particular part outright or it will order the property sold and divide the proceeds of the sale among the cotenants. Creditors may reach the interest of a tenant in common by bringing a lawsuit against a cotenant and, if successful, having the cotenant's interest sold to pay the debt.

By statute in most states, co-ownership of property by two or more persons is considered to be a tenancy in common unless the relationship is expressly indicated as a joint tenancy or a tenancy by the entirety.

Joint Tenancy

When two or more persons own real property as **joint tenants,** the estate created is a single estate with multiple ownership. Each tenant owns the entire estate, subject to the equal rights of the other joint tenants. All joint tenants' interests in the property are equal, and all have the right to possession of the entire estate. Upon the death of one joint tenant, the entire ownership remains in the other joint tenants and does not pass to the heirs or devisees of the deceased cotenant. For this reason, joint tenants are often identified as *joint tenants with the right of survivorship.*

If Ingalls and Carpenter, in the previous example, had owned the parcel of real property as joint tenants instead of as tenants in common, Carpenter would have owned the entire property outright when Ingalls died. Ingalls' three children would not have been entitled to any interest in the real property whatsoever.

Joint tenants may deed away their interest to new owners without permission of the other joint tenants. The new owner, in such a case, becomes a tenant in common with the remaining joint tenants. As in the case of a tenant in common, a joint tenant may petition the court for a partition of the estate, which would end the joint tenancy. Creditors may levy upon the interests of a joint tenant on execution and take over the joint tenant's interest as a tenant in common with the remaining joint tenants. To **levy in execution** means to collect a sum of money by putting into effect the judgment of a court.

Tenancy by the Entirety

A **tenancy by the entirety** may be held only by a husband and wife and is based upon the common law doctrine known as **unity of person.** Under this doctrine, a husband and wife are regarded, in law, as one. In theory, each spouse owns the entire estate, which neither can destroy by any separate act. The husband, however, has the entire control over the estate, including the exclusive right to possession and the right to all rents and profits. Upon the death of either spouse, the surviving spouse owns the entire estate outright. Advantages of this type of tenancy are that both parties must agree to any sale or conveyance of the property, and an execution by a judgment-creditor resulting from an action against a husband or wife alone may not be placed against the property.

The DeVoes owned their home together as a tenancy by the entirety. While driving a car titled in her name alone, Mrs. DeVoe caused an accident resulting in serious injury to another person. The injured person obtained a judgment against Mrs. DeVoe that far exceeded her insurance coverage. The house owned jointly by the DeVoes would not be subject to sale to recover the judgment.

Another important aspect of a tenancy by the entirety is that no administration of the estate is necessary upon the death of one of the parties. This eliminates the costly and time-consuming details of making a settlement of the property, as required in the probate of a will.

In the event that husband and wife are separated by a divorce, the tenancy by the entirety no longer exists and they then become tenants in common, with separate and equal rights in the property.

Some states have done away with the tenancy by entirety by statute. Still other states have enacted statutes giving equal rights to husbands and wives who own property as tenants by the entirety.

Tenancy in Partnership

Ownership of real property by partners is called a tenancy in partnership and is governed by the Uniform Partnership Act in those states which have adopted it. This type of co-ownership of real property is discussed in Chapter 35.

21-5 METHODS OF ACQUIRING TITLE TO REAL PROPERTY

Title to real property may be acquired by sale or gift, will or descent, or occupancy.

Title by Sale or Gift

Ownership and title to real property are most frequently transferred from one owner to another by sale or by gift. This is done by transferring a written instrument called a **deed.** The person transferring the title to the realty in the deed is the **grantor.** The person to whom the title is transferred is the **grantee.** A deed becomes effective when it is delivered to the grantee or an agent of the grantee. A deed to real property may be bestowed as a gift from the owner or through a sale. In the case of a gift, consideration is not given by the grantee for the deed.

General Warranty Deed A **general warranty deed,** sometimes called a **full covenant and warranty deed,** contains express warranties under which the grantor guarantees the property to be free of encumbrances created by the grantor or by others who had title previously. It is the most desirable form of deed from the point of view of the grantee because it warrants (gives assurances) that title is good.

Special Warranty Deed A **special warranty deed** contains express warranties under which the grantor guarantees that no defect arose in the title during the time that the grantor owned the property. No warranties are made as to defects which arose before the grantor owned the property. The warranties do not extend beyond the seller, and they do not guarantee the title against claims arising from situations existing prior to the seller's title interest.

Harkness sold a vacant lot to Grahm. The lot had been left to Harkness through the will of a distant relative. Harkness had never had the title searched, but she could guarantee Grahm that no liens or claims against the property had been created since she inherited the property. Harkness would be safe in granting title under this special warranty deed. Likewise, the buyer would be protected, but only by making a title search that would disclose claims not covered by the seller's warranty.

Bargain-and-Sale Deed A **bargain-and-sale deed** is one which transfers title to property but contains no warranties. The form of the deed is the same as a warranty deed's except that the covenants are omitted. Since a bargain and sale necessarily involves the idea of a valuable consideration, this type of deed is not valid without consideration. It could not be used to convey a gift of real property.

Quitclaim Deed A **quitclaim deed** (also called a **deed without covenants**) is one that transfers to the buyer only the interest that the seller may have in a property. This type of deed merely releases a party's rights to the property. It contains no warranties. It is used when one gives up some right in the property, such as an easement or dower and curtesy, or to cure a defect in the chain of title.

Title by Will or Descent

When people die owning real property solely in their own name or with others as tenants in common, title passes to their heirs at the moment of death. If they die with a will, title passes to the people named in the will. If they die without a will, title passes to the heirs, as tenants in common, according to the laws of intestacy discussed in Chapter 23. A deed is not used when title passes to heirs in this manner. Instead, the records of the Probate Court establish title to the property.

Title by Occupancy

Title to real property may be obtained by taking actual possession of the property openly, notoriously, exclusively, under a claim of right, and continuously for a period of time set by state statute. This method of obtaining title to real property is called **adverse possession.** To establish such ownership rights, claimants must prove that they have had continuous use of the property for 20 years or a period set by state statute. They must also prove that this use has been without interruption by the owner, without the owner's permission, and with the owner's knowledge. Proof of these facts in court will give a person superior rights over the one in whose name a deed is recorded. A court of equity has the power to declare the one claiming under adverse possession to be the new owner.

Wilhelm and Kupersmith were next-door neighbors. Not realizing where the true property line was, Wilhelm built a garage and driveway 2 feet onto Kupersmith's land. He used the garage and driveway continuously, with Kupersmith's knowledge, for the next 22 years. The error was discovered when Kupersmith sold her property to a new owner who had it surveyed. Wilhelm, through court action, will be able to obtain title to the land on which the garage and driveway are located, by adverse possession.

21-6 ZONING LAWS

Zoning laws are laws which regulate the uses that may be made of properties within specified geographical areas or districts. Residential zoning prohibits properties from being used for commercial purposes within a given area. Multifamily zoning permits construction of apartment buildings. Limited-commercial zoning allows the construction of small stores but restricts the building of large shopping malls and commercial centers. Industrial zoning allows the building of factories, and agricultural zoning allows farming in a particular area. Zoning laws help to keep property values from declining. In addition, they protect against the undesirable use of neighboring property.

Newly passed zoning laws do not apply to existing uses of the land. Such uses are called **nonconforming uses** if they are not allowed under the new zoning law. They may continue in existence but may not be enlarged or expanded.

By appeal to the local zoning board, variances may be given to individuals or businesses when justified and reasonable. A **variance** is an exemption or an exception permitting a use that differs from those permitted under the existing ordinance. Variances are granted in special circumstances to protect citizens who might otherwise suffer a hardship if zoning laws were applied and enforced arbitrarily.

Decisions of a local zoning commission may be appealed to county commissioners, a county court, and to the highest court in the state.

21-7 EMINENT DOMAIN

All ownership of private property is subject to the government's superior rights if property is needed for purposes of public good. **Eminent domain** is the right of federal, state, and local governments, or other public bodies, to take private lands, with compensation to their owners, for public use. The right is exercised for such purposes as new highway construction, public parks, state hospitals, and other facilities.

The right of eminent domain is not available to persons or businesses when taken for private profit. In such situations, property may be acquired only through mutual agreement and for consideration acceptable to the owner. Eminent domain is at times extended to public utilities when it can be shown that denial of a right-of-way for electric, telephone, gas, or other lines may interrupt construction of installations providing needed services to an entire community.

When private property is taken by eminent domain proceedings, the owner must be paid the fair value of what has been taken. The owner is not required to accept an amount offered by those assessing the value of the property. But if an offer is refused, the owner must then seek greater compensation through action in the state or federal courts.

Interstate 95 was designed to cut a swath through a residential section of Chester. Hundreds of homes, businesses, and churches lay in the path of the new highway. Kovach refused to accept the $89,500 offered by assessors for his property. An appeal was made through the county court, with Kovach claiming a fair value of $115,000; this amount would provide the family with a similar home in a comparable neighborhood of the same city. The court might accept the assessors' figure as final; might increase the amount offered; or, in some instances, might reduce the $89,500 if it was considered excessive when reviewed.

In 1987, the U.S. Supreme Court held that property owners must be compensated by the government when regulations which are unduly burdensome deprive them of the use of their land.

The First English Evangelical Lutheran Church of Glendale sought compensation from the County of Los Angeles, claiming that a flood control ordinance deprived the church of the use of a 21-acre parcel of land in a canyon alongside a creek. The ordinance had been passed after a forest fire denuded the hills upstream from the property, and a flood had killed several people and destroyed some buildings on the land. The church had previously used the land as a campground and recreational area for handicapped children.

The Supreme Court held that the church was entitled to compensation if it could prove that the regulation preventing the use of the land was unduly burdensome. The court's decision was based on the Fifth Amendment to the U.S. Constitution which states that private property may not "be taken for public use, without just compensation."

SUMMARY

21-1. Real property is the ground and everything permanently attached to it. It includes the airspace above the surface to as high as the owner can use and the ground under the surface. Although property owners may own the land under a stream, they do not own the water itself. Their rights to use of the water vary, depending on the doctrine of law followed in their state. Property owners may use only that amount of subterranean water that is reasonably required to satisfy their needs. Rainwater may not be artificially channeled to an abutter's property without permission of the abutter. Fixtures are personal property that are so permanently attached to real property that they become part of the real property.

21-2. Easements give people the right to pass over another's land, to run wires through another's airspace, to drain water onto another's property, and to run pipes underneath another's ground. Easements run with the land.

21-3. An estate in fee simple is the greatest interest that one can have in real property. It descends to one's heirs upon death and can be disposed of in any manner during one's lifetime. In contrast, a life estate lasts only for someone's life. At the owner's death, the estate either reverts to the former owner or passes on to someone else.

21-4. People may own real property individually or with others. When two or more people own real property as tenants in common, the interest of a deceased owner's share passes to the heirs upon death. In contrast, when two or more people own real property as joint tenants or tenants by the entirety, the interest of a deceased owner's share passes to the other cotenant(s) upon death. Only a husband and wife can own property as tenants by the entirety, and the property is protected from creditors unless both the husband and wife are debtors.

21-5. A deed is used to transfer real property by sale or gift. The records of the probate court, instead of a deed, establish title to property when an owner dies. Title to real property may be gained by adverse possession. This requires possession of another's property openly, notoriously, exclusively, under a claim of right, and continuously for a period of time set by state statute.

21-6. Zoning laws regulate the uses that may be made to properties within specified geographical areas. Newly passed zoning laws do not apply to nonconforming uses, which are uses that were in existence before the zoning law was passed. Nonconforming uses may not be enlarged or expanded. Variances may be issued by boards of appeals to people who suffer undue hardship from zoning laws.

21-7. Eminent domain is the right of federal, state, and local governments, or other public bodies, to take private lands, for public use. Owners must be paid the fair value of the property taken.

Understanding Key Legal Terms

adverse possession (p. 293)
bargain-and-sale deed (p. 293)
curtesy (p. 290)
dower (p. 290)
easement (p. 288)
easement by prescription (p. 288)
eminent domain (p. 294)
estate in fee simple (p. 289)
fixture (p. 287)
general warranty deed (p. 292)
grantee (p. 292)
grantor (p. 292)
joint tenants (p. 291)
life estate (p. 289)
navigable airspace (p. 285)
nonconforming use (p. 294)
quitclaim deed (p. 293)
real property (p. 284)
riparian owners (p. 285)
special warranty deed (p. 293)
tenancy by the entirety (p. 291)
tenants in common (p. 290)
trade fixtures (p. 288)
variance (p. 294)

Questions for Review and Discussion

1. What type of vegetation is considered real property? What type is considered personal property?
2. Under modern court decisions, to what extent do landowners own the airspace above their land?
3. What three questions are asked in deciding whether an item is a fixture?
4. In what three ways may an easement be created?
5. How does a freehold estate differ from a leasehold estate?
6. What is the difference between common law dower and curtesy?
7. In each of the following tenancies, who succeeds to the deceased's title interest? (*a*) tenancy in common, (*b*) joint tenancy, and (*c*) tenancy by the entirety.
8. In what three ways may title to real property be acquired?
9. Describe a nonconforming use of real property, and explain when a variance might be given.
10. Define eminent domain.

Analyzing Cases

1. Anderson and Barton owned a parcel of real property as joint tenants. Without permission of Anderson, Barton deeded her one-half interest in the property to Cooper. One year later, Cooper died. Cooper's heirs claim that they own Cooper's one-half interest in the property. Anderson claims that he now owns Cooper's half interest because he was a joint tenant with Barton. For whom would you decide? Why?
2. When its lease expired, Londonderry Frameworks made plans to move to another building. Preparations were made to remove shelving, mat and glass cutters, display boards, benches, and other fixtures that had been built into the store when the lease first started. All the shelves and fixtures were specially designed for the picture framing business. The landlord told the owners of Londonderry Frameworks to stop removing the items from the property. May they remove the shelves and other fixtures that were paid for and installed by them during their tenancy? Why or why not? See also *George v. Town of Calais,* 373 A.2d 553 (Vermont).
3. Smith and Dudley are next-door neighbors. The branches of a large maple tree on Smith's property hangs over Dudley's driveway, dripping sap onto Dudley's car. Smith refuses to trim the branches overhanging Dudley's driveway, saying that she does not want to spoil the beauty of the tree. What are Dudley's legal rights in this situation?
4. The Eisenmanns purchased a 90-acre tract of land on which they drilled a 179-foot deep irrigation well. When the well was completed, they began pumping water at the rate of 650 gallons per minute. Two of the surrounding landowners, the Prathers (whose well was 121 feet 10 inches deep) and the Furleys, lost the use of their wells the next day. A third neighbor, the Zessins, lost the use of their well three days later. The surrounding landowners seek money damages for the loss of the use of their wells from the Eisenmanns. Will they recover? If so, how much? Explain. *Prather v. Eisenmann,* 261 N.W.2d 766 (Nebraska).
5. Two years after Jean Russell was divorced from Billy Russell, Jean signed a quitclaim deed conveying her interest in their jointly owned real property to Billy. Later, she tried to have the deed set aside on the ground that Billy gave her no consideration. Will she be successful? Why or why

not? *Russell v. Russell,* 361 So.2d 1053 (Alabama).

6. Soon after Walter and Elsie Wienke were married, Walter conveyed property on Ridgewood Drive that was owned by him to himself and Elsie as tenants by the entirety. At the same time, Elsie conveyed property on Harlan Street that was owned by her to herself and Walter as tenants by the entirety. Twelve years later, Elsie conveyed the Harlan Street property by warranty deed to Colonial Discount Corporation. Walter objected to this sale and did not sign the deed. Colonial Discount Corporation sold the property to Danny and Glenda Lynch. Walter Wienke contends that a conveyance by one tenant by the entirety is inoperative. Do you agree with Walter? Why or why not? *Wienke v. Lynch,* 407 N.E.2d 280 (Indiana).

7. Walter and Emma Barrett jointly executed a warranty deed conveying three lots of land to Chandler and Jean Clements as joint tenants with the right of survivorship. Six years later, Jean Clements conveyed her one-half undivided interest in the property to Wheeler. Chandler claims that Jean could not sell her interest to another person without his approval. Is he correct? *Clements v. Wheeler,* 314 So.2d 64 (Alabama).

8. Richard and Olive Misner began to develop a campground on land that they owned on Olive Lake. The zoning law in existence at the time allowed campgrounds to be built in that area. A year later, however, the county rezoned the area to "agricultural and lake resort" use, which did not permit campgrounds. At the time the new law went into effect, the Misners had constructed ten campsites with facilities and three primitive campsites on their property. When they continued to use and expand the campground after the new zoning law was passed, neighbors complained that they were violating the law. Can the Misners continue to use and expand the property as a campground? Explain. *Misner v. Presdorf,* 421 N.E.2d 684 (Indiana).

CHAPTER 22
Landlord and Tenant

OUTLINE

22-1 The Landlord-Tenant Relationship

22-2 Leasing Versus Other Relationships
- Leasing Compared With Licensing
- Leasing Compared With Lodging

22-3 Types of Leasehold Interests
- Tenancy at Will
- Tenancy for Years
- Periodic Tenancy
- Tenancy at Sufferance

22-4 The Lease Agreement
- Parties to a Lease
- Security Deposits
- Option to Renew
- Option to Purchase
- Assignment and Subletting

22-5 Rights and Duties of Landlords and Tenants
- Landlord's Duty to Refrain from Discrimination
- Warranty of Habitability
- Landlord's Rights
- Tenant's Rights
- Responsibility for Repairs
- Tort Liability

22-6 Dispossess Actions

COMMENTARY

In their junior year of college, Martha Savage and Rose Tamburello decided to rent an apartment rather than to continue to live in the dormitory. They knew two students who were leaving college with six months remaining on their lease and decided to take over their apartment. After the first month, things started going wrong. They came home from school late one afternoon to find their landlord in their apartment waiting for them. When they rejected the landlord's improper advances, he demanded the rental payment that was due, and declared that the rent would be double after that. Savage and Tamburello paid the rent that was due. When they returned home the next day, they found that the electricity had been shut off. This time, the landlord told them that they had been evicted. He said that he had leased the apartment to the prior occupants and had not given his permission for Savage and Tamburello to live there. This scenario may appear farfetched, yet it illustrates real problems that can arise in landlord-tenant relationships.

OBJECTIVES

1. List the five elements necessary to create the landlord-tenant relationship.
2. Compare the landlord-tenant relationship with licenses and lodging.
3. Define the four types of leasehold interests.
4. Discuss the law regarding options to renew, options to purchase, assignments, and subletting.
5. Explain the rights and duties of landlords and tenants.
6. Describe the methods used to evict tenants.

22-1 THE LANDLORD-TENANT RELATIONSHIP

The landlord-tenant relationship is a contractual arrangement whereby the owner of real property allows another to have temporary possession and control of the premises in exchange for consideration. The agreement that gives rise to the landlord-tenant relationship is called a **lease.** The property owner who gives the lease is the **lessor** or **landlord,** and the person to whom the lease is given is the **lessee** or **tenant.** There are five elements necessary for the creation of the landlord-tenant relationship:

1. Consent of the landlord to the occupancy by the tenant.
2. Transfer of possession and control of the property to the tenant in an inferior position (in *subordination*) to the rights of the landlord.
3. The right by the landlord to the return of the property, called the right of *reversion*.
4. The creation of an ownership interest in the tenant known as a **leasehold estate.**
5. Either an express or implied contract between the parties that satisfies all the essentials of a valid contract (mutual assent, competent parties, consideration, lawful purpose).

Although rent is usually paid by the tenant to the landlord for the arrangement, it is not essential to the creation of the landlord-tenant relationship.

22-2 LEASING VERSUS OTHER RELATIONSHIPS

Other relationships that may be compared with the landlord-tenant relationship are licensing and lodging.

Leasing Compared With Licensing

A lease differs from a license in that a lease gives an interest in real property and transfers possession, whereas a **license** gives no property right or interest to the land but merely allows the licensee to do certain acts that would otherwise be a trespass.

The city of Topeka was given a gift of 80 acres of land for use as a public park by the heirs of Guilford G. Gage. The deed that was signed by the heirs contained a condition that the property would revert to them if the property were ever deeded or leased to a third party. After the park was established, the city granted the exclusive right to McCall to construct and operate, for a period of five years, a miniature train on the premises. Under the agreement, McCall was subject in virtually all respects to the control of the city, and either party could end the arrangement by giving 30 days' notice. The heirs of Gage claimed that the transaction was a lease and that the property should be returned to them. In holding that McCall had a license rather than a lease, the court said that all McCall had was "the exclusive right to operate as the City may dictate."

Since a license confers a personal privilege to act, and not a present possessory estate, it does not run with the land and is usually not transferable. It may be made orally or in writing and may be given without consideration. In addition, a license need not delineate the specific space to be occupied.

In contrast, a lease gives the tenant exclusive possession of the premises as against all the world, including the owner. It describes the exact property leased and states the term of the tenancy and the rent to be paid. In addition, in some states, a lease must be in writing.

Union Travel Associates operated a gift shop in the lobby of the International Inn. Under the terms of the agreement, Union was permitted "for the convenience of the guests of the hotel" to sell gifts, tobacco, packaged food, reading materials, and artwork, and to give out tour and travel information. Union was required to promote actively guest business for the hotel and to provide the hotel with a key to each entrance to the gift shop. The hotel had the right "to use space in and through the premises for pipes, wires and conduits, to approve the selection of the gift shop employees, and to regulate the appearance of all gift shop signs, merchandise, and fixtures." In addition, the hotel retained the right to substitute at any time in its discretion any equivalent part of the hotel for its gift shop. The court held the arrangement to be a license rather than a lease, saying that the agreement did not grant an estate in real property. Rather, it conferred the limited privilege to occupy a portion of the hotel lobby to conduct services as a nonleasehold concession.

Permission to sell Christmas trees at a gas station, to hold dance parties in a hall, and to place a sign on the outside of a building have all been held to be licenses rather than leases.

Leasing Compared With Lodging

A **lodger** is one who has the use of property without actual or exclusive possession of it. A lodger is a type of licensee, with a mere right to use the property. The landlord retains control of the premises and is responsible for its care and upkeep. Unlike a tenant, a lodger has no right to bring suit for trespass or to eject an intruder from the premises. One who lives in a spare room of a house, for example, whose owner retains direct control and supervision of the entire house, is a lodger.

22-3 TYPES OF LEASEHOLD INTERESTS

The interest conveyed by a lease is called a **leasehold estate,** or a **tenancy.** There are four kinds of leasehold estates: (1) tenancy at will, (2) tenancy for years, (3) periodic tenancy, and (4) tenancy at sufferance.

Tenancy at Will

A **tenancy at will** is an ownership interest (estate) in real property for an indefinite period of time. No writing is required to create this tenancy, and it may be terminated at the will of either party by giving proper notice. The notice requirement to terminate a tenancy at will varies from state to state. It ranges from no notice at all to 30 days' written notice from the next day that rent is due.

The rule generally followed in this country is that a tenancy at will comes to an end when the property is sold by the landlord to a third party.

Tenancy for Years

A **tenancy for years** is an ownership interest (estate) in real property for a definite or fixed period of time. It may be for one week, six months, one year, five years, ninety-nine years, or any period of time, as long as it is definite. Such a tenancy automatically terminates on the expiration of the stated term. A tenancy for 100 years or more creates an estate in fee simple, transferring absolute ownership to the tenant. For this reason, leases are sometimes written for 99-year periods.

In some states, a tenancy for years may be oral if the term is shorter than one year, otherwise it must be in writing. Other states require all tenancies for years to be in writing. A tenant who remains in possession of the premises at the expiration of the term with permission of the landlord, but without a new lease, is a tenant at will in some states. In others, such a tenant is known as a periodic tenant, described below.

Periodic Tenancy

A **periodic tenancy,** which is also known as a **tenancy from year to year** (or month to month, or week to week), is a tenancy which continues for successive periods until one of the parties terminates it by giving notice to the other party.

Unless the landlord or the tenant gives advance notice of an intention to terminate the lease, it will be automatically renewed at the end of each period for the same term. Advance notice varies from state to state, but it generally is defined as a period of three months for periodic tenancies of one year or longer and "one period" for periodic terms of less than a year.

Pasco's year-to-year lease expires on December 31. On November 15, she gave her landlord notice of her intention to terminate the lease. In her state, three months' notice is necessary to terminate a year-to-year tenancy. Pasco's landlord, therefore, can hold her to an additional year.

The death of a tenant who holds a periodic tenancy does not terminate the tenancy. Rather, the interest of the tenant passes to the personal representative of the deceased's estate.

Wilson was in possession of rental property originally leased to his father on a month-to-month basis. After the father's death, the landlord notified Wilson to vacate the premises on the ground that the tenancy had ceased automatically. When Wilson refused to leave, criminal trespass charges were filed against him. He was found not guilty. The court held that his father's interest in the premises passed to him and that he was entitled to proper notice to end the month-to-month tenancy.

A periodic tenancy may be created impliedly by a landlord accepting rent from a tenant for years whose lease has expired or who is wrongfully in possession. Some states treat the latter situation as a tenancy at will.

Tenancy at Sufferance

A **tenancy at sufferance** arises when tenants wrongfully remain in possession of the premises after their tenancy has expired. It often comes about at the expiration of the term of a tenancy for years or when a tenancy at will has been properly terminated and the tenant remains in possession. Such a tenant is a wrongdoer, having no estate or other interest in the property. A tenant at sufferance is not entitled to notice to vacate and is liable to pay rent for the period of occupancy. A periodic tenancy or a tenancy at will may come about, however, instead of a tenancy at sufferance if a landlord accepts rent from a tenant whose tenancy has expired.

Sutherland, an attorney, rented a suite of rooms in the Metropolitan Building in Chicago which she used for law offices. When her two-year lease expired, she negotiated with the owner of the building for a new lease. The negotiations extended over a period of several months, and the parties could not reach agreement. The landlord accepted rent each month from Sutherland during the period of negotiations. Sutherland was not a tenant at sufferance during the negotiation period because the landlord accepted rent from her during that time. A month-to-month tenancy was created. The landlord was required to give Sutherland a month's notice to end the tenancy.

22-4 THE LEASE AGREEMENT

The agreement between a lessor and a lessee, called a lease, creates the landlord-tenant relationship. It provides the tenant with exclusive possession and control of the real property of the landlord. Since the lease is a contract, the general rules of contract law apply to it.

Piccarelli, a representative of Mister Donut, expressed interest in leasing Tull's property. He sent a letter to Tull describing the "rudiments of our deal" and concluding with an expression of hope "that in the very near future preliminaries will be completed." This was followed by a form of lease sent by Piccarelli to Tull for the latter's approval. Tull signed the lease, after changing it materially, and returned it to Mister Donut for a countersignature. Nothing further was done, and the transaction never materialized. Tull's building was vandalized and burned after his tenants were evicted in anticipation of leasing the property to Mister Donut. When Tull sued Mister Donut, the court held that no contract and, thus, no lease came about. The initial letter was no more than an agenda for further discussion. The first draft of the lease sent by Piccarelli to Tull was an offer, and the revised document a counteroffer, never accepted by Mister Donut.

The essential requirements of a lease are: (*a*) a definite agreement as to the extent and bounds of the leased property, (*b*) a definite and agreed term, and (*c*) a definite and agreed price of rental and manner of payment. (See Figure 22-1.)

Schumacher leased a retail store to a tenant for a five-year term. The renewal clause stated that "the Tenant may renew this lease for an additional period of five years at annual rentals *to be agreed upon;* Tenant shall give Landlord thirty (30) days written notice, to be mailed certified mail, return receipt requested, of the intention to exercise such right." The tenant gave timely notice to renew the lease, but the parties could not agree on the rent for the new term. The court held that the agreement to renew the lease was unenforceable because the amount of rent was uncertain.

Parties to a Lease

A lease must be entered into by the property's owner or agent and the tenant who will actually occupy the leased premises. Often the property owner delegates the authority to execute leases to a rental or management agent. Typically, the management company collects all rents and performs all building services for the property owner in exchange for a percent of the rent it collects.

An agent may execute the lease for the lessee, but must disclose who the actual tenant will be. That is because the landlord will usually ask for references, that is, a list of the prospective tenant's business contacts or former landlords. The purpose is to help in deciding whether the prospective lessee would be a responsible tenant.

Since a lease is a contract, it may be disaffirmed by a party who did not have the capacity to execute the contract when it was first entered into. (See Chapter 8.) Similarly, if a person adjudged to be incompetent has entered into a lease, that lease may be disaffirmed by someone who has the authority to govern the affairs of the incompetent. A minor may also disaffirm a lease, unless it is shown to be a necessity. Minors who are married cannot disaffirm their contracts in some states and may be held responsible for all unpaid rents.

Security Deposits

In addition to the first month's rent, landlords often require either a security deposit or the last month's rent, or both, to be paid at the beginning of a tenancy. This protects landlords against damages to their property as well as nonpayment of rent. Due to abuses of such deposits by landlords, state legislatures have passed laws regulating security deposits on residential property. Such laws spell out the rights of tenants and make it easier for tenants to prevail in court. Although these laws differ from state to state, the following characteristics are commonly found:

1. Most states limit security deposits to 1, 1½, 2, or 2½ months' rent.
2. Most states require that security deposits be placed in interest-bearing accounts. The interest is either paid to tenants on an annual basis or accrued in their favor.
3. The landlord is given a specific period, usually 30 days after the lease ends, to account for the security deposit and return the balance due to a tenant.

LEASE

This lease made the 20th day of August, 1988, between ROBERT VICKERS herein called Landlord, and ETHEL LOPAZ, herein called Tenant, witnesseth:

The Landlord leases to the Tenant the following described premises: Four rooms and a bath on the first floor of the premises located at 17 Rosebud Terrace, Ashmont, New Hampshire, for the term of one year commencing at noon on the first day of September, 1988, and ending at noon on the 31st day of August, 1989.

The Tenant agrees to pay to the Landlord the sum of $4,800 for the said term, in eleven (11) monthly payments as follows: The first and last months' rent of $800 payable on September 1, 1988, and $400 on the first day of each month thereafter.

The Landlord agrees that the Tenant on paying the said rent and performing the covenants herein contained shall peaceably and quietly have, hold, and enjoy the premises for said term.

The Tenant agrees that at the expiration of the time mentioned in this lease she will give peaceable possession of the said premises to the Landlord in as good a condition as they now are, the usual wear, unavoidable accidents and loss by fire excepted, and will not make or suffer any waste thereof, nor assign this lease, nor sublet, nor permit any other person to occupy the same, nor make or suffer to be made any alteration therein, without the consent of the Landlord in writing having been first obtained, and that the Landlord may enter to view and make improvements, and to show the premises to prospective tenants or purchasers.

The covenants herein shall extend to and be binding upon the heirs, executors, and administrators of the parties to this lease.

IN WITNESS WHEREOF, the parties have hereunto set their hands and seals the day and year first above written.

Robert Vickers
Robert Vickers

Ethel Lopaz
Ethel Lopaz

Figure 22-1 A lease.

4. Many states have now "put teeth" into the law by providing for double damages, court costs, and attorney's fees for tenants whose security deposits were wrongfully withheld.

Santos rented a $450-per-month apartment from Hollis for a term of two years. When Santos's tenancy ended, Hollis refused to return any of the $450 security deposit to Santos, claiming that the damages to the apartment fully offset the amount of the deposit. Santos hired a lawyer, who brought suit against Hollis. The landlord was able to demonstrate only $70 in damages to Santos's apartment. The court found that Hollis had wrongfully withheld $380 of Santos's security deposit. The court awarded Santos a judgment for double damages of $760 plus attorney's fees of $200. With court costs, the landlord was forced to pay over $1,000.

Landlords of commercial property may also require security deposits, but the statutes do not usually cover commercial leases.

Option to Renew

Many leases contain a provision allowing the lessee to have the option to renew the lease for one or more additional terms. An **option to renew** gives the lessee the right, at the end of the lease, to a new lease for an additional period. The new lease is on the same terms as the old one with the possible exception of an increase in the rent. To exercise the option, the lessee must notify the lessor on or before the date set forth in the lease to do so. If there is more than one lessee to a lease agreement, an option-to-renew provision in the lease must be exercised by the lessees jointly to be effective.

Option to Purchase

A lessee may, if the lease so provides, be given an **option to purchase** the property. This is an agreement by the lessor to sell the property to the lessee for a stated price. To exercise the option, the lessee must notify the lessor, within the time period stated in the lease, of the decision to purchase the property.

Larson purchased a parcel of real property for $19,140 and leased it to the Panhandle Rehabilitation Center. The lease was for ten years and contained an option to buy for $19,000. After leasing the premises for five years and spending $5,000 to improve it, Panhandle notified Larson of its intention to exercise its option. By this time, the property was worth $38,000. Larson refused to sell the property to Panhandle for $19,000. The court ordered her to do so.

Assignment and Subletting

An *assignment* of a lease occurs when the interest in the leased premises is transferred by the lessee to another person for the balance of the term of the lease. The new party, called the *assignee,* steps into the shoes of the tenant, or *assignor,* and is liable for all the old tenant's obligations and entitled to all the old tenant's rights under the lease. It is called a **sublease,** or **underlease,** if the transfer is for a part of the term but not for the remainder of it.

A lease may be assigned or sublet unless the lease states otherwise. Many leases are written so that they require landlord approval for an assignment or a sublease. However, in some states the landlord cannot withhold such approval unreasonably. An assignment or sublease will be held valid if the landlord accepts rent over a period of time from either an assignee or a subtenant.

22-5 RIGHTS AND DUTIES OF LANDLORDS AND TENANTS

A good lease agreement will carefully spell out the respective rights and duties of landlord and tenant. However, appropriate laws may restrict or expand upon what is set forth in the lease.

The standard lease at Helmsly Arms provides that residential tenants may renew automatically after expiration of their standard two-year leases at a new rental rate 12 percent higher than the previous rental. A local "rent-leveling" ordinance limits rent increases in such circumstances to 8 percent. When the ordinance was first passed, a group of landlords brought suit to attack its constitutionality. The matter went all the way to the highest court in the state, where the ordinance was upheld. Helmsly cannot impose its terms despite the clear language of the lease.

Landlord's Duty to Refrain From Discrimination

A landlord may not discriminate in selecting tenants on the grounds of race, creed, color, or sex. In most states a landlord may restrict rentals to persons without children, but may not restrict a married couple's freedom to bear children during the leasehold.

The Stimsons, a married couple, rented a luxury apartment from Chester Realty Associates. A condition inserted in the lease read, "The lessee agrees that if a child or children are born to the tenants during the period of the lease, the lease will be automatically terminated without the necessity of notice from the landlord." This condition is not enforceable against the Stimsons. Persons may not be denied the freedom of bearing children through contracts made with a landlord or others.

Warranty of Habitability

When real property is rented for single- or multiple-family dwelling purposes, there is an implied warranty in most states that the premises are fit for human habitation. This means that the landlord warrants that there are not defects vital to the use of the premises for residential purposes.

Jefferson leased an apartment for one year from Berman. A series of breaks in underground heating pipes caused the tenant to receive intermittent heat for two months. Finally, in early October, the pipe burst completely, and the tenant was without heat and hot water for two weeks. The court held that even though the landlord was not at fault, the warranty of habitability had been breached. Jefferson was not required to pay rent during the period that the apartment had no heat.

Landlord's Rights

The landlord has the right to collect rent from the tenant. In addition, the landlord has the right to remove a tenant for nonpayment of rent, disorderliness, or illegal or unpermitted use of the premises.

Harrison had been a tenant of Driscoll for 13 years, and rent control laws prevented his eviction without good cause. One morning Harrison was late for work. As he was going to his car, which was in the parking lot of the building, he saw that a truck was blocking the exit from the lot. Frank Driscoll, the landlord's son, had arrived in the truck a short time earlier to collect rubbish. Harrison asked Frank Driscoll to move his truck, and Frank Driscoll asked Harrison why he had failed to report a leak in his apartment which had caused water to seep into the unit below his. Harrison denied knowledge of the leak, and a shouting and pushing match ensued. The light pushing as well as the shouting ended when Harrison took a 4-foot closet pole from the trunk of his car and hit Frank Driscoll on the shoulder with it. The court allowed the landlord to evict the tenant for striking his son, saying that the tenant "used excessive force and committed a serious act of violence."

A tenant does have the duty to observe the restrictions contained in the lease. Leases may impose duties of all kinds as long as they are legal and do not deny a tenant's constitutional rights. Failure to abide by the restrictions agreed to at the time of the signing of the lease gives the landlord the right to seek eviction of the tenant.

Boggs's lease states that he cannot paint any exterior woodwork or walls without first getting written permission from the landlord. Painting these surfaces, even though doing so improves the property, gives the landlord the right to terminate Boggs's lease.

The landlord has the right to keep fixtures (except trade fixtures belonging to a business) that have been made a permanent part of the real property by the tenant during the leasehold.

Dr. Hembly installed partitions in the rented house, dividing the living room for consultation offices. New lighting fixtures were installed, as well as a built-in air-conditioning system. Hembly would be barred from removing the additions at the expiration of her lease or upon her eviction, as they had become real property.

Tenant's Rights

The tenant is entitled to the peaceful possession and quiet enjoyment of the rental premises. **Quiet enjoyment** is the right of a tenant to the undisturbed possession of the property. This includes both the physical and legal rights of possession. The landlord may not interfere with the tenant's rights of possession as long as the tenant abides by the conditions of the lease and those imposed by law.

Smith Grocery & Variety, Inc., leased one store in a two-store mall from Northern Terminals, Inc. The lease entitled Smith to the use of the parking areas (between 14 and 20 spaces) abutting the leased premises. Five months after Smith opened for business, Northern Terminals added an additional store to the mall without increasing the mall's parking facilities. Smith's business declined due to the severe parking shortage caused by the opening of a Triple-S Blue Stamp Redemption Center in the new addition. The court held that Northern Terminals, Inc., breached the covenant of quiet enjoyment. There was a substantial interference with the lessee's use of the premises, which was caused by the lessor's taking away of the parking spaces.

The right to exclusive possession by the tenant makes the landlord a trespasser should there be any unauthorized entry by the landlord into the rented premises.

Benson & Childs rented a skylight suite for their architecture offices. The lease gave the owner permission to enter only when a request had been made or in the event of extreme emergency. The landlord entered the offices late one evening for what he termed was his regular safety and fire inspection. Benson & Childs may treat the landlord's trespass as a breach of their right to sole possession, giving them the right to terminate the lease and charge the landlord in either a civil or a criminal complaint.

A tenant who is wrongfully evicted is not required to return and may consider the lease as ended. An **eviction** is an act of the landlord that deprives the tenant of the enjoyment of the premises. It is called an **actual eviction** when the tenant is physically deprived of the leasehold. When the tenant is deprived of something of a substantial nature that was called for under the lease, it is termed a **constructive eviction.** The tenant is justified in abandoning the premises without paying rent when a wrongful eviction occurs. The tenant must mitigate (lessen) any damages, however, if possible.

Sound City, U.S.A., was interested in renting space in a shopping center. An inspection of the premises disclosed portions of the ceiling tile missing or hanging loose, water marks on the ceiling, and bare fluorescent light fixtures. As a result, Sound City included in its one-year lease an addendum (addition) whereby the landlord agreed to repair and paint the ceiling tile, cover the light bulb fixtures, panel the south wall, and erect a partition. Sound City moved into the shopping center, but after three months and many complaints the repairs were never completed. It then moved out. The landlord brought suit for the remaining nine months' rent. The court held against the landlord, saying that there had been a constructive eviction. The physical appearance of the store was an important factor in the successful operation of Sound City's business. The failure to repair the premises properly in accordance with the lease rendered the premises unsuitable for the purpose for which they were rented.

Responsibility for Repairs

The obligation for repairs to rental property has been the subject of much legislation over the past decade. What was formerly regulated by common law practices and court decisions is now under the supervision of public housing authorities in many states and municipalities.

Obligations of Tenant Under earlier law, a tenant was obligated to return premises to the owner in the same condition as when delivered to the tenant. Normal wear and tear and depreciation are not included in this definition. Some states have in the past interpreted this duty in the strictest way, requiring tenants to rebuild structures that have been destroyed for whatever reason during the leasehold. Other states have taken a milder view of the tenant's obligations through judicial interpretation or the passing of laws that limit the tenant's obligations. A lease may be written to contain a more thorough description of the tenant's obligations in the matter of repairs, rather than leaving decisions to judicial decision and statute. In any case, tenants will be held responsible for repairs for damages caused by their negligence, illegal use, or uses not permitted by the lease.

Turner rented a house in Westminster. The lease contained the usual statements covering repairs by tenant and landlord. When Turner negligently plugged in an electric space heater with a defective thermostat and left the house, a serious fire resulted. Turner is responsible for all repairs necessary because of his negligent act.

Obligations of Landlord Traditionally, a landlord needed to make only those repairs that were required by the terms of the lease. But certain parts of a structure have also been considered the landlord's responsibility. Outside walls, foundations, and structural parts of a building are examples. Most leases forapartments or office suites require the landlord to make all repairs to stairways, halls, outside walls, roof, heating and air-conditioning systems, plumbing, and the like. The tenant's obligations would be confined to the areas assigned to the tenant under the lease.

Daniels and Cohen, attorneys, rented a suite of offices in the Farmers Bank Building. Excellent management kept the offices clean, well decorated, and comfortable. But leaking water from the roof was reported to the bank management, which made no effort to remedy the situation. A heavy storm resulted in serious water damage to the office, ruining $10,000 worth of law books. The landlord, not the tenant, was responsible for this loss.

Many municipalities have adopted ordinances to protect tenants from unsafe or unhealthy conditions created by a landlord's refusal to make necessary repairs. Building inspectors, health authorities, and other public officials are empowered to make inspections and demand improvements when they are contacted by dissatisfied tenants. In many cases, ordinances permit the tenant to cease payment of rent for the period during which the landlord fails to make the repairs or improvements needed.

Tort Liability

When a person is injured on leased property, the one who is in control of that part of the premises where the injury occurs, in most cases, is responsible if the injury was caused by that person's negligence. The landlord, for example, is responsible for injury to others caused by a defect in the common areas, such as hallways and stairways.

Wilson sustained serious injuries when she fell on a defective step while descending the front stairway of her apartment building. The landlord was held liable for Wilson's injuries because he was negligent in failing to keep the steps in a reasonably safe condition.

In contrast, tenants are responsible, in most cases, for injuries to persons caused by defects in the portion of the premises over which they have control.

While visiting a friend's second-floor apartment, Ward fell down a single step leading to the bathroom. In a suit brought against the landlord for her injuries, Ward lost the case. The court said that the tenant was the responsible occupier of the premises. Any duty owed to the tenant's guest relative to the step was owed by the tenant, not the landlord.

The majority of states hold that a landlord has a duty to clear common entryways of natural accumulations of snow and ice. Some states nevertheless still follow the older rule that the landlord owes no duty to tenants to clean common entryways of ice and snow unless there is an agreement on the part of the landlord to do so.

22-6 DISPOSSESS ACTIONS

Three principal methods are available to landlords to regain possession of premises when tenants fail to leave at the end of a tenancy: peaceable entry of the premises by the landlord, ejectment, and unlawful detainer.

Most states today do not allow landlords to use force to evict tenants. Instead, they must make use of statutory remedies that are available to them. Some states do, however, recognize the right of landlords to enter wrongfully held premises and take over possession if it can be done peacefully.

Ejectment is the common law name given to the lawsuit brought by the landlord to have the tenant evicted from the premises. This older remedy is still available in many states; however, it is time-consuming, expensive, and subject to long delays.

Unlawful detainer is a legal proceeding that provides landlords with a quick method of evicting a tenant. The proceeding is referred to by different names in different states, including the following: **summary process, summary ejectment, forcible entry and detainer,** and **dispossessory warrant proceedings.** The remedy provides landlords with a quick method of regaining possession of their property and protects tenants from being ousted by force and violence. Strict notice requirements must be followed by the landlord, after which both parties are given their day in court. If a forcible eviction becomes necessary, it is done by the sheriff under the supervision of the court.

Several months after Koonce fell behind in her rent payments, her landlord brought summary process proceedings against her. The court issued an execution (an order to carry out its judgment) giving the landlord possession, rent arrearages, and costs. Armed with the execution, a sheriff went to the premises and removed three fans, a stereo system, a record collection, a digital clock radio, a double-bed quilt, an iron, and a portable tape recorder. He also left a note saying that execution would be carried out if the rent were not paid up. The court held that this was an improper procedure. It was the duty of the sheriff, once the execution was placed in his hands, to remove all Koonce's possessions, sell such of them as were necessary to satisfy the execution, and make the rest of her possessions available to her. Piecemeal exercise of an execution is not permissible.

SUMMARY

22-1. The landlord-tenant relationship is a contractual arrangement whereby the owner of real property allows another to have temporary possession and control of the premises in exchange for consideration.

22-2. A lease differs from a license in that a lease conveys an interest in real property and transfers possession, whereas a license conveys no property right or interest but merely allows the licensee to do certain acts which would otherwise be a trespass. A lodger, a type of licensee, has the use of property without actual or exclusive possession of it.

22-3. A tenancy at will is an ownership interest (estate) in real property for an indefinite period of time. A tenancy for years is an estate for a definite period of time, no matter how long or how short. A periodic tenancy is a tenancy that continues for successive periods until one of the parties terminates it by giving notice to the other party. A tenancy at sufferance arises when tenants wrongfully remain in possession of the premises after their tenancy has expired.

22-4. The lease creates the landlord-tenant relationship. Since it is a contract, the general rules of contract law apply to it. State laws often regulate security deposits on residential property. A lease may be assigned or sublet unless the lease states otherwise.

22-5. A landlord may not discriminate in selecting tenants on the grounds of race, creed, color, or sex. Premises that are rented for residential purposes must be fit for human habitation. Landlords have the right to evict tenants for nonpayment of rent, disorderliness, and unpermitted use of the premises. Tenants are entitled to peaceful possession and quiet enjoyment. Tenants are responsible for repairs for damages caused by their negligence, illegal use, or uses not permitted by the lease. Landlords are usually responsible for repairs to the outside of the building, stairways and hallways, the plumbing and heating system, and the like. When someone is injured, the person in control of that part of the premises where the injury occurs is responsible if negligent.

22-6. Peaceable entry, ejectment, and unlawful detainer are the principal methods available to landlords to regain possession of their premises. Of these, unlawful detainer (called by different names in different states) is the most commonly used method. This remedy provides landlords with a quick method of regaining possession of their property and protects tenants from being ousted by force and violence.

Understanding Key Legal Terms

actual eviction (p. 309)
constructive eviction (p. 309)
ejectment (p. 312)
eviction (p. 309)
landlord (p. 300)
lease (p. 300)
leasehold estate (p. 301)
lessee (p. 300)
lessor (p. 300)
license (p. 300)
lodger (p. 301)
periodic tenancy (p. 302)
quiet enjoyment (p. 309)
sublease (p. 306)
tenancy (p. 301)
tenancy at sufferance (p. 303)
tenancy at will (p. 302)
tenancy for years (p. 302)
tenancy from year to year (p. 302)
tenant (p. 300)
underlease (p. 306)
unlawful detainer (p. 312)

Questions for Review and Discussion

1. Name the five elements that are necessary for the creation of the landlord-tenant relationship.
2. How does a lease compare with a license and with lodging?
3. In what ways do the following tenancies differ: (*a*) tenancy for years, (*b*) periodic tenancy, (*c*) tenancy at will, (*d*) tenancy at sufferance?
4. What are the three essential requirements of a lease?
5. How does the assignment of a lease compare with the subletting of a lease?
6. When and by whom is the implied warranty of habitability made?
7. What rights do landlords have under a lease?
8. What rights do tenants have under a lease?

9. Discuss the obligations of the tenant and the landlord in the matter of repairs to rented premises.

10. Describe the three principal methods available to landlords to regain possession of premises when tenants fail to leave at the end of a tenancy.

Analyzing Cases

1. Gallo rented an apartment from Kennedy as a tenant at will. She paid her rent on time and took good care of the premises; she was never disorderly. Kennedy decided to evict Gallo and rent the apartment to a college friend who was moving to the area. He sent Gallo a proper eviction notice. Gallo claims that she cannot be evicted because she had done nothing wrong. Do you agree with Gallo? Explain. See also *Ralo, Inc. v. Jack Graham, Inc.*, 362 So.2d 310 (Florida).

2. Sarah H. Brown and Sandy F. Soverow agreed to rent separate apartments from Osborn, the owner of an apartment complex called Nob Hill Apartments, which was being constructed. Since their single apartments were not yet completed, Brown and Soverow agreed to rent one larger apartment in the complex and live in that until their separate apartments were finished. A fire occurred in the apartment shortly after Brown had put some leftover livers and gizzards for her dogs on the electric stove and had left the apartment. In the lawsuit that followed, the contention was made that Brown and Soverow were lodgers rather than tenants. Do you agree with the contention? Explain. *Osborn v. Brown,* 361 So.2d 82 (Alabama).

3. Alabama Outdoor Advertising Co., Inc., leased part of a lot from All State Linen Service Co. to erect a commercial advertising sign. The term of the lease was for "indefinite years, beginning 1st day of January, 1973 and ending year to year thereafter." When All State sold the lot, it was argued that Alabama's lease was a tenancy at will and, therefore, came to an end when the lot was sold. Do you agree with this argument? Why or why not? *Industrial Mach., Inc. v. Creative Displays, Inc.*, 344 So.2d 743 (Alabama).

4. O'Connell rented an apartment from Parisi for $500 a month. Up until losing his job, O'Connell always paid his rent on time. He fell behind, however, when his company went out of business and he lost his job. At a point when the amount in arrears reached $1,000, Parisi pushed O'Connell out of the apartment and padlocked the door. O'Connell claims that Parisi violated the law by using force to evict him. Parisi claims that he had a right to do so. For whom would you decide? Why? See also *Sempek v. Minarik,* 264 N.W.2d 426 (Nebraska).

5. Friedman's tenancy came to an end on June 30. His landlord did not return or account for any portion of Friedman's security deposit until the following September 1. A statute in that state requires landlords to either return or account for security deposits within 30 days after the termination of a tenancy. Failure to do so entitles the tenant to an award of damages equal to three times the amount of the security deposit plus 5 percent interest from the date when the payment became due, together with court costs and reasonable attorney's fees. Is Friedman entitled to recover from the landlord? *Friedman v. Costello,* 412 N.E.2d 1285 (Massachusetts).

6. Elmer and Bonnie Cummings, as lessors, entered into a lease with Leo and Glen Ward for the rental of a building from March 16, 1966, to July 31, 1974. The lease provided that there could be no assignment

without the written consent of the lessors. In October, 1966, the Wards assigned the lease to Robert and Alice Smith with no written consent from the Cummingses. The Cummingses accepted rent from the Smiths for five years without objection. Was the assignment valid? Why or why not? *Smith v. Hegg,* 214 N.W.2d 789 (South Dakota).

7. Sorrells rented a single-family dwelling house from Pole Realty Company. When eviction proceedings were brought against her for nonpayment of rent, Sorrells claimed that there had been a breach of the implied warranty of habitability. Pole Realty Company argued that the warranty of habitability does not apply to the rental of single-family residences. Do you agree? Explain. *Pole Realty Co. v. Sorrells,* 417 N.E.2d 1297 (Illinois).

8. The Kings leased a residential dwelling from a partnership called JA-SIN. The lease agreement provided that the tenants were to "take good care of the house" and "make, at their own expense, the necessary repairs caused by their own neglect or misuse." A guest of the Kings, Sharon Ford, tripped on a loose tread on one step while descending an outside stairway and sustained personal injuries. Who was responsible, the landlord or the tenant? Give the reason for your answer. *Ford v. JA-SIN,* 420 A.2d 184 (Delaware).

CHAPTER 23
Wills, Intestacy, and Trusts

OUTLINE

COMMENTARY

Elliott Preston lived alone all his adult life. He lived in a well-kept house in the suburbs. When Preston grew too old to care for himself, two special friends, Dana and Ida Long, took care of him. They cooked his meals, cleaned his house, and took care of his personal needs. Preston told the Longs on several occasions that when he died, his house would belong to them. Preston never made a will, however, and the house was inherited by several distant cousins who hardly knew him.

Lawsuits and family arguments often follow the death of a person who has not made a will or who has made a will carelessly without seeking competent legal advice. In some cases, an entire estate dwindles to nothing because of such litigations. This chapter explains some basic law involving the making of a will, dying without a will, and the importance of trusts.

OBJECTIVES

1. Describe, generally, the disposition of property of a deceased person.
2. Judge whether a person who makes a will has the capacity to do so.
3. Explain the formal requirements for executing a will.
4. Compare the protection of children with the protection of spouses under the law of wills.
5. Identify the different methods of revoking or changing a will.
6. Decide, in different situations, who will inherit the property of someone who dies without a will.
7. Describe the steps to be taken by an executor or administrator in settling an estate.
8. Differentiate among the various types of trusts, and determine when they might be used.

23-1
TESTAMENTARY DISPOSITION OF PROPERTY

When people die, their property passes to their heirs. If they die leaving a **will** (a formal document that governs the transfer of property at death), their property will go to the individuals or institutions named. If they die without leaving a will, their property will be distributed according to the law of the state where they resided prior to death. A person who dies with a will is said to die **testate.** A person who dies without a will is said to die **intestate.** The giving away of one's property by will is known as **testamentary disposition.**

A person who makes a will is called a **testator** if a man or a **testatrix** if a woman.* Personal property that is left by will is called a **bequest,** or **legacy.** Real property that is left by will is known as a **devise.** Those who receive property by will are referred to as **beneficiaries.** They are also known as **legatees** if they receive personal property and as **devisees** if they receive real property under a will. The term **heir** is a broader term referring to one who inherits property either under a will or through someone dying intestate.

23-2
WHO MAY MAKE A WILL

Any person who has reached the age of adulthood (18 years) and is of sound mind may make a will. The issue of soundness of mind is raised only when someone contests a will on that ground. In determining whether a testator was of sound mind when making a will, the court asks the following questions:

1. When making the will, did the testator know, in a general way, the nature and extent of the property he or she owned?
2. Did the testator know who would be the natural recipients of the estate?
3. Was the testator free from delusions which might influence the disposition of the property?
4. Did the testator know that he or she was making a will?

If all of the above questions are answered in the affirmative, the court will find that the testator was of sound mind when making a will.

At the time of the execution of his will, Zdanowicz was suffering from loss of memory. His son observed his father's failing health and mental illness over a period of time. He once observed his father's failure to recognize his own wife. Zdanowicz's daughter observed her father's failure once to recognize her and another relative, both of whom he saw frequently. The court disallowed the will, saying, "The testator did not have mind and memory sound enough to know and understand the businesses upon which he was engaged at the time of execution."

---

*The masculine forms of terms like *testator* are used for purposes of discussion. They refer to people of either sex.

Undue Influence

A will may be attacked and held invalid if a probate court finds that the testator made the will under circumstances of undue influence. When persons come under the influence of another to the degree that they are unable to express their real intentions in a will, the will may be declared invalid. The court must distinguish between undue influence and the kindnesses, attention, advice, guidance, and friendliness shown toward the testator by the one named in the will.

Smolak executed a will prepared by a lawyer whom he had selected and with whom he had conferred several times before the date on which the will was signed. His niece, Sandra, was the major beneficiary under that will. A week later, he executed another will under which his nephew Michael and Michael's brother were named principal beneficiaries. This was done at the same time that he executed a deed conveying his farm to Michael and Michael's brother (which conveyance he promptly sought to rescind, claiming that it was procured by fraud). The second will was executed at the office of a lawyer employed by Michael. Michael had made arrangements for a conference between his lawyer and Smolak. Michael attended that conference and also attended the execution of the resulting will. Smolak never conferred privately with Michael's lawyer concerning the second will and therefore never had an opportunity to express his true intentions out of earshot of his nephew. The court held that the second will was procured through undue influence and was, therefore, void.

23-3 EXECUTING A WILL

The laws governing the making and signing of wills are not uniform throughout the United States since they are a product of state statute. Nevertheless, a will that is properly executed according to the laws of one state will be given full faith and credit in another state. The laws are highly technical and require strict adherence to detailed formalities. Many lawsuits have occurred over the years because people have attempted to make their own wills without consulting a lawyer. Often, in such cases, a technicality causes the will to be disallowed by the court, and the true wishes of the deceased are not carried out.

Formal Requirements

With the exception of an oral will discussed below, a will must be in writing, signed by the testator, and attested in the testator's presence by the number of witnesses established by state law. Each of the particular statutory requirements of the state where the will is made must be met for a will to be valid.

Dugan's will contained the following clause: "All United States Savings Bonds in safety deposit box #559 Farmers Bank 10th and Market Sts. Wilmington Del. to be given to the people and places as marked." When Dugan died, a number of U.S. Savings Bonds were found in his safe-deposit box. There was also a handwritten list of the names of various individuals and organizations, and beside each name were serial numbers, dates, and face amounts corresponding to specific bonds. Further specific notations were written on small slips of paper and attached to each bond with a rubber band. The court held that there was no effective testamentary transfer of the bonds. Neither the list, the envelopes, nor the small slips of paper satisfied the statutory requirements for executing a will. They were not properly signed and witnessed. Dugan's wishes as stated in the will were never carried out.

Written Instrument A will may be typewritten, handwritten, or consist of a filled-in form. It need not be under seal. The will offered for probate must be the original copy, not a carbon, unless the carbon is fully executed with the same formalities as the original. In a case in which a testator executed both an original and a carbon copy of a will and then later canceled only the carbon, the court held that it could be presumed that the testator also intended to cancel the original. Problems of this nature can be avoided by executing only the original copy of a will.

Signature of the Testator A will must be signed by the testator. The place of the signature on the will and the requirement as to who must be present at the signing vary from state to state. In some states, a will must be signed at the end of the instrument; in other states, the signature may be placed anywhere on the paper. Similarly, some states require a will to be signed in the presence of the witnesses, whereas others allow a will to be signed privately if the testator acknowledges to the witnesses when they sign that it is his or her signature. Testators who are not able to write may make a mark, such as an X, attested to by the required number of witnesses. If the testator's condition makes movement impossible, as in paralysis, another person may sign for the testator. This must be done at the request of the testator, in the testator's presence, and in the presence of the witnesses.

Witnesses The number of witnesses varies according to local statutes. Usually two or three are required. Witnesses must sign in the presence of the testator and, in some states, in each others' presence. Since the witnesses may be called upon to attest to the genuineness of the testator's signature and soundness of mind, it is advisable that witnesses be young persons. In most states, minors may witness a will as long as they are of sufficient understanding and competent to testify in court as to the facts relating to the execution of the will. The law also states that persons and their spouses who witness a will may not receive gifts under the will unless there are still other witnesses. The failure to observe this provision may result in their being disinherited.

Elliott executed a will leaving all his property to his three daughters, Jane, Noreen, and Frances. Jane's husband was one of the subscribing witnesses to the will. When Elliott died, Jane received nothing from her father's estate. A statute in that state makes void any testamentary gift to a subscribing witness or spouse of such a witness.

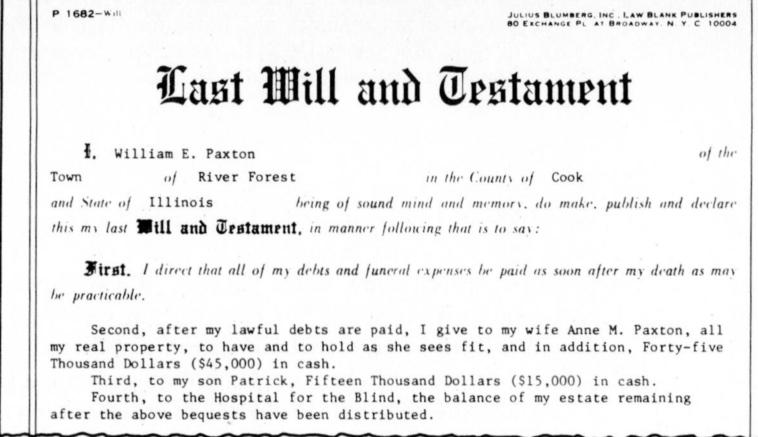

P 1682—Will

JULIUS BLUMBERG, INC., LAW BLANK PUBLISHERS
80 EXCHANGE PL. AT BROADWAY, N. Y. C. 10004

Last Will and Testament

I, William E. Paxton of the Town of River Forest in the County of Cook and State of Illinois being of sound mind and memory, do make, publish and declare this my last **Will and Testament,** in manner following that is to say:

First. I direct that all of my debts and funeral expenses be paid as soon after my death as may be practicable.

Second, after my lawful debts are paid, I give to my wife Anne M. Paxton, all my real property, to have and to hold as she sees fit, and in addition, Forty-five Thousand Dollars ($45,000) in cash.

Third, to my son Patrick, Fifteen Thousand Dollars ($15,000) in cash.

Fourth, to the Hospital for the Blind, the balance of my estate remaining after the above bequests have been distributed.

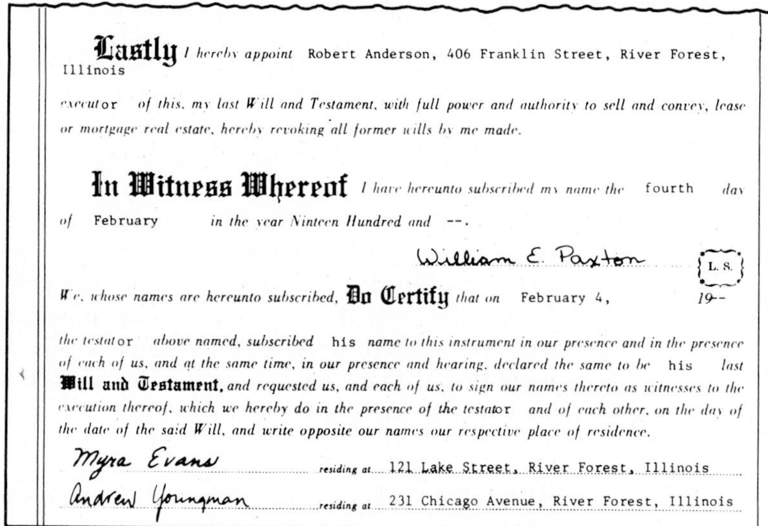

Lastly I hereby appoint Robert Anderson, 406 Franklin Street, River Forest, Illinois

executor of this, my last Will and Testament, with full power and authority to sell and convey, lease or mortgage real estate, hereby revoking all former wills by me made.

In Witness Whereof I have hereunto subscribed my name the fourth day of February in the year Nineteen Hundred and --.

William E. Paxton (L. S.)

We, whose names are hereunto subscribed, **Do Certify** that on February 4, 19--

the testator above named, subscribed his name to this instrument in our presence and in the presence of each of us, and at the same time, in our presence and hearing, declared the same to be his last **Will and Testament,** and requested us, and each of us, to sign our names thereto as witnesses to the execution thereof, which we hereby do in the presence of the testator and of each other, on the day of the date of the said Will, and write opposite our names our respective place of residence.

Myra Evans residing at 121 Lake Street, River Forest, Illinois

Andrew Youngman residing at 231 Chicago Avenue, River Forest, Illinois

Figure 23-1 A formal will.

Need for Accuracy

Certain words often used in wills may have a legal interpretation that is different from their everyday meaning. Care must be taken to describe each bequest and devise in a manner that will satisfy the legal definition. For instance, a testator may use the word *heirs* when really meaning *children*. The difference in the meaning of the two words could result in much dispute and expensive litigation. It is also important to avoid ambiguous language.

Sparacio made a will leaving his property to his daughter, Mary, and his friend, Eileen, "as in their mutual agreement they decide." The court held that the will was invalid. It was impossible to determine, under the terms of the will, how much to give Mary and how much to give Eileen.

Informal Wills

A **holographic will** is one written entirely in the handwriting of the testator. In some states, no formalities are necessary when a holographic will is made. Even witnesses are not required under the laws of some states.

Sedmak resided in Pennsylvania. The following handwritten document was found among his papers when he died:

My Brother Mil Oct 6-72

Please see that Zella Portenar receives $5000 from my Savings account—it is in the Western Savings Bank.

George A. Sedmak
or Alexander Sedmak

The court held the document to be a valid holographic will.

Oral wills made by persons in their last illness or by soldiers and sailors in actual combat are **nuncupative wills.** Nuncupative wills are not valid in all states and, when valid, are restricted to the giving of personal property only. Testators must indicate their bequests and must state that those hearing the statements are to be considered witnesses to the oral will.

23-4 PROTECTION OF CHILDREN AND SPOUSES

Children who can prove that they were mistakenly (rather than intentionally) left out of a parent's will are protected by the laws of most states. Forgotten children will receive the same share that they would have received had their parent died without a will. This does not mean that a parent may not disinherit a child. Parents are not obligated to leave children anything, but to avoid litigation, such an intention should be shown in the will. A testator who wishes to disinherit a child should name the child in the will and make the statement that the child was intentionally omitted. By doing so, the omitted child cannot claim to have been mistakenly omitted from the will.

Adopted children, under modern laws, are given the same legal rights as natural children. They inherit from their adopting parents. In contrast, stepchildren, unless they have been adopted by a stepfather or stepmother, do not inherit from a stepparent. Children who have been taken into the family for one reason or another, but never legally adopted, have no right of inheritance.

The Abelys took into their home three preschool children whose parents had been killed in an accident. The couple developed a special closeness toward one of the children, adopting him through legal proceedings. Only the adopted child would have rights equal to those of the Abelys' natural children.

Surviving spouses are assured a share of the deceased spouse's estate. A surviving spouse who does not like the provisions of a deceased spouse's will may choose to take a portion of the estate set by state statute rather than accept the amount provided in the will. In some states, the right of dower and curtesy (discussed in Chapter 21) is also available to surviving spouses.

23-5 REVOKING OR CHANGING A WILL

With variations from state to state, a will may be revoked (canceled) in any of the following ways: (1) burning, tearing, canceling, or obliterating the will with the intent to revoke it, (2) executing a new will, and (3) subsequent marriage of the testator. In addition, the divorce or annulment of a marriage automatically revokes all gifts made under a will to the former spouse and revokes the appointment of the former spouse as executor of the will.

Sometimes testators wish to make slight changes in a will. They may do this by executing a new will or by executing a **codicil,** which is a formal document used to supplement or change an existing will. A codicil must be executed with the same formalities as a will. It must be signed by the testator and properly witnessed. In addition, it must refer to the existing will to which it applies.

Rueda's will provided that her entire estate would pass to her husband at the time of her death. Rueda enjoyed unusual financial success and felt inclined to leave $100,000 toward a new church building under construction in her parish. Rueda's attorney prepared a codicil which Rueda formally executed in the presence of two witnesses. The bequests contained in the codicil became an integral part of the will itself.

A properly executed codicil has the effect of *republishing* a will. It is said that a codicil breathes new life into a will. This means that the codicil will reestablish a will that had been formerly revoked or improperly executed. If, for example, a will is witnessed by only one person in a state that requires two witnesses, the will is invalid. However, if a properly signed and witnessed codicil is added at a later date, the will becomes valid.

23-6 DYING WITHOUT A WILL

Intestacy is a term given to the quality or state of one who dies without having prepared a valid will. The deceased's property will be distributed according to the laws of intestate succession of the state where the deceased was domiciled (permanently resided) at the time of death. These laws vary slightly from state to state, although they all have their origin in a statute that was passed in England in 1670. Under that early statute, real property passed di-

If the Deceased Is Survived by:	A Surviving Spouse (If Any) Receives:	Any Remainder Is Distributed:
Issue (lineal descendants such as children, grandchildren, great grandchildren)	One-half of the estate	Equally to the deceased's children. If any children are also deceased, their children divide their deceased's parent's share equally.
No issue but by kindred (blood relatives)	$50,000 plus one-half of the remainder of the estate	Equally between the deceased's father and mother or to the survivor of them. *However, if the parents are deceased or have no survivor, then:* Equally among the deceased's brothers and sisters. If any brothers or sisters are also deceased, their children divide their deceased parent's share equally. *However, if there are no living brothers or sisters or nieces or nephews, then:* Equally among the deceased's *next of kin* (those who are most nearly related by blood including aunts, uncles, and cousins)
No issue, and no kindred	The entire estate *However, if there is no surviving spouse, issue or kindred, then:* The entire estate *escheates* to (becomes the property of) the state.	

Figure 23-2 Distribution of intestate property under a typical state statute (Massachusetts).

rectly to the heirs upon the death of the owner, whereas personal property passed to the executor or administrator to be distributed to the heirs. This practice is still followed in the United States today.

Rights of the Surviving Spouse

Under a typical statute, if a person dies intestate, the rights of the surviving spouse are as follows:

1. If the deceased is survived by **issue** (children, grandchildren, great grandchildren), the surviving spouse is entitled to one-half of the estate.
2. If the deceased is survived by no issue but by blood relatives, the surviving spouse is entitled to $50,000 plus one-half of the remainder of the estate.
3. If the deceased is survived by no issue and no blood relatives, the surviving spouse is entitled to the entire estate.

Rights of Other Heirs

Under the same typical statute, if a person dies intestate, the property will pass, subject to the rights of the surviving spouse mentioned above, as follows:

1. If the deceased is survived by issue, the property passes in equal shares to the deceased's children, with the issue of any deceased child taking that child's share.
2. If the deceased is survived by no issue, the property passes in equal shares to the deceased's father and mother or the survivor of them.

3. If the deceased is survived by no issue and no father or mother, the property passes to the deceased's brothers and sisters, with the issue of any deceased brother or sister taking that brother's or sister's share.
4. If the deceased is survived by no issue and no father, mother, brother, or sister, or issue of any deceased brother or sister, the property passes to the deceased's **next of kin** (those who are most nearly related by blood).
5. If the deceased is survived by no blood relatives and no surviving spouse, the estate **escheats** to (becomes the property of) the state.

Henrietta Johnson died intestate. She was survived by her husband, Arnold, a daughter, Bertha, and two grandchildren, Candice and Daniel, who were the children of her deceased son. Under the laws of intestate succession, Arnold will inherit 50 percent of the estate, Bertha will inherit 25 percent, and Candice and Daniel will each inherit 12½ percent.

23-7 SETTLING AN ESTATE

When people die owning assets, their estates must be **probated,** that is, settled under the supervision of the court. The court that supervises the procedure is called a **probate court** is some states, and a **surrogate court,** or **orphan's court**, in others.

The first step in probating an estate is to determine whether the deceased left a will. If a will exists, it usually names a personal representative called an **executor** (male) or **executrix** (female) who is the person named in the will to carry out its terms. If there is no will, or if the executor or executrix named in the will fails to perform, someone must petition the court to settle the estate. That person, if appointed, is called an **administrator** (male) or **administratrix** (female).

Before an executor or administrator is appointed, notice of the petition for appointment is published in a newspaper and sent to all heirs, legatees, and devisees. Anyone with grounds to object may do so. Witnesses are sometimes asked to testify or to sign affidavits about their knowledge of the execution of the will. Testimony is not necessary when all heirs and next of kin assent to the allowance of the will and no one contests it.

To ensure faithful performance, the executor or administrator is required to post a bond. A **bond** is a promise by the executor or administrator (and the sureties, if any) to pay the amount of the bond to the probate court if the duties of the position are not faithfully performed. **Sureties** are persons or insurance companies that stand behind executors or administrators and become responsible for their wrongdoing. In some states, a bond is not required if the will indicates that the executor or administrator need not post bond. In other states, a bond is always necessary, but sureties are not required if the will so dictates.

When a satisfactory bond has been filed, the court issues a certificate of appointment called **letters testamentary** to an executor or **letters of adminis-**

tration to an administrator. The executor or administrator, called a **fiduciary** (one in a position of trust), is then authorized to proceed. The fiduciary's job consists of gathering the assets, paying the debts and taxes, and distributing the remaining assets in accordance with the will or the law of intestate succession.

23-8 TRUSTS

A **trust** is a legal device by which property is held by one person (the **trustee**) for the benefit of another (the **beneficiary**). The person who sets up the trust is called the **settlor.** The property that is held in trust is known as the **corpus,** or **trust fund.**

When a trust is established, title is split between the trustee, who holds legal title, and the beneficiary, who holds equitable, or beneficial, title. This allows the trustee to manage the trust property for the benefit of the beneficiary. Trusts are established to save taxes, to provide for the needs of young children, and to prevent money from being squandered, among other reasons.

Property is often placed in trust so that it will be preserved for future generations. In such cases, only the income is given out during the life of the trust, the principal being held in relatively safe investments. The **rule against perpetuities** prevents trusts (except charitable trusts) from lasting indefinitely. This rule requires trust property to become owned by the beneficiary outright not later than 21 years after the death of some person alive at the creation of the trust.

Types of Trusts

The two principal types of trusts are testamentary trusts and living trusts. A **testamentary trust** is a trust that is created by will. It comes into existence only upon the death of the testator. The terms of the trust together with the names of the trustee and beneficiaries are set out in the body of the will itself.

Urie died, leaving four grown sons and daughters. His children had never demonstrated any real ambition and had depended heavily on prospects of receiving large legacies from the estate. Urie feared that his heirs would quickly spend their inheritances and have nothing to support them in the years ahead. He therefore provided for this possibility in his will by placing all assets in trust. The assets would remain intact, safely invested, and a small income would be paid from the trust income to the children. Urie's purpose was realized in that the estate would be preserved and the surviving children would not squander their inheritance.

In a trust such as the one illustrated, provision must be made for final distribution of the trust assets when the purpose of the trust has been served. For example, Urie could have the trust property go to a church, college, or some other worthy nonprofit organization on the death of the last surviving child.

He also could have designated a grandchild or grandchildren as the ultimate beneficiaries.

A **living trust,** also called an ***inter vivos* trust,** comes into existence while the settlor is alive and is established by either a conveyance in trust or a declaration of trust. In a **conveyance in trust,** the settlor conveys away the legal title to a trustee to hold for the benefit of either the settlor or another as beneficiary. In a **declaration of trust,** the settlor holds the legal title to the property as trustee for the benefit of some other person (the beneficiary) to whom the settlor now conveys the equitable title. A living trust may be either irrevocable or revocable. If it is *irrevocable,* the settlor loses complete control over the trust and cannot change it. The advantage of an irrevocable trust is that the income from the trust is not taxable to the settlor, and estate and inheritance taxes are avoided. The disadvantage of such a trust is that it can never be rescinded. The settlor can never get back that which has been put in an irrevocable trust regardless of the circumstances. A *revocable* living trust may be taken back or changed at any time during the settlor's lifetime. It has neither estate tax nor income tax advantages; however, it can serve the purpose of relieving the cares of management of money or property as well as other purposes.

A **spendthrift** is one who spends money profusely and improvidently. A **spendthrift trust** is designed to provide a fund for the maintenance of a beneficiary and, at the same time, to secure the fund against that person's improvidence or incapacity. In some states, all trusts are considered to be of this type. In others, a clause must be placed in the trust instrument to the effect that the beneficiary cannot assign either the income or the principal of the trust, and neither the income nor the principal can be reached by the beneficiary's creditors. Spendthrift trusts are not permitted in some states.

A **charitable,** or **public, trust** is one established for charitable purposes, such as the advancement of education; relief to the aged, ill, or poor; and the promotion of religion. To be valid, the person to be benefited must be uncertain. The rule against perpetuities does not apply to a charitable trust.

A **sprinkling,** or **spray trust** allows the trustee to decide how much will be given to each beneficiary rather than have the settlor make the decision. The advantage is that the trustee can compare the tax brackets of the beneficiaries, long after the settlor is dead, and cause a smaller tax liability to occur by giving more money to those beneficiaries in the lowest tax brackets. It also has built-in spendthrift provisions. The chief objection to this type of trust is that it gives the trustee too much control.

Obligations of the Trustee

The trustee is obligated by law to use a high standard of care and prudence in the investment of funds held by the trust. If real property is held in trust, it is the trustee's obligation to supervise and care for the property. When economic and other reasons indicate the need to shift trust assets to safer areas of investment, it becomes the duty of the trustee to make such changes. If investments selected by the trustee fail, the trustee is held liable unless a court rules that the action was taken with prudence and caution.

The trustee relationship is one of great and continuing responsibility. Appointment as a trustee should not be accepted by those without the knowledge and background that would afford prudent and good management. Banks, trust companies, and other kinds of fiduciary corporations offer professional services in the administration of trusts. They provide professional investment services and generally give maximum security and benefit for the fees charged.

SUMMARY

23-1. When people die leaving a will, their property passes to those named in the will. When they die without leaving a will, their property is distributed according to the law of the state where they reside.

23-2. Any person who has reached the age of adulthood and is of sound mind may make a will. The following questions are asked to determine soundness of mind: (*a*) Did the testator know, in a general way, the nature and extent of the property he or she owned? (*b*) Did the testator know who would be the most natural recipients of the estate? (*c*) Was the testator free from delusions which might influence the disposition of the property? (*d*) Did the testator know that he or she was making a will? Undue influence can cause a will to be declared invalid.

23-3. Wills must be in writing, signed by the testator, and attested in the testator's presence by either two or three witnesses, depending on state law. In some states, no formalities are necessary when a holographic will is made. Oral wills by soldiers and sailors in combat may be used to bequeath personal property.

23-4. Children who can prove that they weremistakenly (rather than intentionally) omitted from a parent's will may be able to receive an intestate share of their parent's estate. Adopted children, under modern laws, are given the same legal rights as natural children. Surviving spouses are assured a share of the deceased spouse's estate.

23-5. A will may be revoked in the following ways: (*a*) By the burning, tearing, canceling, or obliterating the will with the intent to revoke it, (*b*) By executing a new will, (*c*) By the subsequent marriage of the testator. In addition, the divorce or annulment of a marriage automatically revokes all gifts made under a will to the former spouse. A codicil must be executed with the same formalities as a will. It has the effect of republishing a will that was formerly revoked or improperly executed.

23-6. When a person dies without a will, the person's property will be distributed according to the laws of intestate succession of the state where the deceased was domiciled.

23-7. When people die owning assets, their estates must be probated. Heirs are notified, and an executor or administrator is appointed by the probate court. This fiduciary then gathers the assets, pays the debts and taxes, and distributes the remainder in accordance with the will or the law of intestate succession.

23-8. Trusts are used, among other reasons, to save taxes, to provide for the needs of young children, and to prevent money from being squandered easily. They may be created to take effect while a person is alive or after a person dies. When a trust is established, title is split between the trustee, who holds legal title, and the beneficiary, who holds equitable or beneficial title. The trustee manages the trust fund for the benefit of the beneficiary.

Understanding Key Legal Terms

administratrix (p. 324)
administrator (p. 324)
bequest (p. 317)
bond (p. 324)
codicil (p. 322)
conveyance in trust (p. 326)
declaration of trust (p. 326)
devise (p. 317)
devisee (p. 317)
escheat (p. 323)
executor (p. 324)
executrix (p. 324)
fiduciary (P. 324)
heir (p. 317)
intestate (p. 317)
issue (p. 323)
legatee (p. 317)
living trust (p. 326)
next of kin (p. 323)
probated (p. 323)
sureties (p. 324)
testamentary trust (p. 325)
testate (p. 317)
testator (p. 317)
testatrix (p. 317)
trust (p. 325)
trustee (p. 325)
will (p. 317)

Questions for Review and Discussion

1. Who may make a valid will?
2. What questions does the court ask in determining whether a testator was of sound mind when making a will?
3. In general, what are the formal requirements for executing a will?
4. What must omitted children prove in order to inherit under a parent's will? What provisions should be made in a will by a testator who wishes to disinherit a child?
5. How are adopted children protected under modern inheritance laws?
6. What right is available to a surviving spouse who does not like the provisions of a deceased spouse's will?
7. In what ways may a will be revoked?
8. Who will inherit, and in what amount, from the estate of a person who dies intestate survived by (*a*) a spouse and two children ($30,000 estate), (*b*) a spouse and a father and mother ($75,000 estate), (*c*) a spouse and no blood relatives ($90,000 estate), (*d*) three children ($90,000 estate), (*e*) a brother and two children of a deceased sister ($90,000 estate), (*f*) no blood relatives and no surviving spouse ($90,000 estate), and (*g*) a spouse and a 90-year-old aunt ($200,000 estate).
9. Summarize the steps that must be taken to settle an estate.
10. Describe how and for what reason title to property is split when a trust is established.

Analyzing Cases

1. Lazer, a wealthy 17-year-old, learned that he was suffering from AIDS. He wrote a will leaving everything he owned to a friend he had met in school. Two years later, when Lazer died, his parents claimed that the will was not valid. Do you agree with Lazer's parents? Explain.
2. Santiago, a widower, made a will leaving $1 to his son, Carlos, and the balance in equal shares to his other children, Benito and Angelita. The estate, after deducting debts, taxes and expenses, amounted to $90,000. When Santiago died, Carlos claimed that he was legally entitled to $30,000 from his father's estate. Is Carlos correct? Why or why not.
3. Harris, who had two children, made a will leaving $1 to her husband, Dennis, and the

balance in equal shares to her two children. When Harris died, her husband, Dennis, claimed that he was legally entitled to more than $1. Do you agree with Dennis? Explain.

4. D.W. Elmer, a hospital patient, was seriously ill and unable to write his name. He executed his will, however, by making a belabored "X" on the paper in the presence of witnesses. Can a signature on a will made by an "X" be valid? Explain. *In Re Estate of Elmer,* 210 N.W.2d 815 (North Dakota).

5. Julia Dejmal executed her will while a patient in St. Joseph's hospital. The will was witnessed by Lucille and Catherine Pechacek. Catherine was 19 years old and was employed as an assistant x-ray technician at the hospital. The age of majority at the time in that state was 21. It was contended that the will was not valid because one of the witnesses to it was a minor. Do you agree with the contention? Why or why not? *Matter of Estate of Dejmal,* 289 N.W.2d 813 (Wisconsin).

6. The seventh clause of Jennie Wielert's will provided that if any of her children died before her, leaving "issue of their body" surviving, the issue would take the child's share. (The word *issue* is synonymous with the word descendant, and the phrase *heirs of the body* has commonly referred to heirs borne by the person referred to.) Jennie's son, Clarence, died before her, survived by an adopted daughter, Jan. Will Jan take Clarence's share under the will? Why or why not? *Wielert v. Larson,* 404 N.E.2d 1111 (Illinois).

7. Evidence was introduced in court to show that, at the time she executed her will, Blanch Robinson suffered from schizophrenia. She had delusions as to having had a love affair with Nelson Eddy and was suspicious, mistrustful, and perhaps deluded about her friends and acquaintances. Dixon, who had been left out of her will, contended that she lacked the mental capacity to make a will. Do you agree with Dixon? Explain. *Dixon v. Fillmore Cemetery,* 608 S.W.2d 84 (Missouri).

8. Walsh, as settlor, executed a declaration of trust, naming himself as trustee and giving him the income from the trust during his lifetime. After his death, the income was to be paid to his second wife for her life, and upon her death to his two children, Edward and Margot. Upon their deaths, the income was to be paid to the children of Edward and Margot, after which it terminated. The trust expressly provided that the settlor had not made any provisions for his third child, Patricia, because "previous provisions had been made in her behalf." After executing the instrument, Walsh transferred to the trust the family residence, three farms, and a checking account. Patricia argued that the trust was testamentary and therefore invalid because it failed to comply with the statute of wills. Was this a testamentary or an *inter vivos* trust? Explain. *First Nat'l Bank v. Hampson,* 410 N.E.2d 1109 (Illinois).

PART 4
CASE STUDY
Rambend Realty Corp. v. Backstreets Band

Court of Appeals of Indiana
482 N.E.2d 741 (Indiana)

SUMMARY

On March 18, the Backstreets Band entered into a contract with Rambend Realty Corp. which operates a Ramada Inn at South Bend, Indiana. By the terms of the contract the band was to perform in the Ramada lounge from 9:30 p.m. until 2:00 a.m. on June 1 through June 13. The band was to be paid $2,300 and its members were to be furnished rooms at the inn for the duration of their engagement.

The band arrived at the inn about 11:00 p.m. on May 31, the evening before they were scheduled to begin performing. They had played there before, and so the band members unloaded their equipment from their vans and took it to the stage area as they had done in the past. They asked the food and beverage manager, Mr. Beal, to let them into the lounge and to turn on the lights. Beal propped open the lounge door to allow the band to bring in the equipment and turned up the lights.

By midnight or 12:30 a.m. the band had moved its instruments and equipment to the bandstand in the lounge. Burch, the bandleader, asked Beal to lock up the lounge and was told that a woman was working back in the kitchen but that the doors would be secured when the woman left. The band members then retired for the night.

The next morning it was discovered that during the night someone had broken into the liquor cabinet in the bar. Then the band discovered that some of its equipment was missing.

The band sued the operator of the inn for the loss of the instruments. The lower court judge found in favor of the band. The operator of the inn brought this appeal.

THE COURT'S OPINION: GARRARD, JUDGE

Rambend asserts that the court erred in determining that a bailment was created and that Rambend was negligent. Included is the contention that the court should have applied the provisions of [an Indiana law which limits the liability of innkeepers to their guests. The law states: "A *guest* within the meaning of this act shall include transient guest, permanent guest, tenant, lodger, or boarder."]

We believe the term "guest" as used in the context of the statute ordinarily refers to one who is a paying patron of the inn or hotel. Although this may not always be the case, the term does denote one who is staying at the inn for his own purposes as opposed to the business purposes of the inn. *Cf. Nicholson's Mobile Home Sales, Inc. v. Schramm* (1975), 164 Ind. App. 598, 330 N.E.2d 785.

More importantly, it is apparent that the band instruments and equipment were not brought onto the premises in consequence of any guest or quasi-guest capacity of the members of the band. The equipment was there for the performance of the contractual services engaged by Rambend. It was not taken to the band-members' rooms, or left in their vehicles. Under the evidence the court could correctly conclude that the claim was not governed by [the innkeeper law mentioned above].

Moreover, and contrary to Rambend's assertion, the evidence sustained the finding of a bailment. In *Stubbs v. Hook* (1984), Ind. App. 467 N.E.2d 29, 31 the court noted that to create a bailment the property must be delivered into the bailee's exclusive possession and must be accepted by the bailee. The evidence before the court was sufficient to support as a reasonable inference that this is what occurred when the manager opened the lounge area and permitted the band to place its instruments and equipment there signifying that he would secure the area.

In *Hainey v. Zink* (1979), 182 Ind. App. 192, 394 N.E.2d 238, 241, the court stated that when goods were delivered in good condition and were returned in damaged condition, an inference arises that the damage was caused through the fault or neglect of the bailee. *See also Spencer v. Glover* (1980), Ind. App. 412 N.E.2d 870. Here, of course, the goods were not returned at all. Furthermore, the court could have found negligence on the part of Rambend. The police investigation disclosed that none of the locked outer doors had been tampered with. The only unlocked door to the lounge was the entrance from the lobby which was about 30 feet from the hotel desk where a clerk was supposedly on duty throughout the night. In addition it appears that a security guard employed by Rambend was absent from the premises for about 45 minutes.

Under *Hainey* the burden was upon Rambend to establish its lack of negligence. We cannot say the court erred in concluding it failed to do so.

Finally, Rambend argues there was insufficient evidence of value of the missing equipment to support the damage awards. Again we must disagree.

As the court pointed out in *Floyd v. Jay Co. REMC* (1980), Ind. App., 405 N.E.2d 630, 633, less certainty is required to prove the amount of a loss than the fact that some loss occurred. In addition, on appeal uncertainty as to the exact amount of damages will be resolved against the wrongdoer. *Charlie Stuart Oldsmobile, Inc. v. Smith* (1976), 171 Ind. App. 315, 357 N.E.2d 247, 252.

Here the missing items were specifically established. There was evidence of the price paid for each item, its age and condition, and its replacement cost at the time of trial. In addition there was testimony from an insurance adjuster detailing depreciation factors the insurance company would apply on such equipment. It appears that the judgment entered by the court was within the evidence and was adequately supported by the evidence....

Affirmed.

QUESTIONS FOR ANALYSIS

1. Why did Rambend want the Indiana innkeeper's law to apply in the case?
2. For what reasons did the court say the innkeeper's law did not apply?
3. What did the court say is necessary to create a bailment?
4. What evidence was sufficient to infer that a bailment existed?
5. Why could the court have found negligence on the part of Rambend?
6. What and upon whom was the burden of proof in this case?
7. What evidence was used in the case to support the damage award?

PART 5
Commercial Paper

CHAPTER 24
Nature and Kinds of Commercial Paper

OUTLINE

COMMENTARY

One of the first things that Leona Nesbitt did when she went away to college was to open a checking account. This allowed her to have spending money available without the risk of carrying around large sums of cash. In addition, it provided her with a means of handling the checks her parents sent her from home.

Another thing that Leona did when she went to college was to take out a student loan. Before receiving the money, Leona was required to sign a note, promising to pay the money back with interest, within a certain period of time.

The use of checks, notes, electronic banking, and buying on credit has mushroomed in recent years. More and more people and businesses have opened checking accounts and signed drafts and promissory notes than ever before. These instruments are examples of commercial paper that is used conveniently and safely as a substitute for money and to obtain credit in today's society.

OBJECTIVES

1. State the purpose of commercial paper.
2. Explain the concept of negotiability.
3. Identify the three kinds of negotiable instruments.
4. Name the parties to each kind of negotiable instrument.
5. Judge, upon the examination of various negotiable instruments, whether all the requirements of negotiability have been met.
6. Describe the effect of dates on negotiable instruments and determine which words control.

24-1 PURPOSE OF COMMERCIAL PAPER

Throughout history there has been a need to transact business without carrying around large sums of money. In the Middle Ages, for example, merchants at first carried gold and silver with them as they traveled from one fair to another buying goods. They were in constant danger of being robbed, and needed a safer and more convenient method of exchanging their gold and silver for the goods they bought. A system was developed by which merchants could deposit their precious metals with goldsmiths or silversmiths for safekeeping. When the merchants bought goods, instead of paying for them with gold or silver, they simply filled out a piece of paper, called a bill of exchange. The bill of exchange ordered the goldsmith or silversmith to give a certain amount of the precious metal to the person who sold the goods. That person would then take the bill of exchange to the goldsmith or silversmith and receive payment. There also developed a need to borrow money in order to buy things at one time and pay for them at a later time.

Today, commercial paper circulates freely in the business world as an instrument of credit, allowing millions of people to borrow money easily. The law of commercial paper has developed in recognition of the need to transact business without carrying around large sums of money and to borrow money easily. This law is also referred to as the law of negotiable instruments.

24-2 THE CONCEPT OF NEGOTIABILITY

The concept of negotiability is one of the most important features of commercial paper. Largely because of this feature, negotiable instruments are highly trusted and used daily by millions of people. A **negotiable instrument** is a written document signed by the maker or drawer, containing an unconditional promise or order to pay a certain sum of money on delivery or at a definite time to the bearer or to order. The concept is simple: When an instrument is transferred by negotiation, the person receiving the instrument is provided with more protection than was available to the person from whom it was received. The person receiving the instrument is able, in many instances, to recover money on the instrument even when the person from whom the instrument was received could not have done so. These special rights that are sometimes available to transferees of negotiable instruments are discussed in detail in the chapters that follow.

24-3 KINDS OF NEGOTIABLE INSTRUMENTS

UCC 3-104(2) (see p. 638)

There are three basic kinds of negotiable instruments: drafts (including checks), notes, and certificates of deposit. These are described below.

Drafts

A **draft** (also known as a **bill of exchange**) is an instrument by which the party creating it orders another party to pay money to a third party. The one who draws the draft (that is, the one who orders money to be paid) is called the **drawer.** The one who is requested to pay the money is called the **drawee.** The one who is to receive the money is known as the **payee.**

Ahearn owed Bickum $500, payable in 60 days. Bickum owed Connors the same amount. Bickum wrote out a draft ordering Ahearn to pay Connors $500 in or within 60 days and gave the draft to Connors. When the 60 days elapsed, Connors presented the instrument to Ahearn for payment.

Drafts may be presented to the drawee for payment, as above, or for **acceptance.** When a draft is presented for acceptance, the drawee is requested to become liable on the instrument. To accept a draft, the drawee writes "accepted" across the face of the instrument and dates and signs it. By doing this, the drawee agrees to pay the instrument at a later date when it becomes due. An acceptance must be written on the draft, but it may consist of the drawee's signature alone. Instead of waiting for the 60 days to elapse before making presentment, in the above case, Connors could have asked Ahearn to accept

UCC 3-410 (see p. 645)

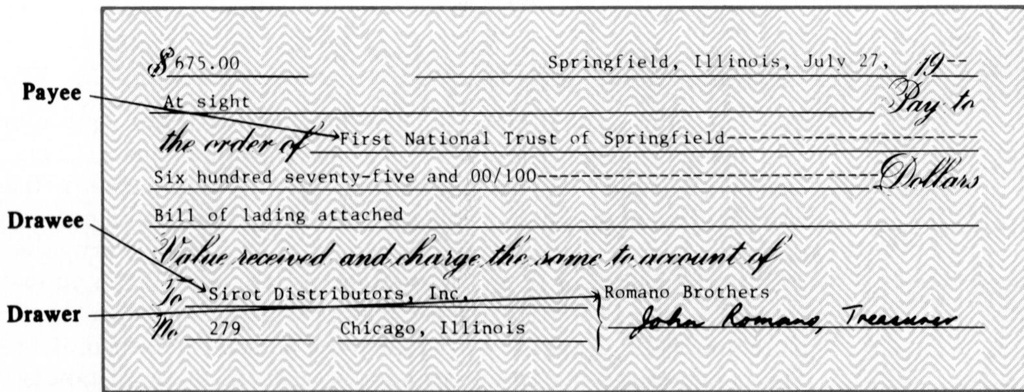

Figure 24-1 A sight draft.

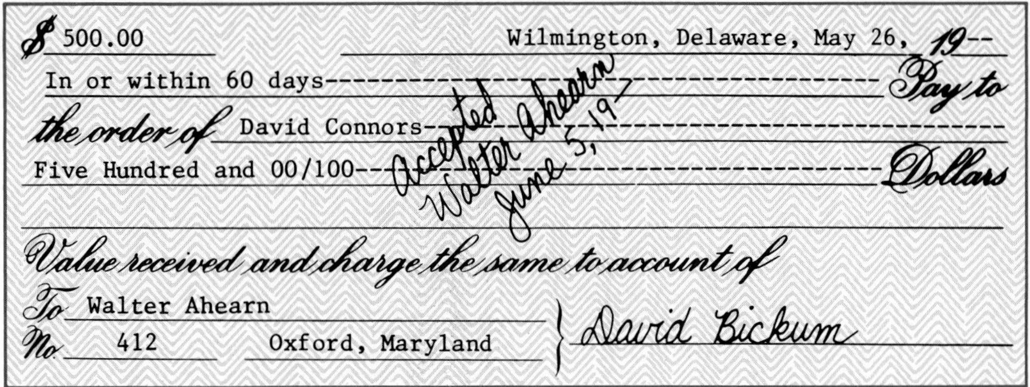

$500.00 Wilmington, Delaware, May 26, 19--

In or within 60 days Pay to

the order of David Connors

Five Hundred and 00/100 Dollars

Accepted Walter Ahearn June 5, 19--

Value received and charge the same to account of

To Walter Ahearn

No. 412 Oxford, Maryland

David Bickum

Figure 24-2 An accepted time draft.

the instrument at any time before its due date. A draft is said to be **dishonored** when a drawee refuses to accept it before its due date or to pay it on its due date.

UCC 3-104 (2)(b) (see p. 638)

Checks A **check** is a special kind of draft that is drawn on a bank and payable on demand. Since a check is also the most common type of draft, it is discussed in more detail in Chapter 27.

Sight and Time Drafts A **sight draft** is a draft that is payable as soon as it is presented to the drawee for payment. A **time draft** is a draft that is not payable until the lapse of a particular time period stated on the draft. Drafts that are payable "30 days after sight" and "60 days after date" are examples of time drafts.

Trade Acceptances A **trade acceptance** is a draft used by a seller of goods to receive payment and also to extend credit. It is often used in combination with a bill of lading, which is a receipt given by a freight company to someone who ships goods. For example, a seller ships goods to a buyer and sends a bill of lading, with a trade acceptance attached, to a bank in the buyer's city. The trade acceptance is drawn by the seller ordering the buyer to pay the money either to the seller or to someone else. If it is a sight draft, the buyer must pay the draft immediately to receive the bill of lading from the bank. If it is a time draft, the buyer must accept the draft to receive the bill of lading from the bank. The freight company will not release the goods to the buyer unless the buyer has the bill of lading.

In Figure 24-3, Walker is the seller and drawer of the trade acceptance, which is a time draft because it is not due until August 2. Palmieri, the buyer, has accepted the trade acceptance by signing and dating it. Thus, she will be able to receive possession of any goods accompanying the trade acceptance. Walker may discount the instrument at a bank for cash or use it as collateral on a short-term loan. **Discounting** means that the bank will buy the instrument at a price below its face amount with the aim of ultimately collecting the face amount.

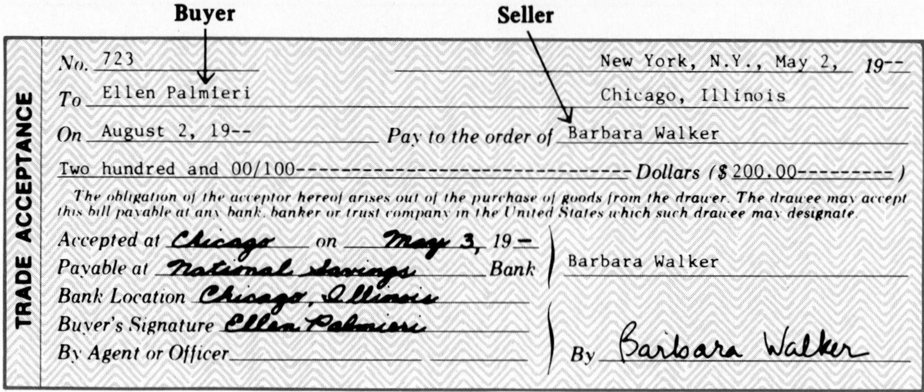

Figure 24-3 A trade acceptance.

Domestic and International Bills of Exchange A **domestic bill of exchange** is a draft that is drawn and payable in the United States. A draft that is drawn in one country but payable in another is called an **international bill of exchange** or **foreign draft.**

Notes

A **note** (often called a **promissory note**) is a written promise by one party, called the **maker,** to pay money to the order of another party, called the *payee*. In contrast with drafts, notes are promise instruments rather than order instruments and involve only two parties instead of three. They are used by people who loan money or extend credit as evidence of debt. When two or more parties sign a note, they are called **comakers.**

A **demand note,** as its name implies, is payable whenever the payee demands payment. A **time note,** on the other hand, is payable at some future time, on a definite date named in the instrument. Unless a note is payable in installments, the principal (face value) of the note plus interest must be paid on the date that it is due. In an **installment note,** the principal together with interest on the unpaid balance is payable in installments (series of payments) at specified times.

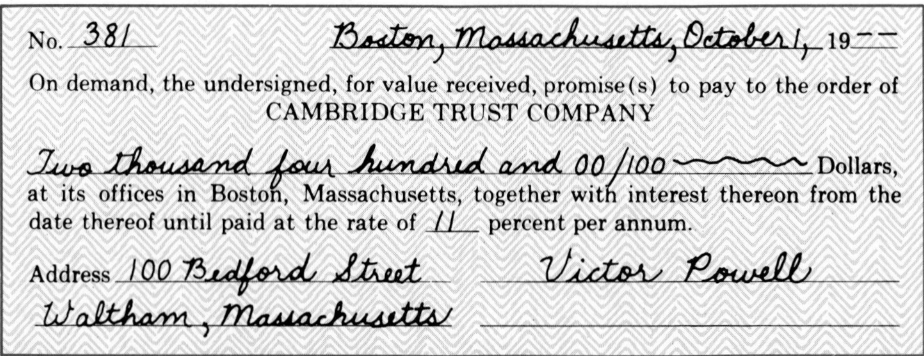

Figure 24-4 A demand note.

Certificates of Deposit

UCC 3-104(2)(c) (see p. 638)

A **certificate of deposit (CD)** is an acknowledgment by a bank of the receipt of money and a promise to pay the money back on the due date, usually with interest. Certificates of deposit generally pay more interest than regular savings accounts because the depositor cannot withdraw the money before the due date without penalty.

24-4 PARTIES TO COMMERCIAL PAPER

In addition to drawers of drafts and checks, makers of notes, and payees of both types of instruments, there are other parties to commercial paper. They are the bearer, the holder, the holder in due course, the indorser, the indorsee, and the acceptor.

UCC 1-201(20) (see p. 613)

A **bearer** is a person who is in possession of a negotiable instrument that is payable to bearer or to cash. A person who is in possession of an instrument that has been indorsed in blank (by the payee's signature alone) is also a bearer.

A **holder** is a person who is in possession of a negotiable instrument that is issued or indorsed to that person's order or to bearer.

A **holder in due course** is a holder of a negotiable instrument who is treated as favored and is given immunity from certain defenses. A detailed discussion of holders in due course can be found in Chapter 26.

An **indorser** is a person who indorses a negotiable instrument. This is done in most cases by signing one's name on the back of the paper. The different kinds of indorsements are discussed in Chapter 25.

An **indorsee** is a person to whom a draft, note, or other negotiable instrument is transferred by indorsement.

An **acceptor** is a drawee of a draft who has promised to honor the draft as presented by signing it on its face.

24-5 REQUIREMENTS OF NEGOTIABILITY

UCC 3-104 (see pp. 637–638)

To be negotiable, an instrument must be:

1. In writing and have the signature of the maker or drawer
2. An unconditional promise or order to pay
3. Made out for a sum certain in money
4. Payable on demand or at a definite time
5. Payable to order or to bearer

Aetna Acceptance Corp. signed a promissory note which stated, "Buyer agrees to pay to seller" a certain amount of money. The note was not negotiable because it lacked certain requirements of negotiability (it was not payable to order or to bearer). The person to whom the note was transferred was not entitled to the special protection that would have been available had the note been negotiable.

The essentials of negotiability, illustrated in Figure 24-5, are discussed in the following paragraphs.

Written Instrument

A negotiable instrument must be in writing. This is broadly understood to include printing, typewriting, pen or pencil writing, or even painting. A negotiable instrument written in pencil is, however, an invitation to alteration by forgery. If this should happen, the person who drew the instrument would be responsible for any loss caused by the negligent drawing of the instrument.

Most negotiable instruments are written on paper, but this is not a requirement. Oddly drawn checks are sometimes presented to and paid by banks. Since negotiable instruments must be capable of circulating, they should not be written on any nonmovable object; for example, they should not be painted on a wall. Neither should they be written on anything unstable and unable to retain writing for a lasting period of time.

Signature of Maker or Drawer

To be negotiable, an instrument must be signed by the maker or drawer. Any writing or executed symbol is accepted as a signature. It may be handwritten, typewritten, printed, or produced in any way that will make a lasting impression. The writing can be done with ink or with anything that makes a mark. For proof of authority or genuineness, however, it is good judgment on the part of the receiver of an instrument to insist on a written signature.

UCC 3-401 (p. 643)

A signature may be made by an **agent** (one who represents and acts for another) or other representative. No particular form of appointment is necessary to establish such authority. Agents who sign their own name to an instrument are personally obligated if the instrument neither names the person represented nor shows that the agent signed in a representative capacity. The signature may appear in the body of the instrument as well as at the end.

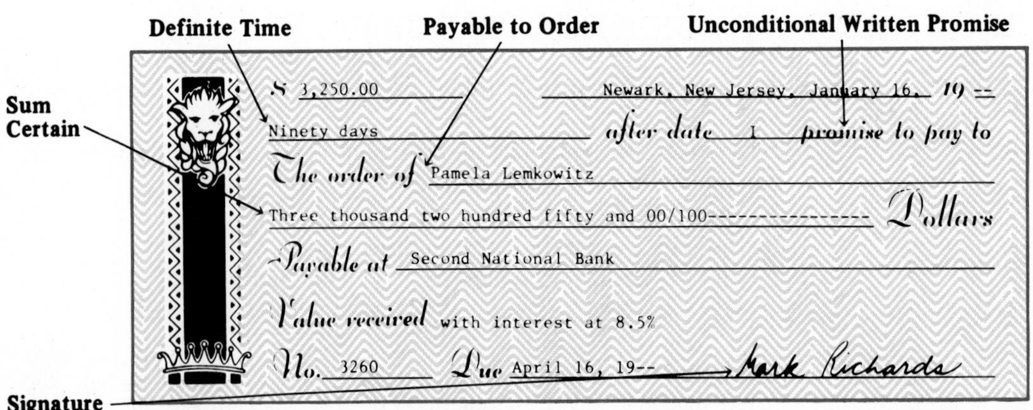

$ 3,250.00 Newark, New Jersey, January 16, 19 --

Ninety days after date I promise to pay to

The order of Pamela Lemkowitz

Three thousand two hundred fifty and 00/100---------------- Dollars

Payable at Second National Bank

Value received with interest at 8.5%

No. 3260 Due April 16, 19-- Mark Richards

Figure 24-5 Requirements of negotiability.

Unconditional Promise or Order to Pay

To be negotiable, an instrument must contain no conditions that might in any way affect its payment. Statements requiring that certain things be done or that specific events take place prior to payment make the instrument a simple contract rather than negotiable paper.

Chung signed the following note to the Chu-Tai Appliance Co.: "I promise to pay to the order of Chu-Tai Appliance Co. $550 sixty days after the delivery of my new refrigerator." This instrument is not negotiable because it is conditional upon the delivery of the refrigerator.

UCC 3-105(2) (see p. 638)

An instrument is conditional, and thus not negotiable, if it states that it is subject to any other agreement. The same is true if an instrument states that it is to be paid only out of a particular fund. This latter rule does not apply to instruments issued by government agencies. An instrument may state that it "arises out of" another agreement without being conditional. Similarly, a negotiable instrument may indicate a particular account that is to be charged.

Florence Durant loaned $150 to a neighbor. The neighbor gave Durant the following note: "Sixty days after date, I promise to pay to the order of Florence Durant $150 out of the proceeds of a garage sale." The note is not negotiable because it is conditional. Payment will be made only if the garage sale takes place and the proceeds of the sale are sufficient. The note could be made negotiable if it were changed to read, "to be charged to the proceeds of a garage sale." This wording does not affect negotiability, since the neighbor's general credit is relied upon and the reference to the garage sale is simply a recordkeeping instruction following payment.

In addition to being unconditional, a negotiable instrument must contain a promise to pay (as in a note) or an order to pay (as in a draft). A writing that says "Due Karen Osgood $600" or "IOU $600" is not negotiable because it is neither a promise nor an order to pay.

Sum Certain in Money

UCC 1-201 (see pp. 612–613)

A negotiable instrument must be payable in a **sum certain** in money. This means an amount of money that is clearly known. **Money** is defined as a medium of exchange adopted by a domestic or foreign government as part of its currency. Thus, a sum certain in money need not be money of the United States.

In exchange for a painting by a well-known American artist, Emil Hauser, of Stuttgart, Germany, sent a note to Ann Maggio, of New York City, which read, "Ninety days after date, I promise to pay to the order of Ann Maggio 5,000 deutsches marks (signed) Emil Hauser." The note was negotiable. On the due date, it would probably be paid in American dollars according to the exchange rate of marks and dollars as of the date of payment.

UCC 3-106
(see p. 638)

The sum payable is a sum certain even though it is to be paid (1) with stated interest or by stated installments, (2) with stated different rates of interest before and after default or a specified date, (3) with a stated discount or addition if paid before or after the date fixed for payment, (4) with exchange or less exchange, whether at a fixed rate or at the current rate, or (5) with costs of collection or an attorney's fee or both upon default.

Payable on Demand or at a Definite Time

Negotiable instruments must be made payable on demand or at a definite time. This requirement makes it possible to determine when the debtor or promisor can be compelled to pay. Without this information, the present value of an instrument cannot be determined.

Demand Paper An instrument is payable *on demand* when it so states, or when it is payable "on sight" or "on presentation." The key characteristic of demand instruments is that the holder can require payment at any time by making the demand upon the person who is obligated to pay.

UCC 3-109
(see pp. 638–639)

Definite-Time Paper Certainty as to the time of payment of an instrument is satisfied if it is payable on or before a definite date. Instruments payable at a fixed period after a stated date or at a fixed period after sight are also considered to be payable at a definite time. In each instance, a simple mathematical calculation makes the maturity date certain. The expressions "one year after date" and "30 days after sight" are definite as to time. An undated instrument payable 60 days after date is negotiable as a demand paper.

A promise to pay only upon an act or event, the time of whose occurrence is uncertain, is not payable at a definite time. Thus, an instrument payable when a person marries, reaches a certain age, or graduates from college, or one payable within a specific period of time after a named person's death, is not negotiable.

Acceleration An *acceleration clause* on the face of an instrument hastens the maturity date. For example: "In case of default in payments of interest (or of an installment of the principal), the entire note shall become due and payable." Instruments payable at a fixed time but subject to acceleration are negotiable.

Extension *Extension clauses* give the maker of a note the opportunity to extend the payment date to a further definite time. For example, a maker may make a note payable in six months, but may include the right to extend it to one year without loss of negotiability.

Payable to Order or to Bearer

The chief characteristic of a negotiable instrument is its capacity to circulate freely as an instrument of credit. This function is achieved, and the intention of the maker (i.e., ease of transferability and payment of the amount indicated to a holder) is expressed, by the words "to the order of" or "to bearer." They are called the words of negotiability. Instruments not payable to order or to bearer are not negotiable.

UCC 3-110 (see p. 639)

Payable to Order An instrument is *payable to order* when it states that it is payable to the order of any person with reasonable certainty. The maker or drawer may state "Pay to the order of Mary Doe," "Pay to Mary Doe or order," or "Pay to Mary Doe or her assigns." An instrument may be payable to the order of the maker or drawer; the drawee; a payee who is not the maker, drawer, or drawee; two or more payees; an estate, trust, or fund; an office or officer by title; or a partnership or unincorporated association.

UCC 3-111 (see p. 639)

Payable to Bearer An instrument is *payable to bearer* when it states that it is payable to bearer or the order of bearer, a specified person or bearer, cash or the order of cash, or any other indication which does not designate a specific payee. An instrument made payable both to order and to bearer, such as "Pay to the order of Anthony Andrews or bearer," is payable to order unless the bearer words are handwritten or typewritten.

24-6 DATES AND CONTROLLING WORDS

UCC 3-114 (see p. 639)

The omission of the date does not affect the negotiability of an instrument. When the date is omitted, the date on which the instrument is received is considered to be the date of issue. An instrument may be predated or postdated without affecting its negotiability. Any instrument lacking one or more elements of negotiability, however, cannot be enforced until it is completed. Handwritten terms control typewritten and printed terms, and typewritten terms control printed terms. Words control figures, except where words are ambiguous (capable of being understood in more than one way). The numbering of, or the failure to number, an instrument does not affect its negotiability.

SUMMARY

24-1. The purpose of commercial paper is to allow people to transact business without carrying around large sums of money and to allow them to borrow money more easily.

24-2. When an instrument is transferred by negotiation, the person receiving the instrument may obtain more protection than was given to the person from whom it was received.

24-3. There are three basic kinds of negotiable instruments. A draft is an instrument by which the party creating it orders another party to pay money to a third party. A note is a written promise by one party to pay money to another party. A certificate of deposit is the acknowledgment by a bank of the receipt of money and a promise to pay the money back on the due date, usually with interest.

24-4. The parties to a draft are the drawer, drawee, and payee. The parties to a note are the maker and payee. A bearer is a person who is in possession of a negotiable instrument that is payable to bearer or to cash. A holder is a person who is in possession of an instrument which is issued or indorsed to that person's order or to bearer. A holder in due course is a holder of a negotiable instrument who is treated as favored and is given immunity from certain defenses. An indorser is a person who indorses a negotiable instrument. An indorsee is a person to whom an instrument is transferred by indorsement. An acceptor is a drawee of a draft who has promised to honor the draft by signing it on its face.

24-5. To be negotiable, an instrument must be (*a*) In writing and have the signature of the maker or drawer. (*b*) An unconditional promise or order to pay. (*c*) For a sum certain in money. (*d*) Payable on demand or at a definite time. (*e*) Payable to order or to bearer.

24-6. Predating, postdating, or the omission of the date does not affect the negotiability of an instrument. Words control figures, except where words are ambiguous.

Understanding Key Legal Terms

acceptance (p. 334)
acceptor (p. 337)
bill of exchange (p. 334)
certificate of deposit (p. 337)
comakers (p. 336)
demand notice (p. 336)
discounting (p. 335)
domestic bill of exchange (p. 336)
draft (p. 334)
drawee (p. 334)
drawer (p. 334)
holder (p. 337)
indorsee (p. 337)
indorser (p. 337)
installment note (p. 336)
international bill of exchange (p. 336)
maker (p. 336)
negotiable instrument (p. 333)
note (p. 336)
payee (p. 334)
sight draft (p. 335)
time draft (p. 335)
trade acceptance (p. 335)

Questions for Review and Discussion

1. What is the purpose of commercial paper?
2. Describe the concept of negotiability. What protection is available in many instances to a transferee of an instrument that has been negotiated?
3. Name the three basic kinds of negotiable instruments. Which of these are order instruments and which are promise instruments?
4. Name the parties to (*a*) a draft and (*b*) a note.
5. Explain how the following notes differ from one another: (*a*) demand note, (*b*) time note, and (*c*) installment note.
6. Contrast a bearer of a negotiable instrument with a holder.
7. Name the essential requirements for an instrument to be negotiable.
8. Explain the manner in which the maker or drawer of a negotiable instrument may sign it.
9. When an amount written in words on an instrument differs from an amount written in figures, which amount controls?
10. How would each of the following affect the negotiability of an instrument: (*a*) omission of the date, (*b*) failure to number the instrument?

Analyzing Cases

1. Frank Oliva, a silver collector, ran short of cash. He borrowed $700 from David Kaplan, giving Kaplan the following note: "Thirty days from date, I promise to pay to the order of David Kaplan $700 worth of silver (signed) Frank Oliva." Was the note negotiable? Why or why not?

2. Bessie Patterson wanted to give her niece, Myrna James, a gift of money for her twenty-first birthday, which was two weeks away. Since she was leaving for a trip to Europe the next day, Patterson gave James a check dated that day reading, "Pay to the order of Myrna James when she reaches the age of 21 (signed) Bessie Patterson." Was the check negotiable? Why or why not?

3. Locke gave two promissory notes to Consumer Food, Inc., which stated, "Buyer agrees to pay to seller. . . ." Consumer Food, Inc., assigned the notes to Aetna Acceptance Corporation. Were the notes negotiable? Explain. *Locke v. Aetna Accept. Corp.,* 309 So.2d 43 (Florida).

4. Jon and Rita How gave the Fulkersons a postdated check for $2,000 as their acceptance of an offer to sell a trailer park. The Fulkersons claim that no contract came into existence because the postdated check created a qualified acceptance. Is the negotiability of an instrument affected by the fact that it is postdated? Explain. *How v. Fulkerson,* 528 P.2d 853 (Arizona).

5. Barton signed a promissory note promising to pay to the order of Scott Hudgens Realty & Mortgage, Inc., the sum of $3,000. The note stated "This amount is due and payable upon evidence of an acceptable permanent loan...and upon acceptance of the loan commitment." Was the note negotiable? Why or why not? *Barton v. Scott Hudgens Realty & Mortg.,* 222 S.E.2d 126 (Georgia).

6. In exchange for legal services rendered to her by the law firm of Westmoreland, Hall, and Bryan, Barbara Hall wrote the following letter: "I agree to pay to your firm as attorney's fees for representing me in obtaining property settlement agreement and tax advice, the sum of $2,760, payable at the rate of $230 per month for twelve (12) months beginning January 1, 1970. Very truly yours, Barbara Hall Hodge." Was the letter a negotiable instrument? Give the reason for your answer. *Hall v. Westmoreland, Hall & Bryan,* 182 S.E.2d 539 (Georgia).

7. James Ahmed gave William Cooper a draft which read: "To Esther Blum: Ninety days from date, pay to the order of William Cooper $5,000 (signed) James Ahmed." Cooper telephoned Blum to see if she would honor the draft. Blum said that she would and, to show her good faith, wrote Cooper a letter saying that she would honor the draft. Was the draft accepted by Blum? Explain.

8. Norek reported to his insurance company that his car had been stolen. The insurance company delivered to Norek a draft drawn on itself and payable through the First Pennsylvania Bank in the amount of $5,878.63. The draft was payable to Norek and to General Motors Acceptance Corporation (GMAC), which held a security interest on the car. Upon receiving the draft, GMAC released its lien on the vehicle and gave Norek the title certificate. Soon thereafter, it was discovered that the automobile had not been stolen and that Norek's claim was fraudulent. The insurance company stopped payment on the draft. GMAC claims that the draft was a check. Do you agree with GMAC? Why or why not? *Gen. Motors Accept. v. Gen. Acc. Fire & Life,* 415 N.Y.S.2d 536 (New York).

CHAPTER 25
Negotiation of Commercial Paper

OUTLINE

COMMENTARY

Have you ever indorsed a check before cashing it or depositing it in a bank account? Few people realize the legal significance of signing their name on the back of a negotiable instrument. By this simple act, indorsers agree to pay any subsequent holder the face amount of the instrument. Indorsers also make five implied warranties, if they received consideration, to all future holders of the instrument. For these and other reasons, commercial paper is passed freely from one person to another for the payment of debts and the purchase of goods and services, taking the place of money.

OBJECTIVES

1. Differentiate between an assignment and a negotiation of commercial paper.
2. Name and describe four kinds of indorsements.
3. Identify the implied warranties that are made when people indorse negotiable instruments.
4. Explain the contract that is made when people indorse negotiable instruments.
5. Determine the indorsements required on instruments with more than one payee.
6. Describe the legal effect of a forged or unauthorized indorsement.
7. Recognize three exceptions to the unauthorized indorsement rule.

25-1 ASSIGNMENT VERSUS NEGOTIATION

Commercial paper that does not meet all the requirements of negotiability cannot be negotiated. It can only be transferred by assignment, which is governed by the ordinary principles of contract law. People who receive instruments by assignment are not given the special protection given to those who receive instruments by negotiation.

Assignment

An **assignment** is the transfer of a contract right from one person to another. Commercial paper is *assigned* either when a person whose indorsement is required on an instrument transfers it without indorsing it or when it is transferred to another person and does not meet the requirements of negotiability. In all such transfers, the transferee has only the rights of an assignee and is subject to all defenses existing against the assignor. (See Chapter 12.)

Arnette sold 100 cases of beans to Brodie for $12 a case. In exchange, Brodie gave Arnette a promissory note, promising to pay the $1,200 in six months at 14 percent per annum interest. The note was not negotiable, however, because it read "I promise to pay to Arnette" instead of "I promise to pay to the order of Arnette." To obtain needed cash, Arnette transferred the note to her bank. This transfer was an assignment rather than a negotiation because the note did not contain the proper words of negotiability. Brodie refused to pay the bank the amount due on maturity because the beans he had received from Arnette were defective. They were not merchantable. Since the transfer of the note was an assignment rather than a negotiation, the bank was subject to the same defense as Arnette and could not enforce payment of the note. Its only recourse is against Arnette. Had the note been negotiable, the bank could have received greater rights than its transferor had. It could have forced Brodie to pay the note even though Brodie received bad beans.

An assignment of commercial paper also occurs by operation of law when the holder of an instrument dies or becomes a bankrupt. In such cases, title to the instrument vests in the personal representative of the estate or the trustee in bankruptcy.

Negotiation

UCC 3-202 (see p. 641)

Negotiation is the transfer of an instrument in such form that the transferee becomes a holder. A holder, you will remember, is a person who is in possession of an instrument issued or indorsed to that person or to that person's order or to bearer or in blank.

Mildred Liles sold Myers some restaurant equipment for $5,000. In payment for the equipment, Liles received $500 cash and a promissory note payable to her order for $4,500. Liles was a holder because she was in possession of an instrument issued to her.

If an instrument is payable to order, such as "pay to the order of," it is known as **order paper.** To be negotiated, order paper must be indorsed by the payee and delivered to the party to whom it is transferred. If an instrument is payable to bearer or cash, it is called **bearer paper** and may be negotiated by delivery alone, without an indorsement. When order paper is indorsed with a blank indorsement (defined below), it is turned into bearer paper and may be further negotiated by delivery alone.

25-2 NEGOTIATION BY INDORSEMENT

An instrument is indorsed when the holder signs it, thereby indicating the intent to transfer ownership to another. Indorsements may be written in ink, typewritten, or stamped with a rubber stamp. They may be written on a separate paper (rider, or ***allonge***) as long as the separate paper is so firmly affixed to the instrument that it becomes part of it. Although the UCC does not require indorsements to be on any particular side of the paper, for convenience purposes they are usually placed on the back of the instrument. Anyone who gives value for an instrument has the right to have the unqualified indorsement of the person who transferred it unless it is payable to bearer.

UCC 3-202(2) **(see p. 641)**

Negotiation is effective to transfer an instrument even when it is: (*a*) transferred by an infant, a corporation exceeding its powers, or any other person without capacity; (*b*) obtained by fraud, duress, or mistake of any kind; (*c*) part of an illegal transaction; or (*d*) made in breach of duty. Any such negotiations, however, may be rescinded except as against a holder in due course (defined and explained in Chapter 26).

UCC 3-207 **(see p. 642)**

There are four commonly used types of indorsements. They are blank indorsements, special indorsements, restrictive indorsements, and qualified indorsements.

Blank Indorsements

UCC 3-204(2) **(see p. 641)**

A **blank indorsement** consists of the signature alone written on the instrument. No particular indorsee (person to whom an instrument is indorsed) is named. When an instrument is indorsed in blank, it becomes payable to bearer and may be transferred by delivery alone. If the instrument is lost or stolen and gets into the hands of another holder, the new holder can recover its face value by delivery alone. For this reason, a blank indorsement should be used only in limited situations, such as at a bank teller's window. Figure 25-1 shows a blank indorsement.

Carol Barcley received her first paycheck from the restaurant where she worked as a part-time hostess. She took the check to the bank, where she indorsed it in blank at the teller's window. This was a proper time and place to use a blank indorsement, since there was no likelihood that the check would get lost or stolen.

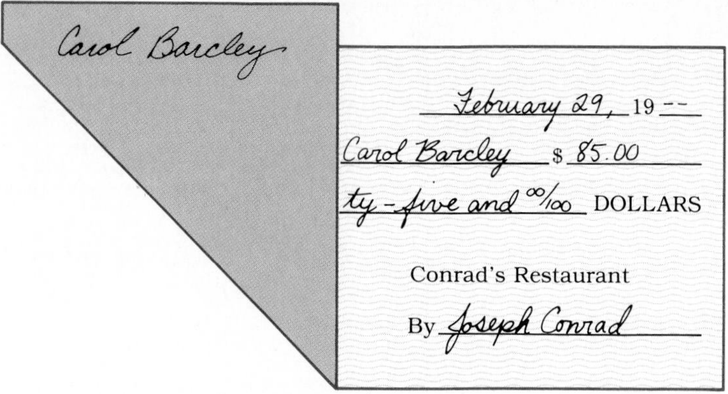

Figure 25-1 A blank indorsement turns order paper into bearer paper and may be transferred by delivery alone.

UCC 3-203 (see p. 641)

When an instrument is made payable to a person under a misspelled name or a name other than that person's own, the payee may indorse in the incorrect name or in the correct name, or in both. Signatures in both names may be required by a person paying or giving value for the instrument.

Special Indorsements

UCC 3-204(1) (see p. 641)

A **special indorsement** (also called an **indorsement in full**) is made by writing the words "pay to the order of" or "pay to" followed by the name of the person to whom it is to be transferred (the indorsee) and the signature of the indorser. When indorsed in this manner, the instrument remains an order instrument and must be indorsed by the indorsee before it can be further negotiated.

Frank Cully withdrew $3,500 from his savings account to buy a car from Glendale Motors, Inc. When he made the withdrawal, Cully received a check from the bank payable to him for $3,500. He took the check to Glendale Motors, indorsed it with a special indorsement (see Figure 25-2), and received title to the car. Since the check cannot be legally transferred or negotiated further until Glendale indorses it, all parties are protected.

UCC 3-204(3) (see p. 641)

The holder of an instrument may convert a blank indorsement into a special indorsement by writing the same words ("pay to the order of" or "pay to") over the indorser's signature.

Restrictive Indorsements

UCC 3-205 (see p. 641)

A **restrictive indorsement** limits the rights of the indorsee in some manner in order to protect the rights of the indorser. An indorsement is restrictive if it (*a*) is conditional, (*b*) purports to prohibit further transfer of the instrument, (*c*) includes the words "for collection," "for deposit," "pay any bank," or like terms signifying a purpose of deposit or collection, or (*d*) otherwise states that it is for the benefit or use of the indorser or of another person.

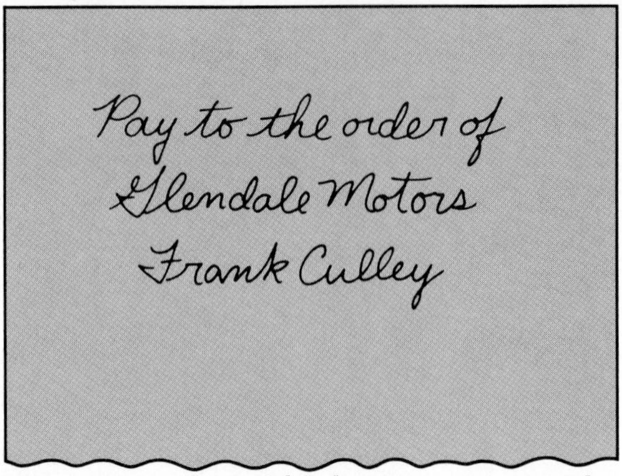

Pay to the order of
Glendale Motors
Frank Culley

Figure 25-2 A special indorsement creates order paper, which requires the signature of the indorsee.

A **conditional indorsement**, a type of restrictive indorsement, makes the rights of the indorsee subject to the happening of a certain event or condition.

Gallo wished to transfer a dividend check that he received to his grandson, James Ingram, as a birthday gift. Since Gallo did not want Ingram to cash the check before his eighteenth birthday, a conditional indorsement (such as the one illustrated in Figure 25-3) was used. Until the condition presented in the indorsement has been satisfied, Ingram does not have the right to cash the check.

Indorsements for deposit or collection are designed to get an instrument into the banking system for deposit or collection. When a check is indorsed "for deposit only," as in Figure 25-4, the amount of the instrument will be credited to the indorser's account before it is negotiated further. Retail stores often stamp each check "for deposit only" when it is received. This provides protection in

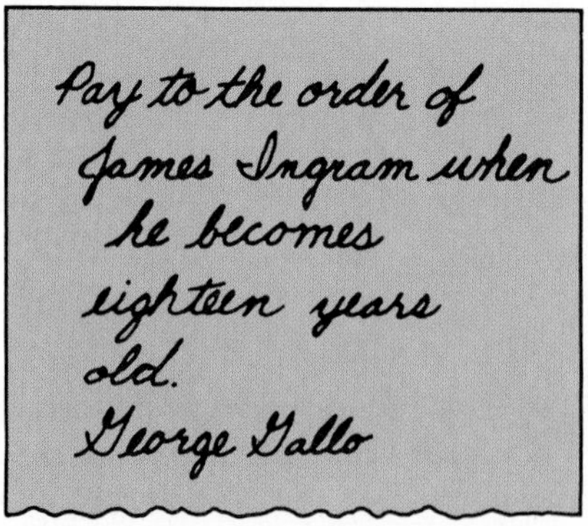

Pay to the order of
James Ingram when
he becomes
eighteen years
old.
George Gallo

Figure 25-3 Conditional indorsement.

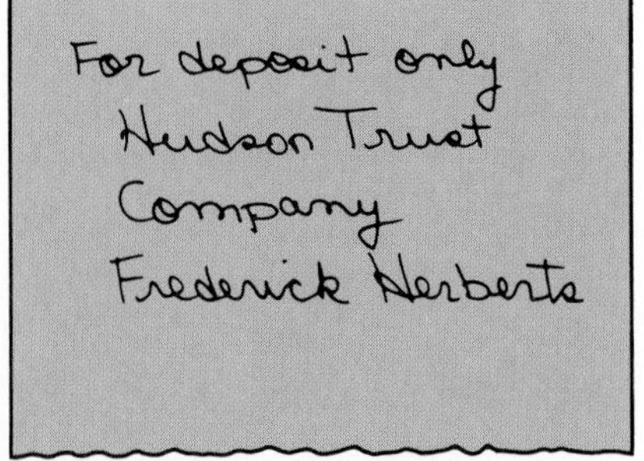

Figure 25-4 A restrictive indorsement limits the subsequent use of the instrument.

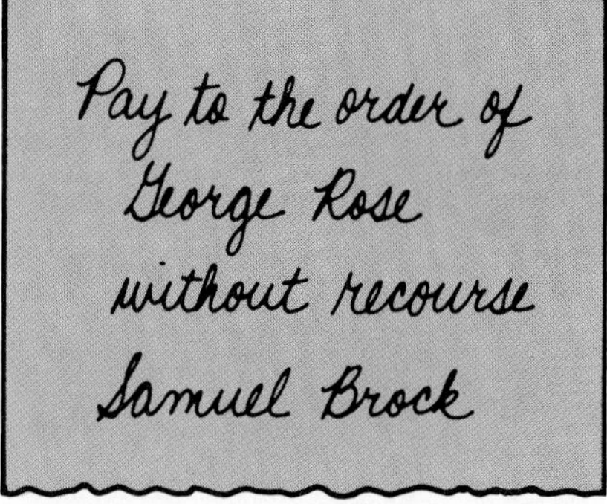

Figure 25-5 A qualified indorsement limits the contractual liability of the indorser.

the event the check is stolen. Checks mailed to the bank for deposit should always be indorsed in this way.

An indorsement that purports to prohibit further transfer, such as "pay Olga Peterson only," may be further negotiated after the directions in the indorsement are carried out. Thus, after Olga Peterson is paid, any holder of the instrument may continue to negotiate it. A restrictive indorsement does not prevent further transfer or negotiation of the instrument.

Qualified Indorsements
UCC 3-414
(see p. 645)

A **qualified indorsement** is one in which words have been added to the signature that limit the liability of the indorser. By adding the words "without recourse" to the indorsement, the indorser is not liable in the event the instrument is dishonored, that is, not paid by the maker or drawer.

A $25,000 check was made payable to Attorney Samuel Brock in payment of a client's claim. Brock indorsed the check to the client, George Rose, "without recourse." By using this indorsement, Brock will not be responsible for payment if the check fails to clear.

25-3 SIGNIFICANCE OF INDORSEMENTS

Indorsements have a threefold significance. In addition to being necessary to negotiate order paper, they create obligations on the part of the indorser. These obligations come in the form of implied warranties and a contractual promise to pay subsequent holders of the instrument.

Warranties of Indorsers

An indorser who receives consideration for an instrument makes five warranties to subsequent holders of the instrument. These warranties are as follows:

UCC 3-417
(see p. 646)

1. The indorser has good title to the instrument. This warranty gives assurances to subsequent holders that the person indorsing it did not steal it or come into possession of it in an unlawful manner.

State National Bank accepted a check from Lawless for deposit to her account. The check contained a blank indorsement by Anthony Fiore. The bank later discovered that Lawless had found the check in a supermarket. A stop payment order had been issued by the real owner, Anthony Fiore. Lawless, by her indorsement, had warranted that she was the true owner of the check. She would be held liable on this warranty for any loss suffered by the bank.

---

2. All signatures are genuine or authorized.

A check made payable to Jones was indorsed by his stepmother, who forged his signature and cashed the check at the Commonwealth Bank & Trust Co. The bank has a cause of action for the recovery of the money from Jones's stepmother on the ground of breach of warranty that all signatures are genuine or authorized.

---

3. The instrument has not been materially altered. The indorser warrants that there has been no alteration or other irregularity.

Cushing wrote a check payable to the order of Daly for $5 and delivered it to Daly. Daly altered the check to read $500, indorsed it, and cashed it at a bank. Cushing will have to pay only the original amount of the check ($5) unless it can be shown that she was negligent in writing it so that it could be easily altered. The bank's recourse is against Daly for breach of this warranty.

---

4. No defense of any party is good against the indorser.

Emerson, who was 17 years old, bought a boat from Flynn for $300, paying for it by personal check. The transaction took place on Friday afternoon. Flynn kept the check over the weekend. On Monday morning she indorsed the instrument and cashed it at her local bank. Meanwhile, Emerson had used the boat over the weekend and had decided that he did not like it. He stopped payment on the check, and it was returned to the bank that had cashed it marked "payment stopped." The bank could not recover the $300 from Emerson because he was a minor when he entered into the contract. He may use the defense of minority against anyone who sues him on the contract. The bank, however, can recover the $300 from Flynn. By indorsing the check, she impliedly warranted that there were no defenses that she could use to defend herself, including Emerson's defense of minority.

A qualified indorser (one who uses the words "without recourse" as shown in Figure 25-5) does not make this warranty. Such an indorsement warrants only that the indorser has no knowledge of a defense that may be used, such as Emerson's defense of minority in the above case.

5. The indorser has no knowledge of the bankruptcy of the maker, acceptor, or drawer.

Contract of Indorsers

Unless an indorsement states otherwise (as by such words as "without recourse"), every indorser agrees to pay any subsequent holder the face amount of the instrument if it is **dishonored** (not paid by the maker or drawee). To enforce this obligation, it is necessary for the holder to do two things. The holder of an instrument must first present it for payment to the maker or drawee when it is due. If that person refuses to pay the instrument, it is said to be dishonored. The holder must then notify the indorser or indorsers of the dishonor. The notice must be given before midnight of the third full business day after the date of the dishonor. Failure by the holder to make presentment and to give timely notice of dishonor to an indorser has the effect of discharging that indorser from liability on the contract to pay subsequent holders of the instrument.

UCC 3-414 (see p. 645)

Unless they otherwise agree, indorsers are liable to one another in the order in which they indorse. This is presumed to be the order in which their signatures appear on the instrument.

The Security Loan company received a check indorsed and delivered to it by Diana Sklar in payment of a loan. When presented for payment at the drawer's bank, the check was returned for want of sufficient funds. Security Loan would have the right to demand payment from any or all of the indorsers shown on the back of the check (see Figure 25-6), if it gave them proper notice, starting with Diana Sklar. To be assured of maximum safety, the holder should demand payment from the indorsers in reverse of the order in which their names appear—Sklar, Allen, Jones, and Brownlee—until payment is received from one of them.

Accommodation Parties

An **accommodation party** is one who signs an instrument in any capacity for the purpose of lending his or her name to another party to the instrument.

Ralph Brownlee
Sandra Jones
Robert Allen
Diana Sklar

Figure 25-6 Indorsers are liable to subsequent holders in the form of implied warranties and contractual promises.

UCC 3-415
(see p. 645)

Thus, an accommodation party who signs on the front of a promissory note below the signature of the maker, assumes the same liability of the maker. On the other hand, an accommodation party who signs on the back of the instrument assumes the same liability as an indorser. An accommodation party is not liable to the party accommodated. The party accommodated is liable to the accommodation party if the latter pays the instrument.

Callaghan applied for a loan at his local bank. The bank would agree to lend the money to him only if someone else would be a co-signer, that is, sign the promissory note along with Callaghan. Williamson agreed to do this and signed the instrument on the front. She was an accommodation party. Callaghan was the party accommodated. The bank could demand payment from either Callaghan or Williamson. Callaghan would be liable to Williamson for the amount of the note if she should pay the amount to the bank.

25-4 MULTIPLE PAYEES AND MISSING INDORSEMENTS

If an instrument is payable to either of two payees, as in "pay to the order of Eric Foss *or* Betty Foss," the indorsement of only one of the payees is necessary to negotiate it. On the other hand, if an instrument is payable to both of two payees, as in "pay to the order of Eric Foss *and* Betty Foss," the indorsement of both payees is necessary for a proper negotiation.

UCC 3-116
(see p. 640)

Middle States Leasing Corporation drew a check payable to the order of two payees, Interpace Corporation and United Leasing Services, Inc., in the sum of $150,000. United Leasing Services, Inc., indorsed the check and received the entire proceeds from the drawee bank without the indorsement of Interpace Corporation on the instrument. Because the instrument was not indorsed by both payees,the bank was held responsible to Middle States Leasing Corporation for the entire amount of the check.

UCC 4-205

A depository bank which has taken in an item for collection may supply any indorsement of the customer which is necessary to title. This rule is designed to speed up bank collections by eliminating the necessity to return to a depositor any items that were not indorsed. Such an indorsement may not be supplied by a bank, however, if the instrument contains the words "payee's indorsement required."

25-5 FORGED OR UNAUTHORIZED INDORSEMENTS

UCC 3-404
(see p. 644)

An unauthorized signature or indorsement is one made without actual, implied, or apparent authority. With three exceptions and unless ratified (approved afterward), an unauthorized or forged signature does not serve as the signature of the person whose name is signed. It has no effect. In addition, when an instrument is paid on a forged indorsement, the tort of conversion takes place. To illustrate, when a bank pays proceeds to a forger and the payee's wishes are not carried out, the bank is held liable for converting the payee's funds. The tort of conversion is explained in Chapter 4.

Seventeen checks payable to the Mott Grain Company, totaling $40,520.93, were deposited to the personal bank account of Baszler, the company's manager. Baszler disappeared with the money but was later found and convicted of embezzlement. Nine of the checks contained restrictive indorsements, requiring them to be deposited in the company's bank account. The remainder of the checks bore blank indorsements, such as "Mott Grain Co./Verson Baszler." Baszler's only authority was to deposit the checks in the Mott Grain Co.'s account. The bank was held liable to the grain company, in conversion, for the amount of all the checks.

UCC 3-405
(see p. 644)

There are three exceptions to the general rule that an unauthorized indorsement has no effect. The exceptions are designed primarily to promote negotiability of commercial paper. They are as follows:

Imposters

An imposter is someone who impersonates another. When an instrument is issued to an imposter on the false belief that the imposter is the payee, the indorsement by any person in the name of the payee is treated as an effective indorsement. This rule places the loss, in such a case, on the one who is in the best position to prevent it—the maker or drawer of the instrument.

Covington was induced in a fraudulent oil-land scheme to issue a cashier's check to an imposter under the false belief that the imposter was a person named Baird. The imposter's indorsement of the name "Baird" on the check was held by the court to be effective to negotiate the instrument. The bank that paid the check was not held liable in conversion, and the check was considered to be properly negotiated. The indorsement by the imposter was treated as an effective indorsement.

No Interest Intended

When the maker or drawer of an instrument intends the payee to have no interest in the instrument, an indorsement by any person in the name of the payee is effective.

Gordon loaned $5,000 to Wolf, intending Wolf to have the entire interest in the money. He made the check payable jointly, however, to Wolf and Wolf's wife Norma. When the check was cashed, Norma's indorsement was forged. The court held that the forged indorsement was valid because Gordon did not intend Norma to have any interest in the instrument.

Padded Payrolls

When an agent or employee of the maker or drawer pads the payroll by supplying the employer with fictitious names, an indorsement by any person in the name of each fictitious payee is effective. This rule places the burden of preventing this type of fraud on the drawer or maker, the party in the best position to prevent it.

Harrison, the payroll clerk for Industries, Inc., made out payroll checks for ten employees who did not exist and had her employer sign them. She negotiated the ten checks by indorsing them in the names of the fictitious payees. The indorsements by Harrison were effective. Industries, Inc., not the bank, had the burden of preventing this type of fraud, which it was in a position to avoid. Industries, Inc., would be liable for any losses suffered as a result of the padding of the payroll.

SUMMARY

25-1. Commercial paper that does not meet all the requirements of negotiability cannot be negotiated. It can only be transferred by assignment. People who receive instruments by assignment are not given the special protection given to those who receive instruments by negotiation. To be negotiated, order paper must be indorsed by the payee and delivered. In contrast, bearer paper may be negotiated by delivery alone.

25-2. When an instrument is indorsed in blank, it becomes bearer paper. Whenan instrument is indorsed in full, it becomes order paper. A restrictive indorsement limits the subsequent use of an instrument. A qualified indorsement limits the liability of the indorser.

25-3. An indorser who receives consideration for an instrument warrants that (*a*) he or she has good title to the instrument, (*b*) all signatures are genuine or authorized, (*c*) the instrument has not been materially altered, (*d*) no defense of any party is good against the indorser, and (*e*) he or she has no knowledge of any insolvency proceedings of the maker, acceptor, or drawer. Unqualified indorsers agree to pay subsequent holders the amount of an instrument if timely presentment is made, if the instrument is dishonored, and if they are given proper notice. Accommodation parties are responsible either as indorsers or makers, depending upon where they sign the instrument.

25-4. Instruments payable to one payee *or* another payee require the indorsement of only one of the payees. In contrast, instruments payable to one payee *and* another payee must be indorsed by both payees. A bank taking an instrument for deposit may supply a customer's missing indorsement.

25-5. With three exceptions and unless ratified, an unauthorized or forged signature does not serve as the signature of the person whose name is signed. A bank commits the tort of conversion when it pays money to a forger. Exceptions occur when (*a*) an instrument is issued to an imposter, (*b*) a payee is not intended to have an interest in an instrument, and (*c*) a payroll is padded with fictitious names.

Understanding Key Legal Terms

accommodation party (p. 351)
allonge (p. 346)
assignment (p. 345)
bearer paper (p. 346)
blank indorsement (p. 346)
conditional indorsement (p. 348)
dishonored (p. 351)
indorsement in full (p. 347)
negotiation (p. 345)
order paper (p. 346)
qualified indorsement (p. 349)
restrictive indorsement (p. 347)
special indorsement (p. 347)

Questions for Review and Discussion

1. What is the difference between an assignment and a negotiation of commercial paper?
2. Identify two ways an instrument may be negotiated so that the transferee becomes a holder.
3. What is the difference between a blank indorsement and a special indorsement?
4. Why should a blank indorsement be used only in limited situations, such as at a bank teller's window?
5. How does a restrictive indorsement differ from a qualified indorsement?
6. What warranties are made by an indorser who receives consideration for an instrument?
7. What contract does an indorser make with subsequent holders of a negotiable instrument?
8. What indorsements are necessary to negotiate an instrument that is payable (*a*) to one person *and* another person (*b*) to one person *or* another person?
9. Explain the legal consequences that arise when an instrument is paid on a forged indorsement.
10. What are the three exceptions to the general rule that any unauthorized indorsement is not effective?

Analyzing Cases

1. Powell, intending to write a check to Thompson Electric, Inc., instead made it payable to the order of "Thompon Electric." Thompson Electric, Inc., indorsed the check with its name correctly spelled. Was the indorsement valid? Why or why not? *State v. Powell,* 551 P.2d 902 (Kansas).
2. Tufi forged the payee's name on the front of a U.S. Treasurer's check. When convicted of a forgery he appealed, contending that a signature on the front of a check cannot be an indorsement. May an indorsement be written on the front of an instrument? Explain. *United States v. Tufi,* 536 F.2d 855 (Hawaii).
3. Morse wrote a check for $2,500 payable to Reynolds for services rendered. Reynolds fraudulently raised the check to $5,500, indorsed it "without recourse," and deposited it in her bank account. Later, when the alteration was discovered, Reynolds argued that she was not responsible because her indorsement was qualified. Do you agree with Reynolds? Why or why not? See also *Wolfram v. Halloway,* 361 N.E.2d 587 (Illinois).

4. Sanders borrowed $5,000 from Waskow, giving Waskow a promissory note which read, "One year from date, I promise to pay to the order of James Waskow $5,000, without interest (signed) Mary Sanders." Six months later, Waskow died. The unindorsed note was in the possession of Waskow's landlord, who claimed that Waskow had given him the note in payment of back rent. Was the landlord a holder of the note? Why or why not? See also *Smathers v. Smathers,* 239 S.E.2d 637 (North Carolina).

5. When checks were received by Palmer & Ray Dental Supply, Mrs. Wilson, a company employee, indorsed them with a rubber stamp reading: "Palmer & Ray Dental Supply" (followed by the company's address). Mrs. Wilson deposited some of the checks in the company's account but cashed the rest, keeping the money for herself. The company contends that the indorsements were restrictive and, therefore, that the bank should not have cashed them. Were the indorsements restrictive? Explain. *Palmer & Ray Dental Supply, Inc. v. First Nat'l Bank,* 477 S.W.2d 954 (Kansas).

6. Commercial Credit Corporation issued a check payable to Rauch Motor Company. Rauch indorsed the check in blank and delivered it to a bank. The bank typed a very long special indorsement payable to Lamson on two legal-size sheets of paper and stapled them to the checks. May an indorsement be written on a separate paper and stapled to the checks? Explain. *Lamson v. Commercial Credit Corp.,* 531 P.2d 966 (Colorado).

7. The indorsement of the payee of a check drawn by Funding Systems Leasing Corporation was forged. Below the forged indorsement was added the signature of another person which was not forged. The check was deposited with the Sumiton Bank, which claims to be a holder. Was the bank a holder? Why or why not? *Sumiton Bank v. Funding Sys. Leasing Corp.,* 512 F.2d 774 (Cir. Ct.).

8. The United States of America issued a check of the U.S. Treasury in the amount of $49,314.47 payable to two companies, Floors, Inc., and American Fidelity Fire Insurance Company. Floors, Inc., indorsed the check with a rubber stamp indorsement, "For Deposit Only, Floors, Inc.," deposited it in its account in the Peoples National Bank, and later withdrew the money. Was the check properly negotiated? Why or why not? What tort, if any, did the Peoples National Bank commit? Explain. *Peoples Nat'l. Bank v. American Fidelity Fire Ins.,* 386 A.2d 1254 (Maryland).

CHAPTER 26
Holders in Due Course, Defenses, and Liabilities

OUTLINE

COMMENTARY

Horowitz bought a stereo system from Sea Crest Stereo Sales for $1,450, paying for it by check. That same day, Sea Crest negotiated the check to Stereo Supply Co. in payment of a debt that was long overdue. That evening, Horowitz tried out the stereo and discovered that it would not work. When he attempted to return the stereo to Sea Crest, the company refused to take it back and would not repair it. Horowitz stopped payment on the check. He discovered, to his surprise, that he was responsible for paying the full amount to Stereo Supply Co., the holder. This was because Stereo Supply was a *holder in due course* and had not dealt directly with Horowitz.

Had Sea Crest deposited the check in its bank account instead of negotiating it to Stereo Supply, the stop-payment order would have been effective. Horowitz would have been able to use the defense of breach of warranty of merchantability against Sea Crest. The same defense could not have been used against Stereo Supply, however, because that company was a holder in due course. This chapter explains the special protection that is given to holders in due course like Stereo Supply Co.

OBJECTIVES

1. State the requirements of being a holder in due course.
2. Describe the special protection given to a holder in due course.
3. Name six personal defenses.
4. Discuss the protection given to people who sign consumer credit contracts.
5. Explain the significance of a real defense.

6. Name six real defenses.
7. Differentiate between primary liability and secondary liability.
8. List the parties who are (*a*) primarily liable and (*b*) secondarily liable.
9. Describe the conditions that must be met to hold a secondary party liable.

26-1 HOLDER IN DUE COURSE

UCC 3-302
(see p. 642)

A **holder in due course** is a holder who takes the instrument for value, in good faith, without notice that it is overdue or has been dishonored and without notice of any defenses against it or claim to it. Holders in due course are treated favorably under the UCC. They receive more rights in negotiable instruments than their transferors had. Largely for this reason, negotiable instruments are passed freely from one person to another almost in the same way as money. A payee may be a holder in due course.

Holder

To be a holder in due course, the person in possession of the instrument must first be a **holder.** This means that the instrument must have been issued or indorsed to that person or to that person's order, to bearer, or in blank.

John and Nancy Augustine contracted with Hanover Homes Corporation for the construction of a house. They obtained a commitment for a mortgage loan from a bank, which issued checks periodically as the construction progressed. The checks were made payable to John, Nancy, and Hanover Homes Corporation. The last check that was issued was deposited in Hanover's bank account without Nancy's indorsement on it. The bank that received the check for deposit was not a holder because, without Nancy's indorsement, the check was not issued or indorsed to it or to bearer or in blank.

Value

UCC 3-303
(see p. 642)

A person must give value for an instrument in order to qualify as a holder in due course. Thus, if an instrument is transferred to a person as a gift, that person would not qualify as a holder in due course. People give value for instruments when they give the consideration that was agreed upon or when they accept instruments in payment of debts.

Good Faith

UCC 1-201
(see pp. 612–613)

To be a holder in due course, the holder must take the instrument in good faith. Good faith, as defined in Chapter 17, is "honesty in fact." It requires that the taker of a commercial instrument act honestly in its acquisition. If the taker is negligent in not discovering that something was wrong with the paper, this does not establish lack of good faith.

Leo's Used Car Exchange purchased three cars at a car auction from Villa, paying for them with two checks totaling $15,150. Villa presented the checks to a bank and asked the teller to give him cash, since he was going to another auction and needed it. The teller did so without obtaining the bank manager's approval, which was against the bank's policy. Shortly thereafter, Leo's Used Car Exchange stopped payment on the checks because title to the three cars was not clear. The lower court held that the bank that cashed them was not a holder in due course because of the teller's negligence in not obtaining the manager's approval before cashing the checks. The appellate court reversed the lower court's decision, holding that good faith means honesty in fact. The court said, "Nothing in the definition suggests that in addition to being honest, the holder must exercise due care to be in good faith." Since the bank was a holder in due course, it was able to recover the $15,150 from the drawer of the checks, Leo's Used Car Exchange.

Without Notice

UCC 3-304(2) (see p. 642)

To be a holder in due course, a holder must not have notice of any claim or defense to an instrument or notice that an instrument is overdue or has been dishonored. A holder has notice of a claim or defense if the instrument bears visible evidence of forgery or alteration. The same is true if the instrument is so incomplete or irregular as to make its legal acceptance doubtful. Notice of a claim or defense is also considered given if the holder knows that the obligation of any party is voidable.

Ann Lovino, who was 17 years old, borrowed $250 from George Minkus. She gave Minkus a promissory note, promising to pay the money back in 90 days. Minkus was not a holder in due course because he knew that Lovino was a minor and could disaffirm the contract to pay back the money.

UCC 3-304(3) (see pp. 642–643)

A holder has notice that an instrument is overdue when more than a reasonable length of time has elapsed since it was issued. A reasonable time to negotiate a check is 30 days. For other instruments, such as a note or draft, a "reasonable time" depends upon the circumstances of each case.

Parks misplaced a check that he had received for cleaning out a neighbor's attic. He found the check two months later and cashed it at a nearby video shop. The video shop was not a holder in due course because it took the instrument when it was more than 30 days old.

Anyone taking an installment note with knowledge of an overdue installment on principal has notice that the instrument is overdue and therefore cannot be a holder in due course. Past-due interest, however, does not give notice of any defect in the instrument.

Knowledge of some facts does not of itself give the holder notice of a defense or claim. For example, the fact that an instrument is postdated or antedated does not prevent someone from being a holder in due course; neither does completing an incomplete instrument constitute having such notice, unless the holder has notice of any improper completion.

Holder Through a Holder in Due Course
UCC 3-201
(see p. 641)

A holder who receives an instrument from a holder in due course acquires the rights of the holder in due course even though he or she does not qualify as a holder in due course. This is called a **shelter provision.** It is designed to permit holders in due course to transfer all rights they have in the paper to others.

Karpinski gave McGraw a $150 check in payment for an antique chair. Since McGraw took the check for value, in good faith, and without notice, he was a holder in due course of the instrument. McGraw indorsed the instrument with a special indorsement and gave it to his niece as a graduation present. McGraw's niece is not a holder in due course because she did not give value for the instrument. However, she has the rights of a holder in due course because she received the check from a holder in due course.

The shelter provision does not apply to a holder who has committed fraud or an illegal act.

26-2 PERSONAL DEFENSES

UCC 3-305
(see p. 643)

A holder in due course takes an instrument free from all claims to it on the part of any person and free from all personal defenses of any party with whom the holder has not dealt. **Personal defenses** (sometimes called **limited defenses**) are defenses that can be used against a holder, but not a holder in due course, of a negotiable instrument. When an instrument is negotiated to a holder in due course, personal defenses are cut off; that is, one cannot use personal defenses against a holder in due course unless one has first dealt with the holder in due course. The most common personal defenses are breach of contract, lack or failure of consideration, fraud in the inducement, lack of delivery, and payment.

UCC 3-306
(see p. 643)

Breach of Contract

Negotiable instruments are often issued in exchange for property, services, or some other obligation as part of an underlying contract. Sometimes, when this occurs, the party to whom the instrument was issued breaches the contract by failing to perform or by doing so in an unsatisfactory manner. If suit is brought on the instrument by a holder against the maker or drawer, the latter may use breach of contract as a defense. Since this is a personal defense, however, it may not be used if the holder of the instrument is a holder in due course unless the parties dealt with one another.

Lack or Failure of Consideration

Lack of consideration is a defense that may be used by a maker or drawer of an instrument when no consideration existed in the underlying contract for which the instrument was issued. The ordinary rules of contract law, discussed in Chapter 9, are followed to determine the presence or absence of consideration in such a case.

Gruel executed a note in favor of Searle as a birthday gift. Searle indorsed the note to Chard in payment of an obligation. As against Searle, Gruel has a defense of lack of consideration. Chard has furnished value and can enforce the note against Gruel in spite of his defense.

Failure (want) of consideration is different. This is a defense that the maker or drawer has available when the party dealt with breaches the contract by not furnishing the agreed consideration.

National Radio Company, Inc., sold to Frequency Electronics, Inc., its product line known as Atomichron, an atomic clock said to be the most accurate commercially available means for keeping time. The sale included certain patent rights valued at $325,000. As part of the purchase price, Frequency Electronics gave National Radio a $325,000 promissory note. The note was subsequently acquired by Lerner, who was chairperson of the board, treasurer, and principal stockholder of National Radio Company. When one of the patents turned out to be void, Frequency Electronics refused to pay the note. The court held that a note given in payment for an invalid patent is void for failure of consideration. In addition, the court said that Lerner was not a holder in due course because he had knowledge of the invalid patent. He was subject to the defense of failure of consideration. Had Lerner been a holder in due course, the defense would have been cut off.

Both lack of consideration and failure of consideration are limited defenses. They may not be used against a holder in due course.

Fraud in the Inducement

There are two kinds of fraud: fraud in the inducement and fraud as to the essential nature of the transaction. The first is a personal defense, discussed here; the second is a real defense, discussed below. The five elements of fraud are explained in depth in Chapter 7. When someone is induced by a fraudulent statement or act to enter into a contract, that person may have the contract rescinded. Likewise, the defense of fraud in the inducement may be used against a holder of a negotiable instrument issued as part of the transaction. Since the defense is limited, it may not be used against a holder in due course.

Lack of Delivery

Every commercial instrument may be revoked by its maker or drawer until it has been delivered to the payee. **Delivery** is the transfer of possession from one person to another. If the transfer of possession is not intended to give the transferee rights, delivery is made in a physical sense, but the instrument has not been "issued." Thus, in the event a payee forcibly, unlawfully, or conditionally takes an instrument from a drawer, the drawer has the defense of conditional delivery. The payee therefore may be denied the right to collect on the instrument. If the payee negotiates the instrument to a holder in due course, however, this defense is cut off.

Morse wrote out a check payable to the order of Smith, intending to give it to Smith after Smith had completed a certain amount of work. Smith discovered the check on Morse's desk, and took it without doing any work at all. Smith is not entitled to the check; however, if she negotiates the check to a bank, store, or private party for value, in good faith, and without notice (a holder in due course), Morse will have to honor the check even though Smith failed to do the required work.

Payment

Payment of an instrument by a maker or drawee usually ends the obligations of the parties. However, if a negotiable instrument is negotiated to a holder in due course after it has been paid, it will have to be paid again. This is because payment is a personal defense, which cannot be used against a holder in due course. Because of this rule, anyone who pays a demand instrument should have it marked "paid" and take possession of it. This requirement is not as important with a time instrument, unless it is paid before its due date, because no one can be a holder in due course of a past-due instrument.

Consumer Protection

The protection that is given to holders in due course was not always fair, in the past, to consumers who bought on credit.

In 1975, Ruby Merlin bought a car from a used-car dealer. She paid a small amount down and signed a consumer sales contract agreeing to pay the balance in 24 monthly installments. The used-car dealer negotiated the contract (which was actually a promissory note) to a finance company and received payment immediately. The next day, the car's transmission stopped working, and the dealer refused to fix it. Merlin would still have to pay the finance company the full amount due on the note because the finance company was a holder in due course and was not subject to personal defenses.

In 1976, the Federal Trade Commission ruled that holders of consumer credit contracts who are holders in due course are subject to all claims and defenses that the buyer could use against the seller, including personal defenses. Thus, if the situation described above were to occur today, Merlin's defense that the car's transmission did not work could be used against the finance company even though it was a holder in due course. When sellers of consumer products have arrangements with financial institutions to finance their customer's purchases, the financial institutions are subject to the customer's personal defenses. They lose their holder-in-due-course protection.

26-3 REAL DEFENSES

UCC 3-305(2) **(see p. 643)**

Some defenses can be used against everyone, including holders in due course. These are known as **real,** or **universal, defenses.** No one is required to pay an instrument when they have a real defense. Real defenses include infancy and mental incompetence, illegality and duress, fraud as to the essential nature of the transaction, bankruptcy, unauthorized signature, and alteration.

Infancy and Mental Incompetence

A minor or mental impotent need not honor a negotiable instrument if it was given in payment for a contract which the minor or mental incompetent may disaffirm on the grounds of minority or incompetency. This is true even if the instrument comes into the hands of a holder in due course. Similarly, persons who have been found insane by a court are not liable on a negotiable instrument since their contracts are void.

Illegality and Duress

An instrument which is associated with an illegal act, such as gambling, smuggling, or duress, would be void and uncollectible by anyone, even a holder in due course. This is true even though the holder in due course is unaware of the illegal acts or conditions.

The Condado Aruba Caribbean Hotel loaned Tickel, who resided in Colorado, $20,000. The money was loaned for the purpose of gambling at the hotel's casino in Aruba, Netherlands Antilles, where gambling is legal. Tickel wrote two checks to repay the debt, each of which was returned for insufficient funds. When suit was brought on the checks, the Colorado court held that gambling debts are unenforceable in that state even against a holder in due course. Tickel was not liable on the checks that he had written to the hotel.

Fraud as to the Essential Nature of the Transaction

Fraud as to the essential nature of the transaction is more serious than fraud in the inducement. Because of its seriousness, it is a real defense and may be used against anyone, even a holder in due course.

Duffy, who was almost blind, was asked by Ingram to sign a receipt. Duffy signed the paper without having had it read to him. The paper was actually a note promising to pay Ingram $2,500. Duffy would not be required to pay the note, even to a holder in due course.

Bankruptcy

Bankruptcy may be used as a defense to all negotiable instruments, even those in the hands of a holder in due course. Holders of such instruments will receive equal treatment with other similar creditors when the debtor's assets are collected and divided according to the bankruptcy law. This law is explained in more detail in Chapter 30.

Unauthorized Signatures

UCC 3-404 **(see p. 644)**

Whenever someone signs another's name on an instrument without authority, it is a forgery. Unless ratified, it does not operate as the signature of the person whose name is signed. Instead, it operates as the signature of the person who signed it, that is, the wrongdoer.

With no authority to do so, Parks signed Brown's name on a note, promising to pay Rivera $3,000 in 90 days. The note was negotiated to a holder in due course.

Brown would not have to pay the money to the holder in due course because the unauthorized signature is a real defense. Parks, however, would be required to pay the money to a holder in due course when the note became due.

Alteration

UCC 3-407 (see p. 644)

Sometimes negotiable instruments are altered after they leave the hands of the maker or drawer. Usually the alteration involves changing the payee's name or raising the amount of an instrument. The alteration of an instrument may be used as a real defense. Unless an instrument is written negligently so that it can be easily altered, makers and drawers are not required to pay altered amounts. They must pay only the amount for which the instrument was originally written.

Maxwell wrote out a check for $315 and gave it to Video Sales in payment for a VCR. Video Sales raised the check to read $815. Maxwell's bank honored the altered check. Maxwell may seek reimbursement from his bank for $500, the difference between the original and the altered amount.

UCC 3-406 (see p. 644)

Any person who negligently contributes to a material alteration of an instrument or an unauthorized signature may not exercise the defense of alteration or lack of authority against a holder in due course, a drawee, or other payor who pays the instrument in good faith. For example, using a pencil to write a check or not being careful to keep the figures compact and clear gives a dishonest holder an opportunity to alter the amount. The careless writer would be without defense.

26-4 LIABILITY OF THE PARTIES

No person is liable on an instrument unless that person's signature or the signature of an authorized agent appears on the instrument. Parties to negotiable instruments are either primarily or secondarily liable.

Primary Liability

UCC 3-413(1) (see p. 645)

Primary liability is an absolute liability to pay. A party with primary liability promises to pay the instrument without any reservation of any kind. Two parties have primary liability: the maker of a promissory note and the acceptor, if any, of a draft.

Secondary Liability

UCC 3-403(2) (see p. 644)

Secondary liability is a liability to pay only after certain conditions have been met. Two types of parties are secondarily liable on negotiable instruments: the drawer of a draft (a check, you will remember, is the most common kind of draft) and the indorsers of either a note or draft. The conditions that must be met are as follows:

1. The instrument must be properly presented to the primary party or drawee and payment must be demanded.
2. The instrument must be dishonored, that is, payment refused.

UCC 3-508
(see p. 649)

3. Notice of the dishonor must be given to the secondary party within the time and in the manner prescribed by the UCC. If all three of the above conditions are not met, indorsers are discharged from their obligations. If the drawee cannot pay because of insolvency and all three conditions are not met, the drawer is discharged from all obligation.

If all three of the above conditions are not met, indorsers are discharged from their obligations. If the drawee cannot pay due to insolvency and all three conditions are not met, the drawer is discharged from all obligation.

Presentment for Payment In order to be sure that a secondary party (drawer or indorser) will be liable on an instrument, the holder must make proper **presentment** for payment unless excused. This means that the holder must present the instrument to the maker or drawer and ask for payment. Presentment must be made on the date that the instrument is due.

Novak indorsed a note as an accommodation to a friend. When the note became due, the holder did not present it to the maker for payment. Two weeks after the date of maturity, when the note was dishonored, the holder attempted to hold Novak liable. Because the holder delayed presentment beyond the time when the note was due without excuse, Novak's liability as an indorser would be discharged.

If no due date is stated on the instrument, presentment must be made within a reasonable time after the maker or drawee became liable on it. The definition of a reasonable time for instruments other than checks will vary, depending on the circumstances and banking and trade practices. A reasonable time for a check is 30 days with respect to the liability of the drawer and 7 days with respect to the liability of an indorser.

A check was drawn by Sarr on June 15. It was indorsed and delivered to Stabler on June 22 by the payee. Stabler then indorsed it to Roche on June 28. When Roche presented the check to Sarr's bank for payment on July 18, he learned that the bank had been ordered closed by bank examiners. Should the bank be unable to pay off its depositors and other liabilities, Roche would have no recourse against either Sarr, the drawer, or Stabler, an indorser. A reasonable period of time within which to initiate bank collection had been exceeded.

When the date that an instrument is payable is not a full business day for either person making the presentment or the party paying, presentment is due on the next following full business day for both parties. To be sufficient, presentment must be made at a reasonable hour. If presentment is made at a bank, it must take place during the banking day.

The party from whom payment is demanded can request to see the instrument. If payment is made, the instrument must be handed over then and there. This is important because if the party paying does not get the instrument back, it might show up later in the hands of a holder of due course, and the paying party would have to pay it again.

Presentment for Acceptance A draft may be presented to the drawee for acceptance as well as for payment. This is particularly important when a draft is not yet due. The holder is given the opportunity to test the drawee's willingness to honor the instrument. When a draft is presented for acceptance, the drawee is asked to become primarily liable on the instrument. The drawee is asked to agree now to pay the amount of the draft when it is presented for payment at a later date. To accept a draft, the drawee signs the instrument (usually perpendicularly) across its face. It is customary, also, to write the word "accepted" and the date along with the drawee's signature. When a drawee bank accepts a check, it stamps the word "certified" across the face of the instrument and signs it. This is known as a certified check. (See Chapter 27.)

Although in most cases a draft may be presented for either payment or acceptance, there are three situations in which a draft *must* be presented for acceptance. They are where the draft states that it must be presented for acceptance, where the draft is payable elsewhere than at the residence or place of business of the drawee, and where the date of payment depends upon presentment, for example, when the draft contains a statement like: "Thirty days after sight pay to the order of ...."

Dishonor As defined in Chapter 25, *dishonor* means to refuse to pay a negotiable instrument when it is due or to refuse to accept it when asked to do so. An instrument is dishonored when proper presentment is made and acceptance or payment is refused. Dishonor also occurs when presentment is excused and the instrument is past due and unpaid. The presenting party has recourse against indorsers or other secondary parties after notice of dishonor has been given.

A note was presented to Baker for payment on the date specified. Baker refused to honor it, claiming the note was a forgery. The holder would have to proceedagainst the indorsers in order to obtain payment. The note was dishonored when Baker refused to pay it.

UCC 3-508(2) **(see p. 649)**

Notice of Dishonor If an instrument has been dishonored, the holder must give notice of the dishonor to the drawer and to the indorsers before midnight of the third full business day after the date of dishonor. Unless notice is excused, any indorser who is not given notice within the specified time is discharged. A drawer who is not given notice within the specified time is discharged if the drawee cannot pay because of insolvency. Notice of dishonor may be given, by or on behalf of the holder, to any person who may be liable. It may also be given by any party who has received notice or by any other party who can be compelled to pay the instrument. Also, an agent or bank in whose hands the instrument is dishonored may give notice to the principal or customer or to another agent or bank from which the instrument was received. Necessary notice must be given by a bank before its midnight deadline and by any other person before midnight of the third business day after dishonor or receipt of notice of dishonor.

UCC 3-508(3) (see p. 649)

Notice may be given in any reasonable manner that conveys the information to the liable parties. It may be given orally or in writing. Written notice is effective when properly sent, even though it is not received. In the event the party to be given notice is involved in insolvency proceedings, notice may be given either to the party or to the court-appointed representative of the bankrupt estate. The banking practice of returning an instrument bearing a stamp to the effect that acceptance or payment has been refused is sufficient notice of dishonor.

Proper notice operates for the benefit of all parties who have rights on an instrument against the party notified.

Karl, Kalish, Janik, and Kunes are indorsers of a dishonored note in that order. The holder gave notice only to Karl and Janik. Janik is not required to give additional notice to Karl. Should Janik be compelled to pay, he would have recourse against Karl. Both Kalish and Kunes are discharged if they are not notified by the holder or by one of the indorsers.

UCC 3-511 (see p. 650)

Delay in giving notice of dishonor or in making presentment is excused when the holder has acted carefully and the delay is due to circumstances beyond the holder's control. The conditions of giving notice or making presentment must be complied with as soon as the cause of the delay ceases.

UCC 3-501 (see p. 647)

Unless excused, protest of any dishonor is necessary to charge the drawer and indorsers of any draft which on its face appears to be drawn or payable outside the states and territories of the United States and the District of Columbia. A **protest** is a certificate of dishonor which states that a draft was presented for acceptance or payment and was dishonored. It also states the reasons given for refusal to accept or pay. It is required for drafts drawn or payable outside the United States and optional in all other cases with the holder. A protest is made under the hand and seal of a United States consul or vice-consul, or of a notary public or other person authorized to certify dishonor by the law where dishonor occurs.

Indorsers who write "demand and notice waived" or "protest waived" above their indorsements or across the face of an instrument are liable for payment without subsequent presentment or notice of dishonor. Prior indorsers are excused from their liability to such indorsers.

If a waiver of notice or protest is stated on the face of the instrument, it is binding upon all parties; when written above the signature of an indorser, it binds only the indorser.

SUMMARY

26-1. A holder in due course is a holder who takes the instrument for value, in good faith, without notice that it is overdue or has been dishonored, and without notice of any defenses against it or claim to it. Good faith means honesty in fact. A holder who receives an instrument from a holder in due course receives all the rights of the holder in due course.

26-2. Personal defenses can be used against a holder, but not a holder in due course. The most common personal defenses are breach of contract, lack or failure of consideration, fraud in the inducement, lack of delivery, and payment. Holders of consumer credit contracts who are holders in duecourse are subject to all claims and defenses that the buyer could use against the seller including personal defenses.

26-3. Real defenses can be used against anyone, including a holder in due course. Real defenses are infancy and mental incompetence, illegality and duress, fraud as to the essential nature of the transaction, bankruptcy, unauthorized signature, and alteration.

26-4. Primary liability is an absolute liability to pay. Makers of notes and acceptors of drafts have primary liability. Secondary liability is a liability to pay only if the following happen: (*a*) an instrument is presented properly for payment, (*b*) the instrument is dishonored, and (*c*) proper notice of dishonor is given to the secondary party. Drawers of drafts and indorsers have secondary liability.

Understanding Key Legal Terms

failure of consideration (p. 361)
holder (p. 358)
holder in due course (p. 358)
lack of consideration (p. 360)
limited defense (p. 360)
personal defense (p. 360)
presentment (p. 365)
primary liability (p. 364)
protest (p. 367)
real defense (p. 362)
secondary liability (p. 364)
shelter provision (p. 360)
universal defense (p. 362)

Questions for Review and Discussion

1. What are the requirements for being a holder in due course?
2. What is the purpose of the shelter provision, and when will it not apply?
3. Why are personal defenses sometimes called limited defenses? Identify the most common personal defenses.
4. What protection is given to consumers who sign consumer credit contracts?
5. Identify and explain the significance of real defenses.
6. Name the parties to an instrument who are (*a*) primarily liable and (*b*) secondarily liable, and explain the differences in their liability.
7. (*a*) Indicate the time when presentment of a negotiable instrument must be made when there is a due date on such an instrument. (*b*) Indicate the time when presentment of a negotiable instrument must be made in the event that there is no due date on such an instrument.
8. When is an instrument dishonored, and what is meant by prompt and proper notice of dishonor?
9. Explain the method of giving notice of dishonor of an instrument drawn or payable outside the United States. How is it accomplished?
10. Under what circumstances will the holder of an instrument be excused from giving notice of dishonor to prior indorsers or to a drawer?

Analyzing Cases

1. Refrigerated Transport Co., Inc., employed a collection agency to collect some of its overdue accounts. The collection agency indorsed, without authority, checks made payable to Refrigerated and deposited them in the agency's own checking account. Was the bank that accepted the checks for deposit a holder in due course? Why or why not? *National Bank v. Refrigerated Transp.,* 248 S.E.2d 496 (Georgia).

2. Andersen entered into a franchise agreement with Great Lake Nursery, under which Andersen was to grow and sell nursery stock and Christmas trees. Great Lake was to provide trees, chemicals, and other items. Andersen signed an installment note which read in part: "For Value received, Robert Andersen promises to pay to Great Lake Nursery Corp. $6,412." Great Lake indorsed the note and transferred it to First Investment Company. Later, Andersen stopped making payments because Great Lake filed bankruptcy and failed to perform its part of the franchise agreement. May Andersen use "failure of consideration" as a defense when sued by First Investment Company on the note? Why or why not? *First Inv. Co. v. Andersen,* 621 P.2d 683 (Utah).

3. In exchange for an asphalt paving job, Paulick gave Bucci a note promising to pay to the order of Bucci $7,593 in six months with 10 percent per annum interest. Payment was not made on the due date, and Bucci brought suit. Paulick claimed failure of consideration as a defense, claiming that the paving job was improperly done. The court held that Bucci was a holder in due course because he had taken the instrument for value, in good faith, and without notice of any claims or defenses of Paulick. Can Paulick use the defense of failure of consideration against Bucci? Why or why not? *Bucci v. Paulick,* 149 A.2d 1255 (Pennsylvania).

4. Carolyn Brazil wrote a check to a contractor who agreed to make certain improvements on her home. She wrote the check in reliance on the contractor's false representation that the materials for the job had been purchased. They, in fact, had not been purchased. Brazil had the bank on which the check was drawn stop payment on it. Another bank, which cashed the check and became a holder in due course of the instrument, attempted to recover the amount of the check from Brazil. Can it do so? Explain. *Citizens Nat'l Bank v. Brazil,* 233 S.E.2d 482 (Georgia).

5. As part of the purchase price for a 9,040-acre ranch, Kirby gave Bergfield a $20,000 check drawn on the Bank of Bellevue. Bergfield had her banker telephone the Bank of Bellevue to inquire about Kirby's account balance to be sure that the check was good. It was learned that there was not enough money in Kirby's account to cover the check. Bergfield continued to hold the check and did not present it to the Bank of Bellevue for payment. Later, Bergfield argued that the telephone call to the bank was a presentment and demand for payment of the check. Do you agree? Why or why not? *Kirby v. Bergfield,* 182 N.W.2d 205 (Nebraska).

6. Haik transferred his stock in Petrocomp, an oil exploration company, to Rowley in exchange for five $10,000 promissory notes. The notes were signed by Rowley and indorsed by Rowley's son, Stephen. Rowley failed to pay the notes when they became due. No presentment for payment was made by Haik on the due date nor was a timely notice of dishonor given to Rowley's son, Stephen. May Haik hold Stephen liable on the notes as an indorser? Explain. *Haik v. Rowley,* 377 So.2d 391 (Louisiana).

7. David and Nettie Weiner signed seven promissory notes, totaling $89,000, in their capacity as president and secretary of NMD

Realty Co. In addition, they indorsed each note on the reverse side with their individual signatures. Each note contained the following provision: "The Maker and endorser or endorsers each hereby waives presentment, demand and notice of dishonor." The Weiners claim that, because they are secondarily liable, the bank may not proceed against them individually until after presentment, notice of dishonor, and protest have occurred. Do you agree with the Weiners? Explain. *Bank of Delaware v. NMD Realty Co.,* 325 A.2d 108 (Delaware).

8. Rutherford purchased real property from Ethel Stokes for $35,000. He paid $5,000 down and signed a promissory note for the balance. The note was secured by a deed of trust (a type of security interest, discussed in detail in Chapter 29). When payments on the note were overdue, Stokes considered foreclosing on the property. Prior to doing so, however, she negotiated the note to Craig, who purchased it at a discount with notice that it was in default. Was Craig a holder in due course of the note? Why or why not? *Matter of Marriage of Rutherford,* 573 S.W.2d 299 (Texas).

CHAPTER 27
Checks and Bank Collections

OUTLINE

COMMENTARY

Rebecca Hockmeyer made most of her bank deposits and withdrawals from an automatic teller machine located near her home. On one occasion, the bank deducted more than it should have from her account. On another occasion, her card was stolen, and the thief learned of her secret number and withdrew $800 from her account. Hockmeyer did not realize that a federal law protected her in both of these situations. More importantly, she did not know that she could lose the protection of the federal law if she did not take action within specific time frames. This law and others dealing with checks and bank collections are discussed in this chapter.

OBJECTIVES

1. Explain the form necessary for an instrument to be a check.
2. Differentiate between a bank draft and a cashier's check.
3. Compare the liability of parties to a check certified by the drawer with that of a check certified by the payee.
4. Discuss the protection given to consumers by the Electronic Fund Transfer Act.
5. Outline a check's life cycle.
6. Explain the duties of a bank relative to (*a*) honoring orders, (*b*) death of a customer, (*c*) forged and altered checks, and (*d*) the bank's midnight deadline.
7. Explain the duties of a depositor relative to bad checks and examining accounts.
8. Compare an oral stop-payment order with a written stop-payment order.

27-1 CHECKS

UCC 3-104(2)(b) **(see p. 638)**

A **check** is a draft drawn on a bank and payable on demand. It is the most common form of a draft. It is drawn on a bank by a drawer who has an account with the bank, to the order of a specified person or business named on the check or to the bearer. A check is a safe means of transferring money, and it serves as a receipt after it has been paid and canceled by the bank.

In the check shown in Figure 27-1, Evans is the drawer; she has an account in the Western National Bank. Alicia Adams Fashions, Inc., is the payee. Western National Bank, on whom the check is drawn, is the drawee.

Ownership of a check may be transferred to another person by indorsement by the payee. In this manner, checks may circulate among several parties, taking the place of money. A bank must honor a check when it is properly drawn against a credit balance of the drawer. Failure to do so would make the bank liable to the drawer for resulting damages.

Requirements as to Form

UCC 3-104(2)(b) (see p. 638)

Banks provide regular and special printed check forms. These check forms display a series of numbers printed in magnetic ink, which makes it possible to process checks speedily and accurately by computers. The first set of figures is the bank's Federal Reserve number. This is followed by the bank's own number. The second set of numbers is the depositor's account number. The use of printed forms is not required. Any writing, no matter how crude, may be used as a check if it is a draft drawn on a bank and payable on demand.

While on a fishing trip in the Maine woods, Nichols lost his belongings when the canoe in which he was riding tipped over. A camper sold Nichols a jacket, some camping equipment, and enough food to make it to the nearest town. Since Nichols had lost his money, he wrote out a check on a piece of notebook paper ordering his bank to pay to the order of the camper $50. Although unusual, this writing amounted to a valid check which would have to be honored by Nichols's bank.

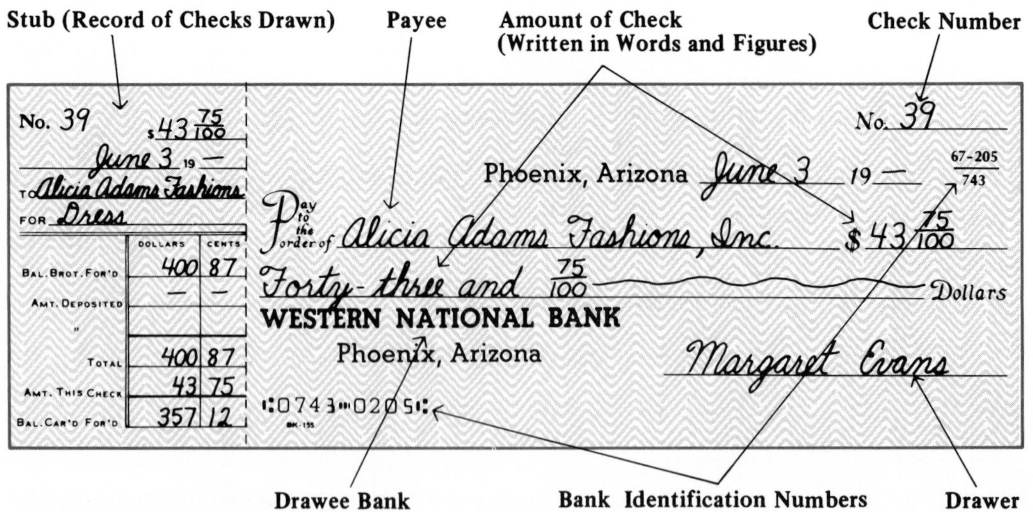

Figure 27-1 A check.

Special Types of Checks

Special types of checks have been developed for use in particular situations. These checks include bank drafts, traveler's checks, and cashier's checks.

Bank Drafts A **bank draft,** sometimes called a **teller's check,** is a check drawn by one bank on another bank in which it has funds on deposit, in favor of a third person, the payee. Many banks deposit money in banks in other areas for the convenience of depositors who depend upon the transfer of funds when transacting business in distant places. When the buyer is unknown to the seller, such checks are more acceptable than personal checks.

Cashier's Checks A **cashier's check** is a check drawn by a bank upon itself. The bank, in effect, lends its credit to the purchaser of the check. Courts have held that payment cannot be stopped on a cashier's check because the bank, by issuing it, accepts the check in advance. In that sense, it is similar to a certified check, discussed below. People who will not accept personal checks will often accept cashier's checks. Such a check may be made payable either to the depositor, who purchases it from the bank, or to the person who is to cash it. If the check is made payable to the depositor, it must be indorsed to the person to whom it is transferred.

Traveler's Checks **Traveler's checks** are similar to cashier's checks in that the issuing financial institution is both the drawer and the drawee. The purchaser signs the checks when they are purchased, in the presence of the issuer. To cash a check, the purchaser writes the name of the payee in the space provided and countersigns it in the payee's presence. Only the purchaser can negotiate traveler's checks, and they are easily replaced by the issuing bank if they are stolen.

Traveler's checks are issued in denominations of $10 and up, and the purchaser of the checks ordinarily pays a fixed fee to the issuer.

Certified Checks

A **certified check** is a check which is guaranteed by the bank. At the request of either the depositor or the holder, the bank acknowledges and guarantees that sufficient funds will be withheld from the drawer's account to pay the amount stated on the check. A prudent person would request a certified check when involved in a business transaction with a stranger rather than accept a personal check.

UCC 3-411 (see p. 645)

The UCC provides that "certification of a check is acceptance." This means that a drawee bank that certifies a check becomes primarily liable on the instrument just the same as the acceptor of a draft. The bank has absolute liability to pay. Whether anyone is secondarily liable depends upon who had the check certified. If the drawer had the check certified, the drawer and all indorsers remain secondarily liable on the instrument. If, on the other hand, the holder had the check certified, the drawer and all prior indorsers are discharged. The UCC places no obligation on a bank to certify a check if it does not want to do so. Figure 27-2 illustrates a certified check.

UCC 3-411(2) (see p. 645)

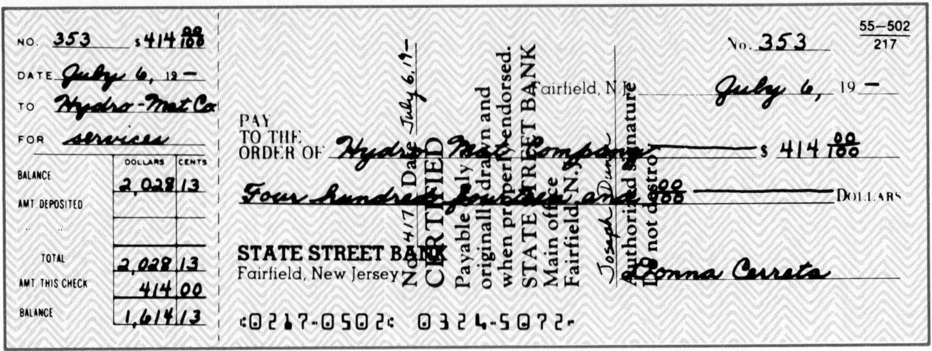
NO. 353 $414 00/100
DATE July 6, 19–
TO Hydro-Mat Co
FOR services

	DOLLARS	CENTS
BALANCE	2,028	13
AMT DEPOSITED		
TOTAL	2,028	13
AMT THIS CHECK	414	00
BALANCE	1,614	13

No. 353 55–502/217
Fairfield, N.J. July 6, 19–
PAY TO THE ORDER OF Hydro-Mat Company $ 414 00/100
Four hundred fourteen and 00/100 DOLLARS
STATE STREET BANK
Fairfield, New Jersey
Donna Curreta
⑆0217-0502⑆ 0324-5072⑈

CERTIFIED
Date July 6, 19–
No. 417
Payable only when properly endorsed.
STATE STREET BANK
Main office
Fairfield, N.J.
Joseph Dunn
Authorized signature

Figure 27-2 A certified check.

Postdated Checks

A check may be postdated when the drawer has insufficient funds in the bank at the time the check is drawn but expects to have sufficient funds to cover the amount of the check at a future date. Postdating is also practiced when some act or performance is to be completed before the date for payment of the check. Such a check, at the time it is drawn, has the effect of turning a demand instrument into a time instrument. This is because it is an order to pay a specified amount of money at the future date stated.

UCC 3-114 **(see p. 639)**

In 1969, Gentilotti wrote a check payable to the order of his five-year-old son for $20,000. The check was postdated to 1984. It was delivered to the child's mother, who kept it for the child. The check was indorsed by the father as follows: "For Edward Joseph Smith Gentilotti / My Son / If I should pass away / The amount of $20,000.00 dollars / Shall be taken from / My Estate at death. / S. Gentilotti 11-25-69." Gentilotti died in 1973. The court held that the negotiability of the check was not affected by the fact that it was postdated 15 years. In addition, the court said that the indorsement modified the check by providing for acceleration (advancement) of the time for payment. The court, therefore, ordered that the $20,000 be paid to the son.

27-2 ELECTRONIC FUND TRANSFERS

A popular method of banking, known as **electronic fund transfers (EFTs),** uses computers and electronic technology as a substitute for checks and other banking methods. People can go to an automatic teller machine 24 hours a day to make bank deposits and withdrawals. They can pay bills by phone, have deposits made directly to their bank accounts, and pay for retail purchases directly from their bank account.

To protect consumers against the possibility of fraud, Congress passed the Electronic Fund Transfer Act in 1978. The law governs the use of 24-hour teller machines, pay-by-phone systems, direct deposits or withdrawals, and point-of-sale transfers. Under the act, consumers are entitled to receive a written receipt whenever they use an automated teller machine. In addition, the transaction must appear on the periodic statement sent to the consumer. The consumer has 60 days to notify the bank of any error on the periodic statement or terminal receipt. After being notified, the bank has 10 business days to investigate the error. If the bank needs more time, it may take up to 45 days to complete the investigation, but only if the money in dispute is returned to the consumer's account.

Consumers are also protected when an EFT card is stolen or used without authority. Under the act, a consumer's liability for the unauthorized use of an EFT card is limited to $50 if notice of the loss or theft of a card is given the issuer within two business days. The consumer's liability increases to $500 when notice is withheld beyond two business days and becomes unlimited when notice is not given within 60 days. The unauthorized use of an EFT card is a criminal offense punishable by a $10,000 fine and/or ten years in prison.

A thief stole Hockmeyer's purse from a grocery store shopping carriage. Three days later, Hockmeyer notified her bank that her EFT card was missing. By then, however, the thief had found the card along with Hockmeyer's secret identification number and had withdrawn $800 from her account. Because the bank was notified within three days of the theft, Hockmeyer lost $500. Had she notified the bank within two business days of the theft, she would have lost only $50.

27-3 BANK DEPOSITS AND COLLECTIONS

The tremendous number of checks handled by banks and the countrywide nature of the bank collection process require uniformity in the law of bank collections. For this reason, Article 4 of the UCC contains rules and regulations for handling bank deposits and collections.

Bank Descriptions

During the bank collection process, banks are described by different terms, depending on their particular function in a transaction. Sometimes a bank takes a check for deposit. At other times, it pays a check as a drawee. At still other times, it takes a check for collection only. The different terms that are used to describe banks and their meanings are as follows:

UCC 4-105

Depositary bank means the first bank to which an item is transferred for collection even though it is also the payor bank.

Payor bank means a bank by which an item is payable as drawn or accepted. It includes a drawee bank.

Intermediary bank means any bank to which an item is transferred in the course of collection except the depositary or payor bank.

Collecting bank means any bank handling the item for collection except the payor bank.

Presenting bank means any bank presenting an item except a payor bank.

Remitting bank means any payor or intermediary bank remitting for an item.

A Check's Life Cycle

UCC 4-213

The life cycle of a check begins when the drawer writes a check and delivers it to the payee. The payee may take the check directly to the payor bank (the bank on which it was drawn) for payment. If that bank pays the check in cash, its payment is final, and the check is returned to the drawer with the next bank statement. However, it is more likely that the check will be deposited in the payee's own account in another bank. That bank, known as the depositary bank, acts as its customer's agent to collect the money from the payor bank. Any settlement given by the depositary bank in this case is **provisional** (not final). It may be revoked if the check is later dishonored. The check is sent (sometimes through an intermediary bank) to a collecting bank, which presents the check to the payor bank for payment. If it is honored by the payor bank, the amount will be deducted from the drawer's account and the check will be returned to the drawer with the next bank statement. If the check is dishonored for any reason, it will be returned to the payee via the same route that it was sent and all credits given for the item will be revoked. (See Figure 27-3, page 377.)

UCC 4-201

27-4 THE BANK-DEPOSITOR RELATIONSHIP

The relationship between the drawee bank and its customer is that of both (1) debtor and creditor and (2) agent and principal. The relationship arises out of the express or implied contract that occurs when the customer opens a checking account with the bank. The bank becomes a debtor when money is deposited in the bank by the customer. At this time, the customer is owed money by the bank and is therefore a creditor. When an **overdraft** occurs, that is, when the bank pays out more than the customer has on deposit, the debtor-creditor role reverses, and the bank becomes the creditor.

UCC 4-201

The bank acts as the customer's agent when it collects or attempts to collect checks or other negotiable instruments made payable to the customer. If the items are deposited in the customer's account, any settlement made by the bank with the customer is provisional. A provisional settlement may be revoked by the bank if an item that the bank is attempting to collect is dishonored. The bank may charge back the amount of any credit given for the item to its customer's account or obtain a refund from its customer.

UCC 4-212

Baker Company deposited in its checking account a check it had received in the mail from a customer. Baker Company's bank credited its account for the amount of the check and sent it through the clearinghouse for collection. The check was returned to the bank because of insufficient funds. Baker Company's bank charged back (debited) the amount it had credited to Baker Company's account.

Moriarty, who lived in Oakland, CA, ordered some custom-made upholstery for her 1932 Ford from Antique Auto, Inc. in Rowley, MA. She sent a check drawn on her Oakland bank along with the order. This chart traces the check through its collection and clearing house route.

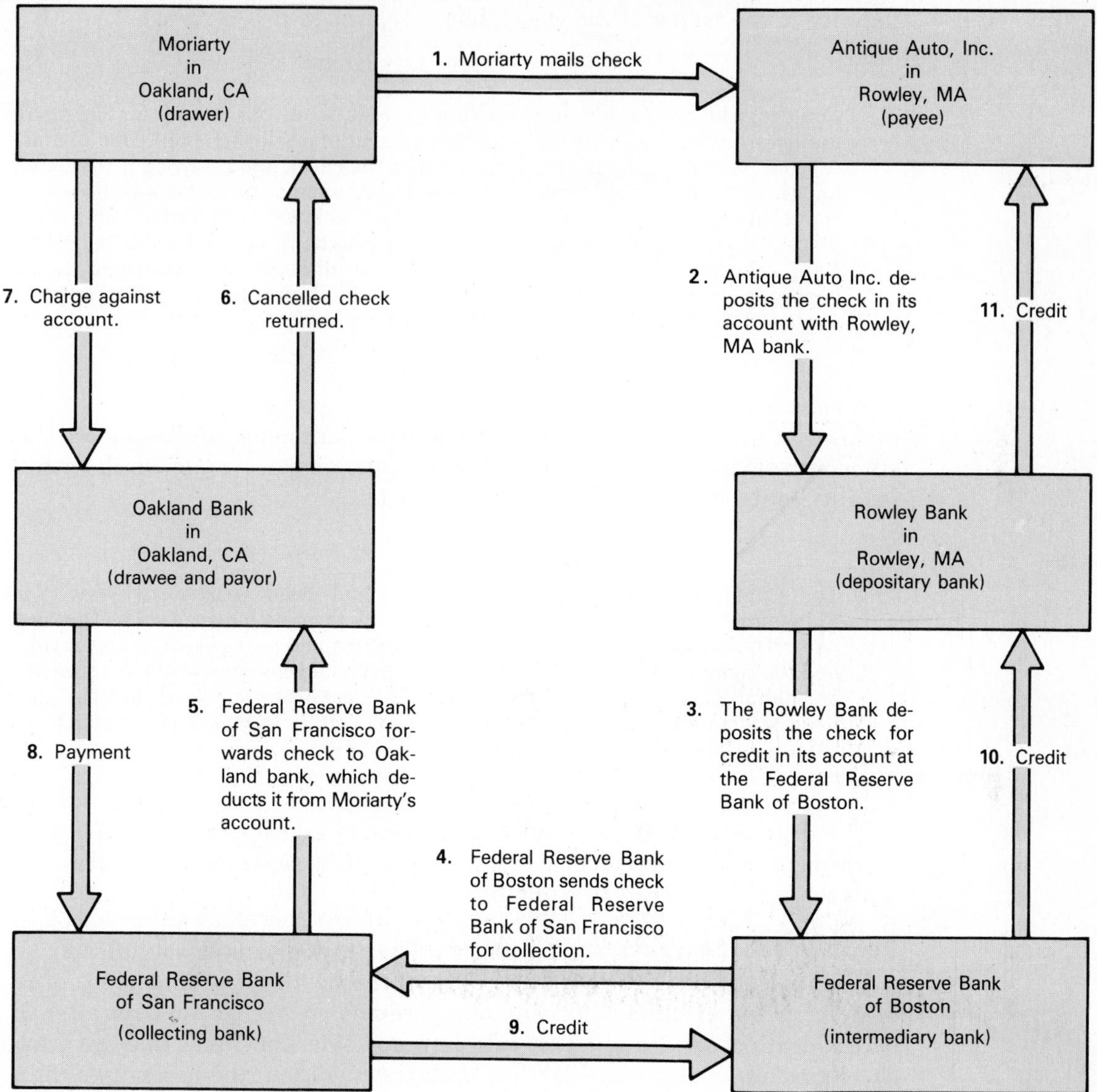

Figure 27-3 The life cycle of a check.

The Bank's Duties

The bank's duties to its customers are as follows:

UCC 4-401

Duty to Honor Orders The drawee bank is under a duty to honor all checks drawn by its customers when there are sufficient funds on deposit in the customer's account. If there are not sufficient funds on deposit, the bank may

UCC 4-402 charge the customer's account even if it creates an overdraft. If a bank fails to honor a check because of a mistake on its part, the bank is liable to the customer for any actual damages the customer suffers. The drawee bank has no liability to the holder of the check, however, unless it is certified.

Rougier, who had $178 in her checking account, wrote out a check for $78.42 and mailed it to the telephone company in payment of a telephone bill. Due to a mistake on its part, Rougier's bank dishonored the check and returned it to the telephone company marked "insufficient funds." As soon as the error was discovered, the telephone company was notified and the check was redeposited and honored by the bank. Since Rougier suffered no loss, the bank was not liable for dishonoring the check. Had Rougier's telephone been disconnected because of the dishonored check, the bank would have been liable to her for the cost of restoring service. The bank is not liable to the telephone company.

UCC 4-404 A bank is under no obligation to a customer to pay a stale check unless it is certified. A **stale check** is a check which is presented for payment more than six months after its date. A bank, however, may honor a stale check without liability to its customer if it acts in good faith.

The Chemical Bank paid a check that had been written by New York Flameproofing Co. ten years earlier on a check form no longer used by that company. The account on which the check was drawn had been closed for seven years, and the company's address written on the check had changed seven years earlier. In holding against the bank for paying the check, the court said that such payment was a reckless disregard of due care so much as to constitute bad faith. The bank was liable for the amount paid.

The drawee bank is not liable to a holder of a check for dishonoring the instrument unless it is certified. The holder's recourse is against the drawer or indorsers on their secondary liability.

UCC 4-405 **Death or Incompetence of Customer** The drawee bank is not liable for the payment of a check before it has notice of the death or incompetence of the drawer. In any event, a bank may pay or certify checks for ten days after the date of death of the drawer. This rule permits holders of checks that are drawn shortly before the drawer's death to cash them without the necessity of filing a claim with the court handling the deceased's estate.

Forged and Altered Checks A **forgery** is the fraudulent making or alteration of a writing. A forgery is committed when a person fraudulently writes or alters a check or other form of commercial paper to the injury of another. The commission of forgery is a crime, subject to a fine and imprisonment. The offering of a forged instrument to another person when the offeror knows it to be forged is also a crime, known as **uttering.** If a bank, in good faith, pays the altered amount of a check to a holder, it may deduct from the drawer's account only the amount of the check as it was originally written.

Lane wrote out a $400 check, in a nonnegligent fashion, to the order of Robinson in payment for repairs to Lane's house. Robinson raised the check to $4,000. If Lane's bank pays the full $4,000 to Robinson, it can deduct $400 from Lane's account, but no more. The bank must either get the money back from the wrongdoer, Robinson, or suffer the loss. The bank would be able to deduct the full $4,000 from Lane's account if the alteration was facilitated by Lane's carelessness in writing the check.

The depositor is also protected against a signature's being forged. When a checking account is opened, the depositor must fill out a signature card, which is permanently filed at the bank. Thereafter, the bank is held to know the depositor's signature. The bank is liable to the depositor if it pays any check on which the depositor's signature has been forged.

UCC 4-302

Midnight Deadline Payor banks are required to either settle or return checks quickly. If they do not do so, they are responsible for paying them. If the payor bank is not the depositary bank, it must settle for an item by midnight of the banking day of receipt.

LaPierre wrote a check to Kimberly Motors for $2,500 in payment for a secondhand car. The payor of the check (the bank on which it was drawn) was the National Bank & Trust Co. Kimberly Motors deposited the check into its account in the Southwest Mutual Bank (the depositary bank), which sent it on for collection. LaPierre's car broke down before she reached home that evening. She immediately stopped payment on the check. The National Bank & Trust Company must return the check to the Southwest Mutual Bank, with a notation that payment has been stopped, before midnight of the day that it received the check. If it keeps the check longer than that, it will be liable for payment.

UCC 4-104(h)

If the payor bank is also the depositary bank, it must either pay or return the check or send notice of its dishonor on or before its midnight deadline. In this case, the bank's **midnight deadline** is midnight of the next banking day following the banking day on which it receives the relevant item.

In the above case, if the National Bank & Trust Company had also been the depositary bank, it would have had an extra day to handle the check. The bank would have had until midnight of the next banking day to return the check to Kimberly Motors with the notation that payment had been stopped.

The Depositor's Duties

Depositors, in general, owe a duty to the banks in which they have checking accounts to have sufficient funds on deposit to cover checks that they write. They must also examine their bank statements and canceled checks promptly and with reasonable care and notify the bank quickly of any discrepancies.

Bad Checks Most states have statutes making it larceny or attempted larceny for a person to issue a check drawn on a bank in which the person has insufficient funds. Such statutes usually have the following provisions, which must be observed in the prosecution of anyone issuing a bad check:

1. The payee has the obligation of informing the drawer of the nonpayment of the check, together with notice of the provisions of the bad-check law and of the party's legal rights and obligations.
2. After receiving notice of nonpayment, or dishonor, the drawer is given a specified number of days, usually five or ten, in which to make the check good, without fear of prosecution.
3. Failure to make full payment of the check within the number of days allowed by statute serves as presumption of guilt that the drawer issued the check with full knowledge of the facts and with intent to defraud.

State National Bank received Yoder's check for $120 due on an installment note it held. After it was deposited, the check was returned to State National with the notification "insufficient funds." The bank's collection department sent a registered letter to Yoder in which responsibility under the bad-check statute was explained. Failure on the part of Yoder to make the check good within the period of time indicated would result in a criminal complaint being lodged against Yoder through the office of the state's prosecuting attorney.

Bad-check statutes are effectively used as a means of collection. Most bad-check writers make an effort to make full payment of the check when advised that they are subject to prosecution.

Many banks now offer overdraft protection service to their depositors, which covers small overdrafts that are usually caused by the mistake of the drawer in balancing the checkbook. With this service, the bank honors small overdrafts and charges the depositor's account. This saves the drawer the inconvenience and embarrassment of having a check returned to a holder marked "insufficient funds."

UCC 4-406

Duty to Examine Accounts The UCC imposes a duty on depositors to examine their bank statements and canceled checks promptly and with reasonable care when they are received from the bank. They must report promptly to the bank any forged or altered checks. If they do not do so, depositors cannot hold the bank responsible for losses due to the bank's payment of a forged or altered instrument.

The exact time within which a depositor must notify a bank is not established except in the case of the same wrongdoer forging or altering more than one check. In that case, the bank must be notified of the wrongdoing within 14 days after the depositor receives the bank statement and canceled checks.

Applegard's checkbook was stolen from her desk without her knowledge. The thief filled out three of the stolen checks, forged Applegard's signature, and cashed them. Applegard must notify the bank of the forgery at least within 14 days after she receives the bank statement and canceled checks. If she does not do so, her bank will not be liable for paying the forged checks.

The absolute limit for notifying a bank of a forged or altered check is one year from the time the depositor receives the bank statement. The limit is three years, however, in the case of a forged indorsement on a check.

Stop-Payment Rights Drawers may order a bank to stop payment on any item payable on their account.

UCC 4-403
UCC 4-403(3)

Manner of Stopping Payment The *stop-payment order* must be received in time and in such a manner as to afford the bank a reasonable opportunity to act on it. An oral order is binding upon the bank for 14 calendar days only, unless confirmed in writing within that period. A written order is binding for only six months, unless renewed in writing. The burden of establishing the fact and amount of loss resulting from the payment of an item contrary to a binding stop-payment order is on the customer.

UCC 4-407

Bank's Right of Subrogation If a bank fails to stop payment on a check, it is responsible for any loss suffered by the drawer who ordered the payment stopped. The bank, however, may take the place of any holder, holder in due course, payee, or drawer who has rights against others on the underlying obligation. This right to be substituted for another is known as the bank's right of **subrogation.** It is designed to prevent loss to the bank and unjust enrichment to other parties.

Jervey was induced by fraud to enter into a contract with Glidden. As part of the transaction, Jervey wrote and delivered a check to Glidden for $1,500. When Jervey discovered the fraud, she immediately ordered her bank to stop payment on the check. The bank, by mistake, ignored the stop-payment order and paid the $1,500 to Glidden. The bank must return the $1,500 to Jervey but may sue Glidden for fraud under its right of subrogation.

SUMMARY

27-1. The use of a printed form to write a check is not required. Any writing, no matter how crude, may be used as a check if it is a draft drawn on a bank and payable on demand. If the drawer of a check has it certified, the drawee bank becomes primarily liable and the drawer and indorsers remain secondarily liable on the instrument. However, if the holder has the check certified, the drawee bank becomes primarily liable and the drawer and indorsers are discharged. Checks may be postdated; this turns a check into a time instrument.

27-2. Consumers who use electronic fund transfers have 60 days to notify the bank of an error, after which the bank must investigate. A consumer's liability for the unauthorized use of an EFT card is limited to $50 if notice of the loss or theft of a card is given the issuer within two business days. The consumer's liability increases to $500 when notice is withheld beyond 2 business days and becomes unlimited when notice is not given within 60 days.

27-3. If a payee cashes a check at a payor (drawee) bank, the payment is final. If, instead, the payee deposits a check in his or her bank which sends it to the payor bank for collection, any payment is provisional.

27-4. The drawee bank must honor all checks (except stale checks) drawn by its customers when there are sufficient funds on deposit. Failure to do so makes the bank liable to the customer for any actual damages the customer suffers. The drawee bank has no liability to the holder of a check unless it is certified. Banks may pay checks for ten days after the death of a drawer. Banks are responsible for paying altered or forged checks. Banks must pay or return checks on or before their midnight deadline. Depositors must examine their bank statements and canceled checks promptly. It is a crime to write a check with insufficient funds in the bank. Oral stop-payment orders are binding upon the bank for 14 days; written stop-payment orders are binding for 6 months.

Understanding Key Legal Terms

bank draft (p. 373)
cashier's check (p. 373)
certified check (p. 373)
check (p. 371)
collecting bank (p. 375)
depositary bank (p. 375)
electronic fund transfers (p. 374)
forgery (p. 378)
intermediary bank (p. 375)
midnight deadline (p. 379)
overdraft (p. 376)
payor bank (p. 375)
presenting bank (p. 375)
provisional (p. 376)
remitting bank (p. 376)
stale check (p. 378)
subrogation (p. 381)
teller's check (p. 373)
traveler's check (p. 373)
uttering (p. 378)

Questions for Review and Discussion

1. What form must be used to write a check?
2. How does a bank draft differ from a cashier's check?
3. Explain the liability of the parties (*a*) when the drawer has a check certified and (*b*) when a holder has a check certified.
4. In what way are consumers protected by the Electronic Fund Transfer Act?
5. Describe the life cycle of a check that is deposited in the payee's bank.
6. Explain the liability of a bank for dishonoring an uncertified check due to a mistake on its part (*a*) to its customer, (*b*) to a holder of the check, (*c*) in the case of a stale check.
7. What is the bank's responsibility as to (*a*) the payment of checks after the death of the drawer and (*b*) the payment of forged and altered checks?
8. Explain the significance of the bank's midnight deadline.

9. What crimes may occur when someone writes a check with insufficient funds? Why is it important for depositors to examine their bank statements promptly?

10. How does an oral stop-payment order compare with a written stop-payment order as it affects the bank's obligations?

Analyzing Cases

1. Kelco bought a truck from Felton, paying for it with a cashier's check she had obtained from her bank. On her way home, the truck broke down. Kelco immediately telephoned her bank and told it to stop payment on the cashier's check. Later, Kelco discovered that her bank had not stopped payment on the cashier's check and instead had paid it. Does Kelco have a claim against the bank? Explain. See also *Taboada v. Bank of Babylon,* 408 N.Y.S.2d 734 (New York).

2. Granite Corp. sent a check to Overseas Equipment Co. When the check was reported lost, Granite wrote to its bank telling it to stop payment on the check. Granite then sent the money to Overseas Equipment Co. by wire. Thirteen months later, the check turned up and Granite's bank paid it. Did the bank violate its duty to stop payment on the check? Explain. *Granite Equip. Leasing Corp. v. Hempstead Bank,* 326 N.Y.S.2d 881 (New York).

3. On Monday, Morales gave Tanner a $125 check for a secondhand VCR. Since he had only $50 in the account but would be paid on Thursday, Morales postdated the check to the following Saturday and told Tanner that he was doing so. Tanner deposited the check the day he received it. It was returned marked insufficient funds. Did Morales violate the law? Explain.

4. While in the hospital during his final illness, Norris wrote out a check and gave it to his sister. She deposited it in her bank account. Norris died before the check cleared, and his bank refused to pay it. May a bank honor a check when it knows of the death of the drawer? Explain. *In Re Estate of Norris,* 532 P.2d 981 (Colorado).

5. On June 18, Templeton deposited in his bank account a $5,000 check that was payable to his order. The check reached the drawee bank through normal banking channels on June 22. That bank had received a stop-payment order on the check on May 15 and therefore refused to honor it. It kept the check until June 28, when it returned it to Templeton with the notification that payment had been stopped. Did the drawee bank violate a duty it owed to Templeton? Explain. *Templeton v. First Nat'l. Bank,* 362 N.E.2d 33 (Illinois).

6. In payment for services rendered, one of Stewart's clients gave him a check for $185.48 which had been drawn by the client's corporate employer and made payable to the order of the client. Although properly indorsed by the client, the drawee bank flatly refused to cash the check for Stewart. The bank acknowledged that the check was good, that is, that there were sufficient funds in the account. Can Stewart sue the bank for refusing to honor the check? Why or why not? *Stewart v. Citizens & Nat'l Bank,* 225 S.E.2d 761 (Georgia).

7. Fitting wrote an $800 check on her account with Continental Bank. A bank employee had mistakenly placed a "hold" on the account, causing the bank to dishonor the check when it was presented for payment. Fitting was unable to prove that she suffered damages because of the dishonor. Can she recover from the bank? Explain. *Continental Bank v. Fitting,* 559 P.2d 218 (Arizona).

PART 5
Case Study
Bank of New York v. Welz

Supreme Court, Special Term
460 N.Y.S.2d 867 (New York)

SUMMARY

Anne Welz purchased a teller's check (a bank draft) from the Greater New York Savings Bank (GNYSB) for $1,900. The check was drawn on the Manufacturer's Hanover Trust (MHT) and, at Welz's request, was made payable to the Bank of New York (BONY). By mistake, GNYSB wrote the check for $19,000 instead of $1,900. The next day, Welz's husband delivered the check to BONY in exchange for shares of Dreyfus Liquid Assets. GNYSB discovered its error and issued a stop payment order to MHT, the drawee bank. BONY kept the check for a month before sending it to MHT for collection and discovering that payment had been stopped. Meanwhile, Welz had redeemed the $19,000 worth of Dreyfus shares for cash. BONY and GNYSB argue that as between themselves, the other is liable for the loss. BONY contends that payment cannot be stopped on a teller's check. GNYSB argues that the loss was caused by BONY waiting more than one month before presenting the check to the drawee bank.

THE COURT'S OPINION: SEYMOUR SCHWARTZ, JUSTICE

If GNYSB is not entitled to stop payment, BONY's delay in presenting the check and its rapid redemption of Robert Welz's Dreyfus shares would not relieve GNYSB from liability to BONY. Therefore, the court will first address the question whether a teller's check may be stopped in these circumstances.

U.C.C. § 4-403(1) provides that "[a] customer may by order to his bank stop payment of any item payable for his account..." As defined in U.C.C. § 4-104(1)(e) "'Customer'...includes a bank carrying an account with another bank." Here, GNYSB carried an account with MHT and is therefore entitled to stop payment on teller's checks.

The Code distinguishes between teller's checks (drawn by a bank on an account carried with another bank) and cashier's checks (drawn by a bank where the bank is both drawer and drawee). A cashier's check is accepted in advance by the act of issuance... and once a check is accepted, which occurs when a bank issues a cashier's or certified check, it cannot stop payment even on its customer's order.

While the Code allows a teller's check to be stopped, New York courts nevertheless have frequently imposed liability on the drawer bank where it has stopped payment....In those cases, the courts dealt with the effect of U.C.C. § 3-802(1) which provides that an "obligation is discharged if a bank is drawer...and there is no recourse on the instrument against the underlying obligor." Thus, where a party accepts a check where the bank is the drawer (a teller's check), the party (the underlying obligor) giving it in payment is discharged if he does not endorse the teller's check.

The effect of U.C.C. 3-802(1) is that when Mr. Welz gave BONY the teller's check he became discharged on the underlying obligation to pay for the Dreyfus Liquid Assets. Thus, as payee, BONY's only remaining recourse is against GNYSB which stopped payment.

A teller's check may also be stopped where it is endorsed to a third party who sues on the instrument....

Limiting a bank's right to stop payment on a teller's check to instances where the payee is a party to the transaction with the bank, or where the payee endorses the check to a third party is unnecessary.... A payee such as BONY has a cause of action against the drawer (GNYSB) on the instrument even if the drawer stops payment. U.C.C. § 3-413. Moreover, a payee who has not dealt directly with the drawer may take the instrument as a holder in due course free from all defenses of any party to the instrument with whom the holder has not dealt with certain exceptions not relevant here. See U.C.C. 3-305.

In other words, the Code permits stop payment of a teller's check but the stop payment does not automatically preclude recovery on the instrument. Defenses may be raised by the endorser where an instrument is endorsed to a third party. Where the payee is a party to the transaction, defenses may be raised to recover on the instrument against the drawer. But where the payee is the holder in due course a stop payment does not permit defenses to be raised because such a payee has exchanged the underlying obligation for the instrument and must be protected.

GNYSB argues that BONY is not a holder in due course because of its failure to present the instrument for payment for more than a month after it was received. The argument lacks merit. U.C.C. 3-302(1)(b) provides that good faith requires honesty only. It does not require the exercise of due care....

None of the defenses available against a holder in due course (U.C.C. 3-305) are applicable here. Therefore, summary judgment is granted to BONY against GNYSB. Robert Welz is discharged from his obligation to pay BONY the amount of the teller's check.

QUESTIONS FOR ANALYSIS

1. What type of check was involved in this case?
2. What is the difference between a teller's check (bank draft) and a cashier's check?
3. Can a bank stop payment on: (*a*) a cashier's check? (*b*) a teller's check?
4. Why was Mr. Welz discharged on the underlying obligation to pay for the Dreyfus Liquid Assets?
5. May a payee be a holder in due course of an instrument?
6. Did the fact that BONY failed to present the instrument for payment for more than a month prevent it from being a holder in due course?
7. Who won the case? Why?
8. What was Welz's obligation to BONY?

PART 6
Insurance, Secured Transactions, and Bankruptcy

CHAPTER 28
The Nature of the Insurance Contract

OUTLINE

28-1 The Insurance Contract
- Parties to an Insurance Contract
- Contractual Elements

28-2 Types of Insurance
- Insurable Interests
- Life Insurance
- Property Insurance

28-3 Form of the Insurance Contract
- Application
- Binders
- Premiums
- Lapse

28-4 Cancellation of Insurance Policies
- Warranties
- Concealment
- Misrepresentation
- Estoppel

COMMENTARY

Phyllis Nirdlinger arranged for her husband to take out a life insurance policy. In the event of his death, she would receive $25,000. Under the policy's double indemnity clause, the insurance company, General Fidelity of California, would double the amount of the benefits in case of accidental death. Mrs. Nirdlinger then arranged for her husband's "accidental" death. What she didn't know was that a person who is supposed to receive benefits under an insurance policy forfeits those benefits if she murders the insured person. This rule motivated an agent of General Fidelity to investigate the possibility that Mrs. Nirdlinger had murdered her husband. After some determined investigative work, the truth came out and justice was done. If the plot sounds familiar, that's because it comes from James M. Cain's famous novel *Double Indemnity*. What Cain was able to accomplish in his novel was to educate the reading public to the intricacies of insurance law, while keeping them interested and entertained. This chapter has the same aspirations.

OBJECTIVES

1. Identify the contractual elements that are necessary to make an insurance agreement binding.
2. Contrast the requirements for an insurable interest for life insurance with that for property insurance.
3. Determine whether a beneficiary may or may not receive benefits under a life insurance policy involving exemptions from risks.
4. Identify the optional provisions that may be purchased as part of a life insurance policy.
5. Describe the kinds of losses that are covered by fire insurance and homeowner's insurance.
6. Differentiate among the principal kinds of automobile insurance and determine which insurance covers a particular loss.
7. List the steps to be followed in applying for, obtaining, and maintaining an insurance policy.
8. Judge whether an insurance policy can be canceled in given situations.

28-1 THE INSURANCE CONTRACT

Life is full of risks and uncertainties. Hazards such as accidents, fire, and illness pose a constant threat to our well-being. The principal protection against losses from such hazards is insurance. **Insurance** is a transfer of the risk of economic loss from the buyer to the seller, or the insurance company. The principle underlying insurance is the **distribution of risk**—that small contributions made by a large number of individuals can provide sufficient money to cover the losses suffered by a few as they occur each year. The function of insurance is to distribute each person's risk among all others, who may or may not experience losses.

Parties to an Insurance Contract

The parties to an insurance contract are the insurer, or underwriter; the insured; and the beneficiary. The **insurer** accepts the risk of loss in return for a **premium** (the consideration paid for a policy) and agrees to **indemnify,** or compensate, the insured against the loss specified in the contract. The **insured** is the party (or parties) protected by the insurance contract. The contract of insurance is called the **policy.** The period of time during which the insurer assumes the risk of loss is known as the **life of the policy.** A third party, to whom payment of compensation is sometimes provided by the contract, is called the **beneficiary.**

Contractual Elements

Insurance policies, like other contracts, require offer, acceptance, mutual assent, capable parties, consideration, and legally valid subject matter. The application filled out by the insured is an offer to the insurer who may then accept or reject the offer. To have mutual assent, the parties must have reached agreement on the terms of the contract. A party to a contract must also be capable of understanding the terms of the agreement. Consideration arises from the premiums paid by the insured and the promise of the insurer to pay money to the beneficiary upon the happening of a certain event. Finally, the subject matter must not be tainted with illegality. For example, a fire insurance policy written on a building where the owners permitted the illegal manufacture of fireworks would be void in the event of a fire.

28-2 TYPES OF INSURANCE

It is possible to obtain insurance against almost any risk if an individual or business is willing to pay the price. The premium charged will depend on the risk involved. **Life insurance** is available to provide indemnity for losses suffered by another's death. **Property insurance** can be obtained to cover the risk of loss or damage to real or personal property. For either type of insurance to be effective, the beneficiary must have an insurable interest in the person or property insured.

Insurable Interests

A person or business applying for insurance must have an insurable interest in the subject matter of the policy. An **insurable interest** is the financial interest that a policyholder has in the person or property that is insured. Generally, an insurable interest will exist if the insured has a financial interest in the insured person or property. The nature and duration of insurable interests vary with the type of insurance purchased.

Insurable Interests and Life Insurance A life insurance contract provides funds to a beneficiary on the death of the person insured. An individual has an insurable interest in the life of another if a financial loss will occur if the insured dies. An insurable interest exists if the insurer is dependent on the insured for education, support, business (partners), or debt collection. A life insurance policy will remain valid and enforceable even if the insurable interest terminates. It is necessary only that the insurable interest exist at the time the policy was issued.

Lorna and Alex Karamon were married in 1987. Lorna took out a life insurance policy on Alex's life, naming herself as beneficiary. She continued to pay the premiums even after they were divorced in 1988. When Alex died in 1989, Lorna was able to collect on the insurance policy. Although Lorna no longer had an insurable interest in Alex's life at the time of his death, she had an insurable interest at the time the policy was originally issued.

If an individual takes out insurance on himself, it is not necessary for the beneficiary to have an insurable interest in the insured's life. However, if a person takes out life insurance on someone else, the insurer must have an insurable interest.

Insurable Interests and Property Insurance To establish the existence of an insurable interest in property, the insured must demonstrate a monetary interest in the property. This monetary interest means that the insured may suffer a financial loss if the property is damaged or destroyed. Unlike life insurance, this insurable interest must exist when the loss occurs.

Terrell purchased an automobile insurance policy to cover his classic 1935 Dusenberg. Before the insurance policy had run its complete term, Terrell sold the car to Streseman. After the purchase was complete and title to the Dusenberg had been transferred, Streseman purchased his own insurance for the car. Two days later the Dusenberg was sideswiped by a drunk driver. Both Streseman and Terrell filed claims to recover monetary benefits for the damage to the car under their respective insurance contracts. Streseman's claim would be honored because he had an insurable interest when the loss occurred. Terrell, however, no longer had an insurable interest. His claim would be denied.

Life Insurance

As noted previously, life insurance provides funds to a beneficiary on the death of the insured. Often insurance policies will include exemption clauses to protect the insurance company from unreasonable risks. Most insurance policies are similar to one another. However, several optional provisions can be included in a life insurance policy that will make it more attractive to the purchaser. Exemptions from risk and optional provisions are covered here.

Exemptions from Risk Many life insurance policies contain clauses which exempt the insurance company from liability in certain situations. For example, policies often do not cover the insured when riding in an airplane, violating the law, or working in certain dangerous occupations. The four most common exemptions from risk are legal execution, causing the death of the insured, suicide of the insured, and war activities.

1. **Legal execution of insured** A number of courts have held that beneficiaries cannot receive the benefits from a life insurance policy when the insured is legally executed. These courts base their reasoning on the theory that it would be against public policy for beneficiaries to receive insurance proceeds in such cases. They also note that death by legal execution is not one of the risks assumed by the insurance company. In contrast, other courts do not allow beneficiaries to receive life insurance benefits in cases of execution because denial of recovery is not a deterrent to crime.
2. **Causing death of insured** In most cases, the courts allow a beneficiary to receive benefits under a life insurance contract when the insured is murdered, except when the murderer is also the beneficiary. A beneficiary who murders the insured forfeits all rights under the life insurance policy.
3. **Suicide of the insured** Most courts allow named beneficiaries other than the insured or his or her estate to recover the proceeds of a life insurance policy when the insured commits suicide provided that the policy contains no provision preventing such recovery and provided that the life insurance was not purchased by someone planning suicide. One primary example of a named beneficiary falling in this category would be a creditor of the insured.

   Generally, suicide exemption clauses will protect the insurance company against all beneficiaries even if the insured was "insane" at the time of the suicide. However, some jurisdictions will allow the beneficiaries to recover under the policy if the insured was so mentally disturbed at the time of the act that he or she had no understanding that death would result. To prevent recovery in such cases, insurance companies frequently include insanity provisions in the suicide exemption clause. Such provisions say that the company will not be required to pay beneficiaries if the insured commits suicide, regardless of whether he or she is sane at the time of death. A majority of courts have held that this type of "insanity" provision completely eliminates any issue as to the mental health of the insured at the time of death. A minority of jurisdictions, however, will still allow recovery if the insured was so mentally disturbed that he or she had no understanding that the act would result in death. These courts would characterize the suicide as an accident. Finally, most policies provide that beneficiaries can recover for a death caused by suicide if the suicide occurs more than two years after the policy was taken out.

4. **War activities** Life insurance policies usually include an exemption from liability in times of war. The exemption states that the insurer will not be liable on the policy if the insured is killed (*a*) while a member of the armed forces, generally outside the continental United States and (*b*) from service-connected causes.

Optional Provisions Life insurance policies have many optional provisions that may be purchased by the insured. Three popular options are double indemnity, waiver of premium, and guaranteed insurability.

1. **Double indemnity** For an additional premium the insured may purchase a benefit known as **double indemnity,** or accidental death benefit. This provides that if the insured dies from accidental causes, the insurer will pay double the amount of the policy to the beneficiary. Death must occur within 90 days of the accident, however, for this benefit to apply.
2. **Waiver of premium** The **waiver-of-premium** option excuses the insured from paying premiums if he or she becomes disabled. Some insurance policies automatically include the waiver in their provisions; others offer it as an extra-cost option.
3. **Guaranteed insurability** A **guaranteed-insurability** option allows the insured to pay an extra premium initially in exchange for a guaranteed op-

Table 28-1 LIFE INSURANCE: OPTIONAL PROVISIONS

Provision	*Explanation*
Double indemnity	Insurer pays double the amount of the policy to the beneficiary if the insured dies from accidental causes
Waiver of premium	Insurer excuses insured from paying premiums if insured becomes disabled
Guaranteed insurability	Insured pays extra initial premium in exchange for a guaranteed option to buy more insurance later with no questions asked

tion to buy more insurance at certain specified times later on. The additional insurance can be purchased with no questions asked; thus no new medical examination is required even if the insured develops a serious illness before exercising the option.

Property Insurance

Property insurance can be purchased to protect both real and personal property. Some property insurance policies protect the insured against a specific danger, as in the case of fire insurance. Other policies are designed to protect certain items of property against a variety of losses. Such is the case with fire, homeowner's, and automobile insurance.

Fire Insurance A fire insurance policy is a contract in which the fire insurance company promises to pay the insured if some real or personal property is damaged or destroyed by fire. A fire insurance policy is effective on delivery to the insured, even before the premium is paid. Even an oral agreement will make fire insurance effective.

The insurer's liability under a fire policy usually covers losses other than those directly attributed to fire. Under most policies, claims may also be made for losses from (1) water used to fight the fire, (2) scorching, (3) smoke damage to goods, (4) deliberate destruction of property as a means of controlling a spreading fire, (5) lightning, even if there is no resultant fire, (6) riot or explosion, if a fire does result, and (7) losses through theft or exposure of goods removed from a burning building.

Homeowner's Insurance Many of the leading insurance companies offer a new combination policy known as the **homeowner's policy.** This insurance gives protection for all types of losses and liabilities related to home ownership. Among the items covered are losses from fire, windstorm, burglary, vandalism, and injuries suffered by other persons while on the property.

Automobile Insurance Automobile insurance provides for indemnity against losses resulting from fire, theft, or collision with another vehicle and damages arising out of injury by motor vehicles to the person or property of another.The most common types of automobile insurance are bodily injury liability, property damage liability, collision, comprehensive coverage, medical payments, uninsured motorist, and no fault.

1. **Bodily injury liability insurance** covers the risk of bodily injury or death to pedestrians and to the occupants of other cars arising from the negligent operation of the insured's motor vehicle. Under liability insurance the insurer is liable for damages up to the limit of the insurance purchased. The insurance company must also provide attorneys for the insured's defense in any civil court action.
2. **Property damage liability insurance** provides protection when other people bring claims or lawsuits against the insured for damaging property such as a car, a fence, or a tree. The person bringing the claim or suit must prove that the driver of the motor vehicle was at fault.

3. **Collision insurance** provides against any loss arising from damage to the insured's automobile caused by accidental collision with another object or with any part of the roadbed. Liability under collision insurance is limited to the insured's car.
4. **Comprehensive coverage** provides protection against loss when the insured's car is damaged or destroyed by fire, lightning, flood, hail, windstorm, riot, vandalism, or theft. The insurance company's liability is limited to the actual cash value of the vehicle at the time of the loss.
5. **Medical payments insurance** pays for medical (and sometimes funeral) expenses resulting from bodily injuries to anyone occupying the policyholder's car at the time of an accident. In some states it pays for the medical bills of all family members who are struck by a car or who are riding in someone else's car when it is involved in an accident.
6. **Uninsured-motorist insurance** provides protection against the risk of being injured by an uninsured motorist. The coverage applies when the person who caused the accident was at fault and had no bodily injury liability to cover the loss. It protects the insured, the insured's spouse, relatives in the same household, and any other person occupying an insured automobile. It also protects people who are injured by hit-and-run drivers. No coverage is provided to persons injured in an automobile used without the permission of the insured or the insured's spouse. Uninsured-motorist insurance provides no reimbursement for damages to the insured's property.
7. **No-fault insurance** allows drivers to collect damages and medical expenses from their own insurance carriers regardless of who is at fault in an accident. This helps to cut down on fraudulent and excessively high claims. It also eliminates costly litigation needed to determine the negligence or lack of negligence of people involved in automobile accidents.

28-3 FORM OF THE INSURANCE CONTRACT

In most states, insurance contracts come in a standard form. These standard forms are carefully drafted by an insurance commissioner with help from the state's legal advisers. In this way, the consumer-buyer is protected from deception or fraud. As an additional protection to consumers, some states now require that insurance contracts must be written in clear, understandable language and printed in a readable typeface.

Application

The first step in obtaining an insurance policy is to fill out an **application.** The application is an offer made by the applicant to the insurance company. As with any offer, the offeree, in this case the insurance company, may accept or reject the offer.

Binders

The waiting period between the offer and the acceptance opens the insured to potential risk. To avoid this risk, the insured can arrange to have the insurer issue a binder. A **binder,** or binding slip, will provide temporary insurance coverage until the policy is formally accepted. The binder will include all the usual terms that would be included in the actual policy to be issued. The key phrase here is "the usual terms." If the final policy excludes something that is usually covered in such policies, that exclusion would not be effective during the binder period.

The owners of the Culver City Soccer Stadium signed an application for a fire insurance policy covering the stadium and its contents. The agent accepted the application and issued a binder for the insurance. Before the policy was issued, the stadium burned down. Usually, when such policies are issued, the coverage extends to all contents, including trophies, awards, plaques, souvenirs, and other similar Hall of Fame material. In this case the insurance company refused to reimburse the stadium owners for the loss of their Hall of Fame material because the value of the trophies, awards, plaques and souvenirs vastly exceeded what most similar trophy rooms would be worth. Nevertheless, since such policies usually cover Hall of Fame material, the insurance company would have to reimburse the stadium owners for their loss.

Premiums

An insurance contract differs from most other contracts in that it requires the payment of premiums. The amount of the premium is determined by the nature and character of the risk and by how likely the risk is to occur. The premium increases as the chance of loss increases. Thus, a premium on a fireproof building in a city with a fire department will be much lower than the premium on a barn located where fire-fighting equipment is not available.

Lapse

When the insured stops paying premiums, an insurance contract is said to *lapse.* This does not mean, however, that the contract will terminate automatically on the date that the last premium is paid. It will also not lapse automatically if the insured makes a delayed payment. Most contracts allow for a *grace period* of 30 or 31 days in which the insured may make payments to keep the policy in force. Beyond this period, however, the insurance contract will lapse and the policy terminate.

28-4 CANCELLATION OF INSURANCE POLICIES

Under certain conditions, the insurer is given a legal right to forfeit, or cancel, an insurance policy. Proof of a forfeiture permits cancellation either before a loss or at the time the claim is made on a policy. Among grounds permitting forfeiture are the breach of warranty and the concealment or misrepresentation of a material fact by the insured. Neither the insured nor the insurer may deny statements or acts previously made or committed that might affect the validity of the policy.

Warranties

A **warranty** is an insured's promise to abide by restrictions especially written into a policy. By statute in many states, an insurance company has the burden of proof in establishing that a warranty has been breached (broken) by the insured. If this is proven, the insurer may cancel the contract or refuse payment of loss to the insured or to a beneficiary.

Encarnacion, a famous European racing car driver, applied for life insurance after being involved in several racing accidents. Community Life was aware of these accidents, and Encarnacion agreed to do no more racing while the policy remained in force. Encarnacion was killed while racing in the Grand Prix. Community Life can rescind any obligation to pay Encarnacion's beneficiaries.

Concealment

Fraudulent **concealment** is any intentional withholding of a fact that would be of material importance to the insurer's decision to issue a policy. The applicant need only give answers to questions asked. However, the insured may not conceal facts that would be material in acceptance of a risk.

VanDorn, an insurance agent for Canadian Life, inspected Kalintor's building before issuing a fire insurance policy. Kalintor did not show VanDorn the basement, which was filled with flammable chemicals. After the policy was issued, Kalintor's building burned to the ground. Canadian Life later learned of the secret lab and would be permitted to cancel Kalintor's policy.

Misrepresentation

If an insured party gives false answers, or **misrepresentations,** to questions in an insurance application which materially affect the risk undertaken by the insurer, the contract is voidable by the insurer. A representation is material if the facts represented influence the insurer's decision to issue the policy or the rate of premium to charge.

The Clark family applied for fire insurance from the Alabama Farm Bureau Mutual Casualty Insurance Company. The Clarks answered "no" when asked whether they had ever been arrested. When their house was destroyed by fire and they attempted to collect under the policy, an investigation revealed that the Clarks had both been arrested on previous occasions. The court upheld the Farm Bureau's denial of benefits due to this deliberate material misrepresentation.

Although all jurisdictions agree on the effects of a deliberate deception, there is disagreement as to the effects of an innocent misrepresentation. A majority of the states hold that the intent of the insured is irrelevant. Even an innocent misrepresentation would make the policy voidable by the insurer. A minority of the states would not allow the insurer to deny coverage to an insured whose misrepresentation was unintentional.

Folk took out an insurance policy with Countryside Casualty. When asked if he had any physical impairments, Folk, who suffered from epilepsy, said no. When

Table 28-2 CANCELLATION OF INSURANCE POLICIES

Grounds for Cancellation	*Explanation*
Warranty violation	Insured fails to abide by restrictions especially written into the policy
Concealment	Insured deliberately withholds fact of material importance to insurer's decision to issue a policy
Misrepresentation	Insured gives false answers to questions in the insurance application which materially affect the insurer's risk

Folk was killed in an automobile accident, his estate attempted to collect the insurance. Countryside, which had discovered Folk's epilepsy, refused to pay, claiming he had misrepresented his physical health. Evidence indicated that Folk genuinely did not consider his epilepsy, which was controlled by drugs, to be a physical impairment. In a majority of states, Folk's belief would make no difference. The policy would still be voidable by Countryside. In a minority of states, Folk's innocent misrepresentation would not allow Countryside to deny recovery under the policy.

Estoppel

An insurer may not deny acts, statements, or promises that are relevant and material to the validity of an insurance contract. This bar to denial is called an **estoppel.** When an insurer has given up the right to cancel a policy under certain circumstances by granting the insured a special dispensation, the insurer cannot deny that dispensation when the chance to cancel or deny liability does arise.

Maxwell, an insurance agent for Fidelity, called on MacLaine, who wanted fire insurance to cover her new cabin. The cabin was heated by a woodburning stove that, according to Fidelity's specifications, was located too close to a wooden wall. Maxwell told MacLaine not to worry about those specifications. He then falsified the measurements on the application. Two weeks later, MacLaine's cabin burned to the ground. Due to Maxwell's behavior, Fidelity would be estopped from denying its liability to MacLaine under the policy.

When the insurance company gives up one of its rights in order to help the insured, the company has issued a **waiver.** A waiver, which is actually a form of estoppel, can be implied from the conduct of the insurance company. For example, when an insurance company cashes the check of a lapsed policy, it has, in effect, given up or waived its right to cancel that policy. Once a right has been waived, the insurer may not later deny its waiver.

SUMMARY

28-1. Insurance is a transfer of the risk of economic loss from the insured to the insurer. Insurance policies require the elements of a contract: offer, acceptance, mutual assent, capable parties, consideration, and legality. The parties to an insurance contract include the insurer, the insured, and the beneficiary.

28-2. It is possible to obtain insurance for a variety of risks. Among the most common forms of insurance are life insurance and property insurance. (*a*) Life insurance provides funds to a beneficiary on the death of the insured. A beneficiary must have an insurable interest when the policy is issued, but need not have that interest when the insured dies. (*b*) Property insurance can cover real property, automobiles, and many other types of goods. In the case of property insurance, the insured must have an insurable interest when the loss occurs. Principal types of property insurance include fire, homeowner's, and automobile insurance.

28-3. The first step in obtaining an insurance policy is to fill out an application. A binder provides temporary insurance coverage between the time the application is made and the time the policy becomes effective. Premiums are the consideration or payment an insured gives the insurer for its acceptance of risk. A lapse occurs when the insured stops paying premiums.

28-4. Under certain conditions, the insurer is given a legal right to cancel an insurance policy. Grounds permitting cancellation include breach of warranty, concealment of material facts, and misrepresentation on a policy. Under the estoppel rule, an insurer is not allowed to deny certain statements, activities, or waivers.

Understanding Key Legal Terms

beneficiary (p. 387)
binder (p. 392)
bodily injury liability insurance (p. 391)
collision insurance (p. 392)
comprehensive coverage (p. 392)
concealment (p. 394)
double indemnity (p. 390)
estoppel (p. 395)
guaranteed-insurability (p. 390)
homeowner's policy (p. 391)
insurable interest (p. 388)
insurance (p. 387)
insured (p. 387)
insurer (p. 387)
life insurance (p. 388)
medical payments insurance (p. 392)
misrepresentation (p. 394)
no-fault insurance (p. 392)
policy (p. 387)
premium (p. 387)
property damage liability insurance (p. 391)
uninsured-motorist insurance (p. 392)
waiver (p. 395)
waiver of premium (p. 390)
warranty (p. 393)

Questions for Review and Discussion

1. In many respects, insurance policies resemble other contractual relationships. What elements would an insurance policy require under contract law?
2. In what ways do requirements of insurable interests differ in property insurance and life insurance?
3. Discuss four situations that might permit the insurer to deny paying life insurance claims.
4. Why are the waiver-of-premium option and the guaranteed-insurability option popular optional provisions of life insurance policies?

5. List and define the seven situations in which an insurer's liability under a fire insurance policy may extend beyond the damage caused directly by the fire. List the five examples of the losses that might be covered by a homeowner's policy.
6. Name seven kinds of automobile insurance, and discuss the risks covered by each of these policies.
7. Identify the first step in obtaining an insurance policy. Describe the device used to protect the insured between the time of this first step and the time the policy is actually obtained by the insured.
8. Why do insurance premiums differ from one insured to another? What happens when an insured fails to maintain a policy by missing a premium payment?
9. Discuss how breach of warranty, concealment, and misrepresentation can be used by an insurance company to cancel a policy.
10. How does the estoppel doctrine work to limit an insurance company's ability to cancel a policy?

Analyzing Cases

1. Victory Container Corporation was owned by the three Radin brothers. Two of those brothers also owned the Warrensburg Paper and Board Corporation. Victory, however, had no direct ownership of the Warrensburg property. Nevertheless, Victory took out a fire insurance policy on the Warrensburg plant. When the Warrensburg property was damaged, Victory attempted to collect under the policy. Does Victory have an insurable interest in the Warrensburg property? Explain. *Victory Container Corporation v. Calvert Fire Insurance Company,* 486 N.Y.S.2d 211 (N.Y. Sup. Ct. App. Div.).
2. Avrit and Schuring entered an agreement to purchase a certain property. Each paid $1,000 as a down payment. They were later to pay an additional $25,000. The seller of the property was to maintain insurance until the deal was finalized. Avrit and Schuring also obtained an insurance policy on the property. Before the deal was finalized, fire damaged the property. Avrit and Schuring attempted to collect on their policy, but the insurance company claimed that Avrit and Schuring had no insurable interest at the time of the fire. Do Avrit and Schuring have an insurable interest between the time of the down payment and the time the deal is finalized? Explain. *Avrit v. Forest Industries Insurance Exchange,* 696 P.2d 583 (Or. App. Ct.).
3. Martin Searle's life insurance policy contained a standard suicide clause. Under the clause, Allstate would not be liable to the beneficiary, Alice Searle, should Martin commit suicide within the first two years of the policy even if Martin were insane at the time of his death. Martin committed suicide ten months after the policy went into effect. Allstate refused to pay Alice any benefits under the policy. Alice sued the company, claiming that her husband had been mentally deranged at the time of the suicide and he did not realize the consequences of his action. Allstate argued that the "sanity" clause removed the issue of mental incapacity from the case. Who would prevail in a majority of states? Explain. *Searle v. Allstate Life Insurance Company,* 212 Cal. Rptr. 466 (Calif. Sup. Ct.).
4. Bayer took his car to Whitaker's auto repair shop for repairs. Whitaker took the car for a test drive, with Bayer seated in the passenger seat. During the test drive, a car operated by another person drove on the wrong side of the road and collided with Bayer's vehicle, injuring Bayer. Neither the Bayer vehicle nor the vehicle owned by the

wrongdoer was insured. Whitaker carried insurance on his own vehicles, including uninsured-motorist insurance. Can Bayer recover from Whitaker's insurance company under the uninsured-motorist provision of the policy? Why or why not? *Bayer v. Travelers Indemnity Co.,* 267 S.E.2d 91 (Va. Sup. Ct.).

5. Riggins contacted the Hartford Insurance Company and asked for an "all-risk" policy for his truck. An underwriter for Hartford agreed to the policy and issued a binder on March 28. On April 2, before the full policy had been executed, Riggins left on a trip, hauling liquor. Sometime during the trip, the liquor was stolen. Hartford refused to pay, arguing that the final policy that would have been issued would not have covered the hauling of liquor. Riggins argued that the "all-risk" binder was in effect at the time of the theft, and that he is, therefore, covered even though the final policy would not have covered him. Is Riggins correct? Explain. *Hilt Truck Lines, Inc. v. Riggins,* 756 F.2d 676 (8th Cir. Ct.).

6. When Sidney Henry applied for insurance with State Farm, he was asked whether he had ever had recurrent indigestion or a hernia. Henry answered "no" to each question. In fact, he had experienced recurring indigestion, and it had been diagnosed as either an ulcer or a hernia. The policy was issued. Eight months later, Henry died of cancer of the esophagus. When Eula Henry applied for benefits, State Farm denied her request. Eula argued that the misrepresentations were not material since her husband died from cancer, not the illnesses he was questioned about. Is Mrs. Henry correct? Explain. *Henry v. State Farm,* 465 So.2d 276 (La. App. Ct.).

7. On January 13, Lax made out a check to State Farm Insurance to pay for her automobile insurance which had lapsed 62 days earlier. Unfortunately, she forgot to mail the check. On January 22, Lax was killed when trying to pass a truck. The check was found in the wreckage and taken to a State Farm agent who mailed it to the main office. The main office, with knowledge of the accident, cashed the check. The beneficiaries argued that State Farm's conduct in cashing the check with knowledge of the accident constituted a waiver of its right to cancel the policy due to her failure to pay by the due date. Are the beneficiaries correct? Explain. *VanHulle v. State Farm,* 254 N.E.2d 457 (Ill. Sup. Ct.).

CHAPTER 29
Security Devices

OUTLINE

COMMENTARY

When Harold Brozowski got engaged to Norma Wilmington, he wanted to buy her an engagement ring. Because he had little money, Brozowski gave the jewelry store a small down payment and financed the rest. Shortly after making the purchase, he was forced to declare bankruptcy. Displeased with Brozowski's financial prospects, Wilmington broke the engagement. She then turned the ring over to the bankruptcy trustee, who intended to convert it to cash to satisfy Brozowski's creditors. The jewelry store, however, claimed it had a monetary interest in the ring that superseded anyone else's claim. Who do you think would get custody of the ring? Questions such as this are answered by the law of security agreements, as you will soon see by reading this chapter.

OBJECTIVES

1. Differentiate between a secured and an unsecured loan, and explain why a creditor needs a security interest when lending money or extending credit.
2. Identify six types of mortgages, and decide which will best suit a particular fact situation.
3. Outline the legal effect of recording a mortgage and the priorities involved when more than one mortgage is held and recorded on the same property.
4. Describe and distinguish between the rights and duties of the mortgagor and the rights and duties of the mortgagee.
5. List the requirements of a security agreement, and describe the events that must occur for a security agreement interest to attach.
6. Decide whether security interests are perfected in cases involving various kinds of collateral.
7. Determine who will have priority when several parties claim a security interest in the same property.
8. Discuss what rights a secured party has when a debtor defaults by failing to make payments when due.

29-1
NECESSITY OF SECURITY DEVICES

Security is the assurance that a creditor will be paid back for any money loaned or credit extended to a debtor. Debts are said to be secured when creditors know that somehow they will be able to recover their money. Lenders of money and people who extend credit often require a security device to protect their financial interests. A **security device** is a way for creditors to get their money back in case the borrower or debtor does not pay. A **secured loan** is one in which creditors have something of value, usually called collateral, from which they can be paid if the debtor does not pay. Generally, if creditors aren't paid the debt owed to them, they can legally gain possession of the collateral. It is then sold, and the money is used to pay the debt. The right to use the collateral to recover a debt is called the creditor's **security interest.** If creditors lend money but do not require collateral, they have made an unsecured loan. An **unsecured loan** is one in which creditors have nothing of value which they can repossess and sell to recover the money owed to them by the debtor. Both real property and personal property can be used to secure a debt.

29-2
REAL PROPERTY AS SECURITY

A **mortgage** is a transfer of an interest in property for the purpose of creating a security for a debt. The one who borrows the money (the **mortgagor**) conveys all or part of his or her interest in the property to the lender (the **mortgagee**) while at the same time retaining possession of the property. A mortgage on real estate creates a legal claim to the property. This legal claim, also called a lien, gives the lender the right to have the property sold if the debt is not paid. Once the land is sold and the debt satisfied, the mortgagor's obligation to the mortgagee is over. However, if the sale of the property does not satisfy the whole debt, the mortgagor will still owe the balance.

Mwanza bought a house for $144,000. Of this sum, he put up $50,000 in cash. Mwanza then took out a $95,000 loan from the Unicorp Bank to cover the rest of his purchase. When Mwanza could not meet his mortgage payments, Unicorp foreclosed and sold the house for $6,593 less than was owed. Mwanza will be personally liable for the $6,593, plus interest, until the debt is paid.

Types of Mortgages

There are many different types of real property mortgages. Some of the most common mortgages are the conventional, the variable-rate, the graduated-payment, the balloon-payment, the FHA and VA, and deeds of trust.

Conventional Mortgage A **conventional mortgage** involves no government backing by either insurance or guarantee. The loan is made by private lenders, and the risks of loss are borne exclusively by them. In the past, conventional mortgages had fixed interest rates which stayed the same during the life of the mortgage regardless of fluctuations in the economy. Changes in recent years, however, have resulted in the creation of variations to the fixed-interest-rate mortgage.

Variable-Rate Mortgage A **variable-rate mortgage** has a rate of interest which changes according to fluctuations in the index to which it is tied. The index rate may be the bank's prime rate or the Federal Reserve Board discount rate. As the index rate goes up and down, so does the rate of interest charged on the loan. This rate may be more or less than the index rate, but varies with it.

The obvious advantage of the variable-rate mortgage is the drop in the amount of the mortgage payment when the rate drops. However, mortgage payments can also rise when the rate rises. Generally, a change in payments, either up or down, does not occur without some advance warning. Also, variable-rate mortgage agreements must include a maximum rate which cannot be exceeded. In addition, the frequency of these changes in the rate is usually restricted by the terms of the mortgage agreement.

Graduated-Payment Mortgage A **graduated-payment mortgage** has a fixed interest rate during the life of the mortgage; however, the monthly payments made by the mortgagor increase over the term of the loan. In the first years of the mortgage, the payments are low. The payments gradually increase over time, usually reaching a plateau at which the payments remain fixed. This type of mortgage is advantageous for young people, whose income may be expected to increase as their mortgage payments increase.

Balloon-Payment Mortgage A **balloon-payment mortgage** has relatively low fixed payments during the life of the mortgage followed by one large final (balloon) payment. The mortgage has a fixed interest rate but is written for a short time period, such as five years. At the end of the time period, the mortgagor usually must find new financing, either with the same or with a different lender, at the current interest rate.

FHA and VA Mortgages Some mortgages, although given by private lenders, are backed by federal agencies. The Federal Housing Administration (FHA) and the Veterans Administration (VA) are responsible to the lending institution in the event of a mortgagor's default and foreclosure on an FHA or VA mortgage. The U.S. government, through these agencies, reimburses the mortgagee for any loss and takes over the property. Such properties are then offered for sale to interested buyers to recover the government's loss.

Deed of Trust In some states, a deed of trust is used instead of a mortgage. In a conventional mortgage, the mortgagor conveys all or part of his or her interest in the property directly to the mortgagee. Under a **deed of trust**, the mortgagor conveys his or her interest in the property to a disinterested third party, known as a trustee. The mortgagor remains on the property, but the trustee holds certain rights to that property as security for the mortgagor's creditors. If the debtor defaults, the trustee can sell the property for the benefit of those creditors. The provisions of many deeds of trust allow the trustee to sell the property without going to court. For this reason, some legal authorities do not consider a deed of trust a true mortgage, since true mortgages require a foreclosure action for the sale of the property (see page 404).

Recording the Mortgage

Like a deed, a mortgage must be in writing and delivered to the recorder's office in the county where the property is located. Recording a mortgage notifies any third party who may be interested in purchasing the property or in lending money to the owner that the mortgagee has an interest in the real property covered by the mortgage. If the mortgage is not recorded and a later mortgage is given on the same property, the new mortgage is superior to the first provided the second mortgagee paid for the property, did not know about the first mortgage, and recorded the mortgage properly. A failure to record the first mortgage, however, would not remove the obligation of the first mortgagor to the first mortgagee.

Niedermier needed $20,000 to cover several bad investments. He obtained the money from the Newman Financial Bank by giving the bank a first mortgage on his house. The bank failed to have the mortgage properly recorded. Silverstern later bought the house from Niedermier. Since Silverstern found no mortgage against the property recorded in the county recorder's office, he took the house free of the mortgage. Niedermier, however, still owes the bank $20,000 plus interest.

Sometimes an owner of real property may execute second and subsequent mortgages on the property. For example, if a mortgagor wants to improve the mortgaged property and needs a loan to do so, he may use the property as security for that loan. If this occurs, the mortgagor is said to have executed a second mortgage on the property. If all the mortgages are recorded, the holders of second and subsequent mortgages may exercise their rights against the property only after prior mortgages have been paid off. Thus, if the first mortgagee causes the property to be sold and is paid off in full, the second and subsequent mortgages are paid out of the proceeds that remain.

Zelentz wanted to add a new bedroom onto his house but did not have the ready cash. His house was already mortgaged to Mercedes Savings and Loan for $80,000. Nevertheless, he decided to take out a second mortgage with Cuyahoga Savings. Cuyahoga loaned Zelentz $10,000 because he pledged his home as security should he fail to repay the loan. When Zelentz defaulted on the mortgage to Mercedes and the loan from Cuyahoga, Mercedes caused the house to be sold for $90,000. Since Mercedes held the first mortgage, it was paid first. After Mercedes had its $80,000, Cuyahoga would collect its $10,000.

Rights and Duties of the Mortgagor

By law and by agreement, the mortgagor has certain rights and certain duties in conjunction with the mortgage. First, under the rule followed by a majority of the states, the mortgagor has the right to possession of the property. In these

Table 29-1 THE MORTGAGOR: RIGHTS AND DUTIES

Rights	*Duties*
Right to possession of the mortgaged property	Duty to pay all installment payments as they fall due
Right to any income produced by the property (often assigned to the mortgagee)	Duty to preserve and maintain the mortgaged property for benefit of the mortgagee
Right to use the property for subsequent mortgages	Sometimes required to insure the property to the amount of the mortgaged debt
Right to redemption, i.e., to pay off the mortgage in full	Duty to pay all taxes and assessments levied against the property

states, the mortgagor holds title to the property despite the financial interest of the mortgagee. In states following the old common law rule, the mortgagee has title to the premises but the mortgagor retains possession.

Furthermore, the mortgagor has the right to any income produced by the property. For instance, the mortgagor would be entitled to any rent proceeds gained from leasing all or part of the property. Of course, the mortgagor could also assign this right to the mortgagee. Sometimes this right is assigned to the mortgagee as a condition to executing the original mortgage agreement.

In addition, the mortgagor has the right to use the property for a second or third mortgage. Finally, the mortgagor has the right of redemption, that is, the right to pay off the mortgage in full, including interest, and to thus discharge the debt in total.

In addition to these rights, the mortgagor also has certain duties. Chief among these duties is to pay installment payments on time. Mortgagors must also preserve and maintain the mortgaged property for the benefit of the mortgagee's interest and security. Similarly, the mortgagor is often required to insure the property for the benefit of the mortgagee to the amount of the mortgaged debt.

The mortgagor must pay all taxes and assessments that may be levied against the property. Frequently, the mortgagor will ease the burden of these obligations by paying a percentage of the insurance premium and taxes each month along with the mortgage payment. The mortgagee holds the money in an escrow account. An **escrow account** is a special account into which money is deposited before the payment of the insurance or taxes is due. The money stays in the account until the time comes to pay the insurance or tax. The mortgagee then takes the money out of the account and makes the payments.

Rights and Duties of the Mortgagee

The mortgagee has the unrestricted right to sell, assign, or transfer the mortgage to a third party. Whatever rights the mortgagee had in the mortgage are then the rights of the assignee. The only way the mortgagor could stop the mortgagee from assigning the mortgage is to pay the mortgagee everything owed on the mortgage. Sometimes an assignment by the mortgagee to another mortgagee can cause unforeseen problems for the mortgagor.

The Chamberlins financed the purchase of their house through the Midway Savings Bank, a local bank with only four branches, all in the city of Bromfield. The

Chamberlins made their mortgage payments faithfully each month, in person, at the branch on their street. Without warning, they received notice that Midway had assigned their mortgage to the Unicorp Mortgage Corporation, a multimillion dollar financial institution headquartered in New York. Although the Chamberlins had no desire to deal with Unicorp, they have no choice in the matter. The only way they could avoid dealing with Unicorp would be to make full payment of the mortgage debt.

Mortgagees have the right to receive each installment payment as it falls due. Frequently, mortgagees will include a term in the mortgage agreement allowing an **acceleration** of the debt if the mortgagor fails to meet an installment payment. This means that a default on one installment payment will make the entire balance due immediately, giving the mortgagee the right to collect the full amount. In general, a clause allowing acceleration must be executed in good faith. In other words, before invoking the acceleration clause, the mortgagee must genuinely believe that the mortgagor will not be able to make good on the debt and that the mortgagee's security interest is therefore threatened. If the matter ends up in court, the mortgagor will have the burden of proving that the mortgagee did not act in good faith.

If the mortgagor has defaulted or has failed to perform some other agreement in the mortgage, such as a condition to pay money into an escrow account for insurance and property taxes, and cannot pay the accelerated amount, the mortgagee has the right to apply to a court to have the property sold. This right is called **foreclosure.** Since in a majority of jurisdictions a mortgage is a lien on the land, a foreclosure is an equitable action. The mortgagor does not have a right to a jury trial in a foreclosure action.

A mortgage is foreclosed when the mortgagee proves the amount of the unpaid debt (including interest and other charges) and the property is sold by and under the direction of a court. The proceeds from the sale are then applied to the payment of the debt. Any money remaining after the claims of the mortgagee have been satisfied goes to the mortgagor or to the second and subsequent mortgagees.

The mortgagee's financial interest in mortgaged property gives rise to certain constitutional rights. Under Amendment 14 to the U.S. Constitution, mortgagees cannot lose their interest in property without due process of law.

Table 29-2 THE MORTGAGEE: RIGHTS AND DUTIES

Rights	*Duties*
Right to receive all installment payments as they fall due	Duty to respect the mortgagor's right to possession
Right to sell, assign, or transfer the mortgage to a third party	Duty not to discriminate against mortgagors because of race, creed, color, sex, or ethnic background
Right to acceleration of the debt coupled with the right to foreclose on the default of the debtor	Duty not to accelerate or to foreclose in the absence of a genuine belief that mortgagor will not pay off the debt
Right to not be deprived of the property without due process of law as guaranteed by Amendment 14, U.S. Constitution	Duty to respect all other rights granted to the mortgagor by law

---

Northmore Bank and Trust made a $456,000 loan to Prendergast. It secured that loan with a mortgage on a warehouse owned by Prendergast. The county commissioners wanted the Prendergast property for an expansion of the county airport. The county paid Prendergast a nominal amount for the warehouse and then had it demolished. Northmore received no notice of the demolition until after the building had been torn down. Northmore sued the county, claiming that its constitutional due process rights had been violated. The court agreed with Northmore's claim.

Mortgagees also have certain duties imposed by law. Both state and federal legislation prohibits lenders from discriminating against borrowers because of race, creed, color, sex, or ethnic background. Such legislation imposes a duty to use nondiscriminatory criteria in approving and disapproving mortgage applications. For example, a lender may not refuse a mortgage to a prospective borrower simply because that borrower is a woman. Similarly, a lender could not refuse a mortgage to a borrower because that borrower is Hispanic. The mortgagee also has the duty to respect all rights properly claimed by the mortgagor.

Purchase by Mortgage Takeover

Mortgages often contain a clause providing that if the property is sold, the mortgage becomes due and payable. If the mortgage does not contain such a clause, the property may be sold with the mortgage remaining on it. In such takeovers, the transfer of title to a new buyer is subject to the buyer's payment of the seller's mortgage at the existing rate of interest.

In purchasing a property already mortgaged, the buyer will either **assume the mortgage** or take the property **subject to the mortgage.** When buyers decide to assume the mortgage, they agree to pay it. When they take the property subject to a mortgage, the seller agrees to continue paying the debt.

29-3 PERSONAL PROPERTY AS SECURITY

Article 9 of the UCC brings all personal property security devices, or security interests, together under one law. The property that is subject to the security interest is called **collateral.** A security interest is created by a written agreement, called a **security agreement,** which identifies the goods and is signed by the debtor. The lender or seller who holds the security interest is known as the **secured party.** A security interest is said to **attach** when the secured party has a legally enforceable right to take that property and sell it to satisfy the debt. It is said to be **perfected** when the secured party has done everything that the law requires to give the secured party greater rights to the goods than others have.

Security Agreements
UCC 9-105(1)

A **security agreement** is an agreement which creates a security interest. It must be in writing, signed by the debtor, and contain a description of the collateral that is used for security.

Montmartre Industries contracted to purchase certain robotics equipment from Universal Bioengineering. Montmartre's president signed a promissory note identifying Universal Bioengineering as a secured party. When Montmartre filed for bankruptcy, Universal Bioengineering claimed to have a security interest in the robotics equipment. Since the promissory note did not describe the collateral, Bioengineering did not hold a valid security interest in the equipment.

If Universal had provided enough information about the collateral to allow the court to identify it even without a detailed description, the result would have been different. Had Universal made reference to the equipment by including certain purchase-order or invoice numbers, the court could have identified the equipment and would have upheld the validity of the security agreement.

Attachment of a Security Interest

To be effective, a security interest must be legally enforceable against the debtor. This is known as **attachment.** Attachment occurs when three conditions are met. First, the debtor has some ownership or possessive rights in the collateral. Second, the secured party (or creditor) transfers something of value, such as money, to the debtor. Third, the secured party takes possession of the collateral or signs a security agreement which describes the collateral.

Conroy loaned Lightfoot $5,000 for six months at 8 percent interest. Lightfoot secured the debt by giving Conroy several uncut diamonds that Lightfoot owned. Conroy agreed to return the diamonds when Lightfoot paid the debt. The security interest is legally enforceable because all three conditions were met. First, Lightfoot had ownership rights in the diamonds. Second, Conroy gave Lightfoot something of value, the $5,000. Finally, Conroy took possession of the diamonds.

UCC 9-204

Creditors may obtain security interests in property acquired by the debtor after the original agreement is entered. The creditor does this by placing a provision in the security agreement that the security interest of the creditor also applies to goods the debtor acquires at a later time. This is important to creditors who take security interests in goods, such as food items, that are sold and replaced within short periods of time. As soon as the debtor takes possession of the new property, the creditor also has a right to that property.

Perfection of a Security Interest

When a security interest attaches, it is effective only between debtor and creditor. Such creditors, however, will want to make certain that no one else can claim that collateral before they do, if the debtors fail to pay them back. To preserve the right to first claim on the collateral, creditors must perfect their interest. A security interest can be perfected in one of three ways: by attachment alone, by possession of the collateral, or by filing a financial statement in the appropriate government office. Sometimes the secured party has a choice as to which of the three methods to use. At other times, no choice exists.

UCC 9-302(1)(d)

Perfection by Attachment Alone In limited situations, a security interest is perfected the moment it attaches; that is, as soon as the security interestbecomes legally enforceable. One situation in which this occurs is when someone lends money to a consumer and then takes a security interest in the goods that the consumer buys. This is called a **purchase money security interest** and applies only to consumer goods. Consumer goods are items bought for personal, family, or household purposes.

UCC 9-109(1)

Napier purchased a new VCR from Steinbeck's Radio & T.V. Outlet. To pay for the VCR, he borrowed $295 from the Security Atlantic Finance Corporation, which took a security interest in the VCR by entering a security agreement with Napier. Since the VCR would be considered consumer goods, the security interest would become perfected the moment it attached, or became legally enforceable.

UCC 9-313(1)(a)

Exceptions to Perfection by Attachment Alone Two exceptions to perfection by attachment alone are the purchase of automobiles and fixtures. Purchase money security interests in neither cars nor fixtures can be perfected by attachment alone.

UCC 9-305
UCC 9-207

Perfection by Possession A security interest may be perfected when the secured party (the creditor) takes possession of the collateral. This is called a *pledge*. The borrower, or debtor, who gives up the property, is the *pledgor*. The secured party, or creditor, is the *pledgee*. A secured party who has possession of the collateral must take reasonable care of the property. The debtor must reimburse the secured party for any money spent to take care of the property. The debtor assumes the risk of accidental loss beyond any insurance coverage.

After Napier paid off the debt to the Security Atlantic Finance Corporation, he decided to buy a compact disk player. This time he borrowed the money from his cousin, Lisa. Lisa agreed to lend Napier the money only if she could have his VCR as security until he repaid her. Lisa's security interest in the VCR became perfected when she took possession of it.

Perfection by Filing Security interests in most kinds of personal property are perfected by filing a financial statement in a public office. The office may be a central one (secretary of state's office) or a local one (county recorder or city clerk) where the debtor resides or has a place of business. The proper office for filing depends on the type of collateral and varies from state to state. As a general rule, financing statements dealing with consumer goods and farming are filed locally.

UCC 9-402

A financing statement must give the names of the debtor and the secured party. It must be signed by the debtor and give the address of the secured party from which information concerning the security interest may be obtained. It must also give a mailing address of the debtor and contain a statement indicating the types, or describing the items, of collateral. When the financing statement covers such things as crops, timber, minerals, oil, and gas, the statement must also contain a description of the real estate concerned.

Napier paid Lisa the money he owed her and took back his VCR. He then decided to purchase an automobile from Sapolsky's New and Used Car Lot. To pay for the vehicle, he borrowed $8,562.34 from the Monticello Financial Bank. Monticello took a security interest in the car by entering a security agreement with Napier. Monticello filed a financing statement with the county recorder. The security interest was perfected when the financing statement was filed.

Priorities and Claims

UCC 9-312

Frequently two or more parties claim a security interest in the same collateral. At other times, unsecured parties claim that they have better rights than secured parties. The UCC helps resolve these conflicts. Some of the provisions, stating who prevails over whom in particular situations, follow:

1. A perfected security interest prevails over an unperfected security interest.
2. When two or more parties have perfected security interests, the first to perfect prevails over the other parties.
3. When two or more parties have unperfected security interests in the same collateral, the first to attach prevails over the other parties.
4. Perfected security interests, lien creditors, trustees in bankruptcy, and buyers in the ordinary course of business prevail over unperfected security interests.
5. Buyers of goods in the ordinary course of business prevail over security interests in the seller's inventory.
6. Buyers of farm products in the ordinary course of business, to the extent that they pay for and receive collateral without knowledge of the security interest, take precedence over nonperfected security interests.
7. A purchaser of secondhand consumer goods without knowledge of a security interest prevails over a security interest of a seller who perfected without filing.

Default of the Debtor

If a debtor defaults by failing to make payments when due, the secured party may satisfy the debt by taking possession of the collateral. Because of the difficulties of doing this, the perfection of a security interest by possession, as in a pledge, is better than other types of perfection. Collateral may be repossessed without going through the court if it can be done without causing a disturbance. Otherwise, the creditor must use legal process.

After repossessing the goods, the secured party (the creditor) may keep them or sell them. If the secured party decides to keep the goods, the debtor and any other secured creditors must be told of this fact. If any of them object within 21 days, the secured party must sell the collateral and use the money received in the sale to pay herself or himself and the other creditors. If there is money left over after all creditors are paid, the secured party must give the extra money to the debtor. If the sale does not produce enough money to pay all the creditors, the debtor must pay them back out of personal funds.

If there is a sale, it may be public (an auction) or private as long as the terms of the sale are reasonable. If the goods are consumer goods and the debtor has paid 60 percent or more of the cash price, the secured party cannot keep the goods. They must be sold. The debtor must be told about any sale and has the right to buy the goods personally.

SUMMARY

29-1. Individuals and institutions that lend money need some assurance that they will have their money returned to them. Security devices serve as this means of assurance.

29-2. Purchases of real property are generally secured by a mortgage. A mortgage is a transfer of an interest in property for the purpose of creating a security for a debt. Some common types of mortgages include: the conventional mortgage, the variable-rate mortgage, the graduated-payment mortgage, the balloon-payment mortgage, FHA and VA mortgages, and deeds of trust.

29-3. When personal property is purchased on credit, the seller frequently retains a security interest in the property. Property that is subject to a security interest is called collateral. A security interest is created by a written agreement called a security agreement, which identifies the goods and is signed by the debtor. To be effective between debtor and creditor, a security interest must be made legally enforceable. This is known as attachment. To be effective against third parties who might also claim the secured property, the creditor must take possession of the property or file a financing statement. This is known as perfection.

Understanding Key Legal Terms

acceliteration (p. 404)
assume the mortgage (p. 405)
attachment (p. 406)
balloon-payment mortgage (p. 401)
collateral (p. 405)
conventional mortgage (p. 400)
deed of trust (p. 401)
foreclosure (p. 404)
graduated-payment mortgage (p. 401)
mortgage (p. 400)
mortgagee (p. 400)
mortgagor (p. 400)
perfected (p. 405)
purchase money security interest (p. 407)
secured loan (p. 400)
secured party (p. 405)
security agreement (p. 405)
security interest (p. 400)
subject to the mortgage (p. 405)
unsecured loan (p. 400)
variable-rate mortgage (p. 401)

Questions for Review and Discussion

1. Briefly explain why creditors frequently require security devices when lending money or extending credit.
2. In what principal way does a conventional mortgage differ from an FHA or a VA mortgage?
3. What are the differences among a variable-rate mortgage, a graduated-payment mortgage, and a balloon-payment mortgage?
4. Discuss the importance of recording a mortgage in a public office in the county where the property is located.

5. Name four rights that belong to a mortgagor. Do the same for the mortgagee.
6. In the purchase of real property, distinguish between assuming a mortgage and taking property subject to a mortgage.
7. What elements must be included in a security agreement?
8. Explain the reason for perfecting a security interest, and describe the different ways this may be done.
9. What rules are found in the UCC for determining who prevails over whom when secured and unsecured parties lay claim to the same collateral?
10. What rights and responsibilities does a secured party have if a debtor defaults by failing to make payments when due?

Analyzing Cases

1. When the Prestons took out a variable mortgage with the First Bank of Marietta, their interest rate was 9 percent. The agreement allowed First Bank to raise or lower the interest rate at any time, provided that the Prestons received 30 days advance notice. When the bank raised the interest rate to 11 percent, the Prestons refused to pay, arguing that the agreement was unenforceable since it set no limit on what interest rate they might be forced to pay. Are the Prestons correct? Explain. *Preston v. First Bank of Marietta,* 473 N.E.2d 1210 (Ohio App. Ct.).
2. The Woolseys ran a mink farm that was mortgaged to the State Bank of Lehi. The agreement included provisions which allowed acceleration and foreclosure if the Woolseys failed to pay their obligations under the contract. The Woolseys defaulted on several payments, and the bank foreclosed. The couple demanded a jury trial on the foreclosure action. They also argued that the bank had not acted in good faith in its acceleration and foreclosure. Are the Woolseys entitled to a jury trial? Explain. Who has the burden of proof in demonstrating the bank's good faith in accelerating payments and demanding foreclosure? *State Bank of Lehi v. Woolsey,* 565 P.2d 413 (Utah Sup. Ct.).
3. Bloom executed a real estate mortgage in favor of Lakeshore Commercial Finance Corporation on September 16. On October 4, Bloom executed another mortgage on the same described real estate in favor of Northridge Bank. Northridge, without notice of the mortgage to Lakeshore, recorded its mortgage at 9:28 a.m. on October 25. On that same date, at 3:07 p.m., the prior mortgage executed in favor of Lakeshore was recorded. Bloom defaulted on the mortgages. The value of the real estate was insufficient to fully satisfy both mortgages. Which party has first rights to the property, Lakeshore or Northridge? Why? *Northridge Bank v. Lakeshore Com. Fin. Corp.,* 365 N.E.2d 382 (Illinois).
4. Cramer's mortgage contained a provision requiring her to pay monthly tax and insurance payments into an escrow account held by the bank in addition to principal and interest. Cramer paid the principal and interest regularly, but refused to pay the tax and insurance escrow payments. The bank brought foreclosure proceedings. Did it have the right to foreclose on Cramer's mortgage? Explain. *Cramer v. Metro. Sav. & Loan Ass'n.,* 258 N.W.2d 20 (Michigan).
5. Matthews Motors sold a Buick Riviera to Jenkins for $11,500. Matthews then borrowed money from Owensboro National Bank, pledging the Buick as collateral. When Matthews defaulted on the loan, the bank attempted to repossess the Buick from Jenkins. Jenkins refused to surrender the

automobile, claiming he owned it and not Matthews. The bank brought suit, asking the court to force Jenkins to turn over the Buick. Should the court grant the bank's request? Why or why not? *Owensboro National Bank v. Jenkins,* 328 S.E.2d 399 (Ga. App. Ct.).

6. Giant Wholesale agreed to supply Hendersonville Food Center with groceries if the owner, William Page, would guarantee all debts incurred by Hendersonville. Page agreed, and a security agreement was drawn up. The security agreement gave Giant a security interest in Hendersonville's groceries and equipment. Giant failed to properly file a financing statement. When Hendersonville ran into financial difficulty, Page turned over the checking account to Giant. When this did not work, Giant repossessed all Hendersonville's inventory. Page later went bankrupt. Gray, the bankruptcy trustee, brought a suit against Giant, claiming the inventory was part of Page's property and thus subject to the bankruptcy proceeding. Gray argued that since the financing statement had not been filed, Giant's security interest had not been perfected. Is Gray correct? Explain. *Gray v. Giant Wholesale,* 758 F.2d 1000 (4th Cir. Ct.).

7. U. S. Electronics, a Missouri corporation with a place of business in DeKalb County, Georgia, borrowed money from a Missouri bank. The corporation gave the bank a security interest in all its machinery and equipment. The bank filed a financing statement in Fulton County rather than in DeKalb County as required by law. U.S. Electronics defaulted on the loan and fell behind on its rent. The corporation's landlord obtained a judgment against it for past-due rent, becoming a lien creditor. The landlord claimed priority over the bank to the proceeds of a sheriff's sale of the machinery and equipment, arguing that the bank's security interest was not perfected. Do you agree? Why or why not? *United States v. Waterford No. 2 Office Center,* 271 S.E.2d 790 (Georgia).

CHAPTER 30
Bankruptcy and Debt Adjustment

OUTLINE

COMMENTARY

Nia Brailsford left her job as an electronics engineer at DenHeuvel Engineering to open her own electronics firm. Brailsford's firm manufactured and sold a line of new lightweight satellite dishes that could easily be mounted on almost any kind of structure. After a year of only marginally successful sales, Brailsford ran into some unexpected difficulties. First, DenHeuvel Engineering brought suit against her for patent infringement. The litigation process was not only expensive, it was also enormously time-consuming. Secondly, most television networks began to market scramblers that made satellite dishes less attractive as an investment for most consumers. Finally, Brailsford's main supplier, Shaintech Electronics, had labor difficulties that stopped all shipments to Brailsford for six months. Unable to pay her personal debts or the debts of the business, Brailsford turned to federal bankruptcy law, seeking some sort of remedy. Will Brailsford be forced to close down her business or can she make other arrangements under the law? Can Brailsford be forced into bankruptcy by her creditors? Can any of her property be saved, if she is forced into bankruptcy? These and other questions are answered in this chapter.

OBJECTIVES

1. Identify the source of congressional power to create statutory law dealing with bankruptcy and other forms of debt adjustment.
2. Distinguish between the voluntary and involuntary methods of filing for bankruptcy as provided for in the Bankruptcy Code.
3. Defend the automatic suspension feature of the bankruptcy process under the Bankruptcy Code.

4. Name the property exemptions that a debtor is allowed before beginning the sale of property.
5. Recognize those debts which have priority payment status under the Bankruptcy Code.
6. List those debts which cannot be discharged by a bankruptcy debtor.
7. Outline the reorganization process as it pertains to individuals and businesses under Chapter 11 of the Bankruptcy Code.
8. Explain the debt adjustment process available to family farmers under Chapter 12 of the Bankruptcy Code.
9. Summarize the options available to individual debtors in Chapter 13 of the Bankruptcy Code.

30-1 BANKRUPTCY AND THE CONSTITUTION

Bankruptcy is the legal process by which the assets of a debtor are sold to pay off creditors so that the debtor can make a fresh start financially. This definition pinpoints the two most crucial objectives of bankruptcy law. First, the law protects the *creditors* who have lent money or extended credit to the debtor by making certain that the debtor's money is divided fairly. Secondly, the law gives *debtors* an escape from their financial burdens and allows them to build new lives.

Constitutional Authority

U.S. Const., Art. I, Sec. 8 **(see p. 600)**

The U.S. Constitution gives the federal government jurisdiction over bankruptcy proceedings. Article I, Section 8, Clause 4 states that "Congress shall have the Power...To establish...uniform laws on the subject of Bankruptcies throughout the United States." Congress exercised this power when it enacted the Bankruptcy Code. The code is found in Title 11 of the United States Code. The **United States Code (USC)** is a compilation of all the statutes passed by Congress (see Chapter 1, page 6).

Bankruptcy Code Structure

Title 11 is a subdivision of the United States Code (USC) which contains all bankruptcy-related statutes. Title 11 is subdivided into nine chapters. All, except Chapter 12, are odd-numbered chapters. Four of these, the universal Chapters of 1, 3, 5, and 15, contain information and rules that affect all forms of bankruptcy. The other five, Chapters 7, 9, 11, 12, and 13, are operative chapters that create different forms of bankruptcy.

Universal Chapters Chapter 1 of the Bankruptcy Code is entitled General Provisions. It outlines who can and who cannot file under the operative chapters. The second universal chapter, Chapter 3, indicates the distribution of powers and responsibilities among bankruptcy officials. Chapter 5 is an important provision because it sets up guidelines for figuring out what property can and cannot be used to satisfy a debtor's obligations. It also outlines the ways those obligations are to be satisfied. Finally, Chapter 15, a recent addition, sets up a new trustee system, which is still in its experimental stages.

Operative Chapters Each of the operative chapters of the Bankruptcy Code creates a different form of bankruptcy. For example, Chapter 7 covers ordinary bankruptcy. In ordinary bankruptcy, or liquidation, debtors sell all nonexempt assets, pay off their debts proportionally, and begin a fresh life. Chapter 9 affects cities only, allowing them to adjust their debts. Chapter 11 creates a new form of debt adjustment, allowing debtors, including partnerships and corporations, to restructure their payment schedules. Chapter 12 allows family farmers to adjust their debts, and Chapter 13 does the same for individuals.

30-2 ORDINARY BANKRUPTCY—CHAPTER 7, BANKRUPTCY CODE

When most people use the word *bankruptcy,* they are referring to the type of ordinary bankruptcy provided for in Chapter 7 of the Bankruptcy Code. Under ordinary bankruptcy, debtors are forced to sell most of their property and use the cash to pay their creditors a portion of the amount owed each one. This process is also called **liquidation.**

Commencing the Action

Ordinary bankruptcy may begin in one of two ways. Either the debtor files a petition or the debtor's creditors band together and file a petition to force the debtor to sell property and pay them off. The first type of filing is called a voluntary filing. The second type of filing is known as an involuntary filing.

Voluntary Proceedings If debtors are alert enough to realize that their financial position can never improve without some drastic action, they may decide to file a bankruptcy petition on their own. To do so, such debtors would go to the nearest federal district court. The government provides official forms for the filing of a bankruptcy petition. The form asks debtors to name all their creditors and to indicate how much money they owe those creditors. The form also requires a listing of their property and a statement of income and expenses. Finally, the form asks debtors to list all the property that they feel should be exempt from sale when it comes time later in the bankruptcy proceeding to sell what they own.

Involuntary Proceedings Under Chapter 7 of the Bankruptcy Code the creditors of a debtor can force that debtor into an involuntary bankruptcy proceeding if the debtor continuously fails to pay bills as they become due. The ability to pay is not the issue. If the debtor has enough money to pay bills but for some reason refuses to do so, an involuntary petition can be filed. Three creditors must file the petition if the debtor has twelve or more creditors. The combined debt owed the three must exceed $5,000. A single creditor who is owed a debt of more than $5,000 can also file if the debtor has fewer than twelve creditors.

Strasser had an excellent job with a high salary and a promise of continued advancement. However, he made several miscalculations in the stock market which severely damaged his financial picture. Consequently, although he owned a lot of property, he had little cash on hand. This situation caused him to fall behind on his payments to most of his 14 creditors. Three of those creditors, the Bromfield Department Store, the Mariano Oil Company, and the Preston Financial Bank, filed an involuntary bankruptcy petition against Strasser in federal court. Since Strasser owed the three of them more than $5,000, the petition was accepted.

Involuntary petitions cannot be filed against farmers, charities, or cities. Debtors can contest any petition filed involuntarily.

Order for Relief

Under the Bankruptcy Code, after a petition for ordinary bankruptcy is filed, the court will issue an order for relief. An **order for relief** is the court's command that the liquidation begin. In a voluntary filing, the petition itself becomes the order for relief. In an involuntary case, the court does not file the order immediately because the debtor is allowed a certain period of time to contest the filing. At this time a **bankruptcy trustee** is also named by the court. The trustee is charged with the responsibility of liquidating the assets of the debtor for the benefit of all interested parties.

Automatic Suspension

As soon as the order for relief is issued, an **automatic suspension,** or automatic stay, goes into effect. An automatic suspension stops the debtor's creditors from making further moves to collect the money that the debtor owes them. The suspension prohibits creditors from filing lawsuits against the debtor even if the suit is filed in a court other than the court handling the bankruptcy petition. It also protects creditors because it places them all on the same footing. No one creditor can take advantage of another. It is fair to the debtor as well because it gives the debtor more control over the situation. Automatic suspension applies to both voluntary and involuntary petitions. Creditors who ignore the suspension can be held in contempt of court.

Easterbrook found himself so deeply in debt that he could pay very little on his bills. One of his creditors, Lindren Musical Supplies, told him that it was about to file a lawsuit against him. At that point, Easterbrook filed a voluntary bankruptcy petition in federal court. Since he filed voluntarily, the voluntary petition was considered the order for relief. At this time, the automatic suspension provision of the Bankruptcy Code went into effect. If Lindren Musical Supplies carried out its planned action, it could be held in contempt of court.

Federal Exemptions

Under the federal Bankruptcy Code, debtors are permitted to exempt or exclude certain items of property from the bankruptcy process. This means that the property cannot be sold to pay the debtor's outstanding bills. These exclusions include: (1) exemptions for the homestead and for household items, (2) exemptions for necessities, and (3) exemptions for benefits and support payments.

Homestead and Household Exemptions The Bankruptcy Code allows debtors to exclude a maximum of $7,500 in equity in the debtor's place of residence and in property used as a burial ground. This is known as the **homestead exemption.**

Tsufura purchased a home worth $17,000 by placing $5,000 down and borrowing the balance from the Englehart Savings and Loan Association. Englehart held a first mortgage on the property. Tsufura was later forced to file for bankruptcy. Under the homestead exemption, she would be allowed to exempt up to $7,500 in equity in her home. Since she only has $5,000 in equity, she would be limited to that amount. This $5,000 would be safe from her creditors.

Debtors can also exclude a maximum of $200 for any individual item of furniture, household goods, clothes, appliances, books, crops, animals, or musical instruments. The total of all exemptions taken in this category cannot exceed $4,000. Sometimes debtors can exempt a collection or set of household goods by counting one item at a time rather than the entire collection or set. For example, a set of china worth of $1,000 would not be exempt. However, each item listed separately would be exempt. Debtors are also allowed to exempt $500 in jewelry beyond the $4,000 set aside for the other household items mentioned above.

Necessities Congress allows debtors to maintain a maximum standard of living by exempting certain necessary items of property. For example, debtors are allowed to exclude a maximum of $750 in professional tools, instruments, and books. In addition, they can exempt up to $1,200 in any automobile or other motor vehicle. Finally, any medical supplies that have been prescribed for the health of the debtor can be excluded.

Benefits and Support Payments Again, to allow debtors to maintain a minimum standard of living, Congress allows the exclusion of certain benefits and support payments. For instance, both alimony and child support payments can be excluded. Benefits received under social security or a disability program are also exempt. Profits that are due under profit-sharing, pension, and annuity plans my be excluded. Furthermore, debtors are allowed to protect payments due to them under certain court orders. For example, if someone owes a debtor damages resulting from a personal injury tort case, those damages are exempt. Finally, any life insurance contracts carried for the benefit of a relative or approved beneficiary that have yet to mature are protected.

State Exemptions

The Bankruptcy Code allows states to prevent debtors from using this federal list of exemptions. Many states have done so, forcing debtors to use a list of exemptions created by the state legislature. Often the broad categories of exempt property will stay the same. However, the maximum dollar amount allowed under each category will vary from state to state. States that enact their own list of exemptions generally do so to protect their own citizens. The dollar amounts included in the state statutes will usually be a more accurate assessment of property values within each state. This is true because the state legislators are more flexible in such matters than members of Congress who must take the property values across the entire country into consideration.

Property Distribution

After the order for relief is granted, a trustee will be appointed to sell the debtor's property to obtain cash. The trustee then distributes the cash among the debtor's creditors according to set priorities. Recall that the debtor is required to list all creditors and the amounts owed to each on the petition form. The trustee uses this form in the distribution process.

Secured Creditors Some of the creditors on the list will be creditors who have secured loans. (See Chapter 29.)

Auchincloss purchased a compact disk (CD) player from Lubenan Electronics. Auchincloss financed the deal by taking out a loan from the Underwood City Loan Company. Underwood agreed to the loan because Auchincloss entered into a security agreement with the company. Under the agreement Underwood retained a security interest in the property allowing it to repossess the player, if Auchincloss defaulted on the loan. Underwood is a secured creditor. The CD player is the collateral.

Since secured creditors have the right to take the collateral to satisfy the debt, the collateral is not sold by the trustee. Although there are some narrow exceptions to this rule, most secured creditors are protected. In contrast, creditors who are owed unsecured debts are called unsecured creditors. The Bankruptcy Code provides a priority list indicating which categories of unsecured debts are paid first. Each category must be paid in full before moving on to the next category. This priority list begins with administrative debts.

Administrative Debts Debts incurred in the administration of the bankruptcy are paid first. This means that the trustee and any other individuals involved in the bankruptcy process know that they will be paid for their services. If this were not the case, few attorneys, accountants, and other professionals would be willing to handle the bankruptcy process.

Certain Unsecured Debts The second priority applies only to involuntary bankruptcy cases. In such cases, all unsecured debts that occur after the petition was filed but before the order for relief was granted are paid next. This priority protects those creditors who dealt with the debtor in good faith but who were unaware of the debtor's severe financial crisis.

Wages and Benefit Plans The third and fourth categories are designed to protect the debtor's employees. If the debtor is an employer, the employees are paid third. These payments cannot top $2,000 per employee and are limited to wages due 90 days before the petition was filed. Fourth, employers must pay any contributions owed to the employees' benefit plan up to $2,000 each.

Table 30-1 PAYMENT PRIORITIES FOR UNSECURED DEBTS

Debt	*Explanation*
Administrative debts	Bankruptcy trustee and others involved in bankruptcy process are paid first.
Certain unsecured debts	All unsecured debts occurring after an involuntary petition has been filed, but before order for relief has been granted are paid next.
Wages	Employees are paid next. *Maximum:* $2,000 per employee.
Benefit plans	Contributions owed on employee benefit plans are paid next. *Maximum:* $2,000 per employee.
Workers in the fishing and farming industries	Owner-operators of fish storage processing plants pay worker creditors next. Owner-operators of grain storage plants pay farmer creditors next.
Deposits and advances	Deposits made for purchase or lease of property are paid next, as are advances made for personal, family, household services. *Maximum:* $900.
Taxes	Certain taxes are paid next.
Remaining unsecured creditors	All other secured creditors are paid from any balance remaining.
Debtor	If there is anything left, it goes back to the debtor.

Debts Owed to Workers in the Fishing and Farming Industries The fifth priority applies only to bankruptcy debtors who own or operate fish storage or processing plants and those who own or operate grain storage plants. Those involved with the fisheries must pay their workers next. Those involved with grain storage plants must pay their farm producers next. A $2,000 limit per worker applies to this category.

Deposits and Advances The next priority covers deposits made to the debtor for the purchase or lease of property. Also included in this category are advances made to the debtor for personal, family, or household services. There is a maximum of $900 on each of these deposits or advances.

Taxes and Other Unsecured Debts Finally, if the debtor owes certain taxes, they are paid next. Once these seven levels have been paid, all other unsecured creditors will be paid from any balance remaining. If there is anything left after that, it goes back to the debtor.

Exceptions to Discharge

Once the trustee has run through all the aforementioned creditors, the debtor's debts are said to be discharged. This means the debts are wiped away, and the debtor is allowed to begin again. If the bankruptcy debtor does not have enough money to cover the debts, they are, nevertheless, considered discharged. However, there are some exceptions to this general rule. Some debts cannot be discharged. In other words, even though the debtor has gone through the entire bankruptcy proceeding, money may still be owed to certain creditors. This list of nondischargeable debts begins with debts created by misconduct.

Debts Created by Misconduct Certain debts that have fallen into the debtor's lap because of misconduct cannot be discharged in bankruptcy. For example, any debts that arose because of the debtor's fraudulent behavior cannot be discharged. Similarly, the debtor cannot escape legal liability for any debt that arose from willful and malicious misconduct. Finally, if the debtor knew about a debt that was not on the original list of debts, then that unlisted debt cannot be discharged.

Debts Enforced by the Government Certain debts that the debtor owes the government will remain on the books even after the bankruptcy proceeding has ended. These include certain back taxes, certain student loans, and many government fines and penalties. Similarly, several types of court-enforced debts cannot be discharged. These include alimony and child support and any legal liability that resulted from a court-ordered judgment for driving while intoxicated. Finally, any debts that were not discharged under a previous bankruptcy cannot be discharged under the new bankruptcy proceeding.

Debts Created by Excessive Spending Congress also refuses to allow bankruptcy debtors to discharge any excessive expenditures that occur around the time of the bankruptcy filing. This measure prevents people from running up big bills unnecessarily because they think they will not have to pay the full amount due on these bills when their assets are finally distributed. Thus, debts for luxury items that top $500 in value cannot be discharged if those items were purchased within 90 days before the order for relief was granted. Likewise, the debtor cannot discharge any cash advances that total more than $1,000 if those advances were obtained within 20 days of the relief order.

Contreras finally realized that his financial problems were out of control. Consequently, he decided to file for bankruptcy on the following Monday. That Friday, he went to the Monroe-Jefferson National Bank and used his bank card to withdraw a cash advance of $1,500. He spent that money on a weekend in Atlantic City and then filed for bankruptcy on Monday. Contreras would not be allowed to discharge that $1,500, since it is a cash advance that was made within 20 days of the relief order.

30-3 REORGANIZATION—CHAPTER 11, BANKRUPTCY CODE

Chapter 11 of the Bankruptcy Code provides a method for businesses to reorganize their financial affairs and still remain in business. If allowed to continue in operation, companies may be able to overcome their difficulties without having to sell most of their property. In **reorganization,** a qualified debtor creates a plan that alters the repayment schedule. A Chapter 11 filing is available to anyone who could file under Chapter 7. This includes individuals, partnerships, and corporations. In addition, unlike Chapter 7, Chapter 11 also allows railroads to file. The only individuals specifically excluded from Chapter 11 are commodity brokers and stockbrokers.

Chapter 11 is advantageous for partnerships and corporations because it allows them to stay in business while the financial problems are cleared up. Like a Chapter 7 filing, a Chapter 11 filing may be voluntary or involuntary. Chapter 11 also shares the Chapter 7 automatic suspension provision. However, reorganization under Chapter 11 also has some unique features of its own.

Special Features of Chapter 11

One of the most attractive features of Chapter 11 for business debtors is that the business continues to operate after the filing. Under Chapter 11, a debtor is frequently referred to as a **debtor-in-possession** because the debtor continues to run the firm. However, if the problems of the business have been caused by poor judgment, mismanagement, or dishonesty, a trustee may have to step in to perform certain tasks. If appointed, the trustee would have to examine the debtor's financial position and provide the court, creditors, and tax authorities with financial information as necessary.

After the filing of the petition and the issuance of an order for relief, a **primary committee** is set up to work with the debtor on a reorganization plan. Membership on the committee generally consists of the debtor's unsecured creditors. Often the seven creditors to whom the debtor owes the most will make up the committee membership. It is also possible for the court to create other committees if membership on the primary committee fails to represent all those with legitimate claims against the debtor. These secondary committees also work with the debtor and, if appropriate, help set up the reorganization plan.

The Reorganization Plan

When a Chapter 11 petition is filed, the debtor has 120 days to devise a reorganization plan. The plan must outline how the debtor intends to reorganize the payment of debts. If the debtor lets the 120 days pass without taking any action or if the debtor creates a plan that is rejected, then a plan may be proposed by anyone involved in the reorganization effort.

Plan Qualifications The Bankruptcy Code requires fairness, equity, and feasibility in the creation of a reorganization plan. The plan will group various claims against the debtor into classes and explain how each creditor in the class will be treated. The law requires equal treatment for all creditors grouped in a class. In addition, the law requires that the plan be feasible. This means that there must be a good chance that the plan will actually work. The law does not require an absolute guarantee of success. A plan may be difficult to implement because of labor or supply problems and still be feasible within the meaning of the law.

Plan Approval The plan must be approved by the creditors before it can go into effect. However, the code does not require unanimous approval by the creditors. Instead, more than one-half of the creditors in each class must acceptthe plan before it is officially approved. There is one exception to the rule. If the plan has not changed the standard legal rights of the members of a class, then no approval is required from that class. Such a class of creditors is termed an **unimpaired class** because the creditors' collection rights have not been impaired by the reorganization process.

The M'bolo-Ziska Petrochemical Company filed for reorganization under Chapter 11 of the Bankruptcy Code. One class of creditors included unsecured creditors who were owed $200 or less. A second class included unsecured creditors who were owed over $200. The plan called for a complete repayment of all Class 1 creditors according to the terms of their original contracts. This provision made Class 1 an unimpaired class. The Class 2 creditors would have a choice. They could receive either a 60 percent repayment on the date of confirmation or 100 percent repayment extended over four years. The extended repayment plan called for a 30 percent repayment on the date of confirmation and seven 10 percent payments at six-month intervals. More than one-half of the Class 2 creditors would have to approve of the plan. In contrast, the Class 1 creditors have no approval rights since Class 1 is unimpaired.

Confirmation and Discharge The court will hold a hearing on the confirmation of the reorganization plan. A **confirmation** officially places a plan in operation. After confirmation, all property dealt with in the plan is free and clear of all claims of creditors and equity security holders. The debtor is discharged from any debts that arose before the date of confirmation.

30-4 FAMILY FARMER DEBT ADJUSTMENT—CHAPTER 12, BANKRUPTCY CODE

Recognizing the grave financial difficulties facing family farmers, Congress enacted the Family Farmer Debt Adjustment Act in 1986. The act is designed to help farmers create a plan for debt repayment that will allow them to keep their farms running. Thus, Chapter 12 is an alternative to the ordinary bankruptcy procedure provided for by Chapter 7. Under the act, a **family farmer** is defined as one who receives more than one-half of the total income from the farm. In addition, 80 percent of the farmer's debt must result from farm expenses.

Chapter 12 has some important characteristics that distinguish it from Chapter 13, which also allows individuals to file debt adjustment plans. First, the amount owed under Chapter 13 must not exceed $100,000 in unsecured debts or $350,000 in secured debts. In contrast, Chapter 12 sets a $1.5 million debt ceiling. Second, Chapter 13 is open to individuals only. Neither partnerships nor corporations can take advantage of a Chapter 13 filing. On the other hand, Chapter 12 is open to partnerships and corporations as long as a farm family owns at least half of the farm business.

Chapter 12 Procedures Like a filing under Chapters 7 and 11, a filing under Chapter 12 creates an automatic suspension of debt collection as soon as the order for relief is issued.It is possible for creditors to ask the court to exempt them from the suspension. However, a hearing on such a motion would have to be held, and the creditors would have to show why the court should grant any exemptions.

As is the case in Chapters 7 and 11, the court may appoint a trustee to handle the farm's finances. The Chapter 12 trustee has duties similar to those of

Chapter 7 and 11 trustees. In general, under Chapter 12, the farmer remains a debtor-in-possession. If the farmer is removed as debtor-in-possession, the trustee takes over.

The Adjustment Plan

Unlike the Chapter 11 debtor, who has a 120-day deadline to devise a reorganization plan, the Chapter 12 farm debtor is limited to 90 days. The clock starts running toward that 90-day deadline when the order for relief is granted. Debtors can file for an extension, though.

Contents of the Plan The Chapter 12 plan must include several provisions. First, the plan must include a provision which requires the debtor to turn over at least part of any future income to the trustee. Second, the plan must make certain that all priority claims are paid in full. It is possible, of course, for a priority creditor to voluntarily surrender this right. Priority claims for Chapter 12 are identical to those named for Chapter 7. Third, if the claims of creditors are grouped into classes, then each creditor in a class must be treated identically. Fourth, the plan must not take longer than three years to complete unless the time is extended by the court. The maximum extension is for two years.

Plan Confirmation A hearing must be held to confirm the plan. This hearing must be set up no longer than 45 days after the debtor has filed the plan. Unlike Chapter 11 creditors, Chapter 12 creditors have no prior input while the plan is being constructed. Secured creditors have approval power after the plan is written. Unsecured creditors do not have this right. However, unsecured creditors can object to the plan at the hearing. The court may still confirm the plan over the objections.

Breyfogle, who owned a dairy farm, filed for debt adjustment under Chapter 12. Two months after the relief order was issued by the court, Breyfogle filed his adjustment plan. Under the plan, unsecured creditors owed over $300 would receive 100 percent of the amount owed to them over a three-year period. They would receive 20 percent immediately and 10 percent at regular intervals. Kozlowski's Farm and Supply Co. objected to the plan. However, since Breyfogle was turning over 100 percent of his disposable income to the trustee for debt repayment, the court did not support Kozlowski's objection.

The debtor can begin to make payments under the plan before its confirmation. Such payments would go to the trustee who would hold them pending the plan's confirmation.

30-5 ADJUSTMENT OF DEBTS—CHAPTER 13, BANKRUPTCY CODE

Sometimes debtors overextend their credit. They have regular income, but they cannot pay all their bills. If given time, they may eventually be able to pay at least part of the amount they owe to each creditor. Chapter 13 of the Bankruptcy Act permits an individual debtor to develop a repayment plan, and upon completion of payments under the plan, to receive a discharge from most remaining debt.

Only individual debtors can take advantage of Chapter 13 provisions. Neither corporations nor partnerships can file under its provisions. However, soleproprietorships can file under Chapter 13, as long as they meet the statute's other requirements. These requirements hold that the debtor's liabilities cannot surpass $100,000 in unsecured debts or $350,000 in secured debts. Also the debtor must have an already established steady income. Only voluntary filings are permitted under Chapter 13. The automatic suspension provision clicks into place under Chapter 13 when the relief order is issued. A trustee oversees the Chapter 13 process. If Chapter 13 does not work out under certain circumstances, the individual can still file under Chapter 7.

The Chapter 13 Plan

It is the debtor's responsibility to file a debt readjustment plan under Chapter 13. Like Chapter 12, Chapter 13 requires the debtor to transfer future income to the trustee in order to satisfy outstanding debts. Although the debtor need not turn over all future income, some portion of it must go to the trustee. Like a Chapter 12 plan, the Chapter 13 plan must make certain that priority debtors receive full payment.

Also, like Chapter 12, if the plan sets up groups of creditors, all group members must be treated equally. Finally, Chapter 13 debtors must also abide by

Table 30-2 TYPES OF BANKRUPTCY PROCEDURES

Chapter Number/Name	*Who Can File?*	*When Used?*	*Special Features*
Chapter 7: Ordinary Bankruptcy	Everyone is eligible except banks, railroads and insurance companies. Filing can be voluntary or involuntary.	Used when debtor wants to discharge most debts and begin with a clean slate.	Debtor's property is liquidated. Some property is exempt. Some debts cannot be discharged.
Chapter 11: Reorganization	Individuals, partnerships and corporations can file. Railroads can file. Only commodity brokers and stockbrokers cannot. Filing can be voluntary or involuntary.	Used when debtor, usually a business, wants to continue operating, but needs to reorganize and liquidate debts.	Debtor-in-possession feature; debtor files plan within 120 days; plan must be fair, equitable, feasible. Creditors can also file plans. Confirmation needed.
Chapter 12: Family Farmer Debt Adjustment	Family Farmers can file including partnerships and corporations. Debt ceiling of $1.5 million.	Used when debtor is a family farmer who needs a debt adjustment plan to keep the farm running.	Debtor-in-possession feature; debtor files plan within 90 days; plan lasts three years (with two-year possible extension). Plan must be confirmed.
Chapter 13: Individual Debt Adjustment	Individuals only. No corporations or partnerships. No involuntary filings allowed. Debt ceiling of $450,000.	Used when an individual debtor with a steady income voluntarily decides to adopt a debt adjustment plan.	Only the debtor can file a plan. Payments must start 30 days after plan submitted. A few debts cannot be discharged. Plan lasts three years (with two-year possible extension).

the three-year rule requiring that the payment plan must be completed within three years. If the debtor files for an extension, the most the court will grant is two years. Thus, the maximum repayment time is five years.

Plan Confirmation Like Chapter 12 creditors, Chapter 13 creditors have no prior input while the plan is being created. Secured creditors have approval powers, but unsecured creditors do not. Unsecured creditors may, of course, object to the plan at the hearing. However, like Chapter 12, Chapter 13 will not allow the court to uphold an objection if the debtor plans to turn over 100 percent of all disposable income to the trustee for debt repayment.

Payments New amendments to the Bankruptcy Code compel the debtor to start payments within 30 days of submitting the plan to the court. If the court has yet to hold its hearing, the debtor pays the trustee. The trustee holds the money until the court upholds or rejects the plan.

Discharge Once the amounts agreed to under the plan are paid, all remaining debts are discharged. The list of debts that cannot be discharged under Chapter 13 is much shorter than the Chapter 7 list. Only alimony, child support, and priority claims must be satisfied in full under Chapter 13. Every other debt may be discharged one way or the other.

SUMMARY

30-1. Bankruptcy is the legal process that allows a debtor to get a fresh start by selling personal property to pay off creditors. The U.S. Constitution gives the federal government jurisdiction over bankruptcy proceedings. The Bankruptcy Code enacted by Congress is found in Title 11 of the U.S. Code.

30-2. Chapter 7 of the Bankruptcy Code covers ordinary bankruptcy. In ordinary bankruptcy, the trustee sells the debtor's property and uses the cash to pay creditors a portion of the amount owed to each one. Such a process can be either voluntary or involuntary.

30-3. Reorganization under Chapter 11 of the Bankruptcy Code allows debtors to overcome financial difficulties without selling *all* their property. Instead, a reorganization plan is drawn up that changes the debtor's payment schedule. The new schedule allows the debtor to maintain personal property while paying creditors.

30-4. Chapter 12 of the Bankruptcy Code applies to family farmers in financial difficulty. Under Chapter 12, a family farmer can maintain the farm while drawing up a debt adjustment plan to satisfy creditors.

30-5. Chapter 13 of the Bankruptcy Code applies only to individual debtors with established steady incomes. Such debtors can prepare a debt readjustment plan that will provide for repayment of all outstanding debts.

Understanding Key Legal Terms

automatic suspension (p. 415)
bankruptcy (p. 413)
bankruptcy trustee (p. 415)
confirmation (p. 421)
debtor-in-possession (p. 420)
family farmer (p. 421)
homestead exemption (p. 416)
liquidation (p. 414)
order for relief (p. 415)
primary committee (p. 420)
reorganization (p. 419)
unimpaired class (p. 420)
United States Code (p. 413)

Questions for Review and Discussion

1. What is the source of power that enables Congress to create federal statutory law dealing with bankruptcy and other debt adjustment procedures?
2. How does a debtor voluntarily institute a bankruptcy proceeding? Under what conditions can the debtor's creditors institute an involuntary proceeding?
3. Outline the automatic suspension process, and explain how it fulfills the objectives of the Bankruptcy Code.
4. Identify those classes of property which can be exempted from sale when a debtor files for bankruptcy.
5. Indicate the priority of claims on a debtor's assets once the debtor's property has been sold and reduced to cash.
6. Name those debts which cannot be discharged under a bankruptcy proceeding.
7. Discuss the purpose of Chapter 11 provisions of the Bankruptcy Code.
8. Who may approve a Chapter 11 reorganization plan? Name any exceptions to this rule.
9. In what ways does a Chapter 12 debt adjustment procedure differ from a Chapter 13 procedure?
10. List the criteria that must be met in order for a debtor to qualify for a Chapter 13 filing under the Bankruptcy Code.

Analyzing Cases

1. Three creditors filed an involuntary bankruptcy petition against the Manchester Lakes Association alleging that the association was not paying its bills when they came due. Manchester fought the petition, arguing that its general partner, Dominion Federal Savings and Loan, had enough money to pay these bills as they came due, even though it was not doing so. Should the court refuse to grant the order for relief if the debtor proves it has the ability to pay its bills? Explain. *In re Manchester Lakes Association,* 47 B.R. 798 (E.D. Virginia).

2. Finding itself in great financial difficulty, Fidelity Mortgage Investors filed a voluntary bankruptcy petition in a New York bankruptcy court. When the petition was led, the automatic suspension went into effect. Ignoring the suspension, Camelia and Farnale, two of FMI's creditors, filed suit against FMI in a Mississippi federal court. As a result, FMI was forced to pay out enormous sums of money in its own defense on the Mississippi case. FMI then returned to the bankruptcy court in New York and asked that both Camelia and Farnale be held in contempt of court for ignoring the suspension. Should the New York bankruptcy court hold Camelia and Farnale in contempt? Explain. *Fidelity Mortgage Investors v. Camelia Builders, Inc.,* 550 F.2nd 47 (2d Cir. Ct.).

3. When the Rahls filed for bankruptcy, they attempted to exclude their entire silver-

ware set from the bankruptcy sale by listing each piece at a value far under the $200 maximum allowed for each item of individual household goods. Had they listed the silverware as one item it would have been worth more than $6,000. Thus, the entire set would not have been exempt. By listing each piece of silverware separately, the total value did not exceed $4,000 and the entire set could be saved. Should the court force the Rahls to list the silverware set as one item, thus limiting the exemption to $200. Explain. *In the Matter of Rahl,* 14 B.R. 153 (E.D. Wisconsin).

4. Dubuque stole more than $4,000 from his employer, U-Haul. He later pled guilty to "theft by unauthorized taking or transfer." The court sentenced him to pay back the stolen money. When Dubuque filed for bankruptcy, U-Haul claimed that this debt would qualify as an exception to discharge. Is U-Haul correct? Explain. *In Re Dubuque,* 46 B.R. 156 (New Hampshire).

5. U.S. Truck Company, Inc. filed for a reorganization under Chapter 11 of the Bankruptcy Code. When the reorganization plan was presented for confirmation, one creditor objected to the plan. The creditor argued that the debtor was facing a possible strike and a new labor contract both of which could place an additional strain on the debtor's finances. These potential labor problems, the creditor concluded, made the plan unfeasible. U.S. Truck admitted that the labor problems existed but noted that the company had recently rebounded from its financial problems to become very successful. Moreover, the labor union had just ratified two previous labor contracts by a 95 percent majority vote. U.S. Truck concluded that these factors made the plan workable and that that was enough under the code, since the code did not require a guarantee of success. Is the conclusion correct? *In the Matter of U.S. Truck Co., Inc.,* 47 B.R. 932 (E.D. Michigan).

PART 6
Case Study
Superior Savings Association v. City of Cleveland

United States District Court
Northern District of Ohio
501 F. Supp. 1244

SUMMARY

Superior Savings held a properly recorded first mortgage on a two-story brick apartment building located at 6802 Superior Avenue in Cleveland. The mortgagor, Hughes, failed to keep the building in an appropriate state of repair. As a result, the city condemned the building. The city gave Hughes more than two months to make the needed repairs before the building would be demolished. When Hughes failed to comply, the building was torn down. At no time during the two months' grace period did Superior Savings receive any notice of the impending demolition by the city. Superior Savings sued, claiming that the city had violated the association's constitutional due process rights by depriving it of the mortgaged property without proper notice.

THE COURT'S OPINION: BEN C. GREEN, SENIOR DISTRICT JUDGE

The Fourteenth Amendment to the United States Constitution reads, in pertinent part: "...nor shall any State deprive any person of...property without due process of law;..."

Under circumstances such as those presented here, communities have been held liable to landowners for destruction of buildings without either notice or opportunity for a hearing. *Miles v. District of Columbia,* 510 F.2d 188 (C.A.D.C., 1975). But the nature of the interests held by a mortgagor landowner differs from those held by his mortgagee, and it has not been suggested that the interests of the mortgagor are subrogated to the mortgagee. Therefore, it will be necessary to examine the nature of the mortgagee's interests and determine to what extent constitutional protection should attach thereto.

In *Louisville Joint Stock Bank v. Radford,* 295 U.S. 555 at 594-95, 55 S.Ct. 854 at 865-866, 79 L.Ed. 1593 (1934), Justice Brandeis listed five property rights in a mortgage on real property which could not be taken from the mortgagee by Congress absent due process... Those attributes were set forth as follows:

"1. The right to retain the lien until the indebtedness secured is paid;
2. The right to realize upon the security by a judicial public sale;
3. The right to determine when such sale shall be held, subject only to the discretion of the court;
4. The right to protect its interest in the prop-

erty by bidding at such sale wherever held, and thus to assure having the mort gaged property devoted primarily to the satisfaction of the debt, either through receipt of the proceeds of a fair competitive sale or by taking the property itself.

5. The right to control meanwhile the property during the period of default, subject only to the discretion of the court, and to have the rents and profits collected by a receiver for the satisfaction of the debt...."

When plaintiff filed the mortgage on 6802 Superior Avenue for record, it thereby gave notice to the City of Cleveland and the whole world of its interest in the land and the building thereon. When the city failed to observe its own ordinances and did not give plaintiff notice of its intent to demolish the building, it denied plaintiff the due process of law. Since the denial of due process deprived plaintiff of a property interest protected by the Due Process Clause of the Fourteenth Amendment, the defendant city is liable to plaintiff for the damages caused.

It is axiomatic that the purpose of monetary damages is, to the extent that the payment of money can do it, to place the damaged party in the same position he would have been in had the wrongful act not occurred. *See* 22 Am.Jur.2d, *Damages,* § 12, n. 11, and cases cited therein. Where compensation and not punishment is the function, the law will not put him in a better position than he would be in had the wrong not been done. *See id.,* at § 13 and cases cited therein. "[T]he law... remains true to the principle that substantial damages should be awarded only to compensate actual injury." *Carey v. Piphus, supra,* 435 U.S. at 266, 98 S.Ct. at 1054.

It thus appears to the court that the proper measure of damages in this case would be the difference in value of plaintiff's mortgage just prior to the demolition of the building, and the value of that mortgage just after the structure was razed. The precise assessment of those damages is not possible on the present record. Further actions by the parties will be required to identify the standard by which that worth may be measured, and, through application of the standard through the fact-finding process, the measure of the loss.

An order will be entered granting partial summary judgment for plaintiff and against defendant on the issue of liability, reserving for later ruling the issues of the measure and amount of damages.

QUESTIONS FOR ANALYSIS

1. Why is it significant that Superior Savings properly recorded the mortage held on the Hughes property?
2. If another mortgagee held a mortgage on the property but did not record it, could that mortgagee use the same arguments used by Superior Savings to recover damages from the city? Explain.
3. What duty owed to Superior Savings has Hughes violated in this case?
4. Identify the constitutional amendment that gives Superior Savings its due process rights.
5. Did Superior Savings have an insurable interest in the property located at 6802 Superior Avenue?

PART 7
Agency and Employment

CHAPTER 31
The Principal and Agent Relationship

OUTLINE

COMMENTARY

When Elvis Presley reigned as the king of the pop-music world, practically every professional move he made—recording songs, giving performances, making movies—was managed by another person, Tom Parker. Parker's role was that of manager. Although Elvis did the actual performing, Parker handled just about everything else, from scheduling tours and negotiating contracts to selling souvenirs and photos.

Presley as performer and Parker as the manager of all business matters illustrates a common legal relationship known as *agency.* It exists when one person, known as the *principal,* authorizes another person, known as the *agent,* to act on the behalf of the principal in dealing with a third person.

Agency is of critical importance to business because it allows delegation of the authority to enter into a contract. By delegating contractual responsibilities to others, it is possible for individuals and companies to carry on business at many different places with many different persons at the same time. This chapter discusses various kinds of agency relationships, the nature of an agent's authority, and the actions or conduct that establish an agency.

OBJECTIVES

1. Describe the nature of the agency relationship.
2. Determine when an agency relationship exists between principal and agent, employer and employee, principal and independent contractor, and between officials of business organizations and third parties.
3. Distinguish among the express, implied, and apparent authority of an agent.
4. Explain the circumstances under which an agency is created by appointment, implication, necessity, operation of law, estoppel, and ratification.

31-1 NATURE OF THE AGENCY RELATIONSHIP

Agency is a legal agreement between two persons, whereby one person is designated the agent of the other. In the relationship, one party, the **agent,** is authorized to act for and under the control of the other, the **principal,** in negotiating and making contracts with a third party. The principal must in some manner indicate that the agent is to act for and under the control of the principal, and the agent must consent to act on behalf of and subject to the control of the principal.

The agency relationship is *fiduciary* in that the person with the duty to act does so in trust for the benefit of the principal. The relationship may or may not arise as a result of an actual contract.

When an agency relationship is created, specific obligations, rights, and liabilities arise which relate to the principal, the agent, and the third party.

Home Products hired sales representatives to introduce its products to homeowners. These representatives called at the homes, interviewed prospective customers, and in many instances obtained orders for products. This arrangement constituted an agency agreement in which Home Products (principal) is liable for the acts of its sales representatives (agents) in their dealings with homeowners (third parties).

When the agent is authorized to contract with third parties on behalf of the principal, the contract that the agent negotiates is between the principal and the third parties. As shown in Figure 31-1, the principal is bound to perform the contract as if the principal had personally executed the agreement.

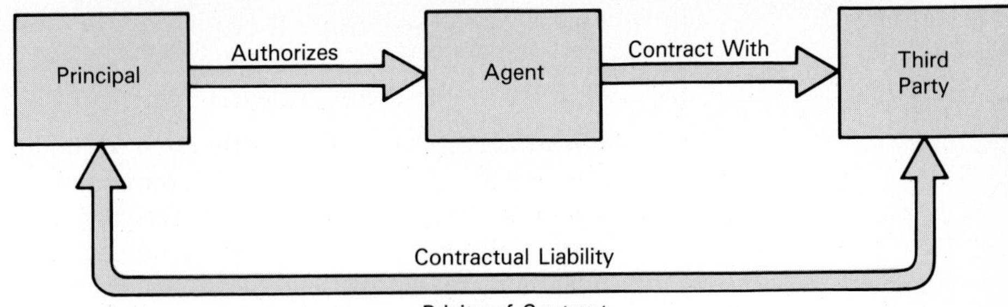

Figure 31-1 Agency relationship.

31-2 AGENCY AS DISTINGUISHED FROM OTHER RELATIONSHIPS

The courts are often called upon to distinguish between principal and agent relationships, employer and employee relationships, independent contractor, and business organization relationships.

Principal-Agent Relationship

In an agency relationship, the agent has the authority to represent the principal. This means that the principal is liable for the agent's acts when the agent deals with third parties for the principals. In the principal-agent relationship, the agent performs duties for the principal that require the exercise of judgment and discretion and that result in a contract.

Any person legally capable of entering into a contract may be a principal. Anyone appointed by the principal may be an agent. Even a minor or one who is mentally limited may be an agent, inasmuch as the acts of such persons are considered to be those of the principal.

Kinds of Principals There are three kinds of principals. A **disclosed principal** is one whose identity is known by third parties dealing with that principal's agent. When an agent does not reveal the existence of an agency relationship but appears to act in the agent's own behalf rather than for another, an **undisclosed principal** exists. A **partially disclosed principal** exists when the agent, in dealing with third parties, reveals the existence of an agency relationship but does not identify the principal.

Kinds of Agents Agents are generally classified according to scope of their responsibility.

A **general agent** is a person given broad authority to act on behalf of the principal, conducting the bulk of the principal's business activity on a daily basis.

Semlak, manager of a Reliable Oil Company service station, hired A-1 Painting Company to paint the interior office and work areas. Semlak also employed two extra attendants to monitor the self-service pumps. As a general agent for Reliable Oil Company, Semlak has the authority to take these independent actions which protect and promote the interest of Reliable Oil Company.

A **special agent** is a person who is authorized to conduct only a particular transaction or to perform only a specified act for the principal. Examples are real estate brokers, lawyers, and accountants who are retained to do a specific job and whose authority is restricted to those acts necessary to accomplish it.

A **factor,** or common merchant, is a special agent employed to sell merchandise consigned for that purpose. The factor has possession of the goods and sells them for and in behalf of a principal. A factor who guarantees the credit of a third party to a principal and guarantees the solvency of the purchaser and performance of the contract is known as ***del credere*** **agent.** In the event of default, the *del credere* agent is liable to the principal.

Lutz employed Saverine to act as her agent in selling merchandise. The contract of agency included a guaranty by Saverine that Lutz would not suffer loss because of sales on credit that Saverine made with third parties. Shortly after Saverine sold merchandise to Malloy valued at $12,000, Malloy declared bankruptcy. As a *del credere* agent, Saverine guaranteed the credit of Malloy and is liable to Lutz for the value of the merchandise.

Liability of Principal The principal is liable on all contracts that a general or special agent may enter into with third parties, as long as the agent acts within the actual or apparent authority conferred by the principal. The principal is also liable for torts or damages of the agent while performing the duties of the agency. This includes criminal acts if conspired in, commanded, or authorized by the principal.

An undisclosed principal can be held liable for the acts of the agent once the identity of the principal is disclosed. Once the identity of the principal is revealed, a third party may sue either the principal or the agent. Once this election is made, however, the third party cannot later decide to sue the other, unless the principal was undisclosed at the time the choice was made.

Liability of Agent When an agent is not known to be an agent and is acting as a principal, the agent can be held as a principal. When a person is known to be an agent, but it is not known for whom the agent acts, the third party can also hold the agent liable.

In addition, when an agent exceeds the authority conferred by the principal, the agent can be made personally liable.

An agent is liable for torts or damages, but if they are committed while the agent is acting within conferred authority, the principal is also liable.

Minors and Agency Law A principal may not use the infancy of an agent as a reason for avoiding a contract made by that agent. The principal who is a minor may generally avoid or accept a contract made by an agent to the same extent that he could had he dealt directly with the third party. However, state statutes are not universal in the way they treat the business contracts of minors. Some state courts have held that a minor who is sufficiently mature to run a business may not avoid business-related contracts made while running the business.

Davis, a minor who owned a stationery store, hired Craig, an adult, as store manager. Craig contracted with a supply house to purchase a new cash register for the store. Davis refused to accept delivery or to pay for the register. In the event the court interprets this transaction to be reasonably related to the carrying on of Davis's business, it could hold that the purchase agreement was binding on Davis.

Employer-Employee Relationship

The legal principles governing the relationship of principal and agent and of employer and employee are basically the same. The main difference between the two relationships is the agent's authority to contract. Whereas an agent contracts on behalf of a principal, an employee has no such rights or powers. An employee merely performs mechanical acts for the employer under the employer's direction and subject to the employer's control. The employer controls not only what shall be done by the employee but also how it shall be done.

A person who is an employee, however, may be required to perform duties for the employer that require the exercise of judgment and discretion and that result in the establishment of a contractual relationship between the employer and a third party. The employee then has the status of an agent even without a formal contract of agency.

Mayer, an estate manager, frequently sent an employee to a building supply center for needed hardware, with instructions to charge them to the estate's account. These purchases were paid for without question. When the employee charged items for personal use, without Mayer's knowledge or consent, the building and supply company could collect from the estate. The employer was liable for the acts of the employee performed within the scope of the employee's apparent duties.

The terms **master** (employer) and **servant** (employee) are now outdated, but continue to be used in some legal circumstances.

Borrowed Servant The term "servant" retains significance in tort liability cases where the employee serves as a borrowed servant. This condition arises when an employer loans an employee to another employer. Which employer should bear the loss caused by the employee's tort depends on which one had control of the worker when the tort occurred.

In dealing with the borrowed-servant doctrine and the general master-servant relationship, the courts refer to the appropriate section of the ***Restatement (Second) of Agency,*** an authoritative compilation of the common law of agency throughout the United States, referred to in judicial decisions and opinions. This compilation defines a servant as an agent who is employed to perform service in the affairs of a master and who with respect to the physical conduct in the performance of the service is controlled or is subject to the right to control by the master. The same *Restatement* also states various circumstances that are helpful in applying this definition. Circumstances such as whose work is being performed and who supplies the tools and the place of work are relevant. The skill of the worker and the manner in which the worker is paid may also be relevant to the ease with which control over a worker may be shifted from one master to another. And the length of time that the nominal servant of one master has been aiding in the business of another is indicative of a shift in control.

Casey, an iron worker for Phalen Steel at a construction site, was standing on the back of a truck driven by Koch, an employee of Cattani Gravel. Cattani had leased the truck and its driver to Phalen Steel for a set hourly amount. The lease required Cattani to maintain the truck and pay its driver. Koch, like other Cattani drivers, was responsible for inspecting his truck and keeping it repaired and serviced during the term of the lease. Suddenly and without warning, the truck jerked forward and Casey was injured. Casey sued Koch and Cattani, seeking damages for negligence. The court found that Koch remained an employee of Cattani, despite his loan to Phalen Steel. Therefore, Cattani was liable for Koch's negligence.

Independent Contractor

An **independent contractor** is a party who contracts to do a job and retains complete control over the methods employed to obtain final completion. Independent contractors are not subject to the control of the party they are serving. In this capacity, independent contractors are neither employees nor agents. They maintain all required business licenses and permits and pay all job-related expenses; they are obligated only to get the job done. They are liable for all wrongs or injury resulting from any breach of their legal duties. The other party has the right, however, to inspect and approve, or disapprove, the results of the independent contractor's performance.

The degree of control or supervision over the matter and means by which work is performed is the principal element that differentiates independent contractors and employees. Employers have the right to control employees. They do not have the right to control independent contractors.

Other guidelines are helpful in establishing an independent contractor relationship. Independent contractors, not the principal, have the power to choose their own workers and to discharge them on the job. They provide their own equipment and tools and are responsible for performing the entire job, including cleaning up. Architects, painters, physicians, nurses, and plumbers are examples of independent contractors when they are in business for themselves. They can lose this status and become employers, however, if they are hired as members of an employer's staff. The independent contractor and not the hiring party is liable to third parties for negligence.

National Development Corp. awarded a contract to Case Utility Equipment to transport temporary structures and erect them on a new building site. Owing to Case Utility's negligence, one of the trailers broke loose en route and crashed into a passenger bus. The bus was heavily damaged, and a number of passengers were injured. Since Case Utility was using its own truck and exercised complete control over the loading and transport of the structures, it was operating as an independent contractor. Case Utility rather than National Development Corp. would be held liable for the property damage and injuries caused by this act of negligence.

Business Organization

Almost every executive of a company acts as the company's agent in some capacity. A purchasing agent is authorized to make agreements to buy equipment and supplies. A salesperson may be authorized to complete sales agreements. The treasurer can dispense the company's money.

The operation of partnerships and corporations (see Part 8, Business Organization and Regulation) illustrates the application of agency laws.

Partnerships The Uniform Partnership Act and the partners' agreement govern partnership operations. Every partner in a partnership is an agent of that partnership, for the purpose of its business. Thus, partners as agents are liable for the contracts that each makes in behalf of the business. The appointment of an agent by one partner is binding on all other partners.

Bianco and Gilman operated the Polka Dot Shop as partners. During Bianco's vacation, Gilman ordered a large selection of maillots and bikinis in stretch velvet and one-piece beach suits in black cotton knit. Although Bianco was not present and might disagree with the selection, she will be liable for her share of the expense. Gilman was acting as agent for the partnership, representing both herself and Bianco.

Corporations The corporation is an artificial person created by state statute authorizing it to provide and deliver products and services by means of agents acting in its behalf. (See Chapter 36.)

All aspects of agency law pertaining to wrongful acts committed by agents against third parties or their property also apply to corporations. A corporation, being a legal entity only, cannot act for itself. All officers and employees are either agents or servants of the corporation, the principal.

The manager of a grocery store sued the National Biscuit Company because one of its agents, a salesperson, had assaulted him. The salesperson got into a furious argument with the store manager over the stocking of Nabisco products on shelf space reserved for other brands. The Nabisco salesperson challenged the manager to fight. When the challenge was refused, the salesperson beat up the grocery store manager in full view of customers. In the subsequent lawsuit, the court concluded that since the assault occurred while the salesperson was officially on duty and the dispute clearly related to his job as agent of Nabisco, the company was liable for the harm done to the store manager.

31-3 SCOPE OF THE AGENT'S AUTHORITY

Agents may perform only acts that have been authorized by the principal. Agents who exceed their delegated authority become personally liable. Unauthorized actions do not bind the principal unless those actions can be reasonably assumed by a third party to be within the scope of the agent's authority. Authority granted an agent may be express, implied, or apparent.

Express Authority

The agent's **express authority** is that authority which the principal voluntarily and specifically sets forth as instructions in the agency agreement, orally or in writing. Sometimes referred to as *actual authority,* express authority may also be indicated by conduct as when a sales representative informs the principal of travel plans and no objection to them is expressed.

Implied Authority

Implied authority is the authority of an agent to perform acts which are necessary or customary to carry out expressly authorized duties. It stems from the reasonable effort of an agent to understand the meaning of the principal's words describing what the agent is to do. Implied authority can be described as *incidental authority* when the acts performed are reasonably necessary to carry out an express authority. For example, an agent might have incidental authority to contract for the repair of the principal's van that broke down while being used to deliver perishable products that the agent had express authority to sell and deliver. Implied authority may be described as *customary authority* when the agent acts in conformity with the general trade or professional practices of the business.

Apparent Authority

Apparent authority is an accountability doctrine whereby a principal, by virtue of words or actions, leads a third party to believe that an agent has authority but no such authority was intended. The principal may make known to the third party in a variety of ways that authority exists. It may be generated by a direct statement to the third party or by permitting someone to have a meaningful business title, occupy a position, or perform duties that give a third party reason to believe that the person has the authority to act for the principal. The doctrine of apparent authority protects innocent third parties who rely on the impression created by the principal's words, acts, or conduct that appropriate authority has been conferred on the agent.

The party with whom the agent is dealing must reasonably believe that the agent has authority to so act, must have had no notice of a lack of such authority, and must act or rely upon the agent's appearance of authority. Once the principal clothes an agent with the semblance of authority, the principal cannot deny that the authority exists when another person has relied upon that appearance.

Meeks parked his car in Poole's garage. Wishing to sell the car, Meeks gave the necessary title papers to Poole, but instructed Poole not to make a final sale without first consulting him regarding the price. Having found a prospect who offered a good price, Poole sold the car and transferred the title papers. Meek's act of giving the title papers to Poole would be viewed by the court as conduct that would reasonably lead a third party to conclude that Poole had apparent authority to sell the car. Thus Meeks could not rescind the sale, because he is bound by the contract made by his agent.

Appointment of Subagents

Agents are appointed by principals because of their assumed fitness to perform some particular job. Since principals rely on the agent's personal skill and integrity, they do not ordinarily give agents the power to delegate someone else to do the job they have agreed to do. Should an agent delegate authority without authorization, the acts of the subagent do not impose any obligation or liability on the principal to third parties.

In some instances, the agent is permitted to delegate authority even though the agency agreement does not contain an express power of delegation. Such an intention may be implied from the nature of the employment or custom and usage. A real estate broker, for example, has the implied authority to delegate authority to salespersons. The nature of the business is such that it is presumed that the principal (seller) contemplates that the authority given to the agent (broker) would be exercised through the broker's agents (subagents).

Exceptions to the Delegation of Authority

The purpose of agency cannot be criminal or contrary to public policy. In addition, some acts must be performed in person, not delegated to an agent. Nondelegable acts include, but are not limited to, voting, serving on juries, testifying in court, making a will, and holding public office. However, forms required by law, such as tax returns and license applications, may be executed by an agent provided that the identity of the principal as well as the identity and capacity of the agent are clearly shown.

31-4 CREATION OF THE AGENCY RELATIONSHIP

An agency is created by some action or conduct on the part of the principal. A would-be agent cannot by conduct alone or by any statement establish an agency relationship. It is therefore wise for a third party when dealing with an agent to determine the nature and extent of the agent's authority.

Kildall looked at a secondhand car at Lovell's used-car lot. Lovell permitted Kildall to take the car out to show his wife. While driving the car to his home, he became involved in an accident with another auto which resulted in injuries to Crockett. In a suit against Lovell, Crockett argued that Kildall was Lovell's agent and was therefore responsible for his negligence. The court held that one cannot be an agent unless empowered to represent the principal. Lovell merely allowed Kildall to take the car to show his wife. Kildall was not authorized to represent Lovell in any way.

An agency relationship is generally created by appointment, implication, necessity, operation of law, estoppel, or by ratification.

Agency by Appointment

The usual agency relationship is created by an expressed agreement in which the agent is appointed to act for and on behalf of the principal.

The agreement may be oral or written in the form of a **power of attorney.** As shown in Figure 31-2, a power of attorney is an instrument in writing by which one person, as principal, appoints another as agent and confers the authority to perform certain specified acts on behalf of the principal. It establishes the authority of the agent to third parties with whom the agent may deal.

Know all Men by these Presents,

THAT I, Fred Herberts, of the City of Elizabeth, in the County of Union, and State of New Jersey, --------------------------------
have made, constituted and apppointed, and by these presents do make, constitute and appoint George Rose, of the City of Hillside, in the County of Union, and State of New Jersey, ---
my ------- *true and lawful attorney for* me ---- *and in* my --- *name, place and stead* to represent me in the management of my property at 15 Essex Avenue, Hillside, New Jersey -- *giving and granting unto* my ------ *said attorney full power and authority to do and perform all and every act and thing whatsoever requisite and necessary to be done in and about the premises, as fully, to all intents and purposes, as* I -------- *might or could do if personally present, with full power of substitution and revocation, hereby ratifying and confirming all that* my ----- *said attorney or* his ------- *substitute shall lawfully do or cause to be done by virtue hereof.*

This instrument may not be changed orally.

In Witness Whereof: I -- *have hereunto set* my ----- *hand and seal the* fourteenth ------- *day of* October -------------------- *in the year one thousand nine hundred and* --.

Sealed and delivered in the presence of

William Pastor

David Gordan

Fred Herberts (L.S.)

STATE OF New Jersey
COUNTY OF Union } *ss:*

BE IT KNOWN, *That on the* fourteenth ----------- *day of* October ----- *one thousand nine hundred and* ----------- *before me* Thomas S. Trainer --------------------- *a Notary Public in and for the State of* New Jersey ----------- *duly commissioned and sworn, personally came and appeared* -------- Fred Herberts --------------------------------- *to me personally known, and known to me to be the same person described in and who executed the Power of Attorney, and* he ------------ *acknowledged the within Power of Attorney to be* his --- *act and deed.*

IN TESTIMONY WHEREOF, *I have hereunto subscribed my name and affixed my seal of office, the day and year last above written.*

THOMAS S. TRAINER
Notary Public, State of New Jersey
No. 404912284
Qualified in Union County
Certificate Filed in New Jersey
Commission Expires November 9, 19...

Thomas S. Trainer
Notary Public

Figure 31-2 Power of attorney.

Sarokhan employed an agent to develop land she owned by drilling for gas and oil. She executed a power of attorney authorizing the agent to contract for the purchase or sale of any property and to execute any necessary leases affecting the interest of Sarokhan. The power of attorney did not give the agent authority to make a loan to drillers in order that their work would continue. In an interpretation of the terms of the power of attorney, the court would reason that the agent's power to purchase, sell, and lease does not include the power to make a loan.

Equal-Dignities Rule In most states, the equal-dignities rule provides that when a principal authorizes an agent to enter into a written contract on behalf of the principal, the agent's authority to do so must also be in writing. The rule generally applies when the type of contract which the authorized person is to negotiate for another is required by the Statute of Frauds to be in writing (see Chapter ll).

Agency by Implication

An agency by implication may be created voluntarily by any conduct or actions of the principal and agent that reflect the intent to create an agency relationship, even though such intent is not expressed orally or in writing.

Any conduct or words of the principal that give another cause to believe that the principal approves of that person's acting as agent is sufficient to create an agency. Allowing a person to act as an agent knowingly and without objection will also be viewed as permission to act as an agent.

Agency by Necessity

An agency by necessity is created lawfully when circumstances make such an agency necessary. If, for example, a real estate broker contracts for the repair of burst water pipes in the absence of the owner whose property the broker has been employed to sell, the court would hold that an agency of necessity had been created in order to prevent loss to the owner (principal).

Agency by Operation of Law

The courts may create or find an agency when there is none if it appears from the facts that a necessity or desired social policy is involved. A child to whom a parent has failed to provide the necessities of life may be declared by the court an agent of the parent for the purpose of purchasing necessaries the parent failed to provide. Under such an agency relationship, the parent would be bound by such contracts as long as they are reasonable.

Gustavson, the father of three children, abandoned his family after placing an advertisement in the classified section of the local newspaper stating that he would no longer be responsible for any bills unless contracted by himself. Mrs. Gustavson bought food, clothing, and medical care for the children and herself, charging everything to her husband. Mrs. Gustavson is an agent by necessity, and her husband is responsible for contracts made by her for all reasonable necessaries of life.

Agency by Estoppel

An agency by estoppel is created when one person is falsely represented to be an agent when no such agency relationship exists. The conduct of the agent alone cannot create an agency by estoppel. The principal must willfully or negligently or by silence give the false impression that another is the principal's agent. Further, having dealt with the alleged agent in reliance on the false impression, the third party must be damaged by the fact that an actual agency relationship did not exist. In such a case, the principal is barred (estopped) from denying the apparent agency relationship.

Weingart, manager of Rusty Bug Restorations, permitted an employee of Spray Painting to use one of the uniforms worn by Rusty Bug Restorations employees. Without authority, the Spray Painting employee sold four new tires to a customer at a reduced price that was excessively low. Since Weingart had allowed the Spray Painting employee to give the customer the impression that he was a regular Rusty Bug employee, Weingart would be barred from denying that Rusty Bug Restorations was liable on the contract for the tires or their replacement warranty.

Agency by Ratification

Agents sometimes perform acts on behalf of the principal that exceed their authority. In such cases, the principal for whom the agent claimed to act may either ignore the transaction or ratify it. **Ratification** occurs when the principal approves the unauthorized act performed by an agent or by one who has no authority to act as an agent. Although an agent generally is personally liable to third parties for actions in excess of the agent's authority, this is not true when the third party knows that the agent has exceeded the proper level of authority.

In addition to an intent to ratify, certain other conditions must be fulfilled for ratification to be valid: The principal must have the capacity to ratify, and the act to be ratified must be legal. The principal must have knowledge of all the material facts. The ratification must apply to the entire act of the agent. The act must have been done on behalf of the principal. Ratification must occur before the third party withdraws.

The principal cannot accept the benefits of an unauthorized act and then refuse to accept the obligations that are part of it. The principal becomes bound as though the agent had authority to act.

Bateman placed an order with a salesperson from a wholesale beef company for weekly shipments of beef. Bateman mailed a purchase order containing the terms of the agreement and was informed by the beef company that it was their intention to honor the transaction. However, the beef company defaulted and attempted to repudiate the contract by contending that its salesperson lacked the authority required to accept the order. The court reasoned that even though its contention was true, the beef company nonetheless had ratified the agreement and rendered itself liable.

SUMMARY

31-1. Agency is the legal fiduciary relationship that exists when the principal authorizes the agent to create, modify, or end contractual relations involving the principal and third parties. The contracts that the agent negotiates are between the principal and third parties, and the principal is bound to perform them as if the principal had personally executed the agreement.

31-2. Only an individual capable of entering into a contract may be a principal. There are three kinds of principals—disclosed, undisclosed, or partially disclosed. Anyone may be appointed an agent. Agents are commonly classified as general agents, special agents, or factor and *del credere* agents.

An employee (servant) performs acts for the employer (master) and is subject to the employer's control. Some employees are also agents.

Independent contractors are neither employees nor agents. They are hired to accomplish a particular result and are not under the direct supervision and control of the hiring party. Partnerships, corporations, and other businesses all act through agents.

31-3. An agent's authority may arise expressly from the written or spoken words of the principal to the agent or implied from the agent's reasonable effort to understand the meaning of the principal's words describing what the agent is to do. Apparent authority results from impressions by the principal to a third party that give the party reason to believe that an individual has authority to act for the principal. Principals do not ordinarily give agents the power to delegate authority to appoint subordinates.

31-4. An agency relationship generally may be created by appointment, implication, necessity, or operation of law. Under certain circumstances, the principal may be legally prevented (estopped) from asserting that the agent's act was unauthorized. Ratification by the principal of an unauthorized act by another person does not create agency, but it has the effect of agency. When the principal does not ratify another's unauthorized act, the agent or other person is personally liable on the contract.

Understanding Key Legal Terms

agency (p. 430)
agent (p. 430)
apparent authority (p. 436)
del credere agent (p. 432)
disclosed principal (p. 431)
express authority (p. 436)
factor (p. 432)
general agent (p. 431)
implied authority (p. 436)
independent contractor (p. 434)
master (p. 432)
partially disclosed principal (p. 431)
power of attorney (p. 438)
principal (p. 430)
ratification (p. 440)
servant (p. 432)
special agent (p. 432)
undisclosed principal (p. 431)

Questions for Review and Discussion

1. Define the position of the three parties involved in the principal-agent relationship.
2. Differentiate between general agents and special agents according to the scope of their responsibilities.
3. Describe the liability of both principal and agent.
4. Distinguish between principal and agent relationships and employer and employee relationships.
5. Identify the principal element that differentiates independent contractors and employees.
6. Contrast the agent's express authority and implied authority.
7. Discuss how apparent authority is conferred on an agent and the manner by which it must be established by the party with whom the agent is dealing.
8. Explain the purpose of a power of attorney in an agency by appointment.
9. What are the circumstances under which an agency is created by appointment, implication, operation of law, estoppel, and ratification?
10. Describe the conditions that must be fulfilled for an agency by ratification to be valid.

Analyzing Cases

1. Food Caterers, Inc., had a franchise agreement with Chicken Delight, Inc. Carfiro was employed by Food Caterers to deliver hot chicken bearing the trademark "Chicken Delight." While making a delivery, Carfiro was involved in an accident that killed McLaughlin. In a suit naming Chicken Delight, the franchisor, as defendant, the McLaughlin estate argued that Carfiro was an agent of Chicken Delight since Carfiro was acting for the benefit of that company. There was no evidence, however, that Carfiro was hired, paid, instructed by, or even known by Chicken Delight. Decision for whom and why? *Estate of McLaughlin v. Chicken Delight, Inc.* 321 A.2d 456 (Connecticut).

2. Stahl was having trouble with her Volkswagen. She brought it to the service station of LePage, where it was examined and the trouble diagnosed. LePage informed Stahl that he would not be able to do the work, but that his employee Donley wanted to take the job on his own and could make use of the garage facilities for this purpose. A new engine was required, and Donley installed the wrong engine. The entire job had to be done over at a cost of hundreds of dollars. Stahl brought suit against LePage. She argued that she should be allowed to recover against LePage for the misdeed of Donley, because Donley had apparent authority to act as LePage's agent. LePage disputed this, arguing that the facts did not warrant a finding of agency under any theory. How should the court find in this dispute? Why? *Stahl v. LePage,* 352 A.2d 682 (Vermont).

3. Castle Fabrics, Inc., sold fabric to Fortune Manufacturers, Inc. A dispute arose as to the acceptability of the fabric received and Fortune returned the fabric to Castle for full credit. Castle gave Fortune only partial credit and sued Fortune for recovery of its loss. In court, Fortune showed a credit memorandum from a Castle employee indicating that Fortune would be given full credit for the fabric. Although it was within the regular responsibility of the Castle employee to send the memorandum, on this occasion

management had specifically instructed the employees not to send one. Fortune argued that the employee was an agent of Castle and thus chargeable with any mistake the agent made. Castle claimed it was not chargeable with the action of its employee because the employee had disobeyed specific instructions not to send the memorandum. Judgment for whom and why? *Castle Fabrics, Inc., v. Fortune Furniture Mfrs.,* 459 F. Supp. 409 (N.D. Mississippi).

4. Ross needed a grinding mill and consulted Clifton, who on occasion repaired such mills but who did not sell them. Ross and Clifton together selected a mill from a catalog that Clifton happened to have on hand which they decided would meet Ross's purposes. Ross instructed Clifton to order the mill they had selected and Clifton did so in his own name and with his own money. When the mill arrived, Ross refused to accept it, stating that it was too small and would not do the job he intended it to do. Clifton brought suit to recover the amount he had spent. Judgment for whom and why? *Clifton v. Ross,* 28 S.W. 1085 (Arkansas).

5. Nielson had limited authority to purchase cattle for his principal, Hauser Packing Company. Christensen, who knew of Nielson's limited authority and who also knew that Nielson was exceeding that authority, nevertheless contracted with Nielson to sell cattle to the packing company. When the packing company refused to accept the cattle, Christensen brought suit against Nielson for damages, showing that Hauser Packing Company refused to ratify the unauthorized act of its agent. Judgment for whom and why? *Christensen v. Nielson,* 276 P.645 (Utah).

6. Ketter Engineering Inc. accepted a contract to enlarge the plant of Canberra Laboratory. The laboratory owners supplied all blueprints and gave instructions to Ketter Engineering to proceed with the job. During construction, a section of exterior wall fell and several passing pedestrians were injured. Suit was brought by the injured pedestrians against the laboratory owners for all damages suffered. Judgment for whom and why?

7. Higgins appointed Barkley as agent to manage her appliance outlet. On display was a special manufacturer's sample of a new television set which Barkley was instructed not to sell. Lambert, who was not aware of these instructions, offered to purchase the set. Barkley sold it to Lambert, promising delivery the following day. Higgins refused to deliver the set and Lambert sued for breach of contract. Higgins argued that since Barkley had exceeded his authority as agent, the agreement was void. Judgment for whom and why?

8. Krider often sent her gardener to Bruce's Garden Mart to make purchases on credit for items needed in the care of her property. On one occasion the gardener bought a large quantity of bulbs, and Krider refused to pay for them. Krider claimed that she had not instructed the gardener to purchase the bulbs. In the suit that followed Krider argued that the gardener did not have expressed or implied authority to purchase bulbs on her behalf. Judgment for whom and why?

CHAPTER 32
Operation and Termination of Agency

OUTLINE

32-1 Agent's Obligations to Principal
- Obedience to Instructions
- Loyalty
- Judgment, Prudence, and Skill
- Duty to Account
- Personal Service
- Communicate Information
- Remedies Available to Principal

32-2 Principal's Obligations to Agent
- Compensation
- Reimbursement
- Indemnification
- Cooperation
- Duration of Agent's Employment
- Remedies Available to Agent

32-3 Tort and Criminal Liability in an Agency
- Tort Liability
- Criminal Liability

32-4 Termination of Agency
- Termination by Act of the Parties
- Termination by Operation of the Law
- Agency Coupled With An Interest
- Notice of Termination to Third Parties

COMMENTARY

Ignatuk, the manager of a rock group, contracted to furnish music for a college dance. The operation of this contractual relationship involves mutual obligations of the rock group, the manager of the group, and the college dance committee. Ignatuk, the agent, acts on behalf of the group and only in the group's best interests. Among other obligations, Ignatuk must obey all instructions, perform assigned duties with reasonable care and skill, and account for money owed the group. The rock group, the principal, must pay Ignatuk for services rendered, reimburse him for money spent on behalf of the group, and make good for any damage suffered in acting for the group's benefit. The dance committee, the third party, has the obligation to live up to the terms of the agency agreement.

What if one of the parties to the agency relationship violates an obligation? What remedies are available to the damaged party? This chapter examines the legal effects of acts that are within and without the agency relationship—those which involve the liabilities of the principal, the authority of the agent, and the rights of third parties.

OBJECTIVES

1. Identify the major duties imposed upon the agent in compliance with the agency agreement and the fiduciary relationship with the principal.
2. Summarize the duties the principal owes to the agent that are created by the agency relationship.

3. Explain the underlying rationale for the concept of vicarious liability and the doctrine of *respondeat superior,* and discuss the extent of liability that they impose upon a principal or employer.
4. Differentiate between agency terminations accomplished by actions of the parties and those accomplished by operation of the law.
5. Recognize when notice of agency termination must be communicated individually to third parties and when a public notice is sufficient.

32-1 AGENT'S OBLIGATIONS TO PRINCIPAL

The agency relationship between agent and principal establishes rights and obligations that may be expressed in the agreement or merely implied. As noted in Chapter 31, an individual who acts as agent for another has a fiduciary relationship with the principal. This relationship implies the placement of trust and confidence in the agent that the agent will serve the principal's interests before all others. Thus, an agent may not enter into any agency transaction in which the agent has a personal interest. An agent must also not take a position in conflict with the interest of the principal.

In compliance with the agency contract and the fiduciary relationship, various obligations are imposed upon the agent. These obligations generally involve the duty (1) to obey all instructions, (2) to be loyal to the principal, (3) to exercise reasonable judgment, prudence, and skill, (4) to account for money and property received, (5) to perform work personally, and (6) to communicate fully all facts that affect the subject matter of the agency.

Obedience to Instructions

The agent, whether being paid or acting gratuitously, must obey all reasonable and legal instructions issued by the principal that relate to the agency agreement. In obeying the instructions of the principal, the agent is duty-bound to remain within the **scope of authority**, or **scope of employment** (i.e., range of acts done while performing one's job duties). For example, if the agent were to sell equipment to a third party in violation of the principal's instructions, the agent is liable for any injury suffered by the principal.

Loyalty

An agent may not engage in any activity that would result in a conflict of interest with the business of the principal. This duty of *loyalty* implies strict and continuing faithfulness to the principal's best interests at all times. Hence, the agent must resist any temptation to use acquired confidential information to advance the agent's own interest at the expense of the principal.

Browner, purchasing agent for Compudata, using her own funds, purchased jumper wires from Wire Products, Inc., at a special discount. Each time Compudata needed additional jumper wires, Browner supplied them from her personal supply at the regular price. She recorded the transaction as if the wires were purchased from an acceptable supplier and pocketed the difference. This practice represented a breach of Browner's fiduciary relationship to Compudata since agents have a duty to act in the best interests of the principal at all times. Compudata could sue to recover the profits made by Browner.

Judgment, Prudence, and Skill

Agents imply that they possess the required knowledge, training, and skill to properly perform and carry out their agency obligations with reasonable care, skill, and diligence. Unless an agent claims to be an expert, the principal is entitled to expect that the agent has the degree of skill commonly displayed by others employed in similar work. An expert such as a person in a profession requiring specific education and a special license must use the expert judgment, prudence, and skill possessed by others who have been admitted to those professions. Whether an expert or not, the agent may be liable to the principal for losses resulting from personal neglect or incompetence.

Duty to Account

The agent has a duty to keep a separate account of the principal's funds. Whatever money the agent receives during and as a result of the agency relationship is held in trust for the principal. An accounting must be given the principal within a reasonable period of time after money or property is received or disbursed.

Money collected by the agent must be held separate from funds belonging to the agent. If deposited in a bank, the money must be deposited in a separate account and so identified that a trust is apparent. Failure to keep such funds separate is known as *commingling*, and the agent may be held personally liable for any resulting losses.

Browne sold equipment for Dart Dental Supply. Whenever a cash collection was made, Browne would mix the money with his own. Should he fail to keep an accurate record of customer payments or be unable to account for all money collected during the working day, Dart Dental Supply would have the right to demand all Browne's commingled money.

Personal Service

The agency relationship is usually one involving an agreement for personal services. In the absence of authority to do so, an agent may not delegate duties to others unless such duties are purely mechanical in nature, requiring no particular knowledge, training, skill, or responsibility.

Communicate Information

The agent is duty-bound to keep the principal fully informed of all facts which materially affect the subject matter of the agency and which come to the agent's attention when acting within the agent's scope of authority or employment. The law assumes that if an agent receives either notice or information, it was communicated to the principal. Therefore, the rights and liabilities of the principal to any third party are the same as if the principal had personally received the notice or information.

Karcher instructed Woolf to purchase a used bulldozer for use in his business. Ellis offered to sell Woolf a bulldozer. On a test run, Woolf discovered that the bulldozer did not operate correctly in reverse speeds. Believing that the bulldozer was an excellent buy and could be repaired easily, Woolf bought it for Karcher. Shortly after delivery, Karcher demanded the return of the purchase price because the equipment did not operate properly in reverse speeds. Since Woolf had knowledge of the bulldozer's defect in the course of carrying out his duties and before purchasing it, the law assumes that Karcher had the same information. He cannot use the bulldozer's defect as the basis for withdrawing from the deal.

Remedies Available to Principal

Remedies are always available when an agent fails to observe a duty owed to a principal. For instance, the principal may do one or more of the following:

1. Terminate the agent's contract of employment
2. Withhold compensation otherwise due the agent
3. Recover profit the agent made in violation of agency obligations
4. Recover money or property gained or held by the agent to which the principal is entitled
5. Restrain the agent from continuing to breach the agency obligations
6. Recover damages from the agent for breach of the contract of employment or assessed against the principal for the agent's wrongdoing
7. Rescind a contract entered into by the agent based on an improper relationship between the agent and the third party

32-2 PRINCIPAL'S OBLIGATIONS TO AGENT

The agreement between a principal and an agent creates the duties the principal owes to the agent. Even when the agency agreement is silent, there are implied obligations that are owed to the agent. Among the principal's actual and implied duties are the obligations (1) to compensate the agent for work or services performed, (2) to reimburse the agent for authorized advances and expenses, (3) to indemnify the agent against liability to third parties, and (4) to allow the agent to perform without interference.

Compensation

The principal is under a duty to pay an agent an agreed amount or the fair value of work or services that the agent performs within the scope of authority or employment, unless the agent agrees to perform gratuitously. In addition, the principal must make salary deductions and payments to the government as are required by law. All states have statutes which provide for the enforcement of the payment of wages and which place penalties on delinquent employers.

The agent may not recover compensation for illegal services, even though they were rendered at the request of the principal. The agent may also forfeit rights to compensation when the agent breaches his or her duties to the principal.

Balfour employed Hunan to find a buyer for her coin collection. Hunan found a buyer and sold the collection for $15,000. Hunan told Balfour the coins sold for $11,000 and kept $4,000 for himself. Hunan breached his duty to Balfour, and would forfeit his right to compensation, as well as to the illicit gain.

Reimbursement

The principal is obligated to reimburse the agent for any reasonable expenses incurred while working on the principal's behalf and within the scope of the agent's authority or employment. The agent cannot recover for expenses due to the agent's own negligence. Recovery is also barred when expenses incurred by an agent are unnecessary or unreasonable in the discharge of the agency.

Torres, while on a business trip for his company, attended a professional basketball game. Although his attendance at the game was made possible by the business trip, the expense did not relate directly to the purpose of the agency. The expense was of a personal nature, and Torres would not be reimbursed.

Indemnification

Agents are entitled to **indemnification** (i.e., payment for loss or damage suffered) if they incur a loss or are damaged as a result of a request made by the principal.

Boynton hired Pasqua to sell a rare stamp. Pasqua sold the stamp to Grubbs and turned over the purchase price, less commission, to Boynton who remained unknown to Grubbs. Discovering that the stamp was not authentic, Grubbs obtained a judgment against Pasqua for the purchase price. Boynton must indemnify Pasqua for the loss resulting from the lawsuit.

The obligation to pay for the agent's personal loss or damage, which may occur in the future or is already suffered, is avoidable if the loss or damage results from an action the agent knew to be illegal or from the agent's negligence.

Public policy also requires employers to indemnify employees for personal injury sustained in the course of employment, except for self-inflicted injury or intoxication. State workers' compensation laws hold that the cost of paying for such injury should be a part of the operating expense of the business.

Cooperation

The principal, having granted the agent the duty to perform certain tasks, must not interfere with the performance of those tasks. Should the principal make the agent's job difficult or impossible, the principal has breached the duty of cooperation.

Soto hired Vaughan to be his agent in selling home window replacements. Soto told Vaughan that she would have exclusive rights to sell the line of replacement windows in Stamford, Connecticut. Vaughan was also told that she must make a monthly profit of at least $4,000 in order to remain Soto's agent. Within a week, Vaughan discovered that Soto had also hired three additional agents to sell replacement windows in Stamford. The other agents made it impossible for Vaughan to meet the $4,000 profit requirement. Soto had breached his duty of cooperation to Vaughan due to his interference with Vaughan's exclusive right to sell the replacement windows in Stamford for Soto.

Duration of Agent's Employment

An agent who is employed by the principal for a specified period of time is entitled to that term of employment unless discharged for **good cause**. Good cause may be defined as a substantial or legally sufficient reason for doing something. An employer who discharges an employee without good cause must pay wages or commissions that would have been earned if the employee's or agent's term of employment had continued for the period specified.

Hurta gave a real estate broker the exclusive right to sell her home for 90 days, excluding all other brokers as well as herself from finding a buyer. If Hurta were to employ another broker or sell the house on her own behalf during the specified period of time, she would not be complying with the terms of the agency agreement. Hurta would be obligated to pay a commission to the broker with whom the exclusive right to sell her home was initially given for a specified period of time.

Remedies Available to Agent

The remedies of an agent against a principal are based upon the principal's breach of express or implied contract obligations. Where appropriate, the agent has the option of exerting one or more of the agent's rights:

1. Terminate employment
2. Recover damages for the principal's breach of contract
3. Recover the value of services rendered
4. Obtain reimbursement for payments made for the principal
5. Secure indemnity for personal liability sustained while performing an authorized act for the principal

32-3 TORT AND CRIMINAL LIABILITY IN AN AGENCY

The three parties to an agency transaction are each liable for any wrongful acts that may injure the person or property of one of the others. In addition to the liabilities that contract law imposes upon a principal or employer for the acts of an authorized agent or employee to third parties, there are liabilities for torts and related business crimes.

When an agent or employee causes harm to a third person, the principal or employer is ordinarily liable, although personally free from fault and innocent of any intentional wrong. This concept of laying responsibility or blame upon one person for the actions of another is known as **vicarious liability**. However, it must be shown that the agent was acting within the scope of authority or the employee within the scope of employment. There is no vicarious liability if the agent or employee was not so acting. For example, if an employee were to steal property from a customer, the employer would not be liable even though it was the authorized work of the employer that placed the employee in position to steal the customer's property.

The wrongful act of an employee or agent may be one of negligence, fraud, or a violation of a government regulation. When the act is a threat to private interest or when it offends such interest, a civil lawsuit for damages may result. Criminal prosecution may result when the act violates a public law.

Tort Liability

The law of agency specifies under what circumstances a principal must pay damages to a third party for the tortious act of an agent.

Respondeat Superior The rule of law that imposes vicarious liability upon an innocent employer for the wrong of an agent or employee is also referred to as the doctrine of *respondeat superior*—"Let the master respond." As shown in Figure 32-1, although an employee has joint liability with the employer and, similarly, the agent with the principal, liability generally falls exclusively on the principal or employer. *Respondeat superior* results from the logic that the principal or employer has the obligation to exercise control over the physical conduct of agents or employees who are acting within their scope of authority

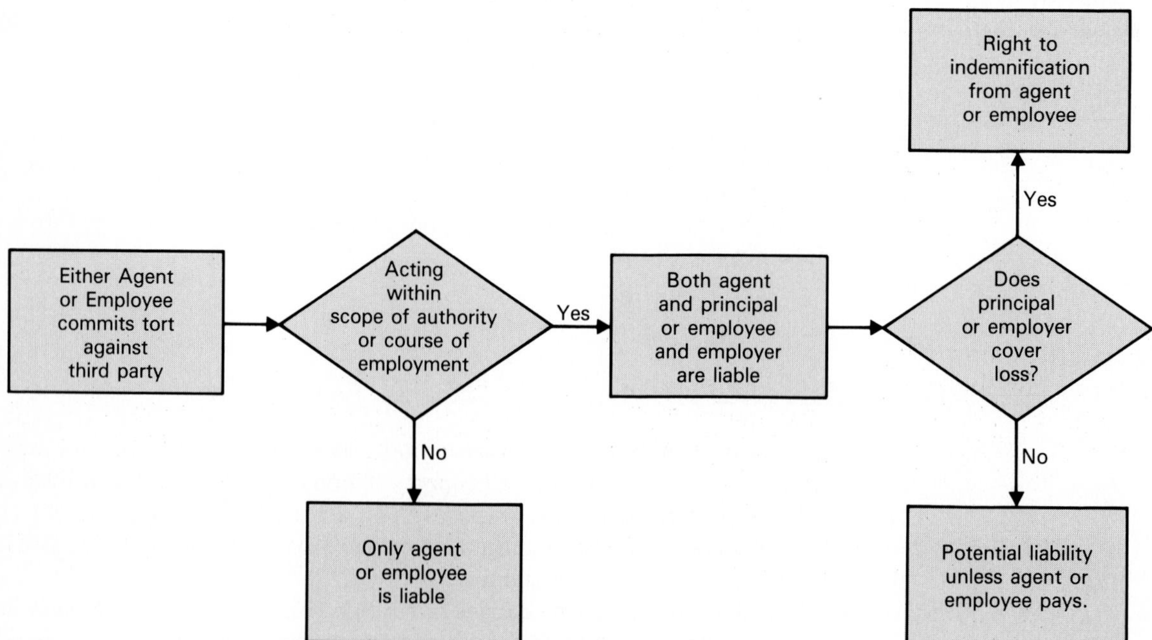

Figure 32-1 Principal/employer tort liability under *respondeat superior* doctrine.

or employment. In making this determination, the courts generally hold that the tortious harm to third parties and property is a hazard of doing business and the principal or employer has a public responsibility to stand behind the actions of an agent or employee.

Donoughue, a passenger in a taxicab owned by LaPenna Company, brought a suit for damages suffered when the taxi driver assaulted her. Donoughue argues that a common carrier is liable to a passenger who is assaulted by one of its employees before the transportation has been completed under the doctrine of *respondeat superior*. The court would hold for Donoughue. The taxi driver's willful and intentional misconduct was directly related and incidental to the performance of duties for which the driver was employed. LaPenna Company would have the right to seek recovery against the driver for any losses it sustains as a result of the wrongful act.

Whether the principal or employer is liable to a third party for the torts committed by the agent or employee does not affect the agent's or employee's liability. The person who actually commits the tort is always liable to the victim.

In addition to the liability imposed by the doctrine of *respondeat superior,* the principal or employer may be held for damages to third parties due to personal negligence in conducting business by means of employees or agents. Such negligence or recklessness may stem from giving improper or ambiguous orders or from failing to make proper regulations. The principal or employer is also liable for damages to third parties for the employment of improper persons in work involving risk of harm to others and in the supervision of the activity.

Sovereign Immunity **Sovereign immunity,** a doctrine preventing a lawsuit against government authority without the government's consent, is nolonger as important a defense for government torts as it once was. It no longer protects government from liability, at least where the injury is caused by the government acting in its capacity as a commercial being rather than that ofsupreme government. The doctrine has been abolished in some states by judicial decision and in others by legislation.

Federal Tort Claims Act The Federal Tort Claims Act of 1946 limits the federal government's sovereign immunity. Whenever a federal employee harms a third party or private property while driving a motor vehicle in the course of employment, the federal government is liable.

However, the 1946 law explicitly preserves governmental immunity for a vaguely defined category of "discretionary" actions by officials. The U.S. Supreme Court has also carved out another exception, barring virtually all damage suits against the federal government for injuries to military personnel.

Agent Orange litigation grew out of complaints by many thousands of veterans who believed their cancers and other illnesses were caused by exposure to the herbicide, which was sprayed over wide areas of Vietnam during the war to deprive Communist troops of cover and food. In 1988, the U.S. Supreme Court refused to hear the appeals of the veterans and others suing the federal government for deaths and injuries they linked to the herbicide. In refusing the appeal, the Court left standing the lower court's ruling that claims by the veterans and their families against the federal government were barred by sovereign immunity.

In 1982, a federal district court judge held that radioactive fallout from aboveground nuclear tests had caused at least nine people and perhaps dozens of others to die of cancer. The judge ruled that the federal government must pay damages under the Federal Tort Claims Act, explaining that while the high-level decision to conduct the tests had been discretionary, and thus was immune from liability, officials had conducted the tests in a negligent manner by failing to monitor radiation adequately or to warn residents of neighboring areas in Nevada, southern Utah, and northern Arizona who lived downwind from the test site about radiation hazards and how to reduce them. A federal appeals court, however, held that all aspects of the testing program were conducted in accordance with discretionary decisions of the Atomic Energy Commission and were thus immune from liability. The U.S. Supreme Court in 1988 refused to hear an appeal from the appellate decision.

Criminal Liability

The principal or employer ordinarily is not liable for an agent's or employee's crimes, unless the principal or employer actually aids or participates in their commission. The commission of a crime usually requires **intent**—a state of mind wherein the person knows and desires the consequences of an act at the time it is committed. Thus, if the principal or employer has not authorized the crime, the courts would conclude that the necessary criminal intent has not been shown.

A principal or employer will be held criminally liable for acts done by an agent or employee to further an illegal business. In addition, most states have enacted statutes that hold a principal or employer liable for certain crimes committed by their agents or employees, even though they acted disobediently. Examples of such statutes are those which penalize the sale of impure foods or alcoholic beverages. Principals or employers may also be penalized for the acts of managerial or advisory persons who are acting in the scope of authority or employment, unless they act in disobedience of instructions and not for the purpose of serving the principal or employer.

32-4 TERMINATION OF AGENCY

The agency agreement may be terminated by the acts of one or both parties to the agency agreement or by operation of the law. When the authority of the agent is terminated, the agent loses the right to act for the principal.

Termination by Act of the Parties

Both principal and agent may terminate an agency relationship by their acts. Most agency relationships are terminated when the parties have satisfied their contractual obligations. The relationship may also be discharged by mutual consent as well as when either the agent or the principal breaches the agency contract.

Fulfillment of Purpose When the purpose for which the agency was created is achieved, the agency is terminated. If an agent is appointed for a specific period of time, the arrival of that time terminates the agency. In short, when the contract is performed, the agency is at an end.

Mutual Agreement The parties to an agency relationship may terminate it at any time by agreement, even before the contract is fully performed.

Revocation or Renunciation The principal or the agent usually has the power (not necessarily the right) at any time to terminate the agency relationship. Acting with or without cause, the principal may terminate by simply recalling the agent's authority to act (i.e., **revocation**). Even though the principal's act of revocation may be a violation of contract, the agent's authority is terminated. Agents may terminate by simply giving notice to principals that they are quitting (i.e., **renunciation**). Unless the terms of the agency agreement permit termination "at will," agents and principals who end their relationship may be liable for damages resulting from the violation of the contractual promise. Nevertheless one cannot be forced to work against one's will.

Termination by Operation of the Law

The termination of the agency agreement by operation of the law results when significant events make the continuance of the agency impossible or impractical. Termination by operation of the law occurs in instances of death, insanity, bankruptcy, or impossibility of performance.

Death The death of the principal or agent ordinarily terminates the agency relationship automatically, even without notice. Hence, any agreement made between the agent and a third party is ineffective upon the death of the principal. Although the agent may be liable to third parties for breach of the implied warranty that the agent has authority so to act, third parties cannot recover from the estate of the principal because the contract is not binding.

Insanity The insanity of either the principal or the agent usually terminates the authority of the agent. In some states, however, the courts have held that an agent has power to bind a principal who has become insane if the principal has not been legally declared insane and if the third party had no knowledge of the insanity. If the principal is only incapacitated briefly, the agent's authority may be suspended rather than terminated.

Bankruptcy In the event of the bankruptcy of the principal, the agency is ended. All the bankrupt's ordinary contracts are canceled, and title to the principal's property passes to a trustee for the benefit of creditors.

The bankruptcy of the agent sometimes terminates the agency for the same reasons, but the principal and the agent may continue the relationship if they choose. Usually the bankruptcy of the agent does not prevent the agent from doing the job in the regular way, provided the agent is not using personal funds.

Impossibility of Performance An agency relationship terminates when it is impossible for the agent to accomplish the purpose of the agency for any reason. Destruction of a house by fire ends the real estate broker's agency to sell the property. A broker authorized to sell a principal's boat loses that authority if the boat is destroyed in a storm.

An agent's loss of a license required to conduct the principal's business ends the authority of the agent. A change in the law which causes authorized acts to be illegal terminates the agent's authority. The authority of the agent is also terminated by notice or knowledge of a change in business conditions or values that substantially affects the agent's exercise of authority. For example, an agent hired to sell property at a specified price would have that authority terminated when the value of the property increases substantially because of zoning changes.

Agency Coupled With an Interest

The only exception to the rule that either the principal or the agent may terminate an agency relationship at any time arises in the situation of an agency coupled with an interest. An **agency coupled with an interest** is an agency agreement in which the agent is given an interest in the subject matter of the agency, in addition to the amount of compensation for services rendered the principal.

The concept protects the agent's interest in specific property belonging to the principal. The principal lacks power to revoke agencies of this kind without the consent of the agent.

Greco borrowed $3,000 from a bank. He put up as security 100 shares of stock which he authorized the bank to sell to satisfy the loan obligation should he default on the loan. In the event that it becomes necessary to sell the stock, the bank serves as Greco's agent. Greco may not terminate the agency except by paying off the $3,000 loan.

Notice of Termination to Third Parties

The principal has the duty to notify third parties with whom the agent has done business when the agency relationship has been terminated by the act of the parties. There is an exception to this rule when the agency is terminated by operation of the law. In such instances, the principal is not required to notify anyone and no subsequent act by the agent will bind the principal.

The type of notice required depends on how the former business relations were conducted. When the third party has given credit to the principal through the agent, the third party is entitled to actual notice of termination of authority. This may be done by regular mail or by telephone. The safest way, however, is by certified mail, because a receipt of the notice can be obtained from

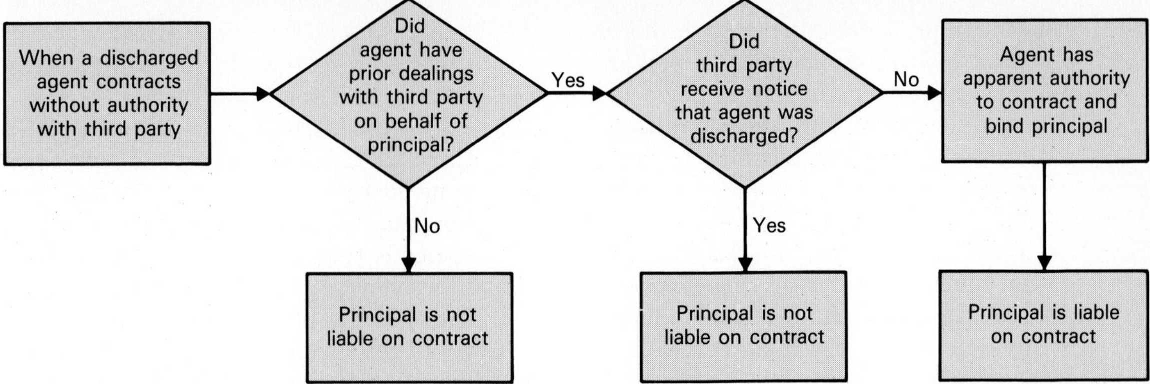

Figure 32-2 How liability is determined after termination of an agency relationship.

the post office. A notice in the classified advertisement section in a newspaper of general circulation is sufficient for third parties who have never given credit, but have had cash transactions with the agent or know that other persons have dealt with the principal through the agent.

As diagramed in Figure 32-2, the failure to give third parties appropriate notice would make the principal liable on contracts made by a former agent with third parties.

Cassone discharged the manager of his Electronic Supply Outlet. Following the firing, the manager ordered electronic games and a car stereo from Electronic Components, Inc., which he kept for himself. Electronic Components had prior credit dealings with Cassone's manager and had not been given actual notice of his discharge. In a suit to recover the value of the items, the court would reason that Electronic Components, without actual notice of the agent's discharge, had the right to presume that the manager had apparent authority to order items on Cassone's behalf. Cassone would be held liable for the former agent's act.

SUMMARY

32-1. As a result of the fiduciary relationship, the agent owes the principal the duty of (*a*) obedience to instructions, (*b*) loyalty, (*c*) reasonable judgment, prudence, and skill, (*d*) accounting for agency money and property, (*e*) performance of agency work personally, and (*f*) communication of all facts that affect the subject matter of the agency.

32-2. In addition to the duties that the principal owes to the agent under the agency agreement, there are certain implied obligations. These include the duty to (*a*) compensate the agent, (*b*) reimburse the agent for authorized expenses incurred, (*c*) indemnify the agent for losses caused by the agency relationship through no fault of the agent, and (*d*) comply with the terms of the agency contract.

32-3. In addition to the liabilities that contract law imposes upon a principal or employer for the acts of an authorized agent or employee to third parties, there are liabilities for torts and related crimes. The principal is liable for the nonphysical torts of the agent or employee and for any tortious physical harm to third parties when they are committed within the course and scope of authority or employment.

32-4. An agency agreement generally terminates when its purposes are accomplished. The agency may also terminate at any time by the principal's revocation of the agent's authority or by the agent's renunciation of the agency relationship. If either party dies, becomes insane, goes bankrupt, or ceases to be qualified to act, the agency relationship is terminated by operation of the law.

The principal has the duty to notify third parties with whom the agent has done business when the agency has been terminated by acts of the parties. Actual notice is required when the third party has given credit to the principal through the agent. A public notice in a newspaper of general circulation is sufficient for third parties who have never given credit but have had cash transactions with the agent.

Understanding Key Legal Terms

agency coupled with an interest (p. 459)
good cause (p. 449)
indemnification (p. 448)
intent (p. 452)
renunciation (p. 453)
revocation (p. 453)
scope of authority (p. 445)
scope of employment (p. 445)
sovereign immunity (p. 451)
vicarious liability (p. 450)

Questions for Review and Discussion

1. Explain the fiduciary duty that arises out of the agency relationship.
2. What duties other than fiduciary are imposed upon the agent in compliance with the agency relationship?
3. Describe the principal's obligations to the agent who is acting within the scope of authority.
4. What is meant by the doctrine of vicarious liability and what effect does theagent's scope of authority have on its application?
5. What are the remedies of an agent against a principal who fails to observe the obligations owed an agent?
6. Explain the extent and logic of liability imposed on a principal or employer by the doctrine of *respondeat superior*.
7. Why are principals and employers ordinarily not liable for the agent's or employee's crimes, the commission of which they did not participate in or aid?
8. In what ways may the agency relationship be terminated?
9. When may an agent who has declared bankruptcy continue to serve as an agent?
10. Discuss the notice required when the termination of any agency results from the acts of the parties.

Analyzing Cases

1. Mularchuk was employed as a part-time reserve police officer for the Borough of Keansburg, New Jersey. He was never given any training, and he was not required to submit to any training with respect to the revolver he carried. A quarrel arose between McAndrew, who had car trouble, and a tow-truck driver who McAndrew had called for assistance. Mularchuk proceeded to make arrests and in the course of events shot and seriously injured McAndrew. Was the Borough of Keansburg liable to McAndrew under the doctrine of *respondeat superior?* Explain? *McAndrew v. Mularchuk,* 162 A.2d 820 (New Jersey).

2. Horn was appointed as agent by Pinchuk to sell Pinchuk's house in Atlanta. The following day, while in Boston, Pinchuk was killed in an automobile accident. After Pinchuk's death but before receiving notice of it, Horn entered into a contract with Devaul for the sale of Pinchuk's house. The executor of Pinchuk's estate refused to honor the contract, and Devaul brought suit for damages. Judgment for whom and why?

3. Flight Unlimited, Inc., hired Haight as its pilot to deliver airplanes to customers located throughout the country. While delivering a plane to a buyer in Florida, Haight buzzed the home of an acquaintance. He lost control of the plane and crashed into the house, which was destroyed. Flight Unlimited was sued for damages. Its defense was that, at the time of the accident, Haight was flying in an unauthorized manner and the company was therefore not responsible for the loss of the house. Judgment for whom and why?

4. Yankee Realty was engaged by Molinari to find a $112,000 house. After selecting a house, Yankee Realty learned that the house was in the center of a plot that a utility company intended to purchase for expansion of its operations. Yankee Realty bought the house itself, placing it in the name of one of its agents, and later sold it to the utility company for $300,000. Molinari sued Yankee Realty for the difference between $112,000 and the $300,000, claiming lack of good faith. Judgment for whom and why?

5. LaRoche worked as a driver-salesperson for Beverage Barn, maker of bottled waters and flavored beverages. While making a delivery, LaRoche was attacked by a pit bull. LaRoche sued his employer for damages for injuries inflicted by the dog. Beverage Barn denied responsibility, claiming that the owner of the pit bull was the only one responsible. Judgment for whom and why?

6. Nam instructed Middleton, her financial consultant, to invest $10,000 in conservative-growth stock. Middleton purchased speculative mining stock with Nam's money. The stock proved to be worthless. Nam sued Middleton for her loss. Judgment for whom and why?

7. Marchant was driving an automobile that collided with a gravel truck owned by Columbia County, Oregon. Marchant alleged negligence and brought suit for personal injuries against Clark, the driver of the truck. He argued that Clark was operating the truck on the left side of the road. Clark defended by stating that he had been ordered to so operate the truck by his employer, the instructions having been conveyed to him by the road supervisor. How should the court dispose of this case? Why? *Marchant v. Clark,* 273 P.2d 541 (Or.S. Ct.)

CHAPTER 33
Employment Law

OUTLINE

33-1 Nature of the Employment Relationship
- Termination of the Employment Contract

33-2 Working Conditions
- Fair Labor Standards Act
- Health and Safety Laws
- Identity and Employment Eligibility

33-3 Worker Benefits
- Social Security
- Unemployment Insurance
- State Workers' Compensation Laws
- Pension Plan Regulation

33-4 Equal Employment Opportunity
- Civil Rights and Equal Employment Acts
- Pay and Age Discrimination
- Discrimination on the Basis of Pregnancy or Handicap
- Drug Testing and Alcoholism
- Acquired Immune Deficiency Syndrome
- Polygraph Testing

COMMENTARY

Learning of a job opening, Cheryl McNeely applied to the employer. Her application represented an offer; the employer's approval of her application was an acceptance. An employment contract resulted, even though the terms of employment were not in writing. Since there is no general law that prohibits the employer from firing Cheryl at any time without good cause, what job rights and security does she have?

There are federal, state, and local laws, presidential orders, and court decisions which deal with Cheryl's employment rights. She is guaranteed a minimum wage and a maximum number of hours of work, safe working conditions, compensation for any injury she may suffer as a result of her work, payments should she become unemployed, and, if provided, protection of her pension plan interests after retirement. Cheryl is also protected should her employer discriminate against her on the basis of sex, race, color, religion, or citizenship status with respect to her wages, fringe benefits, promotion, training, discharge, or any other terms, conditions, or privileges of her employment. This chapter will discuss employment law as it relates to the employment contract, working conditions, worker benefits, and equal employment opportunity.

OBJECTIVES

1. Discuss what provisions are generally contained in simple employment contracts.
2. Explain the "at-will" doctrine, and indicate some of the methods devised to evade or limit its authority.

3. Describe the standards as provided by the Fair Labor Standards Act for (*a*) minimum wages, (*b*) maximum hours of employment, and (*c*) child labor.
4. Describe how the Occupational Safety and Health Act works to reduce hazards to employees and to provide safe and healthful working conditions.
5. Identify the major provisions of the Immigration Reform and Control Act.
6. Explain how both federal and state statutes provide for workers while they are working, when unemployed, and following retirement.
7. Indicate what kinds of employment discrimination are prohibited by federal, state, and local laws; presidential executive orders; and court decisions.
8. Understand the major provisions of the Equal Pay and Age Discrimination in Employment Act.
9. Discuss the acts enforced by the Equal Employment Opportunity Commission (EEOC) against pregnancy and handicap discrimination.

33-1 NATURE OF THE EMPLOYMENT RELATIONSHIP

The employment relationship evolves from the **employment contract** between an employer and an employee. Employment contracts, either oral or written, specify the terms of employment that the employee and employer have negotiated. The terms of the contract may be either express or implied. Although the parties are free to agree to any reasonable terms they wish, simple employment contracts generally contain provisions designating length of employment, title and responsibilities, hours and/or base salary, benefits, and no-compete conditions when appropriate. Employment contracts are subject to all the elements that are applicable to other types of contracts: (1) offer, (2) acceptance, (3) mutual assent, (4) capacity, (5) consideration, and (6) legality.

Holle was hired by Superior Drug Co. as a licensed pharmacist. He was to be paid a salary of $2,500 a month and would work eight hours a day, six days a week. Holle agreed to dispense drugs only on prescriptions signed by physicians. This employment agreement designates the base salary, the hours of work, and a description of the position. Employee benefits are not specified.

Employees may be required to sign employment contracts that restrict them from competing with an employer for a reasonable period of time after leaving their present job. A no-compete provision is not uncommon where the most valuable assets of a business are its secret methods of production and the formulas used in the manufacture of highly competitive consumer goods.

Yeager, a research scientist in nuclear physics, obtained a position in the research and development laboratory of Continental Fuels Inc. Her employment contract covered a period of three years. A provision of the agreement stated that Yeager was to be restricted from working with any other company or government agency engaged in competitive nuclear research for a period of five years following fulfillment of her Continental Fuels employment contract. The restriction was reasonable, given Yeager's freedom and capacity to secure employment in other research fields.

Termination of the Employment Contract

The traditional American rule with respect to termination of employment provides that, without an employment contract or a collective bargaining agreement, employers are free to discharge employees **at will** (e.g., for any reason or even no reason). The rationale for the at-will doctrine is that both the employer and employee should be free to terminate the employment relationship at any time. This allows each to take advantage of new opportunities or end an unsatisfactory work situation. However, state courts in a number of jurisdictions have substantially reduced an employer's discretion to discharge an employee. Several basic judicial theories have been developed by state courts to evade or limit the traditional employment at-will doctrine.

Implied Contract Exception Several state courts, including those in New York and Michigan, have overcome the at-will doctrine by finding implied employment contracts in job applications, employee handbooks, and personnel manuals. These documents state in words or substance that employees shall not be discharged unless their job performance is unsatisfactory or, in the case of reductions in force, unless other jobs are not available within the company.

Good Faith and Fair Dealing Exception Courts in California and Massachusetts have further eroded the at-will doctrine by imposing a duty of good faith and fair dealing in all employment relationships.

In a California case involving American Airlines, the court of appeals held that the discharge of an employee after 18 years of service without good cause "offends the implied in law promise of good faith and fair dealing contained in all contracts, including employment contracts." Further, the court ruled that such conduct breached American Airlines' own personnel policies, which stated that the airline would engage in good faith and fair dealings rather than arbitrary conduct toward its employees. The court concluded that the longevity of the employee's services, together with theexpress policy of the employer, operate as a form of estoppel, precluding any discharge of such an employee by the employer without just cause."

Public Policy Limitations Another exception to the at-will doctrine prevents employers from discharging an employee for reasons that violate clearly defined and well-established fundamental principles of public policy. Examples include: employees who were fired by employers for refusing to give false testimony at a trial, employees who were "whistle blowers" with respect to allegedly illegal conduct of their employers, employees who were fired for filing workers' compensation claims, and employees who were fired for refusing to violate the law.

Phipps, a gas station employee, claimed that he had been let go after refusing to put leaded gasoline in a car that used unleaded gas. The court held that since the firing may have been motivated by Phipps's refusal to violate the law, it was then up to the employer to demonstrate that the termination was due to other reasons.

33-2 WORKING CONDITIONS

Employment conditions can be divided into two major areas: the compensation received by employees and the actual physical situation in which employees must work. In addition, there is a national employment verification system that affects all newly hired employees. The federal government regulates these working conditions to protect workers.

Fair Labor Standards Act

The principal federal law affecting the wages and hours of employees is the Fair Labor Standards Act of 1938 (FLSA). Frequently amended, and commonly known as the Wage-Hour law, the act provides that workers in interstate commerce or in an industry producing goods for interstate commerce must be paid no less than a specified minimum wage. Further, it specifies that employees cannot work for more than 40 hours a week unless they are paid time and a half for overtime. The act also prohibits the employment of children under the age of 14 and the employment of "oppressive child labor" in any enterprise engaged in commerce or in the production of goods for commerce. Provisions of the FLSA have been duplicated by a number of states in order to regulate intrastate commerce and industry not covered by the federal law.

Wage and Hour Exceptions and Exemptions The wage and hour provisions of the FLSA permit the employment of learners, apprentices, messengers, and handicapped persons at less than the minimum wage rate. However, the employer must obtain express permission from the Wage and Hour Division of the U.S. Department of Labor and is subject to conditions set by it governing wages and hours. Full-time students are permitted to be employed under the same conditions in retail and service stores, outside school hours.

The wage and hour provisions of the FLSA do not apply, with certain exceptions, to those employed in an executive, administrative, or professional capacity. These exempt workers are generally identified as those who manage and direct the work of two or more other employees. At least 50 percent of their primary duties must be in the performance of office or nonmanual work relating to the operations of the company or in the performance of work requiring scientific or specialized study.

State, local, and federal employees; self-employed persons; and armed forces personnel are exempted from the wage and hour provisions. Also exempted are outside salespeople, employees of certain seasonal amusement or recreational businesses, and employees of small retail or service establishments with gross sales of less than $250,000 annually.

Child Labor Sixteen is the minimum age for employment in nonhazardous work. Minors between the ages of 14 and 16, in accordance with various regulations, may be employed in a few occupations such as office and clerical work, cashiering, selling, and dispensing gasoline. Minors between 14 and 16, however, cannot be employed in occupations involving the operation of machines or work in rooms where processing and manufacturing take place. Minors under 14 years of age may be employed on farms and by parents, outside school hours, provided the work is nonhazardous. Minors may sometimes work for less than the minimum wage to gain experience where opportunities are limited and a savings to the employer results.

Ansley, a 15-year-old, was employed as a roofer helper. He carried bundles of roofing shingles and supplies up and down extension ladders to workers engaged in the task of waterproofing roofs. He worked four hours a day, six days a week, outside of school hours. A school official charged the work was hazardous and thus violated the provisions of the FLSA that regulate child labor. The attorney general ruled the work to be hazardous. In a willful violation of the provisions of the FLSA, the employer would be subject to a criminal prosecution and fine of up to $10,000.

Child labor prohibitions apply almost universally. The only exemptions are newspaper delivery youths, child actors, children working on farms outside school hours, and children working for local retail and service businesses that make no deliveries across state lines.

Health and Safety Laws

Various state and federal laws and administrative rules and regulations are designed to reduce preventable hazards to employees in the workplace and to provide for safe and healthful working conditions. On the state level, departments of labor and/or health may be charged with determining whether an employer is complying with state health and safety laws. On the federal level, the Occupational Safety and Health Act of 1970, as amended, assures all workers in a business in or affecting interstate commerce a safe and healthful place of employment.

Occupational Safety and Health Administration The Occupational Safety and Health Administration (OSHA), an agency responsible to the Department of Labor, establishes federal health and safety standards for the workplace and enforces them.

OSHA establishes and publishes occupational safety and health standards with which employers must comply. To withstand court challenge, however, it must be shown that the OSHA standards and regulations reasonably reduce the frequency or severity of employee injuries or illnesses. Employers are required to keep records of illnesses, injuries, and deaths suffered by employees and to submit requested reports to the secretary of labor.

A corps of OSHA inspectors enforce compliance with its many and varied health and safety regulations. Employees are permitted to request an inspection if they believe that a violation exists. The U.S. Supreme Court has ruled, however, that an OSHA inspector must produce a search warrant if the employer refuses to admit the inspector to the job site voluntarily.

When a violation of a standard is observed, the inspector issues a **citation** (i.e., a notice commanding the appearance of the employer in a proceeding) and possible penalty. Employers may appeal citations received to the OSHA Review Commission. If this effort fails, they may seek relief in the U.S. Court of Appeals.

Inspectors for OSHA cited the Bath Iron Works Corp. for unsafe practices including exposing workers to asbestos-laden dust, radiation, and raw sewage in some work areas. A fine of $4.2 million, the largest ever proposed against one concern, also listed 641 record keeping violations. These included failure of shipyard officials to record serious injuries and illnesses such as amputations, fractures, and respiratory diseases resulting from overexposure to toxic substances. The shipyard had 15 working days to appeal the citations and penalty to the Independent Occupational Safety and Health Review Commission.

Identity and Employment Eligibility

The federal Immigration Reform and Control Act of 1986 created a national employment verification system which placed responsibility for verification of the identity and employment of all employees on the employer. The act provided that alien workers hired on or before November 6, 1986, had until May 5, 1988, to seek temporary resident status. Those who do not have **documentation** (i.e., evidence supplied by writings) of their right to work in this country are not entitled to help from the NLRB in labor disputes.

Employers are required to request and examine documentation of identity and employment eligibility of all new hires and rehires, including U.S. citizens, permanent residents, and nonimmigrant visa (official passport indorsement) holders. Job applicants must present original documentation set forth in Figure 33-1.

After the original documents are reviewed by the employer, individuals who accept an offer of employment are required to complete and sign an Employment Eligibility Verification Form (Form I-9) in the presence of a supervisor or human resources officer. (See Figure 33-2 on page 465.)

An operator of motels and nursing homes filed a petition with the Immigration and Naturalization Service (INS) for a hearing to overturn a fine imposed on the company for hiring illegal alien workers and for failing to document the employment eligibility of the workers on Form I-9. The fine had been imposed after INS agents staged a surprise inspection of a company-owned motel and arrested 17 undocumented workers, after previously issuing a warning and citations to the motel. Prior to the hearing, the INS lowered the fine in exchange for (1) the company's admission that it had employed illegal aliens, (2) a promise not to violate the Immigration Reform and Control Act again, and (3) an agreement to drop the request for a hearing.

One of these **ORIGINAL** documents to establish identity and employment eligibility:

- U.S. passport;
- Certificate of U.S. citizenship (INS Form N-560 or N-561);
- Certificate of naturalization (INS Form N-550 or N-570);
- Unexpired foreign passport with unexpired official stamp or valid form I-94;
- Alien registration receipt card with bearer's photograph (''green card''– INS Form I-151)'
- Resident alien form with bearer's photograph (Form I-551);
- Temporary resident card (INS Form I-688);
- Employment authorization card (INS Form I-688A).

If you do not have any of the above documents, then you must present one document from each of the next two sections:

One of these **ORIGINAL** documents to establish identity:

- State-issued driver's license or state-issued identification card containing a photograph or if the document does not contain a photograph, identifying information such as name, date of birth, sex, height, color of eyes, and address;
- School identification card with photograph;
- Voter's registration card;
- U.S. military card or draft record;
- Identification card issued by federal, state, or local government agencies or entities;
- Military dependent's identification card;
- Native American tribal documents;
- U.S. Coast Guard Merchant Mariner card;
- Driver's license issued by a Canadian government authority.

AND

One of these **ORIGINAL** documents to establish employment eligibility:

- Social security number card other than one which has printed on its face ''not valid for employment purposes'';
- Certification of birth issued by Dept. of State (Form FS-545);
- Original or certified copy of a birth certificate issued by a state, county, or municipal authority bearing a seal;
- Certification of birth abroad issued by Dept. of State (Form DS-1350);
- Unexpired reentry permit (INS Form I-327);
- Unexpired Refugee Travel document (INS Form I-571);
- Employment authorization document issued by the INS;
- Native American tribal document;
- U.S. citizen identification card (INS Form I-197);
- Identification card for use of resident citizen in the U.S. (INS Form I-179).

Figure 33-1 Original documents required for employment eligibility verifications.

EMPLOYMENT ELIGIBILITY VERIFICATION (Form I-9)

1 EMPLOYEE INFORMATION AND VERIFICATION: (To be completed and signed by employee.)

Name: (Print or Type) Last	First	Middle	Birth Name
Address: Street Name and Number	City	State	ZIP Code
Date of Birth (Month/Day/Year)		Social Security Number	

I attest, under penalty of perjury, that I am (check a box):

- ☐ 1. A citizen or national of the United States.
- ☐ 2. An alien lawfully admitted for permanent residence (Alien Number A ____________).
- ☐ 3. An alien authorized by the Immigration and Naturalization Service to work in the United States (Alien Number A ____________, or Admission Number ____________, expiration of employment authorization, if any ____________).

I attest, under penalty of perjury, the documents that I have presented as evidence of identity and employment eligibility are genuine and relate to me. I am aware that federal law provides for imprisonment and/or fine for any false statements or use of false documents in connection with this certificate.

Signature	Date (Month/Day/Year)

PREPARER/TRANSLATOR CERTIFICATION (To be completed if prepared by person other than the employee). I attest, under penalty of perjury, that the above was prepared by me at the request of the named individual and is based on all information of which I have any knowledge.

Signature	Name (Print or Type)		
Address (Street Name and Number)	City	State	Zip Code

2 EMPLOYER REVIEW AND VERIFICATION: (To be completed and signed by employer.)

Instructions:
Examine one document from List A and check the appropriate box, ***OR*** examine one document from List B ***and*** one from List C and check the appropriate boxes.
Provide the ***Document Identification Number*** and ***Expiration Date*** for the document checked.

List A
Documents that Establish
Identity and Employment Eligibility

- ☐ 1. United States Passport
- ☐ 2. Certificate of United States Citizenship
- ☐ 3. Certificate of Naturalization
- ☐ 4. Unexpired foreign passport with attached Employment Authorization
- ☐ 5. Alien Registration Card with photograph

Document Identification

____

Expiration Date (if any)

____

List B
Documents that Establish
Identity

- ☐ 1. A State-issued driver's license or a State-issued I.D. card with a photograph, or information, including name, sex, date of birth, height, weight, and color of eyes. (Specify State) ____________)
- ☐ 2. U.S. Military Card
- ☐ 3. Other (Specify document and issuing authority) ____________

Document Identification

____

Expiration Date (if any)

____

and

List C
Documents that Establish
Employment Eligibility

- ☐ 1. Original Social Security Number Card (other than a card stating it is not valid for employment)
- ☐ 2. A birth certificate issued by State, county, or municipal authority bearing a seal or other certification
- ☐ 3. Unexpired INS Employment Authorization Specify form # ____________

Document Identification

____

Expiration Date (if any)

____

CERTIFICATION: I attest, under penalty of perjury, that I have examined the documents presented by the above individual, that they appear to be genuine and to relate to the individual named, and that the individual, to the best of my knowledge, is eligible to work in the United States.

Signature	Name (Print or Type)	Title
Employer Name	Address	Date

Form I-9 (05/07/87)
OMB No. 1115-0136

U.S. Department of Justice
Immigration and Naturalization Service

Figure 33-2 Employment eligibility verification (Form I-9).

33-3 WORKER BENEFITS

The law not only protects workers while they are on the job but also helps workers who have retired or who have been injured or disabled while working.

Social Security

Federal and state governments participate in programs designed to reduce the financial risk to workers by reason of their unemployment, disability, hospitalization, retirement, or death. The principle federal law covering these risks is the Social Security Act of 1935. Under the Federal Insurance Contributions Act (FICA), both employers and employees are taxed equally to help pay for loss of income on retirement at age 65 or earlier at age 62 at a reduced amount. There is a limit on how much an individual can earn while receiving retirement benefits. At the age of 70, a full monthly benefit is received no matter how much the retired person earns. Only earnings from a job or self-employment are considered when figuring allowable income, not pension benefits, interest, annuities, or dividends.

Income benefits are assured under the FICA when workers under the age of 65 become unable to work because of an illness or other physical disability. Covered workers are considered **disabled** when a physical or mental condition prevents the performance of any substantial gainful work and when the condition is expected to last or has lasted at least 12 months, or is expected to result in death.

Survivor benefits are provided on the death of a covered worker. The benefits are payable to widows, widows with a disabled child, dependent children, dependent parents, and divorced spouses under certain conditions. In most cases, when a child reaches 18 years of age, any social security benefits he or she is receiving will stop. However, if the child does not marry and is either disabled or is a full-time student in an elementary or secondary school, he or she can continue to receive benefits. The term "disability" in this situation means that the individual had a physical or mental condition which stopped him or her from being gainfully employed. Such a condition must also be expected to last for a minimum of one year. If a child's benefits do stop when he or she reaches 18, the benefits can be started once more if the child becomes a full-time student in an elementary or secondary school before becoming 19 or if the child becomes disabled before becoming 22. Under social security regulations, an individual reaches a particular age at the beginning of the day before his or her birthday.

Unemployment Insurance

The unemployment insurance section of the Social Security Act provides for a joint federal and state system of unemployment insurance. Temporary financial assistance is available to individuals who are unemployed through no fault of their own and who have earned sufficient credits from prior employment. Under the Federal Unemployment Tax Act, each state operates its own unemployment insurance system, subject to conditions established by the federal government.

In addition to meeting state requirements regarding length of time employed and amount of wages, former employees must be ready, able, and willing to take a suitable full-time job that becomes available. Thus, claimants are ineligible to receive unemployment benefits when they refuse offers of suitable work without good cause. Good cause for refusing suitable work must be real, not imaginary; substantial, not trifling; and reasonable, not whimsical. For example, a desire to avoid a small cut in pay does not constitute good cause to refuse an employer's offer of employment in a reasonably similar position.

Wilkins, a machinist, was laid off from his job with Hughes Helicopters because of economic conditions. He registered with the state employment agency and requested unemployment compensation. The interviewing official told him about a job opening for a machinist with United Technologies. Wilkins refused it on the grounds that he needed a rest before accepting another job. Wilkins would be ineligible for compensation for any week in which his unemployment resulted from failure to accept suitable work offered to him by the employment office or by any employer without good cause.

An employee who quits a job without cause or is discharged for misconduct or theft generally does not qualify for unemployment benefits. Most states disqualify workers from receiving benefits if they are on strike because of a labor dispute. Domestic workers, agricultural employees, and state and local government employees are not covered by this federal-state program. Separate federal unemployment programs exist for railroad workers and for federal civilian workers.

State Workers' Compensation Laws

Workers' compensation laws are in effect in all states; these statutes compensate covered workers or their dependents for injuries, disease, or death resulting in the course of employment. One form provides a fund operated only by the state government. Employers pay into a state-controlled fund. When employees suffer injuries, they apply to the state to receive their benefits. In another form of workers' compensation insurance, companies are required to carry insurance for their workforce, but they have the option of contributing to a state fund or purchasing such insurance from a private insurer. In a third form, all employers are required to purchase workers' compensation insurance from private insurers.

Employer Liability Prior to the enactment of current state workers' compensation laws, the common law gave employers a number of defenses to use against employees who sued for damages to compensate for employment-related injuries. Employers could, for example, avoid liability by contending that the worker was negligent and had caused the injury, that a fellow employee was responsible for the worker's injury, or that the injured employee had assumed the risk of injury when accepting the job in the first place.

Under current state workers' compensation statutes, the common law defenses that were at the disposal of employers are no longer effective, and employees generally give up the right to sue the employer. Even if an employee ignores an employer's instructions and is injured as a result, the employee receives a guarantee of compensation. As long as injured employees are engaged in activity for the benefit of the employer, the state workers' compensation board would rule that they are acting in the scope of their employment and entitled to workers' compensation benefits.

> Palma was an employee of a nuclear power plant. He was exposed to high levels of radiation and developed radiation poisoning after he had ignored a posted warning and negligently entered the restricted area. Palma claimed workers' compensation benefits for the injury, and the state workers' compensation board awarded them. On appeal, the employer argued that Palma had caused the injury by refusing to take notice of the warning not to enter the restricted area. The court ruled that since the injury arose within the course of Palma's work from a risk involved in that work, Palma was entitled to the benefits awarded, notwithstanding the employer's defense.

Employer Defenses The workers' compensation laws provide employers with some defenses. Employees who intentionally injure themselves are denied compensation benefits. Those who suffer injury or death due to drugs or alcohol are denied benefits. Temporary workers and independent contractors are not covered by most workers' compensation laws.

Benefit Awards Employees must notify their employers within a specified period of time when they are accidentally injured on the job or develop an occupationally related disease. The state law sets the amount of the benefit and the length of time that payments are to be made. The actual amount depends on the type of injury or disease and the injured employee's average weekly income. Acceptance of an offered award will usually bar the complaining employee from later court action for further damages.

In several states, including Ohio, a statute allows employees who have been *intentionally injured* by their employers to sue in court. Intentionally injured has been defined to mean that the employer proceeds despite a perceived threat of harm to others, with deliberate intent to cause an employee to suffer injury. However, any award won by the employee in an intentional tort suit is offset by the amount the employee received under the state workers' compensation law.

Pension Plan Regulation

The Employee Retirement Income Security Act (ERISA) of 1974 provides needed supervision over employee pension plans established by many employers. Under the act, employers must place their pension contributions on behalf of their employees into a pension trust, independent of the employer. Under the rules of **vesting,** workers are guaranteed the right to receive future pension benefits regardless of whether they are working under the plan at the time of retirement. The law requires all pension plans to have minimum vested benefits. Beginning in 1989, all pension plans must vest after five years on the job.

33-4 EQUAL EMPLOYMENT OPPORTUNITY

A variety of federal, state, and local laws; executive orders, federal guidelines; as well as court decisions and rulings deal with **employment discrimination.** This is defined as any employment practice that results in the unemployment, nonemployment, or underemployment of minorities and women, either through conscious action or from unintentional actions.

The equal employment opportunity laws make it illegal to discriminate on the basis of race, color, religion, sex, age, or national origin in all employment practices. Covered practices include hiring, promoting, compensating, training, discharging, as well as all other terms, privileges, and conditions of employment.

Libbey Owens Ford Co., in a suit charging discrimination based on sex, agreed to open bidding for all jobs to women, including those previously barred because of state laws requiring overtime pay and weightlifting restrictions. The company agreed to begin a training program to aid women employees in transferring to better jobs, to undertake recruitment and advertising that would attract women applicants, and to select two women out of the next four supervisors hired.

Civil Rights and Equal Employment Acts

The Civil Rights Act of 1964, as amended by the Equal Employment Act of 1972, was enacted to ensure equality of employment opportunity. Title VII of the Civil Rights Act makes it unlawful for anyone acting in interstate commerce who employs 15 or more regular employees to practice discrimination in hiring or employment practices. Employers, unions, and employment agencies may not refuse to hire, discharge, or restrict the employment status of any person on the basis of sex, race, color, religion or national origin.

Two California women brought suit in federal district court against State Farm Insurance Company. They charged job discrimination on the basis of sex under the Civil Rights Act of 1964. The women had worked as office managers for State Farm for 13 years, a job that paid about $20,000 a year, and were repeatedly rejected for sales jobs, which paid about $75,000 a year. The women had been told a college degree was a requirement for sales agents even though men were hired without degrees. They were also told that agents might be required to work at night and that the company could not guarantee the safety of female agents. At the time, less than 1 percent of the people hired for sales positions in State Farm's offices were women. The court held that State Farm had discriminated against women in recruiting and hiring sales agents. Those who brought the suit were each awarded more than $400,000, plus legal fees. In addition, State Farm was required to hire women to fill 50 percent of the sales vacancies in the next 10 years.

The Civil Rights Act created the Equal Employment Opportunity Commission (EEOC) to enforce its provisions. The EEOC has the authority to investigate job discrimination complaints and to reach agreements with violators through conciliation arrangements. The Equal Employment Opportunity Act of 1972 gave the EEOC authority to compel an employer to obey the Title VII provisions.

Aggrieved employees must seek relief under a state law. If a state law does not exist or if relief is not achieved, suffering employees can then pursue a federal remedy through the EEOC.

To establish a violation of Title VII, an employee must show that an employer failed to hire, retain, or promote on the basis of race, color, sex, religion, or national origin. Employees must show that (*a*) they received different treatment from that applied to other employees or (*b*) that a particular employment practice had a harmful effect on a racial, ethnic, sexual, or religious group.

Rawlins filed a complaint with the EEOC, claiming that she was denied a promotion by H & L Plastics on the basis of her sex. In a subsequent court action charging promotion discrimination, Rawlins can rely on evidence based on facts from which a conclusion may be drawn. That is, she must show that the employer has comparatively few minority workers in leadership positions within the company.

Once the employee establishes that the employer has discriminated, the burden shifts to the employer to prove that it had a legitimate, nondiscriminatory business necessity for so acting. Courts interpret **business necessity** very narrowly. Convincing evidence is required to show that a discriminatory practice is essential to the safe and efficient operation of the business and/or that without it an extreme adverse financial loss would result.

***Bona Fide* Occupational Qualification** It is not unlawful employment practice to discriminate where a ***bona fide* occupational qualification (BFOQ)** is reasonably necessary to the normal operation of a particular business. A BFOQ is a good faith requirement for employment that does not deceptively prevent certain groups of persons from qualifying. For example, it would be permissible for a Presbyterian church to hire only Presbyterian ministers and refuse employment to individuals of other denominations. Discrimination exemptions are also given where there is a need for authenticity (i.e., a male model, a female actress, etc.). Employers working under government security programs can deny employment to individuals because of their inability to obtain security clearance. Laws also give preferential status to veterans and Native Americans.

Uniform Guidelines The EEOC has the authority to issue guidelines, rules, and regulations and to require employers and unions who are covered by Title VII to report regularly on the race, ethnic origin, and sex of their employees and members.

Guidelines adopted by the EEOC counsel employers on the effect of preemployment tests on equal employment opportunity. The U. S. Supreme Court has ruled that any tests used which result in discrimination against minority group members must be related to the requirements of the jobs involved. To be acceptable, tests or other performance standards must be fair measures of qualities needed to handle specific jobs.

Duke Power Company required applicants for most jobs to have a high school education and satisfactory scores on two professionally prepared general aptitude tests. The record showed that white applicants fared far better than black applicants on the tests. The court found that this consequence appeared to be directly traceable to race and inferior education. No evidence was presented that proved the tests to be related to successful performance of the specific jobs for which they were used as predictors. The court ruled that neither of the tests used was intended to measure the ability to learn or to perform a particular job or category of jobs, and both tests were therefore restricted from continued use.

Affirmative Action The EEOC publishes affirmative action guidelines to help employers voluntarily write an **affirmative action plan.** The plan analyzes the employer's work force and sets forth goals and timetables to remedy any situation where minorities and women are not adequately represented.

The fundamental principle underlying the guidelines is that employer practices which have an adverse impact on employment opportunities of any race, sex, or ethnic group are illegal. The guidelines adopt a rule of thumb for detecting the existence of adverse impact. The rule, known as the "80 percent rule," is not a legal definition of discrimination. It is a practical device to focus attention on serious discrepancies in hiring or promotion rates. By the rule, an adverse impact on employment opportunity may exist when the selection rate for any protected group is less than 80 percent of the rate of the highest selection group. For example, when 60 percent of white applicants are selected, at least 48 percent of minority applicants (i.e., 80 percent of 60 percent) should be selected.

Once it is established that there is adverse impact, the employer can modify or eliminate the procedure which produces it. Failing to do this, the employer must justify the use of the procedure on grounds of *business necessity*. This means showing a clear relation between performance on the selection procedure and performance on the job.

Reverse Discrimination Since the enactment of Title VII, many employers have developed programs to improve employment opportunities for groups that previously suffered from discrimination. Some of these programs and actions have been challenged. These so-called **reverse discrimination** cases charge that affirmative action programs are in conflict with requirements that employment decisions not be based on race, color, religion, sex, or national origin. That is, the law itself provides that no employer is required to grant preferential treatment to correct racial imbalance.

In the 1978 case of *Regents of the University of California v. Bakke,* the U.S. Supreme Court held that affirmative action based on a strict **quota**, which sets aside a fixed number of positions for a particular group, may be illegal.

With his application to the University of California at Davis Medical School twice rejected, Allan P. Bakke sued, charging that the medical school's special admissions policy unconstitutionally set aside 16 of 100 positions for racial minorities and that he was better qualified for admission than some of the students admitted under the special program. The trial court ruled that the university's program was invalid on the grounds that it discriminated against Bakke because of his race, but refused to order the school to admit him. On appeal, the California Supreme Court ruled that the university's affirmative action program was unconstitutional because it violated the equal-protection rights of whites. The court ordered the university to admit Bakke as a medical school student. The university sought and obtained a review by the U.S. Supreme Court. The justices, by a 5-to-4 vote, held that the method of the medical school was an illegal classification of applicants by race. The Court also ruled that professional schools are not legally barred from making race *one* of the criteria upon which to accept applicants.

Pay and Age Discrimination In addition to administering the Civil Rights Act, as amended, the EEOC enforces the Equal Pay Act of 1963 and the Age Discrimination in Employment Act of 1967.

Equal Pay Act The federal Equal Pay Act requires all employers subject to the FLSA to provide equal pay for both men and women performing similar work. Coverage was extended in 1972 to include executive, administrative, and professional employees (including academics, administrative personnel, and teachers in elementary and secondary schools) as well as outside salespeople.

Specifically, the act provides that no employer shall discriminate against employees on the basis of sex by paying wages at a rate less than that paid to employees of the opposite sex for equal work on jobs which require equal skill, effort, and responsibility and which are performed under similar working conditions. Males and females must be treated equally in areas such as base pay, opportunity for overtime, raises, bonuses, commissions, and fringe benefits such as health and life insurance, pensions, profit-sharing and bonus plans, and credit union benefits.

A state university compared the average salaries paid to male faculty members with those paid to female faculty members, using a formula based on levels of education, specialization, experience, and merit. It was found that 30 female faculty members were underpaid. The university promptly raised the minimum pay of these females to the formula level. Ninety male faculty members also discovered that they were receiving salaries below the average. In a court action, it was found that the university violated the provisions of the Equal Pay Act. The court ruled that the same formula must be applied to raise the minimum pay of the lower-paid males to the formula level.

The Equal Pay Act is also concerned with the more subtle kinds of unequal wage problems, such as the existence of different base rates for equal jobs where women are predominantly in the lower-paid category.

Anaconda Aluminum Company was ordered to pay $190,000 in back wages and court costs to 276 women who charged that the company had sex-segregated job categories. Jobs classified "female" and "male" had been reclassified as "light" and "heavy," but women were prevented from transferring to heavy jobs. After layoffs, the company hired new male employees for heavy jobs rather than recalling females with seniority in light jobs. The company was ordered to ensure opportunity for all jobs to anyone who could qualify.

The Equal Pay Act mandates that the sexes must be treated equally, but does not provide that they be treated *the same*. There are exceptions for a *bona fide* seniority system, a merit system, a training program, a system measuring earnings by quantity or quality of production, or a differential based on any factor other than sex.

Payment of different wage rates to permanent employees and temporary employees does not violate the Equal Pay Act. Another provision is that state or other laws regarding hours of work, jobs requiring physical strength, rest periods, and the like do not make work "unequal."

Age Discrimination in Employment Act The federal Age Discrimination in Employment Act (ADIEA) of 1967 outlaws discrimination against workers or potential workers aged 40 and over because of age. The act applies to private employers of 20 or more workers who are engaged in a business in or affecting interstate commerce; federal, state, and local governments; employment agencies; and labor unions with 25 or more members. The ADIEA makes it unlawful for an employer to

1. Refuse to hire or discharge any individual or otherwise discriminate against any individual with respect to compensation, terms, conditions, or privileges of employment, because of the individual's age.
2. Place limits, segregate, or classify individuals so as to deprive any individual of employment opportunities equal to those of younger employees, because of the individual's age.
3. Advertise for job applicants in such a way as to indicate or suggest a preference or limitation on age. Phrases such as "prefer recent graduate," "25 to 35," "young girl," or "young boy" that imply an age preference are forbidden.

There are subtleties in the age discrimination law which moderate the full effect of its broad goal of prohibiting discrimination of any kind against older employees. Employers may discriminate where age is a *bona fide* occupational qualification. For example, FAA regulations bar pilots from carrier operations as pilots after they reach the age of 60. Employers may also observe the terms of any *bona fide* seniority system or employee retirement, pension, or insurance plan. However, no such system or plan can be used as the reason for not hiring any individual or for requiring or permitting the involuntary retirement of any employee because of the age of such person. Thus, if the normal retirement age is 65, employees between the ages of 65 and 70 do not have to retire.

Discrimination on the Basis of Pregnancy or Handicap

The federal Pregnancy Discrimination Act forbids employers to discriminate against unmarried or married women on the basis of pregnancy or giving birth and recovery. Sick leave for an abortion must be provided if it is allowed for childbirth. These conditions are considered temporary disabilities for the period in which an employee cannot or should not on medical advice perform her job. Employers may neither require a woman to stop working if she is still capable of performing her job adequately nor set a fixed time that a woman must be away from work after giving birth. Employers are also not permitted to exclude coverage for pregnancy and childbirth from an employee health care policy if the employer offers comprehensive medical coverage to male employees.

An employer's policies and practices on pregnancy and maternity matters—such as the start and duration of leave, accrual of seniority, reinstatement, payment, or extension of leave—must apply to pregnant employees on the same basis as to other employees physically unable to work.

In a lawsuit brought by the EEOC and individual women, a federal district court ruled that AT&T Technologies Inc. had discriminated against pregnant employees in policies that treated maternity leave differently from other medical-related leaves. The judge ruled that the company had discriminated over a 12-year period through three policies: (1) women were forced to begin unpaid maternity leave at the end of their sixth month of pregnancy; (2) employees taking maternity leave could receive only 30 days of seniority credits, whereas others on disability leave received full credit while they were out of work; (3) women on maternity leave were given no guarantee they could return to their jobs or to similar ones. Monetary damages were awarded to an estimated 20,000 current or former workers.

Rehabilitation Act The federal Rehabilitation Act, as amended, requires every employer doing $2,500 or more business with the government each year to take affirmative action to hire and promote handicapped individuals. The term **handicapped** refers to any individual with a physical or mental impairment which limits one or more of the person's major life functions. Handicapped employees must be given reasonable opportunities to perform a job, with accommodations made by the employer including the installation of wheelchair ramps, special restroom facilities, and reserved parking areas.

Drug Testing and Alcoholism

Random drug testing in the workplace can be a legal problem, unless employers limit their drug testing to employees with jobs that involve the public safety.

Southern Pacific Railroad fired a computer-programmer who refused to submit to a drug test. In a subsequent suit, the railroad argued that the test was required because the employee worked on programs to repair defective rails, a compelling public safety issue. A California court disagreed, finding that the employee's job was not critical to safe train operation. In this instance, requiring a drug test was an invasion of personal privacy guaranteed by California law.

Unionized companies who want to institute a drug testing program must negotiate with the union before implementing the plan. The NLRB can issue an order revoking drug testing where the employer unilaterally puts it into effect without first bargaining with the union. Should the negotiators reach a good faith impasse, the employer may begin drug testing.

The federal Rehabilitation Act bars discrimination based on a handicap. Alcoholism is considered a handicap, if it does not constitute a direct threat to property or to the safety of others.

Acquired Immune Deficiency Syndrome

Legal issues related to acquired immune deficiency syndrome (AIDS) in the workplace are beginning to appear on the dockets of courts. However, no clear legal guidelines on handling them have emerged. One reason is that few cases have yet been decided, largely due to the swift and devastating mortality rates of the disease. Another reason lies in the complexity of AIDS and the widespread ignorance about the means of its transmission. Nevertheless, employers must take into account the legal rights of AIDS victims on their payroll, those of their coworkers, and those of the customers their AIDS-stricken employees serve.

A current legal issue is whether sufferers are protected under federal and state laws that bar job discrimination against handicapped employees by federal contractors. It is not clear whether the federal Rehabilitation Act applies to AIDS. The U.S. Supreme Court's one ruling on the protection the act affords workers with contagious diseases is open to question. In *School Board of Nassau County v. Arline*—a case decided in 1987 involving tuberculosis, not AIDS—the court held that victims are "not necessarily" denied protection unless they pose a real risk of infection or cannot perform their jobs. Logic would indicate that since AIDS is not normally transmitted at the workplace, the federal Rehabilitation Act would protect its victims. But the court did not address the question of whether its ruling applied to AIDS.

State courts, however, have recognized AIDS as a handicap. In Michigan, for example, in *Doe v. Sinacola & Sons Excavating, Inc.*, decided in 1987, AIDS was held to be a handicap under the state disability law. Antidiscrimination laws in California, Colorado, Maine, Massachusetts, New York, New Jersey, and Oregon include AIDS as a handicap.

Polygraph Testing

Lie detector testing is now banned or restricted in 22 states. A 1984 Oregon decision (*State v. Lyon*) tightened state control over polygraph, barring the use of lie detector results if one side in a trial objects.

Retailers are the largest polygraph users. They give millions of lie detector tests a year, primarily in preemployment screening. Efforts to go further can trigger legal difficulties.

Alexander's department store ordered companywide polygraph testing after experiencing widespread inventory loses. One employee objected to taking the test. He claimed he suffered from high blood pressure, throat problems, and a nervous condition, all likely to influence the outcome. Alexander's ignored the claims, made him take the test, and fired him when he failed. In a subsequent suit in which the employee claimed discrimination based on his disabilities which made him fail the test the court ruled in favor of the employee. The court held that the employee must be given an opportunity to demonstrate that the health conditions claimed did, in fact, represent a disability under the law.

SUMMARY

33-1. Like other contracts, employment agreements are subject to all the elements that apply to contracts. Although most employment contracts that are not written may be terminated at any time by either party, many courts have held that an employer may not discharge an employee without some kind of just cause. Both state and federal laws prohibiting discrimination also restrict the employer's power to discharge an employee.

33-2. Freedom of contract is a qualified, not an absolute, right. Federal law establishes maximum hours of employment, minimum wages, and fair standards for the employment of child labor.

State and federal laws serve to reduce preventable hazards to employees in the workplace and to provide for safe and healthful working conditions.

A national employment verification system places responsibility for verification of the identity and employment of all employees on the employer.

33-3. Federal law covers risks of workers by reason of their unemployment, disability, hospitalization, retirement, or death. The principal federal law covering these risks is the Social Security Act of 1935. Federal law also provides supervision over employee pension plans provided by employers.

33-4. Equal employment opportunity laws make it illegal to discriminate on the basis of sex, race, color, religion, or national origin in all employment practices. The equal Employment Opportunity Commission receives and investigates job discrimination complaints. The Commission also issues guidelines to assist employers in making sure their employment practices are in accord with the law. Commission guidelines require employers to furnish a self-analysis, setting goals and timetables for recruiting, hiring, training, upgrading, and promoting minorities and women.

The Equal Employment Opportunity Commission enforces federal law that requires employers to provide equal pay for both men and women performing similar work and legislation which outlaws discrimination against workers aged 40 and over because of age.

Employers are barred from discriminating against married and unmarried women on the basis of pregnancy and related conditions. Employers doing business with the government are required to employ handicapped workers who can perform a given job, with reasonable accommodations.

Random drug testing in the workplace can be a legal problem, unless employers limit tests to employees with jobs that involve the public safety. Alcoholism is considered a handicap, if it does not constitute a direct threat to property or to the safety of others in the workplace.

State courts have recognized AIDS as a handicap, but it is not clear whether federal legislation applies. Lie detector testing is banned or restricted in 22 states, but such testing is conducted widely in preemployment screening by retailers.

Understanding Key Legal Terms

affirmative action plan (p. 471)
at will (p. 460)
bona fide occupational qualification (p. 470)
business necessity (p. 470)
citation (p. 462)
disabled (p. 466)
documentation (p. 463)
employment contract (p. 459)
employment discrimination (p. 468)
handicapped (p. 474)
quota (p. 471)
reverse discrimination (p. 471)
vesting (p. 468)
workers' compensation laws (p. 467)

Questions for Review and Discussion

1. What are the provisions generally expressed in a simple employment contract?
2. Define the "at-will" doctrine, and indicate some of the methods devised by state courts to evade or limit its authority.
3. Describe the standards as provided by the Fair Labor Standards Act for wage and hour exceptions and exemptions.
4. How does the Occupational Safety and Health Act work to reduce hazards to employees and to provide safe and healthful working conditions?
5. List the major provisions of the Immigration Reform and Control Act of 1986.
6. How are workers provided for while they are working, when unemployed, and following retirement?
7. Describe pension plan regulation as enacted by the Employee Retirement Income Security Act.
8. Indicate what kinds of employment discrimination are prohibited by law.
9. Discuss the major provisions of the Equal Pay Act and the Age Discrimination in Employment Act.
10. What acts are enforced by the EEOC to counter discrimination of pregnant or handicapped individuals?

Analyzing Cases

1. Upshaw worked as a chemical engineer for the Urban Chemical Company. Spehar, Upshaw's supervisor, ordered him to remove the old labels from several hundred steel drums which had once contained a severely corrosive acid. Spehar told Upshaw that they intended to reuse the drums to ship a new chemical fertilizer. Upshaw refused to remove the labels because reusing the old drums would violate both federal and state law. When Spehar had another employee remove the labels and reuse the drums, Upshaw reported the company's activities to state and federal authorities.

Upshaw was fired for his refusal to follow orders and for his report to the authorities. In a lawsuit against Urban, which legal exception to the employment-at-will doctrine will Upshaw use? Explain. Will he succeed in his suit?

2. Rice, a black female, was denied employment as a public health representative by the city of St. Louis for lack of a college degree. Failing to obtain relief after filing a complaint with the EEOC charging race discrimination, she brought suit in the U.S. District Court.

   Rice took the position that the degree requirement for employment more heavily burdened blacks than whites. She pointed out that blacks were only approximately 55 percent as likely as whites in the St. Louis area to have a college degree. This requirement, she argued, had an "adverse impact" upon blacks and was invalid under Title VII. Testimony showed that the satisfactory performance of public health representatives required the ability to communicate with others, frequently in an emotional situation, and the ability to speak and write intelligibly. There was also risk to the public health and safety in the employment of unqualified applicants. Judgment for whom and why? *Rice v. City of St. Louis,* 607 F.2d 791 (8th Cir. Ct.).

3. The Commonwealth of Virginia required all applicants for state troopers to be between 21 and 29 years of age, to be at least 5 feet 9 inches tall, and to weigh at least 156 pounds. The height and weight requirements eliminated 98 percent of female applicants. The basic employment requirements also required that all employment applicants, including applicants for civilian dispatcher positions, complete and pass written mental ability tests. Blacks were more likely than whites to fail the tests. The tests for dispatcher positions were not valid predictors of job performance. Tests for trooper positions were not shown to be predictors of job performance. The United States brought suit charging that Virginia engaged in a "pattern and practice" of discrimination against black applicants for civilian positions with the state police and against both black and women applicants for trooper positions. In light of Title VII charges, judgment for whom? Why? *United States v. Com. of Va.,* 620 F.2d 1018 (4th Cir. Ct.)

4. The Security Bank and Trust Company employed a number of men and women as tellers and cashiers. The male workers were paid higher salaries than their female counterparts. The Secretary of Labor brought action to enjoin the bank from violating the equal pay provisions of the Equal Pay Act.

   The bank claimed that the male employees performed extra and more difficult duties which rendered the jobs unequal and that the male employees were not regarded as permanent tellers but were being trained in all aspects of the banking business for future placement in management positions. Judgment for whom and why? *Marshall v. Security Bank & Trust Co.,* 572 F.2d 276 (10th Cir. Ct.)

5. Aetna Insurance Company employed Barratt as a casualty underwriter and paid her a salary of $11,900 a year. She had received a number of raises. Aetna subsequently hired a male who had eight years of underwriting experience to perform the same duties and assume the same responsibilities as Barratt, at a rate of $14,700 a year.

   The Secretary of Labor, on behalf of Barratt, brought suit based upon sex discrimination in violation of the Equal Pay Act, contending that Barratt had been paid less for the same work. Aetna, on the other hand, attributed the differential to a dual merit system and the superior qualifications and greater potential for promotion of Archer. With respect to the merit system of incoming employees, the company assessed the merit of prospective employees by evaluating their job application information and their responses to a number of interviews by supervisory personnel. The merit system for persons already employed at the company was in writing and made periodic salary adjustments for employees who had accumulated service with the company according to past performance and the company's goals and objectives. Judgment for whom and why? *Equal Employment Etc. v. Aetna Ins. Co.*, 616 F.2d 719 (4th Cir. Ct.)

6. Green, 15 years of age, got a job with Butler Concrete Products Co. as a materials checker. The company did not ask Green his age, nor did it request a certificate of age from the Wage and Hour Division of the Labor Department. Green was seriously injured in a fall while in the performance of his duties. He and his parents now seek compensation for his injuries. Will they recover? Explain.

7. Bennerson was employed by the Checker Garage Service Corp. as an auto mechanic. His duties included both assisting mechanics in the garage and making road calls to service vehicles owned and operated by his employer. During his lunch hour, Bennerson used one of his employer's taxicabs to drive to a restaurant. En route to the restaurant, he was seriously injured when the taxicab struck a pole. Bennerson filed a claim before the workers' compensation board for compensation, which was granted. Checker Garage appealed, claiming among other things that the taxicab Bennerson drove did not "go out of control" but that Bennerson "lost control." Judgment for whom and why? *Bennerson v. Checker Garage Serv. Corp.*, 388 N.Y.S. 2d 374.

8. Nancy Barillaro and Nancy Fotia were employed in the inspection and trimming departments at Elwood Knitting Mills for approximately 16 years. Barillaro was laid off in September and Fotia in November. Both were offered the option of returning to work in March of the following year as knitting machine operators, but at an 18 percent reduction in pay. Neither accepted the offer. (*a*) They argued that the offered work would have involved a loss of seniority and a substantial reduction in pay. (*b*) Fotia claimed lack of familiarity with the machine, and Barillaro claimed she was "too short" to operate the machine. The Pennsylvania Unemployment Compensation Board decided that the claimants were ineligible to receive benefits because they refused offers of suitable work without good cause. On appeal to the court, judgment for whom? Why? *Barillaro v. Unemployment Compensation Bd. of Review*, 387 A.2d 1324 (Pennsylvania).

CHAPTER 34
Labor-Management Relations Law

OUTLINE

34-1 Source of Labor-Management Relations
- Labor Unions

34-2 Major Federal Labor Legislation
- Norris-LaGuardia Act
- Wagner Act
- Taft-Hartley Act
- Landrum-Griffin Act

34-3 Collective Bargaining Process
- National Labor Relations Board
- Union Certification Procedure
- Unfair Labor Practice Procedure

34-4 Right to Strike in the Public Sector

COMMENTARY

After Gerow got a job with the Brown Construction Co., he learned that several of his fellow workers were organizing the employees into a labor union. The company management objected to the action and enclosed a notice in each employee's pay envelope to the effect that anyone joining the union would be immediately fired. Since there is a constitutional right of assembly, can Gerow's employer fire him or any other employee because of union activity?

The fact is that an employer cannot prohibit workers from union activity. Federal and state labor laws give workers the right to form, join, or assist a labor organization. Employers may not encourage or discourage membership in a union by discriminating in regard to hiring, job tenure, or any other condition of employment. In addition, employers cannot refuse to bargain collectively with the representatives of the majority of employees. Gerow is also protected by law from any union attempt to cause Brown Construction to discriminate against him for not becoming a union member, unless there is a membership agreement in effect. And once a union member, Gerow has the right to attend union meetings, have a voice in them, and to vote in union elections. These rights, and others relating to labor-management relations law, are discussed in this chapter.

OBJECTIVES

1. Explain the inherent conflict of interest that exists between labor and management, and make clear the results of this conflict.
2. Relate the three basic aims of labor unions in response to workers' needs.
3. Summarize the major provisions of the Norris-LaGuardia Act, the Wagner Act, the Taft-Hartley Act, and the Landrum-Griffin Act.
4. Describe the procedure followed by the National Labor Relations Board upon receiving a complaint of an unfair labor practice.
5. Determine the position taken by federal courts in denying employees in the public sector the right to strike.

34-1 SOURCE OF LABOR-MANAGEMENT RELATIONS

Historically, employees have fought to unite in organizations which could bargain effectively with employers in matters involving wages, hours of work, and working conditions. Employers, on the other hand, have viewed these attempts to unionize by employees as a threat to their rights to make all decisions that affect their businesses. The resulting conflicts have often resulted in the disruption of the free flow of commerce and in serious social and economic problems for the general public.

Labor Unions

U.S. Const., Article I **(see p. 599)**

A **labor union** is an organization that acts on behalf of all employees in negotiations with the employer regarding terms of their employment. It is a lawful assembly, protected by Amendment 1 of the U.S. Constitution and by federal and state laws.

Labor unions grew as businesses expanded and technological change altered the nature of work. Workers demanded some protection to help them cope with changes that made the workplace increasingly less personal. In response to the needs of workers, labor unions developed three aims: (1) to create a seniority system to protect workers' jobs from arbitrary layoffs and replacement with cheaper wage earners, (2) to upgrade worker status through wage and fringe-benefit increases, and (3) to sponsor laws to improve social, economic, and political conditions for workers.

Employers resisted the demands of labor organizations, arguing that their actions were restraints of trade prohibited by federal law. The courts supported this argument and declared unions illegal.

Connecticut hatmakers in 1915 attempted to unionize their employer. They began a boycott of the employer's hats. This action to persuade others to refuse to work for, purchase from, or handle the hats of the employer caused the hatmaker to bring an action against the union under the Sherman Antitrust Act. The hatmaker charged that the boycott was a conspiracy in restraint of trade. Agreeing with the hatmaker, the court reasoned that the hatters union by its actions had obstructed the flow of commerce and, that as a result, the hatmaker was unable to conduct its business as effectively as it might have.

The response to such employer and court resistance to union actions was strikes and economic slowdowns. Violence, and later political pressure, created a popular demand to amend the laws.

34-2 MAJOR FEDERAL LABOR LEGISLATION

Federal labor legislation has been enacted over the years to assist labor and management in settling disputes, to safeguard national interests by insuring a stable economic system, and to protect the public's right.

The first federal statute relating to labor was the Clayton Act of 1914. It attempted to prohibit federal courts from forbidding activities such as picketing and strikes in disputes over terms or conditions of employment. **Picketing** involves the placement of persons for observation, patrol, and demonstration at the site of employment as part of employee pressure on an employer to meet a demand. A **strike** is a stoppage of work by employees as a means of enforcing a demand made on their employers. The Clayton Act also stated that the antitrust laws did not apply to labor unions or their members in carrying out their lawful objectives.

In 1926 Congress passed the Railway Labor Act, which provided procedures for dealing with labor disputes in the railroad industry. It encouraged **collective bargaining,** that is, a good faith meeting between representatives of employees and employers to discuss the terms and conditions of employment. Its provisions were later extended to the airline industry.

Norris-LaGuardia Act

After the passage of the Railway Labor Act, Congress passed four other major labor acts (see Table 34-1). The Norris-LaGuardia Act was passed by Congress in 1932. Among its major provisions was the outlawing of **yellow-dog contracts,** which forbid the joining of a union as a condition of employment. It also specified acts which, during participation in labor disputes, were not subject to federal court injunctions. These acts included striking, picketing, and boycotting. A **boycott** is a concerted refusal to have dealings with someone to force acceptance of certain conditions. While the statute did restrict the use of injunctions in labor disputes, it did not prohibit them entirely.

Wagner Act

The passage of the National Labor Relations Act (known as the Wagner Act) in 1935 opened the door for the rapid growth of the union movement. It is probably the most significant labor relations statute in that it expressly sets forth the unfair labor practices prohibited for both employers and unions.

The Wagner Act gave workers the right to organize by allowing them to form, join, or aid labor unions. It also established procedures for representative elections and for collective bargaining.

The Wagner Act is known as well for the creation of the National Labor Relations Board (NLRB), which hears and rules on charges that unfair labor practices have been committed by employers or by unions.

Various activities are prohibited by the Wagner Act as **unfair labor practices,** that is, improper employment practices by either an employer or union. These activities include interference with employees' right to organize, domination or interference with the formation or administration of any union, discrimination to encourage or discourage union membership, discharge for charges filed or testimony given, and refusal to bargain collectively.

Interference with Employees' Right to Organize An employer cannot interfere with employees when they are forming a union, selecting their representatives, voting, striking, picketing, or engaging in any other protected and legal acts. For example, an employer cannot threaten to fire or discipline a worker for union activity or reward workers who do not participate in union activities. Threats to eliminate certain benefits or privileges, to close down the business, or to discharge workers for union activity are prohibited.

Table 34-1 FEDERAL LAWS GOVERNING LABOR-MANAGEMENT RELATIONS

Year	*Law*	*Major Provisions*
1914	Clayton Act	Exempted union activity from the antitrust laws.
1926	Railway Labor Act	(1) Provided for supervision of collective bargaining for railroads and airlines. (2) Established the National Mediation Board to conduct union elections and mediate employer-union disputes.
1932	Norris-LaGuardia Act	(1) Outlawed yellow-dog contracts. (2) Limited the power of federal courts to issue injunctions to halt labor disputes. (3) Guaranteed employees the right to organize into unions and to engage in collective bargaining.
1934	Wagner Act	(1) Created the National Labor Relations Board (NLRB). (2) Authorized NLRB to conduct representative elections and to determine the bargaining unit. (3) Outlawed certain conduct by employers as unfair labor practices. (4) Authorized NLRB to hold hearings on unfair labor practice petitions.
1947	Taft-Hartley Act	(1) Outlawed certain practices by unions as unfair labor practices. (2) Allowed states to legislate right-to-work laws. (3) Provided an 80-day cooling-off period in strikes that endanger national health or safety. (4) Created a mediation and conciliation service to assist in the settlement of labor disputes.
1959	Landrum-Griffin Act	(1) Established a bill of rights for union members. (2) Required unions to adopt constitutions and bylaws. (3) Required unions to submit annual reports detailing assets, liabilities, payments, and loans. (4) Added further provisions to the list of unfair labor practices.

In her five years with a telephone-answering service, Sebas might have been fired on a number of occasions for violating the work rules. She had an abrasive personality that made it difficult for her to get along with coworkers. When a union began organizing the telephone operators, Sebas strongly supported the effort. During this organizing effort, Sebas apparently acted in an insubordinate manner and was fired. At a subsequent NLRB hearing her discharge was found to be "tainted." On appeal, the court reasoned that although Sebas was far from the valued and trusted employee the union said she was, the company had tolerated her all along. The court held that Sebas's discharge was more a result of her union activities than her work performance and reinstated her with back pay.

Domination or Interference With the Formation or Administration of Any Union An employer cannot form a company-run union for its employees. The purpose of this prohibition is to bar company-owned unions from bowing to the wishes of management. It is also an unfair practice to aid one union over another, place employer spies at union meetings, reward some union officials, or agree with a union that a closed shop will be maintained. A **closed shop** is a work site in which the employer, by agreement, hires only union members in good standing. It is usually lawful, however, to have a union shop contract provision. A **union shop** is a place of employment where nonunion workers may be employed for a trial period of not more than 30 days, after which the nonunion workers must join the union or be discharged.

Discrimination to Encourage or Discourage Union Membership Intentional discrimination by the employer toward an employee to encourage or discourage union membership is an unfair labor practice. Such discrimination may involve assigning an employee to less desirable work or denying an employee the opportunity to participate in overtime work. Also viewed as discriminatory is **constructive discharge;** this occurs when an employee is demoted to a job with lesser pay or authority or poorer working conditions than the previous job, or when the employee is subjected to supervisory harassment. To avoid employee complaints of intentional discrimination, employers must rely on meaningful business reasons when bestowing or denying employment opportunities.

Draper was selected by the union members to serve as their representative in collective bargaining meetings with Detroit White Line Company. After his selection, Draper was harassed by the production manager and the general manager for trivial matters concerning work schedules and productivity. Draper has the right to file a complaint with the NLRB charging constructive discharge due to his union activities.

Discharge for Charges Filed or Testimony Given It is an unlawful act for employers to discharge or otherwise discriminate against employees because they file charges or give testimony under the Wagner Act. The courts interpret discrimination under this provision to include discharge, layoff, failure to rehire or recall, and transfer of covered employees.

Refusal to Bargain Collectively An employer must sit down and negotiate with employee representatives over wages, hours, the effects of business changes on employees, grievance procedures, health benefits, seniority systems, dues checkoffs, and vacations.

Issues must be discussed willingly, free of delaying tactics, coercion, or harassment by both sides. The employer has no duty to agree to any union demands, but must meet with employee representatives at reasonable times and places to bargain in good faith. Neither party can bargain about a closed shop contract, politics, religious issues, management functions, or foreign affairs.

The NLRB does not have jurisdiction over religious schools, both on labor relations grounds and by virtue of the religion clauses of the First Amendment of the U.S. Constitution. The U.S. Supreme Court has ruled that the requirements of collective bargaining would represent an encroachment upon the freedom of church authorities to shape and direct teaching in accord with requirements of their religion.

Taft-Hartley Act

The Labor-Movement Relations Act of 1947, popularly named the Taft-Hartley Act, established a means to protect employers in collective bargaining and labor organization matters. A detailed list of unfair labor activities that unions as well as employers were forbidden to practice was added to those of the Wagner Act.

State Right-to-Work Laws **Right-to-work laws** are state laws which prohibit labor-management agreements requiring union membership as a condition of getting or keeping a job. These laws, in effect, outlaw both the closed shop and the union shop.

Ordinarily, state labor relations laws do not apply to unions and businesses which are involved in interstate commerce and which are governed by federal labor laws. The Taft-Hartley Act, however, created special rules with regard to state right-to-work laws. It provided that a union shop contract would be legal only in states that did not forbid them. As a result, state right-to-work laws, where they exist, are applicable to most unions and businesses. All employees in the **bargaining unit,** i.e., a unit formed for the purpose of collective bargaining, are benefitted by the collective bargaining agreement negotiated by the union, even though they have not paid union dues. However, nonunion employees lose all right to vote on union officers or on collective bargaining agreements.

Free Speech Provision The Taft-Hartley Act includes a free speech provision that allows employers to comment more freely on union organizing activities. The provision states that employers would not commit an unfair labor practice by speaking to employees about unions unless they threaten reprisal or promise some benefit to employees. For instance, an employer might properly inform its employees that they should not vote for a union, but a threat to fire anyone for favoring a union shop would be an unfair labor practice.

Employee Coercion Provision It is also an unfair labor practice for a labor union to try to coerce employees to join the union, to block the employment of individuals who refuse to support a union, or to encourage an employee to withdraw an unfair labor practice charge.

A union can set rules for its internal operations and can punish any member who refuses to follow them, but it cannot use force, violence, or intimidation against an employee. A union is also not permitted to discipline one of its members without good cause. The union has a duty to represent all its members on an equal basis.

Colton was a member of the union representing Dalmar Ken Films, Inc. She learned that another union member was stealing blank tape and reels from the company warehouse. She warned the person that the theft would be reported. When informed of the warning, the union representative revoked Colton's membership and asked the company personnel officer to have her fired. Colton filed a complaint with the NLRB, charging the union with illegal restraint in the exercise of her legal rights. The NLRB ruled that Colton's union membership could not be withdrawn and ordered the union to restore her membership.

Secondary Boycott It is also prohibited for a union to engage in a **secondary boycott.** This is a conspiracy in which a union places pressure on a neutral customer or supplier with whom the union has no dispute in order to cause the neutral entity to cease doing business with the employer with whom the union has a dispute. Under the Taft-Hartley Act provision, it is an unfair labor practice for a union (1) to strike against an employer because another employer uses nonunion employees, (2) to strike against a general contractor to force the contractor to stop dealing with a subcontractor, (3) to ask employees of another company not to load trucks carrying the products of a company the union is striking, or (4) to refuse to work on products made by nonunion employees.

Steel Specialists, Inc., sold strip steel to Thomas Spring Company. The steel is transported by Roadway Express, Inc., whose employees are nonunion. The union representing Steel Specialists instructed its members to refuse to load Roadway Express trucks with steel in order to force Steel Specialists to stop using Roadway Express. This form of secondary boycott is an unfair labor practice because it involves an innocent employer in a union tactic intended to harm another employer.

National Emergency Strikes The Taft-Hartley Act gives the President of the United States special powers to deal with actual or threatened strikes which affect interstate commerce or which endanger the nation's health and safety. On the basis of a board of inquiry's findings, the President can order the Attorney General to petition a federal district court to issue an injunction stopping the strike for 60 days. The board of inquiry may then require the union members to vote on the most recent offer within an additional 15-day period, and the results are sent to the Attorney General within 5 days after balloting. The injunction ends and the employees may strike at the end of this 80-day period. However, the President can then make legislative recommendations to Congress that appear to be appropriate in resolving the dispute.

Other Prohibited Union Practices Under other provisions of the Taft-Hartley Act, unions cannot refuse to bargain collectively with an employer and must give notice to the employer of an intention to strike prior to the termination date of a collective bargaining contract.

It is also an unfair labor practice for a labor union to require an employer to keep unneeded employees, to pay employees for not working, or to assign more employees to a given job than are needed (i.e., **featherbedding**).

Another provision of the law prohibits a union from requiring employees who join a union to pay excessively high dues, fees, and related expenses. To determine what is excessive, the courts consider the amounts other unions charge and the employee's wages.

Landrum-Griffin Act

The Labor Management Reporting and Disclosure Act of 1959, known as the Landrum-Griffin Act, is a tough anticorruption law. It was designed to clean up the corruption and violence that had been uncovered in the internal affairs of unions. The law requires all unions to adopt constitutions and bylaws and to register them with the Secretary of Labor. In addition, unions are required to submit annual reports detailing assets, liabilities, receipts and sources, payments to union members exceeding $10,000, loans to union members and businesses, and other monies paid out.

Bill of Rights Provision An important part of the Landrum-Griffin Act is the "bill of rights" provision for union members. This provision assures all union members of the opportunity to participate in the internal affairs of their union. They are guaranteed the right to vote in union elections, to speak at union meetings, and to receive union financial reports.

Hot-Cargo Agreement The Landrum-Griffin Act amended the Taft-Hartley Act, making it an unlawful labor practice to become involved in a **hot-cargo contract.** This is an agreement in which an employer voluntarily agreed with a union not to handle, use, or deal in nonunion-produced goods of another employer.

34-3 COLLECTIVE BARGAINING PROCESS

The Taft-Hartley Act established a system for helping labor and management settle their disputes without causing a major disruption in the economy or endangering the public health and safety. Central to this collective bargaining process is the National Labor Relations Board (NLRB) and the procedures it follows in settling labor-management disputes.

National Labor Relations Board

The National Labor Relations Board (NLRB) is a governmental commission that has the exclusive jurisdiction to enforce the Taft-Hartley Act and related laws. It has the power to act when cases are brought before it, but only in cases where the employer's operation or the labor dispute affects commerce.

Like most government regulatory agencies, the NLRB has investigative, regulatory, administrative, enforcement, and judgmental powers. It can make its own rules of procedure, conduct investigations into unfair labor practice charges, compel individuals to appear with papers relevant to the controversy, hold hearings, and issue orders. Appeal from the five-member board orders go first to the appropriate U.S. court of appeals and then to the Supreme Court.

Unfair Labor Practice Procedure A person, union, or employer can file notice with the NLRB of an alleged unfair labor practice within six months after it occurs. If the charge has merit, a complaint is issued notifying the offending party that a hearing is to be held concerning the charges. Efforts are made through arbitration to resolve the dispute before the hearing date. **Arbitration** involves the submission of the dispute to selected persons and the substitution of their decision for the judgment of the NLRB. If arbitration efforts fail, the hearing is held.

In the event that the complaint is found to be valid, a cease and desist order may be issued restoring the parties to the state existing before the unfair practice began. For example, wrongfully discharged employees may be reinstated with or without back pay. Where evidence at the hearing does not support the complaint, it is dismissed. Either party to the hearing may subsequently appeal the NLRB action to the appropriate U.S. Court of Appeals and then to the Supreme Court.

Mediation The Taft-Hartley Act encourages labor and management to agree freely on the settlement of disputes. To further this effort to preserve labor peace and promote prompt settlements, Congress formed the Federal Mediation and Conciliation Service. This body can act by itself or upon the request of either side to a labor dispute. Its mediation role is to offer nonbinding suggestions for settling the dispute, require the parties to negotiate, and force a vote by employees on an employer's offers.

34-4 RIGHT TO STRIKE IN THE PUBLIC SECTOR

In the public sector, where the general welfare, safety, health, and morals of the public is involved, the right to strike is restricted. Consequently, strikes by police, fire fighters, refuse collectors, air traffic controllers, postal workers, and other public employees who perform vital services are generally illegal, unless specifically authorized by statute.

The U.S. Code states that "an individual may not accept or hold a position in the government of the United States or the government of the District of Columbia if he participates in a strike or asserts the right to strike against the government." The U.S. Supreme Court has affirmed lower court rulings that there is no constitutional right to strike against the federal government. Thus, strikes by federal employees are substantially more than merely unfair labor practices; they are crimes.

The air traffic controllers, employees of the Federal Aviation Administration, went on strike. The controller's union, the Professional Air Traffic Controllers Organization, demanded that the controllers be removed from the civil service designation which prohibited them from striking. They argued that prohibition of the right to strike was a violation of a fundamental civil liberty. A federal district court ruled that government employees do not have the right to strike because

Congress had not given them such a right. The controllers persisted in their strike. As a result, all striking controllers were fired and the union was fined $100,000 an hour for the duration of the strike. The union was subsequently decertified, removing its rights to bargain on behalf of the controllers.

SUMMARY

34-1. Lacking bargaining power with their employers, employees have fought to unite in organizations that can bargain effectively in labor disputes.

34-2. Federal labor legislation has been enacted over the years to assist labor and management in settling disputes, to safeguard national interest, and to protect the public's rights.

The first federal statute relating to labor was the Clayton Act, which attempted to prohibit federal courts from forbidding activities such as picketing and strikes in disputes over the terms and conditions of employment.

The Norris-LaGuardia Act outlawed yellow-dog contracts and specified acts, such as striking, picketing, and boycotting, which were not subject to federal injunctions.

The Wagner Act opened the door for the growth of the labor union. It set forth specific unfair labor practices which were prohibited for employers and unions, established procedures for representative elections and for collective bargaining, and created the National Labor Relations Board (NLRB), which hears and rules on charges that unfair labor practices have taken place.

The Taft-Hartley Act outlawed specific conduct by unions as unfair labor practices, provided for an 80-day cooling-off period in strikes that endanger national health or safety, and created a mediation and conciliation service to assist in the settlement of labor disputes.

The Landrum-Griffin Act (*a*) established a bill of rights for union members, (*b*) required union reports to the Secretary of Labor, and (*c*) added to the list of unfair labor practices.

34-3. The NLRB has exclusive jurisdiction to enforce labor-management relations laws with investigative, regulatory, administrative, enforcement, and judgment powers.

Any person, union, or employer can file notice with the NLRB of an alleged unfair labor practice. If the complaint has merit, a hearing is held before the NLRB. If the complaint if found to be valid, an order may be issued restoring the parties to the state existing prior to the unfair practice. Appeals to NLRB action can be taken to the appropriate U.S. circuit court of appeals and then to the U.S. Supreme Court.

The Federal Mediation and Conciliation Service was formed to encourage labor and management to agree freely on the settlement of their disputes. Its mediation role is to offer nonbinding suggestions for settling the dispute, require the parties to negotiate, and force a vote by employees on employers' offers.

34-4. In the public sector, the right to strike is restricted. The U.S. Code states that "an individual may not accept or hold a position in the government of the United States or the government of the District of Columbia if he participates in a strike or asserts the right to strike against the government."

Understanding Key Legal Terms

arbitration (p. 488)
bargaining unit (p. 485)
boycott (p. 482)
closed shop (p. 484)
collective bargaining (p. 482)
constructive discharge (p. 484)
featherbedding (p. 487)
hot-cargo contract (p. 487)
labor union (p. 481)
picketing (p. 482)
right-to-work laws (p. 485)
secondary boycott (p. 486)
strike (p. 482)
unfair labor practices (p. 482)
union shop (p. 484)
yellow-dog contracts (p. 482)

Questions for Review and Discussion

1. What is the basis of the historical conflict of interest that exists between workers and their employers?
2. Summarize the three aims that labor unions developed in response to the needs of workers.
3. Identify the four major federal labor laws and state the three objectives they are designed to accomplish.
4. What are the major provisions of the Norris-LaGuardia Act?
5. List some of the activities forbidden to employers under the provisions of the Wagner Act.
6. What is the significance of state right-to-work laws as provided for by the Taft-Hartley Act?
7. Discuss the central purpose of the Landrum-Griffin Act and the scope of its major provisions.
8. Discuss the role of the National Labor Relations Board and explain its major functions.
9. What is the procedure followed after an unfair labor practice notice is filed with the NLRB?
10. Discuss the rights of private and public employees to strike.

Analyzing Cases

1. Carabetta worked as a printer for the St. Clair Printing Company. When the employees of St. Clair Printing decided to form a union, Carabetta was selected by union members to serve as their representative in collective bargaining meetings. Immediately after this appointment, management demoted Carabetta from printer to bindery worker. This demotion meant Carabetta had to take more than a twenty percent cut in pay. He was also frequently harassed by the bindery supervisor who assigned him to the most menial jobs in the bindery. Later, Carabetta was demoted even further to a position on the loading dock. This demotion reduced his pay by another five percent. Explain the grounds upon which Carabetta could file a complaint with the NLRB.

2. The union representing employees of the Consolidated Manufacturing Company elected Franco and Allanson to act on their behalf at a collective bargaining session with management. At the session, Franco and Allanson demanded that the new collective bargaining agreement include terms that would require management to hire only union members in good standing. Management disagreed with this proposal. Instead, management proposed a term in the agreement that would allow the company

to hire non-union workers for a trial period lasting no more than 30 days. After the 30 day trial period the non-union worker would then have to join a union. Which of these two contradictory terms in the proposed collective bargaining agreement would be allowed under federal labor law? Explain. Management also proposed that the employee union be disbanded and replaced by a company-run union. Management argued that the new company-run union would not only be more efficient, but also more economical. Would this proposal be allowed under federal labor law?

3. The NLRB certified a union as bargaining agent for lay teachers in schools operated by the Diocese of Fort Wayne-South Bend, Ind. Its five parochial high schools provided a traditional secular education but were oriented to the beliefs of the Roman Catholic faith. The diocese refused to recognize or bargain with the union, which represented only the lay teachers and nonteaching employees, not religious faculty. The diocese argued that the NLRB had no jurisdiction over religious schools both on statutory grounds and on the basis of the religion clauses of the First Amendment. Do you agree with the diocese? Why or why not? *NLRB v. Catholic Bishop of Chicago,* 440 U.S. 490.

4. A newspaper publisher hired nonunion newsroom employees to write copy and perform general editorial work. They were underpaid, considering the education and experience required of them. Bozza, a copy editor, called a meeting at his home where the newsroom employees discussed salaries and working conditions. They designated Bozza as their representative to meet with the owner of the newspaper and to discuss improvements in working conditions. The publisher heard of the meeting and immediately fired Bozza for insubordination. Bozza filed a petition with the NLRB, charging the publisher with an unfair labor practice. Judgment for whom and why?

5. An employee was discharged for violation of the company's no-solicitation rule in its factory and offices. The employee had persisted in soliciting union membership on company property during lunch periods. The company argued that its no-solicitation rule would have been enforced not merely against union solicitation but against any solicitation. How would you decide? Why? *Republic Aviation Corp. v. NLRB,* 324 U.S. 793.

6. Having advised Exchange Parts Co. that it was conducting an organizational campaign, the union petitioned the NLRB for an election to determine whether it would be certified as the bargaining agent of the company's employees. During the organizational campaign, while the granted certification election was pending, the company announced five additional benefits for the employees, two of which were announced only a few days before the election. In the election, the employees voted against being represented by a union. The union then filed a complaint with the NLRB charging the company with an unfair labor practice because it granted benefits while the campaign was taking place and the election was pending. The union argued that the company's actions interfered with the freedom of choice of the employees to determine whether they wished to be represented by the union. For whom would you decide? Why? *NLRB v. Exchange Parts Co.,* 375 U.S. 405.

7. Darlington Manufacturing Co. operated one textile mill that was controlled by Deering Milliken, who operated 27 other such mills. The union began an organizational campaign, which Darlington resisted. The employees filed charges of unfair labor practices with the NLRB. The board found in a subsequent hearing that the different mills controlled by Deering Milliken represented an integrated enterprise and that the closing of the Darlington mill was due to the antiunion hostility of Deering Milliken. The NLRB ordered Deering

Milliken to provide back pay to the workers until they obtained similar work. The court of appeals denied enforcement of the NLRB order, holding that an independent employer has an absolute right to close a business regardless of notice. On review by the U.S. Supreme Court, how should the Court rule on the question of whether an employer has the absolute right to close part of a business, no matter what the reason? Why? *Textile Worker's Union v. Darlington Mfg. Co.*, 380 U.S. 263.

8. The NLRB conducted an election among employees of Savair Manufacturing Co. to determine whether the union would represent the employees. During the election, "recognition slips" were distributed. The employees were told by the union that if they signed the slips before the election they would not have to pay an initiation fee if the union won. At least 35 employees signed the slips before the election, which the union won by a vote of 22 to 20. The company refused to bargain with the union, contending that the union, by offering possible benefits to employees for signing the recognition slips, was guilty of an unfair labor practice. Did the practice of the union prevent a fair and free choice of a bargaining representative? Why or why not? *NLRB v. Savair Mfg. Co.*, 414 U.S. 270.

PART 7
Case Study
Gary H. Davis v. Steven L. DelRosso, et al.

Supreme Judicial Court of Massachusetts
359 N.E.2d 313 (Massachusetts)

SUMMARY

The plaintiff, thirty-one years old, an executive of a computer service company, on finishing end-of-month work on Friday, about 11:15 P.M., drove a few blocks to Millbury's cafe. In the evenings the cafe provided music, dancing, and other entertainment, besides food and drink. The place was crowded as the plaintiff entered. He stood at the bar and ordered a beer, his only alcoholic drink of the day. He recognized a young woman with whom he was casually acquaintedand began to chat with her at the bar.

A man approached and asked the young woman for a dance. She declined. He returned in a few minutes, and, on being again refused, took the young woman by the arm. The plaintiff said, "Leave her alone." At this point the man grabbed the plaintiff by his shirt. The plaintiff pushed him away. Neither landed any blows or, it seems, attempted any.

Almost instantly—perhaps in response to a call by a bartender for "Stevie" —DelRosso, evidently in uniform, appeared and stepped between the two. Without inquiring into the merits, he pushed the plaintiff against a wall, and as the plaintiff rebounded, or was pulled from the wall by DelRosso, DelRosso struck him a blow on the mouth with his right fist. This did considerable damage to the plaintiff's upper teech and bridgework and he began to bleed profusely. DelRosso seized the plaintiff by the hair, pulled or dragged him outside, and shoved him to the ground. The young woman followed outside and asked DelRosso whether she might help the plaintiff; DelRosso rebuffed her and ordered her back into the cafe. After perhaps ten minutes, a police wagon arrived and the plaintiff wa driven to a hospital where, after waiting a half hour, he was given medication, and a cut in his upper lip was stitched. He was then driven to the Waldo Street jail; there he spent the night in a cell. (The record does not indicate on what charges he was held. DelRosso said he had "arrested" the plaintiff in the cafe for disturbing the peace, and outside the cafe for drunkenness.)

Reconstruction of the plaintiff's teeth required visits to a dentist over a period of several months. The medical bills came to about $3,000.

The jury found in favor of the plaintiff against both DelRosso and Millbury Cafe in the amount of $45,000 each. The lower court judge reduced the plaintiff's award to $25,000 from each defendant. Both defendants appealed.

THE COURT'S OPINION: KAPLAN, JUSTICE

On this evidence, DelRosso's own liability for the use of force or excessive force, and for his subsequent behavior, is clear enough. The jury could find the involvement of Millbury was as follows. Millbury had an informal arrangement with the Worcester police department by which the department cooperated in supplying the cafe with an off-duty policeman for the hours from about 9 P.M. to closing each night, Tuesdays through Saturdays. Millbury paid for these services at an hourly rate by checks to the order of the police department; after tax withholding, the policemen received their shares... It was understood, without need for express instructions, that the policeman was there to inhibit disturbances and, if any arose, to quell them.

Whether one who uses the services of policemen on paid detail may be held responsible as a principal for their particular conduct has been made to depend on whether the policemen were properly classified, in respect to conduct of the sort as "independent contractors" or as "servants" or "employees." This in turn has depended on a multifactored estimate which expresses itself mainly in a conclusion regarding the principal's "right to control" the policemen's activities. See *Luz v. Stop & Shop, Inc. of Peabody*, 202 N.E.2d 771.

In reaching verdicts for the plaintiff, the jury were entitled to attach significance to the circumstances, among others, that DelRosso's task (as the jury might believe) was similar to that which has been customarily confided to the bartender or "bouncer"; that his work was to be performed on the principal's premises though it might spill over to the sidewalk... and that he was engaged alone and not, as in some decided cases, in company with other policemen under the command of a superior officer. See *Luz, supra*... The jury could find that DelRosso was "acting not as [a] public [officer] in a public place but as [an employee] of the defendant for its private purposes on its private premises." That DelRosso, implicitly authorized by the principal to use force in appropriate situations, in fact used force inappropriately or excessively, would not relieve the principal here by putting those tortious acts beyond the scope of the employment.

Nor was there error in the denial of a new trial. It is argued that a verdict of $45,000 was so far excessive that it showed a bias in the jurty that could extend as well to their other findings, and so a new trial should have been ordered. The judge must be taken to have believed otherwise, and there is no basis for overriding his judgment in the matter. In protesting the size of the verdicts and of the judgments, the defendants seem to suggest that the recovery should have been measured by reference only to the physical damage to the plaintiff and the cost of the physical repairs, as in an action for negligent injury. But more was involved—the shock and humiliation of a sudden deliberate assault, not to speak of the jailing that followed. As Justice Holmes put it, "even a dog distinguishes between being stumbled over and being kicked."

Judgments affirmed.

QUESTIONS FOR ANALYSIS

1. Why do you think the court wrote, "DelRosso's own liability for the use of force or excessive force, and for his subsequent behavior is clear enough?"
2. What factor determines whether the policeman is an independent contractor or a servant in a case such as this?
3. What evidence caused the court to say that the jury could find that DelRosso was acting as an employee?
4. From your reading of the textbook, what is the name of the doctrine that makes an employer responsible for the wrongful acts of an employee?
5. How much money did the plaintiff recover (a) from DelRosso? (b) from Millbury's cafe?
6. Why did the court disagree with the defendant's suggestion that recovery should have been measured by reference only to the physical damage to the plaintiff and the cost of the physical repairs?
7. For what reason do you think this decision was fair or unfair to Millbury's cafe?

PART 8
Business Organization and Regulation

CHAPTER 35
Partnership

OUTLINE

COMMENTARY

When Frank Wells died, he bequeathed his farm to his three sons and five daughters. The sons claimed that they alone were entitled to the property as surviving partners. They argued that they had worked the farm together and that their father had always called them his "partners." The daughters disagreed, saying that their brothers had been employees who had taken home weekly paychecks that never fluctuated with the profits made by the business. Who is correct? The five satisfied sisters or the three begrudging brothers? Issues such as this are determined by partnership law.

OBJECTIVES

1. Distinguish between the entity theory and the aggregate theory of partnership law.
2. Describe the evidence used by the courts to determine whether a partnership exists.
3. Distinguish between partnership property and property belonging to individual partners.
4. Outline the various rights, duties, and liabilities of partners.
5. Describe and distinguish between dissolution by acts of the partners, dissolution by operation of law, and dissolution by court decree.
6. Judge the liability of partners to third persons who have no actual or constructive notice that a partnership has been dissolved.
7. Determine the ranking of partnership liabilities in settling accounts after the dissolution of a partnership.
8. Compare the advantages found by a limited partner in a limited partnership to those found by a general partner.

35-1 PARTNERSHIP CHARACTERISTICS

General partnerships are all governed by the Uniform Partnership Act (UPA). Most states have enacted provisions from the UPA. The UPA defines **partnership** as "an association of two or more persons to carry on a business for profit."

Elements of a Partnership

The UPA definition emphasizes the two essential elements of a partnership. First, partnerships must involve at least two persons. (Note that the term *person* need not be limited to flesh and blood individuals, but can also be expanded to include corporations, and other legally created organizations.) Secondly, a partnership must involve a sharing of profits. This point is so crucial that the sharing of profits is considered *prima facie* evidence (sufficient evidence) of the existence of a partnership. ***Prima facie* evidence** in this context means that the law presumes, in the absence of evidence to the contrary, that an individual receiving profits is a partner. Unless specified otherwise, profits are shared equally by the partners.

Partnership Losses

Another partnership characteristic is that all partners share in the losses of the partnership. Losses are shared in the same way that profits are shared. If the agreement says nothing about the sharing of profits and losses, then losses, like profits, are shared equally. However, if the agreement specifies only that profits are shared according to a certain ratio, then losses are shared according to the same ratio.

Unlimited Liability

Perhaps the most unattractive feature of a partnership is each partner's unlimited liability. Unlimited liability places the partner's own property at risk.

This means that the partner's nonpartnership property can be used to satisfy debts owed by the partnership. Generally, a partner's individual nonpartnership property cannot be tapped until the partnership runs out of assets. It is also possible to stipulate in a given contract that nonpartnership property will never be used to satisfy a debt arising out of that agreement. Finally, partners can take out insurance to protect themselves against the loss of individual property due to partnership indebtedness.

Entity and Aggregate Theories

There is some dispute over whether a partnership should be considered an "entity" or an "aggregate." Under the entity theory, a partnership exists as an individual unit with its own identity. This unique, individual entity is separate from the identities of the partners. In contrast, under the aggregate theory, the partnership is seen simply as an assembly or a collection of partners who do business together. Under certain circumstances, a partnership is considered an entity or individual unit. For example, a partnership can own property in its own name as an individual. In contrast, if the partnership is viewed as simply an aggregate or assembly of all the partners, a tort committed by one partner may be attributed to all the other partners. Some states have solved this problem by defining a partnership in statutory law as either an entity or an aggregate. For instance, Nebraska has defined a partnership as an entity. Under Nebraska law, a partnership is "an association of persons organized as a separate entity to carry on a business for profit."

35-2 PARTNERSHIP FORMATION

A partnership can be formed (1) by contract, (2) by proof of existence, or (3) by estoppel (see Table 35-1).

Formation by Contract

One of the most common ways for a partnership to be formed is by an express agreement between the parties. Although the agreement can be oral, it is generally best to put the terms in writing to prevent misunderstanding and disputes later in the life of the partnership. If the partnership activities cannot be carried out within one year, the Statute of Frauds requires a written contract if the agreement is to be enforceable in a court of law. The Statute of Frauds also requires a written agreement if the partnership is formed to buy and sell real estate.

The written agreement that establishes a partnership is called the partnership agreement, or **articles of partnership.** In addition to the date of formation, the identity of the parties, and the purpose of the partnership, the agreement generally includes the following information:

1. Name and duration of the partnership
2. Amount of **capital** (net assets) each partner contributed to the partnership
3. Amount of **reserve funds** (retained earnings) from profits to be accumulated

4. Location and withdrawal procedure for all partnership funds
5. Duties of partners
6. Location and accessibility of a full and accurate account of partnership transactions
7. The times and amounts each partner is entitled to withdraw from partnership earnings
8. Provision for the preparation of an annual balance sheet and income statement; and the distribution of net profits or net losses between partners
9. Limitations on partners
10. Termination notice procedure

Formation by Proof of Existence

Sometimes a partnership will be created simply on the basis of the way in which people do business with one another. If one party claims that a partnership exists and the other party denies its existence, the court will look at a series of elements to solve the problem. Chief among these elements is the sharing of profits. The sharing of profits is *prima facie* (i.e., at first sight) evidence of the existence of a partnership. In other words, once one party has shown that the alleged partners shared the profits of the enterprise, the court will hold that a partnership exists unless the other party can present evidence to the contrary.

A person may receive a share of the profits and avoid the label "partner" if the share is paid (1) as repayment of a debt, (2) as wages to an employee or rent to a landlord, (3) as an **annuity** (i.e., a guaranteed retirement income), (4) as interest on a loan, or (5) as consideration for the sale of **goodwill** (i.e., the expected continuance of public patronage).

Slabaugh owned a warehouse which she leased to Horowitz and Fowler, partners in a printing firm. Rent was paid to Slabaugh out of the partnership's profits. When Horowitz and Fowler decided to dissolve the partnership, Slabaugh claimed she was a partner and presented evidence of the monthly checks she had received from the partnership. However, Horowitz and Fowler were able to demonstrate that their payments represented rent and thus defeated her partnership claim.

Formation by Estoppel

Partnership by estoppel occurs when an individual says or does something that leads a third party to the reasonable belief that a partnership exists. A

Table 35-1 PARTNERSHIP FORMATION

Form	*Definition*
Partnership by contract	Express agreement drawn up by partners Articles of partnership
Partnership by proof of existence	Individuals form partnership because of their method of doing business Sharing of profits is *prima facie* evidence
Partnership by estoppel	Third party led to believe a partnership exists No true partnership created

person's silence despite a duty to speak may also result in a partnership by estoppel. Partnership by estoppel does not create a true partnership. It is a doctrine used by the courts to prevent injustice. However, it benefits only innocent, misled third parties, never the alleged partners themselves.

Oppenheimer and Young's partnership needed a loan to remain solvent. Oppenheimer and Young prevailed upon Rader to accompany them to the bank to help them obtain a loan. Rader cooperated in the charade, pretending to be a partner. Since the bank's loan officer knew Rader had a solid credit rating, he extended the loan to Oppenheimer and Young's partnership. When the loan was not paid back, the bank could hold Rader liable. Rader would not be allowed to deny her participation in obtaining the loan.

35-3 THE ACQUISITION OF PARTNERSHIP PROPERTY

At times it is relatively easy to distinguish between partnership property and individually owned property. For example, the **capital contributions** of all partners are considered to be the property of the partnership. Capital contributions are sums which are contributed by the partners as permanent investments and which the partners are entitled to have returned when the partnership is dissolved. In contrast, loans or later advances that partners make to the partnership and accumulated, but undivided, profits belong to the partners on an individual basis.

Partnership Property Versus Individual Property

When it is difficult for a court to determine whether a particular piece of property belongs to the partnership or to a partner, the court may ask the following questions: Has the partnership consistently used the property? Has the partnership included the property in its account books? Has the partnership expended its own funds to improve or to repair the property? Has the partnership paid taxes on the property? Has the partnership paid other expenses, such as maintenance costs? The more of these questions which are answered affirmatively, the more likely it is that the court will declare the disputed item to be the property of the partnership.

Intellectual Property and Partnerships

The U.S. Constitution allows individual authors and inventors to secure the exclusive right to publish their works or use their discoveries. This right creates a new category of property known as **intellectual property.**

Intellectual property, such as a copyright or patent, can also be contributed to the partnership by a partner. However, determining the extent of the partnership's ownership of intellectual property is often more complex than in the case of tangible property. For example, a copyright owner generally transfers not the copyright itself, but the license to use the copyright. This means that, without evidence to the contrary, the partnership must use the copyrighted material as directed by the copyright owner.

Bryztwa entered a partnership with McMahon, Selan, and Lauretig to publish a book of historical vignettes on the founding of Willowick. Bryztwa had written the vignettes and held the copyrights. She transferred a license to use the vignettes to the partnership. McMahon, Lauretig, and Selan altered Bryztwa's vignettes and published them in a newspaper instead of a book. The court held that the partnership had appropriated Bryztwa's personal property. The partnership owned the license to use Bryztwa's vignettes only as she directed.

35-4 PARTNER RIGHTS, DUTIES, AND LIABILITIES

Partners have a variety of rights and duties and are, as a result, open to potential liability. The rights and duties of partners are determined by provisions found in the Uniform Partnership Act (UPA). It is possible, however, for partners to alter UPA provisions when they draw up the details of their partnership agreement.

Tenancy in Partnership

Each partner has a property interest in specific terms of partnership property, making him or her a co-owner of that property. This form of ownership is known as **tenancy in partnership.** Under the UPA, a tenancy in partnership has the following characteristics:

1. A partner has an equal right with partners to possess and use specific partnership property for partnership purposes, but not for that partner's personal use.
2. A partner's interest in partnership property may not be **assigned** (i.e., transferred by sale, mortgage, pledge, or otherwise) to a nonpartner, unless the other partners agree to the transfer.
3. Partners' rights in partnership property are not subject to **attachment** for personal debts or claims against the partners themselves.
4. A deceased partner's interest in real property held by the partnership passes to the surviving partners.
5. Partners' rights in specific partnership property are not subject to any allowances or rights to widows, heirs, or next of kin.

Interest in the Partnership

A partner's interest in the partnership is his or her share of profits and surplus. **Surplus** includes any funds that remain after a partnership has been dissolved and all other debts and prior obligations have been settled. Partners share profits and surplus equally, unless the articles of partnership specify otherwise.

Partners may voluntarily assign their interests in the partnership to another party without dissolving the partnership. The assignee in such an action is not entitled to take part in the management of the partnership business. The assignee is entitled to receive, in keeping with the assignment contract, the profits that the assigning partner would have received.

Kirchensteiner was a partner in Kowalski Enterprises. Rueber sued Kirchensteiner in his individual capacity and won a personal judgment against him. Rueber attempted to collect her money by forcing a judicial sale of several personal computers belonging to Kowalski Enterprises. Kirchensteiner successfully blocked this attempt because the personal computers were specific partnership property and could not be used to satisfy a personal judgment. However, Rueber could ask the court to hold Kirchensteiner's share of the partnership profits.

Management Rights

All partners have equal rights in the management of partnership business. Participation is not limited by the proportional value of the partner's contribution. Any differences arising as to ordinary matters connected with the business may be decided by a majority vote of the partners. If a vote is split among an even number of partners, then the status quo before the vote remains. If deadlocks persist to the extent that they interfere with the day-to-day operation of the business, the only solution is to dissolve the partnership.

Spanier and Hernandez operated a bakery in Bakersville known as the Bakersville Baker. Spanier believed that the firm could benefit from an extensive advertising campaign, including radio spots and newspaper advertisements. Hernandez, however, disagreed. Unable to convince Hernandez to change his position in this regard, Spanier used his own money to finance the campaign. After the advertising campaign was over, Spanier tried to get Hernandez to agree to reimburse him for his expenditures. After failing repeatedly to convince Hernandez, Spanier brought suit trying to force the partnership to reimburse him. The court ruled that Spanier was not entitled to reimbursement. Since the decision to advertise was an ordinary business matter, it required a majority vote. Since the vote was split, Spanier had no authority to run the advertising campaign.

Some decisions require the unanimous consent of the partners. These decisions are outlined in the UPA and include: admitting a new partner to the firm, disposing of the firm's goodwill, submitting a partnership claim to arbitration, using partnership property as collateral, and selling or otherwise disposing of the partnership's real property.

Right to the Books and an Accounting

Partnership books must be kept at the partnership's principal place of business and must be available for the inspection of all partners. Partners also have the right to copy the books. Any partner has the right to a formal accounting of partnership affairs whenever a dissolution of the partnership is decreed by the court. An **accounting** is a statement detailing the financial transactions of the partnership and the status of its assets. The Uniform Partnership Act also gives partners the right to a formal accounting whenever they have been wrongfully excluded from the partnership business or from possession of partnership property by copartners.

Fiduciary Duties

A **fiduciary** is a person who has a duty to act for the benefit of another. Because of their joint undertaking, partners are fiduciaries to one another. As a fiduciary, each partner has a duty to act in the highest good faith, fairness, and trust when conducting partnership business. Partners must account to the partnership for any benefit received while acting for the partnership. A partner may not use partnership funds or property secretly for personal benefit. In addition, a partner may not compete with the partnership business.

Liabilities

The liability for torts committed by a partner or an employee of the partnership is joint and several. Each partner is liable and may be sued in a separate action or in a joint action. A judgment may be levied against one or more partners. The release of one partner in one action does not necessarily release the others. Partners who commit crimes are separately liable.

Partners are jointly liable on all contractual obligations of the partnership. This means that in a suit brought jointly against all partners, each partner is a defendant. A judgment must be against all or none of the partners, and a release of one partner releases all of them.

35-5 DISSOLUTION OF PARTNERSHIP

A partnership comes to an end by way of a two-part process: (1) dissolution, and (2) winding up. The UPA defines **dissolution of partnership** as a change in the relation of the partners caused by any partner ceasing to be associated in the carrying on of the business. Dissolution is to be distinguished from the winding up and termination of the partnerships, which effectively puts it out of business. Winding up involves completing all ongoing business and selling the partnership property to obtain cash to satisfy all debts owed by the firm. If anything is left, it is distributed to the partners according to the partnership agreement or the rules set down by the UPA.

Methods of Dissolution

A partnership's dissolution can occur in a number of different ways. In general, partnerships dissolve by the acts of the partners, by operation of law, and by court decree (see Table 35-2 on page 503).

Dissolution by Acts of the Partners A partnership may be dissolved without partner liability by the termination of a time period specified in the agreement; the occurrence of an agreed-upon event; or the completion of a purpose called for in the partnership agreement. If no definite term or particular undertaking is designated in a partnership agreement, a partnership at will exists. A **partnership at will** is one which any partner may dissolve at any time without liability. By the mutual consent of all the partners, a partnership maybe dissolved without violating the partnership agreement. Dissolution is also brought about if a partner is expelled by the other partners for cause, when such a power is conferred by the agreement between the partners.

Dissolution by Operation of Law A dissolution by operation of law means that a partnership dissolves automatically under certain circumstances specified by the law. Dissolution of the partnership is caused automatically by the death of a partner. The deceased partner's estate has the right either to have the partnership ended within a reasonable time or to be paid the value of the deceased partner's share in cash.

Bankruptcy of the partnership or of one of the partners also causes a dissolution by operation of law. However, **insolvency** (i.e., inability or failure to pay debts as they fall due) of the partnership or of one or more partners alone does not cause a dissolution.

Certain events also operate to dissolve a partnership by operation of law. For example, the disbarment of a law partner would prevent the excluded attorney from practicing law, thereby dissolving the partnership.

Dissolution by Court Decree When partners cannot work out their differences by agreement, one or more of them may petition a court for a decree ordering a dissolution or recognizing that one has taken place. A partner may apply to the court for a dissolution because of the insanity or incapacity of a partner to perform part of the partnership agreement. Decrees are also granted when a partner acts in a way that is harmful to the partnership or when a partner willfully and persistently breaches the partnership agreement. Where the partnership can be carried on only at a loss or where other circumstances render a dissolution just and fair, a court will decree a dissolution.

Notice of Dissolution

Until they are given notice or have knowledge that a partnership has been dissolved, third persons who deal with a partnership are justified in continuing to deal with it in their usual manner. Actual notice of a dissolution rather than an implied one must be given directly to persons who have extended credit to the partnership.

Table 35-2 DISSOLUTION OF A PARTNERSHIP

Method of Dissolution	*Explanation*
Acts of the parties	Any of these acts can dissolve a partnership: Termination of time period specified in the agreement An agreed-upon event Mutual consent Expulsion of a partner
Operation of law	Automatic dissolution by law under these circumstances: Death of a partner Bankruptcy of a partner Bankruptcy of the partnership Events such as the disbarment of a law partner
Court decree	A court can decree a dissolution in these situations: Insanity of a partner Incapacity of a partner Breach of partnership agreement Partnership can continue only at a loss Other circumstances making a dissolution just and fair

Persons who know of a partnership's existence, but have not extended credit, may be given constructive notice. Constructive notice may be in the form of an advertisement placed in a newspaper of general circulation in the area in which the partnership business was carried on.

Winding Up of Partnership Affairs

When a partnership terminates, there must be a winding up of the partnership business following dissolution. This action involves the orderly sale of the partnership's assets, the payment of creditors, and the distribution, if any, of the remaining surplus to the partners according to their profit-sharing ratios. Until this action is accomplished, the partnership continues. The partners continue to owe a fiduciary duty to one another, but they have only limited authority to bind the partnership through acts that are reasonably necessary to carry out the winding up.

In settling accounts between the partners after dissolution, unless otherwise agreed, the assets of the partnership include its property and the contributions of the partners necessary for the payment of its liabilities. The liabilities of the partnership are ranked in the following order:

1. Those owing to creditors other than partners
2. Those owing to partners for loans or advances made to the partnership
3. Those owing to partners as repayment for their capital contributions
4. Those owing to partners for their share of profits, if any

35-6 LIMITED PARTNERSHIPS

Limited partnerships are governed by the Revised Uniform Limited Partnership Act (RULPA). The revised act defines a **limited partnership** as "a partnership formed by two or more persons...having one or more general partners and one or more limited partners." **General partners** take an active part in the management of the firm and have unlimited liability for the firm's debts. **Limited partners** are nonparticipating investors. They contribute cash, property, or services to the partnership, but do not take part in the management of the firm.

A limited partnership is advantageous for both the limited partner and the general partner. The general partner can accumulate additional capital without admitting another general partner who would be entitled to management rights. Thus, the general partner maintains control while strengthening the firm's treasury. The limited partner also benefits because limited partnership means limited liability. **Limited liability** means that the limited partner's nonpartnership property cannot be used to satisfy any debt owed by the partnership. Thus, limited partners receive a return on their investment while risking only that original investment.

Limited partnerships must follow strict filing requirements. Usually, a **certificate of limited partnership** must be filed with the appropriate state or county official. The purpose of the certificate is to warn third parties of the limited liability of some partners. Limited partners must guard against becoming too involved in the business. A limited partner who exercises too much control over partnership affairs will lose the protective mantle of limited liability. A failure to file a certificate of limited partnership will deprive a limited partner of limited liability if third parties attempting to hold the limited partner liable did not know that they were dealing with a limited partnership.

SUMMARY

35-1. A partnership is an association of at least two persons who have joined to carry on a business for profit. At times a partnership is considered an "entity," or individual unit, separate from the partners. At other times it is considered an "aggregate," or assembly of its partners, having no separate existence of its own.

35-2. A partnership can be formed by contract, by proof of existence, or by estoppel.

35-3. Capital contributions of the partners are considered property of the partnership, whereas loans advanced beyond the initial capital contribution remain individual property.

35-4. Partnership rights include tenancy in partnership, the partner's interest in the firm, management rights, a right to the books, and a right to an accounting. All partners have a fiduciary duty to act primarily for the partnership's benefit. The liability for contracts made by partners is joint whereas the liability for torts is both joint and several.

35-5. A partnership dissolution can take place by the acts of the partners, by operation of law, and by court decree. Creditors are entitled to actual notice of a dissolution, whereas noncreditors are entitled to constructive notice.

35-6. A limited partnership consists of one or more limited partners, or nonparticipating investors. General partners benefit from the limited partnership structure because they gain capital without giving up control. Limited partners benefit because they receive a return on their investment while not risking any nonpartnership property.

Understanding Key Legal Terms

accounting (p. 501)
articles of partnership (p. 497)
assigned (p. 500)
attachment (p. 500)
capital (p. 497)
capital contributions (p. 499)
dissolution of a partnership (p. 502)
fiduciary (p. 502)
general partner (p. 504)
goodwill (p. 498)
limited liability (p. 504)
limited partners (p. 504)
limited partnership (p. 504)
partnership (p. 496)
partnership at will (p. 502)
partnership by estoppel (p. 498)
prima facie evidence (p. 496)
reserve funds (p. 497)
surplus (p. 500)
tenancy in partnership (p. 500)

Questions for Review and Discussion

1. Discuss the difference between the entity theory and the aggregate theory of partnership existence.
2. Explain how the existence of a partnership is determined by law, if there are no articles of partnership.
3. Indicate how a partnership by estoppel is created.
4. What questions would a court ask when attempting to determine whether a given piece of property belongs to the partnership or to an individual partner?
5. Differentiate between the partner's rights in specific partnership property and the partner's interest in the partnership.
6. List five decisions that require unanimous consent of the partners.
7. How may a partnership be dissolved by acts of the partners? By operation of law? By court decree?
8. On dissolution of a partnership, who is entitled to actual notice? Constructive notice?
9. Indicate the ranking of liabilities when a partnership has been terminated.
10. Compare the advantages found by a general partner in a limited partnership to those found by a limited partner.

Analyzing Cases

1. McCoy and Gugelman borrowed money from State Security Bank for their partnership, Antiques, Etc. When McCoy and Gugelman failed to pay back the debt, the bank sued them as individuals. At trial, McCoy and Gugelman argued that their partnership, Antiques, Etc., was an entity, not an aggregate, of the partners. Therefore, they concluded, the bank would have to show that the partnership funds were sufficient to answer the judgment before it could proceed against them individually. Are they correct? Why or why not? *Security State Bank v. McCoy,* 361 N.W.2d 514 (Neb. Sup. Ct.).
2. Shane ran a liquid fertilizer business. As part of the operation of the business, Shane paid Svoboda a specified amount per acre to spread the fertilizer on his clients' crops. Svoboda's per-acre payments remained steady, despite Shane's profits or losses. Frisch was injured while filling a tank truck that was supposed to haul the fertilizer to Svoboda's tractor. Frisch sued both Shane and Svoboda, claiming that Svoboda was sharing in Shane's profits and was, therefore, a partner. Is Frisch correct? Explain. *Frisch v. Svoboda,* 157 N.W.2d 774 (Neb. Sup. Ct.).
3. Ettinger loaned $14,662.59 to Anderson, thinking that Anderson was a partner in B.A.T. Leasing. Unknown to Ettinger, B.A.T. was not a partnership, but a sole proprietorship owned and operated by Anderson's wife, Barbara. Anderson negotiated the loan with Barbara's knowledge and permission. In addition, Anderson shared the same address of B.A.T. and was in the habit of signing B.A.T.'s checks. When Ettinger tried to collect the debt from B.A.T., Anderson argued that Ettinger could not collect from B.A.T.'s treasury because he was not a partner in B.A.T. Is Anderson correct? Why or why not? *M.W. Ettinger, Inc. v. Anderson,* 360 N.W.2d 394 (Minn. App. Ct.).
4. Oddo and Ries entered a partnership, the purpose of which was to publish a book on how to restore Ford pickup trucks. Oddo

was the writer, and Ries was the financial backer. Oddo reworked several of his copyrighted magazine articles and turned them over to Ries. Dissatisfied with Oddo's work, Ries hired another writer to finish the book. When Oddo found out, he filed a copyright infringement action against Ries. Ries claims that the copyrights are partnership property and that he can use the articles and the resulting manuscripts for partnership purposes, that is, for the publication of the book. Oddo claims that the copyrights to the articles are his property and he merely granted the partnership a license to use the property as he directed, that is, as part of the manuscript he had written himself before the ghost writer had made the alterations. Is Oddo correct? Explain. *Oddo v. Ries,* 743 F.2d 630 (9th Cir. Ct.).

5. Summers and Dooley formed a partnership for the purpose of operating a trash collection business. The business was operated by the two men, and when either was unable to work, the nonworking partner provided a replacement at his own expense. Summers approached Dooley and requested that they hire a third worker. Dooley refused. Notwithstanding Dooley's refusal, Summers, on his own initiative, hired a worker. Summers paid the employee out of his own pocket. Dooley, upon discovery that a third person had been hired, objected. He stated that the additional labor was not necessary and refused to allow partnership funds to be used to pay the new employee. After paying out more than $11,000 in wages without any reimbursement from either partnership funds or his partner, Summers brought suit in the Idaho state courts. The trial court held that Summers was not entitled to reimbursement for the wages he had paid the employee. On appeal, should the Supreme Court of Idaho uphold the trial court's decision? Explain. *Summers v. Dooley,* 481 P.2d 318 (Idaho).

6. Hanes entered a partnership agreement with Giambrone, Hayes, and Medley. Hanes was to make an initial capital contribution of $19,875 as were Gambrone and Hayes. Medley was to contribute $39,750. As it turned out, however, only Hanes made his contribution. Hanes's money was deposited in a trust account for the partnership and withdrawn by Medley without the unanimous approval of all the partners as was required under the articles of partnership. In addition, Medley failed to make payments on a partnership mortgage, causing the partnership to default on the loan. Hanes applied for a court-ordered dissolution. Should the court grant Hanes's request for a dissolution? If not, why not? If so, on what grounds? *Hanes v. Giambrone,* 471 N.E.2d 801 (Ohio App. Ct.).

CHAPTER 36
Corporate Formation and Finance

OUTLINE

36-1 The Nature of the Corporation
- Corporate Entity Status
- Corporate Constitutional Rights
- Corporate Citizenship

36-2 Types of Corporations
- Private, Public, Quasi-Public Corporations
- Domestic and Foreign
- Close and S Corporations

36-3 Formation of the Corporation
- Promoters
- Articles of Incorporation
- The Corporate Name
- Approval of the Articles
- Commencement of Business

36-4 Defective Incorporation
- *De Jure* Corporation
- *De Facto* Corporation
- Corporation by Estoppel

36-5 Piercing the Corporate Veil

36-6 Corporate Financing
- Dividends
- Classes of Corporate Stock
- Stock Valuation

COMMENTARY

The corporation is considered by many to be the ideal business structure because it allows for the accumulation of capital from a large number of investors. The investors receive a return on their investment and limited liability. *Limited liability* means that any other property owned by the investors cannot be used to satisfy any debt owed by the corporation. In this way corporate investors risk only their original investment. This assumes, of course, that a corporation really exists. Consider the following case. When Dovenbarger was asked to invest in Bioengetec Pharmaceuticals, he was told that it was a legally formed corporation. In fact, no incorporation papers had ever been filed. Later Dovenbarger became an officer of Biogengetec. In this capacity, he authorized the purchase of an electron microscope from Gunzer-St. Pierre, Inc. When Bioengetec did not pay for the microscope, Gunzer-St. Pierre brought suit to recover the purchase price. Later Gunzer-St. Pierre found out that Bioengetec had never been incorporated. Gunzer-St. Pierre then added Dovenbarger to the suit, seeking to hold him personally liable for the debt. Can Gunzer-St. Pierre recover an award from Dovenbarger's private property? Does Dovenbarger have any way out of this mess? These are some of the issues that this chapter will explore.

OBJECTIVES

1. Distinguish by their characteristics the major forms of business incorporations including public, private, and quasi-public corporations; domestic and foreign corporations; and close and S corporations.

2. Describe what a promoter must do to transform a proposed corporation into a fully and legally incorporated entity.
3. Analyze the rights and duties of promoters and determine the extent of their legal liability under contracts entered on behalf of the corporation.
4. Relate how state incorporation statutes, articles of incorporation, initial organizational meetings, and corporation bylaws each serve to define the legal boundaries within which a corporation may conduct its business.
5. Differentiate between *de jure* corporation, *de facto* corporation, and corporation by estoppel.
6. Explain the activities that would cause courts to go behind the legal status of a corporate entity to pierce the corporate veil.
7. Distinguish between common and preferred stock, and between par value and no par value stock.

36-1 THE NATURE OF THE CORPORATION

A **corporation** is a legal entity (or a legal person) created by either a state or federal statute authorizing individuals to operate an enterprise. The corporation is one of the most important forms of business organization. It came into being to meet the economic needs of an expanding and capital-hungry business economy. It offers a convenient and efficient way to finance a large-scale business operation by dividing its ownership into many units; these units can be sold easily to a large number of investors. The corporate form also offers limited liability to those who share its ownership. This means that the personal assets of the corporation's owners cannot be taken if the corporation defaults on its obligations or commits a tort or a crime. Unlike the legal status of the partnership, the legal status of the corporation is not affected by the death, incapacity, or bankruptcy of an officer or shareholder.

Corporate Entity Status

In partnership law, there is often a dispute over whether a partnership is an independent entity (individual unit) or an aggregate (assembly) of the partners. This problem does not exist in corporate law. Most states settled this issue long ago, deciding to label the corporation as an artificially created legal person. In other words, the corporation exists apart from its owners and is taxed directly on the income it earns. As a legal entity, a corporation can own property and can sue or be sued just as an individual can. Moreover, the existence of a corporation is not affected by the death, incapacity, or bankruptcy of a manager or shareholder.

Corporate Constitutional Rights

U.S. Const., Amendment 14 (see pp. 605–606)

Under provisions of the U.S. Constitution, a corporation is also considered an artificially created legal person. Within the meaning of Amendment 14, a corporation—like a natural person—may not be deprived of life, liberty, or property without due process of law. A corporation may also not be denied equal protection of the laws within the jurisdiction of a state.

The Janwillen Financial Loan Corporation lent $20,000 to Vaughan and secured the loan with a mortgage on Vaughan's hunting lodge located on Meadow Lane Bay. The state decided to build a new highway along the shore line of the bay. Vaughan's lodge was directly in the path of the new highway. The state paid Vaughan the market value of the property, but failed to notify the Janwillen Financial Loan Corporation. Janwillen sued the government, claiming that its constitutional rights had been violated. The court held that Janwillen was correct because the state had deprived the corporation of its property without due process of law.

Corporate Citizenship

U.S. Const., Amendment 14 **(see p. 605–606)**

A corporation is considered a citizen both of the state in which it is incorporated and the state where it has its principal place of business. It can also be sued as a citizen of both these states. By virtue of the due process clause of Amendment 14, a state court may also exercise jurisdiction over a noncitizen corporate defendant as long as that corporation has had an appropriate contact with that state. Such contact can include owning property within the state, doing business in the state, or committing a tort within the state. However, if a corporation performs no services, owns no property, closes no sales, and solicits no business within a state, the courts of that state will have no jurisdiction over that corporation.

While in Atlanta, Georgia, Lermentov purchased a hand-held VCR camera at a local merchandise outlet. The camera was manufactured and marketed by Southern Cross Electronics, Inc., a company that did absolutely no business north of Kentucky and west of Arkansas. When Lermentov returned home to Seattle, Washington, he tried to use the camera, and it exploded in his hands burning him severely. Lermentov sued Southern Cross in a Washington state court. Southern Cross maintained that it had absolutely no contact with Washington, either business or otherwise, and could not, therefore, be sued in Washington. The state court agreed and dismissed Lermentov's complaint.

36-2 TYPES OF CORPORATIONS

Corporations may be classified in various ways in order to emphasize a purpose or characteristic. For clarity, this chapter is limited mainly to a discussion of the major kinds of corporations created by statute and authorized by state-granted charters to incorporate.

Private, Public, and Quasi-Public Corporations

A **private corporation** is a corporation formed by private persons to accomplish a task best undertaken by an entity that can raise large amounts of capital quickly or that can grant the protection of limited liability. Private corporations can be organized for a profit-making business purpose or for a nonprofit charitable, educational, or scientific purpose. If the corporation is organized for profit-making purposes, those profits may be distributed to the shareholders in the form of dividends. **Dividends** are the net profits, or surplus, set aside for the shareholders. **Shareholders** (or stockholders, as they are also known) are the persons who own units of interest (shares of stock) in a corporation.

Large private corporations generally sell their stock to the public at large and are, therefore, often referred to as public corporations. This designation can be confusing because the term **public corporation** is more properly used to describe a corporation created by the federal, state, or local government for governmental purposes. When used in this sense, the term includes incorporated cities, sanitation districts, school districts, transit districts, and so on.

Corporations that are privately organized for profit but also provide a service upon which the public is dependent are generally referred to as **quasi-public corporations.** In most instances, they are public utilities, which provide the public with such essentials as water, gas, and electricity. Although formed under general business corporation statutes, their articles of incorporation must be approved by the appropriate regulatory agency before they are recognized by the state of incorporation. (*Note:* Unless specified otherwise, the discussion in this chapter and those that follow will focus on private corporations.)

Domestic and Foreign Corporations

U.S. Const., Art. I, Sec. 8 **(see pp. 600–601)**

A corporation is a **domestic corporation** in the state that grants its charter. It is a **foreign corporation** in all other states. The right to do business in other states (subject to reasonable regulation) is granted by the commerce clause of the U.S. Constitution. In order to qualify to do business in another state, a foreign corporation must obtain a certificate of authority by providing information similar to the information provided by a domestic corporation applying for a charter. A **certificate of authority** is a document that grants a foreign corporation permission to do business within another state. A registered office and agent must be maintained within the state upon whom **service of process** (notice of a lawsuit) may be made on behalf of the corporation.

A foreign corporation does not have to obtain a certificate of authority in a state if its only business in that state involves an interstate transaction, such as transporting goods across a host state. Most states also allow foreign corporations to maintain bank accounts; generate sales through independent contractors; hold meetings; maintain, defend, or settle lawsuits; solicit or obtain orders; create or acquire indebtedness; secure or collect debts; own property; and conduct an isolated transaction completed within 30 days.

Close and S Corporations

A business corporation may be designated as a **close corporation** when the outstanding shares of stock and managerial control are closely held by fewer than 50 shareholders (often members of the same family) or by one person. State business corporation statutes generally accommodate closely held corporations by allowing them to have a few directors or a sole director and president with no voting shares in the hands of the public.

The Subchapter S Revision Act of 1982 gives small, closely held, business corporations the option of obtaining special tax advantages by becoming an S corporation. An **S corporation** is a corporation in which shareholders have agreed to have the profits (or losses) of the corporation taxed directly to them rather than to the corporation. In this way they avoid double taxation. In order to qualify for S corporation status, a corporation must meet the following criteria:

1. The corporation must have no more than 35 shareholders.
2. The corporation must offer no more than one class of stock.
3. All shareholders must agree to S corporation status.
4. Income and losses are divided among shareholders on a per share basis.
5. All shareholders must be individuals rather than corporations or partnerships.

36-3 FORMATION OF THE CORPORATION

A corporation may be incorporated in any state that has a general incorporation statute. In most states, this general incorporation statute is fashioned after the Model Business Corporation Act (MBCA). The Model Business Corporation Act was written by the American Bar Association Committee on Corporate Laws. It serves as a model law that state legislatures can follow when enacting statutes governing corporate activity. Recently, the MBCA has undergone an extensive revision, resulting in the Revised Model Business Corporation Act (RMBCA). In general, our discussion will follow MBCA principles. However, we will note revisions appearing in the RMBCA whenever those revisions are significant. Keep in mind that corporations are also subject to court decisions and to the state constitution. Federal agencies such as the Securities and Exchange Commission (SEC) also regulate corporate activity. A proper understanding of effective corporate formation necessitates an examination of promoters, the articles of incorporation, the corporate name, the approval of the articles, and commencement of business (see Figure 36-1).

Promoters

The people who want to begin a new corporation or who want to incorporate an existing business are called **promoters.** These people do the actual day-to-day work involved in the incorporation process. **Incorporators** are the people who actually sign the article of incorporation. The promoters may also be the incorporators who may later become shareholders and directors of the corporation. Promoters occupy a fiduciary relationship with the nonexistent corporation and its future shareholders. This means that the promoter must act in the best interests of the new corporation and its shareholders. The promoter must be honest and loyal and must fully reveal all information about any contracts made for the corporation.

Preformation Contracts Often promoters will have to enter contracts for the unborn corporation. For example, it may be necessary to lease office and warehouse space, purchase equipment, and hire employees as preliminary steps in preparing the way for the new corporation. A corporation is not bound by any of the promoter's contracts unless it adopts those contracts. Adoption oc- expressly if the directors pass a resolution agreeing to be bound by a contract.

Adoption can also occur impliedly if the corporation accepts the benefits of a contract or makes any payments called for by the agreement.

Novation Even after adoption of the contracts, promoters are still potentially liable under the preincorporation contracts. One way for promoters to escape potential liability is to have the corporation and the third party agree to release them. The agreement releasing a promoter is known as a **novation.** It is also possible for the promoter to include an automatic release clause in all contracts negotiated for the unborn corporation. However, the release clause must do more than simply include the corporation as a party to the contract. It must also specifically release the promoters from liability.

Popovich was a promoter in the creation of Hopkins Aerospace Transport, Inc. She negotiated a preincorporation contract with Takahira Ishimoto, Inc., for the purchase of an offshore drilling platform. The contract contained a clause which stated that once the new corporation was formed, the sales contract would involve only Hopkins and Takahira and that Popovich would be released from liability. After Hopkins was formed, it defaulted on several payments. Takahira sued Popovich, intending to hold her personally liable for its losses. Popovich quoted the clause and denied her liability. The court upheld her claim.

Articles of Incorporation

The **articles of incorporation** are the written application to the state for permission to incorporate. This written application is prepared by the corporation's **incorporators.** They are the persons who sign the articles of incorporation and submit them to the appropriate state official. The articles, together with the status of incorporation, represent the legal boundaries within which a corporation must conduct its business.

Under the MBCA, the articles of incorporation *must* include:

1. The corporation name
2. The duration of the corporation
3. The purpose(s) of the corporation
4. The number and classes of shares
5. The shareholders' rights in relation to shares, classes of shares, and special shares
6. The shareholders' right to buy new shares
7. The addresses of its original registered (statutory) office and its original registered (statutory) agent
8. The number of directors plus the names and addresses of the initial directors
9. Each incorporator's name and address

The RMBCA has revised this list somewhat and requires only the name of the corporation, the number of shares originally authorized, the address of the original registered (statutory) office, the address of the original registered agent, and the incorporators' names and addresses. All the other items are optional under the RMBCA.

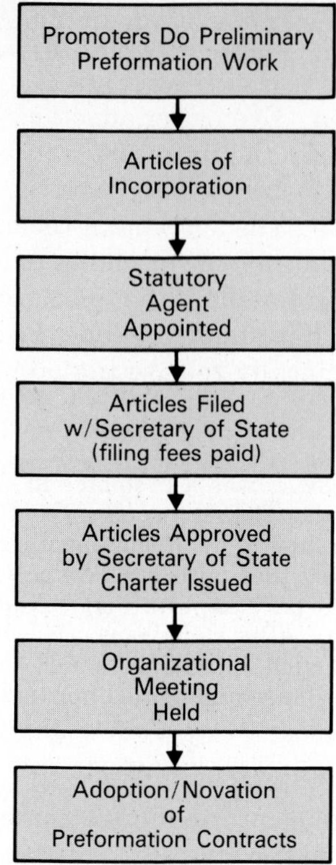

Figure 36-1 Steps in the incorporation process.

The Corporate Name

One of the first steps in forming a corporation is to choose a corporate name. Usually, the words or an abbreviation of the words *corporation, company,* or *incorporated* must appear somewhere in the corporate name. Also, the corporation cannot choose a name that some other corporation already uses or a name that would confuse the new corporation with one already in existence. Even in situations where a specific state statute does not prohibit the use of similar names, the court will prevent such duplication if confusion or unfair competition results.

Health Care, Inc., was incorporated as a nonprofit organization, providing low-cost medical and health care services for the poor. One year after the formation of Health Care, Inc., Nu-Health Care, Inc., was incorporated in the same state. Nu-Health Care, Inc., was an insurance company selling memberships to subscribers. Nu-Health Care ran an aggressive, often obnoxious advertising campaign. After this campaign, Health Care found that people were confusing the two entities. The resulting mixup damaged Health Care's image and threatened its charitable funding sources. Consequently it filed suit, asking for the court to stop Nu-Health Care from using the words "health care" in its corporate name. Because of the confusion that was damaging Health Care, the court granted the request.

Often the secretary of state's office can tell promoters whether a name has been taken. It is also possible to reserve a name. Usually there is a small fee for this service.

Approval of the Articles

After the articles of incorporation are submitted to the state, the appropriate state officer, often the secretary of state, will examine them to make certain that they meet all legal requirements. The secretary of state will also make certain that all filing fees have been paid and that a registered or statutory office and a registered or statutory agent have been appointed. The **registered** or **statutory agent** is an individual who is designated to receive service of process (a complaint plus a summons) when a lawsuit is filed against the corporation. Once satisfied that all legal formalities have been met, the secretary of state will issue the corporation's **charter,** or **certificate of incorporation.** The charter, or certificate of incorporation, is the corporation's official authorization to do business in the state. After the charter is issued, the corporation then becomes a fully and legally incorporated entity. The work of the promoters and incorporators ends, unless they become directors or officers of the corporations.

Commencement of Business

Most state statutes provide that the first order of business upon incorporation is the holding of an organizational meeting. The MBCA requires that the meeting be run by the initial directors designated in the articles. In contrast, the RMBCA, which does not require the naming of directors in the articles, allows the organizational meeting to be run by the incorporators. Nevertheless, the first order of business at an incorporator-run meeting is to elect the directors.

In addition to the appointment of the first directors, the adoption of bylaws, or regulations, also occurs at the organizational meeting. **Bylaws** are the rules which guide the corporation's day-to-day internal affairs. Bylaw provisions usually stipulate the time and place of shareholders' and directors' meetings, quorum requirements, qualifications and duties of directors and officers, and procedures for filling board vacancies.

36-4 DEFECTIVE INCORPORATION

For various liability reasons, the courts may be called upon to decide whether a business entity is a *de jure* corporation, a *de facto* corporation, or a corporation by estoppel (see Table 36-1 on page 516).

***De Jure* Corporation**

A corporation whose existence is the result of the incorporators having fully or substantially complied with the relevant corporation statutes is a ***de jure* corporation.** Its status as a corporation cannot be challenged by private citizens or the state.

***De Facto* Corporation**

Sometimes an error is made in the incorporation process. When this occurs, the corporation does not exist legally. Nevertheless, as long as the following conditions have been met, a ***de facto* corporation** (or a corporation in fact) will exist.

1. A valid state incorporation statute must be in effect.
2. The parties must have made a *bona fide* (good faith) attempt to follow the statute's requirements for incorporation.
3. The business must have acted as if it were a corporation.

Usually, if only some minor requirement has been left unsatisfied, the court will hold that there has been a "good faith" attempt to incorporate. Only the state can directly challenge the existence of a *de facto* corporation. Thus, a *de facto* corporation has the same rights, privileges, and duties as a *de jure* corporation as far as anyone other than the state is concerned.

Tarkington, Nichols, and Teasdale hired Dockstader, an attorney, to file the incorporation papers for their new corporation, TNT, Inc. Unfortunately Dockstader, who was involved in a complex lawsuit at the time, filed an incomplete set of articles that failed to comply with all state law requirements. Nevertheless, TNT acted as if it were a corporation establishing a corporate headquarters and using their trucks to haul cargo across the country for a variety of customers. When one of TNT's trucks was involved in an accident with DeCarlo, he filed suit against TNT. When DeCarlo's attorney discovered that TNT had not been properly incorporated, she filed suit directly against Tarkington, Nichols, and Teasdale, claiming that since no corporation existed, the three of them were personally liable. Since Tarkington, Nichols, and Teasdale had made a good faith attempt to incorporate under a valid state incorporation statute and since TNT had exercised corporate power, the doctrine of *de facto* corporation would protect them from personal liability.

Corporation by Estoppel

In some states, if a group of people act as if they are a corporation when in fact and in law they are not, any parties who have accepted that counterfeit corporation's existence will not be allowed to deny that acceptance. Similarly, those individuals who acted as if they were a corporation will not be able to deny that the corporation exists. This doctrine has been labeled **corporation by estoppel.** Corporation by estoppel does not create a real corporation. Instead, it is a legal fiction used by the courts on a case-by-case basis to prevent injustice. Generally, it is applied in contract cases rather than in tort cases.

Table 36-1 INCORPORATION PROBLEMS

Doctrine	*Definition*
De jure corporation	Legally formed corporation.
De facto corporation	*Bona fide* attempt to incorporate under existing state incorporation law plus an exercise of corporate power.
Corporation by estoppel	No *de jure* corporation. Usually no *de facto* corporation. Persons dealing with the entity as a corporation cannot deny corporate existence.

In the opening commentary, when Dovenbarger became a shareholder and vice president of Bioengetic, he was told it was a corporation when in fact it was not. After the business defaulted on the Gunzel-St. Pierre electron microscope deal, Gunzer-St. Pierre tried to hold Dovenbarger personally liable. Since Gunzer-St. Pierre had dealt with Bioengetic as if it were a corporation, it could not deny that corporation's existence. Dovenbarger was not personally liable.

36-5 PIERCING THE CORPORATE VEIL

Sometimes the court will disregard corporate status to impose personal liability on those who have used the corporation to commit fraud or crimes or to harm the public. In such cases, the court will **pierce the corporate veil** and hold the wrongdoers (usually the controlling shareholders) personally liable for activities committed in the corporation's name. The shareholders of close corporations are more likely to fall victim to piercing the corporate veil than the shareholders of large corporations. This is because the shareholders of a close corporation are usually also the directors and officers of the corporation and thus may neglect to keep corporate property and business separate from their personal property and business.

For years Brimholf ran his clothing store, the Southwood Men's Shoppe by himself. On advice from his accountant, Brimholf decided to incorporate. Brimholf made himself president and chairman of the board of directors. He was also sole shareholder. Despite the incorporation of Southwood, Brimholf continued to run his store as he had before he had incorporated. This meant that he failed to keep a separate corporate account and frequently comingled his own funds with the corporation's funds. In addition, he used corporate property for personal purposes. He also held no director's meetings and kept no corporate records. When he was sued by a creditor, the court allowed that creditor to pierce the corporate veil and held Brimholf personally liable. Brimholf had failed to maintain a distinction between himself and his corporation so that even though they appeared to be separate from one another, in reality they were not.

Large corporations can also fall victim to piercing the corporate veil if they set up subsidiaries, completely control those subsidiaries, and then commit some fraud through the subsidiary. In such cases, however, it is the parent corporation, rather than the individual shareholders, that the courts will hold liable.

Franklin Laboratories, Inc., established a subsidiary named Crawford Chemical Disposal, Inc. Crawford disposed of chemical waste products from all Franklin's plants and laboratories. When a Crawford truck spilled chemical waste in Danville, the townspeople sued both Franklin and Crawford. Franklin claimed waste disposal was Crawford's responsibility. The court discovered, however, that

Crawford's only business was to service Franklin's facilities. In addition, Crawford was a division of Franklin, financed by Franklin, and operated by Franklin's board of directors. Finally, the court found that Crawford had very little money in its treasury and had been set up to prevent large tort recoveries against Franklin, should an accident occur while chemicals were being transported across the country. As a result, the court had no difficulty piercing the corporate veil and holding Franklin liable.

36-6 CORPORATE FINANCING

Corporate financing begins when the original investments are made to set up the corporation. Once the corporation is operating, additional corporate financing may be obtained from earnings, loans, and the issuance of additional shares of stock. The issuing and selling of shares of stock in order to raise capital is known as **equity financing,** and the equity securities give their owners a legal interest in the assets, earnings, and control of the corporation. That part of a corporation's net profits or surplus that is set aside for the shareholders is known as **dividends.**

Classes of Corporate Stock

The number of shares and classes of stock that a corporation is authorized to issue are established in its certificate of incorporation. A shareholder who purchases corporate stock invests money or property in the corporation and receives a stock certificate. A **stock certificate** is written evidence of ownership of a unit of interest in the corporation.

Dividends

The most common type of dividend is the **cash dividend** declared and paid out of current corporate earnings or accumulated surplus at regular intervals. A corporation's board of directors has the sole authority to determine the amount, time, place, and manner of dividend payment. Typically, the directors' declaration of a dividend sets a cutoff date—the date by which a shareholder must hold corporate stock of record in order to receive payment. In a few instances, a distribution of earnings is made in shares of capital stock. This is called a **stock dividend.**

Common Stock The most usual type of corporate stock is **common stock.** Common stock carries with it all the risks of the business, inasmuch as it does not guarantee its holder the right to profits. The shareholder is usually entitled to one vote for each share of stock held. The holders of common stock are paid dividends when the corporation elects to make such a distribution. Holders of common stock risk whatever they invest. There is no guarantee that the corporation will operate profitably, and the common stock purchased may become less valuable or even lose its value entirely. Shareholders of common stock participate in the distribution of capital upon dissolution of the corporation, if capital is available, only after creditors' and preferred shareholders' claims have been satisfied.

Preferred Stock Those classes of stock which have rights or preferences over other classes of stock are known as **preferred stock.** These preferences generally involve the payment of dividends and/or the distribution of assets on the dissolution of the corporation. Preferred stock may be either cumulative or noncumulative. Generally, dividends on **cumulative preferred stock** are paid every year. However, if the dividends are not paid in one year, they will be paid in later years if any dividends at all are paid by the corporation. Dividends on **noncumulative preferred stock** are also usually paid each year. However, with noncumulative preferred stock, dividends that are not paid in one year are lost forever. **Participating preferred stock** is stock that gives its holders a priority on a certain stated amount or percentage of dividends. After a prescribed dividend is paid to the participating preferred shareholders and the common stock shareholders, both participating preferred and common stock shareholders share in any surplus. The holders of **nonparticipating preferred stock** are not entitled to any distribution of surplus dividends along with common stock shareholders. The rights which preferred shareholders enjoy in regard to dividends do not include the inherent right to receive them. They are merely superior rights to dividends over common stock shareholders, when and if dividends are declared by the corporation's board of directors.

Stock Valuation

Par value is the value that is placed on the shares of stock at incorporation. This value, which is the same for each share of stock of the same issue, is stated on the corporation's certificate of incorporation. In the case of par value shares, the amount of the capital stock or stated capital is the total par value of all the issued stock.

The practice of placing a par value on a share of stock has been criticized as misleading. Uninformed buyers often interpret par value printed on the face of the certificate as the actual market value of the shares. To correct this condition, all states have authorized the issuance of **no par value** stock. No par value stock is corporate stock that is issued without any stated price. The advantage of stock without par value has been outlined in a Delaware court ruling:

> If the assets received are $1000 in money, it is of no consequence whether five shares or ten shares, or one thousand shares are given for it. Each share has its one fifth, or one tenth, or one thousandth part of the $1000 as the case may be, and no one is damaged. Everyone knows that under each share is simply its proportionate part of the total assets, unexpressed in terms of money

SUMMARY

36-1. A corporation is a legal entity created by either state or federal statutory law authorizing individuals to operate as an enterprise. As a legal "person," a corporation is due some constitutional rights, including the right to due process.

36-2. Corporations can be classified in many ways, including private, public, and quasi-public corporations; domestic and foreign corporations; and close and S corporations.

36-3. A corporation can be incorporated in any state that has a general incorporation statute. The people who actually start the corporation are the promoters. Promoters are liable on preformation contracts until those contracts are adopted by the corporation. The articles of incorporation are drawn up by the corporation's incorporators. After reviewing the articles of incorporation, the secretary of state will issue the corporate charter and the corporation becomes a legally incorporated entity.

36-4. A *de jure* corporation is a legally formed corporation. Two doctrines, *de facto* corporation and corporation by estoppel, have been developed to deal with the problem of defective incorporation. A *de facto* corporation exists if there has been a good faith attempt to comply with an existing incorporation statute and an exercise of corporate power. The doctrine of corporation by estoppel prevents later denial of corporate existence by those parties willing to deal with an entity as if it were a corporation.

36-5. Under the doctrine of piercing the corporate veil, courts can refuse to recognize a legally formed corporation to prevent injustice and to impose personal liability on the wrongdoers.

36-6. Corporate financing begins when the incorporators give money to set up the business. Subsequent financing takes many forms. The issuing and selling of shares of stock to raise capital is called equity financing. The two most popular classes of stock are common stock and preferred stock. Stock can also be par value or no par value stock. Dividends can be issued as cash or as stock.

Understanding Key Legal Terms

articles of incorporation (p. 513)
bylaws (p. 515)
certificate of authority (p. 511)
certificate of incorporation (p. 515)
close corporation (p. 511)
common stock (p. 518)
corporation (p. 509)
corporation by estoppel (p. 516)
de facto corporation (p. 516)
de jure corporation (p. 515)
dividends (p. 511)
domestic corporation (p. 511)
foreign corporation (p. 511)
incorporators (p. 512)
novation (p. 513)
piercing the corporate veil (p. 517)
preferred stock (p. 519)
private corporation (p. 510)
promoters (p. 512)
public corporation (p. 511)
quasi-public corporation (p. 511)
S corporation (p. 511)
statutory agent (p. 515)
stock certificate (p. 518)
stock dividend (p. 518)

Questions for Review and Discussion

1. Contrast private, public, and quasi-public corporations. Differentiate between domestic and foreign corporations. Distinguish between close and S corporations.
2. Explain the extent to which a corporation is treated as a person within the meaning of Amendment 14 to the U.S. Constitution.

3. Describe the actions that it takes to transform a proposed corporation into a fully and legally incorporated entity.
4. Discuss the nature and extent of a promoter's liability under preformation contracts. Detail how a promoter can avoid such liability.
5. List the items that must be placed in the articles of incorporation according to the MBCA.
6. Distinguish a *de jure* corporation from a *de facto* corporation, and distinguish both of these from corporation by estoppel.
7. Discuss the circumstances under which a court would be likely to pierce the corporate veil in order to hold controlling shareholders personally liable for certain acts carried out in the corporation's name.
8. What are two common rights of preferred shareholders that give them superior standing over holders of common stock?
9. Describe equity securities, and explain the legal interest held by their owners.
10. Differentiate between par value and no par value stock.

Analyzing Cases

1. Harry and Kay Robinson of New York purchased a new Audi automobile from World Wide Volkswagen (WWV) in New York. After having an accident in Oklahoma, they brought a product liability action against WWV. The case was brought to court in Oklahoma. The Robinsons claimed that injuries which they suffered were caused by the defective design and placement of their automobile's gas tank and fuel system. WWV, which was incorporated in New York and did business there, contended that the Robinsons could not sue WWV in Oklahoma because it was not a citizen of Oklahoma. WWV further contended that it performed no services, owned no property, and closed no sales in Oklahoma. It solicited no business in Oklahoma either through salespersons or through advertising. It also did not indirectly through others serve or seek to serve the Oklahoma market. Does the Oklahoma state court have jurisdiction over WWV? Explain. *World Wide Volkswagen Corporation v. Woodson,* 100 S. Ct. 559 (U.S. Sup. Ct.).
2. Zizka and DuCanto were majority shareholders in a close corporation named Zizka-DuCanto, Inc. The remaining common shares were distributed among Zizka and DuCanto's friends and relatives. Shareholders from Zizka's side numbered 20 and DuCanto's numbered 14. In addition, all the preferred shares were held by Polensek, Inc., a separate corporation wholly owned by DuCanto and his brother-in-law, Pavel Polensek. DuCanto and Zizka decided to declare S corporation status under Subchapter S. Although several minority shareholders objected, DuCanto and Zizka owned a majority of the shares and thus controlled the final decision. Nevertheless, Zizka-DuCanto, Inc., did not qualify for S corporation status. Point out all S corporation requirements that Zizka-DuCanto failed to meet.
3. Spence was a promoter in the incorporation of a new business. The new corporation had not yet been formed when he bought Huffman's employment agency to serve as the nucleus of that new corporation. Eventually, the corporation was formed, but it never generated enough cash to pay Huffman for the employment agency. Huffman sued Spence, attempting to hold him personally liable for the amount due. Spence claimed that the corporation was liable and that his personal assets were not a property target of the suit. Is Spence cor-

rect? Explain. *Spence v. Huffman,* 486 P.2d 211 (Arizona).

4. MBI filed its original articles of incorporation under the name Montana Public Employees Benefit Services Co., Inc. After filing the articles, the corporation entered a contract with the Montana Department of Administration. Under the contract, the new corporation would have exclusive administrative control over Montana's public employee deferred-payment pension plan. The articles were not approved by the secretary of state who requested a name change. After the corporation's name was changed to MBI, the charter was issued and the corporation became a legal entity. The Montana Association of Underwriters, a private corporation that wanted a share in administering the state pension plan, challenged the validity of the contract, arguing that at the time the contract was signed, MBI did not legally exist. Is the Montana Association of Underwriters correct? Explain. *Montana Association of Underwriters v. Department of Administration and MBI,* 563 P.2d 577 (Montana).

5. Lamas Company, Inc., was incorporated in Georgia. Baldwin negotiated with Lamas, sole owner of Lamas Company, Inc., to finish some electrical work on a construction site. When Baldwin was dissatisfied with the work, he decided to sue. Unfortunately, the statute of limitations ran out before he could sue Lamas Company, Inc., and so he sued Lamas individually. Baldwin argued that he had dealt only with Lamas, that he did not know Lamas was an agent of the company, that Lamas did not tell him about the company, and that he understood the contract to be with Lamas individually. Lamas pointed out that Baldwin made out and sent checks directly to Lamas Company, Inc., and that Lamas Company, Inc., always appeared as the payee on those checks. Lamas claimed that this evidence alone would be enough to stop Baldwin from denying that he had dealt with Lamas Company, Inc. The trial court rendered judgment against Lamas. On appeal, should the appellate court reverse. Explain. *Lamas v. Baldwin,* 230 S.E.2d 13 (Georgia).

6. Boafo was allegedly injured while giving birth at Parkway Regional Hospital. Boafo sued both Parkway Regional and Hospital Corporation of America (HCA), asking the court to pierce the corporate veil to reach HCA, which Boafo claimed was a parent company. Boafo showed that the two corporations shared the same offices, that they purchased hospital equipment together, that HCA owned 100 percent of Parkway stock, that major financing for Parkway was performed by HCA through a national accounting system, and that Parkway was insured by another wholly owned subsidiary of HCA. In answer, HCA emphasized that Parkway handled its own daily financing, that it was free to negotiate and enter its own contracts, that it had an adequate amount of money in its treasury, and that it was not formed to promote fraud, conceal crime, or evade legal liability. The trial court granted summary judgment, dismissing the claim against HCA. Should the appellate court uphold the trial court's ruling? Explain. *Boafo v. Hospital Corporation of America,* 338 S.E.2d 477 (Georgia).

CHAPTER 37
Corporate Management and Shareholder Control

OUTLINE

COMMENTARY

Philip K. Wrigley, majority shareholder and president of the Chicago Cubs, refused to install lights at Wrigley Field so that the Cubs could play some of their baseball games at night. Shlensky, a minority shareholder who thought this policy foolish, sued Wrigley, and asked the court to force the installation of lights. Shlensky attributed the Cubs' low attendance and loss of profits to Wrigley's decision not to install lights. Shlensky argued that the installation of lights would allow night games that would draw more fans and increase profits. He made comparisons to the Chicago White Sox, who consistently outdrew the Cubs. Wrigley argued that the court should not interfere with his honest, fair, and obviously legal decision. Whether the court should take a hand in such matters is determined by rules outlined in this chapter.

OBJECTIVES

1. Describe the functions of the board of directors and officers of the corporation in regard to the control of corporate affairs.
2. Distinguish between circumstances which call for the application of the business judgment rule and those which call for the fairness rule in the evaluation of management decisions.
3. Judge whether a corporate manager may or may not use inside information in a particular situation.
4. Determine the voting rights of shareholders in regard to proxy solicitations, voting trusts, pooling agreements, and shareholder proposals.
5. Contrast shareholder direct suits with shareholder derivative suits, and explain the prerequisites for each.
6. Analyze the rights of shareholders in regard to the corporation as established by the stock certificate, corporation bylaws, and state corporation statutes.

37-1 MANAGEMENT OF THE CORPORATION

Both the Model Business Corporation Act (MBCA) and the Revised Model Business Corporation Act (RMBCA) provide that a corporation's business affairs are to be "managed under the direction of a board of directors." The board of directors establishes broad policies, and the officers and other employees implement those policies. How to keep the role of the board separate from executive management is related to the challenge of how best to organize the board and select its members. The issues are even more complex today because a single individual will often function as both a director and an officer. Nevertheless, the two roles have distinct functions and should be examined separately.

Board of Directors

The business affairs of a corporation are managed by a board of directors elected by the shareholders. The board's responsibility is to take whatever actions are appropriate, in keeping with the corporation's rules and regulations, to further the corporation's business. Individual board members are supposed to use their own judgment in the corporate decision-making process.

Qualifications of Directors State law and corporate rules set up the qualifications which a person must have to be a corporate director. Unless prohibited by the corporation's certificate of incorporation, membership on the board of directors can be extended to anyone, including aliens, minors, and nonshareholders. Often the certificate will stipulate that at least one director must be a state resident and at least one, a shareholder. A primary consideration in selecting an individual as a director would be the person's ability to bring to the board a calm and objective view of corporate operations.

Time Commitment of Directors Directors are elected at the annual meeting of the shareholders. Generally, directors hold office for one or two years. The number of directors on the board ranges between 8 and 12. Usually, several directors are elected as a group in order to maintain continuity; this procedure permits one-third of the board to be elected annually. The basic time commitment for a director is approximately 30 days per year, but depending upon need, availability, and interest, it can be 40, 60, 80, or even more days. Naturally, directors can resign from the board. However, many states require a handwritten notice of the director's resignation to the corporation. The RMBCA also includes provisions requiring a written notice of resignation.

Meetings of Directors The directors of most large corporations meet on a regular basis at a precise time and place of their choosing. The directors of many smaller corporations meet only when specific items are to be considered. The RMBCA states that small corporations having fewer than 50 shareholders can eliminate the board of directors entirely, as long as someone is assigned the duties that the board would have performed.

Directors are not entitled to be notified about regular board meetings unless notice is required by the corporation's bylaws. (The bylaws, or regulations of a corporation, determine how that corporation will operate.) However, directors must be notified of special meetings of the board. For example, a special meeting of the directors might be called to decide whether the corporation should institute a lawsuit. If any director is not notified of a special meeting, all actions taken at the meeting are void. A director may not specify another person to vote in her or his place. The quorum, or minimum number of directors necessary to conduct business, is usually one more than half the number of directors. Bylaws may require more than a quorum, perhaps 70 percent of the directors, to conduct certain types of business. This "supermajority" might be needed, for instance, to remove a director or to sell a significant portion of the business. Generally, though, the actions of a quorum constitute the official action of the board.

The board of directors of Biotechnicure, Inc. consisted of five persons. At a properly called meeting, one of the directors presented a motion, calling for a 15 percent salary increase for Biotechnicure's president, vice presidents, secretary, and treasurer. Three directors attended the meeting. This constituted a quorum. Two of the three voted for the salary increase. This vote would constitute an official act by the board.

Officers of the Corporation

Directors are not expected to spend all their time and energy managing the corporation. They have authority to appoint officers and agents to run the day-to-day affairs of the corporation. By statute, the usual officers are a president, several vice presidents, a secretary, and a treasurer. Other officers, such as a comptroller, cashier, and general counsel are often provided. The bylaws of the corporation describe the duties of each officer. Officers have the authority of general agents for the operation of the normal business of the corporation. They, in turn, delegate duties to various department heads.

Although the roles of directors and officers differ, they are frequently assumed by the same people. An individual may be both chief executive officer and chairman of the board of the same corporation. For example, in the opening commentary, Philip K. Wrigley was both a director and president of the Chicago Cubs. Directors and officers can also be shareholders in the corporation. Wrigley, for instance, owned 80 percent of the Cubs' stock.

37-2 MANAGEMENT RESPONSIBILITIES

Corporate managers at all levels—from the board of directors and the chief executive officer to department heads and plant supervisors—are "feeling the heat" as new regulatory laws are placed on the books and regulatory agencies take a harder line toward those who err (see Chapter 38).

In addition, the courts have begun to judge officers more harshly, holding them liable for decisions that hurt shareholders and workers. In Illinois, for example, two corporate executives were found guilty of murder in the death of an employee because they deliberately placed that employee in a life-threatening environment without providing appropriate protective gear and without informing the employee of the danger. In Delaware, corporate directors were found personally liable to shareholders when the board approved a merger without making use of "all material information reasonably available to them." When the court is faced with an attack on a manager's decision, it will turn to one of two rules in judging that conduct: (1) the business judgment rule or (2) the fairness rule. Other areas of managerial responsibility are found in the insider trading rule and the corporate opportunity rule.

The Business Judgment Rule

Under the **business judgment rule,** the court will not interfere with most business decisions. The rule protects managers who act (1) with due care and (2) in good faith, as long as (3) their decisions are lawful and (4) in the best interests of the corporation. The rule results from the common sense belief that, based on their education and experience, managers are in the best position to run the corporation. In contrast, shareholders and judges are far removed from the day-to-day operation of the business and should not be allowed to second-guess most management decisions. Protecting directors and officers in this way encourages people to become corporate managers and reassures them that they will be protected when making difficult business decisions.

Cowley was chairman of the board and chief executive officer of the Hybitrust Petro Chemical Corporation. On September 9, a German Processing Plant went on the market for $500 million. The plant appeared to be a guaranteed moneymaker. In considering the plant's purchase, Cowley had to act before September 15. After careful examination of the plant's financial records, consultation with the corporation's legal and financial experts, and a detailed study of the marketplace, Cowley decided to buy. According to the business judgment rule, if the plant fails, Cowley will be protected because he acted (1) with due care, (2) in good faith, (3) within the law, and (4) in the best interests of the corporation.

The Fairness Rule

The business judgment rule assumes that the manager did not personally profit from a decision. If the manager did profit, then the decision is suspect because all managers owe a duty of loyalty to the corporation. To fulfill this duty, managers must place the corporation's interests above their own. When managers enter contracts with the corporation or when they are on the boards of two corporations that are dealing with each other, a different standard is used to judge their conduct. This standard, known as the **fairness rule,** requires managers to be fair to the corporation when they personally benefit from their business decisions. Managers who do benefit from their own decisions are said to be self-dealing. The fairness rule does not automatically declare managers disloyal if they profit from a corporate decision. Rather, it allows the court to examine the decision to determine its basic fairness to the corporation. How fairness is measured is, at best, problematical. At a minimum, it requires corporate managers to disclose all crucial information when they enter contracts with the corporation.

Kazin was chairman of the board of Ross-VanMaulden Pharmaceuticals, Inc. The corporation leased an airstrip from Aerodynamics, Inc. Kazin was also the majority shareholder and CEO of Aerodynamics. Before finalizing the lease agreement, Kazin revealed his relationship to the other board members of Ross-VanMaulden. The rental rate for the airstrip was in keeping with current market rates. Consequently, if the lease were challenged by shareholders of either corporation, a court, using the fairness rule, would uphold its validity.

Two rules that are offshoots of the fairness rule are the insider trading rule and the corporate opportunity rule. Both rules give the courts a specific way to measure a corporate manager's fairness in certain types of situations.

The Insider Trading Rule Because of their role in corporate affairs, directors and officers often possess inside information. This inside information gives them an advantage that they must not abuse when dealing with the corporation or with individuals outside the corporation. Corporate managers act unfairly if they use their inside information to either cheat the corporation or to take unfair advantage of corporate outsiders. Such transactions are referred to as **insider trading** and are forbidden by law. According to the **insider trading rule,** when managers possess important inside information, they are obligated to reveal that information before using it in a transaction. The rule also states when inside information cannot be revealed, the managers must not use that information when trading with the corporation or with those outside the corporation.

As chief executive officer of the Karmen-Lurie Publishing Company, Zimmerman knew that Takasuki Communications, Inc., planned to buy all outstanding shares of K-L at a price far above its current market value. Without revealing this inside information, Zimmerman purchased as much stock as he could and resold it to Takasuki at an enormous profit. Zimmerman has clearly violated the legal prohibition against insider trading.

The Corporate Opportunity Rule As mentioned earlier, corporate managers owe a duty of loyalty to the corporation and its shareholders. One of the outgrowths of this duty is the **corporate opportunity rule.** Under this rule, corporate managers cannot take a business opportunity for themselves if they know that the corporation would also be interested in that opportunity. Before taking the opportunity, managers must first offer it to the corporation by informing the other managers and shareholders. If the corporation rejects the opportunity, the managers are then free to take it for themselves.

Isfahan, vice president of Rammadan, Inc., learned that the Hadith Corporation was offering several oil fields for sale. Isfahan knew that Rammadan had been attempting to acquire these same oil fields for several months. Consequently,

Table 37-1 MANAGEMENT RESPONSIBILITIES

Rule	*Situation*	*Explanation*
Business judgment rule	Manager does not profit from decision.	Decision stands if it is made (1) in good faith, (2) with due care within the law, and (3) in corporation's best interests.
Fairness rule	Manager profits from decision.	The decision must be fair to the corporation because managers must remain loyal to corporation.
Insider trading rule	Manager possesses inside information not available to outsiders.	Manager must either reveal the information or refrain from trading on that information.
Corporate opportunity doctrine	Manager learns of a business opportunity that might reasonably interest the corporation.	Manager must offer the opportunity to the corporation before taking it for personal gain.

Isfahan could not buy the fields for himself before first informing the other managers and shareholders that the oil fields were up for sale.

37-3 SHAREHOLDER CONTROL

The shareholders are the primary reason a corporation exists. They contribute their money to the corporation in hope of a return on their investment. As owners of the corporation, they have a right to some control over management. Just how much control should be given to shareholders has been the source of much debate. The two principal theories that have been offered in response to this question are managerial control and corporate democracy. Individuals who favor **managerial control** would insulate the managers from shareholders by limiting the shareholders' power to vote and by making it difficult for shareholders to sue managers. Individuals who favor **corporate democracy** would make management more responsive to shareholders by giving shareholders greater voting control and by making it easier for them to take managers to court. Today a delicate balance exists between the two positions. Shareholders can influence corporate decision making through their voting powers and through their right to initiate a lawsuit against managers.

Shareholder Voting Control

Shareholders usually receive one vote per share of common stock held. Shareholders who are dissatisfied with management can buy more shares and increase their voting power. With this increased voting power, the dissatisfied or dissident shareholders can influence the election of the board of directors. However, shareholders are not always able to buy more shares of the corporation, either because they cannot afford them or because the other shareholders are not willing to sell. In such cases, shareholders can resort to one of the other voting methods available: cumulative voting, proxy solicitation, voting trusts, pooling agreements, and shareholder proposals.

Cumulative Voting Ordinarily, each share of common stock has one vote. In this manner, only a majority of shareholders can elect directors of the corporation. To give minority shareholders an opportunity to elect one or more directors, some states permit **cumulative voting.** This system allows shareholders to multiply the number of their voting shares by the number of directors to be elected. All these votes may be cast for one candidate or distributed among several candidates. This procedure allows minority shareholders an opportunity to be represented on the board of directors.

Kisselgoff, Collington, Agassiz, and Guertzman were presented to the shareholders as candidates for the board of directors of the Radchenko-Wyeth Publishing Corporation. Three of the four were to be chosen. Since cumulative voting was authorized, the minority shareholders cast all their weighted votes for Guertzman, who had promised to represent the minority voice in corporate affairs. Had the minority voters been allowed only one vote for each share instead of three, they might have failed in their effort to elect a favored director.

Proxy Voting A **proxy** is the ability of one shareholder to cast another shareholder's votes. **Proxy solicitation** is the process by which one shareholder asks another for his or her voting rights. The minority shareholder's voting power increases as the proxies accumulate. Since majority shareholders, including management, can also solicit proxies, a struggle between the two groups, known as a **proxy contest,** often results. Proxy contests involving large, publicly held corporations are closely regulated by the Securities and Exchange Commission (SEC). This regulation is examined in Chapter 38.

Voting Trusts A **voting trust** is an agreement among shareholders to transfer their voting rights to a trustee. A **trustee** is a person who is entrusted with the management and control of another's property or the rights associated with that property. Sometimes the trustee is one of the shareholders; at other times the trustee is an outsider. The trustee votes those shares at the annual shareholders' meeting at the direction of the shareholders. Shareholders surrender only their voting rights. All other rights, including the right to receive profits, remain with them. Generally, once a voting trust has been created, it cannot be ended until the specified time period has run its course. However, state statutes usually place a maximum time limit on the duration of a voting trust. Most state time limits run from 10 to 21 years. Voting trusts must be in writing and must be filed with the corporation.

Pooling Agreements Sometimes shareholders join together in a temporary arrangement agreeing to vote the same way on a particular issue. Such agreements are known as **pooling agreements, shareholder agreements,** or **voting agreements.** They differ from proxies and voting trusts because the shareholders retain control of their own votes. In this sense, pooling agreements are also the weakest voting arrangement because shareholders can change their votes at the last minute. If a member of a pooling agreement changes her or his vote, however, the other members may bring a lawsuit against the shareholder who broke the agreement. Generally, pooling agreements are interpreted by the court under principles of contract law.

Shareholder Proposals A shareholder proposal allows shareholders to exert some influence over corporate affairs, even if they cannot engage in cumulative voting, solicit proxies, create a voting trust, or join in a pooling agreement. Under SEC guidelines, shareholders of large, publicly owned corporations can compel management to communicate their proposals to the corporation's shareholders prior to the next shareholder meeting. A **shareholder proposal,** then, is a suggestion about a broad company policy or procedure that is submitted by a shareholder. The proposal cannot be about the "ordinary business operation" of the corporation. It must concern something that affects all shareholders. A proposal to hire or fire a particular employee would not qualify, whereas a proposal to amend the corporate charter would.

To qualify as a valid shareholder proposal under SEC rules, the proposal must be no more than 500 words long and must be submitted to management at least 120 days before the shareholders' meeting. In addition, the shareholder must own at least 10 percent or $1,000 in market value of the voting stock of the corporation and may submit only one proposal at a time. Even then, managers can reject the proposal if they feel that it does not qualify as a valid shareholder proposal under a lengthy list of disqualifying characteristics cataloged by the SEC. Included on this list are proposals that are personal grievances and those which are beyond the corporation's power.

Kowalski owned 1 percent of the Vista Verde Power and Electric Co. As an avid opponent of nuclear power plants, she submitted the following shareholder proposal to managers of Vista Verde: "Resolved, that nuclear power is dangerous and must be abandoned by all power plants in the United States." The managers rejected the proposal, even though it met length and timing requirements, because it suggested something beyond the company's power.

Shareholder Suits

The battle between management and dissident shareholders may also be waged on a front other than the annual shareholders' meeting. That front is the courtroom. Shareholders can sue management to compel a change in direction or to force management to overturn a decision. The two types of suits available to shareholders are direct suits and derivative suits.

Direct Suits A **direct suit** is brought by shareholders who have been deprived of a right that belongs to them as shareholders. These rights include the right to vote, the right to receive dividends, the right to transfer shares, the right to purchase newly issued stock, and the right to examine corporate books and records. If shareholders have been denied any of these rights, they can bring a direct suit to make up for any loss they have suffered.

Table 37-2 SHAREHOLDER CONTROL

	Explanation
Voting control:	
Cumulative voting	Each share of stock has as many votes as there are directors to be elected.
Proxy voting	The right to vote another shareholder's stock.
Voting trusts	An agreement among shareholders to transfer their voting rights to a trustee.
Pooling agreements	Shareholders join together in a temporary arrangement, agreeing to vote the same way on a particular issue.
Shareholder proposals	A suggestion about a broad company policy or procedure submitted by a shareholder and included in management's proxy solicitation.
Shareholder suits:	
Direct suit	A suit brought by shareholders who have been deprived of a right.
Derivative suit	A suit brought by shareholders based on an injury to the corporation.

Derivative Suits A **derivative suit** allows shareholders to sue corporate management on behalf of the corporation. Unlike a direct suit, a derivative suit is not based on a direct injury to a shareholder. Instead, the injury is to the corporation. The shareholders' right to sue is *derived* from the corporate injury, hence the label *derivative.*

To bring a derivative suit, shareholders must meet certain prerequisites. One prerequisite is the exhaustion of internal remedies. Before bringing suit, the shareholder must attempt to solve the problem by communicating with the board of directors and with other shareholders. In addition, in order to bring a derivative suit, a shareholder must own stock at the time of the injury and at the time of the suit. This is known as the **rule of contemporary ownership.** Frequently, state corporate laws also require derivative suit plaintiffs to pay a security deposit to cover the corporation's potential expenses in defending the derivative suits. All these requirements make it difficult for a shareholder to bring a derivative lawsuit.

L'Auberge was a shareholder of Red Lion Guest Quarters, Inc. L'Auberge discovered that Deschambault, chief executive officer of Red Lion, had sold some of his own land to the corporation at what L'Auberge believed to be excessive prices. After exhausting internal remedies and making the required security deposit, L'Auberge brought a derivative suit, asking the court to compel Deschambault to transfer all profits made from the real estate deal back to Red Lion.

37-4 OTHER SHAREHOLDER RIGHTS

In addition to their voting rights and their right to sue, shareholders have the right to a stock certificate, the right to examine certain corporate records, the right to dividends, the right to transfer shares of stock, and the right to buy newly issued stock.

Right to a Stock Certificate

The **stock certificate** is written evidence of ownership in shares in a corporation. A shareholder must have possession of the certificate and must sign and deliver it to the person to whom title is transferred (the transferee) when selling or pledging shares. Loss of a certificate does not take away the owner's title to the shares of stock represented by the certificate. Shareholders' names and addresses are shown on the books of the corporation, and they receive dividends, notices of meetings, and any distribution of shareholder reports.

Right to Examine Corporate Records

A shareholder's right by statute to inspect the records of the corporation is usually limited to inspections for proper purposes at the proper time and the proper place. Idle curiosity and purposes that unreasonably interfere with or embarrass corporate management would prompt officers or directors to refuse requests of shareholders to examine corporate accounts, minutes, and records. Where the purpose of inspection is proper, it may be enforced by a court order.

Right to Dividends

Shareholders have the right to share in dividends after they have been declared by the board of directors. Once declared, a dividend becomes a debt of the corporation and enforceable by law, as is any other debt. However, shareholders cannot force the directors to declare a dividend unless the directors are not acting in good faith in refusing to do so. Courts are not inclined to order directors to meet and declare a dividend if the court must substitute its own business judgment for that of the directors.

Right to Transfer Shares of Stock

Shareholders have the right to sell or transfer their shares of stock. The person to whom stock shares are transferred has the right to have the stock transfer entered on the corporate books. The transferee becomes a **shareholder of record** and is entitled to vote, receive dividends, and enjoy all other shareholder privileges.

Preemptive Rights

Unless the right is denied or limited by the corporate charter or by state law, shareholders have the right to purchase a proportionate share of every new offering of stock by the corporation. This is known as the shareholder's **preemptive right.** Preemptive rights are more prevalent in small, closely held corporations than in large publicly owned corporations. This prevents management from depriving shareholders of their proportionate control of a corporation simply by increasing the number of shares in the corporation.

DeFalco owns 400 shares of Silvermine Industries, Inc., which has 1,200 shares altogether. The corporation decided to increase its capital stock to 2,400 shares. DeFalco has the preemptive right to protect his proportionate interest in Silvermine by purchasing one share of stock for every share he owns. If he does so, he will have 800 shares out of the total of 2,400. Thus his relative interest in the corporation will not change.

SUMMARY

37-1. The business affairs of a corporation are managed by a board of directors elected by the shareholders. The directors have the authority to appoint officers and agents to run the day-to-day affairs of the corporation.

37-2. Under the business judgment rule, the court will not interfere with most management decisions as long as those decisions are made with due care, in good faith, within the law, and in the best interests of the corporation. If a manager profits personally from a business decision, then the court will use the fairness rule to judge the manager's conduct. Managers are forbidden to use inside information to gain personally at the corporation's expense or at the expense of corporate outsiders. Under the corporate opportunity rule, corporate managers cannot take a business opportunity for themselves if they know the corporation would also be interested in that opportunity.

37-3. Shareholders can increase their voting power by purchasing additional stock. If they cannot purchase additional stock, they may use one of the other devices available to them including cumulative voting, proxies, voting trusts, pooling agreements, and shareholder proposals. Shareholders can also sue the corporation. Direct suits are brought by shareholders to protect their own rights. Derivative suits are brought by shareholders when they feel the corporation has been damaged by a management decision.

37-4. Other shareholder rights include the right to a stock certificate, the right to examine corporate records, the right to dividends, the right to transfer shares of stock, and the right to buy newly issued stock.

Understanding Key Legal Terms

business judgment rule (p. 526)
corporate democracy (p. 528)
corporate opportunity rule (p. 527)
cumulative voting (p. 529)
derivative suit (p. 530)
direct suit (p. 530)
fairness rule (p. 526)
insider trading (p. 527)
insider trading rule (p. 527)
managerial control (p. 528)
pooling agreement (p. 529)
preemptive rights (p. 532)
proxy (p. 529)
proxy contest (p. 529)
proxy solicitation (p. 529)
rule of contemporary ownership (p. 530)
shareholder of record (p. 532)
shareholder proposal (p. 530)
trustee (p. 529)
voting trust (p. 529)

Questions for Review and Discussion

1. What is meant by the fundamental notion that a corporation's business affairs are to be "managed under the direction of a board of directors"?
2. Explain the board of directors' broad power in running the business affairs of the corporation.
3. State the business judgment rule, and outline the court's rationale in using this rule to evaluate management decisions.
4. Discuss the circumstances under which the court will use the fairness rule to judge a corporate manager's decisions.
5. What must a corporate manager do before using inside information in a transaction?
6. Explain the corporate opportunity rule.
7. Describe the process of cumulative voting.
8. Contrast proxy voting with voting trusts, pooling agreements, and shareholder proposals.
9. How does a direct shareholder suit differ from a derivative shareholder suit? Which of the two is more difficult to bring? Explain.
10. Identify five shareholder rights that a shareholder has against a corporation.

Analyzing Cases

1. The bylaws of Cowley Enterprises, Inc., required a 70 percent "supermajority" to establish a quorum sufficient to hold a meeting to remove a director from the board. The bylaws also designated a meeting with such a purpose as a "special meeting." The board consisted of ten directors. Six showed up at the meeting. Of the four who failed to attend, three were in Europe. The fourth, Weinberger, was not notified of the meeting because he was the one to be removed. The six directors attending the meeting first voted to change the bylaws to require only 60 percent of the directors to establish a quorum sufficient to hold a special meeting. The six directors then unanimously voted to remove Weinberger. When Weinberger found out about the meeting, he objected to the vote and claimed that the entire procedure was void. Is Weinberger correct? Explain.
2. Smith, a shareholder, filed suit against the board of directors of a corporation in which he'd owned stock. Smith claimed that he and other shareholders had not received top dollar for their shares when their corporation had merged with another. Consequently, they sought either a reversal of the merger or payment from the directors to make up for their losses. The directors, Smith argued, had violated their duty of due care because they based their decision on a 20-minute speech by the CEO. Also, the directors had not even looked at the merger documents, let alone studied them. Further, the directors had not sought any independent evaluation by outside experts. For their part, the directors argued that since their decision was made in good faith and was legal, they were protected by the business judgment rule. Are the directors correct? *Smith v. VanGorkon,* 488 A.2d 858 (Delaware).
3. Donald Lewis was a shareholder in SLE, a corporation which owned land and a complex of buildings in Rochester, New York. The land and buildings were leased to LGT, a tire manufacturer. Donald's brothers were shareholders and directors of both SLE and LGT. Donald had no financial or managerial interest in LGT. SLE leased the land to LGT at a rate that Donald considered damaging to SLE. He pointed out that SLE collected only $14,000 per year in rent

from LGT while paying out $11,000 in taxes. This, he argued, meant that SLE could never be a profit-making corporation. Should the directors of LGT and SLE be judged by the business judgment rule or the fairness rule? Explain. *Lewis vs. S.L.&E., Inc.,* 629 F.2d 764 (2d Cir. Ct.).

4. Jackson set up a trust for his seven children. Most of the assets in the trust consisted of stock in the two newspapers owned and run by Jackson. Over the course of 18 years, Jackson transferred all but two shares of voting stock in the newspapers. The trustee of the trust was given full power to manage the assets in the fund and to sell or otherwise dispose of the newspaper stock. State law places a strict 10-year limit on voting trusts. The plaintiffs claimed that the trust, which had lasted 18 years, was no longer valid, having passed the 10-year limit 8 years before. The defendants claimed that the 10-year limit did not apply to this trust. Are the defendants correct? Explain. *Jackson v. Jackson,* 420 A.2d 893 (Connecticut).

5. Klinicki and Lundgren incorporated to form an air taxi service known as Berlinair, Inc. Each of them owned one-third interest in the corporation. The final third was owned by Lelco, Inc., a company owned by Lundgren. In his capacity as president of Berlinair, Lundgren learned that the Berlinair Flug Ring (BFR), a business association of Berlin's travel agents, was looking for an air charter service. Lundgren incorporated a new corporate entity called Air Berlin Charter (ABC). ABC then negotiated an air charter contract with BFR. Klinicki brought suit, demanding that Lundgren reimburse Berlinair for any profits made by ABC on the BFR contract. Is this a direct or derivative suit? Explain. Will the business judgment rule or the fairness rule be used by the court to measure Lundgren's performance? Explain. Who should win the suit? Defend your choice. *Klinicki v. Lundgren,* 695 P.2d 906 (Oregon).

6. Naquin, Dubois, and Hoffpauir incorporated to form Air Engineered Systems and Services, Inc. Dubois became president and Hoffpauir became secretary-treasurer. Naquin was employed by the company. Conflicts between the three caused a breakdown in the working relationship. Dubois and Hoffpauir offered Naquin $2,000 a month for ten years for his share of the business if he would sign a noncompetition agreement. Naquin refused to sell until he could examine the corporate records. Dubois and Hoffpauir refused to allow Naquin to see the books until he signed the noncompetition agreement. Can Dubois and Hoffpauir attach such a condition to Naquin's request? Explain. *Naquin v. Air Engineered Systems and Services, Inc.,* 463 So.2d 992 (Louisiana).

CHAPTER 38
Government Regulation of Corporate Business

OUTLINE

COMMENTARY

Ideally, the management and the shareholders of a corporation should be able to control their own affairs without interference. Realistically, this is not always the case. Despite the shareholder controls and the management responsibilities discussed in the last chapter, some corporate decisions hurt employees, investors, customers, other corporations, and even the marketplace itself. When this happens, the government must step in and set things right. This process has been labeled government regulation. Some of the regulatory efforts by the government are aimed at the sale of stock. Others are directed at the sale of one corporation to another. Even if such activities are beneficial to the corporation involved, the government might still step in, since the government must always keep the welfare of the entire society in view. For example, when Ford Motor Company purchased Autolite, the second largest manufacturer of spark plugs in the United States, the financial picture of both corporations improved. Ford purchased all its spark plugs from Autolite at excellent prices and Autolite's share of the market increased dramatically. Nevertheless, the government forced Ford to sell Autolite because the new "buddy system" between the two large corporations hurt competition in the overall marketplace. What activities can the government regulate? How is that regulation carried out? These and other questions are answered in this chapter.

OBJECTIVES

1. Distinguish between the power of the federal government and that of state governments to regulate business.

2. Explain the procedures practiced by the Securities and Exchange Commission to prevent unfair practices.
3. Compare the effectiveness of the Sherman and the Clayton antitrust acts in preventing anticompetitive practices.
4. Describe the various techniques available for corporate expansion and termination.
5. Contrast the Securities and Exchange Commission's interest in the corporate expansion process and the Federal Trade Commission's interest in the process.
6. Identify the major regulatory responsibilities of the federal Environmental Protection Agency and the Federal Energy Regulatory Commission.
7. Discuss how the government is involved in the dissolution of a corporation.

38-1 BUSINESS AND THE CONSTITUTION

U.S. Const., Art. 1, Sec. 8 (see pp. 600–601)

All business organizations are subject to some form of government regulation. The regulatory activities of state governments are based on a state's police power. **Police power** is the state's authority to restrict private rights in order to promote and maintain public health, safety, welfare, and morals. The power of the federal government to regulate business is noted in Article I, Section 8, Clause 3 of the U.S. Constitution. This clause, known as the **Commerce Clause,** states that "Congress shall have Power... To regulate Commerce with foreign Nations and among the several States." In defining the power, the Supreme Court has said, "It is the power... to prescribe the rules by which commerce is to be governed."

Over the years, the Supreme Court has further refined this definition, gradually broadening the federal government's power to regulate business . The power to regulate is so broad today that the federal government can regulate any business activity that affects interstate commerce (commerce among the states) even if that activity takes place solely within the boundaries of a single state.

The Mead-Hiassen Power Corporation owned and operated the Cabel-Bernel Coal Company. Both corporations were based in West Virginia. Cabel-Bernel supplied Mead-Hiassen with about 25 percent of its coal needs, and did no other coal business with anyone. The other 75 percent of Mead-Hiassen's coal came from one in-state producer and two out-of-state suppliers. When the federal government imposed new safety regulations on all coal mines, Cabel-Bernel argued that the regulations did not apply to it since its business was totally within the borders of West Virginia. The court disagreed. The fact that 25 percent of Mead-Hiassen's coal was purchased from Cabel-Bernel meant that Mead-Hiassen did not buy that 25 percent from other corporations, including the two corporations from outside West Virginia. Since the two corporations outside West Virginia could have sold more coal to Mead-Hiassen had Cabel-Bernel not sold its coal to Mead-Hiassen, Cabel-Bernel's business was affecting interstate commerce.

38-2 SECURITIES REGULATION

Two pieces of federal legislation which affect business are the Securities Act of 1933 and the Securities Exchange Act of of 1934. The primary purpose of these acts is to protect business investors by making certain that they are informed about the securities they purchase. The independent regulatory agency which carries out this function is the Securities and Exchange Commission (SEC). The SEC regulates the issuance of securities by corporations and partnerships. A **security** has been defined as a money investment which expects a return solely because of another person's efforts. As the following case demonstrates, a security is a security even if it's called something else.

D'Zungia Industries, Inc., had to raise an enormous amount of capital quickly. One of the directors devised a scheme whereby the corporation would sell to investors parcels of land owned by the corporation and used for mining purposes. In return, the investors would be entitled to a return on their investment. The return would be calculated in relation to the amount of land owned by each investor. To avoid having to comply with SEC regulations, D'Zungia labeled each sale a land contract rather than a security. Since the sales were land contracts, D'Zungia argued, it did not have to follow SEC regulations. The SEC disagreed and brought suit to stop the sale of unregulated securities. The court held that since each investor's profits would be derived solely from the efforts of others, the investments were securities and were, therefore, subject to SEC regulations.

The Securities Act of 1933

The Securities Act of 1933 regulates the issuance of new securities by corporations and partnerships. Offers of securities by mail or through interstate or foreign commerce must be registered with the SEC. A registration statement and a prospectus must be filed with the SEC. A **registration statement** contains detailed information about the corporation, including data about its management, capitalization, and financial condition. A **prospectus** contains much of the same information, but in a condensed and simplified form. The registration statement is designed for the experts at the SEC, whereas the prospectus is designed for potential investors.

The Securities Exchange Act of 1934

The Securities Exchange Act of 1934, which actually established the SEC, deals with the subsequent trading in securities. It requires periodic reports of financial information concerning registered securities, and it prohibits manipulative and deceptive actions in the sale and purchase of securities. The act prohibits insiders, including officers and directors, from realizing profit from any purchase and sale of securities within any period of less than six months. The courts have held that insiders are not permitted to trade on information until that information has been made available to the public.

Under the 1934 act, shareholders, including majority shareholders, who solicit proxies (see Chapter 37) must also follow strict reporting requirements.

The SEC requires a written proxy solicitation to include the identity of the individual or individuals seeking the proxy, any potential conflicts of interest, and specific information about any corporate changes to be voted on. When management solicits proxies, the solicitation must also include information concerning management salaries. The SEC regulations also state quite specifically that all material information must be stated in readable language and displayed prominently, rather than buried in small type somewhere in the back of the document. The regulations also explicitly forbid false or misleading information.

Bulandi, a shareholder in Longbow Enterprise, Inc., was dissatisfied with management's decision to discontinue Longbow's association with Kurasaki Electronics. Since Bulandi did not own enough stock to outvote management and elect himself to the board, he decided to launch a proxy solicitation campaign. In putting together his solicitation, Bulandi failed to mention his controlling interest in Kurasaki. The directors of Longbow filed a suit, asking the court to stop Bulandi's solicitations because he had failed to comply with SEC rules. Since Bulandi had not revealed his conflict of interest, the court ruled in favor of the Longbow directors.

38-3 ANTITRUST REGULATION

Both the federal government and the state have antitrust laws to preserve the values of competition and to discourage monopolies. A **monopoly** is the exclusive control of a market by a business enterprise. At the federal level, the four principal antitrust statutes are the Sherman Anti-Trust Act, the Clayton Act, the Federal Trade Commission Act, and the Robinson-Patman Act.

The Sherman Anti-Trust Act

The Sherman Anti-Trust Act (1890) prohibits contracts, combinations, and conspiracies in restraint of trade. It also prohibits monopolization, attempts to monopolize, and combinations or conspiracies to monopolize any part of interstate or foreign commerce. Violations of the Sherman Act must involve at least two people acting together.

Per Se Violations Some restraint-of-trade practices are so serious that they are prohibited whether or not they harm anyone. These practices are labeled **per se violations.** This means that the practice is so contrary to antitrust policy that harm is presumed and the practice is prohibited. For example, price fixing is inherently unreasonable and is, therefore, considered a per se violation. An agreement between competitors to divide territories among themselves to minimize competition would also be unlawful. This is true even if the agreement helps the parties to compete against other parties outside the agreement.

Similar unlawful activities include agreements among competitors to stop competing with one another in prices, customers, or products.

Rule-of-Reason Standard If an alleged antitrust practice is not considered a per se violation, then, in judging the legality of that practice, the courts will use the rule-of-reason approach. The **rule-of-reason** standard will stop certain practices only if they are an unreasonable restriction of competition. As a result, some practices which, in fact, limit competition may be legal. To determine if an anticompetitive practice is legal, the court considers such facts as the history of the restraint, the harm which results, the reason for the practice, and the purpose to be attained.

Post–Sherman Anti-Trust Legislation

Three principal antitrust statutes made the Sherman Act more specific and, as a result, more effective. The Clayton Act of 1914, the Federal Trade Commission Act of 1914, and the Robinson-Patman Act of 1936 sought to prevent practices that reduced competition or that favored the creation of monopolies.

Clayton Act Congress passed the Clayton Act to police specific business practices that could be used to create a monopoly. One practice outlawed was the **tying agreement.** A tying agreement occurs when one party refuses to sell a product unless the buyer also purchases another product tied to the first product. The issue is the effect of the tie-in on the seller's competitors.

Sinichi Electronics, Inc., manufactured a line of state-of-the-art VHS videocassette recorders that Updike Department Stores wanted to market. Sinichi, however, refused to sell the VCRs to Updike unless the Updike stores also agreed to purchase Sinichi's line of VHS tapes. Since any VHS tape could work with Sinichi's VCRs, the restriction would be ruled an unlawful tying agreement and a violation of the Clayton Act.

Interlocking directorates were also outlawed by the Clayton Act. Interlocking directorates occur when individuals serve as directors of two corporations that are competitors. This provision is not entirely foolproof, however, because banks and common carriers are exempt. To fall under this part of the Clayton Act, at least one of the corporations must have an aggregate worth (capital, surplus, and individual profits) of more than $1 million.

Braunstein was on the board of the Austin-Zircron Medical Supply Corporation and the Biomedical Engineering Corporation of Austin, Texas. The two firms were in direct competition with one another in the sale of biomedical equipment to hospitals and clinics in Texas. While Biomedical had an aggregate worth of only $50,000, Austin-Zircron was worth more than $2 million. Braunstein's activity violated the Clayton Act's prohibition against interlocking directorates.

Table 38-1 SECURITIES AND ANTITRUST REGULATION

Securities regulation:	
Securities Act of 1933	Regulates the issuance of new securities
Securities Exchange Act of 1934	Established the Securities and Exchange Commission; act deals with subsequent trading in securities
Antitrust regulation:	
Sherman Anti-Trust Act	Prohibits contracts, combinations in restraint of trade; also prohibits monopolies, attempts to monopolize, and conspiracies to monopolize
Clayton Act	Prohibits specific practices such as tying agreements and interlocking directorates
Robinson-Patman Act	Deals with product pricing; advertising and promotional allowances
Federal Trade Commission Act	Established the Federal Trade Commission

Robinson-Patman Act The Robinson-Patman Act deals with product pricing, advertising, and promotional allowances. It specifically prohibits a seller from charging different prices to different customers for the same product where such differences might injure competition. However, nothing in the law is intended to prevent price differences due to cost of manufacture, sale, delivery, or bulk purchases. Also permitted are price changes in response to changing conditions affecting the market or the marketability of goods. For example, price changes are allowed to reflect a decline in the quality of perishable goods and the obsolescence of seasonal goods.

Federal Trade Commission Act In addition to establishing the Federal Trade Commission (FTC), the Federal Trade Commission Act, as amended, declared that "unfair methods of competition, and unfair or deceptive practices in or affecting commerce are hereby declared unlawful." The act did not name specific unfair methods of competition. Instead, it allowed the courts and the FTC to determine those unfair practices. The courts do so on a case-by-case basis. The FTC does so by issuing advisory opinions, industry guides, and trade regulation rules. For example, the FTC has ruled that the "bait-and-switch" routine practiced by some sellers is an unfair practice. Under this technique, a seller will offer one item for sale at a very low price. When the customer asks for that one item, the seller steers the customer away from the first product in order to sell something else. Usually, the second product is more expensive and is offered according to terms more advantageous to the seller.

The Federal Trade Commission Act was amended by the Wheeler-Lea Act and amendments in 1938 and 1975. This legislation authorized the FTC to act against unfair or deceptive acts without first proving the existence of anticompetitive behavior. The FTC was also granted the power to challenge false advertising of food, drugs, and cosmetics regardless of the advertiser's knowledge of the advertisement's truth or falsity.

38-4 REGULATION OF CORPORATE EXPANSION

No other area of corporate activity has been scrutinized by the government more closely in recent years than the area of corporate expansion. As previously noted, the two governmental agencies which regulate this activity are the Securities and Exchange Commission and the Federal Trade Commission. The two commissions have different interests in the expansion process. The SEC is concerned with regulating the expansion itself, while the FTC is more concerned with the effects of that expansion. The following discussion covers both areas.

Expansion Techniques and Securities Law

All corporations change in size. Some grow and expand, and others shrink until they dissolve completely or are absorbed by a larger, more successful enterprise. Like all other corporate activities, corporate expansions are looked at very closely by government. The primary expansion techniques include merger, consolidation, asset acquisition, and stock acquisition (takeover).

Merger and Consolidation Traditionally, a **merger** involved two corporations, one of which was absorbed by the other. One of the two corporations continued to carry on business under its original name, and the other simply disappeared into the first. In contrast, in a **consolidation** both companies disappeared and a new company carried on business under a new name. Today, most legal scholars do not make any distinction between merger and consolidation. In fact, the Revised Model Business Corporation Act (RMBCA) makes no reference to consolidation, preferring the term *merger* instead.

A merger requires advance approval from the boards and shareholders of both corporations. In general, a two-thirds majority vote of the shareholders will be required before a merger can be approved, although some states require a supermajority of four-fifths. Shareholders who dissent are entitled to be paid for their stock if they do not wish to be a part of the merger. Written notice of a dissent is required so that the cost of purchasing the dissenter's stock can be figured as a part of the expense involved in the merger.

Most antifraud provisions of the SEC apply to the merger process. Often the merger vote will be preceded by a proxy solicitation battle. All material facts about the merger must be included in the proxy solicitation. In addition, the solicitation must not contain any false or misleading information. Similarly, the SEC prohibits insiders who know of merger plans to take advantage of that knowledge to profit personally before the knowledge is revealed to the public.

Asset Acquisition In an **asset acquisition,** one corporation purchases all the property of a second corporation. Asset acquisition is easy and efficient since the only formality required is approval by the directors and shareholders ofthe corporation that is selling its assets. One advantage of asset acquisition is that, in general, no debts or other liabilities are transferred from seller to buyer.

Again, as in the case of merger, SEC antifraud regulations can be applied to asset acquisitions if a proxy solicitation process is involved or if insider information is used to profit from the sale.

Stock Acquisition **Stock acquisitions** are also known as **takeovers.** In a **takeover bid,** one corporation, the **suitor,** offers to buy the voting stock of another corporation, the **target.** A successful takeover occurs once the suitor has purchased enough voting stock to control the target. One advantage of the stock acquisition process is that it sidesteps the board of directors. The acquiring corporation deals directly with the shareholders. Usually, the shareholders are motivated to sell because the acquiring company has made an offer that is above the current market price of the stock. Frequently, corporations become targets of **unfriendly suitors.** An unfriendly suitor, also known as a **hostile bidder,** is one which intends to change management and shake up the corporation after the takeover. Often to avoid being taken over by an unfriendly suitor, the target company will invite another suitor to outbid the hostile bidder. The second suitor is known as a **friendly suitor** or a **white knight.** A takeover battle usually follows. The winner is generally the suitor who can offer the highest price for the target's stock.

The Ampco Corporation had its eyes set on acquiring the Buffalo Forge Company. Accordingly, Ampco made a $25 per share offer to Buffalo shareholders as part of its takeover bid. Management of Buffalo, fearful of losing their jobs, fought the unfriendly takeover bid by asking the Ogden Corporation to become their "white knight." Ogden agreed and offered Buffalo shareholders $32.75 per share. A takeover battle followed. Ampco countered Ogden's $32.75 offer with $34. Ogden counterattacked with $37 per share. Not to be beaten, Ampco increased its bid to $37.50. Ogden could not match this bid. Accordingly, it surrendered. The "white knight" had been knocked off its horse, and Buffalo went to Ampco.

Takeover bids are closely scrutinized by the SEC. Under recent amendments to federal securities law, whenever a suitor makes an offer to acquire more than 5 percent of a target, that suitor must file a statement with the SEC. The statement must indicate: (1) where the money for the takeover originates, (2) why the suitor is buying the stock, and (3) how much of the target the suitor already owns. These procedures are designed to let shareholders know the identity and intention of a takeover bidder. Bidders who falsify any information on their statement may find their takeover bid stopped by a court order.

Lampert, Levy, and Scuderi purchased more than 12 percent of General Aircraft's stock. Since the purchase topped 5 percent, they filed the necessary statements with the SEC. In their statement, they indicated that the purpose of their purchase was simply to invest in the corporation. For the next year, however, Lampert, Levy, and Scuderi caused a great deal of trouble for the management of General Aircraft. Eventually, they engineered a change in the composition of the board of directors so that the three of them had more influence in corporate decision making. They then entered a proxy contest challenging management control. Man-

Table 38-2 SECURITIES LAW AND CORPORATE EXPANSION

Technique	*Explanation*	*Regulation*
Merger and consolidation	In merger, one company is absorbed by another; in consolidation, two companies join and a new company results.	Most antifraud provisions of the SEC apply here.
Asset acquisition	One corporation buys all the property of another.	Most antifraud provisions of the SEC apply here.
Stock acquisition (takeover)	One corporation (suitor) makes a tender offer to the shareholders of another corporation (target).	Whenever a suitor makes an offer to acquire more than 5 percent of the target, the suitor must file with the SEC.

agement filed a complaint claiming the statement filed with the SEC had been fraudulent because the purchase of the stock had not been for investment purposes but rather for takeover purposes. The court agreed and ordered Lampert, Levy, and Scuderi to refrain from stock purchases and to stop their proxy contest until they filed amendments to the statement.

Expansion Effects and Antitrust Law

Antitrust law does not focus on corporate expansion techniques. Instead, it looks at how an expansion attempt will affect competition in the marketplace. Section 7 of the Clayton Act forbids any corporate expansion if that expansion sets up a monopoly or otherwise hurts competition. The Clayton Act applies to horizontal, vertical, or conglomerate expansion attempts.

Expansion Attempts **Horizontal expansion** occurs between companies that are involved in the same business. For this reason, horizontal expansion attempts are more likely to result in monopolies. Consequently, horizontal expansion schemes are closely scrutinized by the FTC and are more likely to be labeled illegal. A **vertical expansion** occurs between companies that were in a customer-supplier relationship. If a manufacturer of designer jeans were to buy a chain of department stores that carried its jeans, a vertical expansion would result. A **conglomerate expansion** joins two companies that were not in competition with one another, either because they dealt in different products or services or because they operated in different geographical areas.

The board of Koslow Pharmaceuticals, Inc., began a takeover bid for the Kotani-Von Maddox Drug Corporation. This stock acquisition would be watched closely by the FTC since it is a horizontal expansion. Koslow also merged with the Jeijing Vung Chemical Corporation, which had previously supplied Koslow with many of the raw materials for its drugs. Such a move is a vertical expansion and receives less scrutiny from the FTC. Finally, Koslow diversified by purchasing the assets of the Toledo Tornadoes, a professional soc-cer team. This is a conglomerate expansion which, like the vertical expansion, would be less likely to violate antitrust law.

Table 38-3 ANTITRUST LAW AND CORPORATE EXPANSION

Technique	*Explanation*	*Regulation*
Horizontal expansion	Occurs between companies that are involved in the same business	Closely scrutinized by the FTC because of the likelihood of a monopoly
Vertical expansion	Occurs between companies that are in a customer-supplier relationship	Less likelihood of monopoly, therefore less FTC scrutiny
Conglomerate expansion	Occurs between two companies that are not in competition with each other	Least likelihood of monopoly, and so least FTC scrutiny

Hart-Scott-Rodino Like the SEC, the FTC has a chance to step into expansion situations even before they become an established fact. This opportunity is provided by the Hart-Scott-Rodino Antitrust Act. Hart-Scott-Rodino was designed to police any expansion attempts that might harm competition in the marketplace. The act requires corporations that are setting up an expansion attempt to notify the FTC before the deal is completed. This advance notice allows the FTC to investigate the anticompetitive effects of the planned expansion. Should the FTC decide that the expansion will hurt competition, it can go to court and ask for an injunction to prevent the expansion.

38-5 OTHER FORMS OF REGULATION

Corporations are regulated by the government in a variety of ways that extend beyond their involvement in the securities market, the antitrust arena, and the corporate expansion game. Many of these controls were discussed in earlier chapters. Labor regulation, for example, was examined in Chapter 34, Labor Relations, and bankruptcy was covered in Chapter 30, Bankruptcy and Debt Adjustment. Commerce regulation was studied in Chapter 20, Innkeepers, Carriers, and Warehousers, and consumer protection regulation was detailed in Chapter 18, Consumer Protection. Two areas of regulation as yet untouched are energy regulation and environmental protection.

Energy Regulation

The Arab Oil embargo of 1973 and the subsequent "energy crisis" focused national attention on the power industry. In answer to these concerns, Congress created the Department of Energy and the Federal Energy Regulatory Commission. National concern with the problems of nuclear energy has also recently focused attention on the Nuclear Regulatory Commission.

Federal Energy Regulatory Commission The Federal Energy Regulatory Commission (FERC) is responsible for regulating the transportation and the wholesale price of natural gas and electricity sold for use in interstate commerce. State utility commissioners regulate intrastate prices. Rates are calculated to allow companies a specific rate of return on investments (earnings divided by total assets), which they may not exceed. When utilities are confronted with increased costs due to higher fuel prices, they can apply to the commission for permission to pass them on to customers through fuel adjustment charges. A utility that makes more than its allowed rate of return or receives fuel adjustment charges that exceed increased fuel costs may be ordered to rebate the overcharges to customers. Rates for the transportation of electric power, natural gas, and oil through pipelines also fall under FERC's jurisdiction.

Nuclear Regulatory Commission Mandated by the Energy Reorganization Act, the Nuclear Regulatory Commission (NRC) is responsible for the licensing, construction, and operation of nuclear reactors. It is also responsible for regulating the possession, use, transportation, handling, and disposal of nuclear material. The NRC develops and implements rules and regulations governing licensed nuclear activities.

The Office of Inspection and Enforcement inspects nuclear facilities to determine whether they are constructed and operated in accord with NRC regulations. The office investigates accidents, incidents, and charges of improper actions that may adversely affect the production of nuclear materials, the facilities, the environment, or the health and safety of the public.

Environmental Protection Regulation

The Environmental Protection Agency (EPA) is an independent agency in the executive branch of the federal government. It was created to carry out the provisions of the National Environmental Policy Act and other major environmental laws and executive orders dealing with air, water, solid waste, toxic substance, and noise pollution.

National Environmental Policy Act The purpose of the 1969 National Environmental Policy Act is to establish a national policy that will combat pollution and improve the environment. The legislation encourages efforts which prevent or eliminate damage to the environment and which stimulate the health and welfare of the public. The act requires a detailed statement of environmental consequences in every recommendation or proposal for legislation and other major federal actions significantly affecting the quality of the human environment. These **environmental impact statements** describe in detail the expected adverse environmental consequences of a proposed action. The alternatives to the action are also described.

Environmental Protection Agency All major antipollution programs dealing with air, noise, solid wastes, toxic substances, and pesticides were placed under the administrative control of the EPA in 1970. The EPA's primary responsibilities are to conduct research on all aspects of pollution, set and enforce pollution control standards, monitor programs to determine whether pollution abatement standards are being met, and administer grants to assist states in controlling pollution.

The EPA has the power to enforce the standards and programs itinitiates. It encourages voluntary compliance by industry and communities and supports state and local governments' efforts to conduct enforcement actions of their own. When such efforts fail, the EPA conducts enforcement proceedings. Often the EPA must act against companies that pollute the environment, even if the pollution activity is unintentional. For example, the Federal Water Pollution Control Act forbids "*any* addition of *any* pollutants to navigable waters from *any* source." The courts have interpreted this broad prohibition to include even accidental pollution, because to hold otherwise would weaken the statute.

38-6 THE GOVERNMENT AND CORPORATE DISSOLUTION

Just as the government is involved in the birth and the growth (expansion) of a corporation, it is also involved in its death, or dissolution. Whether a corporation ends involuntarily or voluntarily, the government is somehow involved.

Involuntary Dissolution

If a corporation has repeatedly conducted business in an unlawful manner, the secretary of state of the state of incorporation can ask the state attorney general to bring a ***quo warranto*** action against that corporation. Under a *quo warranto* proceeding, the state revokes the corporation's charter. Common examples of illegal actions forming the grounds for revocation include a failure to file annual reports, a failure to pay franchise taxes, or a failure to maintain a registered or statutory agent for service of process. Corporations formed fraudulently and those exceeding their authority may also be subject to a *quo warranto* proceeding.

Courts have the power to liquidate the assets of a corporation when an action is brought by a shareholder. Grounds for involuntary dissolution at the request of a shareholder include: evidence of illegal, oppressive, or fraudulent acts; a misapplication or waste of corporate assets, a deadlock of directors that threatens irreparable harm, or evidence that a dissolution is necessary to protect the rights of the complaining shareholder.

Voluntary Dissolution

Since the government grants corporate charters and regulates corporate activity, it must be informed when a corporation voluntarily dissolves. A corporation can be dissolved voluntarily by the unanimous approval of the shareholders or by a positive vote of the directors with the approval of two-thirds of the shareholders. Once the decision to dissolve has been approved, a statement of intent must be filed with the state government. The corporation will then cease business and notify creditors (by certified mail) and the public (by publication). After all claims have been received, corporate assets will be used first to pay creditors, with the surplus going to shareholders. If the existing assets cannot meet all claims, a **receiver** may be called in to handle matters. A receiver is a person appointed by law to hold property subject to diverse claims. The receiver would divide assets fairly among creditors. Following the distribution of all assets, the corporation must prepare articles of dissolution and present them to the secretary of state.

SUMMARY

38-1. The regulatory activities of state governments are based on each state's police power. The power of the federal government to regulate business is found in the Commerce Clause of the U.S. Constitution.

38-2. The primary objective of the Securities Act of 1933 and the Securities Exchange Act of 1934 is to protect investors by informing them about the securities they purchase. The Securities and Exchange Commission carries out this objective.

38-3. To preserve the value of competition and to discourage monopolies, the government has enacted several antitrust statutes. The Sherman Anti-Trust Act prohibits contracts, combinations, and conspiracies in restraint of trade. The Clayton Act, the Robinson-Patman Act, and the Federal Trade Commission Act make the Sherman Act more specific and more effective.

38-4. While both securities law and antitrust law are concerned with monopolies, they have different areas of concern. Securities law is concerned with regulating corporate expansion techniques including mergers, consolidations, asset acquisitions, and stock acquisition. Antitrust law is concerned with how corporate expansion affects competition in the marketplace. Antitrust law applies to horizontal, vertical, or conglomerate expansion attempts.

38-5. Through the Federal Energy Regulatory Commission and the Nuclear Regulatory Commission, the government regulates businesses involved in energy production. By means of the Environmental Protection Agency, the government also regulates businesses that pollute the environment.

38-6. Corporations can dissolve involuntarily or voluntarily. A corporation that has repeatedly conducted business in an unlawful manner may be subject to involuntary dissolution by the state. A corporation can be voluntarily dissolved by unanimous approval of the shareholders or by a positive vote of the directors with the approval of two-thirds of the shareholders. The government is involved in both involuntary and voluntary dissolution.

Understanding Key Legal Terms

asset acquisition (p. 542)
Commerce Clause (p. 537)
conglomerate expansion (p. 544)
consolidation (p. 542)
horizontal expansion (p. 544)
interlocking directorates (p. 540)
merger (p. 542)
monopoly (p. 539)
per se violations (p. 539)
police power (p. 537)
prospectus (p. 538)
registration statement (p. 538)
rule-of-reason (p. 540)
security (p. 538)
stock acquisition (p. 543)
suitor (p. 542)
takeover bid (p. 543)
target (p. 542)
tying agreement (p. 540)
vertical expansion (p. 544)

Questions for Review and Discussion

1. Indicate the legal basis for a state's regulation of business operating within the state. Identify the constitutional source of the federal government's power to regulate business.
2. Identify the major responsibilities of the Securities and Exchange Commission.
3. Distinguish between a per se violation of antitrust law and a violation determined by the rule-of-reason standard.
4. Name and explain the specific business practices that were outlawed by the Clayton Act of 1914.
5. Describe the changes made to the Federal Trade Commission Act by the Wheeler-Lea Act and other subsequent amendments.
6. Contrast corporate expansion efforts accomplished by merger with those accomplished by asset acquisition and stock acquisition.
7. Differentiate between the Securities and Exchange Commission's interest in the corporate expansion process and the Federal Trade Commission's interest in that process.
8. Discuss the powers and authority of the Federal Energy Regulatory Commission.
9. What are the responsibilities of the Environmental Protection Agency?
10. Under what circumstances can a state government bring a *quo warranto* action to involuntarily dissolve a corporation? Under what circumstances can a court involuntarily dissolve a corporation? How is the government involved in the involuntary dissolution of a corporation?

Analyzing Cases

1. Filburn, a farm owner in Ohio, raised winter wheat primarily to feed his livestock and poultry and to make flour for home use. Under the provisions of the Agricultural Adjustment Act, Filburn was given notice of a wheat acreage and yield allotment. Filburn, however, sowed more acreage and harvested more wheat than he was allowed. As a result, the government fined him $117.11. Filburn sued the government to prevent it from collecting the fine. He argued that the production and consumption of wheat on his own land for his own purposes are outside the reach of Congress because at most, this activity has an indirect effect upon interstate commerce. Is Filburn correct? Explain. *Wickard v. Filburn,* 63 S. Ct. 82 (U.S. Sup. Ct.).

2. The W. J. Howey Co. owned a large citrus grove in Florida. The citrus grove was serviced by Howey-in-the-Hills, Inc., a corporation owned and operated by the same people who ran the Howey Co. When the Howey Co. needed money, it sold tracts of land in the grove. Each buyer had to purchase both land from the Howey Co. and a service contract from Howey-in-the-Hills. The purchasers had no right to enter the land or market the crop. All cultivating and marketing was done by the service company. Most of the buyers were from out of state. In return for their purchase, they received a share of the profits after the crops were harvested and sold. The SEC brought suit against both companies, arguing that the land and service contracts were actually securities that should have been registered with the commission. Is the SEC correct? Explain. *Securities and Exchange Commission v. W. J. Howey Co.,* 66 S. Ct. 1100 (U.S. Sup. Ct.).

3. Topco Associates, Inc., is a cooperative association of small and medium-sized regional supermarket chains. Each of its member chains operates independently. All members are required to operate under "exclusive territorial licenses" issued by Topco. These provide that members will sell Topco-controlled brands only within the marketing territory given them. The government filed suit in federal district court. It argued that this scheme of dividing markets among competing chains violated the Sherman Anti-Trust Act because it prohibited competition in Topco-brand products among grocery chains engaged in retail operations. Topco defended by arguing that the association actually increased competition between the smaller and the larger chains. Is Topco correct? Defend your answer. *United States v. Topco Associates, Inc.*, 92 S. Ct. 1126 (U.S. Sup. Ct.).

4. Enstrom purchased an aircraft from the Interceptor Corporation. When the aircraft crashed due to a design defect, Enstrom sued Interceptor. However, when Enstrom found out that Interceptor's assets had been purchased by Interceptor Company (IC), it asked the court to join IC as a new defendant. IC argued that it was a different corporation involved in a different business. IC further argued that it had simply purchased the assets of Interceptor and was now involved in selling those assets, like the aircraft, to other buyers, like Enstrom. IC concluded that it was, therefore, not liable to Enstrom. Is IC correct? Why or why not? *R.J. Enstrom Corporation v. Interceptor Corporation*, 555 F.2d 277 (10th Cir. Ct.).

5. Earth Sciences, Inc., conducted gold-leaching operations in Colorado. The process involved spraying gold ore with a toxic substance. To prevent pollution, Earth Sciences had installed a reserve sump to catch any toxic runoff. An unexpected early thaw melted a snowbank, covering the ore heap. As a result, the reserve sump overflowed, dumping toxic waste into the Rito Seco Creek. The United States brought suit, alleging that Earth Sciences had violated pollution laws. Earth Sciences argued that it should not be held liable for an unintentional pollution accident. Is Earth Sciences correct? Explain. *United States v. Earth Sciences, Inc.*, 599 F.2d 368 (10th Cir. Ct.).

6. C.E. Stumpf & Sons, Inc., was formed to conduct a masonry and general contracting business. The corporation was owned in equal shares by Stumpf and his two sons, who had previously operated the same business as partners. Hostility between the two sons grew so extreme that one, Donald, ended contact with his family and was allowed no say in the operation of the business. After Donald's withdrawal from the business, he received no salary, dividends, or other revenue from the company. He brought suit seeking involuntary dissolution of the corporation. Should the court of appeals of California uphold the trial court's dissolution order? Why or why not? *Stumpf v. C.E. Stumpf & Sons, Inc.*, 120 Cal. Rptr. 671 (California).

PART 8
Case Study
Rare Earth, Inc. v. Hoorelbeke

United States District Court
Southern District of New York
401 F. Supp. 26

SUMMARY

Rare Earth, Inc., a rock band, instituted a lawsuit against Hoorelbeke to prevent him from performing under the name Rare Earth. The lawsuit had been approved by the directors at a special meeting. Since all shareholders were also directors, the meeting also qualified as a shareholders' meeting. Hoorelbeke, who was still a shareholder and a director of Rare Earth, Inc., had not been notified of the meeting. The other directors and shareholders had not notified Hoorelbeke because they had heard "rumors" that he'd resigned. Hoorelbeke argued that all actions taken at the meeting, including the decision to sue him were invalid. Accordingly, he asked the court to dismiss the case.

THE COURT'S OPINION: DISTRICT JUDGE CANNELLA

Rare Earth, Inc., is not, as one might surmise, an organization dedicated to environmental activism or the preservation of our natural resources. Rather, it is the corporate entity formed by a group of rock and roll musicians who publicly perform as "Rare Earth." From this group "comes the dissonant chord" of an intracorporate battle for control resulting from a schism among the band members....

It is undisputed that Peter Hoorelbeke served as a director and president, as well as a 200 share owner of Rare Earth, Inc. However, in mid-July the Bridges faction became aware (through the musical "grapevine") of Hoorelbeke's purported resignation as band member and as an officer and director of the corporation. Such knowledge did not derive from any written communication from Hoorelbeke to the corporation, but rather resulted from rumor, or, to use a legal term, hearsay. Thereafter, on July 12th, a directors' (or shareholders') meeting of Rare Earth, Inc. was convened in Los Angeles. Hoorelbeke was never notified of such meeting and did not attend; the Bridges faction acting upon "their sincere belief that Hoorelbeke had resigned [concluded that] there was no need to notify him of the meeting." At this July 12th meeting, it was decided that Bridges would replace Hoorelbeke as president of Rare Earth, Inc., and that the corporation would commence this action and retain counsel for its prosecution. As we will show...the actions taken on July 12th were improper.

Under Michigan law, "A director may resign by written notice to the corporation. The resignation is effective upon its receipt by the corporation or a subsequent time as set forth in the notice of resignation." Mich.Comp.Laws Ann. § 450.1505(2). An identical provision pertains with regard to the resignation of officers. Mich.Comp.Laws Ann. § 450.1535(3).

There is no evidence at bar of a written resignation transmitted by Hoorelbeke to the corporation and thus, as of the July 12th meeting, he remained a director, officer and shareholder of Rare Earth, Inc. This being so, the failure to notify Hoorelbeke of the meeting and his absence therefrom renders all actions taken by those present invalid and without effect.

With regard to directors' meetings, Michigan law requires that a "special meeting shall be held upon notice as prescribed in the bylaws" (Mich.Comp.Laws Ann. § 450.1521(2)) and that a "director is entitled to a notice which will give him ample time to attend the meeting." 7 Michigan Law & Practice Encyclopedia, Corporations § 273 at 230. The statutory requirement that the meeting be convened "upon notice" clearly was not met in the present case, as Hoorelbeke received no notice whatsoever. Thus, it is a settled matter of Michigan law that "where a written notice of the meeting of the board of directors is not given although required by either a statute or the corporate bylaws, any action taken by the meeting at which all the directors are not present is void." The import of the foregoing discussion is plain: the failure to notify Director Hoorelbeke of the July 12th meeting and his absence therefrom renders all action thereat invalid, including such action as was required to commence this suit either directly or through the appointment of Bridges as President.

If the July 12th meeting is deemed a shareholders' meeting, the actions taken thereat similarly must fail for noncompliance with the notice requirements contained in Mich. Comp. Laws Ann. § 450.1404(1) or with the consent provisions contained in § 450.1407.

"A corporation has been defined as a body of individuals united as a single separate entity. When corporate powers are vested in the shareholders or members, they repose in them collectively as a body and not as individuals. That is, individuals have no power to act as or for the corporation except at a corporate meeting called and conducted in accordance with law. 6 Callaghan. Michigan Civil Jurisprudence (1958)."

Simply put, as with the case of directors, actions taken at a shareholders' meeting which has not been properly noticed are invalid and without effect.

Thus, we conclude that the meeting of Rare Earth, Inc. which was conducted was a nullity for failure to comply with Michigan law.

QUESTIONS FOR ANALYSIS

1. Is it significant that the failure to notify Hoorelbeke stemmed from a rumor of his resignation, rather than from any official note that he had resigned? Explain.
2. In most situations directors do not have to be notified about board meetings. How can the facts in the Rare Earth case be distinguished from that general rule?
3. What is the legal effect of the directors' failure to notify Hoorelbeke of the directors' meeting?
4. The meeting in the Rare Earth case is characterized as both a directors' meeting and a shareholders' meeting. If it had been characterized simply as a shareholders' meeting, would the outcome have been any different? Explain.
5. Suppose Hoorelbeke had officially resigned as a Rare Earth director prior to this meeting. Under those circumstances, would the result in the case have been any different?
6. Is the suit instituted by Rare Earth, Inc., against Hoorelbeke a direct or a derivative suit? Explain.

PART 9
Emerging Trends and Issues

CHAPTER 39
Professional Legal Liability

OUTLINE

COMMENTARY

Cromwell decided to invest his life savings in Sarnoff Industries, a newly formed business engaged in developing a revolutionary compact disk player. The managers of Sarnoff hired the accounting firm of Windsor-Ogden to audit their records and to give them expert financial advice. Sarnoff told Windsor-Ogden that the audit and advice would be shared with all investors. Cromwell, however, was not actually named as a recipient of this information. Through serious miscalculations and a bungled audit, Windsor-Ogden failed to detect Sarnoff's poor financial condition. When Sarnoff collapsed, Cromwell lost his entire investment. Cromwell found it pointless to bring suit against Sarnoff because the firm had absolutely no assets following the collapse. Somewhat discouraged, but vaguely determined not to be the hapless victim in this financial misadventure, Cromwell sued the accounting firm of Windsor-Ogden. The accountants argued that Cromwell could not sue them because Sarnoff, not Cromwell, had been their client. Can the accountants escape the legal consequences of their bungling simply because the only party willing to bring suit against them is not their client? Issues like this are addressed by the law of professional liability.

OBJECTIVES

1. Differentiate between a certified public accountant and a public accountant.
2. Explain auditing, and identify the various types of auditing opinions that can be issued by auditors.
3. Distinguish between generally accepted accounting principles (GAAP) and generally accepted auditing standards (GAAS).
4. Recognize the duties that accountants owe to their clients, and indicate when third parties are protected from an accountant's misconduct.
5. Outline the registration requirements generally imposed by the state on architects.
6. Identify the ways in which architects can be held liable for injuries suffered by clients and third parties.
7. Determine the duties that attorneys owe clients in a variety of settings and situations.
8. State the standard of care used to judge a health care provider's performance of duties.
9. Contrast the locality rule with the national standard in determining a health care provider's liability.

39-1 THE LIABILITY OF ACCOUNTANTS

A **professional** is an individual who can perform a highly specialized task because of special abilities, education, experience, and knowledge. Business professionals are people who have gained experience and education in one or more areas of business. An accountant is a business professional who can plan, direct, and evaluate a client's financial affairs. Accountants do not simply keep financial records. Their job goes far beyond this relatively routine task. For this reason, among others, accountants are regulated by the state.

Accountant Registration

The regulation of accounting is part of the state's police power. The state's police power allows the state government to regulate various activities in order to promote the general health, safety, welfare, and morals of its citizens.

Types of Accountants There are many different types of accountants. Some accountants work only for one employer. Standard Oil, for example, employs hundreds of accountants to chart the financial fortunes of the corporation. Other accountants hire themselves out to work for a wide variety of different clients. Such accountants generally fall into two categories: certified public accountants and public accountants.

Certified public accountants (CPAs) have met certain age, character, education, experience, and testing requirements. These requirements are generally established by the state. For example, the state government may require CPAs to be at least 18 years old and of good moral character. The state may also require a bachelor's degree, two years of experience, and a passing score on a written examination which covers accounting, auditing, and other related subject areas. Accountants who meet these requirements would be entitled to call themselves certified public accountants.

Public accountants (PAs) are accountants who work for a variety of clients but are not certified. Frequently, states will not allow individuals to call themselves public accountants unless they have met certain requirements that are not as strict as the requirements laid down for CPAs.

The Effect of State Registration State registration requirements are designed to shield citizens against people who practice accounting without the education or experience necessary to do a competent job. The state cannot, however, go so far as to prevent someone from practicing accounting as a profession. The state can stop such individuals only from calling themselves CPAs, PAs, or any other title that might mislead a client into thinking the nonregistered accountant is registered.

The Accountant's Job

Accountants perform a number of functions for their clients. They may balance accounts, reconcile bank records with account books, handle the payroll, fill out income tax returns, and handle other tax matters. Another important job that falls to the accountant is the task of auditing.

Auditing An **audit** is an examination of the financial records of an organization to determine whether those records are a fair presentation of the actual financial health of the institution. Audits are normally conducted by an independent accountant, usually a CPA. The accountant, or **auditor,** handling the audit will go into a business or organization and examine its financial records. The objective of the audit is to see whether the financial records are an accurate reflection of the actual financial health of the institution. Generally, an auditor will present a formal opinion outlining a carefully evaluated perception of the institution's financial records. The auditor is not a guarantor or an insurer of the financial statements. Rather, the auditor renders an opinion as to the fairness of the financial statements and as to their adherence to generally accepted accounting principles (GAAP).

Accounting Principles An independent group known as the Financial Accounting Standards Board (FASB) has established **generally accepted accounting principles (GAAP).** The rules established by the FASB are followed by the American Institute of Certified Public Accountants (AICPA). The rules outline the procedures that accountants must use in accumulating financial data and in preparing financial statements. In general, the procedures facilitate the preparation of reports that are useful, understandable, reliable, verifiable, and comparable.

Auditing Standards The Auditing Standards Board of the AICPA has set up **generally accepted auditing standards (GAAS).** These auditing standards measure the quality of the performance of the auditing procedures.In short, then, the auditing standards explain how an auditor can determine whether proper accounting procedures have been used. In total, there are ten auditing standards. Three of these relate to the auditors, three relate to their work in the field, and four relate to the opinions that they issue.

Types of Opinions An auditor's opinions may be unqualified or qualified. Auditors may also issue adverse opinions and disclaimers.

1. **An Unqualified Opinion** When auditors conclude that the financial records of the company are an accurate reflection of the company's financial status, they will issue an **unqualified opinion.**
2. **Qualified Opinion** When auditors issue a **qualified opinion,** they are saying that as of a given date the books represent the company's financial health. However, auditors may "qualify" the opinion in one of two ways. One type of qualified opinion is the "subject to" opinion. When auditors issue a "subject to" opinion, they are stating that the books represent the company's financial health "subject to" some uncertainty, such as a pending lawsuit, which may affect the company in the future. The second type of qualified opinion is an "except for" opinion. Such an opinion indicates that the financial statements are an accurate reflection of the company's financial health "except for" some minor deviation from GAAP, not serious enough to warrant an adverse opinion.
3. **Adverse Opinion** An **adverse opinion** is rendered when the deviations from GAAP are so serious that an unqualified opinion is impossible and a qualified opinion is not justified. An adverse opinion would be rendered (1) if the financial statements do not fairly present the financial health of the organization, (2) if generally accepted accounting principles are consistently ignored, (3) if financial information has not been adequately disclosed, or (4) if there are major uncertainties which could have a serious impact on the organization and the auditor disagrees with management's presentation of those uncertainties.
4. **Disclaimer** A **disclaimer** declares that the auditor has decided not to give any opinion on the company's financial records. Generally, this situation occurs because the auditor has not had enough time to examine the books properly or was denied access to crucial records. An auditor might also issue a disclaimer if the books indicate that the organization exercised no control at all over the accounting process.

Ethical Rules The AICPA has also established a **Code of Professional Ethics,** which outlines rules that govern the ethical conduct of accountants. These rules are frequently used by the courts to determine whether an accountant has breached a duty to the client in nontechnical matters not covered by GAAP and GAAS. For example, the AICPA's code has established that accountants owe their clients a duty of confidentiality. This means that an accountant cannot reveal information about a client's business to anyone outside the accountant-client relationship unless authorized to do so by the client. Although this privilege does not extend to a court's request for information, it does cover most other situations. The ethical code also covers contingent fees,the independence of the auditor, promotional practices, operational practices, and quality reviews by peers.

Duties Owed to the Client

A client often hires an accountant to take care of all the client's financial affairs. Therefore, the client and the accountant have a contractual arrangement. This imposes a duty on the accountant to live up to the terms of that contract. If an accountant fails to fulfill the terms of the contract, the client could bring a breach of contract suit against the accountant. An accountant might also be liable to clients under common law for negligence and fraud.

Negligence The client has the right to expect the accountant to do a good job in whatever task has been assigned. From this right arises the accountant's duty of due care. The duty of due care means that the accountant must perform the job with the same skill and competence that a reasonable accounting professional would use in the same situation. Accountants failing to do so would be liable to the client for any losses that result from this negligence. How the reasonable accounting professional would handle a given situation would be determined by reference to GAAS and GAAP.

Fraud Accountants must act with the best interests of their clients at heart. If an accountant deliberately misrepresents the client's financial condition or in some way deliberately falsifies a report or audit, that accountant may be liable to that client for fraud. Accountants may also be liable for fraud if they compile a financial report or conduct an audit recklessly.

Liability to Third Parties

It is relatively clear that under common law an accountant can be held liable to some third parties who are damaged by a negligently prepared financial statement. Accountants are also liable to some third parties for deliberately fraudulent statements.

Negligence The right to bring suit for a negligently prepared financial statement will always extend to actually named third parties. Most states also extend this right to any limited classes of specifically foreseen third parties. A few states extend the right to bring suit protection to reasonably foreseeable classes of third parties.

1. **Actually Named Third Parties** If an accountant prepares a financial statement with the actual knowledge that the client is going to show the statement to a particular third party, then the accountant is clearly liable to that *known* third party. If, for example, the client tells the accountant that the statement is for Mr. X, then Mr. X can recover if he suffers actual financial loss due to the accountant's negligence.
2. **Specifically Foreseen Third Parties** Most states have extended this rule even further, holding that accountants are also liable to any limited class of third parties that is specifically foreseen when the financial statement is drawn up. Thus, an accountant who prepares a financial statement knowing that the client intends to show it to existing investors, would be liable to any investor in that limited class of *specifically foreseen* third parties. To recover from the accountant, the investors would have to rely on the statement and would have to suffer financial loss.

Table 39-1 ACCOUNTANT'S LIABILITY TO THIRD PARTIES UNDER COMMON LAW

Liability Theory	*Explanation*
Actually named third parties	When accountants prepare financial statements knowing that the client will show the statement to a named party, then those accountants will be liable to that known third party if through their negligence the third party is injured. Only a few states limit recovery to actually named third parties.
Specifically foreseen third parties	Accountants may also be liable to certain third parties for negligently prepared financial statements if those third parties are members of a limited class that is specifically foreseen when the financial statement is drawn up. Most states follow this theory.
Reasonably foreseeable third parties	Accountants may also be liable for negligently prepared financial statements, if those third parties can be reasonably foreseen as recipients of the statements. Only a few states extend recovery this far.

3. **Reasonably Foreseeable Third Parties** Some courts have extended the class of third parties who can recover to include those people who can be reasonably foreseen as relying on the statement. For instance, if it is reasonable for the accountant to foresee that the financial statement will be shown to bankers, suppliers, and potential investors, then the accountant is liable to anyone in any of these *reasonably foreseeable* classes of individuals. This would be true even though the class was not specifically mentioned when the accountant was hired by the client.

Fraud Since fraud involves a deliberate deception, the courts have no difficulty extending protection to a wide class of third parties. Thus, an accountant who prepares a fraudulent financial statement is liable to anyone who can be reasonably foreseen as relying on that statement.

In the opening commentary, Cromwell brought suit against the accounting firm of Windsor-Ogden when they failed to detect the poor financial health of Sarnoff Industries. Cromwell was an investor who lost his life savings when Sarnoff collapsed. Windsor-Ogden argued that Cromwell could not sue them because Sarnoff, not Cromwell, was their client. Under the named third-parties test, the accountants would be correct because Cromwell was not actually named as a recipient of the financial reports prepared by Windsor-Ogden. However, under the specifically foreseen rule, the accountants would be wrong because Cromwell is a member of a limited class of third parties that was specifically foreseen as a recipient of the information. Significantly, if Cromwell could show fraud it would not matter whether he was actually named as a recipient or simply the member of a specifically foreseen class. If fraud is involved, anyone who can be reasonably foreseenas a recipient of those reports could hold Windsor-Ogden liable for any actual loss caused by reliance on those reports.

Statutory Liability

Accountants may also be sued for violating statutory laws governing their activities. Such suits can arise under the Securities Act of 1933, the Securities Exchange Act of 1934, and various state laws.

The Securities Act of 1933 Under the Securities Act of 1933, the first time a corporation issues stock for sale it must file a registration statement (see Chapter 38). Such statements are prepared by accountants. The 1933 act allows purchasers who have lost money after buying corporate stock based on false or misleading registration statements to sue the accountant who prepared the statement.

The Securities and Exchange Act of 1934 A second federal law, the Securities and Exchange Act of 1934, also contains some provisions that affect accountants. These provisions are designed to prevent the fraudulent filing of various documents with the SEC and the fraudulent manipulation of the securities market. Both acts also contain provisions that impose criminal liability on accountants in some situations.

State Statutes In addition to these federal statutes, most states have enacted similar statutes regulating the activities of accountants as they relate to the sale of stock. State statutes which regulate the sale of stock are frequently referred to as "blue sky" laws because they are set up to stop the sale of securities that are as empty as several feet of blue sky.

39-2 THE LIABILITY OF OTHER PROFESSIONALS

In addition to accountants, two other frequently contacted business professionals are the architect and the attorney. Both are regulated by the state and both must avoid violating certain duties.

The Liability of Architects

An architect is a professional who plans the construction or alteration of a variety of structures from small, single-family dwellings to enormous skyscrapers. Generally, architects do not actually construct the building. However, they may often manage the construction according to their detailed plans.

State Regulation Under its police power, the state can regulate the conduct of architects. States often establish an agency that makes the rules which architects must follow to be officially recognized as professionals in their fieldof expertise. The state will usually establish age, character, education, experience, and testing requirements. Often a state will maintain a list of all architects officially registered as having met all these legal requirements.

Duties of the Architect Like any other professional, an architect owes a duty to exercise due care and skill in carrying out professional duties. This standard of care requires the architect to use the same methods, techniques, and procedures that any architect of ordinary skill would use in a similar situation. The standard does not demand that the architect's design be perfect or that the execution of the design be faultless. Architects can make mistakes, as long as those mistakes do not result from a failure to use appropriate skill and good judgment according to accepted professional standards.

Contractual Liability Sometimes the final version of a building differs from the original plan which existed when the contract was made. If the deviation is actually an error caused by the architect's failure to use due care and skill, then the architect may have to reimburse the client for any extra money spent to correct the error. This is known as the **cost of repair rule.** A different rule is followed if the design is so defective that the structure is unusable for its originally intended purpose. In such situations, the court may declare that the architect owes the client the difference between the market value of the building as it stands and the market value of the intended structure.

Tort Liability Unlike mistakes made by accountants, errors made by architects may injure people or damage property. If the architect has failed to exercise the appropriate standard of care and if, as a result, property is damaged or people are injured, then the architect may have to compensate the victims. Note, however, that the architect's mistake must cause injury or damage.

Architects Dunnewin and Shaeffer were hired to plan the new Camron-Monarchy Hotel to be located in downtown Indianapolis. Shaeffer failed to check the wiring diagrams submitted by the firm's electrical engineering department. Had he made the check, his inspection would have revealed several wiring defects that could easily cause a fire. The construction firm of O'Brien-Delmore, Inc., ignored the Dunnewin-Shaeffer diagrams and used their own plans. However, the O'Brien-Delmore plan contained the same error that the architects' plan had contained. An electrical fire caused by the error injured several people. Because the contractor had ignored the Dunnewin-Shaeffer plan, the architects were not held liable, despite their error.

The Liability of Attorneys

Next to the accountant, one of the most sought-after professionals by a business person is the attorney. An attorney is a professional because of expert knowledge, ability, and education in interpreting and applying the law. Attorneys advise their clients in a variety of different ways, all of which require good faith, loyalty, and the exercise of due care.

State Regulation Like accountants and architects, attorneys are regulated by the state's police power. Also like accountants and architects, attorneys are normally required to be of a certain age (usually 18), and to be of good moral character. They are required to possess a certain educational background and to pass a special examination, demonstrating minimum competency. Unlike architects and accountants, attorneys often do not have any experience requirements. This is true because usually architects and accountants are required to have only a bachelor's degree, whereas attorneys are required to have an advanced degree in law. This extra education usually takes three to four years beyond the bachelor's degree. The experience requirement of architects and accountants is generally only two years.

Duties of the Attorney The attorney has the duty to represent clients with good faith, loyalty, and due care. Usually, however, an attorney is not liable to a third party who is not a client.

1. **Good Faith** When a client hires an attorney, that client has the right to expect the attorney to act in good faith, which basically means to be honest. This right imposes upon the attorney the duty to act in the best interests of the client. In the absence of such good faith conduct, the attorney may face a lawsuit brought by the client and disciplinary action brought by the state.
2. **Loyalty** An attorney's duty is to protect the client and to make certain that the client receives advice and representation which is free of conflicting interests. Thus, an attorney cannot represent two clients on opposite sides of the same dispute, unless both sides have been completely informed of the dual representation and consent to it. Similarly, an attorney violates the duty of loyalty if advantage is taken of the client for personal profit.
3. **Due Care** Like all other professionals, an attorney owes a duty of due care to clients. This means that in giving legal advice, negotiating claims, litigating suits, making out wills, negotiating divorce settlements, and performing any number of other legal tasks, an attorney must exercise the same skill and care that would be expected of other attorneys in the same situation. Again, as in the case of accountants and architects, attorneys are not held to a standard of perfection. This means that attorneys are allowed to make errors. Those errors should not result, however, from a failure to perform the way a competent attorney is expected to perform.

Third-Party Liability In contrast to accountants and architects, attorneys are rarely held liable to third parties because the attorney's responsibilities are tied closely with the interests of that client and that client alone.

Giordano hired the Mirkov Construction Company to pave his driveway. Three days after the job was finished, the driveway began to shift and buckle. When Giordano called Mirkov, the company refused to take any responsibility. Unable to get any satisfaction through normal channels, Giordano contacted Harrigan, a local attorney. Harrigan advised Giordano not to pay Mirkov pending a resolution of the dispute. Eventually the matter was settled in Mirkov's favor. Mirkov then sued Harrigan for advising Giordano not to pay his bill. The court ruled that Mirkov could not hold Harrigan liable for the advice she had given Giordano, even though that advice had proved to be incorrect, because she had acted in good faith and with due care.

39-3 THE LIABILITY OF HEALTH CARE PROVIDERS

Health care providers are professionals who possess the specialized knowledge, abilities, education, and experience that make it possible for them to answer some aspect of a patient's health care needs. Some business people must deal with health care providers on a daily basis. Such contact is routine for hospital administrators, risk management experts, pharmaceutical salespeople, hospital accountants, insurance adjusters, and biomedical equipment salespeople. Even individuals who do not deal regularly with health care providers in the business world may one day have to deal with them as patients. Knowledge of the liability of such professionals may be helpful in these situations.

Professional Status

It should be obvious that physicians are professionals since they must possess the specialized knowledge, abilities, education, and experience needed to perform their jobs. However, dentists, podiatrists, chiropractors, nurses, nurse practitioners, nurse technicians, radiologic technologists, respiratory therapists, and laboratory technicians are also considered health care professionals. All these professions are regulated by the state. In addition, most are regulated by independent professional organizations such as the Joint Commission on the Accreditation of Hospitals (JCAH).

Health Care Liability

Unlike accountants, architects, and attorneys, health care professionals frequently must physically touch their patients. This physical touching can involve routine tests and examinations as well as dangerous and painful procedures. To avoid liability for the intentional tort of battery, health care providers must frequently obtain the patient's consent. In addition to intentional torts, health care providers might open themselves to charges of negligence if they do not follow the appropriate standard of care.

Consent Patients who undergo tests and treatment have the right to know about those procedures and the right to refuse to undergo them if they so desire. This imposes a duty on the health care professional to seek the patient's consent. Consent takes two forms: general consent and informed consent.

1. **General Consent** Upon entering a hospital, a patient automatically gives **general consent** for the routine tests and procedures that are needed for diagnosis and treatment. Although such consent is implied in the situation, many hospitals wisely require patients to sign general consent forms (see Figure 39-1).
2. **Informed Consent** When a diagnostic test or a procedure will be dangerous or painful, the treating physician must obtain the patient's **informed consent.** This means the physician must tell the patient in advance about the procedure and the risks involved. Informed consent must be in writing on a form that is signed by the patient and witnessed by a third party. Generally, such a written consent form will be considered valid by the court and will prevent any suit based on battery unless the patient can prove a lack of understanding of the information on the form or a deliberate misrepresentation as to its content.

Negligence The health care provider must act with the same skill, care, and level of knowledge that a reasonable health care provider would display in a similar situation. Determining how the reasonable health care professional would act in a given situation can be determined in several ways.

CONSENT UPON ADMISSION TO HOSPITAL

Patient ______________________ Date __________ a.m. ____ p.m. ____

(or ______________________ for ______________________)
knowing that I, or the patient (am) (is) suffering from an illness requiring hospital care do hereby voluntarily consent to such hospital care requiring an operation, diagnostic tests or therapeutic treatment by Dr. ______________________,
his/her assistant or his/her designee or as necessary according to his/her judgment.

I also recognize that during the course of my operation, tests, or therapy unforeseen conditions may necessitate additional or different procedures and I am aware that inasmuch as the practice of medicine and surgery is not an exact science, there have been no guarantees made to me as the result of treatments or examinations to be performed in this hospital.

I have read the above statements and I certify that I understand them.

______________________ ______________________

Witness Signature of Patient

Figure 39-1 Many hospitals today require patients to sign general consent forms, like this one, upon admission.

1. **Policy and Procedure Manual** One way to determine whether a health care provider has acted appropriately in a given situation is to refer to the hospital's policy and procedure manual. When professionals follow the standard policies and procedures as written in the manual, they are performing as any reasonable professional would, unless the procedure in the manual can be shown to be out of date or incompetently written.
2. **Similar Locality Rule** If a hospital's manual does not address a particular issue, if the manual is outdated, or if the procedure is incompetently written, the court may judge performance by determining how the same procedure is performed at another hospital located in a similar locality. Under the **similar locality rule,** rural hospitals are compared to other rural hospitals, urban hospitals to urban hospitals, and suburban hospitals to suburban hospitals.
3. **National Standard** Courts today are moving toward a national standard. Under the **national standard** a nurse in metropolitan New York can be held to the same standard of care as one who practices in suburban St. Louis or rural Kansas. Courts who adhere to the national standard feel that mass communication has made it possible for health care providers to keep up to date with the latest trends regardless of where they practice.

Expert Testimony Since many of the tasks performed by the health care provider are highly specialized, determining how the professional should act often requires expert testimony. However, expert testimony is not required if the action under examination is within the common knowledge of all people.

Nurse Ferratti was called away from Edmonson's room by another nurse. Edmonson was sedated, but restless. He was thrashing about and had attempted to leave the bed several times. Despite this, Ferratti left him alone, failing to raise the siderails or restrain Edmonson in any way. While Ferratti was absent, Edmonson tried to get out of bed. He fell and broke his leg. At Ferratti's negligence trial, the judge ruled that no expert testimony was needed to measure Ferratti's standard of care. The judge felt that the issue of whether a sedated and restless patient should be left unsupervised and unrestrained was well within the common knowledge of the jurors.

SUMMARY

39-1. Accountants are business professionals who can plan, direct, and evaluate the complex financial affairs of their clients. The most common types of accountants are certified public accountants and public accountants. Accountants must follow generally accepted accounting principles. Auditors must follow generally accepted auditing standards. They must also follow the Code of Professional Ethics of the AICPA. Accountants can be liable to both their clients and to third parties.

39-2. Both architects and attorneys are considered professionals and are regulated by the state. Architects may find themselves liable to clients and to third parties whereas attorneys are generally responsible to their clients alone. Both architects and attorneys must exercise due care and skill in carrying out their professional duties.

39-3. The term *health care provider* includes not only physicians but also dentists, chiropractors, podiatrists, nurses, nurse practitioners, nurse technicians, radiologic technologists, respiratory therapists, and laboratory technicians. Like other professionals, the health care provider must act with the same skill, care, and level of knowledge that a reasonable health care professional would display in a similar situation.

Understanding Key Legal Terms

adverse opinion (p. 556)
audit (p. 555)
auditor (p. 555)
certified public accountant (CPA) (p. 554)
Code of Professional Ethics (p. 556)
cost of repair rule (p. 560)
disclaimer (p. 556)
general consent (p. 562)
generally accepted accounting principles (GAAP) (p. 555)
generally accepted auditing standards (GAAS) (p. 555)
informed consent (p. 562)
national standard (p. 563)
professional (p. 554)
public accountant (PA) (p. 555)
qualified opinion (p. 556)
similar locality rule (p. 563)
unqualified opinion (p. 556)

Questions for Discussion and Review

1. How does a certified public accountant differ from a public accountant?
2. What does an audit involve, and what types of opinions can be issued by auditors?
3. Differentiate between generally accepted auditing standards (GAAS) and generally accepted accounting principles (GAAP).
4. Identify the duties that an accountant owes to the client, and explain when a third party is protected from an accountant's negligence or fraud.
5. Describe the types of things that a state generally regulates in determining the qualifications of an architect.
6. Contrast the contractual liability with the tort liability of an architect.
7. List the duties that an attorney owes to a client.
8. Discuss an attorney's liability to third parties who are not clients.
9. Explain the standard of care used to measure a health care provider's performance on the job.
10. In what way does the similar locality rule differ from the national standard?

Analyzing Cases

1. The Consolidata Services Company (CDS) was established to provide small businesses with payroll services. All CDS clients were required to provide CDS with an advance deposit equal to the amount of one payroll. When CDS got into a cash flow problem, it tapped some of this deposit money to cover its own debts. Eventually, the accounting firm of Alexander Grant, which had been hired by CDS to advise it on taxes and on other financial matters, discovered that the deposit account was $150,000 short. CDS assured Alexander Grant that it was devising a plan to cover the missing $150,000. Accordingly, CDS asked Alexander Grant not to reveal the deficit. Nevertheless, Alexander Grant, which had several clients using the CDS payroll services, informed those clients and other nonclients of CDS's problem. Was Alexander Grant correct in revealing the information? What guidelines will the court use to answer this question? Explain. *Wagenheim v. Alexander Grant and Co.,* 482 N.E.2d 955 (Ohio).
2. Burke, an energy tycoon, hired the accounting firm of Arthur Young and Company to audit several of his operations. The Securities and Exchange Commission (SEC) brought an action against Burke for fraud and for failure to meet certain SEC reporting requirements. The SEC also named Arthur Young as a defendant, claiming that the accounting firm should have discovered the fraud. Arthur Young argued that it had followed generally accepted auditing standards (GAAS) when it had audited Burke. The accounting firm concluded that this strict adherence to GAAS immunized it from liability under securities law. The SEC argued that Arthur Young should have done more to discover the fraud than what was required under GAAS. Is the SEC correct? Explain? *Securities and Exchange Commission v. Arthur Young and Company,* 590 F.2d 785 (9th Cir. Ct.).
3. Hutchins and O'Neil, as general partners in the Haddon View Investment Co., became limited partners in Car Wash Investments. The general partner in Car Wash was the Minit Man Development Company. Coopers and Lybrand were accountants who handled the accounting work for both

Minit Man and Car Wash. They performed audits and prepared financial statements which allegedly revealed two healthy companies. Nevertheless, both Car Wash and Minit Man went out of business. As a result, Hutchins and O'Neil lost a total of $252,000. They sued Coopers and Lybrand alleging malpractice, breach of contract, concealment, fraud, and deceit in the accountant's work for Car Wash and Minit Man. Coopers and Lybrand argued that Hutchins and O'Neil could not sue them because Car Wash and Minit Man were their clients, not Hutchins and O'Neil. Are the accountants correct? *Haddon View Investment Co. v. Coopers and Lybrand,* 436 N.E.2d 212 (Ohio).

4. Bainbridge hired the architectural firm of Seymour, Shaefer, and Lashutka to draw up plans for the alteration of Bainbridge's office building in Albuquerque, New Mexico. The plans called for the removal of the paneling in parts of the building and its replacement with Maxwell-Plus,a new, more durable material. Maxwell-Plus was specifically recommended by the architects as the best product on the market. From the beginning, the contractor had difficulty with the installation of Maxwell-Plus. In addition, two months after the work was completed, the new paneling began to deteriorate rapidly. Investigation indicated that Seymour, Shaefer, and Lashutka had failed to consider the dry, arid climate of Albuquerque for which Maxwell-Plus was totally unsuitable. Bainbridge had to have the paneling replaced at a cost of $112,532. Subsequently, he sued the architects. Seymour, Shaefer, and Lashutka argued that they were not liable to Bainbridge because the total value of the building had not been altered by their alleged error. Are the architects correct? Explain.

5. Newsome, an attorney at law, represented Landabaugh in her divorce proceedings. As part of the settlement, Newsome arranged to have Landa-baugh's former husband pay her $1,500 per month alimony. Newsome did not arrange for any child support for Landabaugh's three minor children. Six months later Landabaugh remarried and discovered under the agreement that her alimony payments stopped. She also found out that the payments would have continued after her remarriage had they been characterized as child support payments. Landabaugh and her mother joined as plaintiffs in a negligence suit against Newsome. What duties may have been violated by Newsome? What standard of care will be used to judge his conduct? Is the mother a proper party in this lawsuit? Why or why not?

CHAPTER 40
Computer Law

OUTLINE

COMMENTARY

Strohon marketed a set of silicon chips programmed to be used with any Pac-Man video game. Strohon's package, known as Cute-See, completely changed the visual display on the game screen using none of the Pac-Man characters. The computer program, however, was copied directly from the Pac-Man chips. Midway, which owned the Pac-Man copyright, sued Strohon for violating its copyright. Strohon argued that no violation had occurred because his on-screen characters were completely different from the Pac-Man characters. Midway contended that the computer program itself was protected and that Strohon's copying the program was the real copyright violation. Who is correct? The Pac-Man protector? Or the Cute-See copier? Questions like this are addressed by computer law.

OBJECTIVES

1. Recognize the difference between computer hardware and computer software.
2. Judge whether a particular computer program would be protected by labeling it a trade secret.
3. Conclude in a given case whether a particular computer program would be granted patent protection.
4. Determine when the copyright of a computer program has been violated.
5. Decide whether a particular computer-related contract is a sale-of-goods contract or a service contract.
6. Explain how the use of computers to invade privacy rights can be curbed by common law, constitutional law, and statutory law.
7. Outline the various approaches the states have taken in legislation designed to combat computer crime.
8. Name the major provisions of the Counterfeit Access Device and Computer Fraud and Abuse Act and those of the Electronic Funds Transfer Act.

40-1 THE LAW AND THE COMPUTER

Despite the title of this chapter, there really is no such thing as computer law. Computer law—such as it is—has developed by borrowing principles from contract law, tort law, criminal law, and property law. When enough of these principles have been customized to apply to computers, computer law will become a separate legal entity. Until then, we must examine several areas of the law, and apply general principles to the peculiarities created by new computer technology. When discussing computer law, remember that a computer system consists of two distinct components. These components are referred to as *computer hardware* and *computer software.*

Computer Hardware

The term **computer hardware** refers to the actual device known as a computer and its components. The keyboard, screen, disk drive, and the printer, for example, would all be considered computer hardware. If a legal question involves hardware, the answer is usually rather straightforward since computer hardware is essentially electronic equipment. Consequently, a contract for the purchase of a laser printer for use with a personal computer is much the same as a contract for the purchase of a VCR for use with a television set.

Computer Software

The term **computer software** refers to the card, tape, disk, or silicon chip that contains the computer program. The **computer program** consists of the instructions that tell the hardware what to do and when to do it. If a legal question involves software, the answer is often difficult. This difficulty arises because of the peculiar nature of computer software. The software itself is a tangible piece of property, but the particular program on the software is intangible intellectual property. Moreover, it is generally the program that gives the software its inherent value. Nevertheless, the two are often spoken of as one, and the courts are frequently confused about how to deal with this unique type of property. The problem is made worse when hardware and software are sold together as a package. Still, it is the software portion of the package that creates a problem for the courts. For this reason, most of this chapter will focus on the legal questions surrounding computer software. However, when computer hardware is involved and when a **computer package**—hardware plus software—is involved, they will be specifically mentioned. The first problem facing the courts is how to determine ownership rights to the software and to the program that makes the software so valuable.

40-2 THE OWNERSHIP OF A COMPUTER PROGRAM

In the early days of the huge, primitive computers such as ENIAC, BINAC, and UNIVAC, nobody worried about who owned a computer program. Computers were so rare and programming so difficult that few people would have any use for a computer program, even if they could get their hands on one. Today all that has changed. Microcomputer technology has made it possible for every business and many households to own and operate their own personal computers. Consequently, the need to protect the ownership of a computer program has become crucial. Ownership can be protected in four ways: claiming trade secret status, marketing through box-top licenses, obtaining a patent, or securing a copyright.

Trade Secret Protection

A **trade secret** is a plan, process, or device used in a business and known only to employees who need to know that secret to carry out their jobs. Generally, a trade secret is kept confidential because it gives an economic and competitive advantage to the company that owns and uses the secret. With most operations, a business can maintain secrecy by requiring employees to sign secrecy agreements as part of their employment contract. Similarly, customers who are allowed to use a particular process, plan, or formula, generally do so under strict licensing agreements.

Computer Programs Denied Trade Secret Status Computer programs that have been transferred to software and then placed on the open market for wide distribution cannot claim trade secret status. Software which is widely distributed can be easily copied. Thus, it becomes difficult to demonstrate that the company has taken extensive measures to protect the information on the software. Moreover, since the object of placing the software on the open market is to sell it to as many people as possible, the seller must make the software readily available in bookstores and video outlets. This ready availability on the open market defeats the whole trade secret concept. In fact, calling a program a trade secret would be like selling a record album but labeling the lyrics a trade secret. No one would believe that something sold so openly could seriously be considered secret.

Computer Programs Granted Trade Secret Status Trade secret status is available to those companies which distribute their software on a limited, highly selective basis. For example, a computer company that produces and sells a program used to control the distribution of drugs by pharmaceutical firms might be able to call that program a trade secret. Such a company would not actually sell the program to the pharmaceutical firm, but would instead allow the firm to use the program via a **licensing agreement.** A licensing agreement is made when the producer of a product, in this case a computer program, allows a purchaser to use the product only if the purchaser agrees to respect the producer's desire for secrecy. In this situation, in order to use the program the pharmaceutical company would have to agree to respect the computer company's desire for secrecy. In this type of highly selective, strictly controlled transaction, trade secret status works. However, once a company starts to mass-market software, it has lost the right to control the use of the program simply by labeling it a trade secret.

Box-Top License Protection

To protect software products that are distributed in the mass market, some companies use **box-top licenses.** Box-top licenses are generally placed on the software box within the transparent wrapper. The license limits the buyer's right to copy the program, to reveal the contents of the program, and to allow others to use the program. Some legal experts doubt the legality of the box-top license. Under principles of contract law, the inability of buyers to negotiate terms seriously limits their ability to fully consent to the arrangement. There is also some concern about whether the terms are reasonable because buyers give up most of their rights and receive little or nothing in return.

Patent Protection

A *patent* is a property right granted by the federal government to an inventor. A patent gives the inventor the exclusive right to make, use, and sell that invention for a period of years. (See Chapter 19.) To qualify for a patent, an invention must meet two requirements. First, the invention must be a device. Second, that device must consist of some nonobvious, new, and useful feature not known or understood before the invention of this particular device.

The Device Requirement The word **device** has broad application in patent law. The courts have held that a device may be a process, an article of manufacture, or some other object. In contrast, such things as laws of nature, natural phenomena, and abstract ideas are not considered devices and cannot, therefore, be patented. Mathematical formulas are also not considered patentable because they are actually laws of nature. Since many computer programs are based on mathematical formulas or abstract ideas, programs standing alone have so far been declared ineligible for patent protection. On the other hand, if a program is only one part of a larger, more conventional process, then the courts are more willing to allow patent protection for the whole process.

Scientists and engineers at Vasquez-Orlando, Inc., developed a new process for mass producing, synthetic industrial diamonds. The new process allowed Vasquez-Orlando to produce a better-quality diamond at about half the cost of their closest competitors. Part of their success was due to the use of lasers in the process. However, the lasers had to be timed so precisely that each one was controlled by a computer following the directions of a computer program. This portion of the process was only about one-fourth of the entire operation, the rest of which was relatively conventional. The patent examiner denied Vasquez-Orlando's patent application because part of the process involved an unpatentable computer program. A federal court reversed the refusal because the process itself was new and could be patented. The use of the program was only one part of that process.

Usefulness, Novelty, and Nonobviousness The objective of patent law is to encourage inventiveness and to promote progress for the benefit of all society. Thus, a device, to be patentable, must be useful. For this reason, many processes involving computer programs would pass the usefulness test. Passing the usefulness test alone, however, is not enough to qualify for a patent. The new invention must also be novel and nonobvious. To pass the novelty test, the new device or process must be original. Copying someone else's innovation, even unintentionally, will disqualify an invention from patent eligibility. Similarly, to pass the nonobviousness test, the changes or improvements must not be obvious to a person of ordinary skill in the field. If the changes are obvious, then a patent will not be issued. These last two areas would make it difficult for many computer programs to be patentable.

Copyright Protection

Copyrights are intangible-property rights granted by federal statute to authors or originators of literary, musical, or artistic productions. They give to their owners the exclusive right to reproduce, publish, and sell their work for a specific time period. Copyright protection can be secured only for a work fixed in a tangible medium of expression. However, the law extends this protection to include audiovisual displays. While the copyright law does not specifically mention the audiovisual displays produced on a computer screen, the courts have held that such displays are protected. However, the computer program itself was not protected until a 1980 amendment to the copyright act.

The Computer Software Copyright Act of 1980 Congress amended the Copyright Reform Act of 1976 with the Computer Software Copyright Act of 1980. The new act includes computer programs among "writings" to which exclusive rights can be granted. The act defines a computer program as "a set of statements or instructions to be used directly or indirectly in a computer in order to bring about a certain act."

Copyright Infringement Under the amendments to the copyright act, it is not an infringement for the owner of software to make another copy of that software provided that its duplication is essential in the use of a particular computer. However, it would be an infringement to copy the programming of a particular software item, to change the name or a few incidentals, and then to market the copy as an original software package.

In the opening commentary, Strohon copied the Pac-Man program directly from the Pac-Man software. In an attempt to protect himself, he altered the visual display, quickened the pace of the game, and changed the name to Cute-See. Despite these changes, Strohon had violated Midway's copyright interest in the Pac-Man game. Under terms of the Computer Software Copyright Act of 1980, computer programs can be copyrighted.

Although the type of open piracy described in this example is easy to detect, not all copying is quite this obvious. When the copying is more subtle, courts use the substantial similarity test.

The Substantial Similarity Standard The test for determining whether a second work has violated a copyrighted work's integrity does not require absolute word-for-word reproduction. Rather, the courts rely on a **substantial similarity test.** This test asks the following question. Are the two works so like one another that an ordinary reasonable observer would have no recourse other than to conclude that the second was copied from the first? It is important to note that the test uses the ordinary reasonable observer. Although they have different ways of applying this test, most courts hold that this "ordinary

Table 40-1 OWNERSHIP RIGHTS IN COMPUTER PROGRAMS

Protection Device	*Extent of Protection*
Trade secret protection	Trade secret status is available for programs and software that is distributed on a limited, highly selective basis. Licensing agreements are used to protect the owners. Computer programs transferred to software and then put on the open market are not protected by trade secret status.
Box-top license protection	Box-top licenses protect software products that are mass-marketed. Box-top licenses are so-called because they are placed on the software box itself. The license limits the buyer's right to copy the program, to reveal its contents, and to allow others to use it. Some doubts exist as to the legality of box-top licenses.
Patent protection	Computer programs standing alone cannot be patented. However, if a program is part of a larger, more conventional process, the whole process can be patented if it meets the requirements of usefulness, novelty, and nonobviousness.
Copyright protection	The Computer Software Copyright Act of 1980 includes computer programs among the "writings" that can be copyrighted. Audiovisual displays produced on a computer screen by a computer program can also be copyrighted. This copyright would protect the visual display, even if the program producing the display is different from the original program.

reasonable person" is a nonexpert, rather than a professional trained in the art of detecting such piracy. Such a standard poses no difficulty when dealing with conventional works. Passages can be lined up and read to demonstrate substantial similarity as can the entire work. The same is not true of computer software. Consequently, we can expect that courts may be forced to move away from nonexpert observations and move into the use of professional witnesses to determine copyright infringement in computer software cases.

40-3 CONTRACT LAW AND THE COMPUTER

The unique relationship between computer hardware and computer software has caused some interesting problems in contract law. One question facing the courts is whether a contract involving a computer qualifies as a sale-of-goods contract or a service contract. The difference is significant for a variety of reasons. First, if a contract involves a sale of goods, it is governed by the Uniform Commercial Code. (See Chapter 14.) This imposes certain rules that would differ from those applied to service contracts. Second, the statute of limitations is often different for different types of contracts. Thus, whether a contract is a sales or service contract may mean the difference between going to trial and going home after an early dismissal.

Computer Hardware Contracts

A contract for the sale of a computer itself would be considered a sale-of-goods contract. If an individual were to purchase a keyboard, terminal, disk drive, and printer together or separately, that purchase would be a sale-of-goods contract. This would mean that the UCC and its provisions would apply to any dispute that might arise as to that contract.

Computer Software Contracts

Software contracts are not as easily classified. Software can be marketed in three ways. The method of marketing will often determine the nature of the contract and, as a result, the law applicable to the contract.

Software Packages One way for software to be marketed is for the seller to place that software on the open market and allow consumers to purchase it for their own uses. The software is usually preprogrammed to perform a particular function. Such software packages are generally subject to the UCC as a sale-of-goods contract.

Combination Packages Another way software can be marketed is along with the hardware. For example, a company may contract with a computer firm to install its latest computer and to write a series of specialized programs to handle the firm's business. The computer firm would then write customized programs for that company's billing process, payroll records, inventory control, tax payments, and so on. In most cases, the courts have characterized such combination contracts as a sale of goods because the program phase of the arrangement is secondary to the equipment phase.

Customized Program Contracts The final type of computer contract is the one in which a company hires an individual programmer to come into its plant or office and create a unique program designed for that organization alone. Since the contract is primarily service-oriented, it is not characterized as a sales contract but rather as a service contract.

The Culver City Red Cross was having some difficulty keeping track of the distribution of its blood products and maintaining up-to-date records of its blood donors. To solve these problems, the Red Cross took two steps. First, it purchased a Hewlitt-Packard computer. This contract involved only hardware and was, therefore, a sale-of-goods contract. Second, the Red Cross hired Lykins to write a program for blood products distribution and blood donor classification. This contract would be a service contract alone. Had the Red Cross used Hewlitt-Packard people to program the computer, the contract would have been a combination package and, therefore, subject to the UCC as a contract for the sale of goods.

40-4 PRIVACY LAW AND THE COMPUTERS

Computers are capable of storing an enormous amount of information about a vast number of people in very little space. Even though this is a highly effi cient means of keeping records, it also represents a growing threat to the legally protected right of privacy. Privacy rights can be violated when the wrong people gain access to computer records that are supposed to remain secret, when unnecessary information is recorded and stored by an organization, when inaccurate information is kept on file, or when private information is revealed to the public without appropriate authorization. Fortunately, many legal safeguards exist to protect privacy rights. These safeguards are found in common law, in constitutional law, and in statutory law.

Common Law Protection

The common law tort of invasion of privacy is grounded in the people's right to be left alone. Since everyone in our society has the right to be left alone, everyone else has the duty not to violate that right. The right of privacy actually protects two freedoms: (1) freedom from undesired publicity and (2) freedom from unwelcome interference in private matters. Computers can be used to violate both of these freedoms. For example, when one institution reveals a computer-generated list of names to another institution, it has, in effect, made a private record public, thus violating the first aspect of privacy. Similarly, when an unauthorized individual invades a computer system to obtain information on a person's financial situation, employment history, or medical condition, the invader has intruded into a private matter and has, thus, violated the second aspect of the right to privacy.

Constitutional Law Protection

U.S. Const., Articles IV–V **(see pp. 603–604.)**

The U.S. Constitution protects people from governmental intrusion into their private lives. This right to privacy is implied by several provisions in the Constitution. These provisions include the right to be free from an unwarranted search and seizure (Amendment 4) and the right to be free from forced self-incrimination (Amendment 5). Note, however, that the right to privacy established by the Constitution protects the people only from unreasonable governmental intrusions into private matters. It does not apply to nongovernmental parties who perform the same types of intrusive activities. Note also that the Constitution does not prevent the government from gathering information on its citizens if there is a legitimate reason for gathering that information and if reasonable precautions are taken to guard the information.

Statutory Law Protection

Two important federal statutes designed to protect privacy include the Fair Credit Reporting Act and the Right to Financial Privacy Act.

The Fair Credit Reporting Act The Fair Credit Reporting Act of 1970 (see Chapter 18) involves records kept by credit bureaus, most of which now use computers to store data on consumers. Credit reports, by their very nature, include personal information that can be issued to businesses, insurance companies, banks and employers. Under the act, credit bureaus must, on request, inform people about the nature of the information that is in their file. The act also gives people the right to change any inaccurate information found in the file. The credit bu-reau is also responsible for sending notices to businesses and others who have received reports containing the inaccurate data.

The Right to Financial Privacy Act The Right to Financial Privacy Act of 1978 forbids financial institutions from opening customer records, most of which are kept in computer files, to the government without appropriate authorization from the customer or without an official court order of some sort. In addition, if the government does ask for a client's financial information, the institution must inform the client about the request. The client then has the right to contest the request. Naturally, none of this stops either the government or the financial institution itself from investigating allegations of illegal conduct on the part of the client.

40-5 CRIME AND THE COMPUTER

Like most inventions, the computer has improved our way of life. On the negative side, however, it has also introduced new ways of committing crimes. A computer can be used to commit fraud, to steal information, to invade privacy, to destroy records, and to embezzle funds. Many states have enacted legislation to combat these and other computer-related offenses. The federal government has also attempted to deal with the issue by passing the Counterfeit Access Device and Computer Fraud and Abuse Act in 1984.

Computer Crime in the States

Some of the problems created by computer crime are not difficult to solve. Most states have not found it difficult to label computer hardware and software as the type of property that can be stolen. Some states simply use their traditional definitions of property to cover the theft of a computer chip, disk, tape, or card even though it is the program that the thief is really after. In such cases, expert testimony is generally required to demonstrate the value of the property. Other states have created the new category of "intellectual property" to cover such instances. **Intellectual property** includes data, programs, software, computer material, and any confidential information in any form which is stored in or used by a computer. A different type of problem arises when someone uses a computer to commit a crime. States have taken many different approaches in this area. Three common approaches are detailed here.

Computer Trespass One approach used by some states is to create a single, general offense called *computer trespass*. Washington, for example, has defined **computer trespass** as gaining access to a computer with the intent to commit a crime. In effect, in one single stroke, Washington has incorporated the rest of its criminal code into this one crime making it an offense to use a computer to commit any other crime in the code. Thus, the Washington code sections on fraud, embezzlement, blackmail, and theft are all a part of this one crime known as computer trespass.

Borowsky worked as a teller at the Watanabe Financial Bank. As such, he had direct computer access to the savings and checking accounts of all the bank's customers. Unknown to his supervisor, Borowsky began to transfer five cents out of every customer's account and place that money in his own account. After six months of these small undetected transfers, Borowsky had a bank account worth over $120,000. Borowsky was prosecuted under the computer trespass statute in his state. The statute made it a crime to use a computer to commit a crime. The unauthorized transfer of $120,000 was clearly a crime under the state statute prohibiting theft. Borowsky was convicted.

Computer Fraud A second approach is to create a specifically named crime known as computer fraud. **Computer fraud** makes it unlawful to obtain money, property, or services through fraudulent use of a computer. Such use would include adding, deleting, or altering a computer program or data. Both Louisiana and Mississippi use this approach.

McLanahan was assistant director of the computer department at Mazaroft Memorial Hospital. In this capacity, he had access to the computerized billing process. On one occasion, because he was short of funds, he decided to eliminate his hospital bills by accessing his account through the computer and deleting the balance he owed to the hospital. Surprised at how easy it was to alter the billing records undetected, he got into the habit of erasing bills that should have gone to his family and friends. After one year of this practice, McLanahan was caught when one of the beneficiaries of his scheme thanked a hospital administrator for his "free" operation. Although McLanahan never directly stole anything, as Borowsky did in the last case, he was prosecuted, tried, and convicted under the state's computer fraud statute making it an offense to delete or alter any computer program or data.

Computer-Related Crimes A third technique is to develop a list of individually written computer-related crimes. Connecticut, for example, has created five separate computer offenses including: unauthorized access to a computer system, theft of computer services, interruption of computer services, misuse of computer information, and destruction of computer equipment. This third approach allows the creation of crimes that are tied to the type of activity peculiar to the computer. One such crime is known as unauthorized access.

Tutko and Chernay purchased a new modem for their home computer. This device permitted them to use the telephone to connect their computer to any public access computer in the country. They then began to explore the data stored in different computer systems scattered throughout the country. In this way, they learned some highly secretive information about people and institutions that should have been kept secret. Although neither Tutko nor Chernay stole or altered anything, they were prosecuted under a computer access statute which made it a crime to gain access to any computers without appropriate authorization.

In the case above, Tutko and Chernay engaged in a process known as *joyriding*. States are beginning to clamp down on these joyriders, or "hackers," by passing statutes which forbid the unauthorized entry into a computer system.

Table 40-2 COMPUTER CRIME STATUTES IN THE STATES

The Crime	*Explanation*
Computer trespass	Computer trespass is defined as gaining access to a computer with the intent to commit a crime. This technique incorporates a state's entire criminal code into one crime, making it an offense to use a computer to commit any other crime in the code.
Computer fraud	Computer fraud makes it unlawful to obtain money, property, or services through fraudulent use of a computer. Such use would include adding, deleting, or altering a computer program or computer data.
Computer-related crimes	Computer-related crime involves making a long list of individually written computer-related crimes such as unauthorized access to a computer system, theft of computer service, interruption of computer services, misuse of computer information, and destruction of computer equipment.

Federal Computer Crime Legislation

Like state governments, the federal government has also begun to deal with computer-related crime. In general, the federal government has taken two approaches to the problem. First, it has made use of some existing criminal statutes and extended their interpretation to include crimes committed with a computer. Secondly, the federal government has enacted legislation specifically targeted at computer-related crimes. Two of the most prominent computer crime statutes are the Counterfeit Access Device and Computer Fraud and Abuse Act and the Electronic Funds Transfer Act.

Existing Criminal Law Some federal criminal statutes that do not specifically mention computers can still be used, in certain circumstances, to prosecute computer criminals. Chief among these existing statutes are those which prohibit fraud carried out by using the U.S. mail (known as **mail fraud**) or by using the telephone or some other electronic communication device (known as **wire fraud**).

Kelly and Palmer made extensive use of Sperry Univac's computer system to develop a system of computer-generated music which they intended to market on a nationwide basis. Such extensive use of the company's computer system was strictly forbidden by a Sperry Univac policy known to both Kelly and Palmer. As part of their marketing campaign for the new computer-generated music system, Kelly and Palmer sent letters through the mail. The United States prosecuted them under the mail fraud statute for sending information through the mail in furtherance of their scheme to defraud Sperry Univac out of valuable computer time. Both Kelly and Palmer were found guilty of mail fraud.

Kelly and Palmer were found guilty of mail fraud because the federal court was willing to broadly interpret a statute that had been written by legislators who did not have the computer in mind at the time they passed the legislation. However, many situations involving computer-related crimes do not clearly fit within any existing statutes. In an attempt to fill this gap, Congress has passed statutes specifically related to computers. Two such statutes are the Counterfeit Access Device and Computer Fraud and Abuse Act and the Electronic Funds Transfer Act.

The Counterfeit Access Device and Computer Fraud and Abuse Act Activities in five areas are covered by the Counterfeit Access Device and Computer Fraud and Abuse Act. These five areas include: national defense, financial records, government computers, federal interest computers, and interstate commerce.

1. **National Defense** The act makes it unlawful for any unauthorized person to use a computer to gain access to secret information that could compromise national security. The prohibition extends to information considered sensitive under the Atomic Energy Act of 1954. The information must be acquired with the intent to hurt the United States or help a foreign power.
2. **Financial Institutions** The act also prohibits the unauthorized use of a computer to gain access to the financial records of a financial institution. This prohibition includes obtaining consumer information held in any file required by a consumer reporting agency.
3. **Government Computers** In addition, the statute outlaws the unauthorized access to any department or agency computer used exclusively for federal government business. The act extends this prohibition to computers shared with nongovernmental institutions if the unauthorized access affects the government's use of that computer.
4. **Federal Interest Computers** A **federal interest computer** is a computer used only by the federal government or by a financial institution. The term also includes any computer used to commit an offense in tandem with a second computer located in a different state. Congress has forbidden any fraud committed by a federal interest computer. It has also forbidden the alteration, damage, or destruction of information used by a federal interest computer if the offense causes a loss of $1,000 or more during a one-year period or if the offense modifies or impairs medical records.
5. **Interstate Commerce** Finally, the act forbids the transfer of any information that will allow the unauthorized use of any computer, if the transfer of that information affects interstate commerce. This portion of the act requires that the information be obtained with an intent to defraud.

The Electronic Funds Transfer Act The Electronic Funds Transfer Act of 1979 makes it a federal offense to use any device involved in an electronic fund transfer (EFT) to steal money, goods, or services. Devices used in EFT include stolen and counterfeit cards that can be used to activate bank machines. Under the act, it is also a crime to alter data, to intercept wire transmissions, or to use stolen codes, when the object is to obtain something of value unlawfully.

SUMMARY

40-1. Currently, there is no separate area of the law known as computer law. Legal principles governing the ownership, sale, and misuse of computers must be found in other areas of the law. Computer law questions are further complicated by the need to distinguish between computer hardware and computer software. The term *computer hardware* refers to the actual device known as a computer. The term *computer software* refers to the card, tape, chip, or disk that contains the computer program.

40-2. Ownership rights in computer programs can be protected by trade secret, box-top license, patent, and copyright. A *trade secret* is a plan, process, or device used in a business and known only to employees who need to know that secret to perform on the job. A program can be protected as a trade secret only if its distribution is tightly controlled. Box-top licenses protect mass-marketed software. Such licenses limit the buyer's right to copy the program, to reveal the contents of the program, and to allow others to use the program. A *patent* is a property right granted by the federal government to an inventor. A computer program that is part of a larger, more conventional process may be patented, but a program standing by itself cannot be. *Copyrights* are intangible-property rights granted to authors of literary, musical, or artistic productions. Computer programs can be copyrighted under the Computer Software Copyright Act.

40-3. A contract for the sale of a computer itself would be considered a *sale-of-goods contract.* The sale of software by itself on the open market is also considered a sale-of-goods contract. A contract for the sale of a computer package (hardware plus software) is also a sale-of-goods contract. A contract hiring a programmer to create a customized computer program would be a *service contract.*

40-4. The vast amount of information stored in computers represents a potential threat to the right of privacy. Many legal safeguards exist to preserve privacy rights. The common law tort of invasion of privacy guarantees undesired publicity and freedom from unwelcome intervention in private affairs. Amendments 4 and 5 of the U.S. Constitution protect people from government intrusion into private matters. Two federal statutes that protect privacy are the Fair Credit Reporting Act and the Right to Financial Privacy Act.

40-5. State computer crime statutes generally take three forms. They are computer trespass, computer fraud, and computer-related crimes. The federal government has dealt with computer crime under the Counterfeit Access Device and Computer Fraud and Abuse Act and the Electronic Funds Transfer Act.

Understanding Key Legal Terms

computer fraud (p. 576)
computer hardware (p. 568)
computer package (p. 568)
computer program (p. 568)
computer software (p. 568)
computer trespass (p. 575)
device (p. 570)
federal-interest computers (p. 578)
intellectual property (p. 575)
licensing agreement (p. 569)
mail fraud (p. 577)
substantial similarity test (p. 571)
trade secret (p. 569)
wire fraud (p. 577)

Questions for Discussion and Review

1. Differentiate between computer hardware and computer software. Which of the two causes problems in the law today? Explain.
2. Under what circumstances might trade secret protection be available for a computer program?
3. Explain when a computer program can be patented and when such a program would not be eligible for a patent.
4. State the substantial similarity test used to determine whether a copyright infringement has occurred.
5. When is a computer-related contract considered a sale-of-goods contract and when is such a contract labeled a service contract?
6. What two freedoms are protected by the common law of privacy?
7. Does the U.S. Constitution prevent all forms of governmental intrusions into private matters? Explain.
8. How have states dealt with arguments stating that computer programs are not property?
9. Identify three approaches used by the states in handling computer crime.
10. List the areas of computer crime covered by the federal Counterfeit Access Device and Computer Fraud and Abuse Act. What new federal crimes were created by the Electronic Funds Transfer Act?

Analyzing Cases

1. Parrish and Chlarson worked for J & K Computer Systems, Inc. Parrish was a computer programmer, and Chlarson was a trainee. In his capacity as programmer, Parrish wrote an accounts receivable program. Customers of J & K were granted licenses to use the program. A label on the program noted that it was J & K's property and that it could not be used without authorization under a licensing agreement. Parrish, Chlarson, and all other J & K employees were informed that the program was a secret. Nevertheless, Parrish copied it, left J & K's employ, and, along with Chlarson, opened a business similar to J & K. Parrish and Chlarson then sold the copied program to various customers. When J & K sued, Parrish and Chlarson argued that the fact that J & K had revealed the program to their customers meant it was no longer a trade secret. Are Parrish and Chlarson correct? Explain. *J & K Computer Systems, Inc. v. Parrish,* 642 P.2d 732 (Utah).
2. Diehr and Latton applied for a patent toprotect their development of a new process for molding raw, uncured synthetic rubber into cured products. Diehr and Latton argued that their unique contribution was to measure the temperature inside the mold and to feed that temperature into a computer which was programmed to figure the exact time needed for the curing process. The computer would then order a mechanism to open the mold. The process as conceived by Diehr and Latton eliminated the guesswork as to measuring the length of time for the mold to remain closed. The patent office denied the patent because it used a computer program in the process. The office said the program was essentially a mathematical idea and was, therefore, unpatentable. Diehr and Latton argued that the mere fact that a computer program is used as part of a process does not mean the whole process is unpatentable. Are Diehr and Latton correct? Why or why not? *Diamond v. Diehr,* 101 S. Ct. 1048 (U.S. Sup. Ct.).
3. Meyer developed a computer program which would allow neurologists to input patient test results into a computer. The pro-

gram allowed the computer to store and accumulate the patient's test results and, by process of elimination, narrow the possible problem areas so that the neurologist could diagnose a patient's illness. In essence, the program allowed the computer to serve as a memory aid for the neurologist. The patent office refused Meyer's patent application arguing that the program simply provided a mathematical way to duplicate the physician's memory. As such, it was an unpatentable program standing by itself. Was the patent office correct? Explain. *In Re Meyer,* 688 F.2d 789 (U.S. C.C.P.A.).

4. Stern Electronics, Inc., entered a licensing agreement with Konami Industry Co., Ltd., granting Stern exclusive rights to market the video game, Scramble, in the United States. Omni Video Games, Inc., wrote a new program that exactly duplicated the sights and sounds of Scramble. Stern sued Omni in federal court asking for an injunction to prevent Omni from marketing their knockoff of Scramble. Omni argued that Stern could not get a copyright for the Scramble audio visual display because every time a player plays the game, the display is different. The display is not fixed in a tangible medium as required by law. Since Omni had written its own program, Stern could not stop it from marketing the duplicate Scramble games. Is Omni correct? Explain. *Stern Electronics, Inc. v. Kaufman and Omni Video Games, Inc.,* 669 F.2d 852 (2d Cir. Ct.).

5. The owners of Austin's Restaurant were in the market for a cash register. Brown, of Bastrop-Monroe Cash Register Sales and Service, convinced Austin's to purchase a more extensive computerized system. The system, when operational, would not only act as a cash register but would also manage payroll, keep inventory records, monitor the menu, and maintain a mailing list of customers. The system consisted of two microcomputers, three printers, and one disk drive. As part of the contract, Brown agreed to program the system and train Austin's employees in the operation of the computer. From the beginning the programmers had trouble getting the system on-line. After five months of futile attempts, the only part of the system that was operational was the cash register. The owners of Austin's sued Brown asking for their money back. Brown argued that the contract was a service contract and, therefore, not subject to the rescission remedy requested by Austin's. Is Brown correct? Explain. *Austin's of Monroe, Inc. v. Brown,* 474 So.2d 1383 (Louisiana).

6. Hancock worked as a computer programmer for Texas Instruments. In this capacity he wrote and rewrote a variety of computer programs. One package of programs was designed to computerize the process of finding oil. Under false pretenses, Hancock removed some of the programs from Texas Instruments. Through an intermediary, Hancock offered to sell the program to Texaco for $5 million. At his criminal trial, Hancock argued that since the computer programs were abstract in nature, they were not the type of physical personal property that could be subject to theft. He also argued that the only physical part of the program was the paper they were written on, which was worth less than $50. Since grand theft required property valued at over $50, Hancock concluded he could not be tried for grand theft. Texas, at the time, had no definition of intellectual property. How could the Texas prosecutor overcome these objections? *Hancock v. State,* 402 S.W.2d 906 (Texas).

CHAPTER 41
Ethics

OUTLINE

COMMENTARY

The managers of the Pansino Valley Chemical Plant were concerned about unconfirmed, but nevertheless disturbing, reports that several key safety control employees at the plant were drug abusers. To investigate the rumors, the plant managers launched an unannounced drug testing session for all safety control workers. The employees were confined by security guards as they arrived for work on each shift. They were then forced to submit to several drug tests or face discharge. Of the 64 employees confined, eight refused to submit to the admittedly unreliable tests. They were immediately fired. Of the remaining 56 employees, seven tested positively. They were all discharged without further testing even though they protested their innocence. Two months later the Pansino Valley plant suffered a chemical spill when an employee, high on cocaine, failed to perform his job. The employee's tests had shown no drug abuse. Since the law in the area of employee testing is so new, the managers here had no clear legal guidelines to follow. Yet, regardless of the law, they did several things that were clearly "wrong." Determining right from wrong in the absence of law is the function of ethics.

OBJECTIVES

1. Explain how our constantly changing scientific, business, and philosophic environment has created a legal vacuum.
2. Distinguish between ethical and cultural relativism.
3. Explain the doctrine of utilitarianism.
4. Trace the rational basis of moral absolutism, stating the final moral rule which guides absolutist decision making.
5. Apply utilitarian and absolutist principles to solve existing ethical problems.
6. Defend the proposition that states that corporations owe certain social obligations to society and its members.
7. Give examples of how a corporation can live up to its social obligations.

41-1 ETHICAL, MORAL, AND LEGAL DILEMMAS

Ethics can be defined as rules of conduct that transcend legal rules, telling people how to act when the law does not. No business person can truthfully claim to be free from ethical problems. All businesses, large and small, face such problems on a daily basis. Some people face ethical dilemmas head on, welcoming the challenge; others avoid them, preferring to pretend they do not exist. Sometimes the law will provide the answer to such dilemmas. However, in today's world, the law does not always provide appropriate guidelines.

Progress, Change, and the Legal Vacuum

The world today is changing so rapidly that it is difficult for many people to keep pace. New developments in science, engineering, politics, business, and economics leave judges, attorneys, and legislators with no guidelines for making sound legal judgments. This legal "vacuum" simply creates more problems.

Moore became curious when his physician required him to submit to an abnormal number of routine checkups, especially since the doctor gave him a mysterious "waiver" to sign each time he was examined. Upon investigation, Moore discovered that scientists and physicians at the University of California Medical Center were using his unique blood cells in scientific research. He later discovered that his cells were so unique that the medical center had patented them. Moreover, the university had received more than $500,000 from a biogenetic firm for the right to use the patented blood cells. When Moore sued for a share of the money, the judge had no cases, statutes, or regulations to use as guidance. The law had never before dealt with a situation in which a human being's cells were taken, patented, and then used to develop products that reaped enormous profits. Consequently, the judge dismissed the case for failure to state a legally recognizable claim.

Ethical Diversity

Although Moore had no legal claim in the above situation, the medical center's conduct might be viewed as unethical. It could be argued that the scientists had exploited Moore for their own ends with little concern for his welfare, let alone his right for control of his own body. Viewing the situation from a different perspective, the scientists might be praised for their resourcefulness in obtaining the patent and for their business sense in landing such a profitable contract. With no legal guidelines to point the way, which position is correct, and how are such decisions made? Ethics can answer these questions.

Morality and Ethics

Technically, ethics and morality can be distinguished from each other. **Morality** involves the values that govern a society's attitude toward right and wrong. Thus, a person who lives by certain social values is said to be **moral;** one who does not is **immoral;** and one who does not care either way is **amoral.** *Ethics,* in contrast, attempts to develop a means for determining what those values ought to be and for creating rules in line with those values. For the sake of simplicity, however, in this chapter the two terms, morality and ethics, will be used interchangeably to encompass both concepts.

41-2 ETHICAL DECISION MAKING

Ethical decisions are made in a variety of ways. Some people will say that they do not think about ethics, but instead act on instinct when faced with a moral dilemma. Others will say that they try to act rationally and eventually do what they "believe" is right. Still others will say that they follow the rules they learned in school, in their place of worship, or in their family setting. Regardless of the source, most ethical decisions are based on one of three theories: ethical relativism, utilitarianism, or moral absolutism.

Ethical Relativism

Ethical relativism claims that there are no constant standards of right or wrong. Rather, the standards used to distinguish right from wrong change from person to person and from circumstance to circumstance. Thus, ethical rules are relative; that is, the rules vary depending upon the actor, the situation, and innumerable other factors that may affect a person's moral judgments. Since relativism emphasizes the shifting nature of ethical judgments, it is also referred to as **subjective ethics.**

Dreiser works as an agent for Caldwell-Crowly Construction, Inc. He has worked for six weeks hammering out the details of a contract with a South American power company to construct a new hydroelectric power plant at the Iguassu Falls on the Iguassu River at the Brazilian-Argentine border. During the last stages of the negotiations, the power company officials make it quite clear that they expect to receive bribes of $50,000 each to sign the contract. Dreiser would not even think of paying a bribe in the United States. However, as an ethical relativist, he has no scruples about doing so in South America. His ethical judgment has changed because the circumstances have changed.

Those like Dreiser who follow ethical relativism often defend it on the basis of cultural relativism.

Cultural Relativism The recognition of social differences from one social system (culture) to another is known as **cultural relativism.** Cultural relativism is not an ethical belief. Rather, it is a social reality that can be proved by simple observation.

Cultural Relativism as a Defense of Ethical Relativism Some people use cultural relativism to justify their adherence to ethical relativism. Since cultures differ in beliefs, customs, and traditions, what is right for one culture may not be right for another. Thus, the relativist would say that a desert culture which executes an individual for the theft of a quart of water is morally justified in imposing that penalty even though it would seem overly harsh to a culture located on an enormous freshwater lake.

Relativism, Bribery, and Other Practices Cultural relativism makes it easy for the American in a foreign country to bribe government officials without having any misgivings about the immorality of the bribe. If the culture condones the practice of bribery, the executive would argue that there can be nothing wrong with it within that culture.

Other business tactics, such as paying low wages, polluting the environment, establishing monopolies, selling dangerous products, and using substandard building materials—all of which would be not only unethical but also illegal in the United States—can be justified by the ethical relativist. These practices bother some individuals who see them as wrong, no matter what culture is involved. These people may seek other ethical solutions. Some find the solution in utilitarianism.

Utilitarianism

Ethical relativism lacks a solid guiding principle that can create a consistent moral attitude. In contrast, utilitarianism provides a principle that, in many cases, reflects how business people actually make ethical decisions.

Utilitarianism and Consequences Instead of focusing on circumstances, as ethical relativism does, **utilitarianism** focuses on the consequences of an action. Thus, the morality of an action is determined by its ultimate effects. The more good that results, the more ethical the action. Conversely, the more bad that results, the less ethical the action.

Randolph is chief executive officer of Mount Holly Motels, a chain of motels in Texas. The chain has fallen into financial difficulty. An officer suggests that they fire the entire housekeeping staff at all motels and replace them with illegal aliens who will work for one-third the wages. The officer argues that costs could be kept down and the motels would easily recover from their financial problems. Randolph, however, points out the following negative consequences: An injustice would be inflicted upon the fired workers; the fired workers might file wrongful discharge suits against Mount Holly; the corporation might be fined for the hiring of illegal aliens; and bad publicity might cause a drastic loss of revenue. Considering all these negative consequences, Randolph rejects the plan.

The Application of Utilitarianism Unlike ethical relativism, which is constantly shifting, utilitarianism seeks only one stable goal, the greatest good for the greatest number. Determining the greatest good for the greatest number, however, is not always as simple as it sounds. Nevertheless, the process is made easier by following a sequence of steps:

1. The action to be evaluated should be stated in nonemotional terms. (For example, "stealing another's property" is emotional language; "confiscating property for one's own use," is somewhat neutral.)
2. Every participant or class of participants who will be affected by the action should be identified.

3. Good and bad consequences in relation to the major participants must be considered.
4. Good and bad consequences in relation to secondary participants must be considered.
5. All alternatives to the action stated in Step 1 must now be examined.
6. Once Step 5 has been carried out, a conclusion must be reached. Whichever alternative creates the greatest good for the greatest number is the one that ought to be taken.

Some people are uncomfortable with the utilitarian method because it depends on such a complex reasoning process and because, like relativism, it frequently lacks consistency. Moral absolutism attempts to overcome both problems.

Moral Absolutism

In contrast to relativism and utilitarianism, moral absolutism rejects the notion that ethical rules can change. Absolutism replaces the shifting standards of relativism and the result-oriented standards of utilitarianism with a system that is objective, rational, and relatively consistent.

Objectivity According to moral absolutism, actions are either right or wrong regardless of circumstances and regardless of the consequences. The moral absolutist establishes objective rules of behavior that transcend personal preferences, cultural differences, and end results. For this reason absolutism is often referred to as **objective ethics.**

The Prokesch-Harbert Pharmaceutical Company (PHP) is in deep financial difficulty. It has poured millions of dollars into a new oral contraceptive, Prokestrin-2. An FDA advisory panel has recommended approval of Prokestrin-2 for marketing. The marketing of the drug will save PHP from financial ruin. This is doubly important because PHP is the principal business in Rossville, Ohio, employing 5,000 workers out of a population of 15,000. At the last minute, a PHP biochemist informs Wareham, the president of PHP, that he has discovered that Prokestrin-2 has an unacceptably high risk of causing gallbladder disease in about 1 percent of the women who take it for more than six months. As a moral absolutist, Wareham is under a moral obligation to reveal what she has been told and to stop the marketing of Prokestrin-2, despite the small number of women affected and despite the disastrous consequences for PHP and Rossville.

One question which the moral absolutist must answer is "Where do these objective rules come from?" The answer to this question takes several forms.

Theological Ethics Many people believe that all moral rules come from God. This belief is known as **theological ethics.** Theological ethics needs no justification for the existence or validity of the rules beyond the fact that they come from God. Since God has revealed these moral rules they transcend all other rules and stand as the ultimate guide to human behavior. For example, according to theological ethics killing is wrong because God says it's wrong. Although most people would see valid reasons for having such a rule, those who

Table 41-1 ETHICAL THEORIES

Ethical Theory	*Explanation*
Ethical relativism (subjective ethics)	Ethical relativism holds that the standards used to judge right from wrong change from person to person and circumstance to circumstance. It is often justified by reference to cultural relativism.
Utilitarianism	Utilitarianism holds that ethical standards are determined by the consequences of an action. Its basic principle demands the greatest good for the greatest number.
Moral absolutism	Moral absolutism holds that actions are either right or wrong regardless of circumstances and regardless of consequences. Moral absolution is justified through either theological ethics or rational ethics.

believe in the validity of theological ethics would not question God as the rule's authoritative source.

Rational Ethics Other people who believe in objective moral rules have difficulty attributing the origin of the rules to God alone. Many of these people justify the existence of objective rules by referring to the rational nature of human beings. This belief, known as **rational ethics,** begins with the premise that only human beings are morally responsible for their actions. Animals, plants, and inanimate objects might cause injury or harm, but they are never held morally responsible because they are incapable of reason and are therefore incapable of purposeful action. The only thing that separates moral beings from those which are amoral is the rationality of the moral beings.

The Absolutist Rule As rational beings, people think for themselves and, in doing so, recognize their own self-worth as individuals. Along with self-worth comes a belief in certain inherent rights. These rights include the right to life, the right to own property, the right to a good reputation, the right to be free from injury, and so on. Rational beings recognize that they do not want to be killed or cheated. They do not want their property stolen or their reputation damaged. Since they believe in their own inherent rights, they also recognize that all people share those same rights. Thus, each individual has a duty to refrain from violating the right of all other rational beings. The result of this logical pattern is the ultimate rule of the moral absolutist: "Act so that you treat others as you believe you yourself would want to be treated. Be sure to respect those other people as ends in themselves, not as a means to an end."

41-3 MODERN ETHICAL ISSUES

Ethical issues in today's world are so complex and so varied that it is difficult to know where to begin such a study. New issues are created all the time as scientific discoveries are made, as the financial world develops, and as attitudes and beliefs change. Scientific and medical terms like surrogate parenthood, cloning, AIDS, and genetic engineering—all of which were unknown to preceding generations—are commonplace today. The same is true in the business world where new concepts such as insider trading, comparable worth, takeover bids, and drug testing have become part of our standard vocabulary.

Ethical Apathy

In view of these rapid changes it is easy to understand why many business people might "tune out" all such issues and leave them to ethical and legal experts. Given the far-reaching implications of these issues, however, such an attitude is unwise. The business people who abdicate their moral involvement in these issues may find themselves saddled with solutions that they find less than satisfying. Moreover, such an attitude is unnecessary given the ethical theories discussed in this chapter. Both utilitarianism and moral absolutism can impose order on these diverse issues, giving the business person a framework upon which to build an ethical reasoning process.

Utilitarianism and the Pansino Valley Case

Consider the Pansino Valley drug testing case detailed in the Commentary. Clearly, the managers of the chemical plant committed several moral errors. What is not immediately evident is how the managers should have acted when faced with the drug abuse rumor. A utilitarian approach to the Pansino Valley Case would follow the six steps outlined on pages 585–586.

1. **Action Stated in Nonemotional Language** The action examined in the Pansino Valley case could be stated in nonemotional language like this: "All employees in sensitive areas must undergo a series of unannounced drug tests. Employees who choose not to submit to the tests and employees who fail them are to be dismissed."
2. **Participants Identified** The next step in a utilitarian analysis would be to identify all participants affected by the action. In this case that would include the employees, their families, the customers of Pansino Valley, the community in which the chemical plant is located, and the shareholders who own an interest in the chemical company.
3. **Good and Bad Consequences Affecting Major Participants** Clearly, the employees were the major participants in this situation. They were mistreated by the way in which they were apprehended, confined, and forced to undergo several drug tests that are, at the very least, embarrassing. Those who refused, even with good reason, were dismissed without a hearing. Those who failed the admittedly inaccurate tests were also fired. Both groups of dismissed employees could become a burden on the community as unemployed welfare recipients. In addition, their families might suffer economically and psychologically.
4. **Good and Bad Consequences Affecting Secondary Participants** The customers, the shareholders, and the community are less directly affected in such situations. Nevertheless, drug testing programs do cost money that would be passed on to the customer as higher rates and to the shareholders as lower dividends. There could, of course, be positive effects. Many actual drug users could be eliminated from the staff making the plant and the com-

munity safer. This could also translate into a long-range saving for customers and increased profits for the shareholders. However, since the drug users have not been rehabilitated but have, instead, been let loose into the community, they may become public charges or take other jobs where their drug abuse may cause other, perhaps worse, problems.

5. **Alternatives Examined** Since negative results outweigh positive results, alternatives must now be examined. Pansino Valley might institute a drug testing procedure with less drastic consequences. Those employees who test positively might be placed in drug rehabilitation programs. This procedure would eliminate the drug abuse but would prevent the negative effects that come from simply releasing them into the community. Adding an appeal process would also protect those who are innocent victims of inaccurate tests.
6. **Conclusion** What should be obvious from this extended application is that the apparently difficult problems of dealing with drug abuse need not go unresolved simply because the law has no answer and because there are ethical difficulties inherent in the problem. Here the use of utilitarianism gave some focus and direction to the ethical decision-making process. Similar focus can be achieved when absolutism is applied to a difficult problem.

Absolutism and the U.C. Medical Center Case

In the case of *Moore v. University of California Medical Center,* the scientists at the medical center had taken Moore's blood cells, for their own benefit (see page 583). They had patented the unique cells and then sold the rights to a biogenetics firm for $500,000. While the judge in the case could see no legal issues, the ethical questions are obvious. Should the scientists have taken the cells without informing Moore of their true nature? Did the center have the right to patent cells that actually belonged to Moore? Once the cells were patented, did the center have the right to sell the patent rights to the biogenetics firm in exchange for $500,000? Does Moore have a right to any share in that $500,000 profit?

The Absolutist Rule These questions are not easily answered, but addressing them becomes somewhat less complicated when moral absolutism is used to simplify and streamline the issues. Recall that the absolutist rule states, "Act so that you treat others as you yourself would want to be treated. Be sure to respect those other people as ends in themselves, not as a means to an end."

Violations of the Rule The medical center scientists violated the last tenet of this rule by using Moore not as an end in himself but as a means to the ends of scientific research and financial profit. To the scientists, Moore became a vehicle to advance their scientific pursuits and to enhance their economic situation. In short, he was no longer a natural human being; he was a thing to be used and discarded when his usefulness had ended.

Absolutist Conclusions The absolutist would insist, first, that Moore be informed of the true nature of his blood cells. Secondly, the absolutist would say the scientist should have obtained Moore's permission before applying for the patent. Third, the absolutist would conclude that they should have shared their profits with Moore. All these actions would conform to the absolutist rule because Moore would have become a partner in the enterprise, rather than a tool.

41-4 CORPORATE SOCIAL RESPONSIBILITY

Up to this point, we've examined how individuals make moral decisions. As we've seen, there are three basic ethical reasoning patterns: ethical relativism, utilitarianism, and moral absolutism. Clearly, these theories can be used by individuals to judge their own conduct as well as the conduct of other individuals. However, when the focus changes from individual to corporate conduct, new problems arise. Not everyone agrees on whether corporate conduct can be judged from an ethical point of view, let alone which standard to use in making those judgments. A less controversial question is whether the corporation has certain social obligations to society and its members. Many people will agree that corporations owe certain social obligations because of their immense power and because of their special status among business organizations.

Corporate Power

When the issue of social responsibility arises, the corporation, rather than the partnership or the sole proprietorship, takes center stage. Perhaps the most obvious reason for this attention is that today's corporations control 90 percent of the total yearly business receipts of $6.8 trillion. This gives corporations an enormous amount of power. This power is further enhanced because it is concentrated in the hands of a few. Although corporations control 90 percent of the wealth, they represent only 20 percent of the business organizations in the country.

Corporate Status

Society also grants certain privileges to corporations that allow them to operate the way they do. For example, corporate shareholders are granted limited liability. In addition, the corporation as a legal "person" is granted a form of citizenship status and many of the rights and privileges that go along with that status. Finally, corporate managers are granted the protection of the business judgment rule, which means that their business decisions are immune from legal challenges as long as those decisions are made legally, in good faith, with due care, and in the best interests of the corporation. For all these reasons, the corporation owes society some measure of social responsibility.

Corporate Social Obligations

Whether a corporation is living up to its social obligations requires an examination of its relationship to the community. Social responsibility would be reflected by a corporation's involvement in the political and civic life of the community. A corporation that cooperated, for example, with the local chamber of commerce would be demonstrating civic-mindedness. Social responsibility can also be demonstrated by support for educational and cultural projects in the community. Corporations that fight illicit drug traffic, contribute to charitable foundations, and combat poverty would be demonstrating social consciousness. Some companies create their own social programs.

McDonald's has been involved in several self-initiated social programs in recent years. One program involves establishing Ronald McDonald Houses around the country. These houses, located near hospitals, allow parents to stay with their children during critical medical procedures. McDonald's has also joined the fight against the drug crisis by establishing the *Get It Straight* program. As part of this program, McDonald's provides schools with a 20-minute film on the drug problems facing teens today. McDonald's is also involved in helping younger children stay safe through its *Safe Kids Tips* program. This program, which involves in-school speakers, publications, and broadcasts, is designed to prevent the abduction and abuse of children.

In these ways, McDonald's has become a model of social responsibility. It has fulfilled its social duties by contributing to existing charitable programs, by cooperating with community agencies, and by establishing its own special social programs. Naturally, McDonald's benefits from such programs in goodwill and favorable publicity. However, such beneficial spinoffs do not detract from the good that is done for society as a whole.

SUMMARY

41-1. *Ethics* can be defined as rules of conduct that transcend legal rules, telling people how they should act even if the law does not.

41-2. *Ethical relativism* holds that there are no fixed or stable standards of right and wrong. Instead, ethical standards change from person to person and from circumstance to circumstance. *Utilitarianism* holds that the ethical nature of an action is determined by its consequences. *Moral absolutism* holds that certain actions are always right and others always wrong, regardless of the circumstances or the consequences. Moral absolutism can be grounded in either religious faith or rationality.

41-3. Ethical issues in today's world are so complex and varied that many people abandon any hope of understanding them or of making sound ethical decisions. Such an abdication is unnecessary, however, since both utilitarianism and moral absolutism impose order on these diverse issues, giving people a framework upon which to build a consistent ethical reasoning process.

41-4. Corporations have certain social duties because of their enormous power and because society grants them special status in the business world. This special status includes limited liability, many citizenship rights, and the legal protection of the business judgment rule. Social obligations can be fulfilled by contributing to existing charitable institutions, by cooperating with community agencies, and by establishing special social programs.

Understanding Key Legal Terms

amoral (p. 583)
cultural relativism (p. 584)
ethical relativism (p. 584)
ethics (p. 583)
immoral (p. 583)
moral (p. 583)
moral absolutism (p. 586)
morality (p. 583)
objective ethics (p. 586)
rational ethics (p. 587)
subjective ethics (p. 584)
theological ethics (p. 585)
utilitarianism (p. 585)

Questions for Discussion and Review

1. Outline the factors that have combined to create a legal "vacuum" in the world today.
2. Explain the difference between morality and ethics.
3. Distinguish between ethical relativism and cultural relativism.
4. How does utilitarianism differ from ethical relativism as a way of making ethical decisions? Identify the ultimate rule that guides absolutist decision making.
5. List the steps that must be taken in the application of the utilitarian decision-making process.
6. Contrast moral absolutism as an ethical decision-making process with ethical relativism and utilitarianism.
7. What is meant by the term *theological ethics?*
8. Discuss rational ethics as an explanation for the existence of absolute, objective moral rules.
9. Identify two arguments for imposing certain social obligations on corporations.
10. Describe several social activities in which a corporation could involve itself to meet its social obligations.

Analyzing Cases

Special directions: The following cases have been carefully chosen to represent several of the most pressing ethical dilemmas facing American business today. These issues include truth in advertising, employment discrimination, defective products, product recall, insider trading, corporate accountability, surrogate parenting, nuclear energy, and environment deterioration. Even though all the cases are real-life situations, not all have become actual court cases. Some of these cases have ended up in court; others will never be litigated. When answering the questions at the end of each case, first choose the ethical decision-mak-ing process that you feel most comfortable withand apply it according to the explanation in the chapter. Choose either utilitarianism or moral absolutism rather than ethical relativism and be consistent within each answer and from one answer to another. In this way you will learn both the strong and the weak points of your chosen ethical framework. Be less concerned with the "right" answer and more with applying the ethical decision-making process properly.

1. **Truth in Advertising** American Home Products (AHP) was faced with a dilemma. Their new acetaminophen product, Anacin-3, was in direct competition with Johnson and Johnson's acetaminophen product, Tylenol. AHP wanted to demonstrate that hospitals had faith in Anacin-3. Unfortunately, most hospital pharmacies used Tylenol, not Anacin-3. AHP solved the problem by creating an advertising campaign based on the slogan "Hospitals recommend acetaminophen, the aspirin-free pain reliever in Anacin-3, more than any other pain reliever." AHP's campaign failed to mention that the acetaminophen product that hospitals preferred was actually Tylenol. Although technically AHP was stating the truth, it was, nevertheless, deliberately misleading the public. Is such a deception ethically permissible? Why or why not? Would your answer change if you found out that hospitals used Tylenol only because it was cheaper than Anacin-3, not because it was more effective? Defend your answer.

2. **Employment Discrimination** Wirth, a recovering alcoholic, sought employment as an electrician with the Babcock and Wilcox Company. Wirth was not hired because of his handicap. Babcock and Wilcox argued that alcoholism is not a handicap but a legitimate reason for not hiring Wirth because it could hurt his ability to perform on the job. In a similar case, Arline, an elementary school teacher, was fired by the Nassau County school board because she had tuberculosis. Arline argued that she was fired because of her handicap. The board said she was fired because her contagious condition endangered the children. Should employers fire or refuse to hire recovering alcoholics because of their potential for causing problems at work? Defend your response. Should employers fire or refuse to hire individuals with contagious diseases because of the danger to others in the workplace? Why or why not?

3. **Defective Products** Since Bic lighters were first manufactured in 1972, hundreds of people have been injured by lighters that explode into flames, often when they are not even in use. The Bic Corporation has stopped most lawsuits by offering huge settlements to those people injured by the lighters. One such settlement, for example, topped $3 million. In these settlements, Bic inserted a secrecy clause preventing the other party from revealing to the public any part of the incident. Should Bic continue to market lighters knowing of their tendency to explode? Should the corporation settle these claims out of court? Should the secrecy clause be included in each settlement agreement? Are the injured parties acting ethically when they promise to keep quiet knowing what can happen to hundreds of unsuspecting consumers? Defend each answer.

4. **Insider Trading** Investment banker Freeman of Goldman, Sachs and Co., learned about a takeover bid involving Unocal, a Goldman, Sach's client. Freeman told Siegel of Kidder, Peabody, and Co., about the deal. As a result of this information Kidder, which owned stock in Unocal, made an enormous profit. In exchange for this information, Siegel later told Freeman about a takeover bid involving Kohlberg, Kohlberg, Roberts and Company, a Kidder client. Freeman, who owned stock in Kohlberg, sold his shares and made a tremendous profit on the deal. Before answering the following questions, recall that Siegel owed the duties of trust and loyalty to his client, Kohlberg, and that Freeman owed the same duties to his client, Unocal. However, Freeman owed no duty to Kohlberg, and Siegel owed no duty to Unocal. Is the exchange of this inside information ethical? Why or why not? Does it make a difference whether the company profits, as in Kidder's case, or whether the individual profits, as in Freeman's situation? Defend your answer.

5. **Corporate Accountability** The shareholders of TransUnion felt they'd been cheated in the sale of their stock in a take-

over battle. They filed a lawsuit against the board of directors, claiming that the board had not exercised due care in reaching the decision to sell since they'd failed to read any documents filed in the takeover bid and had made the decision after an incredibly short meeting. The court agreed and said that the directors had failed to exercise due care. The ripple effects of this decision were far reaching. Insurance rates for corporate directors soared. People resigned from boards, and other good people refused to serve. In addition, Delaware began to lose corporations because they feared the harsh judgment of the court and began to pack up and move out. In response to this crisis, the Delaware legislature enacted a statute that allows shareholders to change their bylaws and exempt directors from financial liability should they not exercise due care. Is such legislation ethical? Should corporate shareholders support such a change in their bylaws? Defend your answers.

6. **Surrogate Parenting** The Baby M case is one of the most famous surrogate parenting cases in recent years. In response to this case, several state legislatures began to examine legislation involving surrogate parenting. Many of these bills took one of two approaches to the issue. One approach was to legalize surrogate parenthood contracts. These bills also included elaborate standards and regulations to govern the practice. For example, many such bills provided for psychological screening of both parents. At the other end of the legislative spectrum were those bills which would prevent surrogate parents from seeking a remedy for breach of contract in a court of law. The legislatures did not make such contracts illegal because such a move might be unconstitutional. However, they could prevent the state courts from entertaining any litigation seeking to uphold such contracts. In essence, these statutes make the contracts unenforceable as against public policy. Which of these two approaches seems the most ethical? Explain your answer.

7. **Nuclear Energy** At General Electric (GE) an eight-month internal study, known as the Reed Report, revealed serious defects in the company's BWR 6 nuclear reactor and in its Mark III containment design. Management at GE made the changes suggested in the Reed Report at a cost of over $400 million. However, the company never released the report to the public at large or to any of the nine communities served by reactors of that design. Was it ethically permissible for GE to suppress results of the Reed Report? Explain your response.

8. **Environmental Deterioration** From 1942 to 1953 the Hooker Chemical and Plastics Corporation disposed of its chemical waste by dumping it in the Love Canal or burying it in the canal's banks. Eventually, the canal was sold to the local school board, which constructed a school on part of the site. The rest of the land was sold to various development companies, which constructed single-family dwellings in the area. In 1976, after a series of storms, the buried chemicals seeped to the surface. The dangerous chemicals had disastrous effects on the neighborhood. Some mothers bore children with birth defects while others suffered miscarriages. The incidence of liver disease and nervous disorders increased dramatically. Vegetation was destroyed, and the entire area reeked with a terrible odor. Is Hooker Chemical ethically responsible for the environmental disaster that hit the Love Canal area? Before answering, recall that dumping had been legal when Hooker had disposed of its chemicals in the canal. Now defend your answer.

PART 9
Case Study
Atari, Inc. v. North American
672 F.2d 607 (7th Cir. Ct.)

SUMMARY

The exclusive marketing rights for the copyrighted computer game Pac-Man belonged to Atari, Inc., and the Midway Manufacturing Co. K.C. Munchkin, a game based on Pac-Man, was created and marketed by North American. North American did not copy the Pac-Man program. Rather, it developed its own program which created a visual display similar to the Pac-Man display. Both games involved a main figure known as a "gobbler." In each game the gobbler was chased by "ghost monsters." Under the direction of the player, the gobbler character in each game consumed dots and power capsules while running through a maze. The ultimate goal of both games was to accumulate points by consuming dots and ghost monsters. The two games were different in several respects: K.C. Munchkin had one dead-end passage in its maze, whereas Pac-Man had no such dead ends. The K. C. Munchkin dots, which numbered only 12, were randomly spaced and in constant motion. In contrast, the Pac-Man dots, which numbered 200, were evenly spaced and stationary. Both Atari and Midway brought suit against North American asking the court to stop North American from selling K. C. Munchkin. The plaintiffs contended that K. C. Munchkin was so similar to Pac-Man that it constituted a copyright violation. North American argued that the differences between the two games made K. C.Munchkin an original work.

THE COURT'S OPINION: JUDGE HARLINGTON WOOD, JR.

To establish infringement a plaintiff must prove ownership of a valid copyright and "copying" by the defendant. Because direct evidence of copying often is unavailable, copying may be inferred where the defendant had access to the copyrighted work and the accused work is substantially similar to the copyrighted work. The parties stipulated to the validity of plaintiffs' copyright and to access; the district court's ruling turned solely on the question of substantial similarity....

Specifically, the test is whether the accused work is so similar to the plaintiff's work that an ordinary reasonable person would conclude that the defendant unlawfully appropriated the plaintiff's protectible expression by taking material of substance and value. *Krofft,* 562 F.2d at 1164. Judge Learned Hand, in finding infringement, once stated that "the ordinary observer, unless he set out to detect the disparities,would be disposed to overlook them, and regard their aesthetic appeal as the same." *Peter Pan Fabrics, Inc. v. Martin Weiner Corp.,* 274 F.2d 487, 489 (2d Cir. 1960). It has been said that this test does not involve "analytic dissection and expert testimony," *Arnstein,* 154 F.2d at 468....

North American not only adopted the same basic characters but also portrayed them in a manner which made K. C. Munchkin appear substantially similar to Pac-Man. The K. C. Munchkin gobbler has several blatantly similar features, including the relative size and shape of the "body," the V-shaped "mouth," its distinctive gobbling action (with appropriate sounds), and especially the way in which it disappears upon being captured. An examination of the K. C. Munchkin ghost monsters reveals even more significant visual similarities. In size, shape, and manner of movement, they are virtually identical to their Pac-Man counterparts. K. C. Munchkin's monsters, for example, exhibit the same peculiar "eye" and "leg" movement. Both games, moreover, express the role reversal and "regeneration" process with such great similarity that an ordinary observer could conclude only that North American copied plaintiffs' Pac-Man.

Defendants point to a laundry list of specific differences—particularly the concept of moving dots, the variations in mazes, and certain changes in facial features and colors of the characters—which they contend, and the district court apparently agreed, shows lack of substantial similarity. Although numerous differences may influence the impressions of the ordinary observer, "slight differences between a protected work and an accused work will not preclude a finding of infringement" where the works are substantially similar in other respects. ... Exact reproduction or near identity is not necessary to establish infringement....

In comparing the two works, the district court focused on certain differences in detail and seemingly ignored (or at least failed to articulate) the more obvious similarities. The *sine qua non* [essence] of the ordinary observer test, however, is the overall similarities rather than the minute differences between the two works.

To assess the impact of certain differences, one factor to consider is the nature of the protected material and the setting in which it appears.... Video games, unlike an artist's painting or even other audiovisual works, appeal to an audience that is fairly undiscriminating insofar as their concern about more subtle differences in artistic expression. The main attraction of a game such as Pac-Man lies in the stimulation provided by the intensity of the competition. A person who is entranced by the play of the game "would be disposed to overlook" many of the minor differences in detail and "regard their aesthetic appeal as the same."

The district court's conclusion that the two works are not substantially similar is clearly erroneous, and its refusal to issue a preliminary injunction constitutes an abuse of discretion.

For the foregoing reasons, we reverse the district court's denial of plaintiffs' motion for a preliminary injunction and direct the district court to enter a preliminary injunction against continued infringement of plaintiffs' copyright.

QUESTIONS FOR ANALYSIS

1. Since North American did not copy the Pac-Man program, what is the basis for the suit brought by Atari and Midway?
2. Could Atari and Midway protect their ownership rights in any way other than a copyright?
3. What test does the court use to determine whether North American violated the Pac-Man copyright?
4. Would the trial court need expert testimony to apply this test? Explain.
5. Does the court rest its decision on the similarities or the dissimilarities between the two games?
6. What did the winner of this proceeding gain by the court's decision?

APPENDIXES

GLOSSARY

INDEX

APPENDIX A
The Constitution of the United States

PREAMBLE

We the People of the United States, in Order to form a more perfect Union, establish Justice, insure domestic Tranquility, provide for the common defence, promote the general Welfare, and secure the Blessings of Liberty to ourselves and our Posterity, do ordain and establish this Constitution for the United States of America.

ARTICLE I

Section 1. All legislative Powers herein granted shall be vested in a Congress of the United States, which shall consist of a Senate and House of Representatives.

Section 2. [1] The House of Representatives shall be composed of Members chosen every second Year by the People of the several States, and the Electors in each State shall have the Qualifications requisite for Electors of the most numerous Branch of the State Legislature.

[2] No Person shall be a Representative who shall not have attained to the Age of twenty-five Years, and been seven Years a Citizen of the United States, and who shall not, when elected, be an Inhabitant of that State in which he shall be chosen.

[3] Representatives and direct Taxes shall be apportioned among the several States which may be included within this Union, according to their respective Numbers, which shall be determined by adding to the whole Number of free Persons, including those bound to Service for a Term of Years, and excluding Indians not taxed, three fifths of all other Persons. The actual Enumeration shall be made within three Years after the first Meeting of the Congress of the United States, and within every subsequent Term of ten Years, in such Manner as they shall by Law direct. The Number of Representatives shall not exceed one for every thirty Thousand, but each State shall have at Least one Representative; and until such enumeration shall be made, the State of New Hampshire shall be entitled to chuse three, Massachusetts eight, Rhode Island and Providence Plantations one, Connecticut five, New York six, New Jersey four, Pennsylvania eight, Delaware one, Maryland six, Virginia ten, North Carolina five, South Carolina five, and Georgia three.

[4] When vacancies happen in the Representation from any State, the Executive Authority thereof shall issue Writs of Election to fill such Vacancies.

[5] The House of Representatives shall chuse their Speaker and other Officers; and shall have the sole Power of Impeachment.

Section 3. [1] The Senate of the United States shall be composed of two Senators from each State, chosen by the Legislature thereof, for six Years; and each Senator shall have one Vote.

[2] Immediately after they shall be assembled in Consequence of the first Election, they shall be divided as equally as may be into three Classes. The Seats of the Senators of the first Class shall be vacated at the Expiration of the Second Year, of the second Class at the Expiration of the fourth Year, and of the third Class at the Expiration of the sixth Year, so that one third may be chosen every second Year; and if Vacancies happen by Resignation, or otherwise, during the Recess of the Legislature of any State, the Executive thereof may make temporary Appointments until the next Meeting of the Legislature, which shall then fill such Vacancies.

[3] No Person shall be a Senator who shall not have attained to the Age of thirty Years, and been nine Years a Citizen of the United States, and who shall not, when elected, be an Inhabitant of that State for which he shall be chosen.

[4] The Vice President of the United States shall be President of the Senate, but shall have no Vote, unless they be equally divided.

[5] The Senate shall chuse their other Officers, and also a President pro tempore, in the Absence

of the Vice President, or when he shall exercise the Office of President of the United States.

[6] The Senate shall have the sole Power to try all Impeachments. When sitting for that Purpose, they shall be on Oath or Affirmation. When the President of the United States is tried, the Chief Justice shall preside: And no Person shall be convicted without the Concurrence of two thirds of the Members present.

[7] Judgment in Cases of Impeachment shall not extend further than to removal from Office, and disqualification to hold and enjoy any Office of honor, Trust, or Profit under the United States: but the Party convicted shall nevertheless be liable and subject to Indictment, Trial, Judgment, and Punishment, according to Law.

Section 4. [1] The Times, Places and Manner of holding elections for Senators and Representatives, shall be prescribed in each State by the Legislature thereof; but the Congress may at any time by Law make or alter such Regulations, except as to the Places of chusing Senators.

[2] The Congress shall assemble at least once in every Year, and such Meeting shall be on the first Monday in December, unless they shall by Law appoint a different Day.

Section 5. [1] Each House shall be the Judge of the Elections, Returns, and Qualifications of its own Members, and a Majority of each shall constitute a Quorum to do Business; but a smaller Number may adjourn from day to day, and may be authorized to compel the Attendance of absent Members, in such Manner, and under such Penalties as each House may provide.

[2] Each House may determine the Rules of its Proceedings, punish its Members for disorderly Behavior, and, with the Concurrence of two thirds, expel a Member.

[3] Each House shall keep a Journal of its Proceedings, and from time to time publish the same, excepting such parts as may in their Judgment require Secrecy; and the Yeas and Nays of the Members of either House on any question shall, at the Desire of one fifth of those Present, be entered on the Journal.

[4] Neither House, during the Session of Congress, shall, without the Consent of the other, adjourn for more than three days, nor to any other Place than that in which the two Houses shall be sitting.

Section 6. [1] The Senators and Representatives shall receive a Compensation for their Services, to be ascertained by Law, and paid out of the Treasury of the United States. They shall in all Cases, except Treason, Felony and Breach of the Peace, be privileged from Arrest during their Attendance at the Session of their respective Houses, and in going to and returning from the same; and for any Speech or Debate in either House, they shall not be questioned in any other Place.

[2] No Senator or Representative shall, during the Time for which he was elected, be appointed to any civil Office under the Authority of the United States, which shall have been created, or the Emoluments whereof shall have been increased during such time; and no Person holding any Office under the United States, shall be a Member of either House during his Continuance in Office.

Section 7. [1] All Bills for raising Revenue shall originate in the House of Representatives; but the Senate may propose or concur with Amendments as on other Bills.

[2] Every Bill which shall have passed the House of Representatives and the Senate, shall, before it becomes a Law, be presented to the President of the United States; If he approve he shall sign it, but if not he shall return it, with his Objections to the House in which it shall have originated, who shall enter the Objections at large on their Journal, and proceed to reconsider it. If after such Reconsideration two thirds of that House shall agree to pass the Bill, it shall be sent together with the Objections, to the other House, by which it shall likewise be reconsidered, and if approved by two thirds of that House, it shall become a Law. But in all such Cases the Votes of both Houses shall be determined by yeas and Nays, and the Names of the Persons voting for and against the Bill shall be entered on the Journal of each House respectively. If any Bill shall not be returned by the President within ten Days (Sundays excepted) after it shall have been presented to him, the Same shall be a Law, in like Manner as if he had signed it, unless the Congress by their Adjournment prevent its Return in which Case it shall not be a Law.

[3] Every Order, Resolution, or Vote, to Which the Concurrence of the Senate and House of Representatives may be necessary (except on a question of Adjournment) shall be presented to the President of the United States; and before the Same shall take Effect, shall be approved by him, or being disapproved by him, shall be repassed by two thirds of the Senate and House of Representatives, according to the Rules and Limitations prescribed in the Case of a Bill.

Section 8. [1] The Congress shall have Power To lay and collect Taxes, Duties, Imposts and Excises, to pay the Debts and provide for the common Defence and general Welfare of the United States; but all Duties, Imposts and Excises shall be uniform throughout the United States;

[2] To borrow money on the credit of the United States;

[3] To regulate Commerce with foreign Nations,

and among the several States, and with the Indian Tribes;

[4] To establish an uniform Rule of Naturalization, and uniform laws on the subject of Bankruptcies throughout the United States;

[5] To coin Money, regulate the Value thereof, and of foreign Coin, and fix the Standard of Weights and Measures;

[6] To provide for the Punishment of counterfeiting the Securities and current Coin of the United States;

[7] To Establish Post Offices and Post Roads;

[8] To promote the Progress of Science and useful Arts, by securing for limited Times to Authors and Inventors the exclusive Right to their respective Writings and Discoveries;

[9] To constitute Tribunals inferior to the supreme Court;

[10] To define and punish Piracies and Felonies committed on the high Seas, and Offenses against the Law of Nations;

[11] To declare War, grant Letters of Marque and Reprisal, and make Rules concerning Captures on Land and Water;

[12] To raise and support Armies, but no Appropriation of Money to that Use shall be for a longer Term than two Years;

[13] To provide and maintain a Navy;

[14] To make Rules for the Government and Regulation of the land and naval Forces;

[15] To provide for calling forth the Militia to execute the Laws of the Union, suppress Insurrections and repel Invasions;

[16] To provide for organizing, arming, and disciplining, the Militia, and for governing such Part of them as may be employed in the Service of the United States, reserving to the States respectively, the Appointment of the Officers, and the Authority of training the Militia according to the discipline prescribed by Congress;

[17] To exercise exclusive Legislation in all Cases whatsoever, over such District (not exceeding ten Miles square) as may, by Cession of particular States, and the Acceptance of Congress, become the Seat of the Government of the United States, and to exercise like Authority over all Places purchased by the Consent of the Legislature of the State in which the Same shall be, for the Erection of Forts, Magazines, Arsenals, dock-Yards and other needful Buildings;—And

[18] To make all Laws which shall be necessary and proper for carrying into Execution the foregoing Powers, and all other Powers vested by this Constitution in the Government of the United States, or in any Department or Officer thereof.

Section 9. [1] The Migration or Importation of Such Persons as any of the States now existing shall think proper to admit, shall not be prohibited by the Congress prior to the Year one thousand eight hundred and eight, but a Tax or duty may be imposed on such Importation, not exceeding ten dollars for each Person.

[2] The privilege of the Writ of Habeas Corpus shall not be suspended, unless when in Cases of Rebellion or Invasion the public Safety may require it.

[3] No Bill of Attainder or ex post facto Law shall be passed.

[4] No Capitation, or other direct, Tax shall be laid, unless in Proportion to the Census or Enumeration herein before directed to be taken.

[5] No Tax or Duty shall be laid on Articles exported from any State.

[6] No Preference shall be given by any Regulation of Commerce or Revenue to the Ports of one State over those of another: nor shall Vessels bound to, or from, one State be obliged to enter, clear, or pay Duties in another.

[7] No money shall be drawn from the Treasury, but in Consequence of Appropriations made by Law; and a regular Statement and Account of the Receipts and Expenditures of all public Money shall be published from time to time.

[8] No Title of Nobility shall be granted by the United States: And no Person holding any Office of Profit or Trust under them, shall, without the Consent of the Congress, accept of any present, Emolument, Office, or Title, of any kind whatever, from any King, Prince, or foreign State.

Section 10. [1] No State shall enter into any Treaty, Alliance, or Confederation; grant Letters of Marque and Reprisal; coin Money; emit Bills of Credit; make any Thing but gold and silver Coin a Tender in Payment of Debts; pass any Bill of Attainder, ex post facto Law, or Law impairing the Obligation of Contracts, or grant any Title of Nobility.

[2] No State shall, without the Consent of the Congress, lay any Imposts or Duties on Imports or Exports, except what may be absolutely necessary for executing its inspection Laws: and the net Produce of all Duties and Imposts, laid by any State on Imports or Exports, shall be for the Use of the Treasury of the United States; and all such Laws shall be subject to the Revision and Control of the Congress.

[3] No State shall, without the Consent of Congress, lay any Duty of Tonnage, keep Troops, or Ships of War in time of Peace, enter into any Agreement or Compact with another State, or with a foreign Power, or engage in War, unless actually invaded, or in such imminent Danger as will not admit of delay.

ARTICLE II

Section 1. [1] The executive Power shall be vested in a President of the United States of America. He shall hold his Office during the Term of four Years, and, together with the Vice President, chosen for the same Term, be elected, as follows:

[2] Each State shall appoint, in such Manner as the Legislature thereof may direct, a Number of Electors, equal to the whole Number of Senators and Representatives to which the State may be entitled in the Congress; but no Senator or Representative, or Person holding an Office of Trust or Profit under the United States, shall be appointed an Elector.

[3] The Electors shall meet in their respective States, and vote by Ballot for two Persons, of whom one at least shall not be an Inhabitant of the same State with themselves. And they shall make a List of all the Persons voted for, and of the Number of Votes for each; which List they shall sign and certify, and transmit sealed to the Seat of the Government of the United States, directed to the President of the Senate. The President of the Senate shall, in the Presence of the Senate and House of Representatives, open all the Certificates, and the Votes shall then be counted. The Person having the greatest Number of Votes shall be the President, if such Number be a Majority of the whole Number of Electors appointed; and if there be more than one who have such Majority, and have an equal Number of Votes, then the House of Representatives shall immediately chuse by Ballot one of them for President; and if no Person have a Majority, then from the five highest on the List the said House shall in like Manner chuse the President. But in chusing the President, the Votes shall be taken by States the Representation from each State having one Vote; A quorum for this Purpose shall consist of a Member or Members from two thirds of the States, and a Majority of all the States shall be necessary to a Choice. In every Case, after the Choice of the President, the Person having the greater Number of Votes of the Electors shall be the Vice President. But if there shall remain two or more who have equal Votes, the Senate shall chuse from them by Ballot the Vice President.

[4] The Congress may determine the Time of chusing the Electors, and the Day on which they shall give their Votes; which Day shall be the same throughout the United States.

[5] No person except a natural born Citizen, or a Citizen of the United States, at the time of the Adoption of this Constitution, shall be eligible to the Office of President; neither shall any Person be eligible to that Office who shall not have attained to the Age of thirty-five Years, and been fourteen Years a Resident within the United States.

[6] In case of the removal of the President from Office, or of his Death, Resignation or Inability to discharge the Powers and Duties of the said Office, the Same shall devolve on the Vice President, and the Congress may by Law provide for the Case of Removal, Death, Resignation or Inability, both of the President and Vice President, declaring what Officer shall then act as President, and such Officer shall act accordingly, until the Disability be removed, or a President shall be elected.

[7] The President shall, at stated Times, receive for his Services, a Compensation, which shall neither be increased nor diminished during the Period for which he shall have been elected, and he shall not receive within that Period any other Emolument from the United States, or any of them.

[8] Before he enter on the Execution of his Office, he shall take the following Oath or Affirmation: "I do solemnly swear (or affirm) that I will faithfully execute the Office of President of the United States, and will to the best of my Ability, preserve, protect, and defend the Constitution of the United States."

Section 2. [1] The President shall be Commander in Chief of the Army and Navy of the United States, and of the militia of the several States, when called into the actual Service of the United States; he may require the Opinion, in writing, of the principal Officer in each of the Executive Departments, upon any subject relating to the Duties of their respective Offices, and he shall have Power to grant Reprieves and Pardons for Offenses against the United States, except in Cases of Impeachment.

[2] He shall have Power, by and with the Advice and Consent of the Senate to make Treaties, provided two thirds of the Senators present concur; and he shall nominate, and by and with the Advice and Consent of the Senate, shall appoint Ambassadors, other public Ministers and Consuls, Judges of the supreme Court, and all other Officers of the United States, whose Appointments are not herein otherwise provided for, and which shall be established by Law; but the Congress may by Law vest the Appointment of such inferior Officers, as they think proper, in the President alone, in the Courts of Law, or in the Heads of Departments.

[3] The President shall have Power to fill up all Vacancies that may happen during the Recess of the Senate, by granting commissions which shall expire at the End of their next Session.

Section 3. He shall from time to time give to the Congress Information of the State of the Union, and recommend to their Consideration such Measures as he shall judge necessary and expedient; he may, on extraordinary Occasions, convene both Houses, or either of them, and in Case of Disagreement between them, with Respect to the Time of Adjournment, he may adjourn them to such Time as he shall think proper; he shall receive Ambassadors and other public Ministers; he shall take Care that the Laws be faithfully executed, and shall commission all the Officers of the United States.

Section 4. The President, Vice President and all civil Officers of the United States, shall be removed from Office on Impeachment for, and Conviction of, Treason, Bribery, or other high Crimes and Misdemeanors.

ARTICLE III

Section 1. The judicial Power of the United States, shall be vested in one supreme Court, and in such inferior Courts as the Congress may from time to time ordain and establish. The Judges, both of the supreme and inferior Courts, shall hold their Offices during good Behaviour, and shall, at stated Times, receive for their Services a Compensation, which shall not be diminished during their Continuance in Office.

Section 2. [1] The judicial Power shall extend to all Cases, in Law and Equity, arising under this Constitution, the Laws of the United States, and Treaties made, or which shall be made, under their Authority;—to all Cases affecting Ambassadors, other public Ministers and Consuls;—to all Cases of admiralty and maritime Jurisdiction;—to Controversies to which the United States shall be a Party;—to Controversies between two or more States;—between a State and Citizens of another State;—between Citizens of different States;—between Citizens of the same State claiming Lands under the Grants of different States, and between a State, or the Citizens thereof, and foreign States, Citizens or Subjects.

[2] In all Cases affecting Ambassadors, other public Ministers and Consuls, and those in which a State shall be a Party, the supreme Court shall have original Jurisdiction, In all the other Cases before mentioned, the supreme Court shall have appellate Jurisdiction, both as to Law and Fact, with such Exceptions, and under such Regulations as the Congress shall make.

[3] The trial of all Crimes, except in Cases of Impeachment, shall be by Jury; and such Trial shall be held in the State where the said Crimes shall have been committed; but when not committed within any State, the Trial shall be at such Place or Places as the Congress may by Law have directed.

Section 3. [1] Treason against the United States, shall consist only in levying War against them, or, in adhering to their Enemies, giving them Aid and Comfort. No Person shall be convicted of Treason unless on the Testimony of two Witnesses to the same overt Act, or on Confession in open Court.

[2] The Congress shall have Power to declare the Punishment of Treason, but no Attainder of Treason shall work Corruption of Blood, or Forfeiture except during the Life of the Person attainted.

ARTICLE IV

Section 1. Full Faith and Credit shall be given in each State to the public Acts, Records, and judicial Proceedings of every other State. And the Congress may by general Laws prescribe the Manner in which such Acts, Records and Proceedings shall be proved, and the Effect thereof.

Section 2. [1] The Citizens of each State shall be entitled to all Privileges and Immunities of Citizens in the several States.

[2] A Person charged in any State with Treason, Felony, or other Crime, who shall flee from Justice, and be found in another State, shall on demand of the executive Authority of the State from which he fled, be delivered up, to be removed to the State having Jurisdiction of the Crime.

[3] No Person held to Service or Labour in one State, under the Laws thereof, escaping into another, shall, in Consequence of any Law or Regulation therein, be discharged from such Service or Labour, but shall be delivered up on Claim of the Party to whom such Service or Labour may be due.

Section 3. [1] New States may be admitted by the Congress into this Union; but no new State shall be formed or erected within the Jurisdiction of any other State; nor any State be formed by the Junction of two or more States, or Parts of States, without the Consent of the Legislatures of the States concerned as well as of the Congress.

[2] The Congress shall have Power to dispose of and make all needful Rules and Regulations respecting the Territory or other Property belonging to the United States; and nothing in this Constitution shall be so construed as to Prejudice any Claims of the United States, or of any particular State.

Section 4. The United States shall guarantee to every State in this Union a Republican Form of Government, and shall protect each of them against Invasion; and on Application of the Legislature, or of the Executive (when the Legislature cannot be convened) against domestic Violence.

ARTICLE V

The Congress, whenever two thirds of both Houses shall deem it necessary, shall propose Amendments to this Constitution, or, on the Application of the Legislatures of two thirds of the several States, shall call a Convention for proposing Amendments, which, in either case, shall be valid to all Intents and Purposes, as part of this Constitution, when ratified by the Legislatures of three fourths of the several States, or by Conventions in three fourths thereof, as the one or the other Mode of Ratification may be proposed by the Congress; Provided that no Amendment which may be made prior to the Year One thousand eight hundred and eight shall in any Manner affect the first and fourth Clauses in the Ninth Section of the first Article; and that no State, without its Consent, shall be deprived of its equal Suffrage in the Senate.

ARTICLE VI

[1] All Debts contracted and Engagements entered into, before the Adoption of this Constitution shall be as valid against the United States under this Constitution, as under the Confederation.

[2] This Constitution, and the Laws of the United States which shall be made in Pursuance thereof; and all Treaties made, or which shall be made, under the Authority of the United States, shall be the supreme Law of the Land; and the Judges in every State shall be bound thereby, any Thing in the Constitution or Laws of any State to the Contrary notwithstanding.

[3] The Senators and Representatives before mentioned, and the Members of the several State Legislatures, and all executive and judicial Officers, both of the United States and of the several States, shall be bound by Oath or Affirmation, to support this Constitution; but no religious Test shall ever be required as a Qualification to any Office or public Trust under the United States.

ARTICLE VII

The Ratification of the Conventions of nine States shall be sufficient for the Establishment of this Constitution between the States so ratifying the Same.

AMENDMENTS

Articles in addition to, and in amendment of, the Constitution of the United States of America, proposed by Congress, and ratified by the Legislatures of the several States pursuant to the Fifth Article of the original Constitution.

AMENDMENT 1 [1791]

Congress shall make no law respecting an establishment of religion, or prohibiting the free exercise thereof; or abridging the freedom of speech, or of the press; or the right of the people peaceably to assemble, and to petition the Government for a redress of grievances.

AMENDMENT 2 [1791]

A well regulated Militia, being necessary to the security of a free State, the right of the people to keep and bear Arms, shall not be infringed.

AMENDMENT 3 [1791]

No Soldier shall, in time of peace be quartered in any house, without the consent of the Owner, nor in time of war, but in a manner to be prescribed by law.

AMENDMENT 4 [1791]

The right of the people to be secure in their persons, houses, papers, and effects, against unreasonable searches and seizures, shall not be violated, and no Warrants shall issue, but upon probable cause, supported by Oath or affirmation, and particularly describing the place to be searched, and the persons or things to be seized.

AMENDMENT 5 [1791]

No person shall be held to answer for a capital, or other infamous crime, unless on a presentment or indictment of a Grand Jury, except in cases arising in the land or naval forces, or in the Militia, when in actual service in time of War or public danger; nor shall any person be subject for the same offence to be twice put in jeopardy of life or limb; nor shall be compelled in any criminal case to be a witness against himself, nor be deprived of life, liberty, or property, without due process of law; nor shall private property be taken for public use, without just compensation.

AMENDMENT 6 [1791]

In all criminal prosecutions, the accused shall enjoy the right to a speedy and public trial, by an impartial jury of the State and district wherein the crime shall have been committed, which district shall have been previously ascertained by law, and to be informed of the nature and cause of the accusation; to be confronted with the witnesses against him; to have compulsory process for obtaining witnesses in his favor, and to have the Assistance of Counsel for his defence.

AMENDMENT 7 [1791]

In Suits at common law, where the value in controversy shall exceed twenty dollars, the right of trial by jury shall be preserved, and no fact tried by jury, shall be otherwise re-examined in any Court of the United States, than according to the rules of common law.

AMENDMENT 8 [1791]

Excessive bail shall not be required, nor excessive fines imposed, nor cruel and unusual punishments inflicted.

AMENDMENT 9 [1791]

The enumeration in the Constitution, of certain rights, shall not be construed to deny or disparage others retained by the people.

AMENDMENT 10 [1791]

The powers not delegated to the United States by the Constitution, nor prohibited by it to the States, are reserved to the States respectively, or to the people.

AMENDMENT 11 [1798]

The Judicial power of the United States shall not be construed to extend to any suit in law or equity, commenced or prosecuted against one of the United States by Citizens of another State, or by Citizens or Subjects of any Foreign State.

AMENDMENT 12 [1804]

The Electors shall meet in their respective states and vote by ballot for President and Vice-President, one of whom, at least, shall not be an inhabitant of the same state with themselves; they shall name in their ballots the person voted for as President, and in distinct ballots the person voted for as Vice-President, and they shall make distinct lists of all persons voted for as President, and of all persons voted for as Vice-President, and of the number of votes for each, which lists they shall sign and certify, and transmit sealed to the seat of the government of the United States, directed to the President of the Senate;—The President of the Senate shall, in the presence of the Senate and House of Representatives, open all the certificates and the votes shall then be counted;—The person having the greatest number of votes for President, shall be the President, if such number be a majority of the whole number of Electors appointed; and if no person have such majority, then from the persons having the highest numbers not exceeding three on the list of those voted for as President, the House of Representatives shall choose immediately, by ballot, the President. But in choosing the President, the votes shall be taken by states, the representation from each state having one vote; a quorum for this purpose shall consist of a member or members from two-thirds of the states, and a majority of all states shall be necessary to a choice. And if the House of Representatives shall not choose a President whenever the right of choice shall devolve upon them before the fourth day of March next following, then the Vice-President shall act as President, as in the case of the death or other constitutional disability of the President.—The person having the greatest number of votes as Vice-President, shall be the Vice-President, if such number be a majority of the whole number of Electors appointed, and if no person have a majority, then from the two highest numbers on the list, the Senate shall choose the Vice-President; a quorum for the purpose shall consist of two-thirds of the whole number of Senators, and a majority of the whole number shall be necessary to a choice. But no person constitutionally ineligible to the office of President shall be eligible to that of Vice-President of the United States.

AMENDMENT 13 [1865]

Section 1. Neither slavery nor involuntary servitude, except as a punishment for crime whereof the party shall have been duly convicted, shall exist within the United States, or any place subject to their jurisdiction.

Section 2. Congress shall have power to enforce this article by appropriate legislation.

AMENDMENT 14 [1868]

Section 1. All persons born or naturalized in the United States, and subject to the jurisdiction thereof, are citizens of the United States and of the State wherein they reside. No State shall make or enforce any law which shall abridge the privileges or immunities of citizens of the United States; nor shall any State deprive any person of life, liberty, or property, without due process of law; nor deny to any person within its jurisdiction the equal protection of the laws.

Section 2. Representatives shall be apportioned among the several States according to their respective numbers, counting the whole number of persons in each State, excluding Indians not taxed. But when the right to vote at any election for the choice of electors for President and Vice President of the United States, Representatives in Congress, the Executive and Judicial officers of a State, or the members of the Legislature thereof, is denied to any of the male inhabitants of such State, being twenty-one years of age, and citizens of the United States, or in any way abridged, except for participation in rebellion, or other crime, the basis of representation therein shall be reduced in the proportion which the number of such male citizens shall bear to the whole number of male citizens twenty-one years of age in such State.

Section 3. No person shall be a Senator or Representative in Congress, or elector of President and Vice President, or hold any office, civil or military, under the United States, or under any State, who having previously taken an oath, as a member of Congress, or as an officer of the United States, or as a member of any State legislature, or as an executive or judicial officer of any State, to support the Constitution of the United States, shall have engaged in insurrection or rebellion against the same, or given aid or comfort to the enemies thereof. But Congress may by a vote of two-thirds of each House, remove such disability.

Section 4. The validity of the public debt of the United States, authorized by law, including debts incurred for payment of pensions and bounties for services in suppressing insurrection or rebellion, shall not be questioned. But neither the United States nor any State shall assume or pay any debt or obligation incurred in aid of insurrection or rebellion against the United States, or any claim for the loss or emancipation of any slave; but all such debts, obligations and claims shall be held illegal and void.

Section 5. The Congress shall have power to enforce, by appropriate legislation, the provisions of this article.

AMENDMENT 15 [1870]

Section 1. The right of citizens of the United States to vote shall not be denied or abridged by the United States or by any State on account of race, color, or previous condition of servitude.

Section 2. The Congress shall have power to enforce this article by appropriate legislation.

AMENDMENT 16 [1913]

The Congress shall have power to lay and collect taxes on incomes, from whatever source derived, without apportionment among the several States, and without regard to any census or enumeration.

AMENDMENT 17 [1913]

[1] The Senate of the United States shall be composed of two Senators from each State, elected by the people thereof, for six years; and each Senator shall have one vote. The electors in each State shall have the qualifications requisite for electors of the most numerous branch of the State legislatures.

[2] When vacancies happen in the representation of any State in the Senate, the executive authority of such State shall issue writs of election to fill such vacancies: *Provided,* That the legislature of any State may empower the executive thereof to make temporary appointments until the people fill the vacancies by election as the legislature may direct.

[3] This amendment shall not be so construed as to affect the election or term of any Senator chosen before it becomes valid as part of the Constitution.

AMENDMENT 18 [1919]

Section 1. After one year from the ratification of this article the manufacture, sale, or transportation of intoxicating liquors within, the importation thereof into, or the exportation thereof from the United States and all territory subject to the jurisdiction thereof for beverage purposes is hereby prohibited.

Section 2. The Congress and the several States shall have concurrent power to enforce this article by appropriate legislation.

Section 3. This article shall be inoperative unless it shall have been ratified as an amendment to the Constitution by the legislatures of the several States, as provided in the Constitution, within seven years from the date of the submission hereof to the States by the Congress.

AMENDMENT 19 [1920]

[1] The right of citizens of the United States to vote shall not be denied or abridged by the United States or by any State on account of sex.

[2] Congress shall have power to enforce this article by appropriate legislation.

AMENDMENT 20 [1933]

Section 1. The terms of the President and Vice President shall end at noon on the 20th day of January, and the terms of Senators and Representatives at noon on the 3rd day of January, of the years in which such terms would have ended if this article had not been ratified; and the terms of their successors shall then begin.

Section 2. The Congress shall assemble at least once in every year, and such meeting shall begin at noon on the 3rd day of January, unless they shall by law appoint a different day.

Section 3. If, at the time fixed for the beginning of the term of the President, the President elect shall have died, the Vice President elect shall become President. If the President shall not have been chosen before the time fixed for the beginning of his term, or if the President elect shall have failed to qualify, then the Vice President elect shall act as President until a President shall have qualified; and the Congress may by law provide for the case wherein neither a President elect nor a Vice President elect shall have qualified, declaring who shall then act as President, or the manner in which one who is to act shall be selected, and such person shall act accordingly until a President or Vice President shall have qualified.

Section 4. The Congress may by law provide for the case of the death of any of the persons from whom the House of Representatives may choose a President whenever the right of choice shall have devolved upon them, and for the case of the death of any of the persons from whom the Senate may choose a Vice President whenever the right of choice shall have devolved upon them.

Section 5. Sections 1 and 2 shall take effect on the 15th day of October following the ratification of this article.

Section 6. This article shall be inoperative unless it shall have been ratified as an amendment to the Constitution by the legislatures of three-fourths of the several States within seven years from the date of its submission.

AMENDMENT 21 [1933]

Section 1. The eighteenth article of amendment to the Constitution of the United States is hereby repealed.

Section 2. The transportation or importation into any State, Territory, or possession of the United States for delivery or use therein of intoxicating liquors, in violation of the laws therefore, is hereby prohibited.

Section 3. This article shall be inoperative unless it shall have been ratified as an amendment to the Constitution by conventions in the several States, as provided in the Constitution, within seven years from the date of the submission hereof to the States by the Congress.

AMENDMENT 22 [1951]

Section 1. No person shall be elected to the office of the President more than twice, and no person who has held the office of President, or acted as President, for more than two years of a term to which some other person was elected President shall be elected to the office of President more than once. But this Article shall not apply to any person holding the office of President when this Article was proposed by the Congress, and shall not prevent any person who may be holding the office of President, or acting as President, during the term within which this Article becomes operative from holding the office of President or acting as President during the remainder of such term.

Section 2. This article shall be inoperative unless it shall have been ratified as an amendment to the Constitution by the legislatures of three-fourths of the several States within seven years from the date of its submission to the States by the Congress.

AMENDMENT 23 [1961]

Section 1. The District constituting the seat of Government of the United States shall appoint in such manner as the Congress may direct:

A number of electors of President and Vice President equal to the whole number of Senators and Representatives in Congress to which the District would be entitled if it were a State, but in no event more than the least populous state; they shall be in addition to those appointed by the states, but they shall be considered, for the purposes of the election of President and Vice President, to be electors appointed by a state; and they shall meet in the District and perform such duties as provided by the twelfth article of amendment.

Section 2. The Congress shall have power to enforce this article by appropriate legislation.

AMENDMENT 24 [1964]

Section 1. The right of citizens of the United States to vote in any primary or other election for President or Vice President, for electors for President or Vice President, or for Senator or Representative in Congress, shall not be denied or abridged by the United States, or any State by reason of failure to pay any poll tax or other tax.

Section 2. The Congress shall have power to enforce this article by appropriate legislation.

AMENDMENT 25 [1967]

Section 1. In case of the removal of the President from office or of his death or resignation, the Vice President shall become President.

Section 2. Whenever there is a vacancy in the office of the Vice President, the President shall nominate a Vice President who shall take office upon confirmation by a majority vote of both Houses of Congress.

Section 3. Whenever the President transmits to the President pro tempore of the Senate and the Speaker of the House of Representatives his written declaration that he is unable to discharge the powers and duties of his office, and until he transmits to them a written declaration to the contrary, such powers and duties shall be discharged by the Vice President as Acting President.

Section 4. Whenever the Vice President and a majority of either the principal officers of the executive departments or of such other body as Congress may by law provide, transmit to the President pro tempore of the Senate and the Speaker of the House of Representatives their written declaration that the President is unable to discharge the powers and duties of his office, the Vice President shall immediately assume the powers and duties of the office as Acting President.

Thereafter, when the President transmits to the President pro tempore of the Senate and the Speaker of the House of Representatives his written declaration that no inability exists, he shall resume the powers and duties of his office unless the Vice President and a majority of either the principal officers of the executive department or of such other body as Congress may by law provide, transmit within four days to the President pro tempore of the Senate and the Speaker of the House of Representatives their written declaration and the President is unable to discharge the powers and duties of his office. Thereupon Congress shall decide the issue, assembling within forty-eight hours for that purpose if not in session. If the Congress, within twenty-one days after receipt of the latter written declaration, or, if Congress is not in session, within twenty-one days after Congress is required to assemble, determines by two-thirds vote of both Houses that the President is unable to discharge the powers and duties of his office, the Vice President shall continue to discharge the same as Acting President; otherwise, the President shall resume the powers and duties of his office.

AMENDMENT 26 [1971]

Section 1. The right of citizens of the United States, who are eighteen years of age or older, to vote shall not be denied or abridged by the United States or by any State on account of age.

Section 2. The Congress shall have power to enforce this article by appropriate legislation.

APPENDIX B
Uniform Commercial Code
(Articles 1, 2, and 3)

ARTICLE 1: GENERAL PROVISIONS

Part 1: Short Title, Construction, Application and Subject Matter of the Act

§1-101. Short Title. This act shall be known and may be cited as Uniform Commercial Code.

§1-102. Purposes; Rules of Construction; Variation by Agreement.

(**1**) This Act shall be liberally construed and applied to promote its underlying purposes and policies.

(**2**) Underlying purposes and policies of this Act are

(**a**) to simplify, clarify and modernize the law governing commercial transactions;

(**b**) to permit the continued expansion of commercial practices through custom, usage and agreement of the parties;

(**c**) to make uniform the law among the various jurisdictions.

(**3**) The effect of provisions of this Act may be varied by agreement, except as otherwise provided in this Act and except that the obligations of good faith, diligence, reasonableness and care prescribed by this Act may not be disclaimed by agreement but the parties may by agreement determine the standards by which the performance of such obligations is to be measured if such standards are not manifestly unreasonable.

(**4**) The presence in certain provisions of this Act of the words "unless otherwise agreed" or words of similar import does not imply that the effect of other provisions may not be varied by agreement under subsection (3).

(**5**) In this Act unless the context otherwise requires

(**a**) words in the singular number include the plural, and in the plural include the singular;

(**b**) words of the masculine gender include the feminine and the neuter, and when the sense so indicates words of the neuter gender may refer to any gender.

§1-103. Supplementary General Principles of Law Applicable. Unless displaced by the particular provisions of this Act, the principles of law and equity, including the law merchant and the law relative to capacity to contract, principal and agent, estoppel, fraud, misrepresentation, duress, coercion, mistake, bankruptcy, or other validating or invalidating cause shall supplement its provisions.

§1-104. Construction Against Implicity Repeal. This Act being a general act intended as a unified coverage of its subject matter, no part of it shall be deemed to be impliedly repealed by subsequent legislation if such construction can reasonably be avoided.

§1-105. Territorial Application of the Act; Parties' Power to Choose Applicable Law.

(**1**) Except as provided hereafter in this section, when a transaction bears a reasonable relation to this state and also to another state or nation the parties may agree that the law either of this state or of such other state or nation shall govern their rights and duties. Failing such agreement this Act applies to transactions bearing an appropriate relation to this state.

(**2**) Where one of the following provisions of this Act specifies the applicable law, that provision governs and a contrary agreement is effective only to the extent permitted by the law (including the conflict of laws rules) so specified:

Rights of creditors against sold goods. Section 2-402.

Applicability of the Article on Bank Deposits and Collections. Section 4-102.

Bulk transfers subject to the Article on Bulk Transfers. Section 6-102.

Applicability of the Article on Investment Securities. Section 8-106.

Perfection provisions of the Article on Secured Transactions. Section 9-103.

§1-106. Remedies to Be Liberally Administered.

(1) The remedies provided by this Act shall be liberally administered to the end that the aggrieved party may be put in as good a position as if the other party had fully performed but neither consequential or special nor penal damages may be had except as specifically provided in this Act or by other rule of law.

(2) Any right or obligation declared by this Act is enforceable by action unless the provision declaring it specifies a different and limited effect.

§1-107. Waiver or Renunciation of Claim or Right After Breach. Any claim or right arising out of an alleged breach can be discharged in whole or in part without consideration by a written waiver or renunciation signed and delivered by the aggrieved party.

§1-108. Severability. If any provision or clause of this Act or application thereof to any person or circumstances is held invalid, such invalidity shall not affect other provisions or applications of the Act which can be given effect without the invalid provision or application, and to this end the provisions of this Act are declared to be severable.

§1-109. Section Captions. Section captions are parts of this Act.

Part 2: General Definitions and Principles of Interpretation

§1-201. General Definitions. Subject to additional definitions contained in the subsequent Articles of this Act which are applicable to specific Articles or Parts thereof, and unless the context otherwise requires, in this Act.

(1) "Action" in the sense of a judicial proceeding includes recoupment, counterclaim, set-off, suit in equity and any other proceedings in which rights are determined.

(2) "Aggrieved party" means a party entitled to resort to a remedy.

(3) "Agreement" means the bargain of the parties in fact as found in their language or by implication from other circumstances including course of dealing or usage of trade or course of performance as provided in this Act, (Section 1-205 and 2-208). Whether an agreement has legal consequences is determined by the provisions of this Act, if applicable; otherwise by the law of contracts (Section 1-103). (Compare "Contract".)

(4) "Bank" means any person engaged in the business of banking.

(5) "Bearer" means the person in possession of an instrument, document of title, or certificated security payable to bearer or indorsed in blank.

(6) "Bill of lading" means a document evidencing the receipt of goods for shipment issued by a person engaged in the business of transporting or forwarding goods, and includes an airbill. "Airbill" means a document serving for air transportation as a bill of lading does for marine or rail transportation, and includes an air consignment note or air waybill.

(7) "Branch" includes a separately incorporated foreign branch of a bank.

(8) "Burden of establishing" a fact means the burden of persuading the triers of fact that the existence of the fact is more probable than its non-existence.

(9) "Buyer in ordinary course of business" means a person who in good faith and without knowledge that the sale to him is in violation of the ownership rights or security interest of a third party in the goods buys in ordinary course from a person in the business of selling goods of that kind but does not include a pawnbroker. All persons who sell minerals or the like (including oil and gas) at wellhead or minehead shall be deemed to be persons in the business of selling goods of that kind. "Buying" may be for cash or by exchange of other property or on secured or unsecured credit and includes receiving goods or documents of title under a pre-existing contract for sale but does not include a transfer in bulk or as security for or in total or partial satisfaction of a money debt.

(10) "Conspicuous": A term or clause is conspicuous when it is so written that a reasonable person against whom it is to operate ought to have noticed it. A printed heading in capitals (as: NON-NEGOTIABLE BILL OF LADING) is conspicuous. Language in the body of a form is "conspicuous" if it is in larger or other contrasting type or color. But in a telegram any stated term is "conspicuous". Whether a term or clause is "conspicuous" or not is for decision by the court.

(11) "Contract" means the total legal obligation which results from the parties' agreement as affected by this Act and any other applicable rules of law. (Compare "Agreement".)

(**12**) "Creditor" includes a general creditor, a secured creditor, a lien creditor and any representative of creditors, including an assignee for the benefit of creditors, a trustee in bankruptcy, a receiver in equity and an executor or adminsitrator of an insolvent debtor's or assignor's estate.

(**13**) "Defendant" includes a person in the position of defendant in a cross-action or counterclaim.

(**14**) "Delivery" with respect to instruments, documents of title, chattel paper, or certificated securities means voluntary transfer of possession.

(**15**) "Document of title" includes bill of lading, dock warrant, dock receipt, warehouse receipt or order for the delivery of goods, and also any other document which in the regular course of business or financing is treated as adequately evidencing that the person in possession of it is entitled to receive, hold and dispose of the document and the goods it covers. To be a document of title a document must purport to be issued by or addressed to a bailee and purport to cover goods in the bailee's possession which are either identified or are fungible portions of an identified mass.

(**16**) "Fault" means wrongful act, omission or breach.

(**17**) "Fungible" with respect to goods or securities means goods or securities of which any unit is, by nature or usage of trade, the equivalent of any other like unit. Goods which are not fungible shall be deemed fungible for the purposes of this Act to the extent that under a particular agreement or document unlike units are treated as equivalents.

(**18**) "Genuine" means free of forgery or counterfeiting.

(**19**) "Good faith" means honesty in fact in the conduct or transaction concerned.

(**20**) "Holder" means a person who is in possession of a document of title or a certificated instrument or an investment security drawn, issued or indorsed to him or to his order or to bearer or in blank.

(**21**) To "honor" is to pay or to accept and pay, or where a credit so engages to purchase or discount a draft complying with the terms of the credit.

(**22**) "Insolvency proceedings" includes any assignment for the benefit of creditors or other proceedings intended to liquidate or rehabilitate the estate of the person involved.

(**23**) A person is "insolvent" who either has ceased to pay his debts in the ordinary course of business or cannot pay his debts as they become due or is insolvent within the meaning of the federal bankruptcy law.

(**24**) "Money" means a medium of exchange authorized or adopted by a domestic or foreign government as part of its currency.

(**25**) A person has "notice" of a fact when

(**a**) he has actual knowledge of it; or

(**b**) he has received a notice or notification of it; or

(**c**) from all the facts and circumstances known to him at the time in question he has reason to know that it exists.

A person "knows" or has "knowledge" of a fact when he has actual knowledge of it. "Discover" or "learn" or a word or phrase of similar import refers to knowledge rather than to reason to know. The time and circumstances under which a notice or notification may cease to be effective are not determined by this Act.

(**26**) A person "notifies" or "gives" a notice or notification to another by taking such steps as may be reasonably required to inform the other in ordinary course whether or not such other actually comes to know of it. A person "receives" a notice or notification when

(**a**) it comes to his attention; or

(**b**) it is duly delivered at the place of business through which the contract was made or at any other place held out by him as the place for receipt of such communications.

(**27**) Notice, knowledge or a notice or notification received by an organization is effective for a particular transaction from the time when it is brought to the attention of the individual conducting that transaction, and in any event from the time when it would have been brought to his attention if the organization had exercised due diligence. An organization exercises due diligence if it maintains reasonable routines for communicating significant information to the person conducting the transaction and there is reasonable compliance with the routines. Due diligence does not require an individual acting for the organization to communicate information unless such communication is part of his regular duties or unless he has reason to know of the transaction and that the transaction would be materially affected by the information.

(**28**) "Organization" includes a corporation, government or governmental subdivision or agency, business trust, estate, trust, partnership or association, two or more persons having a joint or common interest, or any other legal or commercial entity.

(**29**) "Party", as distinct from "third party", means a person who has engaged in a transaction or made an agreement within this Act.

(**30**) "Person" includes an individual or an organization (See Section 1-102).

(**31**) "Presumption" or "presumed" means that the trier of fact must find the existence of the fact presumed unless and until evidence is introduced which would support a finding of its non-existence.

(**32**) "Purchase" includes taking by sale, discount, negotiation, mortgage, pledge, lien, issue or re-issue, gift or any other voluntary transaction creating an interest in property.

(**33**) "Purchaser" means a person who takes by purchase.

(**34**) "Remedy" means any remedial right to which an aggrieved party is entitled with or without resort to a tribunal.

(**35**) "Representative" includes as agent, an officer of a corporation or association, and a trustee, executor or administrator of an estate, or any other person empowered to act for another.

(**36**) "Rights" includes remedies.

(**37**) "Security interest" means an interest in personal property or fixtures which secures payment or performance of an obligation. The retention or reservation of title by a seller of goods notwithstanding shipment or delivery to the buyer (Section 2-401) is limited in effect to a reservation of a "security interest". The term also includes any interest of a buyer of accounts or chattel paper, which is subject to Article 9. The special property interest of a buyer of goods on identification of such goods to a contract for sale under Section 2-401 is not a "security interest", but a buyer may also acquire a "security interest" by complying with Article 9. Unless a lease or consignment is intended as security, reservation of title thereunder is not a "security interest" but a consignment is in any event subject to the provisions on consignment sales (Section 2-326). Whether a lease is intended as security is to be determined by the facts of each case; however, (a) the inclusion of an option to purchase does not itself make the lease one intended for security, and (b) an agreement that upon compliance with the terms of the lease the lessee shall become or has the option to become the owner of the property for no additional consideration or for a nominal consideration does make the lease one intended for security.

(**38**) "Send" in connection with any writing or notice means to deposit in the mail or deliver for transmission by any other usual means of communication with postage or cost of transmission provided for and properly addressed and in the case of an instrument to an address specified thereon or otherwise agreed, or if there by none to any address reasonable under the circumstances. The receipt of any writing or notice within the time at which it would have arrived if properly sent has the effect of a proper sending.

(**39**) "Signed" includes any symbol executed or adopted by a party with present intention to authenticate a writing.

(**40**) "Surety" includes guarantor.

(**41**) "Telegram" includes a message transmitted by radio, teletype, cable, any mechanical method of transmission, or the like.

(**42**) "Term" means that portion of an agreement which relates to a particular matter.

(**43**) "Unauthorized" signature or indorsement means one made without actual, implied or apparent authority and includes a forgery.

(**44**) "Value". Except as otherwise provided with respect to negotiable instruments and bank collections (Sections 3-303, 4-208 and 4-209) a person gives "value" for rights if he acquires them

(**a**) in return for a binding commitment to extend credit or for the extension of immediately available credit whether or not drawn upon and whether or not a chargeback is provided for in the event of difficulties in collection; or

(**b**) as security for or in total or partial satisfaction of a pre-existing claim; or

(**c**) by accepting delivery pursuant to a pre-existing contract for purchase; or

(**d**) generally, in return for any consideration sufficient to support a simple contract.

(**45**) "Warehouse receipt" means a receipt issued by a person engaged in the business of storing goods for hire.

(**46**) "Written" or "writing" includes printing, typewriting or any other intentional reduction to tangible form. As amended 1962 and 1972.

§1-201. General Definitions *(1977 Amendments).*

Subject to additional definitions contained in the subsequent Articles of this Act which are applicable to specific Articles or Parts thereof, and unless the context otherwise requires, in the Act:

* * *

(**5**) "Bearer" means the person in possession of an

instrument, document of title, or certificated security payable to bearer or indorsed in blank.

* * *

(14) "Delivery" with respect to instruments, documents of title, chattel paper, or certificated securities means voluntary transfer of possession.

* * *

(20) "Holder" means a person who is in possession of a document of title or an instrument or a certificated investment security drawn, issued or indorsed to him or his order or to bearer or in blank.

* * *

§1-202. Prima Facie Evidence by Third Party Documents. A document in due form purporting to be a bill of lading, policy or certificate of insurance, official weigher's or inspector's certificate, consular invoice or any other document authorized or required by the contract to be issued by a third party shall be prima facie evidence of its own authenticity and genuineness and of the facts stated in the document by the third party.

§1-203. Obligation of Good Faith. Every contract or duty within this Act imposes an obligation of good faith in its performance or enforcement.

§1-204. Time; Reasonable Time; "Seasonably".

(1) Whenever this Act requires any action to be taken within a reasonable time, any time which is not manifestly unreasonable may be fixed by agreement.

(2) What is a reasonable time for taking any action depends on the nature, purpose and circumstances of such action.

(3) An action is taken "seasonably" when it is taken at or within the time agreed or if no time is agreed at or within a reasonable time.

§1-205. Course of Dealing and Usage of Trade.

(1) A course of dealing is a sequence of previous conduct between the parties to a particular transaction which is fairly to be regarded as establishing a common basis of understanding for interpreting their expressions and other conduct.

(2) A usage of trade is any practice or method of dealing having such regularity of observance in a place, vocation or trade as to justify an expectation that it will be observed with respect to the transaction in question. The existence and scope of such a usage are to be proved as facts. If it is established that such a usage is embodied in a written trade code or similar writing the interpretation of the writing is for the court.

(3) A course of dealing between parties and any usage of trade in the vocation or trade in which they are engaged or of which they are or should be aware give particular meaning to and supplement or qualify terms of an agreement.

(4) The express terms of an agreement and an applicable course of dealing or usage of trade shall be construed wherever reasonable as consistent with each other; but when such construction is unreasonable express terms control both course of dealing and usage of trade and course of dealing controls usage of trade.

(5) An applicable usage of trade in the place where any part of performance is to occur shall be used in interpreting the agreement as to that part of the performance.

(6) Evidence of a relevant usage of trade offered by one party is not admissible unless and until he has given the other party such notice as the court finds sufficient to prevent unfair surprise to the latter.

§1-206. Statute of Frauds for Kinds of Personal Property Not Otherwise Covered.

(1) Except in the cases described in subsection (2) of this section a contract for the sale of personal property is not enforceable by way of action or defense beyond five thousand dollars in amount or value of remedy unless there is some writing which indicates that a contract for sale has been made between the parties at a defined or stated price, reasonably identifies the subject matter, and is signed by the party against whom enforcement is sought or by his authorized agent.

(2) Subsection (1) of this section does not apply to contracts for the sale of goods (Section 2-201) nor of securities (Section 8-319) nor to security agreements (Section 9-203).

§1-207. Performance or Acceptance Under Reservation of Rights. A party who with explicit reservation of rights performs or promises performance or assents to performance in a manner demanded or offered by the other party does not thereby prejudice the rights reserved. Such words as "without prejudice", "under protest" or the like are sufficient.

§1-208. Option to Accelerate at Will. A term providing that one party or his successor in interest may accelerate payment or performance or require collateral or additional collateral "at will" or "when he deems himself insecure" or in words of similar import shall be construed to mean that he shall have power to do so only if he in good faith believes that the prospect of payment or performance is impaired. The burden of establishing lack of good faith is on the party against whom the power has been exercised.

§1-209. Subordinated Obligations. An obligation may be issued as subordinated to payment of another obligation of the person obligated, or a creditor may subordinate his right to payment of an obligation by agreement with either the person obligated or another creditor of the person obligated. Such a subordination does not create a security interest as against either the common debtor or a subordinated creditor. This section shall be construed as declaring the law as it existed prior to the enactment of this section and not as modifying it. Added 1966.

Note: *This new section is proposed as an optional provision to make it clear that a subordination agreement does not create a security interest unless so intended.*

ARTICLE 2: SALES

Part 1: Short Title, General Construction and Subject Matter

§2-101. Short Title. This Article shall be known and may be cited as Uniform Commercial Code—Sales.

§2-102. Scope; Certain Security and Other Transactions Excluded From This Article. Unless the context otherwise requires, this Article applies to transactions in goods; it does not apply to any transaction which although in the form of an unconditional contract to sell or present sale is intended to operate only as a security transaction nor does this Article impair or repeal any statute regulating sales to consumers, farmers or other specified classes of buyers.

§2-103. Definitions and Index of Definitions.

(**1**) In this Article unless the context otherwise requires

(**a**) "Buyer" means a person who buys or contracts to buy goods.

(**b**) "Good faith" in the case of a merchant means honesty in fact and the observance of reasonable commercial standards of fair dealing in the trade.

(**c**) "Receipt" of goods means taking physical possession of them.

(**d**) "Seller" means a person who sells or contracts to sell goods.

(**2**) Other definitions applying to this Article or to specified Parts thereof, and the sections in which they appear are:

"Acceptance". Section 2-606.
"Banker's credit". Section 2-325.
"Between merchants". Section 2-104.
"Cancellation". Section 2-106(4).
"Commercial unit". Section 2-105.
"Confirmed credit". Section 2-325.
"Conforming to contract". Section 2-106.
"Contract for sale". Section 2-106.
"Cover". Section 2-712.
"Entrusting". Section 2-403.
"Financing agency". Section 2-104.
"Future goods". Section 2-105.
"Goods". Section 2-105.
"Identification". Section 2-501.
"Installment contract". Section 2-612.
"Letter of Credit". Section 2-325.
"Lot". Section 2-105.
"Merchant". Section 2-104.
"Overseas". Section 2-323.
"Person in position of seller". Section 2-707.
"Present sale". Section 2-106.
"Sale". Section 2-106.
"Sale on approval". Section 2-326.
"Sale or return". Section 2-326.
"Termination". Section 2-106.

(**3**) The following definitions in other Articles apply to this Article:

"Check". Section 3-104.
"Consignee". Section 7-102.
"Consignor". Section 7-102.
"Consumer goods". Section 9-109.
"Dishonor". Section 3-507.
"Draft". Section 3-104.

(**4**) In addition Article 1 contains general definitions and principles of construction and interpretation applicable throughout this article.

§2-104. Definitions: "Merchant"; "Between Merchants"; "Financing Agency".

(**1**) "Merchant" means a person who deals in goods of the kind or otherwise by his occupation holds himself out as having knowledge or skill peculiar to the practices or goods involved in the transaction or to whom such knowledge or skill may be attributed by his employment of an agent or broker or other intermediary who by his occupation holds himself out as having such knowledge or skill.

(**2**) "Financing agency" means a bank, finance company or other person who in the ordinary course of business makes advances against goods or documents of title or who by arrangement with either the seller or the buyer intervenes in ordinary course to make or collect payment due or claimed under the contract for sale, as by purchasing or paying the seller's draft or making advances against it or by merely taking it for collection whether or not documents of title accompany the draft. "Financing agency" includes also a bank or other person who similarly intervenes between persons who are in the position of seller and buyer in respect of the goods (Section 2-707).

(3) "Between merchants" means in any transaction with respect to which both parties are chargeable with the knowledge or skill of merchants.

§2-105. Definitions: Transferability; "Goods"; "Future" Goods; "Lot"; "Commercial Unit".

(1) "Goods" means all things (including specially manufactured goods) which are movable at the time of identification to the contract for sale other than the money in which the price is to be paid, investment securities (Article 8) and things in action. "Goods" also includes the unborn young of animals and growing crops and other identified things attached to realty as described in the section on goods to be severed from realty (Section 2-107).

(2) Goods must be both existing and identified before any interest in them can pass. Goods which are not both existing and identified are "future" goods. A purported present sale of future goods or of any interest therein operates as a contract to sell.

(3) There may be a sale of a part interest in existing identified goods.

(4) An undivided share in an identified bulk of fungible goods is sufficiently identified to be sold although the quantity of the bulk is not determined. Any agreed proportion of such a bulk or any quantity thereof agreed upon by number, weight or other measure may to the extent of the seller's interest in the bulk be sold to the buyer who then becomes an owner in common.

(5) "Lot" means a parcel or a single article which is the subject matter of a separate sale or delivery, whether or not it is sufficient to perform the contract.

(6) "Commercial unit" means such a unit of goods as by commercial usage is a single whole for purposes of sale and division of which materially impairs its character or value on the market or in use. A commercial unit may be a single article (as a machine) or a set of articles (as a suite of furniture or an assortment of sizes) or a quantity (as a bale, gross, or carload) or any other unit treated in use or in the relevant market as a single whole.

§2-106. Definitions: "Contract"; "Agreement"; "Contract for Sale"; "Sale"; "Present Sale"; "Conforming" to Contract; "Termination"; "Cancellation".

(1) In this Article unless the context otherwise requires "contract" and "agreement" are limited to those relating to the present or future sale of goods. "Contract for sale" includes both a present sale of goods and a contract to sell goods at a future time. A "sale" consists in the passing of title from the seller to the buyer for a price (Section 2-401). A "present sale" means a sale which is accomplished by the making of the contract.

(2) Goods or conduct including any part of a performance are "conforming" or conform to the contract when they are in accordance with the obligations under the contract.

(3) "Termination" occurs when either party pursuant to a power created by agreement or law puts an end to the contract otherwise than for its breach. On "termination" all obligations which are still executory on both sides are discharged but any right based on prior breach or performance survives.

(4) "Cancellation" occurs when either party puts an end to the contract for breach by the other and its effect is the same as that of "termination" except that the cancelling party also retains any remedy for breach of the whole contract or any unperformed balance.

§2-107. Goods to Be Severed From Realty: Recording.

(1) A contract for the sale of minerals or the like (including oil and gas) or a structure or its materials to be removed from realty is a contract for the sale of goods within this Article if they are to be severed by the seller but until severance a purported present sale thereof which is not effective as a transfer of an interest in land is effective only as a contract to sell.

(2) A contract for the sale apart from the land of growing crops or other things attached to realty and capable of severance without material harm thereto but not described in subsection (1) or of timber to be cut is a contract for the sale of goods within this Article whether the subject matter is to be severed by the buyer or by the seller even though it forms part of the realty at the time of contracting, and the parties can by identification effect a present sale before severance.

(3) The provisions of this section are subject to any third party rights provided by the law relating to realty records, and the contract for sale may be executed and recorded as a document transferring an interest in land and shall then constitute notice to third parties of the buyer's rights under the contract for sale.

Part 2: Form, Formation and Readjustment of Contract

§2-201. Formal Requirements; Statute of Frauds.

(1) Except as otherwise provided in this section a contract for the sale of goods for the price of $500 or more is not enforceable by way of action or defense unless there is some writing sufficient to indicate that a contract for sale has been made between the parties and signed by the party against whom enforcement is sought or by his authorized agent or broker. A writing is not insufficient because it omits or incorrectly states a term agreed upon but the contract is not enforceable under this paragraph beyond the quantity of goods shown in such writing.

(2) Between merchants if within a reasonable time a writing in confirmation of the contract and sufficient against the sender is received and the party receiving it has reason to know its contents, it satisfies the requirements of subsection (1) against such party unless written notice of objection to its contents is given within 10 days after it is received.

(3) A contract which does not satisfy the requirements of subsection (1) but which is valid in other respects is enforceable

(a) if the goods are to be specially manufactured for the buyer and are not suitable for sale to others in the ordinary course of the seller's business and the seller, before notice of repudiation is received and under circumstances which reasonably indicate that the goods are for the buyer, has made either a substantial beginning of their manufacture of commitments for their procurement; or

(b) if the party against whom enforcement is sought admits in his pleading, testimony or otherwise in court that a contract for sale was made, but the contract is not enforceable under this provision beyond the quantity of goods admitted; or

(c) with respect to goods for which payment has been made and accepted or which have been received and accepted (Sec. 2-606.)

§2-202. Final Written Expression: Parol or Extrinsic Evidence. Terms with respect to which the confirmatory memoranda of the parties agree or which are otherwise set forth in a writing intended by the parties as a final expression of their agreement with respect to such terms as are included therein may not be contradicted by evidence of any prior agreement or of a contemporaneous oral agreement but may be explained or supplemented

(a) by course of dealing or usage of trade (Section 1-205) or by course of performance (Section 2-208); and

(b) by evidence of consistent additional terms unless the court finds the writing to have been intended also as a complete and exclusive statement of the terms of the agreement.

§2-203. Seals Inoperative. The affixing of a seal to a writing evidencing a contract for sale or an offer to buy or sell goods does not constitute the writing a sealed instrument and the law with respect to sealed instruments does not apply to such a contract or offer.

§2-204. Formation in General.

(1) A contract for sale of goods may be made in any manner sufficient to show agreement, including conduct by both parties which recognizes the existence of such a contract.

(2) An agreement sufficient to constitute a contract for sale may be found even though the moment of its making is undetermined.

(3) Even though one or more terms are left open a contract for sale does not fail for indefiniteness if the parties have intended to make a contract and there is a reasonably certain basis for giving an appropriate remedy.

§2-205. Firm Offers. An offer by a merchant to buy or sell goods in a signed writing which by its terms gives assurance that it will be held open is not revocable, for lack of consideration, during the time stated or if no time is stated for a reasonable time, but in no event may such period of irrevocability exceed three months; but any such term of assurance on a form supplied by the offeree must be separately signed by the offeror.

§2-206. Offer and Acceptance in Formation of Contract.

(1) Unless otherwise unambiguously indicated by the language or circumstances

(a) an offer to make a contract shall be construed as inviting acceptance in any manner and by any medium reasonable in the circumstances;

(b) an order or other offer to buy goods for prompt or current shipment shall be construed as inviting acceptance either by a prompt promise to ship or by the prompt or current shipment of conforming or nonconforming goods, but such a shipment of nonconforming goods does not constitute an acceptance if the seller seasonably notifies the buyer that the shipment is offered only as an accommodation to the buyer.

(2) Where the beginning of a requested performance is a reasonable mode of acceptance an offeror who is not notified of acceptance within a reasonable time may treat the offer as having lapsed before acceptance.

§2-207. Additional Terms in Acceptance or Confirmation.

(1) A definite and seasonable expression of acceptance or a written confirmation which is sent within a reasonable time operates as an acceptance even though it states terms additional to or different from those offered or agreed upon, unless acceptance is expressly made conditional on assent to the additional or different terms.

(2) The additional terms are to be construed as proposals for addition to the contract. Between merchants such terms become part of the contract unless:

(a) the offer expressly limits acceptance to the terms of the offer;

(b) they materially alter it; or

(c) notification of objection to them has already been given or is given within a reasonable time after notice of them is received.

(3) Conduct by both parties which recognizes the existence of a contract is sufficient to establish a contract for sale although the writings of the parties do not otherwise establish a contract. In such case the terms of the particular contract consist of those terms on which the writings of the parties agree, together with any supplementary terms incorporated under any other provisions of this Act.

§2-208. Course of Performance or Practical Construction.

(1) Where the contract for sale involves repeated occasions for performance by either party with knowledge of the nature of the performance and opportunity for objection to it by the other, any course of performance accepted or acquiesced in without objection shall be relevant to determine the meaning of the agreement.

(2) The express terms of the agreement and any such course of performance, as well as any course of dealing and usage of trade, shall be construed whenever reasonable as consistent with each other; but when such construction is unreasonable, express terms shall control course of performance and course of performance shall control both course of dealing and usage of trade (Section 1-205).

(3) Subject to the provisions of the next section on modification and waiver, such course of performance shall be relevant to show a waiver or modification of any term inconsistent with such course of performance.

§2-209. Modification, Rescission and Waiver.

(1) An agreement modifying a contract within this Article needs no consideration to be binding.

(2) A signed agreement which excludes modification or rescission except by a signed writing cannot be otherwise modified or rescinded, but except as between merchants such a requirement on a form supplied by the merchant must be separately signed by the other party.

(3) The requirements of the statute of frauds section of this Article (Section 2-201) must be satisfied if the contract as modified is within its provisions.

(4) Although an attempt at modification or rescission does not satisfy the requirements of subsection (2) or (3) it can operate as a waiver.

(5) A party who has made a waiver affecting an executory portion of the contract may retract the waiver by reasonable notification received by the other party that strict performance will be required of any term waived, unless the retraction would be unjust in view of a material change of position in reliance on the waiver.

§2-210. Delegation of Performance; Assignment of Rights.

(1) A party may perform his duty through a delegate unless otherwise agreed or unless the other party has a substantial interest in having his original promisor perform or control the acts required by the contract. No delegation of performance relieves the party delegating of any duty to perform or any liability for breach.

(2) Unless otherwise agreed all rights of either seller or buyer can be assigned except where the assignment would materially change the duty of the other party, or increase materially the burden or risk imposed on him by his contract, or impair materially his chance of obtaining return performance. A right to damages for breach of the whole contract or a right arising out of the assignor's due performance of his entire obligation can be assigned despite agreement otherwise.

(3) Unless the circumstances indicate the contrary a prohibition of assignment of "the contract" is to be construed as barring only the delegation to the assignee of the assignor's performance.

(4) An assignment of "the contract" or of "all my rights under the contract" or an assignment in similar general terms is an assignment of rights and unless the language or the circumstances (as in an assignment for security) indicate the contrary, it is a delegation of performance of the duties of the assignor and its acceptance by the assignee constitutes a promise by him to perform those duties. This promise is enforceable by either the assignor or the other party to the original contract.

(5) The other party may treat any assignment which delegates performance as creating reasonable grounds for insecurity and may without prejudice to his rights against the assignor demand assurances from the assignee (Section 2-609).

Part 3: General Obligation and Construction of Contract

§2-301. General Obligations of Parties. The obligation of the seller is to transfer and deliver and that of the buyer is to accept and pay in accordance with the contract.

§2-302. Unconscionable Contract or Clause.

(1) If the court as a matter of law finds the contract or any clause of the contract to have been unconscionable at the time it was made the court may refuse to enforce the contract, or it may enforce the remainder of the contract without the unconscionable clause, or it may so limit the application of any unconscionable clause as to avoid any unconscionable result.

(2) When it is claimed or appears to the court that the contract or any clause thereof may be unconscionable the parties shall be afforded a reasonable opportunity to present evidence as to its commercial setting, purpose and effect to aid the court in making the determination.

§2-303. Allocation or Division of Risks. Where this Article allocates a risk or a burden as between the parties "unless otherwise agreed", the agreement may not only shift the allocation but may also divide the risk or burden.

§2-304. Price Payable in Money, Goods, Realty, or Otherwise.

(1) The price can be made payable in money or otherwise. If it is payable in whole or in part in goods each party is a seller of the goods which he is to transfer.

(2) Even though all or part of the price is payable in an interest in realty the transfer of the goods and the seller's obligations with reference to them are subject to this Article, but not the transfer of the interest in realty or the transferor's obligations in connection therewith.

§2-305. Open Price Term.

(1) The parties if they so intend can conclude a contract for sale even though the price is not settled. In such a case the price is a reasonable price at the time for delivery if

(a) nothing is said as to price; or

(b) the price is left to be agreed by the parties and they fail to agree; or

(c) the price is to be fixed in terms of some agreed market or other standard as set or recorded by a third person or agency and it is not so set or recorded.

(2) A price to be fixed by the seller or by the buyer means a price for him to fix in good faith.

(3) When a price left to be fixed otherwise than by agreement of the parties fails to be fixed through fault of one party the other may at his option treat the contract as cancelled or himself fix a reasonable price.

(4) Where, however, the parties intend not to be bound unless the price be fixed or agreed and it is not fixed or agreed there is no contract. In such a case the buyer must return any goods already received or if unable so to do must pay their reasonable value at the time of delivery and the seller must return any portion of the price paid on account.

§2-306. Output, Requirements and Exclusive Dealings.

(1) A term which measures the quantity by the output of the seller or the requirements of the buyer means such actual output or requirements as may occur in good faith, except that no quantity unreasonably disproportionate to any stated estimate or in the absence of a stated estimate to any normal or otherwise comparable prior output or requirements may be tendered or demanded.

(2) A lawful agreement by either the seller or the buyer for exclusive dealing in the kind of goods concerned imposes unless otherwise agreed an obligation by the seller to use best efforts to supply the goods and by the buyer to use best efforts to promote their sale.

§2-307. Delivery in Single Lot or Several Lots. Unless otherwise agreed all goods called for by a contract for sale must be tendered in a single delivery and payment is due only on such tender but where the circumstances give either party the right to make or demand delivery in lots the price if it can be apportioned may be demanded for each lot.

§2-308. Absence of Specified Place for Delivery. Unless otherwise agreed

(a) the place for delivery of goods is the seller's place of business or if he has none his residence; but

(b) in a contract for sale of identified goods which to the knowledge of the parties at the time of contracting are in some other place, that place is the place for their delivery; and

(c) documents of title may be delivered through customary banking channels.

§2-309. Absence of Specific Time Provisions; Notice of Termination.

(1) The time for shipment or delivery or any other action under a contract if not provided in this Article or agreed upon shall be a reasonable time.

(2) Where the contract provides for successive performances but is indefinite in duration it is valid for a reasonable time but unless otherwise agreed may be terminated at any time by either party.

(3) Termination of a contract by one party except on the happening of an agreed event requires that reasonable notification be received by the other party and in agreement dispensing with notification is invalid if its operation would be unconscionable.

§2-310. Open Time for Payment or Running of Credit; Authority to Ship Under Reservation. Unless otherwise agreed

(a) payment is due at the time and place at which the buyer is to receive the goods even though the place of shipment is the place of delivery; and

(b) if the seller is authorized to send the goods he may ship them under reservation, and may tender the documents of title, but the buyer may inspect the goods after their arrival before payment is due unless such inspection is inconsistent with the terms of the contract (Section 2-513); and

(c) if delivery is authorized and made by way of documents of title otherwise than by subsection (b) then payment is due at the time and place at which the buyer is to receive the documents regardless of where the goods are to be received; and

(d) where the seller is required or authorized to ship the goods on credit the credit period runs from the time of shipment but post-dating the invoice or delaying its dispatch will correspondingly delay the starting of the credit period.

§2-311. Options and Cooperation Respecting Performance.

(1) An agreement for sale which is otherwise sufficiently definite (subsection (3) of Section 2-204) to be a contract is not made invalid by the fact that it leaves particulars of performance to be specified by one of the parties. Any such specification must be made in good faith and within limits set by commercial reasonableness.

(2) Unless otherwise agreed specifications relating to assortment of the goods are at the buyer's option and except as otherwise provided in subsections (1) (c) and (3) of Section 2-319 specifications or arrangements relating to shipment are at the seller's options.

(3) Where such specifications would materially affect the other party's performance but is not seasonably made or where one party's cooperation is necessary to the agreed performance of the other but is not seasonably forthcoming, the other party

(a) is excused for any resulting delay in his own performance; and

(b) may also either proceed to perform in any reasonable manner or after the time for a material part of his own performance treat the failure to specify or to cooperate as a breach by failure to deliver or accept the goods.

§2-312. Warranty of Title and Against Infringement; Buyer's Obligation Against Infringement.

(1) Subject to subsection (2) there is in a contract for sale a warranty by the seller that

(a) the title conveyed shall be good, and its transfer rightful; and

(b) the goods shall be delivered free from any security interest or other lien or encumbrance of which the buyer at the time of contracting has no knowledge.

(2) A warranty under subsection (2) will be excluded or modified only by specific language or by circumstances which give the buyer reason to know that the person selling does not claim title in himself or that he is purporting to sell only such right or title as he or a third person may have.

(3) Unless otherwise agreed a seller who is a merchant regularly dealing in goods of the kind warrants that the goods shall be delivered free of the rightful claim of any third person by way of infringement or the like but a buyer who furnishes specifications to the seller must hold the seller harmless against any such claim which arises out of compliance with the specifications.

§2-313. Express Warranties by Affirmation, Promise, Description, Sample.

(1) Express warranties by the seller are created as follows:

(a) Any affirmation of fact or promise made by the seller to the buyer which relates to the goods and becomes part of the basis of the bargain creates an express warranty that the goods shall conform to the affirmation or promise.

(b) Any description of the goods which is made part of the basis of the bargain creates an express warranty that the goods shall conform to the description.

(c) Any sample or model which is made part of the basis of the bargain creates an express warranty that the whole of the goods shall conform to the sample or model.

(2) It is not necessary to the creation of an express warranty that the seller use formal words such as "warrant" or "guarantee" or that he have a specific intention to make a warranty, but an affirmation merely of the value of the goods or a statement purporting to be merely the seller's opinion or commendation of the goods does not create a warranty.

§2-314. Implied Warranty: Merchantability; Usage of Trade.

(1) Unless excluded or modified (Section 2-316), a warranty that the goods shall be merchantable is implied in a contract for their sale if the seller is a merchant with respect to goods of that kind. Under this section the serving for value of food or drink to be consumed either on the premises or elsewhere is a sale.

(2) Goods to be merchantable must be at least such as

(a) pass without objection in the trade under the contract description; and

(b) in the case of fungible goods, are of fair average quality within the description; and

(c) are fit for the ordinary purposes for which such goods are used; and

(d) run, within the variations permitted by the agreement, of even kind, quality and quantity within each unit and among all units involved; and

(e) are adequately contained, packaged, and labeled as the agreement may require; and

(f) conform to the promises or affirmations of fact made or the container or label if any.

(3) Unless excluded or modified (Section 2-316) other implied warranties may arise from course of dealing or usage of trade.

§2-315. Implied Warranty: Fitness for Particular Purpose. Where the seller at the time of contracting has reason to know any particular purpose for which the goods are required and that the buyer is relying on the seller's skill or judgment to select or furnish suitable goods, there is unless excluded or modified under the next section an implied warranty that the goods shall be fit for such purpose.

§2-316. Exclusion or Modification of Warranties.

(1) Words or conduct relevant to the creation of an express warranty and words or conduct tending to negate or limit warranty shall be construed wherever reasonable as consistent with each other; but subject to the provisions of this Article on parol or extrinsic evidence (Section 2-202) negation or limitation is inoperative to the extent that such construction is unreasonable.

(2) Subject to subsection (3), to exclude or modify the implied warranty of merchantability or any part of it the language must mention merchantability and in case of a writing must be conspicuous, and to exclude or modify any implied warranty of fitness the exclusion must be by a writing and conspicuous. Language to exclude all implied warranties of fitness is sufficient if it states, for example, that "There are no warranties which extend beyond the description on the face hereof."

(3) Notwithstanding subsection (2)

(a) unless the circumstances indicate otherwise, all implied warranties are excluded by expressions like "as is", "with all faults" or other language which in common understanding calls the buyer's attention to the exclusion of warranties and makes plain that there is no implied warranty; and

(**b**) when the buyer before entering into the contract has examined the goods or the sample or model as fully as he desired or has refused to examine the goods there is no implied warranty with regard to defects which an examination ought in the circumstances to have revealed to him; and

(**c**) an implied warranty can also be excluded or modified by course of dealing or course of performance or usage of trade.

(**4**) Remedies for breach of warranty can be limited in accordance with the provisions of this Article on liquidation or limitation of damages and on contractual modification of remedy (Sections 2-718 and 2-719).

§2-317. Cumulation and Conflict of Warranties Express or Implied. Warranties whether express or implied shall be construed as consistent with each other and as cumulative but if such construction is unreasonable the intention of the parties shall determine which warranty is dominant. In ascertaining that intention the following rules apply:

(**a**) Exact or technical specifications displace an inconsistent sample or model or general language of description.

(**b**) A sample from an existing bulk displaces inconsistent general language of description.

(**c**) Express warranties displace inconsistent implied warranties other than an implied warranty of fitness for a particular purpose.

§2-318. Third Party Beneficiaries of Warranties Express or Implied.

Note: *If this Act is introduced in the Congress of the United States this section should be omitted. (States to select one alternative.)*

Alternative A—A seller's warranty whether express or implied extends to any natural person who is in the family or household of his buyer or who is a guest in his home if it is reasonable to expect that such person may use, consume or be affected by the goods and who is injured in person by breach of the warranty. A seller may not exclude or limit the operation of this section.

Alternative B—A seller's warranty whether express or implied extends to any natural person who may reasonably be expected to use, consume or be affected by the goods and who is injured in person by breach of the warranty. A seller may not exclude or limit the operation of this section.

Alternative C—A seller's warranty whether express or implied extends to any person who may reasonably be expected to use, consume or be affected by the goods and who is injured by breach of the warranty. A seller may not exclude or limit the operation of this section with respect to injury to the person of an individual to whom the warranty extends. As amended 1966.

§2-319. F.O.B. and F.A.S. Terms.

(**1**) Unless otherwise agreed the term F.O.B. (which means "free on board") at a named place, even though used only in connection with the stated price, is a delivery term under which

(**a**) when the term is F.O.B. the place of shipment, the seller must at that place ship the goods in the manner provided in this Article (Section 2-504) and bear the expense and risk of putting them into the possession of the carrier; or

(**b**) when the term is F.O.B. the place of destination, the seller must at his own expense and risk transport the goods to that place and there tender delivery of them in the manner provided in this Article (Section 2-503);

(**c**) when under either (a) or (b) the term is also F.O.B. vessel, car or other vehicle, the seller must in addition at his own expense and risk load the goods on board. If the term is F.O.B. vessel the buyer must name the vessel and in an appropriate case the seller must comply with the provisions of this Article on the form of bill of lading (Section 2-323).

(**2**) Unless otherwise agreed the term F.A.S. vessel (which means "free alongside") at a named port, even though used only in connection with the stated price, is a delivery term under which the seller must

(**a**) at his own expense and risk deliver the goods alongside the vessel in the manner usual in that port or on a dock designated and provided by the buyer; and

(**b**) obtain and tender a receipt for the goods in exchange for which the carrier is under a duty to issue a bill of lading.

(**3**) Unless otherwise agreed in any case falling within subsection (1) (a) or (c) or subsection (2) the buyer must seasonably give any needed instructions for making delivery, including when the term is F.A.S. or F.O.B. the loading berth of the vessel and in an appropriate case its name and sailing date. The seller may treat the failure of needed instructions as a failure of cooperation under this Article (Section 2-311).

He may also at his option move the goods in any reasonable manner preparatory to delivery or shipment.

(4) Under the term F.O.B. vessel or F.A.S. unless otherwise agreed the buyer must make payment against tender of the required documents and the seller may not tender nor the buyer demand delivery of the goods in substitution for the documents.

§2-320. C.I.F. and C.&F. Terms.

(1) The term C.I.F. means that the price includes in a lump sum the cost of the goods and the insurance and freight to the named destination. The term C.&F. or C.F. means that the price so includes cost and freight to the named destination.

(2) Unless otherwise agreed and even though used only in connection wtih the stated price and destination, the term C.I.F. destination or its equivalent requires the seller at his own expense and risk to

(a) put the goods into the possession of a carrier at the port for shipment and obtain a negotiable bill or bills of lading covering the entire transportation to the named destination; and

(b) load the goods and obtain a receipt from the carrier (which may be contained in the bill of lading) showing that the freight has been paid or provided for; and

(c) obtain a policy or certificate of insurance, including any war risk insurance, of a kind and on terms then current at the port of shipment in the usual amount, in the currency of the contract, shown to cover the same goods covered by the bill of lading and providing for payment of loss to the order of the buyer or for the account of whom it may concern; but the seller may add to the price the amount of the premium for any such war risk insurance; and

(d) prepare an invoice of the goods and procure any other documents required to effect shipment or to comply with the contract; and

(e) forward and tender with commercial promptness all the documents in due form and with any indorsement necessary to perfect the buyer's rights.

(3) Unless otherwise agreed the term C.&F. or its equivalent has the same effect and imposes upon the seller the same obligations and risks as a C.I.F. term except the obligation as to insurance.

(4) Under the term C.I.F. or C.&F. unless otherwise agreed the buyer must make payment against tender of the required documents and the seller may not tender nor the buyer demand delivery of the goods in substitution for the documents.

§2-321. C.I.F. or C.&F.: "Net Landed Weights"; "Payment on Arrival"; Warranty of Condition on Arrival. Under a contract containing a term C.I.F. or C.&F.

(1) Where the price is based on or is to be adjusted according to "net landed weights", "delivered weights", "out turn" quantity or quality or the like, unless otherwise agreed the seller must reasonably estimate the price. The payment due on tender of the documents called for by the contract is the amount so estimated, but after final adjustment of the price a settlement must be made with commercial promptness.

(2) An agreement described in subsection (1) or any warranty of quality or condition of the goods on arrival places upon the seller the risk of ordinary deterioration, shrinkage and the like in transportation but has no effect on the place or time of identification to the contract for sale or delivery or on the passing of the risk of loss.

(3) Unless otherwise agreed where the contract provides for payment on or after arrival of the goods the seller must before payment allow such preliminary inspection as is feasible; but if the goods are lost delivery of the documents and payment are due when the goods should have arrived.

§2-322. Delivery "Ex-Ship".

(1) Unless otherwise agreed a term for delivery of goods "ex-ship" (which means from the carrying vessel) or in equivalent language is not restricted to a particular ship and requires delivery from a ship which has reached a place at the named port of destination where goods of the kind are usually discharged.

(2) Under such a term unless otherwise agreed

(a) the seller must discharge all liens arising out of the carriage and furnish the buyer with a direction which puts the carrier under a duty to deliver the goods; and

(b) the risk of loss does not pass to the buyer until the goods leave the ship's tackle or are otherwise properly unloaded.

§2-323. Form of Bill of Lading Required in Overseas Shipment; "Overseas".

(1) Where the contract contemplates overseas shipment and contains a term C.I.F. or C.&F. or F.O.B. vessel the seller unless otherwise agreed must obtain a negotiable bill of lading stating that the

goods have been loaded on board or, in the case of a term C.I.F. or C.&F., received for shipment.

(2) Where in a case within subsection (1) a bill of lading has been issued in a set of parts, unless otherwise agreed if the documents are not to be sent from abroad the buyer may demand tender of the full set; otherwise only one part of the bill of lading need be tendered. Even if the agreement expressly requires a full set

(a) due tender of a single part is acceptable within the provisions of this Article on cure of improper delivery (subsection (1) of Section 2-508); and

(b) even though the full set is demanded, if the documents are sent from abroad the person tendering an incomplete set may nevertheless require payment upon furnishing an indemnity which the buyer in good faith deems adequate.

(3) A shipment by water or by air on a contract contemplating such shipment is "overseas" insofar as by usage of trade or agreement it is subject to the commercial, financing or shipping practices characteristic of international deep water commerce.

§2-324. "No Arrival, No Sale" Term. Under a term "no arrival, no sale" or terms of like meaning, unless otherwise agreed,

(a) the seller must properly ship conforming goods and if they arrive by any means he must tender them on arrival but he assumes no obligation that the goods will arrive unless he has caused the nonarrival; and

(b) where without fault of the seller the goods are in part lost or have so deteriorated as no longer to conform to the contract or arrive after the contract time, the buyer may proceed as if there had been casualty to identified goods (Section 2-613).

§2-325. "Letter of Credit" Term; "Confirmed Credit".

(1) Failure of the buyer seasonably to furnish an agreed letter of credit is a breach of the contract for sale.

(2) The delivery to seller of a proper letter of credit suspends the buyer's obligation to pay. If the letter of credit is dishonored, the seller may on seasonable notification to the buyer require payment directly from him.

(3) Unless otherwise agreed the term "letter of credit" or "banker's credit" in a contract for sale means an irrevocable credit issued by a financing agency of good repute and, where the shipment is overseas, of good international repute. The term "confirmed credit" means that the credit must also carry the direct obligation of such an agency which does business in the seller's financial market.

§2-326. Sale on Approval and Sale or Return; Consignment Sales and Rights of Creditors.

(1) Unless otherwise agreed, if delivered goods may be returned by the buyer even though they conform to the contract, the transaction is

(a) a "sale on approval" if the goods are delivered primarily for use, and

(b) a "sale or return" if the goods are delivered primarily for resale.

(2) Except as provied in subsection (3), goods held on approval are not subject to the claims of the buyer's creditors until acceptance; goods held on sale or return are subject to such claims while in the buyer's possession.

(3) Where goods are delivered to a person for sale and such person maintains a place of business at which he deals in goods of the kind involved, under a name other than the name of the person making delivery, then with respect to claims of creditors of the person conducting the business the goods are deemed to be on sale or return. The provisions of this subsection are applicable even though an agreement purports to reserve title to the person making delivery until payment or resale or uses such words as "on consignment" or "on memorandum". However, this subsection is not applicable if the person making delivery

(a) complies with an applicable law providing for a consignor's interest or the like to be evidenced by a sign, or

(b) establishes that the person conducting the business is generally known by his creditors to be substantially engaged in selling the goods of others, or

(c) complies with the filing provisions of the Article on Secured Transactions (Article 9).

(4) Any "or return" term of a contract for sale is to be treated as a separate contract for sale within the statute of frauds section of this Article (Section 2-201) and as contradicting the sale aspect of the contract within the provisions of this Article on parol or extrinsic evidence (Section 2-202).

§2-327. Special Incidents of Sale on Approval and Sale or Return.

(1) Under a sale on approval unless otherwise agreed

(**a**) although the goods are identified to the contract the risk of loss and the title do not pass to the buyer until acceptance; and

(**b**) use of the goods consistent with the purpose of trial is not acceptance but failure seasonably to notify the seller of election to return the goods is acceptance, and if the goods conform to the contract acceptance of any part is acceptance of the whole; and

(**c**) after due notification of election to return, the return is at the seller's risk and expense but a merchant buyer must follow any reasonable instructions.

(**2**) Under a sale or return unless otherwise agreed

(**a**) the option to return extends to the whole or any commercial unit of the goods while in substantially their original condition, but must be exercised seasonably; and

(**b** the return is at the buyer's risk and expense.

§2-328. Sale by Auction.

(**1**) In a sale by auction if goods are put up in lots each lot is the subject of a separate sale.

(**2**) A sale by auction is complete when the auctioneer so announces by the fall of the hammer or in other customary manner. Where a bid is made while the hammer is falling in acceptance of a prior bid the auctioneer may in his discretion reopen the bidding or declare the goods sold under the bid on which the hammer was falling.

(**3**) Such a sale is with reserve unless the goods are in explicit terms put up without reserve. In an auction with reserve, the auctioneer may withdraw the goods at any time until he announces completion of the sale. In an auction without reserve, after the auctioneer calls for bids on an article or lot, that article or lot cannot be withdrawn unless no bid is made within a reasonable time. In either case a bidder may retract his bid until the auctioneer's announcement of completion of the sale, but a bidder's retraction does not revive any previous bid.

(**4**) If the auctioneer knowingly receives a bid on the seller's behalf or the seller makes or procures such a bid, and notice has not been given that liberty for such bidding is reserved, the buyer may at his option avoid the sale or take the goods at the price of the last good faith bid prior to the completion of the sale. This subsection shall not apply to any bid at a forced sale.

Part 4: Title, Creditors and Good Faith Purchasers

§2-401. Passing of Title; Reservation for Security; Limited Application of This Section. Each provision of this Article with regard to the rights, obligations and remedies of the seller, the buyer, purchasers or other third parties applies irrespective of title to the goods except where the provision refers to such title. Insofar as situations are not covered by the other provisions of this Article and matters concerning title become material the following rules apply:

(**1**) Title to goods cannot pass under a contract for sale prior to their identification to the contract (Section 2-501), and unless otherwise explicitly agreed the buyer acquires by their identification a special property as limited by this Act. Any retention or reservation by the seller of the title (property) in goods shipped or delivered to the buyer is limited in effect to a reservation of a security interest. Subject to these provisions and to the provisions of the Article on Secured Transactions (Article 9), title to goods passes from the seller to the buyer in any manner and on any conditions explicitly agreed on by the parties.

(**2**) Unless otherwise explicitly agreed title passes to the buyer at the time and place at which the seller completes his performances with reference to the physical delivery of the goods, despite any reservation of a security interest and even though a document of title is to be delivered at a different time or place; and in particular and despite any reservation of a security interest by the bill of lading

(**a**) if the contract requires or authorizes the seller to send the goods to the buyer but does not require him to deliver them at destination, title passes to the buyer at the time and place of shipment; but

(**b**) if the contract requires delivery at destination, title passes on tender there.

(**3**) Unless otherwise explicitly agreed where delivery is to be made without moving the goods.

(**a**) if the seller is to deliver a document of title, title passes at the time when and the place where he delivers such documents; or

(**b**) if the goods are at the time of contracting already identified and no documents are to be delivered, title passes at the time and place of contracting.

(**4**) A rejection or other refusal by the buyer to receive or retain the goods, whether or not justified, or a justified revocation of acceptance revests title to the goods in the seller. Such revesting occurs by operation of law and is not a "sale".

§2-402. Rights of Seller's Creditors Against Sold Goods.

(**1**) Except as provided in subsections (2) and (3), rights of unsecured creditors of the seller with respect to goods which have been identified to a contract for sale are subject to the buyer's rights to recover the goods under this Article (Section 2-502 and 2-716).

(**2**) A creditor of the seller may treat a sale or an identification of goods to a contract for sale as void if as against him a retention of possession by the seller is fraudulent under any rule of law of the state where the goods are situated, except that retention of possession in good faith and current course of trade by a merchant-seller for a commercially reasonable time after a sale or identification is not fraudulent.

(**3**) Nothing in this Article shall be deemed to impair the rights of creditors of the seller

(**a**) under the provisions of the Article on Secured Transactions (Article 9); or

(**b**) where identification to the contract or delivery is made not in current course of trade but in satisfaction of or as security for a pre-existing claim for money, security or the like and is made under circumstances which under any rule of law of the state where the goods are situated would apart from this Article constitute the transaction a fraudulent transfer or voidable preference.

§2-403. Power to Transfer; Good Faith Purchase of Goods; "Entrusting".

(**1**) A purchaser of goods acquires all title which his transferor had or had power to transfer except that a purchaser of a limited interest acquires rights only to the extent of the interest purchased. A person with voidable title has power to transfer a good title to a good faith purchaser for value. When goods have been delivered under a transaction of purchase the purchaser had such power even though

(**a**) the transferor was deceived as to the identity of the purchaser, or

(**b**) the delivery was in exchange for a check which is later dishonored, or

(**c**) it was agreed that the transaction was to be a "cash sale", or

(**d**) the delivery was procured through fraud punishable as larcenous under the criminal law.

(**2**) Any entrusting of possession of goods to a merchant who deals in goods of that kind gives him power to transfer all rights of the entruster to a buyer in ordinary course of business.

(**3**) "Entrusting" includes any delivery and any acquiescence in retention of possession regardless of any condition expressed between the parties to the delivery or acquiescence and regardless of whether the procurement of the entrusting or the possessor's disposition of the goods have been such as to be larcenous under the criminal law.

(**4**) The rights of other purchasers of goods and of lien creditors are governed by the Articles on Secured Transactions (Article 9), Bulk Transfers (Article 6) and Documents of Title (Article 7).

Part 5: Performance

§2-501. Insurable Interest in Goods; Manner of Identification of Goods.

(**1**) The buyer obtains a special property and an insurable interest in goods by identification of existing goods as goods to which the contract refers even though the goods so identified are non-conforming and he has an option to return or reject them. Such identification can be made at any time and in any manner explicitly agreed to by the parties. In the absence of explicit agreement identification occurs

(**a**) when the contract is made if it is for the sale of goods already existing and identified;

(**b**) if the contract is for the sale of future goods other than those described in paragraph (c), when goods are shipped, marked or otherwise designated by the seller as goods to which the contract refers;

(**c**) when the crops are planted or otherwise become growing crops or the young are conceived if the contract is for the sale of unborn young to be born within twelves months after contracting or for the sale of crops to be harvested within twelve months or the next normal harvest season after contracting whichever is longer.

(**2**) The seller retains an insurable interest in goods so long as title to or any security interest in the goods remains in him and where the identification is by the seller alone he may until default or insolvency or notification to the buyer that the identification is final substitute other goods for those identified.

(**3**) Nothing in this section impairs any insurable

interest recognized under any other statute or rule of law.

§2-502. Buyer's Right to Goods on Seller's Insolvency.

(1) Subject to subsection (2) and even though the goods have not been shipped a buyer who has paid a part or all of the price of goods in which he has a special property under the provisions of the immediately preceding section may on making and keeping good a tender of any unpaid portion or their price recover them from the seller if the seller becomes insolvent within ten days after receipt of the first installment on their price.

(2) If the identification creating his special property has been made by the buyer he acquires the right to recover the goods only if they conform to the contract for sale.

§2-503. Manner of Seller's Tender of Delivery.

(1) Tender of delivery requires that the seller put and hold conforming goods at the buyer's disposition and give the buyer any notification reasonably necessary to enable him to take delivery. The manner, time and place for tender are determined by the agreement and this Article, and in particular

(a) tender must be at a reasonable hour, and if it is of goods they must be kept available for the period reasonably necessary to enable the buyer to take possession; but

(b) unless otherwise agreed the buyer must furnish facilities reasonably suited to the receipt of the goods.

(2) Where the case is within the next section respecting shipment tender requires that the seller comply with its provisions.

(3) Where the seller is required to deliver at a particular destination tender requires that he comply with subsection (1) and also in any appropriate case tender documents as described in subsections (4) and (5) of this section.

(4) Where goods are in the possession of a bailee and are to be delivered without being moved

(a) tender requires that the seller either tender a negotiable document of title covering such goods or procure acknowledgement by the bailee of the buyer's right to possession of the goods; but

(b) tender to the buyer of a non-negotiable document of title or of a written direction to the bailee to deliver is sufficient tender unless the buyer seasonably objects, and receipt by the bailee of notification of the buyer's rights fixes those rights as against the bailee and all third persons; but risk of loss of the goods and of any failure by the bailee to honor the non-negotiable document of title or to obey the direction remains on the seller until the buyer has had a reasonable time to present the document or direction, and a refusal by the bailee to honor the document or to obey the direction defeats the tender.

(5) Where the contract requires the seller to deliver documents

(a) he must tender all such documents in correct form, except as provided in this Article with respect to bills of lading in a set (subsection (2) of Section 2-323); and

(b) tender through customary banking channels is sufficient and dishonor of a draft accompanying the documents constitutes non-acceptance or rejection.

§2-504. Shipment by Seller. Where the seller is required or authorized to send the goods to the buyer and the contract does not require him to deliver them at a particular destination, then unless otherwise agreed he must

(a) put the goods in the possession of such a carrier and make such a contract for their transportation as may be reasonable having regard to the nature of the goods and other circumstances of the case; and

(b) obtain and promptly deliver or tender in due form any document necessary to enable the buyer to obtain possession of the goods or otherwise required by the agreement or by usage of trade; and

(c) promptly notify the buyer of the shipment.

Failure to notify the buyer under paragraph (c) or to make a proper contract under paragraph (a) is a ground for rejection only if material delay or loss ensues.

§2-505. Seller's Shipment under Reservation.

(1) Where the seller has identified goods to the contract by or before shipment:

(a) his procurement of a negotiable bill of lading to his own order or otherwise reserves in him a security interest in the goods. His procurement of the bill to the order of a financing agency or of the buyer indicates in addition only the seller's expectation of transferring that interest to the person named.

(**b**) a non-negotiable bill of lading to himself or his nominee reserves possession of the goods as security but except in a case of conditional delivery (subsection (2) of Section 2-507) a non-negotiable bill of lading naming the buyer as consignee reserves no security interest even though the seller retains possession of the bill of lading.

(**2**) When shipment by the seller with reservation of a security interest is in violation of the contract for sale it constitutes an improper contract for transportation within the preceding section but impairs neither the rights given to the buyer by shipment and identification of the goods, to the contract nor the seller's powers as a holder of a negotiable document.

§2-506. Rights of Financing Agency.

(**1**) A financing agency by paying or purchasing for value a draft which relates to a shipment of goods acquires to the extent of the payment or purchase and in addition to its own rights under the draft and any document of title securing it any rights of the shipper in the goods including the right to stop delivery and the shipper's right to have the draft honored by the buyer.

(**2**) The right to reimbursement of a financing agency which has in good faith honored or purchased the draft under commitment to or authority from the buyer is not impaired by subsequent discovery of defects with reference to any relevant document which was apparently regular on its face.

§2-507. Effect of Seller's Tender; Delivery on Condition.

(**1**) Tender of delivery is a condition to the buyer's duty to accept the goods and, unless otherwise agreed, to his duty to pay for them. Tender entitles the seller to acceptance of the goods and to payment according to the contract.

(**2**) Where payment is due and demanded on the delivery to the buyer of goods or documents of title, his right as against the seller to retain or dispose of them is conditional upon his making the payment due.

§2-508. Cure by Seller of Improper Tender or Delivery; Replacement.

(**1**) Where any tender or delivery by the seller is rejected because non-conforming and the time for performance has not yet expired, the seller may seasonably notify the buyer of his intention to cure and may then within the contract time make a conforming delivery.

(**2**) Where the buyer rejects a non-conforming tender which the seller had reasonable grounds to believe would be acceptable with or without money allowance the seller may if he seasonably notifies the buyer have a further reasonable time to substitute a conforming tender.

§2-509. Risk of Loss in the Absence of Breach.

(**1**) Where the contract requires or authorizes the seller to ship the goods by carrier

(**a**) if it does not require him to deliver them at a particular destination, the risk of loss passes to the buyer when the goods are duly delivered to the carrier even though the shipment is under reservation (Section 2-505); but

(**b**) if it does require him to deliver them at a particular destination and the goods are there duly tendered while in the possession of the carrier, the risk of loss passes to the buyer when the goods are there duly so tendered as to enable the buyer to take delivery.

(**2**) Where the goods are held by a bailee to be delivered without being moved, the risk of loss passes to the buyer

(**a**) on his receipt of a negotiable document of title covering the goods; or

(**b**) on acknowledgement by the bailee of the buyer's right to possession of the goods; or

(**c**) after his receipt of a non-negotiable document of title or other written direction to deliver as provided in subsection (4) (b) of Section 2-503.

(**3**) In any case not within subsection (1) or (2), the risk of loss passes to the buyer on his receipt of the goods if the seller is a merchant; otherwise the risk passes to the buyer on tender of delivery.

(**4**) The provisions of this section are subject to contrary agreement of the parties and to the provisions of this Article on sale on approval (Section 2-327) and on effect of breach on risk of loss (Section 2-510).

§2-510. Effect of Breach on Risk of Loss.

(**1**) Where a tender or delivery of goods so fails to conform to the contract as to give a right of rejection the risk of their loss remains on the seller until cure or acceptance.

(**2**) Where the buyer rightfully revokes acceptance he may to the extent of any deficiency in his effective insurance coverage treat the risk of loss as having rested on the seller from the beginning.

(**3**) Where the buyer as to conforming goods already identified to the contract for sale repudiates or is otherwise in breach before risk of their loss has passed to him, the seller may to the extent of any deficiency in his effective insurance coverage treat the risk of loss as resting on the buyer for a commercially reasonable time.

§2-511. Tender of Payment by Buyer; Payment by Check.

(**1**) Unless otherwise agreed tender of payment is a condition to the seller's duty to tender and complete any delivery.

(**2**) Tender of payment is sufficient when made by any means or in any manner current in the ordinary course of business unless the seller demands payment in legal tender and gives any extension of time reasonably necessary to procure it.

(**3**) Subject to the provisions of this Act on the effect of an instrument of an obligation (Section 3-802), payment by check is conditional and is defeated as between the parties by dishonor of the check on due presentment.

§2-512. Payment by Buyer Before Inspection.

(**1**) Where the contract requires payment before inspection non-conformity of the goods does not excuse the buyer from so making payment unless

(**a**) the non-conformity appears without inspection; or

(**b**) despite tender of the required documents the circumstances would justify injunction against honor under the provisions of this Act (Section 5-114).

(**2**) Payment pursuant to subsection (1) does not constitute an acceptance of goods or impair the buyer's right to inspect or any of his remedies.

§2-513. Buyer's Right to Inspection of Goods.

(**1**) Unless otherwise agreed and subject to subsection (3), where goods are tendered or delivered or identified to the contract for sale, the buyer has a right before payment or acceptance to inspect them at any reasonable place and time and in any reasonable manner. When the seller is required or authorized to send the goods to the buyer, the inspection may be after their arrival.

(**2**) Expenses of inspection must be borne by the buyer but may be recovered from the seller if the goods do not conform and are rejected.

(**3**) Unless otherwise agreed and subject to the provisions of this Article on C.I.F. contracts (subsection (3) of Section 3-221), the buyer is not entitled to inspect the goods before payment of the price when the contract provides

(**a**) for delivery "C.O.D." or on other like terms; or

(**b**) for payment against documents of title, except where such payment is due only after the goods are to become available for inspection.

(**4**) A place or method of inspection fixed by the parties is presumed to be exclusive but unless otherwise expressly agreed it does not postpone identification or shift the place for delivery or for passing the risk of loss. If compliance becomes impossible, inspection shall be as provided in this section unless the place or method fixed was clearly intended as an indispensable condition failure of which avoids the contract.

§2-514. When Documents Deliverable on Acceptance; When on Payment. Unless otherwise agreed documents against which a draft is drawn are to be delivered to the drawee on acceptance of the draft if it is payable more than three days after presentment; otherwise, only on payment.

§2-515. Preserving Evidence of Goods in Dispute. In furtherance of the adjustment of any claim or dispute

(**a**) either party on reasonable notification to the other and for the purpose of ascertaining the facts and preserving evidence has the right to inspect, test and sample the goods including such of them as may be in the possession or control of the other; and

(**b**) the parties may agree to a third party inspection or survey to determine the conformity or condition of the goods and may agree that the findings shall be binding upon them in any subsequent litigation or adjustment.

Part 6: Breach, Repudiation and Excuse

§2-601. Buyer's Rights on Improper Delivery. Subject to the provisions of this Article on breach in installment contracts (Section 2-612) and unless otherwise agreed under the sections on contractual limitations of remedy (Sections 2-718 and 2-719), if the goods or the tender of delivery fail in any respect to conform to the contract, the buyer may

(**a**) reject the whole; or

(**b**) accept the whole; or

(**c**) accept any commercial unit or units and reject the rest.

§2-602. Manner and Effect of Rightful Rejection.

(**1**) Rejection of goods must be within a reasonable

time after their delivery or tender. It is ineffective unless the buyer seasonably notifies the seller.

(**2**) Subject to the provisions of the two following sections on rejected goods (Section 2-603 and 2-604).

(**a**) after rejection any exercise of ownership by the buyer with respect to any commercial unit is wrongful as against the seller; and

(**b**) if the buyer has before rejection taken physical possession of goods in which he does not have a security interest under the provisions of this Article (subsection (3) of Section 2-711), he is under a duty after rejection to hold them with reasonable care at the seller's disposition for a time sufficient to permit the seller to remove them; but

(**c**) the buyer has no further obligations with regard to goods rightfully rejected.

(**3**) The seller's rights with respect to goods wrongfully rejected are governed by the provisions of this Article on Seller's remedies in general (Section 2-703).

§2-603. Merchant Buyer's Duties as to Rightfully Rejected Goods.

(**1**) Subject to any security interest in the buyer (subsection (3) of Section 2-711), when the seller has no agent or place of business at the market of rejection a merchant buyer is under a duty after rejection of goods in his possession or control to follow any reasonable instructions received from the seller with respect to the goods and in the absence of such instructions to make reasonable efforts to sell them for the seller's account if they are perishable or threaten to decline in value speedily. Instructions are not reasonable if on demand indemnity for expenses is not forthcoming.

(**2**) When the buyer sells goods under subsection (1), he is entitled to reimbursement from the seller or out of the proceeds for reasonable expenses of caring for and selling them, and if the expenses include no selling commission then to such commission as is usual in the trade or if there is none to a reasonable sum not exceeding ten per cent on the gross proceeds.

(**3**) In complying with this section the buyer is held only to good faith and good faith conduct hereunder is neither acceptance nor conversion nor the basis of an action for damages.

§2-604. Buyer's Options as to Salvage of Rightfully Rejected Goods. Subject to the provisions of the immediately preceding section on perishables if the seller gives no instructions within a reasonable time after notification of rejection the buyer may store the rejected goods for the seller's account or reship them to him or resell them for the seller's account with reimbursement as provided in the preceding section. Such action is not acceptance or conversion.

§2-605. Waiver of Buyer's Objections by Failure to Particularize.

(**1**) The buyer's failure to state in connection with rejection a particular defect which is ascertainable by reasonable inspection precludes him from relying on the unstated defect to justify rejection or to establish breach

(**a**) where the seller could have cured it if stated seasonably; or

(**b**) between merchants when the seller has after rejection made a request in writing for a full and final written statement of all defects on which the buyer proposes to rely.

(**2**) Payment against documents made without reservation of rights precludes recovery of the payment for defects apparent on the face of the documents.

§2-606. What Constitutes Acceptance of Goods.

(**1**) Acceptance of goods occurs when the buyer

(**a**) after a reasonable opportunity to inspect the goods signifies to the seller that the goods are conforming or that he will take or retain them in spite of their nonconformity; or

(**b**) fails to make an effective rejection (subsection (1) of Section 2-602), but such acceptance does not occur until the buyer has had a reasonable opportunity to inspect them; or

(**c**) does any act inconsistent with the seller's ownership; but if such act is wrongful as against the seller it is an acceptance only if ratified by him.

(**2**) Acceptance of a part of any commercial unit is acceptance of that entire unit.

§2-607. Effect of Acceptance; Notice of Breach; Burden of Establishing Breach After Acceptance; Notice of Claim or Litigation to Person Answerable Over.

(**1**) The buyer must pay at the contract rate for any goods accepted.

(**2**) Acceptance of goods by the buyer precludes rejection of the goods accepted and if made with knowledge of a nonconformity cannot be revoked because of it unless the acceptance was on the reasonable assumption that the non-conformity would be seasonably cured but acceptance does not of itself impair any other remedy provided by this Article for nonconformity.

(**3**) Where a tender has been accepted

(**a**) the buyer must within a reasonable time after he discovers or should have discovered any breach notify the seller of breach or be barred from any remedy; and

(**b**) if the claim is one for infringement or the like (subsection (3) of Section 2-312) and the buyer is sued as a result of such a breach he must so notify the seller within a reasonable time after he receives notice of the litigation or be barred from any remedy over for liability established by the litigation.

(**4**) The burden is on the buyer to establish any breach with respect to the goods accepted.

(**5**) Where the buyer is sued for breach of a warranty or other obligation for which his seller is answerable over

(**a**) he may give his seller written notice of the litigation. If the notice states that the seller may come in and defend and that if the seller does not do so he will be bound in any action against him by his buyer by any determination of fact common to the two litigations, then unless the seller after seasonable receipt of the notice does come in and defend he is so bound.

(**b**) if the claim is one for infringement or the like (subsection (3) of Section 2-312) the original seller may demand in writing that his buyer turn over to him control of the litigation including settlement or else be barred from any remedy over and if he also agrees to bear all expense and to satisfy any adverse judgment, then unless the buyer after seasonable receipt of the demand does turn over control the buyer is so barred.

(**6**) The provisions of subsection (3), (4) and (5) apply to any obligation of a buyer to hold the seller harmless against infringement or the like (subsection (3) of Section 2-312).

§2-608. Revocation of Acceptance in Whole or in Part.

(**1**) The buyer may revoke his acceptance of a lot or commercial unit whose non-conformity substantially impairs its value to him if he has accepted it

(**a**) on the reasonable assumption that its non-conformity would be cured and it has not been seasonably cured; or

(**b**) without discovery of such non-conformity if his acceptance was reasonably induced either by the difficulty of discovery before acceptance or by the seller's assurances.

(**2**) Revocation of acceptance must occur within a reasonable time after the buyer discovers or should have discovered the ground for it and before any substantial change in condition of the goods which is not caused by their own defects. It is not effective until the buyer notifies the seller of it.

(**3**) A buyer who so revokes has the same rights and duties with regard to the goods involved as if he had rejected them.

§2-609. Right to Adequate Assurance of Performance.

(**1**) A contract for sale imposes an obligation on each party that the other's expectation of receiving due performance will not be impaired. When reasonable grounds for insecurity arise with respect to the performance of either party the other may in writing demand adequate assurance of due performance and until he receives such assurance may if commercially reasonable suspend any performance for which he has not already received the agreed return.

(**2**) Between merchants the reasonableness of grounds for insecurity and the adequacy of any assurance offered shall be determined according to commercial standards.

(**3**) Acceptance of any improper delivery or payment does not prejudice the aggrieved party's right to demand adequate assurance of future performance.

(**4**) After receipt of a justified demand failure to provide within a reasonable time not exceeding thirty days such assurance of due performance as is adequate under the circumstances of the particular case is a repudiation of the contract.

§2-610. Anticipatory Repudiation. When either party repudiates the contract with respect to a performance not yet due the loss of which will substantially impair the value of the contract to the other, the aggrieved party may

(**a**) for a commercially reasonable time await performance by the repudiating party; or

(**b**) resort to any remedy for breach (Section 2-703 or Section 2-711), even though he has notified the repudiating party that he would await the latter's performance and has urged retraction; and

(**c**) in either case suspend his own performance or proceed in accordance with the provisions of this Article on the seller's right to identify goods to the contract notwithstanding breach or to salvage unfinished goods (Section 2-704).

§2-611. Retraction of Anticipatory Repudiation.

(**1**) Until the repudiating party's next performance is due he can retract his repudiation unless the aggrieved party has since the repudiation cancelled or materially changed his position or otherwise indicated that he considers the repudiation final.

(**2**) Retraction may be by any method which clearly indicates to the aggrieved party that the repudiating party intends to perform, but must include any assurance justifiably demanded under the provisions of this Article (Section 2-609).

(**3**) Retraction reinstates the repudiating party's rights under the contract with due excuse and allowance to the aggrieved party for any delay occasioned by the repudiation.

§2-612. "Installment Contract"; Breach.

(**1**) An "installment contract" is one which requires or authorizes the delivery of goods in separate lots to be separately accepted, even though the contract contains a clause "each delivery is a separate contract" or its equivalent.

(**2**) The buyer may reject any installment which is nonconforming if the non-conformity substantially impairs the value of that installment and cannot be cured or if the non-conformity is a defect in the required documents, but if the non-conformity does not fall within subsection (3) and the seller gives adequate assurance of its cure the buyer must accept that installment.

(**3**) Whenever non-conformity or default with respect to one or more installments substantially impairs the value of the whole contract there is a breach of the whole. But the aggrieved party reinstates the contract if he accepts a non-conforming installment without seasonably notifying of cancellation or if he brings an action with respect only to past installments or demands performance as to future installments.

§2-613. Casualty to Identified Goods. Where the contract requires for its performance goods identified when the contract is made, and the goods suffer casualty without fault of either party before the risk of loss passes to the buyer, or in a proper case under a "no arrival, no sale" term (Section 2-324) then

(**a**) if the loss is total the contract is avoided; and

(**b**) if the loss is partial or the goods have so deteriorated as no longer to conform to the contract the buyer may nevertheless demand inspection and at his option either treat the contract as avoided or accept the goods with due allowance from the contract price for the deterioration or the deficiency in quantity but without further right against the seller.

§2-614. Substituted Performance.

(**1**) Where without fault of either party the agreed berthing, loading, or unloading facilities fail or an agreed type of carrier becomes unavilable or the agreed manner of delivery otherwise becomes commercially impracticable but a commercially reasonable substitute is available, such substitute performance must be tendered and accepted.

(**2**) If the agreed means or manner of payment fails because of domestic or foreign governmental regulation, the seller may withhold or stop delivery unless the buyer provides a means or manner of payment which is commercially a substantial equivalent. If delivery has already been taken, payment by the means or in the manner provided by the regulation discharges the buyer's obligation unless the regulation is discriminatory, oppressive or predatory.

§2-615. Excuse by Failure of Presupposed Conditions. Except so far as a seller may have assumed a greater obligation and subject to the preceding section on substituted performance:

(**a**) Delay in delivery or non-delivery in whole or in part by a seller who complies with paragraphs (b) and (c) is not a breach of his duty under a contract for sale if performance as agreed has been made impracticable by the occurrence of a contingency the non-occurrence of which was a basic assumption on which the contract was made or by compliance in good faith with any applicable foreign or domestic governmental regulation or order whether or not it later proves to be invalid.

(**b**) Where the causes mentioned in paragraph (a) affect only a part of the seller's capacity to perform, he must allocate production and deliveries among his customers but may at his option include regular customers not then under contract as well as his own requirements for further manufacture. He may so allocate in any manner which is fair and reasonable.

(**c**) The seller must notify the buyer seasonably that there will be delay or non-delivery and, when allocation is required under paragraph (b), of the estimated quota thus made available for the buyer.

§2-616. Procedure on Notice Claiming Excuse.

(**1**) When the buyer receives notification of a material or indefinite delay or an allocation justified under the preceding section he may by written notification to the seller as to any delivery concerned, and where the prospective deficiency substantially impairs the value of the whole contract under the provisions of this Article relating to breach of installment contracts (Section 2-612), then also as to the whole,

(**a**) terminate and thereby discharge any unexecuted portion of the contract; or

(**b**) modify the contract by agreeing to take his available quota in substitution.

(**2**) If after receipt of such notification from the seller the buyer fails so to modify the contract within a reasonable time not exceeding thirty days the contract lapses with respect to any deliveries affected.

(**3**) The provisions of this section may not be negated by agreement except in so far as the seller has assumed a greater obligation under the preceding section.

Part 7: Remedies

§2-701. Remedies for Breach of Collateral Contracts Not Impaired. Remedies for breach of any obligation or promise collateral or ancillary to a contract for sale are not impaired by the provisions of this Article.

§2-702. Seller's on Discovery of Buyer's Insolvency.

(**1**) Where the seller discovers the buyer to be insolvent he may refuse delivery except for cash including payment for all goods theretofore delivered under the contract, and stop delivery under this Article (Section 2-705).

(**2**) Where the seller discovers that the buyer has received goods on credit while insolvent he may reclaim the goods upon demand made within ten days after the receipt, but if misrepresentation of solvency has been made to the particular seller in writing within three months before delivery the ten day limitation does not apply. Except as provided in this subsection the seller may not base a right to reclaim goods on the buyer's fraudulent or innocent misrepresentation of solvency or of intent to pay.

(**3**) The seller's right to reclaim under subsection (2) is subject to the rights of a buyer in ordinary course or other good faith purchaser under this Article (Section 2-403). Successful reclamation of goods excludes all other remedies with respect to them. As amended 1966.

§2-703. Seller's Remedies in General. Where the buyer wrongfully rejects or revokes acceptance of goods, or fails to make a payment due on or before delivery or repudiates with respect to a part or the whole, then with respect to any goods directly affected and, if the breach is of the whole contract (Section 2-612), then also with respect to the whole undelivered balance the aggrieved seller may

(**a**) withhold delivery of such goods;

(**b**) stop delivery by any bailee as hereafter provided (Section 2-705);

(**c**) proceed under the next section respecting goods still unidentified to the contract;

(**d**) resell and recover damages as hereafter provided (Section 2-706);

(**e**) recover damages for non-acceptance (Section 2-708) or in a proper case the price (Section 2-709);

(**f**) cancel.

§2-704. Seller's Right to Identify Goods to the Contract Notwithstanding Breach or to Salvage Unfinished Goods.

(**1**) An aggrieved seller under the preceding section may

(**a**) identify to the contract conforming goods not already identified if at the time he learned of the breach they are in his possession or control;

(**b**) treat as the subject of resale goods which have demonstrably been intended for the particular contract even though those goods are unfinished

(**2**) Where the goods are unfinished an aggrieved seller may in the exercise of reasonable commercial judgment for the purposes of avoiding loss and of effective realization either complete the manufacture and wholly identify the goods to the contract or cease manufacture and resell for scrap or salvage value or proceed in any other reasonable manner.

§2-705. Seller's Stoppage of Delivery in Transit or Otherwise.

(**1**) The seller may stop delivery of goods in the possession of a carrier or other bailee when he discovers the buyer to be insolvent (Section 2-702) and may stop delivery of carload, truckload, planeload or larger shipments of express or freight when the buyer repudiates or fails to make a payment due before delivery or if for any other reason the seller has a right to withhold or reclaim the goods.

(**2**) As against such buyer the seller may stop delivery until

(**a**) receipt of the goods by the buyer; or

(**b**) acknowledgement to the buyer or by any

bailee of the goods except a carrier that the bailee holds the goods for the buyer; or

(**c**) such acknowledgement to the buyer by a carrier by reshipment or as warehouseman; or

(**d**) negotiation to the buyer of any negotiable document of title covering the goods.

(**3**) (**a**) To stop delivery the seller must so notify as to enable the bailee by reasonable diligence to prevent delivery of the goods.

(**b**) After such notification the bailee must hold and deliver the goods according to the directions of the seller but the seller is liable to the bailee for any ensuing charges or damages.

(**c**) If a negotiable document of title has been issued for goods the bailee is not obliged to obey a notification to stop until surrender of the document.

(**d**) A carrier who has issued a non-negotiable bill of lading is not obliged to obey a notification to stop received from a person other than the consignor.

§2-706. Seller's Resale Including Contract for Resale.

(**1**) Under the conditions stated in Section 2-703 on seller's remedies, the seller may resell the goods concerned or the undelivered balance thereof. Where the resale is made in good faith and in a commercially reasonable manner the seller may recover the difference between the resale price and the contract price together with any incidental damages allowed under the provisions of this Article (Section 2-710), but less expenses saved in consequence of the buyer's breach.

(**2**) Except as otherwise provided in subsection (3) or unless otherwise agreed resale may be at public or private sale including sale by way of one or more contracts to sell or of identification to an existing contract of the seller. Sale may be as a unit or in parcels and at any time and place and on any terms but every aspect of the sale including the method, manner, time, place and terms must be commercially reasonable. The resale must be reasonably identified as referring to the broken contract, but it is not necessary that the goods be in existence or that any or all of them have been identified to the contract before the breach.

(**3**) Where the resale is at private sale the seller must give the buyer reasonable notification of his intention to resell.

(**4**) Where the resale is at public sale

(**a**) Only identified goods can be sold except where there is a recognized market for a public sale of futures in goods of the kind; and

(**b**) it must be made at a usual place or market for public sale if one is reasonably available and except in the case of goods which are perishable or threaten to decline in value speedily the seller must give the buyer reasonable notice of the time and place of the resale; and

(**c**) if the goods are not to be within the view of those attending the sale the notification of sale must state the place where the goods are located and provide for their reasonable inspection by prospective bidders; and

(**d**) the seller may buy.

(**5**) A purchaser who buys in good faith at a resale takes the goods free of any rights of the original buyer even though the seller fails to comply with one or more of the requirements of this section.

(**6**) The seller is not accountable to the buyer for any profit made on any resale. A person in the position of a seller (Section 2-707) or a buyer who has rightfully rejected or justifiably revoked acceptance must account for any excess over the amount of his security interest, as hereinafter defined (subsection (3) of Section 2-711).

§2-707. "Person in the Position of a Seller".

(**1**) A "person in the position of a seller" includes as against a principal an agent who has paid or become responsible for the price of goods on behalf of his principal or anyone who otherwise holds a security interest or other right in goods similar to that of a seller.

(**2**) A person in the position of a seller may as provided in this Article withhold or stop delivery (Section 2-705) and resell (Section 2-706) and recover incidental damages (Section 2-710).

§2-708. Seller's Damages for Non-acceptance or Repudiation.

(**1**) Subject to subsection (2) and to the provisions of this Article with respect to proof of market price (Section 2-723), the measure of damages for non-acceptance or repudiation by the buyer is the difference between the market price at the time and place for tender and the unpaid contract price together with any incidental damages provided in this Article (Section 2-710), but less expenses saved in consequence of the buyer's breach.

(**2**) If the measure of damages provided in subsection (1) is inadequate to put the seller in as good a position as performance would have done then the measure of damages is the profit (including reasonable overhead) which the seller would have made from full performance by the buyer, together with any incidental damages provided in this Article (Section 2-710), due allowance for costs reasonably incurred and due credit for payments or proceeds of resale.

§2-709. Action for the Price.

(1) When the buyer fails to pay the price as it becomes due the seller may recover, together with any incidental damages under the next section, the price

(a) of goods accepted or of conforming goods lost or damaged within a commercially reasonable time after risk of their loss has passed to the buyer; and

(b) of goods identified to the contract if the seller is unable after reasonable effort to resell them at a reasonable price or the circumstances reasonably indicate that such effort will be unavailing.

(2) Where the seller sues for the price he must hold for the buyer any goods which have been identified to the contract and are still in his control except that if resale becomes possible he may resell them at any time prior to the collection of the judgment. The net proceeds of any such resale must be credited to the buyer and payment of the judgment entitles him to any goods not resold.

(3) After the buyer has wrongfully rejected or revoked acceptance of the goods has failed to make a payment due or has repudiated (Section 2-610), a seller who is heid not entitled to the price under this section shall nevertheless be awarded damages for non-acceptance under the preceding section.

§2-710. Seller's Incidental Damages. Incidental damages to an aggrieved seller include any commercially reasonable charges, expenses or commissions incurred in stopping delivery, in the transportation, care and custody of goods after the buyer's breach, in connection with return or resale of the goods or otherwise resulting from the breach.

§2-711. Buyer's Remedies in General; Buyer's Security Interest in Rejected Goods.

(1) When the seller fails to make delivery or repudiates or the buyer rightfully rejects or justifably revokes acceptance then with respect to any goods involved, and with respect to the whole if the breach goes to the whole contract (Section 2-612), the buyer may cancel and whether or not he has done so may in addition to recovering so much of the price as has been paid

(a) "cover" and have damages under the next section as to all the goods affected whether or not they have been identified to the contract; or

(b) recover damages for non-delivery as provided in this Article (Section 2-713).

(2) Where the seller fails to deliver or repudiates the buyer may also

(a) if the goods have been identified recover them as provided in this Article (Section 2-502); or

(b) in a proper case obtain specific performance or replevy the goods as provided in this Article (Section 2-716).

(3) On rightful rejection or justifiable revocation of acceptance a buyer has a security interest in goods in his possession or control for any payments made on their price and any expenses reasonably incurred in their inspection, receipt, transportation, care and custody and may hold such goods and resell them in like manner as an aggrieved seller (Section 2-706).

§2-712. "Cover"; Buyer's Procurement of Substitute Goods.

(1) After a breach within the preceding section the buyer may "cover" by making in good faith and without unreasonable delay any reasonable purchase of or contract to purchase goods in substitution for those due from the seller.

(2) The buyer may recover from the seller as damages the difference between the cost of cover and the contract price together with any incidental or consequential damages as hereinafter defined (Section 2-715), but less expenses saved in consequence of the seller's breach.

(3) Failure of the buyer to effect cover within this section does not ban him from any other remedy.

§2-713. Buyer's Damages for Non-Delivery or Repudiation.

(1) Subject to the provisions of this Article with respect to proof of market price (Section 2-723), the measure of damages for non-delivery or repudiation by the seller is the difference betwen the market price at the time when the buyer learned of the breach and the contract price together with any incidental and consequential damages provided in this Article (Section 2-715), but less expenses saved in consequence of the seller's breach.

(**2**) Market price is to be determined as of the place for tender or, in cases of rejection after arrival or revocation of acceptance as of the place of arrival.

§2-714. Buyer's Damages for Breach in Regard to Accepted Goods.

(**1**) Where the buyer has accepted goods and given notification (subsection (3) Section 2-607) he may recover as damages for any non-conformity of tender the loss resulting in the ordinary course of events from the seller's breach as determined in any manner which is reasonable.

(**2**) The measure of damages for breach of warranty is the difference at the time and place of acceptance between the value of the goods accepted and the value they would have had if they had been as warranted, unless special circumstances show proximate damages of a different amount.

(**3**) In a proper case any incidental and consequential damages under the next section may also be recovered.

§2-715. Buyer's Incidental and Consequential Damages.

(**1**) Incidental damages resulting from the seller's breach include expenses reasonably incurred in inspection, receipt, transportation and care and custody of goods rightfully rejected, any commercially reasonable charges, expenses or commissions in connection with effecting cover and any other reasonable expense incident to the delay or other breach.

(**2**) Consequential damages resulting from the seller's breach include

(**a**) any loss resulting from general or particular requirements and needs of which the seller at the time of contracting had reason to know and which could not reasonably be prevented by cover or otherwise; and

(**b**) injury to person or property proximately resulting from any breach of warranty.

§2-716. Buyer's Right to Specific Performance or Replevin.

(**1**) Specific performance may be decreed where the goods are unique or in other proper circumstances.

(**2**) The decree for specific performance may include such terms and conditions as to payment of the price, damages, or other relief as the court may deem just.

(**3**) The buyer has a right of replevin for goods identified to the contract if after reasonable effort he is unable to effect cover for such goods or the circumstances reasonably indicate that such effort will be unavailing or if the goods have been shipped under reservation and satisfaction of the security interest in them has been made or tendered.

§2-717. Deduction of Damages From the Price. The buyer on notifying the seller of his intention to do so may deduct all or any part of the damages resulting from any breach of the contact from any part of the price still due under the same contract.

§2-718. Liquidation or Limitation of Damages; Deposits.

(**1**) Damages for breach by either party may be liquidated in the agreement but only at an amount which is reasonable in the light of the anticipated or actual harm caused by the breach, the difficulties of proof of loss, and the inconvenience or nonfeasibility of otherwise obtaining an adequate remedy. A term fixing unreasonably large liquidated damages is void as a penalty.

(**2**) Where the seller justifiably withholds delivery of goods because of the buyer's breach, the buyer is entitled to restitution of any amount by which the sum of his payments exceeds

(**a**) the amount to which the seller is entitled by virtue of terms liquidating the seller's damages in accordance with subsection (1), or

(**b**) in the absence of such terms, twenty per cent of the value of the total performance for which the buyer is obligated under the contract or $500, whichever is smaller.

(**3**) The buyer's right to restitution under subsection (2) is subject to offset to the extent that the seller establishes

(**a**) a right to recover damages under the provisions of this Article other than subsection (1), and

(**b**) the amount or value of any benefits received by the buyer directly or indirectly by reason of the contract.

(**4**) Where a seller has received payment in goods their reasonable value or the proceeds of their resale shall be treated as payments for the purposes of subsection (2); but if the seller has notice of the buyer's breach before reselling goods received in part performance, his resale is subject to the conditions laid down in this Article on resale by an aggrieved seller (Section 2-706).

§2-719. Contractual Modification or Limitation of Remedy.

(1) Subject to the provisions of subsections (2) and (3) of this section and of the preceding section on liquidation and limitation of damages,

(a) the agreement may provide for remedies in addition to or in substitution for those provided in this Article and may limit or alter the measure of damages recoverable under his Article, as by limiting the buyer's remedies to return of the goods and repayment of the price or to repair and replacement of non-conforming goods or parts; and

(b) resort to a remedy as provided is optional unless the remedy is expressly agreed to be exclusive, in which case it is the sole remedy.

(2) Where circumstances cause an exclusive or limited remedy to fail of its essential purpose, remedy may be had as provided in this Act.

(3) Consequential damages may be limited or excluded unless the limitation or exclusion is unconscionable. Limitation of consequential damages for injury to the person in the case of consumer goods is prima facie unconscionable but limitation of damages where the loss is commercial is not.

§2-720. Effect of "Cancellation" or "Rescission" on Claims for Antecedent Breach. Unless the contrary intention clearly appears, expressions of "cancellation" or "rescission" of the contract or the like shall not be construed as a renunciation or discharge of any claim in damages for an antecedent breach.

§2-721. Remedies for Fraud. Remedies for material misrepresentation or fraud include all remedies available under this Article for non-fraudulent breach. Neither rescission or a claim for rescission of the contract for sale nor rejection or return of the goods shall bar or be deemed inconsistent with a claim for damage or other remedy.

§2-722. Who Can Sue Third Parties for Injury to Goods. Where a third party so deals with goods which have been identified to a contract for sale as to cause actionable injury to a party to that contract

(a) right of action against the third party is in either party to the contract for sale who has title to or a security interest or a special property or an insurable interest in the goods; and if the goods have been destroyed or converted a right of action is also in the party who either bore the risk of loss under the contract for sale or has since the injury assumed that risk as against the other;

(b) if at the time of the injury the party plaintiff did not bear the risk of loss as against the other party to the contract for sale and there is no arrangement between them for disposition of the recovery, his suit or settlement is, subject to his own interest, as a fiduciary for the other party to the contract;

(c) either party may with the consent of the other sue for the benefit of whom it may concern.

§2-723. Proof of Market Price: Time and Place.

(1) If an action based on anticipatory repudiation comes to trial before the time for performance with respect to some or all of the goods, any damages based on market price (Section 2-708 or Section 2-713) shall be determined according to the price of such goods prevailing at the time when the aggrieved party learned of the repudiation.

(2) If evidence of a price prevailing at the times or places described in this Article is not readily available the price prevailing within any reasonable time before or after the time described or at any other place which in commercial judgment or under usage of trade would serve as a reasonable substitute for the one described may be used, making any proper allowance for the cost of transporting the goods to or from such other place.

(3) Evidence of a relevant price prevailing at a time or place other than the one described in this Article offered by one party is not admissible unless and until he has given the other party such notice as the court finds sufficient to prevent unfair surprise.

§2-724. Admissibility of Market Quotations. Whenever the prevailing price or value of any goods regularly bought and sold in any established commodity market is in issue, reports in official publication or trade journals or in newspapers or periodicals of general circulation published as the reports of such market shall be admissible in evidence. The circumstances of the preparation of such a report may be shown to affect its weight but not its admissibility.

§2-725. Statute of Limitations in Contracts for Sale.

(1) An action for breach of any contract for sale must be commenced within four years after the cause of action has accrued. By the original agreement the parties may reduce the period of limitation to not less than one year but may not extend it.

(2) A cause of action accrues when the breach occurs, regardless of the aggrieved party's lack of knowledge of the breach. A breach of warranty occurs when tender of delivery is made, except that where a warranty explicitly extends to future performance of the goods and discovery of the breach must await the time of such performance the cause of action accrues when the breach is or should have been discovered.

(3) Where an action commenced within the time limited by subsection (1) is so terminated as to leave available a remedy by another action for the same breach such other action may be commenced after the expiration of the time limited and within six months after the termination of the first action unless the termination resulted from voluntary discontinuance or from dismissal for failure or neglect to prosecute.

(4) This section does not alter the law on tolling of the statute of limitations nor does it apply to causes of action which have accrued before this Act becomes effective.

ARTICLE 3: COMMERCIAL PAPER

Part 1: Short Title, Form and Interpretation

§3-101. Short Title. This Article shall be known and may be cited as Uniform Commercial Code—Commercial Paper.

§3-102. Definitions and Index of Definitions.

(1) In this Article unless the context otherwise requires

(a) "Issue" means the first delivery of an instrument to a holder or a remitter.

(b) An "order" is a direction to pay and must be more than an authorization or request. It must identify the person to pay with reasonable certainty. It may be addressed to one or more such persons jointly or in the alternative but not in succession.

(c) A "promise" is an undertaking to pay and must be more than an acknowledgment of an obligation.

(d) "Secondary party" means a drawer or endorser.

(e) "Instrument" means a negotiable instrument.

(2) Other definitions applying to this Article and the sections in which they appear are:

"Acceptance". Section 3-410.
"Accommodation party". Section 3-415.
"Alteration". Section 3-407.
"Certificate of deposit". Section 3-104.
"Certification". Section 3-411.
"Check". Section 3-104.
"Definite time". Section 3-109.
"Dishonor". Section 3-507.
"Draft". Section 3-104.
"Holder in due course". Section 3-202.
"Negotiation". Section 3-202.
"Note". Section 3-104.
"Notice of dishonor". Section 3-508.
"On demand". Section 3-108.
"Presentment". Section 3-504.
"Protest". Section 3-509.
"Restrictive Indorsement". Section 3-205.
"Signature". Section 3-401.

(3) The following definitions in other Articles apply to this Article:

"Account". Section 4-104.
"Banking Day". Section 4-104.
"Clearing house". Section 4-104.
"Collecting bank". Section 4-105.
"Customer". Section 4-104.
"Depositary Bank". Section 4-105.
"Documentary Draft". Section 4-104.
"Intermediary Bank". Section 4-105.
"Item". Section 4-104.
"Midnight deadline". Section 4-104.
"Payor bank". Section 4-105.

(4) In addition Article 1 contains general definitions and principles of construction and interpretation applicable throughout this Article.

§3-103. Limitations on Scope of Article.

(1) This Article does not apply to money, documents of title or investment securities.

(2) The provisions of this Article are subject to the provisions of the Article on Bank Deposits and Collections (Article 4) and Secured Transations (Article 9).

§3-104. Form of Negotiable Instruments; "Draft"; "Check"; "Certificate of Deposit"; "Note".

(1) Any writing to be a negotiable instrument within this Article must

(a) be signed by the maker or drawer; and

(**b**) contain an unconditional promise or order to pay a sum certain in money and no other promise, order, obligation or power given by the maker or drawer except as authorized by this Article; and

(**c**) be payable on demand or at a definite time; and

(**d**) be payable to order or to bearer.

(**2**) A writing which complies with the requirements of this section is

(**a**) a "draft" ("bill of exchange") if it is an order;

(**b**) a "check" if it is a draft drawn on a bank and payable on demand;

(**c**) a "certificate of deposit" if it is an acknowledgement by a bank of receipt of money with an engagement to repay it;

(**d**) a "note" if it is a promise other than a certificate of deposit.

(**3**) As used in other Articles in this Act, and as the context may require, the terms "draft", "check", "certificate of deposit" and "note" may refer to instruments which are not negotiable within this Article as well as to instruments which are so negotiable.

§3-105. When Promise or Order Unconditional.

(**1**) A promise or order otherwise unconditional is not made conditional by the fact that the instrument

(**a**) is subject to implied or constructive conditions; or

(**b**) states its consideration, whether performed or promised, or the transaction which gave rise to the instrument, or that the promise or order is made or the instrument matures in accordance with or "as per" such transaction; or

(**c**) refers to or states that it arises out of a separate agreement or refers to a separate agreement for rights as to prepayment or acceleration; or

(**d**) states that is drawn under a letter of credit; or

(**e**) states that it is secured, whether by mortgage, reservation of title or otherwise; or

(**f**) indicates a particular account to be debited or any other fund or source from which reimbursement is expected; or

(**g**) is limited to payment out of a particular fund or the proceeds of a particular source, if the instrument is issued by a government or governmental agency or unit; or

(**h**) is limited to payment out of the entire assets of a partnership, unincorporated association, trust or estate by or on behalf of which the instrument is issued.

(**2**) A promise or order is not unconditional if the instrument

(**a**) states that it is subject to or governed by any other agreement; or

(**b**) states that it is to be paid only out of a particular fund or source except as provided in this section. As amended 1962.

§3-106. Sum Certain.

(**1**) The sum payable is a sum certain even though it is to be paid

(**a**) with stated interest or by stated installments; or

(**b**) with stated different rates of interest before and after default or a specified date; or

(**c**) with a stated discount or addition if paid before or after the date fixed for payment; or

(**d**) with exchange or less exchange; whether at a fixed rate or at the current rate; or

(**e**) with cost of collection or an attorney's fee or both upon default.

(**2**) Nothing in this section shall validate any term which is otherwise illegal.

§3-107. Money.

(**1**) An instrument is payable in money if the medium of exchange in which it is payable is money at the time the instrument is made. An instrument payable in "currency" or "current funds" is payable in money.

(**2**) A promise or order to pay a sum stated in a foreign currency is for a sum certain in money and, unless a different medium of payment is specified in the instrument, may be satisfied by payment of that number of dollars which the stated foreign currency will purchase at the buying sight rate for that currency on the day on which the instrument is payable or, if payable on demand, on the day of demand. If such an instrument specifies a foreign currency as the medium of payment the instrument is payable in that currency.

§3-108. Payable on Demand. Instruments payable on demand include those payable at sight or on presentation and those in which no time for payment is stated.

§3-109. Definite Time.

(**1**) An instrument is payable at a definite time if by its terms it is payable (**a**) on or before a stated date or at a fixed period after a stated date; or

(**b**) at a fixed period after sight; or

(**c**) at a definite time subject to any acceleration; or

(**d**) at a definite time subject to extension at the option of the holder, or to extension to a further definite time at the option of the maker or acceptor or automatically upon or after a specified act or event.

(**2**) An instrument which by its terms is otherwise payable only upon an act or event uncertain as to time of occurrence is not payable at a definite time even though the act or event has occurred.

§3-110. Payable to Order.

(**1**) An instrument is payable to order when by its terms it is payable to the order or assigns of any person therein specified with reasonable certainty, or to him or his order, or when it is conspicuously designated on its face as "exchange" or the like and names a payee. It may be payable to the order of

(**a**) the maker or drawer; or

(**b**) the drawee; or

(**c**) a payee who is not maker, drawer or drawee; or

(**d**) two or more payees together or in the alternative; or

(**e**) an estate, trust or fund, in which case it is payable to the order of the representative of such estate, trust or fund or his successors; or

(**f**) an office, or an officer by his title as such in which case it is payable to the principal but the incumbent of the office or his successors may act as if he or they were the holder; or

(**g**) a partnership or unincorporated association, in which case it is payable to the partnership or association and may be indorsed or transferred by any person thereto authorized.

(**2**) An instrument not payable to order is not made so payable by such words as "payable upon return of this instrument properly indorsed."

(**3**) An instrument made payable both to order and to bearer is payable to order unless the bearer words are handwritten or typewritten.

§3-111. Payable to Bearer. An instrument is payable to bearer when by its terms it is payable to

(**a**) bearer or the order of bearer; or

(**b**) a specified person or bearer; or

(**c**) "cash" or the order of "cash", or any other indication which does not purport to designate a specific payee.

§3-112. Terms and Omissions Not Affecting Negotiability.

(**1**) The negotiability of an instrument is not affected by

(**a**) the omission of a statement of any consideration or of the place where the instrument is drawn or payable; or

(**b**) a statement that collateral has been given to secure obligation either on the instrument or otherwise of an obligor on the instrument or that in case of default on those obligations the holder may realize on or dispose of the collateral; or

(**c**) a promise or power to maintain or protect collateral or to give additional collateral; or

(**d**) a term authorizing a confession of judgment on the instrument if it is not paid when due; or

(**e**) a term purporting to waive the benefit of any law intended for the advantage or protection of any obligor; or

(**f**) a term in a draft providing that the payee by indorsing or cashing it acknowledges full satisfaction of an obligation of the drawer; or

(**g**) a statement in a draft drawn in a set of parts (Section 3-801) to the effect that the order is effective only if no other part has been honored.

(**2**) Nothing in this section shall validate any term which is otherwise illegal. As amended 1962.

§3-113. Seal. An instrument otherwise negotiable is within this Article even though it is under a seal.

§3-114. Date, Antedating, Postdating.

(**1**) The negotiability of an instrument is not affected by the fact that it is undated, antedated or postdated.

(**2**) Where an instrument is antedated or postdated the time when it is payable is determined by the stated date if the instrument is payable on demand or at a fixed period after date.

(**3**) Where the instrument or any signature thereon is dated, the date is presumed to be correct.

§3-115. Incomplete Instruments.

(**1**) When a paper whose contents at the time of signing show that it is is intended to become an instrument is signed while still incomplete in any necessary respect it cannot be enforced until completed, but when it is completed in accordance with authority given it is effective as completed.

(2) If the completion is unauthorized the rules as to material alteration apply (Section 3-407), even though the paper was not delivered by the maker or drawer, but the burden of establishing that any completion is unauthorized is on the party so asserting.

§3-116. Instruments Payable to Two or More Persons. An instrument payable to the order of two or more persons

(a) if in the alternative is payable to any one of them and may be negotiated, discharged or enforced by any one of them who has possession of it;

(b) if not in the alternative is payable to all of them and may be negotiated, discharged or enforced only by all of them.

§3-117. Instruments Payable With Words of Description. An instrument made payable to a named person with the addition of words describing him

(a) as agent or officer of a specified person is payable to his principal but the agent or officer may act as if he were the holder;

(b) as any other fiduciary for a specified person or purpose is payable to the payee and may be negotiated, discharged or enforced by him;

(c) in any other manner is payable to the payee unconditionally and the additional words are without effect on subsequent parties.

§3-118. Ambiguous Terms and Rules of Construction. The following rules apply to every instrument:

(a) Where there is doubt whether the instrument is a draft or a note the holder may treat it as either. A draft drawn on the drawer is effective as a note.

(b) Handwritten terms control typewritten and printed terms, and typewritten control printed.

(c) Words control figures except that if the words are ambiguous figures control.

(d) Unless otherwise specified a provision for interest means interest at the judgment rate at the place of payment from the date of the instrument, or if it is undated from the date of issue.

(e) Unless the instrument otherwise specifies two or more persons who sign as maker, acceptor or drawer or indorser and as a part of the same transaction are jointly and severally liable even though the instrument contains such words as "I promise to pay."

(f) Unless otherwise specified consent to extension authorizes a single extension for not longer than the original period. A consent to extension, expressed in the instrument, is binding on secondary parties and accommodation makers. A holder may not exercise his option to extend an instrument over the objection of a maker or acceptor or other party who in accordance with Section 3-604 tenders full payment when the instrument is due.

§3-119. Other Writings Affecting Instrument.

(1) As between the obligor and his immediate obligee or any transferee the terms of an instrument may be modified or affected by any other written agreement executed as a part of the same transaction, except that a holder in due course is not affected by any limitation of his rights arising out of the separate written agreement if he had no notice of the limitation when he took the instrument.

(2) A separate agreement does not affect the negotiability of an instrument.

§3-120. Instruments "Payable Through" Bank. An instrument which states that is is "payable through" a bank or the like designates that bank as a collecting bank to make presentment but does not of itself authorize the bank to pay the instrument.

§3-121. Instruments Payable at Bank.

Note: *If this Act is introduced in the Congress of the United States this section should be omitted. (States to select either alternative.)*

Alternative A—A note or acceptance which states that is is payable at a bank is the equivalent of a draft drawn on the bank payable when it falls due out of any funds of the maker or acceptor in current account or otherwise available for such payment.

Alternative B—A note or acceptance which states that it is payable at a bank is not of itself an order or authorization to the bank to pay it.

§3-122. Accrual of Cause of Action.

(1) A cause of action against a maker or an acceptor accrues

(a) in the case of a time instrument on the day after maturity;

(b) in the case of a demand instrument upon its date or, if no date is stated, on the date of issue.

(2) A cause of action against the obligor of a demand or time certificate of deposit accrues upon demand, but demand on a time certificate may not be made until on or after the date of maturity.

(3) A cause of action against a drawer of a draft or an indorser of any instrument accrues upon demand following dishonor of the instrument. Notice of dishonor is a demand.

(4) Unless an instrument provides otherwise, interest runs at the rate provided by law for a judgment

> **(a)** in the case of a maker, acceptor or other primary obligor of a demand instrument, from the date of demand;
>
> **(b)** in all other cases from the date of accrual of the cause of action. As amended 1962.

Part 2: Transfer and Negotiation

§3-201. Transfer: Right to Indorsement.

(1) Transfer of an instrument vests in the transferee such rights as the transferor has therein, except that a transferee who has himself been a party to any fraud or illegality affecting the instrument or who as a prior holder had notice of a defense or claim against it cannot improve his position by taking from a later holder in due course.

(2) A transfer of a security interest in an instrument vests the foregoing rights in the transferee to the extent of the interest transferred.

(3) Unless otherwise agreed any transfer for value of an instrument not then payable to bearer gives the transferee the specifically enforceable right to have the unqualified indorsement of the transferor. Negotiation takes effect only when the indorsement is made and until that time there is no presumption that the transferee is the owner.

§3-202. Negotiation.

(1) Negotiation is the transfer of an instrument in such form that the transferee becomes a holder. If the instrument is payable to order it is negotiated by delivery with any necessary indorsement; if payable to bearer it is negotiated by delivery.

(2) An indorsement must be written by or on behalf of the holder and on the instrument or on a paper so firmly affixed thereto as to become a part thereof.

(3) An indorsement is effective for negotiation only when it conveys the entire instrument or any unpaid residue. If it purports to be of less it operates only as a partial assignment.

(4) Words of assignment, condition, waiver, guaranty, limitation or disclaimer of liability and the like accompanying in indorsement do not affect its character as an indorsement.

§3-203. Wrong or Misspelled Name. Where an instrument is made payable to a person under a misspelled name or one other than his own he may indorse in that name or his own or both, but signature in both names may be required by a person paying or giving value for the instrument.

§3-204. Special Indorsement; Blank Indorsement.

(1) A special indorsement specifies the person to whom or to whose order it makes the instrument payable. Any instrument specially indorsed becomes payable to the order of the special indorsee and may be further negotiated only by his indorsement.

(2) An indorsement in blank specifies no particular indorsee and may consist of a mere signature. An instrument payable to order and indorsed in blank becomes payable to bearer and may be negotiated by delivery alone until specially indorsed.

(3) The holder may convert a blank indorsement into a special indorsement by writing over the signature of the indorser in blank any contract consistent with the character of the indorsement.

§3-205. Restrictive Indorsements. An indorsement is restrictive which either

> **(a)** is conditional; or
>
> **(b)** purports to prohibit further transfer of the instrument; or
>
> **(c)** includes the words "for collection", "for deposit", "pay any bank", or like terms signifying a purpose of deposit or collection; or
>
> **(d)** otherwise states that it is for the benefit or use of the indorser or of another person.

§3-206. Effect of Restrictive Indorsement.

(1) No restrictive indorsement prevents further transfer or negotiation of the instrument.

(2) An intermediary bank, or a payor bank which is not the depositary bank, is neither given notice nor otherwise affected by a restrictive indorsement of any person except the bank's immediate transferor or the person presenting for payment.

(3) Except for an intermediary bank, any transferee under an indorsement which is conditional or includes the words "for collection", for deposit", "pay any bank", or like terms (subparagraphs (a) and (c) of Section 3-205) must pay or apply any value given by him for or on the security of the instrument consistently with the indorsement and to the extent that he does so he becomes a holder for value. In addition such transferee is a holder in due course if he otherwise complies with the requirements of Section 3-302 on what constitutes a holder in due course.

(4) The first taker under an indorsement for the benefit of the indorser or another person (subparagraph (d) of Section 3-205) must pay or apply any value given by him for or on the security of the instrument consistently with the indorsement and to the extent that he does so he becomes a holder for value. In addition such taker is a holder in due course if he otherwise complies with the requirements of Section 3-302 on what constitutes a holder in due course. A later holder for value is neither given notice nor otherwise affected by such restrictive indorsement unless he has knowledge that a fiduciary or other person has negotiated the instrument in any transaction for his own benefit or otherwise in breach of duty (subsection (2) of Section 3-304).

§3-207. Negotiation Effective Although It May Be Rescinded.

(1) Negotiation is effective to transfer the instrument although the negotiation is

(a) made by an infant, a corporation exceeding its powers, or any other person without capacity; or

(b) obtained by fraud, duress or mistake of any kind; or

(c) part of an illegal transaction; or

(d) made in breach of duty.

(2) Except as against a subsequent holder in due course such negotiation is in an appropriate case subject to rescission, the declaration of a constructive trust or any other remedy permitted by law.

§3-208. Reacquisition. Where an instrument is returned to or reacquired by a prior party he may cancel any indorsement which is not necessary to his title and reissue or further negotiate the instrument, but any intervening party is discharged as against the reacquiring party and subsequent holders not in due course and if his indorsement has been cancelled is discharged as against subsequent holders in due course as well.

Part 3: Rights of a Holder

§3-301. Rights of a Holder. The holder of an instrument whether or not he is the owner may transfer or negotiate it and, except as otherwise provided in Section 3-603 on payment or satisfaction, discharge it or enforce payment in his own name.

§3-302. Holder in Due Course.

(1) A holder in due course is a holder who takes the instrument

(a) for value; and

(b) in good faith; and

(c) without notice that it is overdue or has been dishonored or of any defense against or claim to it on the part of any person.

(2) A payee may be a holder in due course.

(3) A holder does not become a holder in due course of an instrument

(a) by purchase of it at judicial sale or by taking it under legal process; or

(b) by acquiring it in taking over an estate; or

(c) by purchasing it as part of a bulk transaction not in regular course of business of the transferor.

(4) A purchaser of a limited interest can be a holder in due course only to the extent of the interest purchased.

§3-303. Taking for Value. A holder takes the instrument for value

(a) to the extent that the agreed consideration has been performed or that he acquires a security interest in or a lien on the instrument otherwise than by legal process; or

(b) when he takes the instrument in payment of or as security for an antecedent claim against any person whether or not the claim is due; or

(c) when he gives a negotiable instrument for it or makes an irrevocable commitment to a third person.

§3-304. Notice to Purchaser.

(1) The purchaser has notice of a claim or defense if

(a) the instrument is so incomplete, bears such visible evidence of forgery or alteration, or is otherwise so irregular as to call into question its validity, terms or ownership or to create an ambiguity as to the party to pay; or

(b) the purchaser has notice that the obligation of any party is voidable in whole or in part, or that all parties have been discharged.

(2) The purchaser has notice of a claim against the instrument when he has knowledge that a fiduciary has negotiated the instrument in payment of or as security for his own debt or in any transaction for his own benefit or otherwise in breach of duty.

(3) The purchaser has notice that an instrument is overdue if he has reason to know

(a) that any part of the principal amount is overdue or that there is an uncured default in payment of another instrument of the same series; or

(b) that acceleration of the instrument has been made; or (**c**) that he is taking a demand instrument after demand has been made or more than a reasonable length of time after its issue. A reasonable time for a check drawn and payable within the states and territories of the United States and the District of Columbia is presumed to be thirty days.

(**4**) Knowledge of the following facts does not of itself give the purchaser notice of a defense or claim

(**a**) that the instrument is antedated or postdated;

(**b**) that it was issued or negotiated in return for an executory promise or accompanied by a separate agreement, unless the purchaser has notice that a defense or claim has arisen from the terms thereof;

(**c**) that any party has signed for accommodation;

(**d**) that an incomplete instrument has been completed, unless the purchaser has notice of any improper completion;

(**e**) that any person negotiating the instrument is or was a fiduciary;

(**f**) that there has been default in payment of interest on the instrument or in payment of any other instrument, except one of the same series.

(**5**) The filing or recording of a document does not of itself constitute notice within the provisions of this Article to a person who would otherwise be a holder in due course.

(**6**) To be effective notice must be received at such time and in such manner as to give a reasonable opportunity to act on it.

§3-305. Rights of a Holder in Due Course. To the extent that a holder is a holder in due course he takes the instrument free from

(**1**) all claims to it on the part of any person; and

(**2**) all defenses of any party to the instrument with whom the holder has not dealt except

(**a**) infancy, to the extent that it is a defense to a simple contract; and

(**b**) such other incapacity, or duress, or illegality of the transaction, as renders the obligation of the party a nullity; and

(**c**) such misrepresentation as has induced the party to sign the instrument with neither knowledge nor reasonable opportunity to obtain knowledge of its character or its essential terms; and

(**d**) discharge in insolvency proceedings; and

(**e**) any other discharge of which the holder has notice when he takes the instrument.

§3-306. Rights of One Not Holder in Due Course. Unless he has the rights of a holder in due course any person takes the instrument subject to

(**a**) all valid claims to it on the part of any person; and

(**b**) all defenses of any party which would be available in an action on a simple contract; and

(**c**) the defenses of want or failure of consideration, non-performance of any condition precedent, non-delivery, or delivery for a special purpose (Section 3-408); and

(**d**) the defense that he or a person through whom he holds the instrument acquired it by theft, or that payment or satisfaction to such holder would be inconsistent with the terms of a restrictive indorsement. The claim of any third person to the instrument is not otherwise available as a defense to any party liable thereon unless the third person himself defends the action for such party.

§3-307. Burden of Establishing Signatures, Defenses and Due Course.

(**1**) Unless specifically denied in the pleading each signature on an instrument is admitted. When the effectiveness of a signature is put in issue

(**a**) the burden of establishing it is on the party claiming under the signature; but

(**b**) the signature is presumed to be genuine or authorized except where the action is to enforce the obligation of a purported signer who has died or become incompetent before proof is required.

(**2**) When signatures are admitted or established, production of the instrument entitles a holder to recover on it unless the defendant establishes a defense.

(**3**) After it is shown that a defense exists a person claiming the rights of a holder in due course has the burden of establishing that he or some person under whom he claims is in all respects a holder in due course.

Part 4: Liability of Parties

§3-401. Signature.

(**1**) No person is liable on an instrument unless his signature appears thereon.

(**2**) A signature is made by use of any name, including any trade or assumed name, upon an instrument, or by any word or mark used in lieu of a written signature.

§3-402. Signature in Ambiguous Capacity. Unless the instrument clearly indicates that a signature is made in some other capacity it is an indorsement.

§3-403. Signature by Authorized Representative.

(1) A signature may be made by an agent or other representative, and his authority to make it may be established as in other cases of representation. No particular form of appointment is necessary to establish such authority.

(2) An authorized representative who signs his own name to an instrument

(a) is personally obligated if the instrument neither names the person represented nor shows that the representative signed in a representative capacity;

(b) except as otherwise established between the immediate parties, is personally obligated if the instrument names the person represented but does not show that the representative signed in a representative capacity, or if the instrument does not name the person represented but does show that the representative signed in a representative capacity.

(3) Except as otherwise established the name of an organization preceded or followed by the name and office of an authorized individual is a signature made in a representative capacity.

§3-404. Unauthorized Signatures.

(1) Any unauthorized signature is wholly inoperative as that of the person whose name is signed unless he ratifies it or is precluded from denying it; but it operates as the signature of the unauthorized signer in favor of any person who in good faith pays the instrument or takes it for value.

(2) Any unauthorized signature may be ratified for all purposes of this Article. Such ratification does not of itself affect any rights of the person ratifying against the actual signer.

§3-405. Impostors; Signature in Name of Payee.

(1) An indorsement by any person in the name of a named payee is effective if

(a) an impostor by use of the mails or otherwise has induced the maker or drawer to issue the instrument to him or his confederate in the name of the payee; or

(b) a person signing as or on behalf of a maker or drawer intends the payee to have no interest in the instrument; or

(c) an agent or employee of the maker or drawer has supplied him with the name of the payee intending the latter to have no such interest.

(2) Nothing in this section shall affect the criminal or civil liability of the person so indorsing.

§3-406. Negligence Contributing to Alteration or Unauthorized Signature. Any person who by his negligence substantially contributes to a material alteration of the instrument or to the making of an unauthorized signature is precluded from asserting the alteration or lack of authority against a holder in due course or against a drawee or other payor who pays the instrument in good faith and in accordance with the reasonable commercial standards of the drawee's or payor's business.

§3-407. Alteration.

(1) Any alteration of an instrument is material which changes the contract of any party thereto in any respect, including any such change in

(a) the number or relations of the parties; or

(b) an incomplete instrument, by completing it otherwise than is authorized; or

(c) the writing as signed, by adding to it or by removing any part of it.

(2) As against any person other than a subsequent holder in due course

(a) alteration by the holder which is both fraudulent and material discharges any party whose contract is thereby changed unless that party assents or is precluded from asserting the defense;

(b) no other alteration discharges any party and the instrument may be enforced according to its original tenor, or as to incomplete instruments according to the authority given.

(3) A subsequent holder in due course may in all cases enforce the instrument according to its original tenor, and when an incomplete instrument has been completed, he may enforce it as completed.

§3-408. Consideration. Want or failure of consideration is a defense as against any person not having the rights of a holder in due course. (Section 3-305), except that no consideration is necessary for an instrument or obligation thereon given in payment of or as security for an antecedent obligation of any kind. Nothing in this section shall be taken to displace any statute outside this Act under which a promise is enforceable notwithstanding lack or failure of consideration. Partial failure of consideration is a defense pro tanto whether or not the failure is in an ascertained or liquidated amount.

§3-409. Draft Not as Assignment.

(1) A check or other draft does not of itself operate as an assignment of any funds in the hands of the drawee available for its payment, and the drawee is not liable on the instrument until he accepts it.

(2) Nothing in this section shall affect any liability in contract, tort or otherwise arising from any letter of credit or other obligation or representation which is not an acceptance.

§3-410. Definition and Operation of Acceptance.

(1) Acceptance is the drawee's signed engagement to honor the draft as presented. It must be written on the draft, and may consist of his signature alone. It becomes operative when completed by delivery or notification.

(2) A draft may be accepted although it has not been signed by the drawer or is otherwise incomplete or is overdue or has been dishonored.

(3) Where the draft is payable at a fixed period after sight and the acceptor fails to date his acceptance the holder may complete it by supplying a date in good faith.

§3-411. Certification of a Check.

(1) Certification of a check is acceptance. Where a holder procures certification the drawer and all prior indorsers are discharged.

(2) Unless otherwise agreed, a bank has no obligation to certify a check.

(3) A bank may certify a check before returning it for lack of proper indorsement. If it does so the drawer is discharged.

§3-412. Acceptance Varying Draft.

(1) Where the drawee's proffered acceptance in any manner varies the draft as presented the holder may refuse the acceptance and treat the draft as dishonored in which case the drawee is entitled to have his acceptance cancelled.

(2) The terms of the draft are not varied by an acceptance to pay at any particular bank or place in the United States, unless the acceptance states that the draft is to be paid only at such bank or place.

(3) Where the holder assents to an acceptance varying the terms of the draft each drawer and indorser who does not affirmatively assent is discharged. As amended 1962.

§3-413. Contract of Maker, Drawer and Acceptor.

(1) The maker or acceptor engages that he will pay the instrument according to its tenor at the time of his engagement or as completed pursuant to Section 3-115 on incomplete instruments.

(2) The drawer engages that upon dishonor of the draft and any necessary notice of dishonor or protest he will pay the amount of the draft to the holder or to any indorser who takes it up. The drawer may disclaim this liability by drawing without recourse.

(3) By making, drawing or accepting the party admits against all subsequent parties including the drawee the existence of the payee and his then capacity to indorse.

§3-414. Contract of Indorser; Order of Liability.

(1) Unless the indorsement otherwise specifies (as by such words as "without recourse") every indorser engages that upon dishonor and any necessary notice of dishonor and protest he will pay the instrument according to its tenor at the time of his indorsement to the holder or to any subsequent indorser who takes it up, even though the indorser who takes it up was not obligated to do so.

(2) Unless they otherwise agree indorsers are liable to one another in the order in which they indorse, which is presumed to be the order in which their signatures appear on the instrument.

§3-415. Contract of Accommodation Party.

(1) An accommodation party is one who signs the instrument in any capacity for the purpose of lending his name to another party to it.

(2) When the instrument has been taken for value before it is due the accommodation party is liable in the capacity in which he has signed even though the taker knows of the accommodation.

(3) As against a holder in due course and without notice of the accommodation oral proof of the accommodation is not admissible to give the accommodation party the benefit of discharges dependent on his character as such. In other cases the accommodation character may be shown by oral proof.

(4) An indorsement which shows that it is not in the chain of title is notice of its accommodation character.

(5) An accommodation party is not liable to the party accommodated, and if he pays the instrument has a right of recourse on the instrument against such party.

§3-416. Contract of Guarantor.

(1) "Payment guaranteed" or equivalent words added to a signature mean that the signer engages that if the instrument is not paid when due he will pay it according to its tenor without resort by the holder to any other party.

(**2**) "Collection guaranteed" or equivalent words added to a signature mean that the signer engages that if the instrument is not paid when due he will pay it according to its tenor, but only after the holder has reduced his claim against the maker or acceptor to judgment and execution has been returned unsatisfied, or after the maker or acceptor has become insolvent or it is otherwise apparent that it is useless to proceed against him.

(**3**) Words of guaranty which do not otherwise specify guarantee payment.

(**4**) No words of guaranty added to the signature of a sole maker or acceptor affect his liability on the instrument. Such words added to the signature of one of two or more makers or acceptors create a presumption that the signature is for the accommodation of the others.

(**5**) When words of guaranty are used presentment, notice of dishonor and protest are not necessary to charge the user.

(**6**) Any guaranty written on the insrument is enforcible notwithstanding any statute of frauds.

§3-417. Warranties on Presentment and Transfer.

(**1**) Any person who obtains payment or acceptance and any prior transferor warrants to a person who in good faith pays or accepts that

(**a**) he has a good title to the instrument or is authorized to obtain payment or acceptance on behalf of one who has a good title; and

(**b**) he has no knowledge that the signature of the maker or drawer is unauthorized, except that this warranty is not given by a holder in due course acting in good faith

(**i**) to a maker with respect to the maker's own signature; or

(**ii**) to a drawer with respect to the drawer's own signature, whether or not the drawer is also the drawee; or

(**iii**) to an acceptor of a draft if the holder in due course took the draft after the acceptance or obtained the acceptance without knowledge that the drawer's signature was unauthorized; and

(**c**) the instrument has not been materially altered, except that this warranty is not given by a holder in due course acting in good faith

(**i**) to the maker of a note; or

(**ii**) to the drawer of a draft whether or not the drawer is also the drawee; or

(**iii**) to the acceptor of a draft with respect to an alteration made prior to the acceptance if the holder in due course took the draft after the acceptance, even though the acceptance provided "payable as originally drawn" or equivalent terms; or

(**iv**) to the acceptor of a draft with respect to an alteration made after the acceptance.

(**2**) Any person who transfers an instrument and receives consideration warrants to his transferee and if the transfer is by indorsement to any subsequent holder who takes the instrument in good faith that

(**a**) he has a good title to the instrument or is authorized to obtain payment or acceptance on behalf of one who has a good title and the transfer is otherwise rightful; and

(**b**) all signatures are genuine or authorized; and

(**c**) the instrument has not been materially altered; and

(**d**) no defense of any party is good against him; and

(**e**) he has no knowledge of any insolvency proceeding instituted with respect to the maker or acceptor or the drawer of an unaccepted instrument.

(**3**) By transferring "without recourse" the transfer limits the obligation stated in subsection (2) (d) to a warranty that he has no knowledge of such a defense.

(**4**) A selling agent or broker who does not disclose the fact that he is acting only as such gives the warranties provided in this section, but if he makes such disclosure warrants only his good faith and authority.

§3-418. Finality of Payment of Acceptance. Except for recovery of bank payments as provided in the Article on Bank Deposits and Collections (Article 4) and except for liability for breach of warranty on presentment under the preceding section, payment or acceptance of any instrument is final in favor of a holder in due course, or a person who has in good faith changed his position in reliance on the payment.

§3-419. Conversion of Instrument; Innocent Representative.

(**1**) An instrument is converted when

(**a**) a drawee to whom it is delivered for payment refuses on demand either to pay or to return it; or

(**b**) any person to whom it is delivered for payment refuses on demand either to pay or to return it; or

(**c**) it is paid on a forged indorsement.

(**2**) In an action against a drawee under subsection (1) the measure of the drawee's liability is the face amount of the instrument. In any other action under subsection (1) the measure of liability is presumed to be the face amount of the instrument.

(**3**) Subject to the provisions of this Act concerning restrictive indorsements a representative, including a depositary or collecting bank, who has in good faith and in accordance with the reasonable commercial standards applicable to the business of such representative dealt with an instrument or its proceeds on behalf of one who was not the true owner is not liable in conversion or otherwise to the true owner beyond the amount of any proceeds remaining in his hands.

(**4**) An intermediary bank or payor bank which is not a depositary bank is not liable in conversion solely by reason of the fact that proceeds of an item indorsed restrictively (Sections 3-205 and 3-206) are not paid or applied consistently with the restrictive indorsement of an indorser other than its immediate transferor.

Part 5: Presentment, Notice of Dishonor and Protest

§3-501. When Presentment, Notice of Dishonor, and Protest Necessary or Permissible.

(**1**) Unless excused (Section 3-511) presentment is necessary to charge secondary parties as follows:

(**a**) presentment for acceptance is necessary to charge the drawer and indorsers of a draft where the draft so provides, or is payable elsewhere than at the residence or place of business of the drawee, or its date of payment depends upon such presentment. The holder may at his option present for acceptance any other draft payable at a stated date;

(**b**) presentment for payment is necessary to charge any indorser;

(**c**) in the case of any drawer, the acceptor of a draft payable at a bank or the maker of a note payable at a bank, presentment for payment is necessary, but failure to make presentment discharges such drawer, acceptor or maker only as stated in Section 3-502(1)(b).

(**2**) Unless excused (Section 3-511)

(**a**) notice of any dishonor is necessary to charge any indorser;

(**b**) in the case of any drawer, the acceptor of a draft payable at a bank or the maker of a note payable at a bank, notice of any dishonor is necessary, but failure to give such notice discharges such drawer, acceptor or maker only as stated in Section 3-502(1) (b).

(**3**) Unless excused (Section 3-511) protest of any dishonor is necessary to charge the drawer and indorsers of any draft which on its face appears to be drawn or payable outside of the states, territories, dependencies and possessions of the United States, the District of Columbia and the commonwealth of Puerto Rico. The holder may at his option make protest of any dishonor of any other instrument and in the case of a foreign draft may on insolvency of the acceptor before maturity make protest for better security.

(**4**) Notwithstanding any provision of this section, neither presentment nor notice of dishonor nor protest is necessary to charge an indorser who has indorsed an instrument after maturity. As amended 1966.

§3-502. Unexcused Delay; Discharge.

(**1**) Where without excuse any necessary presentment or notice of dishonor is delayed beyond the time when it is due

(**a**) any indorser is discharged; and

(**b**) any drawer or the acceptor of a draft payable at a bank or the maker of a note payable at a bank who because the drawee or payor bank becomes insolvent during the delay is deprived of funds maintained with the drawee or payor bank to cover the instrument may discharge his liability by written assignment to the holder of his rights against the drawee or payor bank in respect of such funds, but such drawer, acceptor or maker is not otherwise discharged.

(**2**) Where without excuse a necessary protest is delayed beyond the time when it is due any drawer or indorser is discharged.

§3-503. Time of Presentment.

(**1**) Unless a different time is expressed in the instrument the time for any presentment is determined as follows:

(**a**) where an instrument is payable at or a fixed period after a stated date any presentment for acceptance must be made on or before the date it is payable;

(**b**) where an instrument is payable after sight it must either be presented for acceptance or negotiated within a reasonable time after date or issue whichever is later;

(**c**) where an instrument shows the date on which it is payable presentment for payment is due on that date;

(**d**) where an instrument is accelerated presentment for payment is due within a reasonable time after the acceleration;

(**e**) with respect to the liability of any secondary party presentment for acceptance or payment of any other instrument is due within a reasonable time after such party becomes liable thereon.

(**2**) A reasonable time for presentment is determined by the nature of the instrument, any usage of banking or trade and the facts of the particular case. In the case of an uncertified check which is drawn and payable within the United States and which is not a draft drawn by a bank the following are presumed to be reasonable periods within which to present for payment or to initiate bank collection:

(**a**) with respect to the liability of the drawer, thirty days after date or issue whichever is later; and

(**b**) with respect to the liability of an indorser, seven days after his indorsement.

(**3**) Where any presentment is due on a day which is not a full business day for either the person making presentment or the party to pay or accept, presentment is due on the next following day which is a full business day for both parties.

(**4**) Presentment to be sufficient must be made at a reasonable hour, and if at a bank during its banking day.

§3-504. How Presentment Made.

(**1**) Presentment is a demand for acceptance or payment made upon the maker, acceptor, drawee or other payor by or on behalf of the holder.

(**2**) Presentment may be made

(**a**) by mail, in which event the time of presentment is determined by the time of receipt of the mail; or

(**b**) through a clearing house; or

(**c**) at the place of acceptance or payment specified in the instrument or if there be none at the place of business or residence of the party to accept or pay. If neither the party to accept or pay nor anyone authorized to act for him is present or accessible at such place presentment is excused.

(**3**) It may be made

(**a**) to any one of two or more makers, acceptors, drawees or other payor; or

(**b**) to any person who has authority to make or refuse the acceptance or payment.

(**4**) A draft accepted or a note made payable at a bank in the United States must be presented at such bank.

(**5**) In the cases described in Section 4-210 presentment may be made in the manner and with the result stated in that section. As amended 1962.

§3-505. Rights of Party to Whom Presentment Is Made.

(**1**) The party to whom presentment is made may without dishonor require

(**a**) exhibition of the instrument; and

(**b**) reasonable identification of the person making presentment and evidence of his authority to make it if made for another; and

(**c**) that the instrument be produced for acceptance or payment at a place specified in it, or if there be none at any place reasonable in the circumstances; and

(**d**) a signed receipt on the instrument for any partial or full payment and its surrender upon full payment.

(**2**) Failure to comply with any such requirement invalidates the presentment but the person presenting has a reasonable time in which to comply and the time for acceptance or payment runs from the time of compliance.

§3-506. Time Allowed For Acceptance or Payment.

(**1**) Acceptance may be deferred without dishonor until the close of the next business day following presentment. The holder may also in a good faith effort to obtain acceptance and without either dishonor of the instrument or discharge of secondary parties allow postponement of acceptance for an additional business day.

(**2**) Except as a longer time is allowed in the case of documentary drafts drawn under a letter of credit, and unless an earlier time is agreed to by the party to pay, payment of an instrument may be deferred without dishonor pending reasonable examination to determine whether it is properly payable, but payment must be made in any event before the close of business on the day of presentment.

§3-507. Dishonor: Holder's Right of Recourse; Term Allowing Re-Presentment.

(**1**) An instrument is dishonored when

(**a**) a necessary or optional presentment is duly made and due acceptance or payment is refused or cannot be obtained within the prescribed time or in case of bank collections the instrument is seasonably returned by the midnight deadline (Section 4-301); or

(**b**) presentment is excused and the instrument is not duly accepted or paid.

(**2**) Subject to any necessary notice of dishonor and protest, the holder has upon dishonor an immediate right of recourse against the drawers and indorsers.

(**3**) Return of an instrument for lack of proper indorsement is not dishonor.

(**4**) A term in a draft or an indorsement thereof allowing a stated time for re-presentment in the event of any dishonor of the draft by nonacceptance if a time draft or by nonpayment if a sight draft gives the holder as against any secondary party bound by the term an option to waive the dishonor without affecting the liability of the secondary party and he may present again up to the end of the stated time.

§3-508. Notice of Dishonor.

(**1**) Notice of dishonor may be given to any person who may be liable on the instrument by or on behalf of the holder or any party who has himself received notice, or any other party who can be compelled to pay the instrument. In addition an agent or bank in whose hands the instrument is dishonored may give notice to his principal or customer or to another agent or bank from which the instrument was received.

(**2**) Any necessary notice must be given by a bank before its midnight deadline and by any other person before midnight of the third business day after dishonor or receipt of notice of dishonor.

(**3**) Notice may be given in any reasonable manner. It may be oral or written and in any terms which identify the instrument and state that it has been dishonored. A misdescription which does not mislead the party notified does not vitiate the notice. Sending the instrument bearing a stamp, ticket or writing stating that acceptance or payment has been refused or sending a notice of debit with respect to the instrument is sufficient.

(**4**) Written notice is given when sent although it is not received.

(**5**) Notice to one partner is notice to each although the firm has been dissolved.

(**6**) When any party is in insolvency proceedings instituted after the issue of the instrument notice may be given either to the party or to the representative of his estate.

(**7**) When any party is dead or incompetent notice may be sent to his last known address or given to his personal representative.

(**8**) Notice operates for the benefit of all parties who have rights on the instrument against the party notified.

§3-509. Protest; Noting for Protest.

(**1**) A protest is a certificate of dishonor made under the hand and seal of a United States consul or vice consul or a notary public or other person authorized to certify dishonor by the law of the place where dishonor occurs. It may be made upon information satisfactory to such person.

(**2**) The protest must identify the instrument and certify either that due presentment has been made or the reason why it is excused and that the instrument has been dishonored by nonacceptance or nonpayment.

(**3**) The protest may also certify that notice of dishonor has been given to all parties or to specified parties.

(**4**) Subject to subsection (5) any necessary protest is due by the time that notice of dishonor is due.

(**5**) If, before protest is due, an instrument has be noted for protest by the officer to make protest, the protest may be made at any time thereafter as of the date of the noting.

§3-510. Evidence of Dishonor and Notice of Dishonor. The following are admissible as evidence and create a presumption of dishonor and of any notice of dishonor therein shown:

(**a**) a document regular in form as provided in the preceding section which purports to be a protest;

(**b**) the purported stamp or writing of the drawee, payor bank or presenting bank on the instrument or accompanying it stating that acceptance or payment has been refused for reasons consistent with dishonor;

(**c**) any book or record of the drawee, payor bank, or any collecting bank kept in the usual course of business which shows dishonor, even though there is no evidence of who made the entry.

§3-511. Waived or Excused Presentment, Protest or Notice of Dishonor or Delay Therein.

(**1**) Delay in presentment, protest or notice of dishonor is excused when the party is without notice that it is due or when the delay is caused by circumstances beyond his control and he exercises reasonable diligence after the cause of the delay ceases to operate.

(**2**) Presentment or notice or protest as the case may be is entirely excused when

(**a**) the party to be charged has waived it expressly or by implication either before or after it is due; or

(**b**) such party has himself dishonored the instrument or has countermanded payment or otherwise has no reason to expect or right to require that the instrument be accepted or paid; or

(**c**) by reasonable diligence the presentment or protest cannot be made or the notice given.

(**3**) Presentment is also entirely excused when

(**a**) the maker, acceptor or drawee of any instrument except a documentary draft is dead or in insolvency proceedings instituted after the issue of the instrument; or

(**b**) acceptance or payment is refused but not for want of proper presentment.

(**4**) Where a draft has been dishonored by nonacceptance a later presentment for payment and any notice of dishonor and protest for nonpayment are excused unless in the meantime the instrument has been accepted.

(**5**) A waiver of protest is also a waiver of presentment and of notice of dishonor even though protest is not required.

(**6**) Where a waiver of presentment or notice of protest is embodied in the instrument itself it is binding upon all parties; but where it is written above the signature of an indorser it binds him only.

Part 6: Discharge

§3-601. Discharge of Parties.

(**1**) The extent of the discharge of any party from liability on an instrument is governed by the sections on

(**a**) payment or satisfaction (Section 3-603); or

(**b**) tender of payment (Section 3-604); or

(**c**) cancellation or renunciation (Section 3-605); or

(**d**) impariment of right of recourse or of collateral (Section 3-606); or

(**e**) reacquisition of the instrument by a prior party (Section 3-208); or

(**f**) fraudulent and material alteration (Section 3-407); or

(**g**) certification of a check (Section 3-411); or

(**h**) acceptance varying a draft (Section 3-412); or

(**i**) unexcused delay in presentment or notice of dishonor or protest (Section 3-502).

(**2**) Any party is also discharged from his liability on an instrument to another party by any other act or agreement with such party which would discharge his simple contract for the payment of money.

(**3**) The liability of all parties is discharged when any party who has himself no right of action or recourse on the instrument

(**a**) reacquires the instruments in his own right; or

(**b**) is discharged under any provision of this Article, except as otherwise provided with respect to discharge for impairment of recourse or of collateral (Section 3-606).

§3-602. Effect of Discharge Against Holder in Due Course. No discharge of any party provided by this Article is effective against a subsequent holder in due course unless he has notice thereof when he takes the instrument.

§3-603. Payment or Satisfaction.

(**1**) The liability of any party is discharged to the extent of his payment or satisfaction to the holder even though it is made with knowledge of a claim of another person to the instrument unless prior to such payment or satisfaction the person making the claim either supplies indemnity deemed adequate by the party seeking the discharge or enjoins payment or satisfaction by order of a court of competent jurisdiction in an action in which the adverse claimant and the holder are parties. This subsection does not, however, result in the discharge of the liability

(**a**) of a party who in bad faith pays or satisfies a holder who acquired the instrument by theft or who (unless having the rights of a holder in due course) holds through one who so acquired it; or

(**b**) of a party (other than an intermediary bank or a payor bank which is not a depositary bank) who pays or satisfies the holder of an instrument which has been restrictively indorsed in a manner not consistent with the terms of such restrictive indorsement.

(**2**) Payment or satisfaction may be made with the consent of the holder by any person including a stranger to the instrument. Surrender of the instrument to such a person gives him the rights of a transferee (Section 3-201).

§3-604. Tender of Payment.

(**1**) Any party making tender of full payment to a holder when or after it is due is discharged to the extent of all subsequent liability for interest, costs and attorney's fees.

(**2**) The holder's refusal of such tender wholly discharges any party who has a right of recourse against the party making the tender.

(**3**) Where the maker or acceptor of an instrument payable otherwise than on demand is able and ready to pay at every place of payment specified in the instrument when it is due, it is equivalent to tender.

§3-605. Cancellation and Renunciation.

(**1**) The holder of an instrument may even without consideration discharge any party

(**a**) in any manner apparent on the face of the instrument or the indorsement, as by intentionally cancelling the instrument or the party's signature by destruction or mutilation, or by striking out the party's signature; or

(**b**) by renouncing his rights by a writing signed and delivered or by surrender of the instrument to the party to be discharged.

(**2**) Neither cancellation or renunciation without surrender of the instrument affects the title thereto.

§3-606. Impairment of Recourse or of Collateral.

(**1**) The holder discharges any party to the instrument to the extent that without such party's consent the holder

(**a**) without express reservation of rights releases or agrees not to sue any person against whom the party has to the knowledge of the holder a right of recourse or agrees to suspend the right to enforce against such person the instrument or collateral or otherwise discharges such person, except that failure or delay in effecting any required presentment, protest or notice of dishonor with respect to any such person does not discharge any party as to whom presentment, protest or notice of dishonor is effective or unnecessary; or

(**b**) unjustifiably impairs any collateral for the instrument given by or on behalf of the party or any person against whom he has a right of recourse.

(**2**) By express reservation of rights against a party with a right of recourse the holder preserves

(**a**) all his rights against such party as of the time when the instrument was originally due; and

(**b**) the right of the party to pay the instrument as of that time; and

(**c**) all rights of such party to recourse against others.

Part 7: Advice of International Sight Draft

§3-701. Letter of Advice of International Sight Draft.

(**1**) A "letter of advice" is a drawer's communication to the drawee that a described draft has been drawn.

(**2**) Unless otherwise agreed when a bank receives from another bank a letter of advice of an international sight draft the drawee bank may immediately debit the drawer's account and stop the running of interest pro tanto. Such a debit and any resulting credit to any account covering outstanding drafts leaves in the drawer full power to stop payment or otherwise dispose of the amount and creates no trust or interest in favor of the holder.

(**3**) Unless otherwise agreed and except where a draft is drawn under a credit issued by the drawee, the drawee of an international sight draft owes the drawer no duty to pay an unadvised draft but if it does so and the draft is genuine, may appropriately debit the drawer's account.

Part 8: Miscellaneous

§3-801. Drafts in a Set.

(**1**) Where a draft is drawn in a set of parts, each of which is numbered and expressed to be an order only if no other part has been honored, the whole of the parts constitutes one draft but a taker of any part may become a holder in due course of the draft.

(**2**) Any person who negotiates, indorses or accepts a single part of a draft drawn in a set thereby becomes liable to any holder in due course of that part as if it were the whole set, but as between different holders in due course to whom different parts have been negotiated the holder whose title first accrues has all rights to the draft and its proceeds.

(**3**) As against the drawee the first presented part

of a draft drawn in a set is the part entitled to payment, or if a time draft to acceptance and payment. Acceptance of any subsequently presented part renders the drawee liable thereon under subsection (2). With respect both to a holder and to the drawer payment of a subsequently presented part of a draft payable at sight has the same effect as payment of a check notwithstanding an effective stop order (Section 4-407).

(4) Except as otherwise provided in this section, where any part of a draft in a set is discharged by payment or otherwise the whole draft is discharged.

§3-802. Effect of Instrument on Obligation for which It Is Given.

(1) Unless otherwise agreed where an instrument is taken for an underlying obligation

(a) the obligation is pro tanto discharged if a bank is drawer, maker or acceptor of the instrument and there is no recourse on the instrument against the underlying obligor; and

(b) in any other case the obligation is suspended pro tanto until the instrument is due or if it is payable on demand until its presentment. If the instrument is dishonored action may be maintained on either the instrument or the obligation; discharge of the underlying obligor on the instrument also discharges him on the obligation.

(2) The taking in good faith of a check which is not postdated does not of itself so extend the time on the original obligation as to discharge a surety.

§3-803. Notice to Third Party. Where a defendant is sued for breach of an obligation for which a third person is answerable over under this Article he may give the third person written notice of the litigation, and the person notified may then give similar notice to any other person who is answerable over to him under this Article. If the notice states that the person notified may come in and defend and that if the person notified does not do so he will in any action against him by the person giving the notice be bound by any determination of fact common to the two litigations, then unless after seasonable receipt of the notice the person notified does come in and defend he is so bound.

§3-804. Lost, Destroyed or Stolen Instruments. The owner of an instrument which is lost, whether by destruction, theft or otherwise, may maintain an action in his own name and recover from any party liable thereon upon due proof of his ownership, the facts which prevent his production of the instrument and its terms. The court may require security indemnifying the defendant against loss by reason of further claims on the instrument.

§3-805. Instruments Not Payable to Order or to Bearer. This Article applies to any instrument whose terms do not preclude transfer and which is otherwise negotiable within this Article but which is not payable to order or to bearer, except that there can be no holder in due course of such an instrument.

GLOSSARY

abandonment In contract law, the condition that exists when a minor has left home and given up all rights to parental support.

abandonment of contract obligations The situation which exists when a party to a contract stops performance after he or she has begun to perform.

absolute defense A defense that is good against everyone, even a holder in due course of a negotiable instrument. Also called *real defense* or *universal defense*.

absolute liability See *strict liability*.

acceleration A provision in a mortgage agreement that allows the mortgagee to demand the entire balance due when the mortgagor misses a single installment payment.

acceptance A promise or act on the part of an offeree indicating a willingness to be bound by the terms and conditions contained in an offer. In commercial paper, the acknowledgment of a drawee that binds the drawee to the terms of a draft.

acceptor A drawee of a draft who has promised to honor the draft as presented by signing it on its face.

accommodation party A person who signs an instrument as a maker, acceptor, or indorser without receiving value therefor and lends his or her name to another person as a means of guaranteeing payment on the due date.

accord The implied or expressed acceptance of less than what the creditor billed the debtor.

accord and satisfaction An agreement (accord) whereby one party makes payment of money, or some other consideration, of usually less than the amount owed, in return for the elimination of the debt or some other claim.

accounting A statement detailing the financial transactions of a business and the status of its assets.

acknowledgment The official recognition by a notary public that another's signature was made by that party's free will. The acknowledgment is accomplished when the notary has signed the document and added the official seal to it.

act of God In contract law, any natural disaster that is not reasonably foreseeable.

active fraud A false statement made or an action actually taken by one party with the intent to deceive a second party and thus lead that second party into a deceptively based agreement. The innocent party must actually rely on the falsehood and must be damaged as a result of entering into the agreement.

actual damages A sum of money equal to the real financial loss suffered by an injured party; also known as *compensatory damages*.

actual malice The legal test used by the courts to determine defamation against a public official or a public figure. The actual malice test requires the public official or the public figure to prove not only that the statement was false, but also that it was made with the knowledge that it was false or with a reckless disregard for its truth or falsity.

administrative law That body of law, including decrees and legal decisions, generated by administrative agencies.

administrator (male); administratrix (female) A person appointed by the court to settle the estate of someone who died intestate, that is, without a will.

adverse opinion An auditor's opinion which states that deviations from generally accepted accounting principles are so severe that an unqualified opinion is impossible and a qualified opinion is not justified.

adverse possession Title to real property obtained by taking actual possession of the property openly, notoriously, exclusively, under a claim of right, and continuously for a period of time set by state statute.

affirmance See *ratification*.

affirmative action plan Goals and timetables set forth by an employer to remedy any situation where minorities and/or women are not adequately represented in the workplace.

agency A legal agreement between two persons, whereby one is designated the agent of the other.

agency coupled with an interest An irrevocable agency agreement that authorizes an agent to sell specific property, deduct a commission, and apply the proceeds to the credit of a debt that the principal owes the agent. See *irrevocable agency*.

agent A person authorized to act on behalf of another and subject to the other's control in dealing with third parties.

agreements in restraint of trade Agreements which have the effect of removing competition or denying to the public services they would otherwise have or which result in higher prices and resulting hardship.

allonge A strip of paper attached to a negotiable instrument for the writing of additional indorsements.

American Law Institute Test Under this test, criminal defendants will be judged not guilty by reason of insanity if the mental disease from which they suffered at the time of the action prevented them from understanding just how wrong their actions were or stopped them from conforming their conduct to the law.

amoral Acting with indifference toward the values that govern a society's attitude toward right and wrong.

annual percentage rate The effective or actual true cost of credit to the consumer.

annuity A guaranteed retirement income.

answer A defendant's official response to the allegations in the complaint.

antenuptial agreement See *prenuptial agreement*.

anticipatory breach A breach which occurs when a party to a contract either expresses or clearly implies an intention not to perform the contract before actually being required to act. Also known as *constructive breach*.

apparent authority A doctrine involving accountability, whereby a principal, by virtue of words or actions, leads a third party to believe that an agent has authority, but no such authority was intended.

appeal The referral of a case to a higher court for review.

appellate jurisdiction The power of a court to review a case for errors.

application In obtaining an insurance policy, an offer made by the applicant to the insurance company.

arbitration The process by which an outside party settles a dispute between two other parties.

arbitrator An outside party who settles a dispute between two contending parties.

arson The willful or malicious act of causing the burning of another's property.

articles of incorporation A written application to a state for permission to incorporate.

articles of partnership A written agreement that sets up a partnership.

assault An act that places the victim in apprehension of immediate bodily harm.

asset acquisition The purchase of all the property of a corporation.

assign To transfer property by sale, mortgage, pledge, or otherwise.

assignee A person to whom an assignment is made.

assignment The transfer of a contract right from one person to another.

assignor A person who assigns rights under an assignment.

assume the mortgage An agreement whereby

the buyer of real property agrees to pay the mortgage.

at will Discharge of employees for any reason or even for no reason, subject only to statutory and regulatory limitations.

attach The creation of a secured party's legally enforceable right to take the debtor's property and sell it to satisfy the debt.

attachment The act of taking a person's property and bringing it into the custody of law.

auction with reserve An auction at which the auctioneer has the right to withdraw goods and not sell them if acceptable bids are not made.

audit An examination of the financial records of an organization to determine whether those records are a fair presentation of the actual financial health of the organization.

auditor The accountant who examines the financial records of an organization to determine whether those records are a fair presentation of the actual financial health of the institution.

automatic suspension A court order that stops a debtor's creditors from making any further moves to collect the money that the debtor owes them; also known as an *automatic stay.*

bailee The person to whom personal property is delivered under a contract of bailment.

bailor The owner of personal property that has been temporarily transferred to a bailee under a contract of bailment.

bailment Possession of the personal property of another without ownership and for a special purpose, under the express or implied contract that it will be redelivered to the bailor.

bailment by necessity Arises when a customer must give up possession of property for the benefit of both parties; for example, when one purchases a suit or dress and is required to give up possession of one's own property while being fitted.

bailment for the sole benefit of the bailee A transaction in which the possession of personal property is transferred for purposes that will benefit only the bailee.

bailment for the sole benefit of the bailor Occurs when possession of personal property is transferred for purposes that will benefit only the bailor.

bait-and-switch scheme An illegal promotional practice in which a seller attracts consumers by promoting a product (bait) that he or she does not intend to sell and then directs the consumers' attention to a higher-priced product (switch).

balloon-payment mortgage A mortgage that has relatively low fixed payments during the life of the mortgage followed by one large final (balloon) payment.

bank draft An order drawn by one bank directing itself or another bank in which it has funds on deposit to pay a specified sum of money to a named person.

bankruptcy The legal process by which the assets of a debtor are sold (liquidated) to pay off creditors so that the debtor can make a fresh start financially.

bankruptcy trustee A person appointed by the court or elected by creditors who takes legal title to the property and/or money of the debtor and holds it in trust for equitable distribution among creditors.

bargain and sale deed A deed that transfers title to real property but contains no warranties. This type of deed is not valid without consideration.

bargained-for exchange In reference to agreements, when a promise is made in exchange for another promise, in exchange for an act, or in exchange for a forbearance to act.

bargaining unit Employees appropriately joined together for the purpose of collective bargaining.

battery The harmful or offensive, unprivileged touching of another.

bearer A person who is in possession of a negotiable instrument which is payable to "bearer" or "cash" or which has been indorsed in blank.

bearer paper An instrument payable to bearer or cash that may be negotiated by delivery only. Also called *bearer instrument.*

beneficiary A person for whom a trust is created and who owns equitable or beneficial title to the trust property; also, the person named in an insurance policy to receive benefits paid by the insurer in event of a claim.

bequest In a will, a gift of money or personal property. Also called *legacy.*

best evidence rule The legal rule that holds that the courts will accept only the original of a writing into evidence, not a copy.

bilateral contract A contract in which both parties make promises.

bilateral mistake In contract law, a mistake made by both parties to a contract. Bilateral mistake allows a rescission by either party.

bill of exchange See *draft.*

bill of lading A document evidencing the receipt of goods for shipment and issued by a person engaged in the business of transporting or forwarding goods.

bill of sale A written statement evidencing the transfer of personal property from one person to another.

binder An oral or a written memorandum of an agreement for insurance intended to provide temporary insurance coverage until the policy is formally accepted.

binding precedent A previous case that a particular court must follow.

blank indorsement An indorsement made by a signature alone written on a negotiable instrument.

blue laws State statutes and local ordinances which regulate the making and performing of contracts on Sunday.

bodily injury insurance A type of automobile insurance that covers the risk of bodily injury or death to pedestrians and to the occupants of other cars arising from the negligent operation of the insured's motor vehicle.

bona fide occupational qualification (BFOQ) A good faith requirement for employment that does not deceptively prevent certain groups of persons from qualifying for employment.

bond A certificate of indebtedness that obligates a government or corporation to pay the bondholder a fixed rate of interest on the principal at regular intervals and to pay the principal on a stated maturity date; a written instrument with sureties, guaranteeing faithful performance or acts contemplated.

box-top license A license placed on a computer software box that limits the buyer's right to copy the program, to reveal the contents of the program, and to allow others to use the program.

boycott An agreed-upon refusal to have dealings with an employer or handle a product as a way to express disapproval or to force acceptance of certain employee demands.

breach A breaking or violation of a contract.

breach of contract The failure of one of the parties to a contract to do what was previously agreed upon.

bribery The act of offering, giving, receiving, or soliciting something of value to influence official action or the discharge of legal or public duty.

bulk transfer Any transfer in bulk and not in the ordinary course of the transferor's business of a major part of the materials, supplies, merchandise, or other inventory of an enterprise.

burglary The break-in of a dwelling or building for the purpose of carrying out a felony or theft.

business compulsion See *economic duress.*

business judgment rule The rule that a corporate manager's decisions will not be interfered with by a court as long as the decision was made with due care, in good faith, on the basis of legal precepts, and in the best interests of the corporation.

business necessity A business practice that is essential to the safe and efficient operation of the business or that without which an extreme adverse financial loss results.

buyer's guide A window sticker that is required by the Federal Trade Commission Act to be placed in the window of each used car offered for sale by a used-car dealer. The sticker discloses the warranties that are made with the sale of the car.

bylaws Rules that guide a corporation's day-to-day internal affairs (also known as *regulations*).

capacity In contract law, the legal ability to enter a contractual relationship.

capital The money and property that a business needs to operate.

capital contribution The sum invested to receive an interest in a business, either as a purchase of stock in a corporation or the amount contributed by each member of a partnership.

carrier A business that undertakes to transport persons or goods, or both.

cash dividends Dividends paid to shareholders in the form of cash.

cashier's check A check drawn by a bank upon its own funds.

certificate of authority A document that grants a foreign corporation permission to do business within another state.

certificate of deposit (CD) An acknowledgment by a bank of the receipt of money and a promise to pay the money back on the due date, usually with interest.

certificate of incorporation A corporation's official authorization to do business in the state (also known as *charter* or *corporate charter*).

certificate of limited liability A formal document filed with the appropriate state or county office that is placed on file to warn third parties of the limited liability of some partners.

certification The legal assent by the NLRB that a union has fulfilled the legal requirements to qualify as bargaining agent for the employees at a particular employment site.

certified check A check that has been marked, or certified, by the bank on which it was drawn, guaranteeing payment to the holder.

certified public accountants Accountants who have met certain age, character, education, experience, and testing requirements.

charitable trust Established for charitable purposes, such as the advancement of education; relief to the aged, ill, or poor; and the promotion of religion. Also called *public trust.*

charter See *certificate of incorporation.*

check A draft drawn on a bank and payable on demand.

chose in action Evidence of the right to property but not the property itself.

c.i.f. (cost, insurance, and freight) Terms instructing a carrier to collect the cost of goods shipped, insurance, and freight charges.

citation The identification of a court case, consisting of the names of the parties, the volume number, the name of the reporter, and the beginning page number of the case.

citator A book that will show where a case has been referred to by state and federal court decisions.

close corporation A corporation whose shares of stock and managerial control are closely held by fewer than 50 shareholders (often members of the same family) or by one person. Also known as a *closely held corporation.*

closed-end credit Credit that is extended only for a specific amount of money, such as to buy a car or other expensive item.

closed shop A place of employment in which the employer by agreement hires only union members in good standing.

c.o.d. Cash on delivery.

code A compilation of all the statutes of a particular state or of the federal government.

code of professional ethics A set of rules established by the American Institute of Certified Public Accountants which governs the ethical conduct of accountants.

codicil (kód-i-sil) An addition to or change in an existing will.

cognovits (kog-nō-vits) (Also called *confession of judgment.*) Clauses in credit contracts requiring consumers to agree in advance, if they are sued for nonpayment of a debt, to give up their right to be notified of a court hearing. Such clauses are now outlawed by the Credit Practices Rule.

collateral The property that is subject to a security interest.

collecting bank Any bank handling an item for collection except the payor bank.

collective bargaining The good faith meeting between representatives of employees and the employer for purposes of discussing the terms and conditions of employment.

collision insurance A type of automobile protection that protects the insured against any loss arising from damage to the insured's automobile caused by accidental collision with another object or with any part of the roadbed.

comaker A person who signs a promissory note on its face along with another person and becomes primarily liable for its payment if the other defaults.

commerce Trade, traffic, transportation, or communication among the several states or between any foreign country and any state or territory.

commerce clause The clause in the U.S. Constitution that gives the federal government the power to regulate business.

commercial unit A single whole for the purpose of sale, the division of which impairs its character or value on the market, such as a set of furniture.

commingle To put together property and money in one mass.

common carrier A company that transports goods or persons for compensation and offers its facilities to the general public without discrimination. Compare *contract carrier.*

common law The body of recorded court decisions that courts refer to and rely upon when making later legal decisions.

common stock The most usual type of corporate stock, representing the stockholder's share of the corporation's net worth. It carries with it all the risks of the business and does not guarantee its holder the right to profits.

comparative negligence A form of contributory negligence that requires the court to assign damages according to the degree of fault of each party.

compensatory damages See *actual damages.*

compensated bailee A bailee who is paid for his or her services.

complaint A legal document filed by a plaintiff to begin a lawsuit. The complaint sets forth the names of the parties, the facts in the case, and the relief sought by the plaintiff.

complete performance In contract law, the situation that exists when both parties to a contract have fully accomplished every term, condition, and promise to which they agreed.

comprehensive coverage A type of automobile insurance that provides protection against loss when the insured's car is damaged or destroyed by fire, lightning, flood, hail, windstorm, riot, vandalism, or theft.

compromise The settlement of differences or the adjustment of matters in dispute by mutual concessions.

computer fraud Obtaining money, property, or services through the fraudulent use of a computer.

computer hardware In computer science, the actual device known as a computer and its components, including the keyboard, screen, disk drive, and the printer.

computer package In computer science, the combination of the computer hardware and the computer software.

computer program In computer science, the instructions on the software that tell the computer hardware what to do and when to do it.

computer software In computer science, the card, tape, disk, or silicon chip that contains the computer program.

computer trespass Gaining access to a computer with the intent to commit a crime.

concealment In insurance, the intentional withholding of a fact that would be of material importance to the insurer's decision to issue a policy. (See also *passive fraud.*)

condition concurrent A condition in a contract that requires both parties to perform at the same time.

condition precedent A condition in a contract that requires performance of certain acts before the other party is obligated to pay money or give other consideration agreed to.

condition subsequent A condition in a contract by which the parties agree that the contract will be terminated if a prescribed event occurs or does not occur.

conditional indorsement An indorsement which makes the rights of the indorsee subject to the happening of a certain event or condition.

confessions of judgment (Also called *cognovits.*) Clauses in credit contracts requiring consumers to agree in advance, if they are sued for nonpayment of a debt, to give up their right to be notified by a court hearing. Such clauses are now outlawed by the Credit Practices Rule.

confidential relationship A relationship of trust and dependence between persons in a continued relationship, as between doctor and patient or between parent and child.

confirmation In bankruptcy law, the official approval of a reorganization plan.

conforming goods Goods that are in accordance with the obligations under the contract.

conglomerate expansion The joining of two companies that were not in competition with each other, either because they dealt in different products or services or in different geographical areas.

consent order Under the Federal Trade Commission Act, an order under which a company agrees to stop a disputed practice without necessarily admitting that the practice violated the law.

consequential damages Losses that do not flow directly and immediately from an act but only from some of the consequences or results of the act.

consideration In contract law, the mutual promise to exchange benefits and sacrifices between the parties.

consignee The party to whom goods are shipped under a bill of lading.

consignor The party shipping goods under a bill of lading.

consolidation The joining of two corporations.

conspiracy The crime that occurs when people get together with others to talk about, plan, or agree to the commission of a crime.

constitution The basic law of a nation or state.

constitutional law That body of law which involves a constitution and its interpretation.

constitutional supremacy The legal principle that requires all laws to be consistent with the provisions within the constitution.

constructive breach See *anticipatory breach.*

constructive discharge Discriminatory action whereby an employee is demoted to a position of lesser pay or authority or poorer conditions or is subject to supervisory harassment.

constructive eviction An eviction that occurs by the act of the landlord depriving the tenant of something of a substantial nature which was called for under the lease.

consumer Someone who buys or leases real estate, goods, or services for personal, family, or household purposes.

consumer products Tangible personal property normally used for personal, family, or household purposes.

contract An agreement between two or more competent parties, based on mutual promises to do or to refrain from doing some particular thing that is neither illegal nor impossible. The agreement results in an obligation or a duty that can be enforced in a court of law.

contract carrier A carrier that provides transportation for compensation only to those people with whom it desires to do business.

contract of record A special type of formal contract usually confirmed by a court with an accompanying judgment issued in favor of one of the parties.

contract to sell An agreement to pass title to goods from the seller to the buyer for a price at a future time.

contributory negligence The failure of an injured party to be careful enough to ensure personal safety.

conventional mortgage A mortgage that involves no government backing by either insurance or guarantee.

conveyance in trust A trust in which the settlor conveys away the legal title to a trustee to hold for the benefit of either the settlor or another as beneficiary.

copyright Exclusive right of ownership of literary, musical, or artistic creations, granted by the government for a limited period of time.

corporate charter See *certificate of incorporation.*

corporate democracy A theory of corporate management that favors making management more responsive to shareholders by giving shareholders greater voting power and by making it easier for shareholders to sue managers.

corporate opportunity rule The rule that states that corporate managers cannot take a business opportunity for themselves if they know that the corporation would also be interested in the opportunity.

corporation A legal entity (or artificial person) created under the authority of either a state or a federal statute that authorizes individuals to operate an enterprise.

corporation by estoppel The doctrine by which parties who have benefited by dealing with a business as though it were a corporation cannot deny its existence as a corporation.

corpus Property that is held in trust. Also called a *trust fund.*

cost of repair rule The principle that states that an architect or contractor may have to reimburse a client for any extra money spent by the client to correct an error made by the architect or contractor.

cost-plus contract A contract in which the price is determined by the cost of labor and materials plus an agreed-to percentage markup.

cotenants Two or more persons who own real property together.

counterclaim A claim filed by a defendant against a plaintiff in the same lawsuit.

counteroffer A response to an offer in which the terms and conditions of the original offer are changed. A counteroffer acts, in most cases, as a rejection of the original offer.

courts Judicial tribunals that meet in a regular place and apply laws in an attempt to settle disputes fairly.

cover Buying similar goods from someone else when a seller breaches a contract.

credit practices rule A federal rule prohibiting creditors from including certain provisions in their consumer credit contracts.

creditor beneficiary A third party to whom one or both contracting parties owe a continuing debt of obligation arising out of a contract.

crime An offense against the public at large punishable by the official governing body of a nation or state.

cross-claim A claim filed by a defendant in a lawsuit against another defendant in the same lawsuit.

cross-examination The questioning of witnesses by an opposing attorney.

cultural relativism The recognition of social differences from one social system to another.

cumulative preferred stock A class of stock that pays dividends in later years, if dividends are not paid in the present year.

cumulative voting A system of voting corporate shares, designed to benefit minority shareholders, that allows shareholders to multiply their voting shares by the number of directors to be elected.

cure The correction of a defect in goods that caused the goods to be rejected by a buyer.

current market price contract An agreement in which the prices are determined by reference to the market price of the goods as of a specified date.

curtesy Under common law, the estate to which a husband is entitled on the death of his wife, provided they have had children born alive who might have been capable of inheriting the estate. Compare *dower.*

damages Money recovered by a party in a court action to compensate that party for injury or loss.

debtor-in-possession A debtor who continues to operate his or her business after filing for bankruptcy.

declaration of trust A trust in which the settlor holds the legal title to the property as trustee for the benefit of some other person (the beneficiary) to whom the settlor now conveys the equitable title.

deed A written instrument signed, sealed, and delivered in a special form, that is used to pass legal title of real property from one person to another; a conveyance.

deed of trust A formal written instrument that transfers legal ownership of real property to a third party while the mortgagor remains on the property. The third party holds the property for the benefit of a creditor or creditors and has the power to sell the property without going to court.

***de facto* corporation** A corporation defectively incorporated in good faith that exists in fact although not in law through its actual exercise of corporate power.

defamation Any false statement communicated to others that harms a person's good name or reputation.

defective agreement An agreement existing when mutual assent has been destroyed.

defective condition A condition that makes a product unreasonably dangerous to the consumer, the user, or property. See *product liability*.

defendant The person against whom relief is sought in a lawsuit.

***de jure* corporation** A corporation whose existence is the result of having fully or substantially complied with the relevant incorporation statutes.

***del credere* agent** (del kré-de-re agent) A factor who guarantees the credit of a third party, the solvency of the purchaser, and performance of the contract.

delegation The transfer of a contractual duty by a contracting party to a third party.

delivery The transfer of possession from one person to another.

demand note A promissory note which is payable whenever the payee demands payment.

demurrage charge A fee charged by a carrier for the storage of goods still remaining in its possession beyond the time allowed for unloading by the consignee.

depositary bank The bank to which a commercial paper is transferred for collection; the depositary bank may also be the payor bank.

deposition An oral question-and-answer session conducted under oath during which an attorney questions parties or witnesses from the opposition in a lawsuit.

derivative suit A lawsuit brought by shareholders on behalf of the corporation.

destination contract A contract under which the seller is required to deliver goods to a place of destination. Title passes to the buyer when the seller delivers the goods.

detriment In contract law, giving up something (or promising to give up something) that one has a legal right to keep, doing something (or promising to do something) that one has a legal right not to do, or refraining from doing something (or promising not to do something) that one has a legal right to do.

device In patent law, an article of manufacture or some other tangible object.

devise (de-víz) A gift of real property in a will.

devisee (de-viz-eé) One who receives a gift of real property under a will.

direct examination The questioning of witnesses by the lawyer who has called them.

direct suit A lawsuit brought by shareholders who have been deprived of a right that belongs to them as shareholders.

disabled The worker's physical or mental condition that prevents the performance of any substantial, gainful work and is expected to last or has lasted at least 12 months, or is expected to result in death.

disaffirm In contract law, the act of repudiating or giving up contractual rights and obligations.

discharge An act by which a person is freed from performing a legal obligation.

disclaimer A statement declaring that an auditor has decided not to give any opinion on the firm's financial records.

disclosed principal The person known by a third party to be the principal of an agent.

discounting System by which a bank will buy an instrument at a price below its face amount with the aim of ultimately collecting the face amount.

discovery The process by which the parties to a civil suit search for information relevant to the case.

dishonor To refuse to accept or pay a negotiable instrument when it is presented.

dispossessory warrant proceedings A legal proceeding that provides landlords with a quick method of evicting a tenant.

disputed amounts Consideration on which parties to a contract never reach mutual agreement.

dissolution of a partnership A change in the relation of partners caused by any partner ceasing to be associated in the carrying on of business.

distribution of risk The principle which holds that small contributions made by a large number of individuals can provide sufficient money to cover the losses suffered by the few as they occur each year.

diversity cases Federal lawsuits that are between persons from different states, between citizens of the United States and a foreign government, or between citizens of the United States and citizens of a foreign nation. Diversity cases must involve an amount over $10,000.

dividends Net profits or surplus set aside for distribution to shareholders.

document of title A paper that serves as evidence that the person holding the paper has title to the goods mentioned in the document.

documentation Evidence supplied by writings.

domestic bill of exchange A draft that is drawn and payable in the United States.

domestic corporation A corporation created by or organized under the laws of the state where it is operating.

dominant tenement The property to which the right or privilege of easement attaches.

donee One to whom a gift is given.

donee beneficiary A third party who does not provide any consideration for the benefits received and who owes the contracting parties no legal duty.

donor One who gives a gift.

door-to-door rule A Federal Trade Commission rule under which sales of consumer goods or services over $25 made away from the seller's regular place of business, may be canceled within three business days after the sale occurs.

double indemnity An optional provision in life insurance policies that provides that the insurer will pay double the amount due to a beneficiary if the insured dies from accidental causes.

dower By common law, the vested rights of the wife to a one-third lifetime interest in the real property owned by her spouse; a life estate to which a wife is entitled upon the death of her husband. Compare *curtesy*.

draft A written order drawn upon one person by another, ordering payment of money to a designated third party. Also called a *bill of exchange*.

drawee The party named in a draft who is ordered to pay money to the payee.

drawer The party who draws a draft, that is, the party who orders that the money be paid.

dunning letter A letter requesting payment sent by a creditor to a debtor.

duress An action by one party that forces another party to do what need not be done otherwise.

duty An obligation placed on individuals by law.

easement The right to use the land of another for a particular purpose.

easement by prescription An easement that is obtained by passing over another's property openly and continuously for a period of time set by state statute (20 years in many states).

economic duress Threats of a business nature that force another party without real consent to enter a commercial agreement.

ejectment The common law name given to the lawsuit brought by a landlord to have a tenant evicted from the premises.

electronic fund transfer (EFT) A method of banking that uses computers and electronic technology as a substitute for checks and other banking methods.

emancipation In contract law, the condition that exists when a minor has been freed from the laws regulating the rights and obligations of minors on contracts.

embezzlement The act of wrongfully taking property entrusted to one's care or appropriating to one's own use or benefit.

eminent domain The right of federal, state, and local governments, or other public bodies, to take private lands, with compensation to their owners, for public use.

emotional duress Acts or threats that create

emotional distress which lead a person into a contract against his or her will.

employee One who works for an employer for wages or salary. Synonymous with the term *servant.*

employer One who employs others in exchange for wages or salary. Synonymous with the term *master.*

employment contract The agreement of both employee and employer that binds them legally and enforceably to employment terms, conditions, and objectives.

employment discrimination Any employment practice that results in the unemployment, nonemployment, or underemployment of minorities and women, either through conscious action or from the unintentional action of an employer.

entrapment A defense to criminal liability that claims that a previously law-abiding citizen was led into an illegal situation by a government agent.

environmental impact statement Statements that describe in detail the expected adverse environmental consequences of a proposed action and the alternatives to the action.

equal-dignities rule The legal rule which provides that when a party appoints an agent to negotiate an agreement which itself must be in writing, the appointment and authorization of the agent must also be in writing.

equitable remedy A court-imposed remedy that compels the wrongdoer to perform an act or to refrain from performing an act.

equity financing The issuing and selling of shares of stock to raise capital.

escheat (es-chét) The right of the state to title to property when no legal owner may be found.

escrow account A special account into which money is deposited and held for a specified period of time or until a specified date.

espionage The gathering or transmitting of information pertaining to the national defense of the United States for the political or military use of any foreign nation.

estate The interest or right that a person has in land or any other property.

estate in fee simple An estate in which the present owner owns the land for life (i.e., freehold), with the right to use it or dispose of it freely, so long as the use of it does not interfere with the rights of others.

estoppel A legal bar to alleging or denying a fact because of one's own previous action or words to the contrary or because of one's silence, which induced another person to believe something that was not true.

ethical relativism An ethical theory that holds that there are no constant standards of right and wrong. Also known as *subjective ethics.*

ethics Rules of conduct that transcend legal rules, telling people how to act when the law does not.

eviction An act of the landlord that deprives the tenant of the enjoyment of the premises.

exculpatory agreement A clause or condition that excuses a party from any liability, fault, or guilt emanating from the party's negligence or failure to perform in a skillful manner.

executed contract A contract whose terms have been completely and satisfactorily carried out by both parties.

executor (male); executrix (female) The party named in a will to carry out the terms of the will.

executory contract A contract that has not yet been fully performed by the parties.

exemplary damages See *punitive damages.*

express authority The authority that the principal voluntarily and specifically sets forth as instructions in the agency agreement, orally or in writing.

express contract A contract that requires some sort of written or spoken expression indicating the desire to enter the contractual relationship.

express warranty An oral or written statement, promise, or other representation about the quality of a product.

extortion The act of taking another's property with consent when such consent is coerced by threat to injure the victim's person, property, or reputation.

factor A special agent employed to buy or sell consigned goods on another's behalf.

failure of consideration A personal defense that may be used by a maker or drawer of a negotiable instrument when the party with whom the maker dealt breaches the contract by not furnishing the agreed consideration. A holder in due course is not subject to this defense.

fair-use doctrine Copyrighted material may be reproduced without permission if the use of the material is reasonable and not harmful to the rights of the copyright owner.

fairness rule The rule that requires managers to be fair to the corporation when they personally benefit from the business decisions.

false imprisonment An intentional tort involving the unjustified confinement or detention of a person.

family farmer Under Chapter 12 of the Bankruptcy Code, a farmer who receives more than half the total income from the farm. In addition, to qualify as a family farmer, 80 percent of the farmer's debt must result from the farm expenses.

f.a.s. vessel Free alongside vessel.

featherbedding Union rules allegedly made to make jobs or to require more employees to be assigned to a given job than are needed.

federal interest computer A computer used only by the federal government or by a financial institution.

felony A crime punishable by death or by imprisonment in a federal or state prison for a term exceeding one year.

fiduciary A person who acts for another in a position of trust or confidence.

fiduciary relationship A relationship based on trust such as exists between an attorney and a client, a guardian and a ward, a trustee and a beneficiary, or a director and a corporation.

field warehousing The practice of using goods that are stored in a warehouse as security for a loan.

finance charge The sum of all charges that the consumer must pay in order to obtain credit.

firm offer A merchant's written promise to hold an offer open for the sale of goods. No consideration is necessary for the promise to be binding.

fixture An article of personal property physically attached to real property and considered part of the real property.

f.o.b. Free on board.

f.o.b. the place of destination Terms indicating that goods will be delivered free to the place of destination.

f.o.b. the place of shipment Terms indicating that goods will be delivered free to the place from which the goods are to be shipped.

forbearance The act of refraining from doing something (or promising not to do something) that a person has a legal right to do.

forcible entry and detainer A legal proceeding that provides landlords with a quick method of evicting a tenant.

foreclosure The right of a mortgagee to apply to a court to have property sold when the mortgagor defaults or fails to perform some agreement attached to the mortgage.

foreign corporation A corporation created by or organized under the laws of a state other than the one in which it is operating.

forgery The fraudulent making or alteration of a writing.

formal contract Under common law, a contract that had to be (1) written, (2) signed, witnessed, and placed under the seal of the parties, and (3) delivered.

fraud A wrongful statement, action, or concealment pertinent to the subject matter of a contract knowingly made to damage the other party. The innocent party must actually rely on the wrongful statement, action, or concealment, and must be damaged as a result. If proved, fraud destroys any contract and makes the wrongdoer liable to the injured party for all losses that result.

freehold estate An estate in which the holder owns the land for life or forever.

friendly suitor A suitor invited in to outbid a hostile bidder. Also called a *white knight.*

fructus industriales (frúk-tus in-dus-tri-á-lez) Fruit of industry. Crops or garden plantings that produce flowers, vegetables, or other harvest only for the year in which they are planted. They are treated as personal property.

fructus naturales (frúk-tus na-tu-rá-lez) Fruit of nature. Trees, flowers, shrubs, vineyards, and field crops that grow each year without replanting. They are considered part of the real property.

frustration-of-purpose doctrine In contract law, the doctrine that releases a party from a contractual obligation when performing the obligations would be thoroughly impractical and senseless.

full covenant and warranty deed A deed containing express warranties under which the grantor guarantees the property to be free of all encumbrances. Also called *general warranty* deed.

full warranty Under the Magnuson-Moss Warranty Act, a defective product will be fixed or replaced free within a reasonable time after a complaint has been made about the product.

fungible goods Goods of which any unit is, by nature or usage of trade, the equivalent of any like unit; wheat, flour, sugar, and liquids of various kinds are examples.

future goods Goods that are not yet in existence or under the control of people; they include fish in the sea, minerals in the ground, and goods not yet manufactured.

garnishment An execution against the income of the loser in a civil case. Property, wages, salaries, or dividends may be taken to satisfy.

garnishment proceedings The proceedings in an execution against income, or garnishment.

general agent A person given broad authority to act on behalf of the principal, conducting the bulk of the principal's business activities on a daily basis.

general consent Consent which arises automatically when a patient enters a hospital for routine tests and procedures needed for diagnosis and treatment.

general jurisdiction The power of a court to hear any type of case.

general partner A partner who takes an active part in running a business and has unlimited liability for the firm's debts.

general release A document expressing the intent of a creditor to release a debtor from obligations to an existing and valid debt.

general warranty deed See *full covenant and warranty deed.*

generally accepted accounting principles (GAAP) Rules established by the Financial Accounting Standards Board (FASB) which outline the procedure that accountants use in accumulating financial data and in preparing financial statements.

generally accepted auditing standards (GAAS) Standards set up by the Auditing Standards Board of the American Institute of Certified Public Accountants (AICPA) that measure the quality of the performance of the auditing procedures.

gift *in causa mortis* (in ká-za mór-tis) A gift given during one's lifetime in contemplation of death from a known cause.

good cause The substantial or legally sufficient reason for doing something.

good faith Honesty in fact and observance of reasonable commercial standards of fair dealings in the trade.

goods All things (including specially manufactured goods) which are movable at the time of identification to the contract for sale, other than money in which the price is to be paid, investment securities, and intangible items. Goods include growing crops and unborn young of animals.

goodwill The expected continuance of public patronage of a business because of the name under which it is managed.

graduated-payment mortgage A mortgage that has a fixed interest rate during the life of the mortgage; however, the monthly payments made by the mortgagor increase over the term of the loan.

grantee A person to whom title to real property is transferred in a deed.

grantor A person who transfers title to real property in a deed.

gratuitous bailment A bailment for the sole benefit of either the bailor or the bailee, in which the other party receives no consideration for benefits bestowed.

great pond A pond that is ten acres or more in size.

gross negligence Very great negligence.

guaranteed insurability An optional provision in an insurance contract that allows the insured to pay an extra premium initially in exchange for a guaranteed option to buy more insurance at certain specified times later on with no questions asked and no new medical examination required.

guaranty of payment A promise to pay another's bills or to settle for any of another's wrongful acts if that party does not settle them personally.

guilty but mentally ill (GMI) A defense to criminal liability under which defendants are sentenced to prison for a set number of years, during which they generally receive treatment at a state hospital. When they are cured, they are returned to prison to complete their sentences.

handicapped Any individual with a physical or mental impairment that limits one or more of the person's major life functions.

heir One who inherits property either under a will or through someone's dying without a will.

holder A person who is in possession of a negotiable instrument that is issued or indorsed to that person's order or to bearer.

holder in due course A holder who has taken a negotiable instrument in good faith and for value without any knowledge that there is anything irregular about the instrument. Such a holder is treated as favored and is given immunity from certain defenses.

holographic will An informal will written entirely in the handwriting of the testator.

homeowner's policy A type of insurance that gives protection for all types of losses and liabilities related to home ownership. Items covered include losses from fire, windstorm, burglary, vandalism, and injuries suffered by others while on the property.

homestead exemption A provision in the bankruptcy code that allows debtors to exclude a maximum of $7,500 in equity in the debtor's place of residence and in property used as a burial ground.

homicide The killing of one human being by another.

horizontal expansion The joining of companies involved in the same business.

hostile bidder See *unfriendly suitor.*

hot cargo contract A union and employer agreement not to handle the products of an employer with whom the union has a labor dispute.

household goods security clauses Clauses that require consumers to use household and personal items as collateral for a loan. Such clauses are now outlawed by the Credit Practices Rule unless the loan is for the purpose of buying the household and personal items.

identified goods Specific goods that are selected as the subject matter of a contract.

illusory promise A promise that does not obligate the promisor to do anything.

immoral A failure or refusal to conform to the values which govern a society's attitude toward right and wrong.

implied acceptance In contract law, an acceptance that results from the conduct or actions of the offeree.

implied authority The authority of an agent to perform acts that are reasonably necessary or customary to carry out expressly authorized duties.

implied contract A contract created by the actions or gestures of the parties involved in the transaction.

implied-in-fact contract A contract implied by direct or indirect acts of the parties.

implied-in-law contract A remedy imposed by a court in a situation where it can be proved that the parties did not create a written, oral, or implied-in-fact agreement but that one party has unfairly benefited at the innocent expense of another. Also known as *quasi contract.*

implied warranty A warranty imposed by law rather than by statements, descriptions, or samples given by the seller.

incidental beneficiary A third party for whose benefit a contract was not made, but who would substantially benefit if the agreement were performed according to its terms and conditions.

incidental damages Reasonable expenses that indirectly result from a breach of contract. They include such expenses as those incurred in stopping delivery of goods, transporting goods, and caring for goods that have been rightfully rejected by a buyer.

incorporators The people who actually start a corporation.

indemnification Payment for loss or damage suffered as a result of acting at another's request or for another's benefit.

indemnify To compensate for loss or damage or insure against future loss or damage.

independent contractor One who contracts to do a job and retains complete control over the methods employed to obtain final completion.

indorsee A person to whom a draft, note, or other negotiable instrument is transferred by indorsement.

indorsement in full An indorsement made by first writing on the back of a negotiable instrument an order to pay to a specified person and then signing the instrument. Also called *special indorsement.*

indorser A person who indorses a negotiable instrument.

informed consent Written consent given by patients for diagnostic tests or treatments that will involve any danger or pain after being told about the risks and alternative involved in the tests or treatments.

informal contract Any oral or written contract that is not a contract of record or under seal. Also known as a *simple contract.*

injunction A court order preventing someone from performing a particular act or commanding the defendant to do some positive act or particular thing.

innkeeper An operator of a hotel, motel, or inn which holds itself out to the public as ready to entertain travelers, strangers, and transient guests.

in pari delicto (in pa'rī de-lik'tō) In equal fault. A contract relationship when both parties are equally wrong in the intention of carrying out an agreement that is deemed void because it is illegal or against public policy or for any other reason.

insider trading A transaction in which corporate managers or some other corporate insider uses inside information to either cheat the corporation or to take unfair advantage of corporate outsiders.

insider trading rule The rule which states that managers and other corporate insiders who possess important inside information cannot use that information in a transaction unless they first reveal that information.

insolvent Inability of a business entity to pay its debts as they become due in the usual course of business.

installment note A promissory note in which the principal together with interest on the unpaid balance is payable in installments at specified times.

insurable interest The financial interest that a policy holder has in the person or property that is insured.

insurance A contract whereby one party pays premiums to another party who undertakes to pay compensation for losses resulting from risks or perils specified in the contract.

insured A party that is protected by an insurer against losses caused by the risks specified in an insurance policy.

insurer A party that accepts the risk of loss in return for a premium (payment of money) and agrees to compensate the insured against a specified loss.

intangible personal property Property consisting of rights rather than goods and chattels; property not perceptible to the senses; evidenced by documents in some cases. Compare *tangible personal property.*

intellectual property Data, programs, software computer material, and any confidential information in any form that is stored in or used by a computer.

intended beneficiary A third party in whose favor a contract is made.

intent The state of mind wherein the person knows and desires the consequences of an act at the time it is committed.

***inter vivos* gift** (in-ter veé-vos) A real gift; a gift between living persons.

***inter vivos* trust** (in-ter veé-vos) A trust that comes into existence while the person who establishes it is alive. Also called *living trust.*

interference with a contract The intentional tort that results when a person, out of ill will, entices a contractual party into breaking the contract.

interlocking directorates In antitrust law, a situation which occurs when individuals serve as directors of two corporations which are competitors.

intermediary bank Any bank to which an item is transferred in the course of collection except the depositary or payor bank.

international bill of exchange A draft that is drawn in one country but payable in another. Also called a *foreign draft.*

interrogatories Written questions to be answered under oath by the opposite party or parties in a lawsuit.

interstate commerce Commerce or the transportation of persons or property from one state to another state.

interstate shipment A shipment that goes beyond the borders of the state in which it originated.

intestacy The quality or state of one who dies without having prepared a valid will.

intestate Having died without leaving a valid will. Compare *testate.*

intrastate commerce Commerce or the transportation of persons or property between points located within the same state.

intrastate shipment A shipment that is entirely within a single state.

invasion of privacy The intentional tort that occurs when one person unreasonably denies another person the right to be left alone or intrudes into another's private affairs.

invitation to trade An announcement or advertisement published to reach many persons for the purpose of creating interest and attracting responses.

involuntary bailment A gratuitous bailment implied by law; a bailment arising from the leaving of personal property in the possession of a bailee through an act of God, accident, or other uncontrolled phenomenon.

involuntary manslaughter The unlawful killing of one human being by another when that killing results from criminal negligence.

irresistible impulse test Under this rule, criminal defendants are judged not guilty by reason of insanity if at the time of the action in question they suffered from a mental disease that either prevented them from knowing right from wrong or compelled them to commit the criminal act.

irrevocable agency See *agency coupled with an interest.*

issue Descendants (children, grandchildren, great-grandchildren).

joint tenancy Ownership of property by two or more persons wherein the right of any deceased owner is automatically transferred to other surviving owners.

judicial review The process by which a court determines the constitutionality of various legislative statutes, administrative regulations, and executive activities.

jurisdiction The authority of a court to hear and decide cases.

kidnapping The unlawful abduction of an individual against that individual's will.

knowledge In criminal law, the mental state that requires an awareness that a particular result will probably occur.

labor union An organization of employees that acts on behalf of all employees in negotiations with the employer regarding the terms and conditions of their employment contract.

lack of consideration A personal defense that may be used by a maker or drawer of a negotiable instrument.

landlord A person who owns real property and who rents or leases it to someone else; a lessor.

larceny The act of taking and carrying away the personal property of another without the right to do so.

last clear chance The doctrine under which a tortfeasor may be held liable if the injured party can show that the tortfeasor had the last chance to avoid injuring the victim. The injured party's defense to a charge of contributory negligence.

law A set of rules created by the governing body of a society to ensure the orderly maintenance of that society.

law merchant In England, the commercial law developed by merchants who needed a set of rules to govern their business transactions.

lease A contract granting the use of certain real property to another for a specified period in return for the payment of rent.

leasehold estate (Also called *tenancy*.) The creation of an ownership interest in the tenant. An interest in real estate which is held under a lease.

legacy In a will, a gift of money or personal property. Also called *bequest*.

legal tender Coin and currency issued by a government and declared valid for payment of all debts, both public and private.

legatee One who receives a gift of personal property given under the terms of a will.

lessee A tenant under a lease of real property.

lessor See *landlord*.

letters of administration A certificate of appointment authorizing an administrator to proceed with settling an estate.

letters testamentary A certificate of appointment authorizing an executor to proceed with settling an estate.

levy on execution To collect a sum of money by putting into effect the judgment of a court.

liability The legal responsibility of an individual for his or her actions.

liable Legally responsible.

libel Any false statement that harms another person's good name or reputation made in a permanent form, such as movies, writing, and videotape, and communicated to others.

license A grant of permission to do a particular thing, to exercise a certain privilege, to carry on a particular business, or to pursue a certain occupation; a personal privilege or permission with respect to some use of land, revocable at the will of the landowner; a privilege granted by a state or city upon payment of a fee, which is not a contract and may be revoked for cause, conferring authority to perform a designated task, such as operating a motor vehicle.

licensee A person to whom a license is given; a social guest; a person entering or using premises by permission or by operation of the law but without express or implied invitation; a person entering premises by permission only; a person on another's premises solely in pursuit or furtherance of his or her own business, pleasure, or convenience.

licensing agreement An agreement in which the producer of a product allows a purchaser to use a product only if the purchaser agrees to respect the producer's desire for secrecy.

lien A claim that one has against the property of another.

life estate An estate in which the owner owns real property for her or his life or for the life of another.

life insurance An insurance contract that provides money compensation for losses suffered by another's death.

life of the policy A period of time during which an insurer assumes the risk of loss specified in the insurance contract.

limited defense In negotiable-instruments law, a defense that can be used against a holder but not against a holder in due course of a negotiable instrument. Also called *personal defense*.

limited liability Status which specifies that an individual's liability will not go beyond his or her original investment.

limited partner A partner whose liability does not extend beyond the partner's investment.

limited partnership A partnership formed by two or more persons having one or more general partners and one or more limited partners.

limited warranty Under the Magnuson-Moss Warranty Act, a warranty that is not a full warranty.

liquidated damages An amount of anticipated damages, agreed to by both parties and contained in a contract, to be the basis of any award in the event of a breach of the contract.

liquidation The conversion of property into cash.

litigant A person involved in litigation.

litigation The process of bringing a case to court to enforce a right.

living trust A trust that comes into existence while the person who establishes it is alive. Also called *inter vivos trust.*

local option The practice in a state of eliminating uniform statewide laws regulating Sunday activities and allowing the local counties, cities, towns, and villages to adopt their own special Sunday ordinances.

locus sigilli The place of the seal. The abbreviation L.S. is often used in place of the seal itself on formal written contracts.

lodger Any person staying at a hotel, motel, or rooming house for a definite period of time.

M'Naughten Rule Under this rule a criminal defendant is declared not guilty by reason of insanity if at the time of the criminal act he or she suffered from a mental disease that prevented him or her from understanding the difference between right and wrong.

mail fraud Fraud carried out by using the U.S. mail.

maiming Acts done with the intent to injure or disfigure the victim's person.

majority A term used to describe persons who have reached the legal age of adulthood.

maker A person obligated as the payor on a promissory note. See also *comaker.*

managerial control A theory of corporate management that favors insulating managers from shareholders by limiting the shareholders' power to vote and by making it difficult for shareholders to sue managers.

mandatory arbitration Arbitration that is required by state law before two contending parties can go to trial.

manslaughter The unlawful killing of one person by another when the killing is not intended.

master An individual who has the right to control the physical conduct of a servant or employee. See also *employer.*

material fact An essential or important fact; a fact of substance.

mediation The process by which an outside party attempts to help two other parties settle their differences.

mediator An outside party who attempts to convince two contending parties to adjust or settle their dispute.

medical payments insurance A type of automobile insurance that pays for medical (and sometimes funeral) expenses resulting from bodily injuries to anyone occupying the policyholder's car at the time of an accident.

memorandum A written document or series of documents containing the terms of an agreement, an identification of the subject matter of the agreement, the consideration promised, the names and identities of the parties to the agreement and the signature of the party charged to the agreement.

merchant A person who deals in goods of the kind sold in the ordinary course of business or who otherwise claims to have knowledge or skills peculiar to those goods.

merger The acquisition of one corporation by another.

midnight deadline In banking, midnight of the next banking day following the day on which the bank receives a relevant item.

minority A term used to describe persons who have not yet reached the legal age of adulthood.

mirror image rule In contract law, the rule that an acceptance must have exactly the same terms as the offer.

misdemeanor A less serious crime that is generally punishable by a fine or jail sentence of not more than one year.

misrepresentation A false statement innocently or fraudulently made by one party to a contract. In insurance, giving false answers to questions in an insurance application that materially affect the risk undertaken by the insurer.

money A medium of exchange adopted by a domestic or foreign government as part of its currency.

monopoly The exclusive control of a market by a business enterprise.

moral Acting according to the values which govern society's attitude toward right and wrong.

moral absolutism An ethical theory that holds that actions are either right or wrong regardless of circumstances and regardless of consequences. Also known as *objective ethics.*

morality Values that govern a society's attitude toward right and wrong.

mortgage A transfer of an interest in real property for the purpose of creating security for a debt.

mortgagee The party who lends money and takes back a mortgage as security for the loan.

mortgagor The party who borrows money and gives a mortgage to the lender or mortgagee as security for the loan.

motion A request by a party to a lawsuit asking the court to rule on a particular matter.

motive In criminal law, the wrongdoer's reason for committing a crime. Motive is not an element of criminal liability.

murder The unlawful killing of one human being by another when the killing is done with deliberate purpose or intent.

mutual assent In contract law, the state of mind that exists between an offeror and an offeree once a valid offer has been accepted and once the parties know what the terms are and have agreed to be bound by them. Also known as "a meeting of the minds."

mutual-benefit bailment A bailment in which both the bailor and the bailee receive some benefit.

mutual mistake See *bilateral mistake.*

mutual rescission A condition in which both parties to a contract return to the other any consideration already received or pay for any services or materials already rendered.

mutuum (mú-tu-um) A loan of goods with the intention that the goods may be used and later replaced with an equal amount of different goods of the same kind.

national standard A rule that allows a court to judge a health care provider's degree of care by determining how the same procedure is performed on a national basis.

navigable air space Space above 1,000 feet over populated areas, and above 500 feet over water and unpopulated areas.

navigable stream A stream that ebbs and flows with the tide or is capable of being navigated by commercial vessels.

necessaries Goods and services that are essential to a minor's or mental incompetent's health and welfare.

negligence Failure to exercise a degree of care that a reasonable person would exercise under the same circumstances.

negotiable instrument A written document signed by the maker or drawer, containing an unconditional promise or order to pay a certain sum of money on demand or at a definite time to the bearer or to order.

negotiation The transfer of a negotiable instrument in such form that the transferee becomes a holder.

next of kin Those who are most nearly related by blood.

no-fault insurance A type of automobile insurance that allows drivers to collect damages and medical expenses from their own insurance carriers regardless of who is at fault in the accident.

no par value stock Corporate stock that is issued without any stated price.

nonconforming goods Goods that are not the same as those called for under a contract or those which are in some way defective.

nonconforming uses Uses of land permitted to continue in existence even though newly enacted zoning laws no longer permit similar uses.

noncumulative preferred stock A class of stock that does not have the right to be paid dividends in later years if dividends are not paid in the present year.

nondisclosure See *passive fraud.*

nonparticipating preferred stock A class of stock that does not give its holders a priority on a certain stated amount or percentage of dividends.

nonperformance In contract law, failing to fulfill or accomplish a contract according to its terms.

not guilty by reason of insanity (NGRI) A defense to criminal liability which claims that the accused was mentally incompetent at the time the crime was committed. Also known as *insanity defense.*

note A written promise by one party to pay money to another party. Also called a *promissory note.*

novation The substitution of another party for one of the original parties to a contract with the consent of the remaining party; the old contract is extinguished and a new contract is created.

nuisance Anything that endangers life or health, offends the senses, violates the laws of decency, or obstructs the reasonable and comfortable use of property.

nuncupative will (nuńg-ku-pa-tiv wil) An oral will declared in the presence of witnesses by the testator; made by a person in a final illness or by soldiers and sailors in actual combat.

objective ethics. See *moral absolutism.*

obligee In contract law, the party to whom another party owes an obligation or duty.

obligor In contract law, a party who is obligated to deliver on a promise or to undertake some act of performance.

offer In contract law, a proposal made by one party to another indicating a willingness to enter a contract.

offeree In contract law, the person to whom an offer is made.

offeror In contract law, the person who makes an offer.

open-end credit Credit that can be increased by the debtor, up to a limit set by the creditor, by continuing to purchase goods on credit.

open price terms Terms of a sales contract in which the price is to be determined at a later date.

option In contract law, the giving of consideration to support an offeror's promise to hold open an offer for a stated or reasonable length of time.

option contract An agreement that binds the offeror to a promise to hold open an offer to a predetermined or reasonable length of time.

option to purchase An agreement by one party to sell property to the other party for a stated price if the other party accepts within a prescribed time period.

option to renew The right given to a lessee, at the end of a lease, to a new lease for an additional period.

order bill of lading A negotiable bill of lading, containing words of negotiability.

order for relief In bankruptcy law, a court's command that bankruptcy proceedings begin.

order paper A negotiable instrument that is payable to someone's order.

ordinary negligence Failure to use that amount of care that a reasonable person would use under ordinary circumstances.

original jurisdiction The authority of a court to hear a case when it is first brought to court.

orphan's court See *probate court.*

output contract An agreement under which a seller agrees to sell "all the goods he or she manufactures" or "all the crops he or she produces" to a particular buyer. See also *requirements contract.*

outside party See *third party.*

overdraft A payment by a bank on behalf of a customer for more than the customer has on deposit.

par value The value that is placed on the shares of stock at incorporation.

parol evidence rule The rule which states that oral evidence of prior or contemporaneous negotiations between parties is not admissible in court to alter, vary, or contradict the terms of a written agreement.

partially disclosed principal A person, in a transaction conducted by an agent, whose existence is known to the third party but whose specific identity is unknown.

participating preferred stock A class of stock that gives its holder a priority on a certain stated amount or percentage of dividends.

partnership An association of two or more persons to carry on a business for profit.

partnership at will A partnership that may be dissolved at any time by one of the partners without liability.

partnership by estoppel A partnership that occurs because someone says or does something that leads a third party to believe a partnership exists.

passenger A person who enters the premises of a carrier with the intention of buying a ticket for a trip.

passive fraud A failure to reveal some material fact about the subject matter of a contract which one party is obligated to reveal to the other party and which intentionally deceives that second party leading him or her into a damaging contract. Also known as *concealment* and *nondisclosure.*

past consideration A promise to give another something of value in return for goods or services rendered and delivered in the past, without expectation of reward.

patent An official document that gives the owner the exclusive right to make, use, or sell an invention for a limited time period.

pawn The act of giving up personal property as security for performance of a promise or future payment of a debt, usually associated with a loan made by a pawnbroker; a pledge.

payee The party named in commercial paper to whom payment is to be made.

payor bank A bank by which an item is payable as drawn or accepted. It includes a drawee bank.

per se violation In antitrust law, a restraint of trade practice so serious that it is prohibited whether or not it actually harms anyone.

percolating waters Waters that pass through the ground beneath the surface of the earth without any definite channel.

perfected A security interest is said to be perfected when the secured party has done everything that the law requires to give the secured party greater rights to the goods than others have.

performance In contract law, the situation that exists when the parties to a contract have done what they had agreed to do.

periodic tenancy See *tenancy from year to year.*

personal defense See *limited defense.*

personal property All property and property rights, both tangible and intangible, not included within the definition of real property.

persuasive precedent A previous case that a court is free to follow or to ignore.

physical duress Violence or the threat of violence against an individual or against that person's family, household, or property that is so serious that it forces a person into a contract against his or her will.

picketing The placement of persons for observation, patrol, and demonstration at the site of employment as part of employee pressure on an employer to meet a demand.

piercing the corporate veil The doctrine holding the shareholders of a corporation liable when they have used the corporation as a facade to defraud or commit some other misdeed.

plaintiff The person who begins a lawsuit by filing a complaint in a trial court of original jurisdiction.

pledge The giving up of personal property as security for performance of an act or repayment of a debt.

pledgee A person to whom property is given as security for a loan.

pledgor A person who gives property to another as security for a loan.

police power A state's authority to promote and maintain public health, safety, and morals.

policy The contract of insurance.

pooling agreement An agreement made by shareholders whereby they promise to vote the same way on a particular issue. Also known as *shareholder agreements* and *voting agreements.*

power of attorney An instrument in writing by which one person, as principal, appoints another as agent and confers the authority to perform certain specified acts on behalf of the principal.

precedent A model case that a court can follow when facing a similar situation.

preemptive right A shareholder's right to purchase a proportionate share of every new offering of stock by the corporation.

pre-existing duty An obligation that a party is already bound to by law or by some other agreement that the party attempts to use as consideration in a new contract. Such consideration is invalid.

preferred stock A class of stock that carries with it the right to receive payment of dividends and/or the distribution of assets on the dissolution of the corporation before other classes of stock receive their payments.

premarital agreement See *prenuptial agreement.*

premium The consideration paid by the insured to the insurer for insurance protection.

prenuptial agreement An agreement made before marriage in which two people planning marriage agree to change the property rights which usually arise in a marriage. Also known as a *premarital agreement,* an *antenuptial agreement,* and a *marriage settlement.*

presenting bank Any bank presenting an item except a payor bank.

presentment A demand for acceptance or payment of a negotiable instrument made upon the maker, acceptor, or drawee by or on behalf of the holder of the instrument.

***prima facie* evidence** (príma fá-shi-e ev́-idens) Evidence sufficient to support, but not to compel, a certain conclusion by the trier of fact.

primary committee In bankruptcy law, a committee of creditors set up to work with a debtor in drawing up a reorganization plan.

primary liability Absolute liability to pay a negotiable instrument.

principal A person who authorizes an agent to act on her or his behalf and subject to her or his control.

prior appropriation doctrine This doctrine says that of various people whose property is located on a waterway, the first person to make beneficial use of the water has the right to take all he or she is able to use before anyone else has any rights to it.

private carrier A company that transports goods or persons under individual contract with those seeking its services. A private carrier is not required to serve all who apply, unlike a common carrier.

private corporation A corporation formed by private persons to accomplish a task best undertaken by an entity that can raise large amounts of capital quickly or that can grant the protection of limited liability.

private nuisance The interference of one party with the use or enjoyment of land by an individual or the individual's family.

private warehouser A warehouser whose warehouse is not for general public use.

privity In contract law, the relationship that exists between two parties to a contract giving each a recognized interest in the subject matter of the contract so that they are bound to that contract.

probate The proving of a will to the satisfaction of public authorities and the carrying out of the terms of such a will by the executor or administrator.

probate court A court that supervises the procedure of settling estates.

product liability A legal theory that imposes liability on the manufacturer and seller of a product produced and sold in a defective condition.

product-liability laws Laws that make manufacturers and sellers responsible for injuries to consumers caused by defective, unhealthy, or unsafe products.

profit à prendre (pró-fet ah proń-druh) An easement that gives its owner the right to remove something of value from another's property such as the right to enter lands of another for the purpose of cutting hay, harvesting wheat, and the like.

promisee In the making of a contract, the party to whom a promise is made.

promisor In the making of a contract, the party who makes a promise.

promissory estoppel The legal doctrine that restricts an offeror from revoking an offer even though consideration has not been promised to bind an agreement. To be effective, promissory estoppel requires that the offeror know, or be presumed to know, that the offeree might otherwise make a change of position in contemplation of promises contained in the offer.

promissory note A negotiable instrument wherein the maker promises to pay a certain sum at a definite time to the order of the payee.

promoters The people who do the day-to-day work involved in creating a corporation.

property damage liability insurance A type of automobile insurance that provides protection when other people bring claims or lawsuits against the insured for damaging property such as car, a fence, or a tree.

property insurance A type of insurance contract that provides money compensation for losses suffered by the loss, theft, damage, or destruction of real or personal property.

prospectus A document published by a corporation explaining, in simplified fashion for potential investors, the details of a stock issuance and the business making the offer.

protest A formal certification by a notary public (or other authorized party) that an instrument has been refused payment at maturity.

proximate cause In tort law, the causal connection between the unreasonable conduct and the resulting harm. Proximate cause is determined by asking whether the harm which resulted from the conduct was foreseeable at the time of the original negligent act.

proxy The ability of one shareholder to cast another shareholder's votes.

proxy contest A struggle between two factions in a corporation, usually management and a group of dissident shareholders, to obtain the votes of other shareholders.

proxy solicitation The process by which one shareholder asks another for his or her voting rights.

public accountant An accountant who works for a variety of clients but who is not certified.

public corporation A corporation created by the federal, state, or local government for governmental purposes.

public nuisance Annoyances which offend, interfere with, or damage the rights common to all.

public offer An offer made through the public media but which is intended for only one person whose identity or address is unknown to the offeror.

public policy The general legal principle that says no one should be allowed to do anything that tends to injure the public at large.

public trust Established for charitable purposes, such as the advancement of education; relief to the aged, ill, or poor; and the promotion of religion. Also called *charitable trust.*

public warehouser A warehouser who owns a warehouse where any member of the public who is willing to pay the regular charge may store goods.

puffery See *sales puffery.*

punitive damages Damages in excess of losses suffered by the plaintiff awarded as a measure of punishment for the defendant's wrongful acts. Also called *exemplary damages.*

purchase money security interest A security interest which arises when someone lends money to a consumer and then takes a security interest in the goods that the consumer buys.

purpose In criminal law, the intent to cause the result which does, in fact, occur.

qualified indorsement An indorsement in which words, such as "without recourse," that limit or qualify the liability of the indorser to answer for the default of the maker have been added to the signature.

qualified opinion An opinion issued by an auditor saying that as of a given date, the books of a firm represent its financial health; however, the auditor qualifies the opinion either because the firm is facing some uncertainty that might affect the health of the firm or because the firm has deviated from generally accepted accounting principles (GAAP) in some minor way.

quantum meruit (kwoń-tum mé-ru-it) "As much as one has earned;" damages awarded in an amount considered reasonable in return for the benefits derived through a quasi-contractual relationship.

quasi contract. See *implied-in-law contract.*

quasi-public corporation Corporations that are privately organized for profit but which provide a service the public depends on.

quiet enjoyment The right of a tenant to the undisturbed possession of the property that he or she is renting.

quitclaim deed (Also called a *deed without covenants.*) A deed that transfers to the grantee only the interest that the grantor had in the property and which contains no warranties.

quo warranto (kwo wo-rán-to) Literally, "by what authority." A *quo warranto* action is one in which the state revokes a corporation's charter.

quota The fixed number of employment positions for a particular group of persons for affirmative action purposes.

ratification The principal's approval of an unauthorized act performed by an agent or by one who has no authority to act as an agent. Also, an approval of a contract made by a minor after reaching maturity.

rational ethics The ethical belief that ethical and moral rules can be arrived at through reason.

real defense See *absolute defense.*

real property The ground and anything permanently attached to it including land, buildings, and growing trees and shrubs; the air space above the land is also included.

reasonable care The degree of care which a reasonably prudent person would have used under the same circumstances and conditions.

reasonable person test The legal test that determines whether an alleged tortfeasor acted with due care. The test compares the actions of the alleged tortfeasor with those of the reasonable person under the same or similar circumstances.

rebuttable presumption A presumption that a defending party has the right to attack, which is disputable, holding good only until disproved.

receiver A person appointed by law to hold property subject to diverse claims; the receiver divides the assets fairly among creditors.

recklessness In criminal law, the mental state that requires a perverse disregard for a known risk of a negative result.

registration statement A statement required by the Securities and Exchange Commission to indicate details about securities for sale and about the business selling those securities.

rejection The express or implied refusal by an offeree to accept an offer.

release In contract law, a promise made by one party agreeing not to sue a second party.

remainder estate A future interest that occurs when title to real property passes at the end of a life estate to someone other than the grantor or the grantor's heirs.

remitting bank Any payor or intermediary bank remitting for an item.

renunciation A legal act by which a person abandons a right acquired, but without transfering it to another.

reorganization In bankruptcy law, a plan created by a qualified debtor that alters his or her repayment schedule.

request for real evidence A discovery device that asks the opposing party in a lawsuit to produce papers, accounts, correspondence, photographs, tapes, or other tangible evidence.

requirement contract An agreement under which one party agrees to purchase all his or her requirements of a particular product from another. See also *output contract.*

rescission A remedy in contract law that returns both parties to a contract back to their original positions before the contract was entered into.

reserve funds Earnings from a business that are held in reserve.

respondeat superior (re-spón-de-at su-pé-ri-or) The legal theory that imposes liability on employers for torts committed by their employees. Literally translated it means "Let the master respond."

Restatement (Second) of Agency An authoritative general compilation of the common law of agency throughout the United States, referred to in judicial decisions and opinions.

restraint of trade A limitation on the full exercise of doing business with others.

restrictive covenant A promise by an employee in an employment contract not to work for anyone else in the same field of employment for a specified time period within a particular geographical area.

restrictive indorsement An indorsement in which words have been added to the signature of the indorser that specify the purpose of the indorsement or the use to be made of the commercial paper, such as "for deposit only."

reverse discrimination A claim by a member of a majority group that he or she has been discriminated against usually because of an affirmative action program intended to favor a minority group.

reversion estate A future interest that occurs when title to real property passes at the end of a life estate to the grantor or to the grantor's heirs.

revocation A taking back; a withdrawal of an offer; a recalling of authority.

revolving charge account A charge account with an outstanding balance at all times.

right-to-work laws State laws prohibiting labor-management agreements that require union membership to obtain or keep a job.

riparian rights doctrine Under this doctrine, owners of land bordering a stream have equal rights to use the water passing by or through their property.

robbery The act of taking personal property from the possession of another against that person's will and under threat to do great bodily harm.

rule against perpetuities A rule requiring that trust property become owned by the beneficiary outright not later than 21 years after the death of some person alive at the creation of the trust.

rule of contemporary ownership The rule that holds that shareholders must own stock at the time of the injury and at the time of the lawsuit if they wish to begin a derivative suit.

rule of reason In antitrust law, a doctrine that holds that a court should stop certain practices only if they are an unreasonable restriction of competition.

S corporation A corporation in which shareholders have agreed to have the profits (or losses) of the corporation taxed directly to them rather than to the corporation. (Formerly known as a subchapter S corporation.)

sale The passing of title to goods from the seller to the buyer for a price.

sale on approval A conditional sale that becomes absolute only if the buyer approves or is satisfied with the article being sold.

sale or return A sale that allows goods to be returned even though the goods conform to the contract.

sales puffery Persuasive words or exaggerated arguments made by salespeople to induce customers to buy their product. As long as such comments are reserved to opinion and do not misstate facts, they are not actionable as fraud, even if they turn out to be grossly in error.

satisfaction The agreed-to settlement as contained in an accord.

satisfactory performance In contract law, the situation that exists when either personal taste or objective standards determine whether contracting parties have performed their contractual duties according to the agreement.

scope of authority The range of acts done while performing agency duties. Synonymous with *scope of employment.*

scope of employment See *scope of authority.*

seal A mark or impression placed on a written contract indicating that the instrument was executed and accepted in a formal manner.

secondary boycott Any union action against a company that does not have a labor dispute with the employees it is representing.

secondary liability Liability to pay a negotiable instrument only after certain conditions are met.

secured loan A loan in which creditors have something of value, usually called *collateral,* from which they can be paid if the debtor does not pay.

secured party A lender or seller who holds a security interest.

security In secured transactions, the assurance that a creditor will be paid back for any money loaned or credit extended to a debtor. In corporate law, a money investment that expects a return solely because of another person's efforts.

security agreement A written agreement that creates a security interest.

security device A way for creditors to get their money back in case the borrower or debtor does not pay.

security interest A creditor's right to recover a debt.

self-defense A defense to criminal liability available to defendants if they can demonstrate (1) that they did not start the altercation, (2) that they believed they were in danger of death or severe bodily injury, (3) that this belief was reasonable, and (4) that they used only enough force to repel the attack.

servant A person employed to perform services in the affairs of another and who, with respect to the physical conduct in the performance of the service, is subject to the other's control or right to control. Synonymous with the term *employee*.

service of process Notice of a lawsuit.

servient tenement The property through which an easement is created or through which it extends.

settlor A person who establishes a trust.

shareholder agreements See *pooling agreement.*

shareholder of record A person to whom stock has been transferred and whose name has been entered on the corporate books as the owner of that stock. Shareholders of record are entitled to vote, receive dividends and enjoy all other shareholder privileges.

shareholder proposal A proposal by certain shareholders about a broad company policy or procedure that is communicated by management to the corporation's shareholders prior to the next shareholder meeting.

shareholders Persons who own units of interest called *shares of stock* in a corporation. Also known as *stockholders.*

shelter provision A holder who receives an instrument from a holder in due course acquires the rights of the holder in due course even though he or she does not qualify as a holder in due course.

shepardizing Using a set of books called *Shepard's Citations* to determine the subsequent disposition of a case by the court.

shipment contract A contract under which the seller is required to send or ship goods (such as by carrier) to the buyer but not to deliver them directly to the place of destination. Under this type of contract, title passes to the buyer at the time and place of shipment.

sight draft A draft that is payable as soon as it is presented to the drawee for payment.

similar locality rule Rule that allows a court to judge a health care provider's degree of care by determining how the same procedure is performed at another hospital located in a similar locality.

simple contract See *informal contract.*

slander Any false statement that harms a person's good name or reputation that is made in a temporary form, such as speech, and communicated to others.

slight negligence The failure to use that degree of care which persons of extraordinary prudence and foresight are accustomed to.

small pond A pond that is less than ten acres in size.

sovereign immunity The somewhat discredited doctrine preventing a lawsuit against governmental authority without the government's consent.

special indorsement See *indorsement in full.*

special jurisdiction The power of a court to hear only certain kinds of cases.

special-warranty deed A deed containing express warranties under which the grantor guarantees that no defects arose in the title during the time that he or she owned the property.

specific performance A decree from a court of equity ordering a contracting party to carry out the promises made in a contract; available only in those cases where money would not be a satisfactory solution to a wrong.

speculative damages Damage computed on losses that have not actually been suffered and which cannot be proved; they are based entirely on an expectation of losses that might be suffered from a breach; the courts do not allow speculative damages.

spendthrift One who spends money profusely and improvidently.

spendthrift trust A trust designed to provide a fund for the maintenance of a beneficiary and, at the same time, to secure the fund against that person's improvidence or incapacity.

sprinkling trust (Also called a *spray trust.*) A trust which allows the trustee to decide how much will be given to each beneficiary rather than have the settlor make the decision.

stale check A check that is presented for payment more than six months after its date.

stare decisis (stáh-ray dé-si-sis) (Also called the *law of precedent.*) The legal principle that allows a court to rely on the rules of law applied in previous decisions, when deciding a similar case. Literally translated it means "Let the decision stand."

statute A law passed by a legislature.

statute of frauds A law requiring written evidence to support certain contracts if they are to be enforced in court.

statutes of limitations State laws that limit the time within which a party is allowed to bring legal action against another.

statutory law That body of law which includes statutes, ordinances, and by-laws.

stock acquisition The purchase of enough of the voting stock of a corporation to allow the buyer to control the corporation. Also known as *takeover.*

stock certificate Written evidence of ownership of a unit of interest in the corporation.

stock dividends Dividends paid to shareholders in the form of shares of capital stock.

stockholders See *shareholders.*

stoppage in transit A right by the seller, upon learning that the buyer is insolvent, to have the delivery of goods stopped before they reach their destination.

straight bill of lading A bill of lading that does not contain words of negotiability; it may not be negotiated but may be assigned.

strict liability The doctrine under which people may be liable for injuries to others whether or not they have acted wrongfully (also called *absolute liability*).

strike The stoppage of work by employees as a means of enforcing a demand made on their employer.

subject to the mortgage An agreement whereby the seller of real property agrees to continue paying the mortgage payments.

subjective ethics See *ethical relativism.*

sublease A lease given by a lessee to a third person conveying the same interest for a shorter term than the period for which the lessee is holding it.

subrogation The right of one party to substitute itself for another party.

substantial certainty test In copyright law, the test that asks whether two works under scrutiny are so like one another that an ordinary reasonable observer would conclude that the second was copied from the first.

substantial performance In contract law, the situation that results when a party to a contract, in good faith, executes all the promised terms and conditions of the contract with the exception of minor details that do not affect the real intent of their agreement.

subterranean rights Rights to materials below the surface of the land.

subterranean waters Waters that lie wholly beneath the surface of the ground.

suitor A corporation or individual who offers to purchase the voting stock of a corporation with the objective of taking over the corporation.

summary ejectment A legal proceeding that provides landlords with a quick method of evicting a tenant.

summary judgment A motion that asks the court for an immediate judgment for the party filing the motion because both parties agree on the facts in the case and because under law the party who introduced the motion is entitled to a favorable judgment.

summary process See *summary ejectment.*

summons An official legal document issued by a court naming the court, describing the nature of the lawsuit, and demanding that the defendant in the suit answer the complaint within a stated period of time.

surety One who incurs a liability for the benefit of another but who is nevertheless directly and immediately liable for a debt.

surplus Funds that remain after a partnership has been dissolved and all other debts and prior obligations have been settled.

surrogate court See *probate court.*

takeover See *stock acquisition.*

takeover bid In corporate law, the offer to buy the voting stock of a corporation.

tangible personal property Property which may be seen or touched and which may be given an actual physical description. Compare *intangible personal property.*

target In corporate law, a corporation that is the object of a takeover bid.

teller's check See *bank draft.*

tenancy An interest in real estate that is held under a lease. Also called *leasehold estate.*

tenancy at sufferance A leasehold estate, or tenancy, that arises when a tenant wrongfully remains in possession of the premises after his or her tenancy has expired. Such a tenant is a wrongdoer, having no estate or other interest in the property.

tenancy at will A leasehold estate, or tenancy, that continues for as long as both parties desire.

tenancy by the entirety Ownership by husband and wife, considered by law as one, with full ownership surviving to the living spouse on the death of the other.

tenancy for years A leasehold estate, or tenancy, for a fixed period of time.

tenancy from year to year A leasehold estate, or tenancy, that continues for successive periods until one of the parties terminates it by giving notice to the other party. Also called *periodic tenancy.*

tenancy in common Ownership of an undivided interest in property by two or more persons, with each owner's rights going to his or her heirs upon death rather than to the surviving co-owners.

tenancy in partnership Ownership in which each person has an interest in partnership property and is co-owner of such property.

tenant A person who has temporary possession of and interest in the land of another. See *lessee.*

tender An offer or performance by one party to a contract which, if unjustifiably refused, places the other party in default and permits the party making the tender to exercise remedies for breach of contract.

tender of delivery An offer by the seller of goods to turn the goods over to the buyer.

tender of payment An offer by the buyer of goods to turn the money over to the seller.

tender of performance Occurs when the seller offers to turn goods over to the buyer and when the buyer offers to pay for them.

termination by waiver A voluntary relinquishing of one's right to demand the performance of a contract.

testamentary disposition The giving away of one's property by will.

testamentary trust A trust that is created by will.

testate (teś-tate) Having made a valid will. Compare *intestate.*

testator (male); testatrix (female) A person who makes a will.

theological ethics The ethical belief that all moral rules come from God.

third party In contract law, a person who may, in some way, be affected by a contract, even though he or she is not one of the contracting parties. Also known as an *outside party.*

third-party complaint A claim filed by a defendant in a lawsuit that reaches outside the original circle of parties to the suit and brings in a party that heretofore was not a part of the suit.

time draft A draft that is not payable until the lapse of a particular time period stated on the draft.

time note A promissory note that is payable at some future time, on a definite date named in the instrument.

title The right of ownership to goods. A subdivision of a code containing all the statutes that deal with a particular area of law.

tort A private wrong that causes injury to another person's physical well-being, property, or reputation.

tortfeasor A person who commits a tort.

tortious bailee Any party unlawfully in possession of another's personal property.

trade acceptance A draft used by a seller of

goods to receive payment and also to extend credit. It is often used in combination with a bill of lading.

trade fixtures Items of personal property, brought upon the land by a tenant, that are necessary to carry on the trade or business to which the land will be devoted. Contrary to the general rule, trade fixtures remain the personal property of the tenant and are removable at the expiration of the terms of occupancy.

trade secret A plan, process, or device used in a business and known only to employees who need to know the secret to carry out their jobs.

trademark Any word, name, symbol, or device adopted and used by a manufacturer or merchant to identify goods and distinguish them from those manufactured or sold by others.

transient A hotel guest; a person who accepts the services of a hotel or other public accommodation without any obligation to remain a specified length of time.

traveler's check A draft purchased from a bank or express company and signed by the purchaser at the time of the purchase and again at the time of cashing as a precaution against forgery.

treason The levying of war against the United States, or the giving of aid and comfort to the nation's enemies.

trespass Wrongful injury to or interference with the property of another.

trust A right of ownership to property held by one person for the benefit of another.

trust fund Property that is held in trust. Also called the *corpus*.

trustee A person who is entrusted with the management and control of another's property and who is given legal title to that property.

tying agreement In antitrust law, an illegal practice that occurs when one party refuses to sell a given product unless the buyer also purchases another product tied to the first product.

unconscionable contract Contract terms and conditions deemed to be oppressive, overreaching, or shocking to the conscience; under the UCC, grounds for rescission of a contract or parts thereof.

underlease (Also called *sublease*.) A lease given by a lessee to a third person conveying the same interest for a shorter term than the period for which the lessee holds it.

undisclosed principal A person, in a transaction conducted by an agent, whose existence and identity are unknown to the third party.

undisputed amount An amount upon which the parties to a contract have mutually agreed.

undue influence The use of excessive pressure by the dominant member of a confidential relationship to convince the weaker party to enter a contract that greatly benefits the dominant party.

unenforceable contract A contract that cannot be upheld by a court of law because of some rule of law.

unfair labor practices Improper employment practices by either an employer or union.

unfriendly suitor A bidder who intends to change management and shake up a corporation after a takeover. Also called a *hostile bidder*.

Uniform Commercial Code (UCC) A uniform law relating to certain commercial transactions, including the sale of goods, commercial paper, bank deposits and collections, letters of credit, bulk transfers, warehouse receipts, bills of lading, and secured transactions.

unilateral contract An agreement in which one party makes a promise to do something in return for an act of some sort.

unilateral mistake In contract law, a mistake made by one party to a contract. Unilateral mistake does not offer sufficient grounds for rescission.

unimpaired class In bankruptcy law, a group of creditors whose collection rights have not been impaired by a reorganization plan.

uninsured-motorist insurance A type of automobile insurance that provides protection against the risk of being injured by a motorist who does not have any insurance.

union shop A place of employment where nonunion workers may be employed for a trial period of 30 days, after which the nonunion workers must join the union or be discharged.

unity of person Common law doctrine under

which a husband and wife are regarded as one.

unity of possession Occurs when each cotenant is entitled to possession of the entire premises.

universal defense See *absolute defense.*

unlawful detainer See *summary ejectment.*

unqualified opinion An opinion issued by an auditor that indicates that the financial records of a firm are an accurate reflection of the firm's financial status.

unsecured loan A loan in which creditors have nothing of value that they can repossess and sell in order to recover the money owed to them by the debtor.

U.S. code A comprehensive collection of federal laws.

usage of trade Any method of dealing that is commonly used in the particular field.

Used Car Rule A rule established by the Federal Trade Commission requiring used-car dealers to place a sticker, called a Buyer's Guide, in the window of each used car they offer for sale, disclosing the warranties that go with the sale of the car.

usury The practice of charging more than the amount of interest allowed by law.

utilitarianism An ethical theory that focuses on the consequences of an action.

uttering The crime of offering a forged instrument to another person, knowing it to be forged.

valid contract A contract that is legally binding.

variable-rate mortgage A mortgage that has a rate of interest that changes according to fluctuations in the index to which it is tied.

variance An exemption or an exception permitting a use that differs from those permitted under the existing zoning law.

verdict A finding of fact by the jury in a court case; the jury's decision.

vertical expansion The joining of two companies that were in a customer-supplier relationship.

vesting The rules by which workers are guaranteed the right to receive future pension benefits regardless of whether they are working under the plan at the time of retirement.

vicarious liability The laying of responsibility or blame upon one person for the actions of another.

void contract A contract that has no legal effect whatsoever.

void title No title at all.

voidable contract A contract that may be avoided or canceled by one of the parties.

voidable title Title that may be voided if one of the parties elects to do so.

voluntary manslaughter The unlawful killing of one human being by another when the killing results from extreme fright, terror, anger, or blind rage that destroys reason.

voting agreement See *pooling agreement.*

voting trust An agreement among shareholders to transfer their voting rights to a trustee.

wage assignment clauses Clauses that permit consumers to agree in advance among shareholders to transfer their voting rights to a trustee.

waiver The voluntary surrender of some right, claim, or privilege.

waiver of exemption clauses Clauses requiring consumers to give up the state law protection that allows them to keep certain personal belongings even though they are sued for nonpayment of a debt. Such clauses are now outlawed by the Credit Practices Rule.

waiver of premium An optional provision in an insurance contract that excuses the insured from paying premiums if the insured becomes disabled.

warehouse A building or structure in which any goods, but particularly wares or merchandise, are stored.

warehouse receipt A receipt issued by a person engaged in the business of storing goods for hire.

warehouser A person engaged in the business of storing goods for hire.

warehouser's lien The right of a warehouser to retain possession of goods stored in the warehouse until the amount of money owed for storage charges, transportation charges, insurance, and preservation expense is paid.

warranty A statement, promise, or other representation that an item has certain qualities; also, an obligation imposed by law that an item will have certain qualities. Warranties made by means of a statement or other affirmation of fact are called *express warranties;* those imposed by law are *implied warranties.*

warranty of fitness for a particular purpose An implied warranty that goods will be fit for a particular purpose. This warranty is given by the seller to the buyer of goods whenever the seller has reason to know of any particular purpose for which the goods are needed and the buyer relies on the seller's skill and judgment to select the goods.

warranty of merchantability An implied warranty that goods are fit for the ordinary purpose for which such goods are used. Unless excluded, this warranty is always given by a merchant who sells goods in the ordinary course of business.

warranty of title A warranty given by a seller to a buyer of goods which states that the title be-ing conveyed is good and that the transfer is rightful.

white knight See *friendly suiter.*

will A legal document, not valid until the testator's death, expressing the testator's intent in distribution of all real and personal property.

wire fraud Fraud carried out by using the telephone or some other electronic communication device.

workers' compensation law State statute that compensates covered and eligible workers or their dependents for injury, disease, or death resulting in the course of employment.

writ of *certiorari* An order from the U.S. Supreme Court to a lower court to deliver the records of a case to the Supreme Court for review.

writ of execution A court order directing the sheriff of a county to sell the property of a losing defendant to satisfy the judgment against that defendant.

writ of replevin A court order requiring a defendant to turn goods over to a plaintiff because the plaintiff has the right to immediate possession of the goods.

yellow-dog contract An agreement whereby an employer requires, as a condition of employment, that an employee promise not to join a union.

zoning law A local regulation or ordinance which restricts certain areas to specific uses; for example, areas zoned for residential, commercial, agricultural, industrial, or other uses.

Index

M

N

O

P